Why do you need this new edition?

Here are 5 good reasons:

With so much in flux, this continues to be the most exciting time in human history to be studying mass media. Although self-proclaimed gurus are everywhere, nobody knows for certain how or when the commotion will really settle. This new edition of *The Media of Mass Communication* will help you see why the media are in such a tumultuous transition and provide you with tools for understanding the reshaping of the entire media industry.

Reflecting the transformation in the mass media, this 11th edition focuses on the following:

1. The impact of internet-based media and new delivery devices. The changing media landscape is reflected in every chapter, showing the ongoing and accelerating transition of virtually all mass communication online. The expansion of options for consuming media (smartphones and tablet devices, especially) is also taken into consideration throughout this new edition.

2. Greater emphasis on world events and the globalization of mass media. This edition demonstrates how mass media are at the heart of so much that is happening in the world today. Throughout the text you will see how world events are tied into the mass media. Examples include: an internet cafe in Yangzhou City, street protests in Azadi Square, the Thor Data Center outside Reykjavík, the Stryker Brigade leaving Iraq, and the Arab Spring in Tahrir.

3. New and updated features. Chapter features have a new parallelism. Every chapter carries *new* Media Counterpoints that pose contentious issues, offer leading arguments, and ask questions to help you frame your own position; a Media People feature focusing on someone pivotal in our understanding of mass media; as well as a Media Timeline, designed to help you place media developments in a context of social, political and cultural history. Finally, *new* Media Tomorrow features look at where media are headed, usually through technology still in development.

4. Fresh, current examples. New examples throughout the text are used to illustrate enduring points as well as capture new uses of the media to bring about social change, such as Dan Savage's *It Gets Better* video project.

5. Fully updated visual program. This edition offers dozens of powerful photos, sized and cropped for impact in the tradition of the best photojournalism. Captions underscore the key takeaways for each image, allowing you to appreciate the full force of the visual.

PEARSON

to HAROLD VIVIAN, my father, who sparked my curiosity about the mass media at age 5 by asking what was black and white and read all over.

to ELAINE VIVIAN, my mother, who nurtured this curiosity by keeping the house stocked with books, magazines and reading material of every sort.

The Media

of MASS COMMUNICATION

ELEVENTH EDITION

John Vivian

Winona State University

PEARSON

Boston   Columbus   Indianapolis   New York   San Francisco   Upper Saddle River
Amsterdam   Cape Town   Dubai   London   Madrid   Milan   Munich   Paris   Montréal   Toronto
Delhi   Mexico City   São Paulo   Sydney   Hong Kong   Seoul   Singapore   Taipei   Tokyo

Editor-in-Chief, Communication: Karon Bowers
Senior Acquisitions Editor: Melissa Mashburn
Editorial Assistant: Megan Hermida
Director of Development: Sharon Geary
Development Editor: Barbara Heinssen
Associate Development Editor: Angela Mallowes
Marketing Manager: Blair Zoe Tuckman
Senior Digital Editor: Paul DeLuca
Digital Editor: Lisa M. Dotson
Production/Project Manager: Barbara Mack
Project Coordination, Text Design, and Electronic Page Makeup: Integra
Senior Cover Design Manager/Cover Designer: Nancy Danahy
Cover Photos: Top: Old style globe © haveseen/iStock; Middle: Gold world globe © pagadesign/iStock;
    Bottom: © Sean Locke/iStock
Manufacturing Manager: Mary Fischer
Procurement Specialist: Mary Ann Gloriande
Printer/Binder: Courier/Kendallville
Cover Printer: Courier/Kendallville

Library of Congress Cataloging-in-Publication Data
Vivian, John.
    The media of mass communication / John Vivian.—11th ed.
      p. cm.
    ISBN 978-0-205-02958-7
    1. Mass media.   2. Mass media—Technological innovations.   3. Mass media—Social aspects.
4. Communication—Technological innovations.   5. Mass media and culture.   I. Title.
    P90.V53 2011
    302.23—dc23

                                                                    2012001324

10 9 8 7 6 5 4 3 2 1—CRK—15 14 13 12

www.pearsonhighered.com

ISBN 13: 978-0-205-02958-7
ISBN 10:   0-205-02958-2

■ brief contents

contents

■ PART ONE   MASS MEDIA FUNDAMENTALS

contents

3 Media Economics   56

■ PART TWO

2

MASS MEDIA INDUSTRIES

4 Ink on Paper   84

contents

5 Sound Media   120

contents

contents

■ PART THREE   MASS MEDIA CONTENT

8 News   198

contents

contents

11 Advertising 288

■ PART FOUR MASS MEDIA ISSUES

12 Mass Audiences 316

13 Mass Media Effects 342

contents

contents

preface

The mass media was in rapid, dizzying change in 1991 when I first wrote *The Media of Mass Communication* in an attempt help college students make sense of it all. Since then, the change has accelerated exponentially. Indeed, newspapers were still a reigning medium back then. Facebook inventor Mark Zuckerberg was a second-grader. By the day, it seems, the change is more rapid, more dizzying—and more exciting and fascinating. As an author, my task is greater than ever to make sense of it all.

Through *The Media of Mass Communication* and a growing network of colleagues who have adopted the book, my reach as a teacher has been extended far, far beyond the confines of my own classroom. There are editions in several countries, including Canada, China and Indonesia. In all, *The Media of Mass Communication* has been published in 24 variations over the years, each revised specifically to keep students up-to-speed with ever changing media dynamics. I am indebted deeply to professors and their students, who pepper me almost daily with their reactions to the book and with news and tidbits to keep the next edition current.

Most gratifying to me is the community that has grown up around *The Media of Mass Communication.* These are people, many of whom have become valued friends, whose thoughts have made the book an evolving and interactive project. In countless messages, professors have shared what works in their classes and how it might work elsewhere. Students write me the most, sometimes puzzled over something that deserves more clarity, sometimes with examples to illustrate a point. All of the comments, questions and suggestions help add currency and effectiveness to every new edition.

NEW TO THIS EDITION

New editions of textbooks are warranted when the body of knowledge changes significantly and events have rendered old examples weak or wrong. The following list highlights how much change is captured in this edition of *The Media of Mass Communication*:

- **The Mass Media in Transition:** Legacy media receive a more compact treatment in this edition, notably the ink-on-paper media and traditional sound and motion media industries. There was no other way to create space for the flood of new material on internet-based media. The compacting was tortuous but essential. The book remains a manageable length for a semester. Every chapter reflects the ongoing and accelerating transition of virtually all mass communication to the internet and the advent of new delivery methods, most particularly smartphones and tablet devices.

- **The Mass Media and World Events:** More than ever, this new edition reflects the reality that mass media are at the heart of so much that is happening in the world. When the last edition went to press, George W. Bush was still president of the United States. The Arab Spring had not dawned. The rallying chants of the Occupy Wall Street movement were yet to be heard. The BP Gulf oil disaster hadn't happened. The global recession had not yet begun a correction. The Kardashians were barely a blip in the cable television universe.

- **New and Updated Chapter Features:** Every chapter highlights the fast pace of change and rise in controversies accompanying the mass media. New **Media Counterpoints** pose contentious issues, offer key arguments, and provide questions to help readers determine their personal positions on the subject at hand. **Media Tomorrow** features, also new to this edition, examine media's future—especially the impact of budding technologies. Updated **Media People** and **Media Timeline** features examine key personalities in media and the social, political, and cultural historical context of media developments.

- **Current, relevant examples:** Throughout this edition you will find fresh examples that illustrate enduring points, like the gripping and tragic story that opens Chapter 1 with a police raid and media ride-along that went all wrong. In Chapter 7 you will find the World According to Steve Jobs, whose legacy indeed might be less his Apple empire than his insights into how the new Internet Age came to be and is unfolding still. Mark Zuckerberg, of course, has new prominence in this edition. Who, after all, can ignore Facebook? You will find many emerging social issues, as well, including efforts to combat bullying via mass media.

■ **A Fully Updated Visuals Program:**   In the first edition *The Media of Mass Communication* made a landmark contribution to mass communication education with a color photo program. Looking back, it's hard to imagine how the mass communication story can be appropriately told without color. In this edition you will find dozens of powerful photos, sized and cropped for impact in the tradition of the best photojournalism. The potency of media in world-changing street riots in Egypt, Iran and elsewhere peppers this edition. So do the drug lord horrors from Mexico's border cities. And the tsunami that wiped out whole coastlines and thousands of lives in Japan and threatened nuclear disaster.

TEXT OVERVIEW

The Media of Mass Communication covers the important issues that confront students as consumers and purveyors of mass media. Issues such as culture, democracy, the economy and audience fragmentation are addressed in each chapter.

The opening chapter on media literacy establishes the importance of studying the media of mass communication. The rest of the book is organized into four parts.

Part One looks at the fundamentals of media technology and media economics.

Part Two examines media industries. These include legacy ink on paper industries—newspapers, magazines and books. There are chapters on the sound media industries of recordings and radio and on the motion media industries of movies and television. In the chapter on the new media landscape, you will see how internet-based media are subsuming all the others.

Once you have a firm foundation on the shape of mass media, you will move into Part Three on media content, which includes chapters on news, entertainment, public relations and advertising.

The final part examines issues: What is the role of audiences in mass communication? What are mass communication effects? What is the role of mass media in governance? How is globalization affecting the mass media? And vice versa. What are legal issues for mass media? And ethics issues?

To provide a framework for key concepts and help bring these issues together for student understanding and retention, each chapter concludes with a highly visual "Thematic Chapter Summary." These summaries offer a unifying perspective—a kind of cross-referencing of material in every chapter to material in every other chapter.

New and Updated Features

EVERY CHAPTER INCLUDES:

NEW! **MEDIA COUNTERPOINTS.** Each Media Counterpoints feature poses a contentious issue, offers leading arguments to help you understand the controversy being explored, and provides questions to help readers determine their own positions on the topic.

NEW! **MEDIA TOMORROW.** These features look at where media are headed, usually with an emphasis on developing technology. Questions invite you to build on your new understanding.

MEDIA PEOPLE. These features focus on individuals pivotal in our understanding of mass media.

MEDIA TIMELINE. Each timeline casts key developments in the mass media in a graphic chronology and is designed to help you place media developments in a context of social, political and cultural history. You will find the timelines useful in drawing connections between what you are learning about the mass media and what you already know.

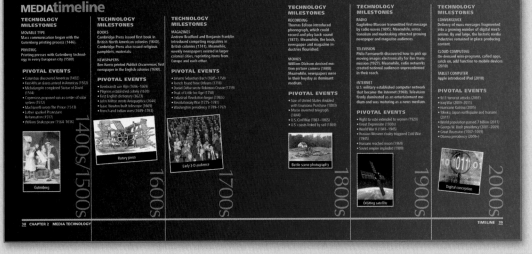

■ How to Use This Book

BY DEFINITION A BOOK IS MEANT FOR READING. A TEXTBOOK, HOWEVER, GOES FURTHER. THE GOAL IS READING FOR THE SAKE OF LEARNING AND UNDERSTANDING AND POSING GOOD QUESTIONS FOR FURTHER EXPLORATION. *THE MEDIA OF MASS COMMUNICATION* IS DESIGNED TO HELP YOU AS NOT MERELY A READER BUT AS A CRITICAL LEARNER.

It all begins with the chapter organization. Chapters are broken into six to eight "bite-size chunks." Each section has a heading to orient you to what is being explored in the section. These sections are divided into subsections, each also with an orienting heading.

CHAPTER OPENING VIGNETTES. ▶

Each vignette serves as a gateway into the chapter. Vignettes are colorful stories that focus on a media personality, industry mover and shaker, or a timely issue of importance.

CHAPTER INSIGHTS

- Mass communication is a technology-based process.
- Mass production of the written word became possible with movable metal type.
- Chemistry is the technological basis of movies.
- Mastery of the electromagnetic spectrum led to radio and television.
- Orbiting satellites and fiber optics have improved media efficiency.
- Traditional media products and new products are emerging from digital technology.
- Models help explain the technology-driven process of mass communication.

◀ CHAPTER INSIGHTS.

At the outset of every chapter you will find one-sentence insights, each geared to the chapter's main sections. These insights serve as springboards to what's ahead.

STUDY PREVIEWS. ▶

To get you started with a chapter's major sections, you will find a brief summary. These not only summarize the next few pages but are also a useful study guide in preparing for exams.

> **STUDY PREVIEW** | Technology is basic in mass communication. If not for the technology of printing presses, books as we know them wouldn't exist. If not for electronic technology, television, radio and the internet wouldn't be.

APPLYING YOUR MEDIA LITERACY

- Explain this assertion: Photography and words are not mass media but are essential for the media to exploit their potential.
- How does persistence of vision work in movies? How about in 3-D movies?

◀ APPLYING MEDIA LITERACY.

Every major section ends with questions that ask you to apply the media experience that you brought to the course to the new material you have learned.

MARGINAL GLOSSARY. ▶

The significance of important terms, institutions and people is established in the text as you read. As an additional study aid, these terms are bold-faced. Also, a definition appears in the margin for your instant reference and as a guide in reviewing material for exams.

Heinrich Hertz
Demonstrated existence of radio waves 1887

vellum
A treated animal skin used in early printing

▲ Frederick Ives.

◀ **Halftone.** *The halftone process, invented by Frederick Ives, uses variously sized dots to transfer ink to paper. The dots are invisible except under close examination. At a reading distance, however, the bigger dots leave darker impressions, the smaller dots a lighter impression. The effect looks like the varying tones in a photograph.*

◀ CAPTIONS.

Although visually catchy, photographs in *MMC* are no mere eye-candy. Each has a pedagogical purpose, either to reinforce a lesson from the text or to make a significant additional point. Don't overlook captions as learning tools.

Chapters end with a suite of valuable review tools:

THINKING CRITICALLY. ▶

These questions ask you to think through what you've learned in a new way. Each question is geared to a major section in the chapter. Parenthetical page references will take you back to the chapter discussion to help you with your response.

■ Thinking Critically

1. What were early effects of Gutenberg's movable type on civilization? Can you speculate on what our culture would be like without Gutenberg's invention?

2. Photography and movies are both rooted in chemical technology, but one is a mass medium and one is not. Please explain this distinction with this paradigm: A photograph is to a book what a script is to a movie.

3. How did the introduction of systems for delivering mass messages

◀ MEDIA VOCABULARY.

Master these chapter terms and you will be on your way to articulating a new level of media literacy. Parenthetical page references will take you back to the chapter discussion of each term if you need further review time.

■ Media Vocabulary

amplification (Page 48)
App (Page 46)
Arthur C. Clarke (Page 40)

digital (Page 43)
downlink (Page 40)
Ed Parsons (Page 41)

filters (Page 48)
Frederick Ives (Page 32)
gatekeeping (Page 48)

MEDIA SOURCES. ▶

These suggested reading lists include both printed and online works to help carry your learning further. Each source includes an annotation with the author's credential and a brief summary of the work.

■ Media Sources

■ Ken Auletta. *Googled: The End of the World as We Know It.* Penguin, 2009. Auletta, media critic for the *New Yorker,* tracks Google from humble origins into an online powerhouse that displaced traditional media, then deals with its profit-driven quest to dominate media delivery and become a major advertising vehicle.

■ Linda Gordon. *Dorothea Lange: A Life Beyond Limits.* Norton, 2009. Gordon, a historian, glimpses with convincing insight into the psychology of Lange to

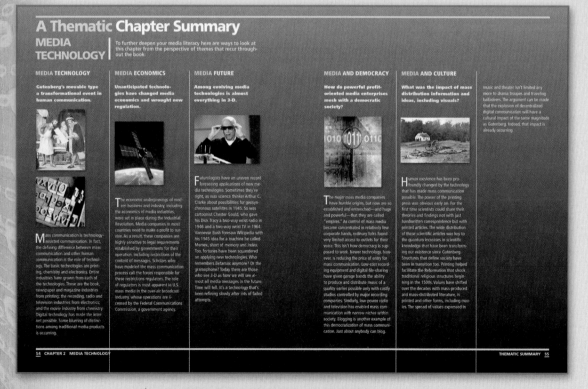

▲ **CHAPTER WRAP-UP.**

Provides a concise review of major themes from the chapter, opportunities for thinking critically, a handy list of key terms, and additional media sources.

▲ **THEMATIC CHAPTER SUMMARY.**

To help you put the chapter in broader perspective, a thematic summary recasts the chapter in terms of overarching themes in the book. Parenthetical page references link back to relevant discussions to help with answering questions.

Instructor Support

Name of Supplement	Available	Instructor or Student Supplement	Description
Instructor's Manual (ISBN: 0205251498)	Online	Instructor Supplement	This comprehensive instructor resource contains Chapter-by-Chapter teaching material organized around six major sections: Chapter Synopsis, Chapter Structure, Key Terms and Figures, Lecture Ideas, Activities, and Additional Resources. Available for download at the Instructor's Resource Center (www.pearsonhighered.com/irc; instructor login required).
Test Bank (ISBN: 020525148X)	Online	Instructor Supplement	The Test Bank contains more than 2500 multiple-choice, true/false, completion, short answer, essay, and matching questions organized by chapter. Each question is referenced by page. Available for download at the Instructor's Resource Center (www.pearsonhighered.com/irc; instructor login required).
MyTest (ISBN: 0205251455)	Online	Instructor Supplement	This flexible, online test-generating software includes all questions found in the *Test Bank*. This computerized software allows instructors to create their own personalized exams, to edit any or all of the existing test questions, and to add new questions. Other special features of this program include random generation of test questions, creation of alternate versions of the same test, scrambling of question sequence, and test preview before printing. Available at www.pearsonmytest.com (instructor login required).
PowerPoint™ Presentation Package (ISBN: 0205251501)	Online	Instructor Supplement	This text-specific package provides a basis for your lecture with PowerPoint™ slides for each chapter of the book. Available for download at the Instructor's Resource Center (www.pearsonhighered.com/irc; instructor login required).
Mass Communication Videos	DVD	Instructor Supplement	Designed to help bring media issues to life in the classroom, this DVD contains videos relevant to a variety of media issues and problems. Please contact your Pearson representative for details; some restrictions apply.
Introduction to Mass Communication Study Site	Online	Student Supplement	Pearson's Introduction to Mass Communication Study Site is an open-access resource featuring learning objectives, practice tests, and weblinks organized around each major topic of your introduction to mass communication course. http://www.pearsonmasscommunication.com
Study Card for Introduction to Mass Communication	In Print	Student Supplement	Colorful, affordable, and packed with useful information, *Pearson Study Cards* make studying easier, more efficient, and more enjoyable. Course information is distilled down to the basics, helping you quickly master the fundamentals, review a subject for understanding, or prepare for an exam. Because they're laminated for durability, you can keep these Study Cards for years to come and pull them out whenever you need a quick review. Available for purchase and packaging with the text.
MyCommunicationLab	Online	Instructor & Student Supplement	MyCommunicationLab is a state-of-the-art, interactive and instructive solution for mass communication courses. Designed to be used as a supplement to a traditional lecture course or to completely administer an online course, MyCommunicationLab combines a Pearson eText, MySearchLab™, MediaShare, Pearson's class preparation tool, multimedia, video clips, activities, research support, tests, and quizzes to completely engage students. See next page for more details.

MyCommunicationLab®
The moment you know.

Educators know it. Students know it. It's that inspired moment when something that was difficult to understand suddenly makes perfect sense. Our MyLab products have been designed and refined with a single purpose in mind—to help educators create that moment of understanding with their students.

MyCommunicationLab can be used by itself or linked to any learning management system. To learn more about how the new MyCommunicationLab combines proven learning applications with powerful assessment, read on!

MyCommunicationLab delivers **proven results** in helping individual students succeed.

- Pearson MyLabs are currently in use by millions of students each year across a variety of disciplines.

- MyCommunicationLab works—but don't take our word for it. Visit our MyLab / Mastering site (www.pearsonhighered.com/mylabmastering) to read white papers, case studies, and testimonials from instructors and students that consistently demonstrate the success of our MyLabs.

MyCommunicationLab provides **engaging experiences** that personalize, stimulate, and measure learning for each student. MyCommunicationLab is available for Mass Communication, Introduction to Communication, Interpersonal Communication, and Public Relations courses.

- **The Pearson eText:** Identical in content and design to the printed text, the Pearson eText lets students access their textbook anytime, anywhere, and any way they want — including downloading to an iPad. Students can take notes and highlight, just like a traditional book.

- **Assessments:** Pre-and Post-Tests for each chapter enables students and instructors to track progress and get immediate feedback. Results from the Pre and Post-Tests generate a personalized study plan that helps students master course content. Chapter Exams allow instructors to easily assign exams online. Results feed into the MyLab grade book.

- **MediaShare:** This comprehensive file upload tool allows students to post speeches, outlines, visual aids, video assignments, role plays, group projects, and more in a variety of formats including video, Word documents, PowerPoint, and Excel. Structured much like a social networking site, MediaShare can help promote a sense of community among students. Uploaded files are available for viewing, commenting, and grading by instructors and class members in face-to-face and online course settings. Integrated video capture functionality allows students to record video directly from a webcam to their assignments, and allows instructors to record videos via webcam in class or in a lab and attach them directly to a specific student and/or assignment. Instructors also can upload files as assignments for students to view and respond to directly in MediaShare. Grades can be imported into most learning management systems, and robust privacy settings allow instructors and students to ensure a secure learning environment.

- **Videos and Video Quizzes**: Interactive videos provide students with the opportunity to watch and evaluate multimedia pertaining to chapter content. Many videos are annotated with critical thinking questions or include short, assignable quizzes that report to the instructor's grade book.

- **Pearson's Class Preparation Tool** collects the very best class presentation resources in one convenient online destination, so instructors can keep students engaged throughout every class.

- **MySearchLab**: Pearson's MySearchLab™ is the easiest way for students to start a research assignment or paper. Complete with extensive help on the research process and four databases of credible and reliable source material, MySearchLab™ helps students quickly and efficiently make the most of their research time.

- **Audio Chapter Summaries:** Every chapter includes and audio chapter summary, formatted as an MP3, perfect for students reviewing material before a test or instructors reviewing material before class.

MyCommunicationLab comes from a **trusted partner** with educational expertise and a deep commitment to helping students, instructors, and departments achieve their goals.

- Pearson supports instructors with workshops, training, and assistance from Pearson Faculty Advisors—so you get the help you need to make MyCommunicationLab work for your course.

- Pearson gathers feedback from instructors and students during the development of content and the feature enhancement of each release to ensure that our products meet your needs

No matter what course management system you use—or if you do not use one at all, but still wish to easily capture your students' grade and track their performance—Pearson has a MyCommunicationLab option to suit your needs. A MyCommunicationLab access code is no additional cost when packaged with print versions of select Pearson Communication texts. To get started, contact your local Pearson Publisher's Representative at www.pearsonhighered.com/replocator.

acknowledgments

This edition of *The Media of Mass Communication*, the 11th, represents the work of more people than I can count. Most significant among them have been Karon Bowers, the Editor in Chief for Communication, who has shepherded the project through recent editions; Jeanne Zalesky, the acquisitions editor, and her successor, Melissa Mashburn; and Angela Mallowes, associate development editor. This project could not have had a more energetic and supportive leadership.

The most hands-on contributor, sometimes being almost a co-author, has been Barbara Heinssen, a veteran development editor across many academic disciplines. Our minds clicked from the start. On many days Barbara was ahead of me with ideas to keep this edition the most current and compelling in a field of worthy competitors. We had much to live up to. Over the previous 10 editions, appearing in 27 variations, more than 1 million students worldwide have used *The Media of Mass Communication*. Thank you, Barbara, for the stamp you have left on these pages.

To ensure that this edition be as up-to-date as possible, freelance writer Kay Turnbaugh, herself a media maven, wrote many of the boxed inserts. These include some new Media Counterpoints boxes that lay out unfolding issues to help you move to new levels of media literacy.

In a real sense the most visible contributor this edition has been Brandi Ford as photo researcher. Brandi picked up on the book's tradition as a visually compelling textbook and applied her imagination to making it more so.

Production manager Barbara Mack and project manager Eric Arima, both with a long record with *The Media of Mass Communication*, honchoed the edition through technical complexities that would confound most normal mortals and certainly me. They bent deadlines and found opportunities to wedge new material and breaking issues into the edition while still getting everything to the press on time.

I am indebted to my students and colleagues at my academic home, Winona State University, who made contributions in ways beyond what they realize. I am indebted too to many students elsewhere who have written thoughtful suggestions that have shaped this edition. They include Niele Anderson, Grambling State University; Krislynn Barnhart, Green River Community College; Michelle Blackstone, Eckerd College; Mamie Bush, Winthrop University; Lashaunda Carruth, Forest Park Community College; Mike Costache, Pepperdine University; Scott DeWitt, University of Montana; John Dvorak, Bethany Lutheran College; Denise Fredrickson, Mesabi Range Community and Technical College; Judy Gaines, Austin Community College; James Grades, Michigan State University; Dion Hillman, Grambling State University; Rebecca Iserman, Saint Olaf University; Scott Wayne Joyner, Michigan State University; David Keys, Citrus College; Chad Larimer, Winona State University; Amy Lipko, Green River Community College; Christina Mendez, Citrus College; Nicholas Nabokov, University of Montana; Andrew Madsen, University of Central Florida; Scott Phipps, Green River Community College; Colleen Pierce, Green River Community College; June Siple, University of Montana; and Candace Webb, Oxnard College.

I am grateful to reviewers who provided guidance for this new edition of *The Media of Mass Communication*:

Patricia Cambridge, Ohio University

Michael Cavanagh, University of Illinois at Springfield

Thomas Gardner, Westfield State College

Nancy Jennings, University of Cincinnati

Eungjun Min, Rhode Island College

Lynn C. Owens, Peace College

I also appreciate the suggestions of other colleagues whose reviews over the years have contributed to the book's success: Edward Adams, Brigham Young University; Ralph D. Barney, Brigham Young University; Thomas Beell, Iowa State University; Ralph Beliveau, University of Oklahoma; Robert Bellamy, Duquesne University; ElDean Bennett, Arizona State University; Lori Bergen, Wichita State University; Michelle Blackstone, Eckerd College; Bob Bode, Western Washington University;Timothy Boudreau, Central Michigan University; Bryan Brown, Missouri State UniversityCambridge, Ohio University; Jane Campbell, Columbia State Community College; Dom Caristi, Ball State University; Michael L. Carlebach, University of Miami; Meta Carstarphen, University of North Texas; Michael Cavanagh, University of Louisiana at Lafayette; Danae Clark, University of Pittsburgh; Jeremy Cohen, Stanford University; Michael Colgan, University of South Carolina; Ross F. Collins, North Dakota State University; Stephen Corman, Grossmont College; James A. Danowski, University of Illinois, Chicago; David Donnelly, University of Houston; Thomas R. Donohue, Virginia Commonwealth University; John Dvorak, Bethany Lutheran College; Michele Rees Edwards, Robert Morris University; Kathleen A. Endres, University of Akron; Glen Feighery, University of Utah; Celestino Fernández, University of Arizona; Donald Fishman, Boston College; Carl Fletcher, Olivet Nazarene University; Laurie H. Fluker, Southwest Texas State University; Kathy Flynn, Essex County College in Newark, New Jersey; Robert Fordan, Central Washington University; Ralph Frasca, University of Toledo; Judy Gaines, Austin Community College; Mary Lou Galician, Arizona State University; Andy Gallagher, West Virginia State College; Ronald Garay, Louisiana State University; Lisa Byerley Gary, University of Tennessee; Donald Godfrey, Arizona State University; Tom Grier, Winona State University; Neil Gustafson, Eastern Oregon University; Donna Halper, Emerson College; Peggy Holecek, Northern Illinois University; Anita Howard, Austin Community College; Jason Hutchens, University of North Carolina at Pembroke; Elza Ibroscheva, Southern Illinois University, Edwardsville; Carl Isaacson, Sterling College; Nancy-Jo Johnson, Henderson State University; Carl Kell, Western Kentucky University; Mark A. Kelley, The University of Maine; Wayne F. Kelly, California State University, Long Beach; Donnell King, Pellissippi State Technical Community College; William L. Knowles, University of Montana; John Knowlton, Green River Community College; Sarah Kohnle, Lincoln Land Community College in Illinois; Jennifer Lemanski, University of Texas-Pan American; Charles Lewis, Minnesota State University, Mankato; Lila Lieberman, Rutgers University; Amy Lignitz, Johnson County Community College in Kansas; Amy Lipko, Green River Community College ;Larry Lorenz, Loyola University; Sandra Lowen, Mildred Elley College; Linda Lumsden, Western Kentucky University; John N. Malala, Cookman College; Reed Markham, Salt Lake Community College; Maclyn McClary, Humbolt State University; Daniel G. McDonald, Ohio State University; Denis Mercier, Rowan College of New Jersey; Timothy P. Meyer, University of Wisconsin, Green Bay; Jonathan Millen, Rider University; Bruce Mims, Southeast Missouri State University; Joy Morrison, University of Alaska at Fairbanks; Gene Murray, Grambling State University; Richard Alan Nelson, Kansas State University; Thomas Notton, University of Wisconsin–Superior; Judy Oskam, Texas State University; David J. Paterno, Delaware County Community College; Terri Toles Patkin, Eastern Connecticut State University; Sharri Ann Pentangelo, Purdue University; Deborah Petersen–Perlman, University of Minnesota–Duluth; Tina Pieraccini, State University of New York at Oswego; Leigh Pomeroy, Minnesota State University, Mankato; Mary-Jo Popovici, Monroe Community College; Thom Prentice, Southwest Texas State University; Hoyt Purvis, University of Arkansas; Jack Rang, University of Dayton; John Reffue, Hillsborough Community College; Benjamin H. Resnick, Glassboro State College; Rich Riski, Peninsula College; Ronald Roat, University of Southern Indiana; Patrick Ropple, Nearside Communications; Marshel Rossow, Minnesota State University, Mankato; Julia Ruengert, Pensacola Junior College; Cara L. Schollenberger, Bucks County Community College; Quentin Schultz, Calvin College; Jim Seguin, Robert Morris College; Susan Seibel, Butler County Community College; Todd Simon, Michigan State University; Ray Sinclair, University of Alaska at Fairbanks; J. Steven Smethers, Kansas State University; Karen A. Smith, College of Saint Rose;Mark Smith, Stephens College; Howard L. Snider, Ball State

University; Brian Southwell, University of Minnesota; Rob Spicer, DeSales University; Alan G. Stavitsky, University of Oregon; Penelope Summers, Northern Kentucky University; Philip Thompsen, West Chester University; Larry Timbs, Winthrop University; John Tisdale, Baylor University; Edgar D. Trotter, California State University, Fullerton; Carl Tyrie, Appalachian State University; Helen Varner, Hawaii Pacific University; Rafael Vela, Southwest Texas State University; Stephen Venneman, University of Oregon; Kimberly Vos, Southern Illinois University; Michael Warden, Southern Methodist University; Hazel G. Warlaumont, California State University, Fullerton; Ron Weekes, Ricks College; Bill Withers, Wartburg College; Donald K. Wright, University of South Alabama; Alan Zaremba, Northeastern University; and Eugenia Zerbinos, University of Maryland.

STAY IN TOUCH

Please feel free to contact me with questions and also ideas for improving the next edition. My e-mail: (jvivian@winona.edu). May your experience with *The Media of Mass Communication* be a good one. Or as Facebook would suggest, click the "like" button.

—John Vivian
Winona State University

1 MASS MEDIA LITERACY

■ Media Tag-Alongs

The Fox television network didn't invent police ride-along news reporting, but Fox's *Cops* polished the journalistic story form into a low-budget, high-drama genre. To be sure, the Fox program and copycat series on other networks attracted controversy from the start. Critics called the shows an assault on civil society—a sign of a new "peep culture." Indeed, there was a tawdriness. Crime isn't pleasant. And journalistically there were questions. Was Fox serious about illuminating crime as a public policy issue? Or was Fox merely into a filthy lucre game with cheap-to-produce programming that was easy to sell to advertisers?

These questions exploded powerfully when a crew for a copycat program, the A&E network's *First 48 Hours,* trailed the cops on a police raid on a Detroit home. Police were searching for a suspect in a convenience store killing. Specifics of what happened may never be known, but police insisted that an officer either collided with the woman of the house, Mertilla Jones, or was jostled by her. For sure, a police gun went off. Mrs. Jones' granddaughter, asleep on a couch, took the bullet. Seven-year-old Aiyana died instantly. Everyone agreed: A tragic mistake.

The immediate questions included whether the A&E television crew had factored into the tragedy. Were the cops conducting themselves differently because they knew the raid was being taped? People do play for the camera, to look better, to be more daring, and also sometimes being more cautious than otherwise. We'll never know those answers.

▲ **A Grandma's Grief.** *At a candlelight vigil Mertilla Jones wails in sorrow over the death of her granddaughter. The 7-year-old girl was killed by a police bullet in a raid on the family home. Was television a factor in the tragedy? A television crew was taping the raid for a network reality show.*

CHAPTER INSIGHTS

- Mass media easily go unnoticed despite their enormous role in our lives.

- Technology distinguishes mass and social media from other human communication.

- Linguistic, visual and film literacy are essential skills for mass communication.

- Media literacy involves not only knowledge but also critical thinking.

- Mass communication is done with a purpose, usually to inform, persuade, amuse or enlighten.

- Mass communication has become simultaneously a unifying and divisive force in society.

There are ways, however, to address important and confounding questions about mass media behavior and effects. This chapter is a primer on media literacy. The purpose is to help you hone your skills at understanding the myriad dynamics that influence media activities, like reporter ride-alongs on police raids. These include economic imperatives and the complicated relationship of building audiences to draw in advertising revenue. These also include ethics questions, like intrusions on privacy and gotcha journalism. And what about consequences of media behavior? Do media messages have effects on us as individuals that are positive? Or insidiously manipulative? Think about monster movies. Think about advertising. What about effects on society? For better or worse, consider corporate public relations campaigns. And what of political campaigns? Are they good for democracy? Or are they part of a path for ruining our way of life?

Tools are available to help assess these issues. They require media literacy—knowing what to look for, and knowing how to evaluate critically. These are tools to defend ourselves against being conned though mass media. More important, these are tools to empower us to use mass media ourselves in our lives to our individual and mutual advantage.

In the death of little Aiyana Stanley-Jones in Detroit one Sunday night, it is important to know that producers of ride-along cop shows defend their work as giving citizens valuable insights into police work. Many police departments note that ride-along shows help recruit young men and women. Some political scientists say that the recording of police activities by non-police entities like television crews enhances police accountability to the public.

At the same time, cases can be made against these so-called ride-along shows. In 1999 the U.S. Supreme Court ruled that media ride-alongs violate a citizen's right to "residential privacy" when reporters follow cops into a home. In the Detroit raid, the A&E crew stayed outside when the cops drew weapons and stormed the house. Thus A&E technically did not violate the law, but questions remain about whether the presence of the television crew heightened tensions or otherwise contributed to the tragedy.

Another question, broader and even more vexing: Do reality cop shows trivialize important issues, reducing everything to mere entertainment? If so, is it conveniently disingenuous for A&E and other carriers of reality shows to cloak their programming in saintly journalistic rationales like public service that heightens public understanding?

And if these are indeed *reality* shows, which suggests a journalistic justification, then why do the producers accede to police department insistence on editing them? Journalists never allow the people in their stories to edit the news, but police departments routinely are allowed the final say on what gets aired on ride-along shows and what doesn't. This even includes minor issues like whether police are wearing their uniforms by the book. One department even took out shots of officers smoking because they reflected poorly on police professionalism.

What is the truth in all this? Media literacy enables us to have the conversation that can steer us to answers. ∎

Media Ubiquity

STUDY PREVIEW

We swim in an ocean of mass communication, exposed 68.8 percent of our waking hours to media messages. So immersed are we in these messages that we often are unmindful of their existence, let alone their influences.

Media Exposure

So awash are we in **mass media** messages that most of the time we don't even think about them. Scholars at Ball State University found that people are intentionally involved in a media activity, like watching television or browsing the internet, 30 percent of their waking hours—almost five hours a day. Additional media exposure is passive, like audio wallpaper. In the 21st century, mass media are essential in most of our daily lives, sometimes in our faces and sometimes, like air, ubiquitous but invisible. Or at least unnoticed, taken for granted.

mass media
Strictly speaking, mass media are the vehicles through which messages are disseminated to mass audiences. The term also is used for industries built on mass media: *the television and book media*. Also, companies in the business of delivering mass messages with mass media: *Viacom is a media company.*

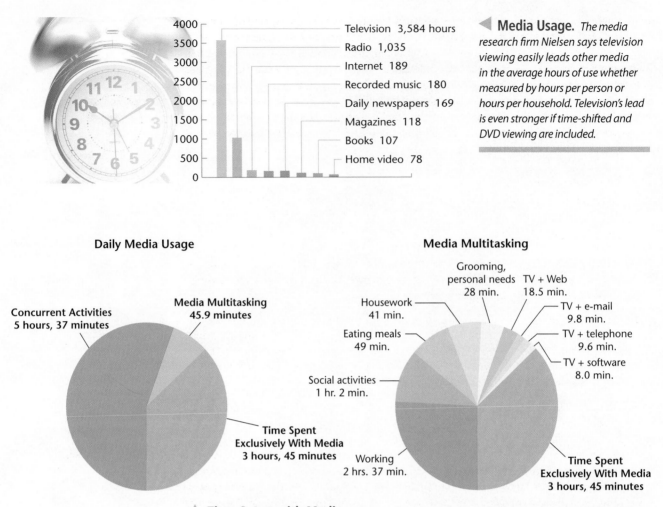

4000	Television 3,584 hours
3500	Radio 1,035
3000	Internet 189
2500	Recorded music 180
2000	Daily newspapers 169
1500	Magazines 118
1000	Books 107
500	Home video 78
0	

◀ **Media Usage.** *The media research firm Nielsen says television viewing easily leads other media in the average hours of use whether measured by hours per person or hours per household. Television's lead is even stronger if time-shifted and DVD viewing are included.*

Daily Media Usage

Concurrent Activities
5 hours, 37 minutes

Media Multitasking
45.9 minutes

Time Spent
Exclusively With Media
3 hours, 45 minutes

Media Multitasking

Grooming, personal needs 28 min.

TV + Web 18.5 min.

Housework 41 min.

TV + e-mail 9.8 min.

Eating meals 49 min.

TV + telephone 9.6 min.

TV + software 8.0 min.

Social activities 1 hr. 2 min.

Working 2 hrs. 37 min.

Time Spent
Exclusively With Media
3 hours, 45 minutes

▲ **Time Spent with Media.** *Mass media are everywhere all the time. An extensive Ball State University study found that we spend 68.8 percent of our waking hours with the media, much of it while doing something else. Also, we sometimes expose ourselves to additional media messages at the same time.*

Concurrent Media Usage

Incredible as it may seem, the Ball State study found that besides five hours of media involvement a day, people average more than an additional six hours with the media while doing something else. That's an additional 39 percent of our waking hours. This includes half-watching television while cooking dinner or catching a billboard while commuting. All tallied, the media are part of our lives about two-thirds of the time we're not sleeping—68.8 percent, to be precise. Perhaps we need the rest.

media multitasking
Simultaneous exposure to messages from different media

Mass media have become so integrated into people's lives that **media multitasking** is no chore. The Ball State researchers found that roughly one-third of the time people spend with mass media involves simultaneous contact with two or more other media. This includes reading a newspaper with one ear tuned to a television program, listening to the radio with the other ear, and simultaneously surfing the internet.

As startling as the Ball State study may seem, the findings are hard to dispute. Researchers tracked 294 Midwesterners for 12 hours a day, 5,000 hours in all, recording their media use every 15 seconds on a handheld device. That's a sample size and methodology that commands respect.

mass communication
Technology-enabled process by which messages are sent to large, faraway audiences

Strictly speaking, the media exposure tracked in the Ball State study was not all mass communication. By definition, **mass communication** is the technology-assisted transmission of messages to mass audiences. The Ball State study included technology-assisted one-on-one communication, such as instant messaging and e-mail, which primarily are forms of interpersonal communication. The fact, however, is that distinctions between mass communication and some interpersonal communication are blurring. Video gaming, for example, can be a solo activity. Video gaming can also be interpersonal, with two people together or apart. Also, video gaming can be a mass activity with dozens, theoretically thousands, clearly making it a form of mass communication. By lumping technology-assisted communication and mass media communication together, the Ball State data merely reflect the emerging reality that we are living a media-saturated existence.

Inescapable Symbiosis

As a demonstration of willpower, someone occasionally goes cold turkey and abstains from exposure to mass media. The oddity makes it news, whether it's a grade-school class exercise or a scientific experiment with careful controls. Usually these media-free demonstrations are short-lived. Except perhaps when we backpack into the remote wilds, most of us have a happily symbiotic dependence on mass media. We depend on media. And media industries, of course, are dependent on having an audience. What would be the purpose of a radio station, for example, if nobody listened?

Personal Dependence.   Most days the most-listened-for item in morning newscasts is the weather forecast. People want to know how to prepare for the day. Not knowing that rain is expected can mean getting wet on the way home. For most of us, modern life simply wouldn't be possible without media. We need media for news and information; for entertainment, amusement and diversion, and for the exchange of ideas.

Media Dependence.   Not only do people in their contemporary lifestyles need mass media, but the industries that have built up around the media need an audience. This is the interdependence—a **symbiosis**. To survive financially, a publishing house needs readers who will pay for a book. A Hollywood movie studio needs people at the box office or signed up for movie downloads. Media companies with television, radio, newspaper and magazine products cannot survive financially unless they can deliver to an audience that advertisers want to reach. Advertisers will buy time and space from media companies only if potential customers can be delivered.

symbiosis
Mutually advantageous relationship

We live in an environment that interconnects with mass media. The interdependence is a generally satisfying although not problem-free fact of modern life.

APPLYING YOUR MEDIA LITERACY

- Take a day or two to track your own media usage. How closely do your results match those of the Ball State University study?
- How does media multitasking affect the way messages are presented?
- What is the impact of the interdependence of mass media and audience on our society?

Mediated Communication

STUDY PREVIEW | Mass communication is a process that targets technologically amplified messages to massive audiences. Other forms of communication pale in comparison in their ability to reach great numbers of people.

Ancient Communication

Human communication has many forms. Cave dwellers talked to each other. When Tor grunted at his neighbor Oop, it was **interpersonal communication**—one on one. Around the campfire, when Tor recounted tales from the hunt for the rest of the tribe, he was engaging in **group communication**. Traditionally, both interpersonal and group communication are face-to-face. Technology has expanded the prehistoric roots of human communication. When lovers purr

interpersonal communication
Between two individuals, although sometimes a small group, usually face to face

group communication
An audience of more than one, all within earshot

sweet nothings via a mobile phone, it's still interpersonal communication. And even though technology-assisted, a rabble-rouser with a megaphone is engaging in group communication.

Communication Through Mass Media

Fundamental to media literacy is recognizing the different forms of communication for what they are. Confusing interpersonal communication and mass communication, for example, only muddles an attempt to sort through important complex issues.

Mass communication is the sending of a message to a great number of people at widely separated points. Mass communication is possible only through technology, whether it be a printing press, a broadcast transmitter or an internet server. The massiveness of the audience is a defining characteristic of mass communication:

Audience.   The mass audience is eclectic and heterogeneous. With sitcoms, for example, the television networks seek mega-audiences of disparate groups—male and female, young and old, liberal and right-wing, devout and nonreligious. Some media products narrow their focus, like a bridal magazine. But a bridal magazine's intended audience, although primarily young and female, is still diverse in terms of ethnicity, income, education and other kinds of measures. It still is a mass audience.

Distance.   The mass audience is beyond the communicator's horizon, sometimes thousands of miles away. This is not the case with either interpersonal or group communication. Even technology-assisted group meetings via satellite or videoconferencing, although connecting faraway points, are not mass communication but a form of group communication.

feedback
Response to a message

Feedback.   The mass audience generally lacks the opportunity for immediate **feedback.** In interpersonal communication, a chuckle or a punch in the nose right then and there is

MEDIAtimeline

MEDIA LITERACY MILESTONES

LANGUAGE
Humans devise structured oral language (pre-history)

CAVE ART
Art on cave walls broadened human communication (17,000 years ago)

PIVOTAL EVENTS

• Human communication (prehistory)
• Homo sapiens originated in Africa (200,000 years ago)

Paleolithic humans left images that communicated among selves and later cave visitors.

Pre-history

MEDIA LITERACY MILESTONES

WRITING AND READING
Reading skills grow

PIVOTAL EVENTS

• Gutenberg's mass production for printing (1446)
• First press in British North American colonies (1639)

Milton encouraged an open forum

1400s–1700s

immediate feedback. With most mass communication, response is delayed—an e-mail to the editor, a canceled subscription, a nasty tweet. Even a text message to a reality television show is delayed a bit and is certainly less potent than that punch in the nose. Also, the recipient of an e-mailed message doesn't necessarily read it right away.

Mass communication cannot exist without technology like printing presses and broadcast transmitters. As such, mass communication was a triumph of the Industrial Age and the rise of machinery. Some people call it **industrial communication.** The term signifies the significant technological resources that are essential for mass communication to work on a large scale. Ever thought about buying a Goss Metro printing press to start a newspaper? Think in the millions of dollars. The Federal Communications Commission won't even consider issuing a television broadcast license to anyone without cash upfront to meet six months of expenses. Again, think millions. Mass communication is an industrial-scale undertaking.

industrial communication
Synonym for mass communication that points up industrial-scale technology that underlines the mass communication process

Communication Through Social Media

Perhaps as revolutionary as the addition of mass communication to human communication is the 21st century phenomenon of **social media.** This too, like mass communication, is mediated. But unlike mass communication, social media are accessible to almost anybody. You don't need costly printing presses or broadcast equipment. With only an internet-ready computer, individuals can create content that can be tapped into worldwide. Social media are internet-based. Through mobile technologies they turn communication into interactive dialogue. This interactive exchange of user-generated content led to the term *social* media. Leading examples: Facebook, Twitter and YouTube, all of which are relatively inexpensive to individuals to publish or find information and to exchange information—in contrast to industrial media. Both mediated forms of communication, whether through mass media or

social media
Internet-based communication platforms for the interactive exchange of user-generated content

MEDIA LITERACY MILESTONES

PUBLIC EDUCATION
First public school in U.S. in Boston (1821)

PHOTOGRAPHY
Joseph Niepcé invented photography (1826)

FREE SCHOOLING
All U.S. states offering free schooling (1870)

PIVOTAL EVENTS

• Illustrations a standard in magazine *Harper's Weekly* (1862)
• First newspaper photograph (1880)
• *National Geographic* magazine featured photos (1899)

Visuals grow in mass communication importance in 20th Century

1800S

MEDIA LITERACY MILESTONES

KINESICS
Julius Fast wrote *Body Language* on non-verbal communication cues (1970)

VISUAL LITERACY
Scott McCloud defined visual literacy in *Understanding Comics* (1993)

ORGANIZING
John Debes founded International Visual Literacy Association (1969)

PIVOTAL EVENTS

• Predecessor to first major movie studio, Paramount, formed (1912)
• *Life* magazine founded (1936)
• Internet invented (1969)

1900S

MEDIA LITERACY MILESTONES

YOUTUBE
Do-it-yourself video on YouTube (2005)

PIVOTAL EVENTS

• Wikipedia founded (2001)
• Facebook founded (2004)
• Great Recession (2007–2009)
• IPad introduced (2010)
• Steve Jobs of Apple died (2011)

Coming to grips with visual literacy

2000S

social media, can reach tiny or huge audiences. A video posted on YouTube can go almost unnoticed, as most do, while others go viral and outdraw the most successful products from the television industry.

Here are useful ways to see differences between social media and industrial media:

Reach.   Social and industrial media both use technologies to give scale to communication. Both are capable of reaching a global audience. However, industrial media typically use a centralized framework for organization, production and dissemination. Social media are more decentralized, less hierarchical, and have many more points of production and access.

Ownership.   Because the means of production are complicated and costly, industrial media typically are owned by corporations or government. In contrast, social media's production tools have low thresholds for entry and are within the economic means of most people.

Access.   The complexity of production for industrial media requires specialized skills and training. Social media production requires only commonly held skills, which means that just about anyone with access to an internet-ready computer can produce messages for potentially wide distribution.

APPLYING YOUR MEDIA LITERACY

- Compare the effectiveness of interpersonal communication, group communication and mass communication.
- What characteristics of social media distinguish it from industrial communication?
- If you see yourself eventually as a communicator with information and ideas to change the world, would you choose to hone your skills now for a career in mass media or social media?

Literacy for Media Consumers

STUDY PREVIEW | Basic components of media literacy are writing and reading skills. But as visuals have become more important in mass communication, visual literacy is needed too. This involves "reading" still and moving images.

Linguistic Literacy

Mass media once were almost entirely word-centric. The act of creating media messages and deriving meaning from them—media literacy, it's called—required vocabulary, grammar and other writing and reading skills. These were acquired skills, both teachable and learnable—not anything innate from birth.

linguistic literacy
Competencies with a written and spoken language

Linguistic literacy today is as much a measure of modern civilization as economic production and prosperity, all of which are interconnected. Although there are exceptions, like Cuba, with a national policy that emphasizes education but which is economically troubled, strong literacy rates correlate roughly to capita income:

	Literacy	Annual income per capita
United States	99.0 percent	$7,132
India	54.2 percent	$1,265
Afghanistan	34.0 percent	$906
Niger	28.7 percent	$381

Visual Literacy

Symbols of communication predate structured and complex human languages. There were messages in animal drawings in ancient caves, such as the one in Lascaux in southwestern France. More than 17,000 years ago, before structured languages, Paleolithic cave-dwellers communicated meaning among themselves through images. Probably the messages were augmented by simple uttered indicators. Whether intended to or not, the images also conveyed meaning to future generations. Just ask anthropologists who are "translating" the cave paintings today. The images are recognizable through **visual literacy.**

Except for occasional crude woodcuts, visual images weren't part of early mass media products. Technology back then was word-centric and didn't lend itself to visuals. This changed gradually with the introduction of photography in the mid-1800s, and then quickly with improved printing processes by the 1900s. People liked pictures, but the process was largely intuitive. Not until the 1960s did anyone think much about whether a systematic intellectual process was at work for interpreting, negotiating and making meaning. The term *visual literacy* was the invention of **John Debes** when he was education projects coordinator at Eastman Kodak in 1969. Debes defined visual literacy as "a group of vision-competencies a human being can develop by seeing and at the same time having and integrating other sensory experiences."*

With technology making visuals increasingly part of human communication, educators recognized that learning visual literacy could be indispensable in increasingly visual modern life. But the multiplicity of academic disciplines involved hindered the development of core principles.

Today the most coherent definitions are from comics author **Scott McCloud.** In a 1993 nonfiction book in the graphic novel format, McCloud proved himself a leading theorist of visual literacy. In *Understanding Comics: The Invisible Art* McCloud described how artists can control core elements of their work, including form, idiom and structure, to convey messages with precision. Savvy media consumers will recognize basics concepts

visual literacy
A competency at deciphering meaning from images

John Debes
Introduced term visual literacy in 1969

Scott McCloud
Comic book author who refined understandings about media literacy

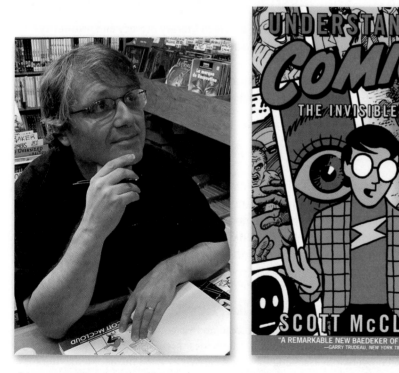

▲ Scott McCloud.

◄ **Agents of Control.** *Mass communicators are effective to the extent that they control their messages. These techniques of control, as theorized by graphic novelist Scott McCloud, include form, idiom and structure. The better the mastery of these techniques by mass communicators, the keener the message—and the stronger the visual as well as linguistic literacy. From the media consumer's perspective, the more that these techniques are recognized, the stronger their participation in the mass communication process.*

---

* "The Loom of Visual Literacy: An Overview" by John L. Debes in *Proceedings: First National Conference on Visual Literacy* by C. M. Williams and J. L. Debes (eds.). Copyright © 1970 by International Visual Literacy Association. Reprinted by permission.

such as right-facing depictions of movement being upward and positive, at least in Western cultures in which reading is ingrained as left to right. Left-moving depictions suggest obstacles, orneriness and tension. Colors affect mood and tone, just as can the pace and juxtapositioning of words in word-centric communication.

Done well, the intended messages in comics and other visuals don't require conscious analysis. But a sophisticated media consumer who recognizes the principles employed by an artist is well-positioned to understand and assess the messages. Picking up an author's intent yields more accuracy and satisfaction from the message.

McCloud and other visual literacy theorists are quick to point out that visual literacy, although necessary to survive and communicate in a highly complex world, cannot be a replacement for linguistic literacy. Rather, visual and linguistic literacies are interlaced and a mastery of both is essential to maximize meaning and understanding.

Film Literacy

film literacy
Competences to assess messages in motion media, such as movies, television and video

The introduction of photography and other still images into mass media content was gradual over decades. Motion pictures dawned explosively. Techniques were subject to immediate exploration, which created conventions known as **film literacy.** Audiences learned, for example, not to be frightened by bigger-than-life heroes and heroines on screen. It took awhile, but audiences eventually overcame confusion about visual clues to flashbacks. White hats were shorthand for good guys, black hats for villains. These techniques of master film-makers were transferred to television, also a motion medium. There are countless other techniques for conveying deep subtleties that aficionados recognize. Film literacy deepens the experience.

Much of the work going on in visual literacy comes from the much more extensive thinking that had been going on in movies for the better part of a century before Debes, McCloud and others began exploring visual literacy.

APPLYING YOUR MEDIA LITERACY

- **How do you explain the rough correlation between literary literacy and prosperity?**
- **Going as far back as you can remember, trace the development of your own visual literacy.**
- **Film literacy has multiple layers of sophistication. What does the use of white and black hats to represent good guys and villains say to you?**

Assessing Media Messages

STUDY PREVIEW

Media literacy is the application of knowledge and critical thinking processes. Fundamentals include recognizing message forms, not confusing messages and messengers, understanding the possibilities and limitations of various media and platforms, and placing media in a framework of history and traditions. Media literacy also requires continued questioning of conventional wisdom.

Fundamentals of Media Literacy

media literacy
Competences that enable people to analyze and evaluate media messages and also to create effective messages for mediated delivery

By literacy, people usually mean the ability to read and write. Literacy also can mean command of a specific discipline such as history or physics. **Media literacy** is possessing the knowledge to be competent in assessing messages carried by mass media. Media literacy is essential in this Age of Mass Communication that envelops our lives dawn to dusk, cradle to grave. Think about not having modern media literacy. Thomas Jefferson, although brilliant and learned in his time, would be in absolute wonderment at hearing a radio for the first time. As foolish as he would seem to you and me today, a resurrected Jefferson might ask how so many little people could fit inside so tiny a box and make so much noise. Jefferson's lack of media literacy would be laughable.

■ Eclipse of the Novel?

Technology begat the novel as long-form storytelling. Before Gutenberg invented mass production for the printed word in the mid-1400s, lengthy fictional prose was a rarity. Hand-scribed and bound books were horribly expensive, produced manually one copy at a time. Further, with low pre-Gutenberg literacy levels, the market was miniscule. The word *novel* itself didn't come about until the 1700s.

Now after a run of 300 or 400 years, the novel as we know it may be at a crossroads. The question is whether technology, which gave birth to the novel as a high form of literary art, may be its comeuppance.

"Cultic Activity." *American novelist Philip Roth is dour about prospects for his craft. Novels, he sees, have peaked as medium for long-form story-telling. He sees novels becoming "a cultic activity."*

- **COMPETING TECHNOLOGY.** Newer media technology has created potent storytelling forms that encroach on the novel's once exclusive province. Movies have emerged as a powerful vehicle for exploring the human condition and great social issues. Television too has potential for serious literary expression. Every medium has unique attributes and shortcomings. As an example, the relative compactness of a movie is limiting. But the compactness hardly means that movies are incapable of yielding literary insights.

- **EASE OF ACCESS.** Technology, also, has made access easier to electronic-based and digital-based media. Going to a movie house for a two-hour experience is easier, far easier, than acquiring a book and committing two weeks to reading. Access could hardly be easier than on-demand movies and television downloaded to a mobile tablet.

- **TIME CONSTRAINTS.** Although novels can be downloaded, the process of consuming long-form literature involves the slow and laborious intellectual process of reading. Most people, when reading for comprehension, move through only 300 words a minute—less than a page. As a learning tool, textbooks are even more labor-intensive. At an extreme, quick reading, like skimming, is typically 600 or 700 words a minute. With easier access to more compact media communication, it seems that people either have shorter attention spans or less patience. For sure, more is competing for people's attention than ever before. And 24 hours a day is not enough for even a fraction of the media involvement most of us would like.

Will the novel disappear? Not overnight, but even some champions of long-form story telling, like novelist Philip Roth, see the sun setting. Roth bemoaned to the *Daily Beast:* "The book can't compete with the screen. It couldn't compete beginning with the movie screen. It couldn't compete with the television screen. And it can't compete with the computer screen. Now we have all those screens."

New media forms are attracting creative people who in earlier times might have chosen the form of the novel for their artistic explorations and expression. At an extreme are episodic Japanese cell phone novels. While 16-character *keitai shosetsu* episodes can hardly be considered good literature, the history of printed and bound full-length books is also littered with lots of weak and even bad stuff. It's probably fairer to evaluate *keitai shosetsu* not as episode but in the complexity of their whole. It may be that the format has yet to mature into any kind of artistic fulfillment.

Episodic delivery—in chunks—exists in television series and to a greater degree in the edited break-downs of shows into mini-segments for downloading and consumption on the run.

▌ What Do You Think?

How much longer will the traditional novel as long-form storytelling be with us either in a print-and-bound or a down-loadable form?

How do you respond to broad-sweeping criticism of new media packaging of literary expression as inferior to the novel?

Most of our media exposure is invisible or at least unnoticed at a conscious level—the background music at a mall store, the advertising blurb on a pen, the overblown entrée description on a menu with the stacked-higher-than-life photo of a burger. Many media messages blur into our landscape as part of the environment that we take for granted. One measure of media literacy is awareness of the presence of media messages.

Some awareness requires broader and deeper media literacy than others.

Message Form.   Fundamental media literacy is the ability to see the difference between a one-on-one message and a mass message. This is not always easy. Consider a mass mailing with a personal salutation: "Hi, Karla." It's naïve—media illiteracy, we could call it—for Karla to infer from the salutation that she's getting a personal letter.

Message vs. Messenger.   Once there was a monarch, as the story goes, who would behead the bearer of bad news. The modern-day media equivalent is faulting a news reporter for telling about a horrible event, or criticizing a movie director for rubbing your face in an unpleasant reality. Media literacy requires distinguishing between messages and messengers. A writer who deals with the drug culture is not necessarily an advocate. Nor necessarily is a rapper who conjures up clever rhymes for *meth.*

Motivation Awareness.   Intelligent use of the mass media requires assessing the motivation for a message. Is a message intended to convey information? To convince me to change brands? To sour me on a candidate? The answer usually requires thinking beyond the message and identifying the source. Is the message from a news reporter who is trying to be detached and neutral about the subject? Or is the message from the Democratic National Committee? It makes a difference.

Media Limitations.   The different technologies on which media are shaped affect messages. CDs, for example, can deliver music superbly but printed books cannot. Both CDs and books are mass media, but they have vastly different potentials.

Someone who criticizes a movie for departing from the particulars of the book on which it's based may well lack sufficient media literacy to recognize that a 100-minute movie cannot possibly be literally true to a 90,000-word novel. Conversely, Matthew Vaughn's 2011 movie *X-Men: First Class* did things visually and audiologically that Stan Lee and Jack Kirby could not have done in their Marvel Comics series *X-Men* back in the 1960s. It's as pointless to criticize a movie for not being a book as it is to criticize tuna for not tasting like spinach, Or vice versa.

Traditions.   The past informs our understanding of the present. A longstanding strain in U.S. journalism, for example, was born in the Constitution's implication that the news media should serve as a watchdog on behalf of the people against government folly and misdeeds. Another tradition is for artistic expression that is free from government restraint. Media literacy is impossible without an appreciation of the traditions that have profoundly shaped the parameters of media performance and reasonable expectations.

Too, media literacy requires an understanding of other cultures and traditions. The role of mass media in China, for example, flows from circumstances and traditions radically different from those in Western democracies. Even among democracies, media performance varies. News reporting about criminal prosecutions in Britain, as an example, is much more restrained than in the United States.

Media Myth.   Video games are the latest whipping boys for violent crime. The fact is that the oft-heard conventional wisdom that media violence begets real-life violence has never been proved, despite hundreds of serious studies by social scientists. In fact, no matter how cleverly criminal defense attorneys have tried to scapegoat violent behavior on video gaming, television or movies, the courts always have rejected the argument. This is not to say that there is no link between violence in the media and violence in real life. Rather, it's to say that a simple, direct lineage has yet to be confirmed.

Media myths galore are afloat, polluting intelligent dialogue and understanding of important issues, including media violence. To separate real phenomena from conjecture and nonsense requires media literacy.

■ Literacy and the Internet

The Neuroscience Question. *Research on how the brain functions is posing questions about whether internet access to so much information is changing how we humans think. Nicholas Carr framed the issue provocatively in the Atlantic magazine.*

Nicholas Carr, a widely published technical writer, thought maybe he was suffering "middle-age mind rot." At 47 he realized he couldn't pay attention to one thing for more than a couple minutes. Back in college at Dartmouth, Carr loved books and spent hours in the library. So what was happening now, almost 30 years later? Indeed, was it mind rot?

No, Carr says. But how he uses his brain has changed drastically—and not necessarily for the better. He blames the internet.

In his book *The Shallows*, Carr notes that the brain is a creature of habit. Just as a rut in a road deepens with traffic, so do the channels of connectivity in the brain. The more he was using the internet over the years, picking up bits and pieces of information, often fragmentary and scattered, the less his brain was working as it once was trained to do. Before the web, he read linearly as the author had intended, going from beginning to end and looking for facts and ideas, making connections, following plots, and assessing rationales.

Carr's history as an internet junkie goes back to 1995 and Netscape, the first web browser. A dozen years later he recognized that the internet had come to exert a strong and broad influence on both his professional habits as a writer and his personal habits. He wanted information in quick, easy chunks, the more the better. It was addictive, he says. And destructive.

Once Carr had enjoyed deep reading. He recalls getting caught up in an author's prose and thinking about twists in plot lines. He would spend hour after hour immersed in a book. No more. Now, he says, his mind drifts after a page or two. He gets fidgety. Deep reading, he says, has become a struggle.

Even so, Carr acknowledges the wonders and efficiencies of the internet. As a writer he has immediate access to unprecedented stores of data. What once took hours in a library now takes seconds or a few minutes. But at what price? The internet, he says, has been chipping away at his capacity for concentration and contemplation. This worries him.

Carr cites friends who have experienced the same phenomenon. And there is research on brain function that supports his theory, although, as he concedes, much more research is needed.

No shortage of scholarship exists, however, about positive cognitive aspects of internet use. Katherine Hayles, a postmodern literary scholar, sees less of a threat in the fragmented and nonlinear processes that the internet encourages. To be sure, Hayles says, this "hyperattention," hopping around screens and hyperlinking, is far from the traditional approach of cloistering yourself off from the world to concentrate on a written work. But as she sees it, switching through information streams quickly and flexibly has its own value. Hayles calls for "new modes of cognition" that bridge traditional deep attention with internet-age hyperattention.

With the superficial engagement of the internet we are losing our ability to pay deep attention. This devaluation of contemplative thought, solitary thought and concentration is a loss not only for us as individuals but also for our culture.

POINT  **COUNTER POINT**

The risk of losing our culture and our abilities to reason are overblown. There are things that traditional linear and literary approaches can do that hyperattention cannot do. And vice versa.

DEEPENING YOUR MEDIA LITERACY

EXPLORE THE ISSUE: From your experience, identify a literary work that has shaped your values or your thinking. A novel that's recognized as important would work well for this exercise. Or a movie. If you have a hard time deciding, consider Dalton Trumbo's 1939 book *Johnny Got His Gun* or the 1971 movie adaptation.

DIG DEEPER: Conduct a web search with words for key details and concepts from the work. If you chose *Johnny Got His Gun*, try the author's name, the title, and terms like World War I, trachea, suffocation, pacifism, Morse code, euthanasia. Be imaginative with search terms. Go to as many additional links as your time allows.

WHAT DO YOU THINK? How did your web search enrich your experience with the work you chose for this exercise? Did you see the author's purpose or point differently after the web search? Were your values shaken? Reinforced? Fine-tuned? Most important, was your web experience adequate as a substitute for your linear, reading experience?

Spheres of Media Literacy

Media literacy takes many forms. People who craft media messages, for example, need technical competence. Competence at a soundboard is essential for music producers. Mastery of editing software is essential for magazine editors. These are skills that a media consumer doesn't need. In fact, the more invisible the technical details of media production are to media audiences, the more effective the messages. At the same time, media consumers can have a deeper appreciation of media messages if they have a sense of what went into making the message. In the same sense, anyone can be awed by a Yo-Yo Ma performance, but someone schooled just a little bit on the cello has a greater feel for Ma's intricacies and range.

Media literacy can be highly specialized. There are so many academic specialties on mass media, for example, that no one can master them all. An award-recognized historian on Federalist Period newspapers may not have the vocabulary to converse with a scholarly theorist on visual communication. We all will have blind spots in our media literacy, which is not a reason to give up or ease off working at improving your media literacy across a broad range. Rather, it's a recognition of the breadth of mass communication and mass media as a field.

Put another way: Because so much media behavior is explained through economics, savvy media consumers need an understanding of media revenue streams and finances and corporate structures. Most of us, however, need not aspire to the level of business acumen to be a high-stakes risk-taker like radio-television entrepreneur David Sarnoff, CNN founder Ted Turner or Fox television creator Rupert Murdoch.

APPLYING YOUR MEDIA LITERACY

- **How do you expect your media literacy to deepen as you proceed through this semester? Think in terms of the preconceptions you bring to the course: Is news biased? Can advertising be trusted? Are media depictions of aberrant behavior contagious? Think in terms of your own media usage: Mostly for information? Mostly for amusement?**
- **About which kind of media messages are you most expert at this point? Music? Political news? Video-production techniques? Movie genres? Celebrity news?**

Purposeful Mass Communication

STUDY PREVIEW | Unless anyone is interested in babble, mass communication has purpose. One purpose is informational, so people can make intelligent decisions in their daily lives and in their participation in society. Persuasion can be a purpose of mass communication. Indeed, media are essential in making most purchases and even embracing points of view. Another purpose is amusement.

To Inform

Mass media-delivered information comes in many forms. Students heading for college, especially if they plan to live in a dorm, receive a brochure about the dread disease meningitis. It's a life-or-death message about reducing the contagion in cramped living quarters. The message "Inoculate Now" is from a mass medium—a printed brochure or a mass-mailed letter or an e-mail attachment from the campus health director.

The most visible mass media-delivered information is news. People look to newscasts and news sites, even Steven Colbert, Bill Maher and David Letterman, to know what's going on beyond the horizon. If not for mass media, people would have to rely on word-of-mouth from travelers to know what's happening in Afghanistan, Hollywood or their state capital.

Information creates awareness in many forms—not just news and health brochures. For example, advertising offers information to help consumers make intelligent decisions. In a democracy, media comprise an essential forum for news and information and the exchange of ideas that promote intelligent citizen participation.

■ Hero of Cairo's Arab Spring

The plainclothes agents of the corrupt Mubarak administration knew who they were after. At a sidewalk café near Tahrir Square in Cairo, the henchmen strong-armed Wael Ghonim and dragged him away. It was a desperate attempt by Mubarak underlings to quell a revolution erupting in Egyptian streets. Ghonim's crime? Ghonim was a computer engineer who at age 27 had become a regional marketing executive for Google. In his spare time Ghonim operated a web site that now, three years later, was encouraging the departure of President Hosni Mabarak after three decades in power. Mubarak recognized that Ghonim's online activism was the fuse for revolution.

As the revolution continued in the streets, Ghonim was locked in a Cairo jail. Eleven days later under severe international pressure, the authorities released Ghonim. Soon, with the Mubarak administration disarrayed and writhing in death throes, Ghonim was back in the streets. And after 14 days of massive protests, Mubarak fled Cairo. It was a new day for Egypt.

In the months leading up to the pivotal 2011 protests, Ghonim was among a handful of activists whose Facebook page became a virtual headquarters for the movement. Ghomin began by documenting case after case of police brutality online, then burst quickly into a passionate voice against human rights abuses. The page also documented fraudulent November parliamentary elections.

Besides Facebook, Ghonim set up a Web site for Nobel Peace Prize winner Mohamed ElBaradei, who was emerging as the leading opponent to the Mubarak regime. Ghonim was not bashful about his connection with ElBaradei. Ghonim posted a photo with him smiling broadly next to ElBaradei with the caption: "My name is Wael Ghonim and I publicly support ElBaradei." His pledge to ElBaradei made Ghonim an obvious target when the government decided to deploy goons to round up ringleaders of the protests. Almost 1,300 people were detained.

Ghonim was less visible with another Facebook page that he and a few techno-activists engineered anonymously to honor a 28-year-old Alexandria blogger, Khaled Said, whom police had beaten to death. The page stirred anti-government sentiments. Khaled Said quickly became a martyr.

Inexplicably, the United States-based Facebook closed down the page, but soon a new replacement page cropped up, even more virulent and angry. The new page, labeled "We are All Khaled Said," included gruesome photos of Said's battered body. Then an English-language Facebook page appeared, explicitly aimed at drawing attention beyond Egypt.

The Arabic Facebook page's following approached 400,000 people as word spread that nationwide anti-government rallies were being organized. Besides news and photos, there was a seemingly unending stream of downloadable flyers and emotional calls for all Egyptians to join the cause. Other political movements joined online for demonstrations.

Under his own name Ghonim tweeted one message in this period: "Pray for Egypt. We are all ready to die."

After being released from jail, Ghonim acknowledged that he had run the "We Are All Khaled Said" page under the nom de plume "El Shaheeed." In Arabic the name means The Martyr.

In the streets, marchers carried homemade posters emblazoned with Ghomin's name. But even as he was being hailed a hero of the revolution, Ghonim displayed a modesty: "Actually, I did the easiest thing, which was writing. At the end of the day, it was about the power of the people."

Despite the modesty, Ghonim was in a media-savvy vanguard that helped spark the massive demonstrations that overthrew an autocratic and abusive government that had been in power 30 years.

▲ Wael Ghonim.

Freed from jail in the final hours of the Egyptian revolution, the revolution's media hero addressed thousands of triumphant protesters. Wael Ghonim diverted the enthusiasm from himself: "This is not the time for individuals or parties or movements. It's a time for all of us to say just one thing: Egypt above all." Ghonim's web activism had been a key in organizing millions of protestors nationwide against a 30-year autocratic reign and in moving the country to democracy.

What Do You Think?

Could the Arab Spring revolutions that began in 2010 have occurred before a pre-internet era?
While it's easy to applaud Wael Ghonim as a hero, would you have had his courage?

If Not Reporters, Then Whom? *Power company executive Akihisa Mizuno leaves a news conference after announcing that the tsunami-damaged Hamaoka nuclear power plant would close. The company and the Japanese government had resisted detailing the accident and widespread contamination but began yielding under insistent news media demands for explanations that detailed public pressure for action.*

To Persuade

marketplace of ideas
The concept that a robust exchange of ideas, with none barred, yields better consensus

People come to conclusions on pressing issues by exposing themselves to competing ideas in what's called the **marketplace of ideas.** In 1644 the thinker-novelist John Milton eloquently stated the concept of the value of competing ideas: "Let truth and falsehood grapple; whoever knew truth put to the worse in a free and open encounter." Today more than ever, people look for truth by exposing their views and values to those of others in a mass media marketplace. Milton's mind would be boggled by the volume. Consider the diversity: talk radio, newspaper editorial pages, anti-war lyrics from iTunes, blogs and tweets.

The role of persuasion is especially important in a democratic society, in which public policy bubbles up from the citizenry over time. Consider the debate for decades on limiting young people's access to alcohol. Should the legal drinking age be 18? 21? None at all? Or should booze be banned entirely? As the debate has worn on, with both sides making their cases, public policy representing a grassroots majority has evolved. The media have been essential in this process. The same for all cutting-edge issues across a broad range. Examples: Abortion, gay marriage, war and peace.

Power to the People. *Protesters against Egyptian autocracy charge their cell phones in a tangle of power bars and extension cords in Cairo's Tahrir Square. It was cell phone communication that organizers of the 18-day 2011 protest used to force the ouster of the country's 30-year ruler in the largest Middle East move to democracy.*

The most obvious persuasion that the mass media carry is advertising. People look to ads to decide among competing products and services. What would you know about Nikes or iPads if it weren't for advertising to which you exposed yourself or heard about from a friend who saw or heard an ad or noted it as a "like" on Facebook?

A major element in persuasion also comes from the public relations industry, which uses media to win people over. General Motors has a staff to make people feel good about GM. The Republican National Committee wants people to feel good about the GOP. The techniques of public relations fall short of advertising's pitches to make a sale, but none-theless have persuasion as the goal.

To Amuse

Before mass media came into existence in the mid-1400s, people created their own diversion, entertainment and amusement. Villagers got together to sing and swap stories. Traveling jugglers, magicians and performers dropped by. What a difference mass media have made since then. More than 75 million people in North America alone saw the James Cameron movie *Avatar* in its first four months. Do you know anyone who hasn't had television or radio on for entertainment in the past week? The past 24 hours?

To Enlighten

Mass media are important in figuring ourselves out. Insights into the human condition come from prose and poetry, both fiction and nonfiction, in every medium. Mass media are powerful vehicles for exploring. Think about listening to a moving obituary on a pivotal person in our society. Or reading a powerful novel—Dalton Trumbo's *Johnny Got His Gun* on the price of war or Alice Walker's *The Color Purple*. Ideas that have changed our worldview gained traction and acceptance as mediated messages—Charles Darwin's *Origin of Species*, Thomas Paine's *Common Sense*, or Rachel Carson's *Silent Spring*. Betty Friedan's *Feminine Mystique* was fundamentally transformative. The whole range of media products, as diverse as sappy television sitcoms, somber radio documentaries and online brooding anime cartoons, can tell us something about ourselves.

▲ **Marketplace of Ideas.** *In his tract* Areopagitica *in the 1600s, English thinker John Milton made an eloquent case for free expression. Milton's idea was that individuals can use their power of reasoning to improve their situation and come to know great truths by exchanging ideas freely. The mass media are the primary vehicle for persuasive discourse.*

APPLYING YOUR MEDIA LITERACY

- **A joker once remarked that the most important item in the news is the weather forecast. What do you think?**
- **How do you distinguish advertising and public relations as persuasive communication?**
- **How do you rank the importance of the informational, persuasive and amusement functions of mass communication?**
- **Explain life-changing media experiences you have had, perhaps challenges to personal values.**

Media and Society

STUDY PREVIEW | Today the mass audience of yore is fragmenting. Media companies cater increasingly to niches, not the whole.

Unifying Influence

Media literacy can provide an overview of mass media's effects on society and culture. A sweeping effect of mass media has been as a cultural unifier. The mass media bind communities with messages that become a shared experience. The first distinctly American novels, appearing in the early 1800s, helped give the young nation a cultural identity. The mass media of the time, mostly books and newspapers, created an awareness of something distinctly American. Shared knowledge, experience and the values flowing therefrom are, after all, what a culture is.

The national radio networks beginning in the 1920s, seeking the largest possible audiences, contributed intensely to cultural cohesion. Pop music became a coast-to-coast phenomenon. It was radio that gave President Franklin Roosevelt a national audience in the Depression from which to rally massive majorities behind daring economic and social reforms.

Later the television networks became major factors in the national identity. Audiences of unprecedented magnitude converged on the networks, all promulgating the same cultural fare. Even network newscasts, when they were introduced, all had a redundancy.

Through most of the 20th century, the most successful mass media companies competed to amass the largest possible audiences. The media, especially those dependent on advertising revenue, had a largely homogeneous thrust that simultaneously created, fed and sustained a dominant monoculture.

The role of mass media as a binding influence is most clear in news coverage of riveting events. Think 9/11. Think Hurricane Katrina. Even the Super Bowl. Onscreen news graphics are a regular binding influence: *America in Crisis, Our Porous Border*

The internet has broadened the binding influence, at least theoretically, beyond national borders. National borders are irrelevant by some measures. Britain's BBC is available all over the planet. So is Czech radio, the New York *Times* and continually updated reference sources like Wikipedia.

Moral Consensus

The mass media contribute to the evolution of what society regards as acceptable or as inexcusable. News coverage of the impeachment of President Clinton did this. You might ask whether the media, in covering controversy, are divisive. The short answer: No. Seldom do the media create controversy. For the most part, media merely cover it. Thorough coverage, over time, helps to bring about societal consensus—sometimes for change, sometimes not. For example, most Americans once opposed legalizing abortion. Today, after exhaustive media attention, a majority belief has emerged that abortion should be available legally in a widening array of circumstances. Racial integration was settled upon as public policy in the latter 20th century. The debate, conducted almost entirely through mass media, is well along on many fundamental issues, such as gun control, universal health care, gay marriage and, never-ending, government budget priorities.

▲ **In Triumph, in Grief.** *Media can be a great unifier. When President Obama announced on television that terrorist leader Osama Bin Laden had been killed, 56.5 million Americans tuned in. Media play a unifying role in moments of national triumph as well as tragedy. A few months earlier, 31 million people watched a televised tribute to Congress member Gabby Giffords in Tucson, Arizona, after an assassination attempt. At the emotional memorial service, Obama embraced astronaut Mark Kelly, Giffords' husband, in a symbol of shared national grief. Audiences of these sizes, pulling together huge swaths of the population, are possible only with mass media.*

▲ **Dan Savage.** *After news coverage rash of gay teen suicides linked to bullying in 2010, newspaper columnist Dan Savage created the internet-based It Gets Better campaign. Within six months, 10,000 people signed on to the web site. Dozens of celebrities, including President Barack Obama, added their videos against bullying. The campaign seemed on its way into media history every much a success like Smokey the Bear campaign against forest fires, A Mind Is a Terrible Thing to Waste for minority educational opportunity, and Friends Don't Let Friends Drive Drunk.*

Fragmentation

The giant Gannett newspaper chain launched a national daily, *USA Today*, in 1982, with editing techniques that pandered explicitly to an American identity. The paper had a first-person "our" tone throughout in referring to national issues. *USA Today* rose to become the largest daily in the nation, reflecting and also fueling a homogeneity in American culture. At the same time, however, a phenomenon was at work elsewhere in the mass media to turn the conventional wisdom about mass audiences on its head. In a process called **demassification,** media companies shifted many of their products from seeking the largest possible audience to focusing on audience segments.

demassification
Media's focus on narrower audience segments

Demassification began on a large scale with radio. In the 1950s the major radio networks, NBC, CBS and ABC, pirated their most popular radio programming and put it on their new television networks. There was an exodus of audience and advertisers from radio. Suddenly, the radio industry was an endangered species. Stations recognized that they couldn't compete with network television for the mass audiences anymore and began seeking audience segments with specialized music. Radio became a demassified medium with a growing number of musical genres. Stations each sought only a local slice of the mass media—**sub-mass audiences,** they could be called. Or niche audiences. The new radio programming was designed not for universal appeal but for audience niches. These were audience segments that television networks didn't bother to seek in their quest to build mass audiences that left no one out.

sub-mass audience
A section of the largest mass audience, with niche interests

Accelerating Demassificaton

Media demassification accelerated in the 1980s with technology that gave the cable television industry the ability to deliver dozens of channels. Most of these channels, while national, were taking the demassified course of magazines and gearing programs to

narrowcasting
Seeking niche audiences, as opposed to broadcasting's traditional audience-building concept

audience niches—sports fans, food aficionados, speed freaks. The term **narrowcasting,** as opposed to broadcasting, entered the vocabulary for media literacy. Then a wholly new technology, the internet, offered people more alternatives that were even narrower.

What has demassification done to the media's role as a contributor to social cohesion? Some observers are quick to link media fragmentation with the political polarization of the country, epitomized by Blue State and Red State divisions. Clearly there are cultural divides that have been nurtured if not created by media fragmentation. Music, as an example, is defined today by generational, racial, ethnic and socioeconomic categories, contrary to the homogenizing of tastes that radio fostered at the national level in its heyday in the 1930s and 1940s. At the same time, there remain media units that amass huge audiences in the traditional sense. A great drama of our times is the jockeying of the mass media for audience in an unpredictable and fast-changing media landscape. In pursuit of audience, whether mass or niche, media companies are experimenting with alternative platforms to deliver content that will find a following—or keep a following. Movies aren't only at the multiplex anymore. You can now easily view them on your computer, your iPod, iPad or many other tablet devices. CBS's *NCIS* series isn't only on prime time but is also downloadable. *USA Today* is online. CNN has multiple online platforms.

APPLYING YOUR MEDIA LITERACY

- **What has been the most society-unifying episode in your own media experience?**
- **What do you see as great social issues that are receiving media attention and moving toward consensus?**
- **What contemporary media content would you define as geared for mass audiences? For sub-mass audiences? For niche audiences?**
- **Do you see a slowing of the media demassification process?**

▲ **Cable Niches.** *The network Shalom TV signed on in 2006 for Jewish viewers in North America. Such sub-mass audiences have become reachable through cable and satellite technology. This is in contrast to the days when ABC, CBS and NBC were the only U.S. national networks, each seeking the biggest possible audiences. Not all latter-day niche networks survive, like the Puppy Channel. Others, like the Wine Network and the Anti-Aging Network, never make it beyond the conceptual stage. Even so, today's diversity of media content fragments audiences and works against the social cohesion when audiences had fewer choices and thus more shared media experiences.*

■ Media Ubiquity (Pages 3–5)

Two-thirds of our waking hours is spent consciously or subconsciously with the mass media. The media is a major part of our environment. Mass media are so ubiquitous in our lives that we multitask with them without even thinking about it. We can be oblivious to the media's effects unless we cultivate an understanding of how the media work and why. This understanding is called media literacy.

■ Mediated Communication (Pages 5–8)

Technology has expanded the original forms of face-to-face human communication. Today, we send amplified messages to great numbers of diverse people through mass communication. This sometimes is called industrial communication because of the underlying technology requires large capital investments. Communication by social media, a 21st century invention, offers low cost of entry for both broad and focused communication and potential for immediate feedback.

■ Literacy for Media Consumers (Pages 8–10)

Media literacy begins with a factual foundation and becomes keener with an understanding of the dynamics that influence media messages. There are degrees of awareness, including abilities to understand and explain media behavior and effects and to identify significant media issues.

■ Assessing Media Messages (Pages 10–14)

Media messages are so embedded into the landscape of our daily lives that it requires a conscious effort to understand how they may be influencing us. Media literacy means recognizing message forms. It also means understanding the possibilities and limitations of various media and platforms, and placing media in a framework of history and traditions. Critical thinking is essential to make sense of it all.

■ Purposeful Mass Communication (Pages 14–17)

People talk with one another with purpose and also listen with purpose. Sometimes it's to be informed, sometimes to be amused, sometimes to be open to persuasion or enlightenment. Such is no less true in mass communication. Mass communicators have purpose—or why do it? Media literacy requires understanding of the purpose of a mass message as part of assessing the content.

CHAPTER WRAP UP

◼ Media and Society (Pages 17–20)

The effect of mass media on society is changing. In the early days of radio and television, the same programs were beamed to everyone. Despite their cultural diversity, audiences across the country all watched and listened to the same comedy, drama and music shows. The result: a strong cultural cohesion. Today that audience is fragmenting and the cultural cohesion is breaking apart. Today's media companies are constantly experimenting to find a following or a new niche audience, and the resulting audience fragmentation is sometimes polarizing, at other times simply diverging.

◼ Thinking Critically

1. **What are risks of weak media literacy?**

2. **How does communicating through mass media and social media differ from other human communication?**

3. **What literacies besides writing and reading are important for people to handle mediated messages?**

4. **How do critical thinking skills figure into media literacy?**

5. **What mass messages have you encountered recently whose purpose is a combination of information, persuasion, amusement and enlightenment?**

6. **How is mass communication both a unifying and divisive force in society?**

◼ Media Vocabulary

demassification (Page 19)

feedback (Page 6)

film literacy (Page 10)

group communication (Page 5)

industrial communication (Page 7)

interpersonal communication (Page 5)

John Debes (Page 9)

linguistic literacy (Page 8)

marketplace of ideas (Page 16)

mass communication (Page 4)

mass media (Page 3)

media literacy (Page 10)

media multitasking (Page 4)

narrowcasting (Page 20)

Scott Mc Cloud (Page 9)

social media (Page 7)

sub-mass audiences (Page 19)

symbiosis (Page 5)

visual literacy (Page 9)

◼ Media Sources

◼ Nicholas G. Carr. *The Shallows: What the Internet Is Doing to Our Brains*. W.W. Norton, 2010. Carr, a technology writer, theorizes that the internet can diminish the capacity for concentration and contemplation.

◼ James W. Potter. *Media Literacy,* 5th edition. Los Angeles, Calif.; Sage Publications; 2010. Potter, a media scholar, makes the case that media literacy enables us to avoid potentially negative media effects and amplify potentially positive effects.

◼ Andreas M. Kaplan and Michael Haenleina. "Users of the World, Unite! The Challenges and Opportunities of Social Media," *Business Horizons 53:1* (January-February 2009), Pages 53, 59–68. The authors, scholars in management and marketing, explore a useful definition for the somewhat faddy and usually slippery term *social media.*

◼ Hal Niedzviecki. *The Peep Diaries: How We're Learning to Love Watching Ourselves and Our Neighbors.* City Lights, 2009. Niedzviecki, a Toronto journalist and novelist, says that modern life is isolating us from old social forums, like neighborhoods, and that, for better or worse, we are replacing our loneliness by seeking meaning by peeping into the private lives of strangers via mass media. He says the web compounds our ability to do this.

◼ Silverblatt, Art, Jane Ferry and Barbara Finan. *Approaches to Media Literacy: A Handbook*, 2nd edition. M. E. Sharpe; 2009. The authors suggest qualitative approaches to decipher mass communication, including photography, film, radio, television, and interactive media.

◼ Gunther R. Kress. *Literacy in the New Media Age*. Routledge, 2003. Sees unimaginable political and cultural implications of the growing role of technology in mass communication.

◼ Benjamin M. Compaine and Douglas Gomery. *Who Owns the Media? Competition and Concentration in the Mass Media Industry,* 3rd edition. Earlbaum, 2000. The authors update the 1979 and 1992 editions with details on further concentration, more attention to the cable and home video business, and the effect of technological convergence.

◼ Eric McLuhan and Frank Zingrone. *Essential McLuhan*. Basic Books, 1997. These scholars have edited the vast scholarship of Marshall McLuhan into this one-volume introduction to his theories and insights about the mass media. These include the global village, hot and cold media, the medium as the message, and media and culture.

◼ Judith Stamps. *Unthinking Modernity: Innis, McLuhan, and the Frankfurt School.* McGill-Queen's University Press, 1995. Stamps compares and contrasts the work of the Canadian theorists Innis and McLuhan and casts them within the larger Frankfurt School of philosophical thought.

◼ Scott McCloud. *Understanding Comics: The Invisible Art.* Tundra, 1993. In this landmark work, McCloud, a theorist of comics, uses the forum of linear comic panels to offer an early explanation of visual literacy.

A Thematic Chapter Summary

MASS MEDIA LITERACY

To further deepen your media literacy here are ways to look at this chapter from the perspective of themes that recur throughout the book:

MEDIA LITERACY

Scott McCloud has taught us the principles for linguistic literacy can be applied also to reading visuals.

Word-centric mass communication dating to the mid-1400s and Johannes Gutenberg's printing press placed a social premium on linguistic literacy. After Gutenberg, people who couldn't read faced a growing barrier in conducting the business of their daily lives and in social interaction. Over the past century, the visual component of mass communication has grown to point that visual literacy is important for both the creators and consumers of mass messages.

MEDIA TECHNOLOGY

President Franklin Roosevelt took to the radio networks in the 1930s, urging calm in the face of a global economic depression. Technology gave him a bigger audience than ever assembled before.

A distinction between mass communication and other forms of communication is technology. Without technology like printing presses and broadcast transmitters, mass communication would not exist. The advantage of mass communication over interpersonal and group communication is the size of the audience that can be reached. Think about how Simon Fuller could possibly parade *American Idol* performances before a national audience if it weren't for the amplifying technology of the mass media.

MEDIA AND DEMOCRACY

Seventeenth century political theorist John Milton favored a robust and unbridled exchange of ideas.

Democracy cannot function without the mass media. Citizens need the information provided by mass media to participate in shaping their common course. This will be even more true in the future. People also need a forum for exchanging their reactions to information and their ideas. The mass media provide that forum.

MEDIA AND CULTURE

Almost one-third of our waking hours are with mass media.

We live in a culture that's increasingly media-saturated. So ubiquitous are mass media that their presence largely is invisible. Occasionally we're jarred by in-your-face content, but mostly the mass media are taken for granted—like air. Just as air affects us, and deserves scientific examination and monitoring, so do media.

AUDIENCE FRAGMENTATION

Demassification has led to media products geared to narrower and narrower audiences, like television networks like the techno CNET cable television network, low-power neighborhood radio stations, and micro-run book publishing.

The American experience became a cohesive one with books in the early 1800s that fostered a sense of nationhood, and later with radio and television networks beaming the same comedies, dramas and newscasts to the country's diverse population. Today, media can still bond people, but increasingly messages are targeted to sub-mass audiences, a practice that is adding to the fragmentation of society.

MEDIA EFFECTS

Media can create huge audiences for events, like 111 million for the 2011 Super Bowl. The effect is a shared experience that has a cultural unifying effect.

Media affect us, and we affect media. Media messages influence our daily decision-making in ways that can be almost invisible. For instance, media influence us when we make a decision about whether to go to Starbucks or McDonald's for coffee. Similarly, we aren't always aware of the ways that we influence the media. Because media are economically dependent on audience, we as media consumers influence the media when we decide which coffee to sip or which web sites to visit or magazines to read.

2 MEDIA TECHNOLOGY

■ A Cyber-War Tool

As an early hacker, John Draper is legendary, bordering on mythical. Maybe that's why they call him Cap'n Crunch. His hacking often had an edge of carefree whimsy. When Richard Nixon was president, a 20-something Draper cracked a White House telephone code and used the password *olympus* for a direct line to the president. Then he proceeded to tell the president about a toilet paper shortage in Los Angeles. Or so goes the story.

With the advent of personal computers, hacking assumed dark proportions—far beyond Draper's sophomoric pranks. Mass-targeted mini-software programs anonymously destroyed the hard drives of personal computers. These programs, known variously as viruses and worms, were more than petty annoyances. Some malware from hackers disdainful of establishment institutions focused on banks and other high-visibility targets like government agencies. They caused widespread damage. Police agencies worldwide created investigative units to catch hackers. Despite wave after wave of new software firewalls to thwart intruders, hackers kept finding weak points and, for their own malicious satisfaction, continued to wreak havoc.

Governments were not only victims but perpetrators. Israel and its ally the United States, for example, had long suspected that Iran was trying to build nuclear weapons to attack Tel Aviv. Although not officially confirming it, Israel and U.S. agencies designed a worm, Stuxnet, to infiltrate controls in Iran's uranium-refining centrifuges. Stuxnet was unleashed secretly in 2010. Within

◀ **Google Tensions.** *When Google's Gmail system was hacked in 2011 for access to messages among U.S. diplomats and other government officials, Google blamed the Chinese government. U.S. Secretary of State Hillary Clinton warned that the United States took the cyber-attack seriously and noted that a new U.S. military doctrine provided for military responses. China denied it had authorized the hacking—a skirmish in a new era of cyber-war.*

CHAPTER INSIGHTS

- Mass communication is a technology-based process.
- Mass production of the written word became possible with movable metal type.
- Chemistry is the technological basis of movies.
- Mastery of the electromagnetic spectrum led to radio and television.
- Orbiting satellites and fiber optics have improved media efficiency.
- Traditional media products and new products are emerging from digital technology.
- Models help explain the technology-driven process of mass communication.

months 384 of Iran's 3,900 centrifuges were wiped out. Israel and the United States took comfort in believing that an Iranian weapons development program had been slowed by years. Coincidentally or not, during the months that Stuxnet was quietly infecting Iran's centrifuges, three Iranian nuclear scientists were targeted, two fatally, by car bombs. This is the stuff on which spy drama scripts are based.

The Stuxnet virus was hardly an isolated case. Among others in 2011:

- Hackers presumably in Jinan, home to the Chinese military intelligence agency, found a way into Google's Gmail servers to target e-mail addresses, including senior U.S. government officials, anti-Chinese activists and journalists. The hackers changed settings on the accounts to tap regularly into other users' messaging.

- Hackers, apparently foreign-based, cracked into a network of U.S. military contractor Lockheed Martin that contained sensitive war technology under development. At risk was state-of-the-art technology, possibly even the stealth helicopter technology used in the 2011 raid that killed terrorist Osama bin Laden in Pakistan.

In ways, the growing military cast of cyber issues is déjà vu. The internet was created in the 1960s when the Pentagon recognized that all-out nuclear war would disrupt their command-and-control networks. Indeed, a first-strike attack could have wiped it all out. Their answer: Build a web of interlinked but independent channels to transport packets of data without central communication hubs that could be targeted. The network went operational in 1969. The network, never tested by all-out nuclear war, grew into today's internet—the backbone for e-mail, the web and all forms of mass communication.

The internet turned out to be vulnerable too—not to bombs as was the original plan but to hacking. Because the internet has evolved into more than a military tool and become integrated into everyday life, a cyber-attack could so unwind our modern computer-centric and intertwined communication system that mass communication as we know it would be in jeopardy. In a 2011 research essay, Chinese scholars Ye Zheng and Zhao Baoxian explained that war has changed. As they see it, nuclear strategies belonged to the industrial era in human history. Cyber-warfare is now the strategic war of the information era. Both can be "massively destructive." The common denominator: Nations can live and die in both nuclear and cyber war.

The United States has developed military doctrine to regard computer sabotage from another country as an act of war that warrants a traditional military response. One Pentagon official, speaking to the *Wall Street Journal* on condition of anonymity, put it this way: "If you shut down our power grid, maybe we will put a missile down one of your smokestacks."

The escalation has moved far beyond Jack Draper's fun-and-games hacking half a century ago.

In this chapter, you will look at the range of technologies that underpin all mass communication. These include print, broadcast and film, as well as digital technology and the internet, which are subsuming traditional delivery platforms and creating new issues, like new cyber battlefields. ■

Media Technology

STUDY PREVIEW | Technology is basic in mass communication. If not for the technology of printing presses, books as we know them wouldn't exist. If not for electronic technology, television, radio and the internet wouldn't be.

Technology Dependence

One defining characteristic of **mass communication** is its reliance on technology. People can communicate face-to-face, which is called **interpersonal communication**, without technological assistance. For centuries people communicated in large groups, as in town-hall meetings and concert halls, without microphones—just the human voice, albeit sometimes elevated to extraordinary volume. For mass communication, however, with audiences much more far-flung than those in the largest auditorium, machinery is necessary.

mass communication
Technology-enabled process by which messages are sent to large faraway audiences

interpersonal communication
Usually two people face-to-face

Evolving Media Landscape

Media technology, the product of human invention, exists in several forms, each one distinctive. Around each of these technologies, industries have been built that are closely allied with each specific technology.

Printing Technology. The printing press, dating to the 1440s, spawned the book, newspaper and magazine industries. After centuries, these industries still exist in largely cubbyholed niches in the media landscape.

Chemical Technology. Photography and movies have relied on chemical technology throughout most of their history.

Electronic Technology. The first of the electronic media, sound recording, actually preceded the widespread use of electricity. But with the wiring of the United States in the early 1900s, sound recording quickly became an electrically powered medium. Radio was electrical early on. Television was electronic from the get-go.

Digital Technology. Traditional mass media all adapted to digital technology to varying degrees beginning in the first decade of the 21st century, but the industries built on the original printing, chemical and electronic forms remain largely distinctive. Book companies like HarperCollins still produce books. CBS is still primarily in the television business. The distinctive newest medium built on digital technology is the internet. Even as companies that were built on older technologies swirled in a frenzy to find ways to capitalize on the new medium, the internet itself created entirely new categories of media companies. Think Facebook. Think Google. Think Wikipedia

Meanwhile, printed and bound books are still with us. So too is Channel 2 on television, Paramount Pictures and talk radio.

APPLYING YOUR MEDIA LITERACY

- What do the four primary technologies of mass communication have in common?
- What industries have been built around the different media technologies?

Printing Technology

STUDY PREVIEW | With the invention of movable metal type in the mid-1440s, suddenly the written word could be mass-produced. The effect on human existence was profound. Incorporating photographic technology with printing in the late 1800s added new impact to printed products.

Movable Metal Type

Although printing can be traced back a couple thousand years to eastern Asia, an invention in the mid-1440s made mass production of the written word possible for the first time. The innovation: **movable metal type**. A tinkerer in what is now the German city of Mainz, **Johannes Gutenberg**, was obsessed with melting and mixing metals to create new alloys. He came up with the idea to cast the individual letters of the alphabet in metal, and then assemble them one at a time into a page for reproduction by pressing paper onto the raised, inked characters. The metal characters were sturdy enough to survive the repeated pressure of transferring the inked letters to paper—something not possible with the carved wood letters that had been used in earlier printing.

In time, industries grew up around the technology, each producing print media products that are still with us today—books, newspapers and magazines. But historically, the impact of Gutenberg's invention was apparent much earlier. Printing with the new Gutenberg technology took off quickly. By 1500 printing presses were in place throughout Europe. Suddenly civilization had the mass-produced written word.

movable metal type
Innovative metal alphabet that made the printing press an agent for mass communication

Johannes Gutenberg
Metallurgist who invented movable metal type in mid-1440s

■ Dawn of Mass Communication

Johannes Gutenberg was eccentric—a secretive tinkerer with a passion for beauty, detail and craftsmanship. By trade he was a metallurgist, but he never made much money at it. Like most of his fellow 15th century Rhinelanders in present-day Germany, he pressed his own grapes for wine. As a businessman, he was not very successful, and he died penniless. Despite his unpromising combination of traits, quirks and habits—perhaps because of them—Johannes Gutenberg wrought the most significant change in history: the mass-produced written word. He invented movable metal type.

Despite the significance of his invention, there is much we do not know about Gutenberg. Even to friends he seldom mentioned his experiments, and when he did, he referred to them mysteriously as his "secret art." When he ran out of money, Gutenberg quietly sought investors, luring them partly with the mystique he attached to his work. What we know about Gutenberg's "secret art" was recorded only because Gutenberg's main backer didn't receive the quick financial return he'd expected on his investment and sued. The litigation left a record from which historians have pieced together the origins of modern printing.

The date when Johannes Gutenberg printed his first page with movable type is unknown, but historians usually settle on 1446. Gutenberg's printing process was widely copied—and quickly. By 1500, presses all over Western Europe had published almost 40,000 books.

Today, Gutenberg is remembered for the Bibles he printed with movable type. Two hundred **Gutenberg Bibles**, each a printing masterpiece, were produced over several years. Gutenberg used the best paper. He concocted an especially black ink. The quality amazed everybody, and the Bibles sold quickly. Gutenberg could have printed hundreds more, perhaps thousands. With a couple of husky helpers he and his modified wine press could have produced 50 to 60 pages an hour. However, Johannes Gutenberg, who never had

▲ **Johannes Gutenberg.**

Applying muscle power, Gutenberg's husky assistants turned a weight down a vertically threaded post, which forced the weight against a sheet of paper. Under the sheet of paper were the raised metal characters, which had been pre-arranged into words and sentences and then been inked. The ink transferred to the paper with ink. Gutenberg took pride in showing the machine to visitors, who marveled as the weight was screwed back up, revealing a printed page. Each page would be hung to air-dry the ink and then the backside was printed. Eventually the pages, each individually printed, would be bound into a book.

much business savvy, concentrated instead on quality. Forty-seven Gutenberg Bibles remain today, all collector's items. One sold in 1978 for $2.4 million.

What Do You Think?

Would Gutenberg make your list of the 10 most important persons in human history? Explain where you would rank him.

Gutenberg's Impact

The impact was transformational. Scientists who earlier had carried on time-consuming hand-written correspondence with colleagues now could print their theories and experiments for wide dissemination. Modern science thus took form. Religious tracts could be mass-produced. So could materials with serious challenges to religion. The growing quantity of printed materials fueled literacy and, slowly, a standardization in written languages. What Gutenberg begat can be called the Age of Mass Communication, but his innovation also spurred Western civilization into the new Age of Science and Age of Reason. Civilization hasn't been the same since.

Gutenberg's invention changed history in numerous ways:

- **Scholarship.** Scholars were enabled to publish multiple copies of their discoveries and theories. By tracking each other's progress, scholars could build on each other's work as never before, Human knowledge made quantum advances that brought on the scientific revolution.

- **Oral Traditions.** With printed materials more widely available, people placed new value on reading. With the growing literacy, the tradition of listening to stories being told or read by others was displaced by reading as a silent and private act.

- **Languages.** Printing fostered a standardization of spelling and syntax in local languages that coalesced into national languages. One upshot was the modern nation-state in which citizens gradually replaced the local variations with a national language. The dominance of Latin as the only pan-European language began slipping.

- **Authorship.** The role of authors gained recognition. Hitherto, the names of authors often were lost as works were reproduced one copy at a time by scribes, often with idiosyncratic changes compounding one another with every new copy. These pre-Gutenberg transcriptions seldom cited the original authors, which made for confusion about authorship that still confounds scholars.

- **Commercialization.** Printed works became profitable, with some authors attracting what today would be called *brand recognition.* For the first time, authorship was profitable, publishing too. Copyright laws were created to protect the financial interests of the author or publisher by discouraging wanton copying.

- **Pagination.** With printing, page numbering became practical and useful. This was in contrast to hand-scribed works in which page breaks were a function of penmanship. Results included the first indexing and tables of content, both essential in optimizing the usefulness of printed material.

- **Religion.** Most written works in Europe before Gutenberg had been produced under church auspices to perpetuate religious beliefs. With secularization and commercialization of the printed word, the church leaders found they had to share their historic dominance in shaping Western civilization and values.

Industrial Revolution Effects

vellum
A treated animal skin used in early printing

The quality of Gutenberg's Bibles was incredible given the elements available. Consider the paper. Gutenberg printed some of his Bibles on **vellum,** a treated animal skin. Ink? From

◼ Chinese as a Problem

The first print culture, far preceding Gutenberg, was in Asia. Sometime before the year 600 the Chinese were using woodblocks, carved in reverse, to apply images with ink. The process is called *negative relief printing.* The Chinese also invented paper, which was an ideal medium.

With woodblock printing the Chinese produced hundreds of books on subjects as diverse as science, math and philosophy. It was printing that added to the influence of Confucius, whose teachings date to 500 years B.C.

But the Chinese printing technology was stalled. The Chinese written language comprised more than 5,000 basic characters. Literacy requires knowledge of 3,000 to 4,000 characters. In contrast, Latin and derivative languages like Gutenberg's German had an alphabet of only 26 characters. For the Chinese, their language had too many components for movable type to be a practical possibility.

charcoal residue and linseed oil he stirred his own concoction. Gutenberg's ink still amazes museum curators for its blackness, even these centuries later.

Pulp Paper.   Although taken for granted today, paper and ink were scarce for centuries. When the **Industrial Revolution** approached its stride in the early 1800s, machines took over production of all kinds of products, including paper. Machine-made paper was introduced in 1803, manufactured from cotton and linen rags. The transition to wood pulp as the main ingredient occurred in 1840 with incredible cost efficiencies. Pulp-based paper helped fuel unprecedented production of printed materials. The term *pulp fiction* took hold for low-cost books for mass audiences. The first newspapers for mass audiences also were dependent on the new factory-produced pulp paper.

The simultaneous development of a petroleum industry made for cheaper inks.

High-Speed Presses.   Products of the Industrial Revolution included presses that, like all the early machinery of the era, were powered by steam. The greatest innovation was the rotary press, which was perfected by **Richard Hoe,** whose name remains synonymous with high-speed printing production. An 1876 Hoe rotary press could produce 30,000 impressions an hour. In contrast, four centuries earlier with Gutenberg-style presses, printers could turn out 500 copies at most on a good day. Today, presses can print 160,000 copies an hour.

Paper Reels.   Production was further accelerated when technology made it possible to manufacture paper in rolls. Paper could be pulled through the press continually and then cut and folded—all in a single operation in presses that were becoming more sophisticated all the time. Earlier, for four centuries going back to Gutenberg, paper was fed into the press one sheet at a time. It was a momentous event in the history of mass media technology when the Philadelphia *Inquirer* installed the first automatic reel-fed rotary press in 1865.

Typesetting.   The Gutenberg process of hand-plucking metal-alloy characters and assembling them into words, paragraphs and pages was automated in 1884 by **Omar Mergenthaler.** With Mergenthaler's **Linotype** machine, a person at a 90-character keyboard could set in motion a process that created a mold for an entire line of type, poured melted lead into the mold and then, after a few seconds of cooling, dropped the lines of type into sequences for assembly into a page. After each line was created, the molds for the individual characters were automatically disassembled for use again.

Industrial Revolution
Use of machinery, notably steam-powered, that facilitated mass production beginning in late 1700s and through 1800s

pulp fiction
Derisive term for cheap novels

Richard Hoe
Perfected rotary press 1840

Omar Mergenthaler
Invented Linotype typesetting machine 1886

Linotype
Complex machine with typewriter-like keyboard to set type into line from molten lead

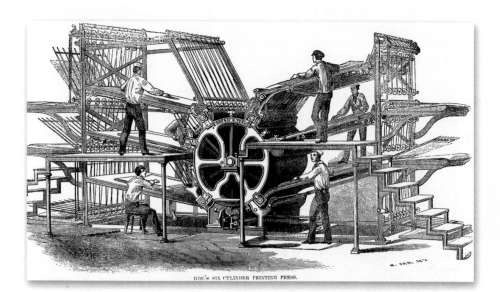

▲ **Rotary Press.** *Perfected by Richard Hoe, rotary presses had type molded onto a cylinder that rolled over sheets of paper that were fed into the press. This 1846 model was for the Philadelphia Ledger. Another major innovation was paper in rolls. Sheets then were not fed individually through the press.*

Post-Industrial Age improvements have included typesetting processes, some similar to a computer printer.

Even so, the printed media have direct lineage from Gutenberg, with enhancements from the Industrial Revolution and evolving technology. Books, newspapers and magazines remain mostly word-driven media. Production, however, now relies on chemical and electronic technology. Steam-powered presses? Electricity replaced steam a long time ago.

Print-Visual Integration

Although visuals are not a mass medium, photography increased the communicative power of the printed word in the late 1800s. Experiments at Cornell University in the 1870s led to technology that could mass-produce images in books, newspapers and magazines. This new technology, pioneered by **Frederick Ives**, was the **halftone**. Ives divided a photograph into a microscopic grid, each tiny square having a raised dot that registered a separate tonal gray from a photograph—the bigger the dot, the more ink it would transfer to the paper and the darker the gray. At the typical reading distance of 14 inches, the human eye can't make out the grid, but the eye can see the image created by the varying grays. Although crude, this was the first halftone.

At the New York *Daily Graphic*, **Steve Horgan** adapted Ives' process to high-speed printing. In 1880, the *Graphic* published a halftone image of Shantytown—a break from the line drawings that were the *Graphic*'s original claim to distinction. Ives later improved on Horgan's process, and visual communication joined the Age of Mass Communication.

Magazines, notably the early *National Geographic*, experimented with halftones too. When *Time* founder **Henry Luce** launched *Life* in 1934, photography moved the magazine industry into new visual ground. The oversize pages with slick, super-white paper gave *Life* photographs an intensity not possible with newsprint. *Life* captured the spirit of the times photographically and demonstrated that a wide range of human experiences could be recorded visually. Both real life and *Life* could be shocking. In 1938 a *Life* photo spread on human birth was so shocking for the time that censors succeeded in banning the issue in 33 cities.

Frederick Ives
Invented halftone in 1876

halftone
Reproduction of an image in which the various tones of gray or color produced by variously sized dots of ink

Steve Horgan
Adapted halftone technology for high-speed newspaper presses

National Geographic
Pioneer magazine in using visuals

Henry Luce
Magazine innovator whose *Life* exploited photographs for their visual impact

▲ **Frederick Ives.**

◄ **Halftone.** *The halftone process, invented by Frederick Ives, uses variously sized dots to transfer ink to paper. The dots are invisible except under close examination. At a reading distance, however, the bigger dots leave darker impressions, the smaller dots a lighter impression. The effect looks like the varying tones in a photograph.*

- Do any media technology innovations since Johannes Gutenberg rival the transformational impact of his movable metal type?
- What was the link between Gutenberg and the scientific revolution of the 1600s and 1700s? And with the later Industrial Revolution?
- How would your study habits be affected if your textbooks had no tables of content? Or indexes?
- What facilitated the integration of word-driven and illustration-driven media messages?

Chemistry Technology

STUDY PREVIEW

Historically, photography is rooted in chemistry. The distinct technology had come of age by the time of the U.S. Civil War, creating a new kind of archival record. When techniques were devised to integrate photography into Gutenberg legacy printing, the mass media suddenly were in a new visual era. Movies also drew on chemical technology but evolved along a separate path.

Photography

The 1727 discovery that light causes silver nitrate to darken was a breakthrough in mass communication. Scientists dabbled with the chemical for the next century. Then in 1826 **Joseph Níepce** found a way to capture and preserve an image on light-sensitive material. Photography was born—a chemical process for creating and recording a visual message. The technology was sufficiently established by the 1860s to create a new type of historical archive. Teams of photographers organized by **Mathew Brady** created an incredible visual record, much of it horrific, of the U.S. Civil War.

Joseph Níepce
Preserved a visual image on light-sensitive material

Mathew Brady
Created photographic record of U.S. Civil War

▲ **Visual Impact.** *With new technology in the late 1800s that could produce photographs on printing presses, newspapers and magazines suddenly had new potency in telling stories. The potential of photography to send printed media in a new direction was illustrated with painfully gory battlefield scenes from the Civil War. This visual perspective on war was mostly the work of teams of photographers organized by entrepreneur Mathew Brady.*

▲ **Mathew Brady.**

■ 3-D: Next Big Thing?

Jeffrey Katzenberg. *He's been called the Evangelist of 3-D. Indeed, as Katzenberg notes, four of the 10 films released in 3-D in 2010 ranked among Hollywood's top money-makers. Expect 3-D TV to blossom next, he says.*

Jeffrey Katzenberg hardly invented 3-D, but the future of three-dimensional media may be in his hands. As chief of Hollywood movie-maker DreamWorks Animation, Katzenberg is in the vanguard promoting 3-D not only in movies but television, video games, cell phone screens, even billboards. To Katzenberg, all our media of the future will be seen through the illusion of 3-D. Except, of course, radio and other sound-alone media.

Is Katzenberg onto something? Or is he ignoring the bumpy history of 3-D?

Just after Christmas 1922, Cornell University inventor **Laurens Hammond** showed *Radio-Man,* the first commercial 3-D movie. Hammond enhanced the illusion of depth perception by flashing two slightly offset images simultaneously, one for the right eye, one for the left. The technology, called **stereoscopy,** had roots almost a century earlier with 3-D illusions imposed on still photography. Despite Hammond's breakthrough work with *Radio-Man,* he ran into an obstacle. Only one theater, the Selwyn in New York was equipped with special projection and viewing devices needed for 3-D. *Radio-Man* had a short run, although it was later released in 2-D. As movie technology, 3-D went dormant.

In the 1950s a rash of 3-D movies were issued. Moviegoers were supplied with throw-away eyeglasses with orange and blue lenses. But it was awkward, plus there were extra production expenses and a mish-mash of rival projection systems. Years later, Katzenberg, at DreamWorks had become fascinated with 3-D. In 2009 the company released the first 3-D movie that was directly produced in a stereoscopic 3-D format— instead of being converted into 3-D after completion. That same year James Cameron's blockbuster *Avatar* was released. With Hollywood abuzz about *Avatar's* success, Katzenberg announced that all DreamWorks animated films would be 3-D henceforth. While banging the drums for more 3-D movies, Katzenberg hedged his bets by also issuing 2-D versions.

Katzenberg's enthusiasm may be a signal of the future. But he faces obstacles. One is the same as doomed *Radio-Man* in 1922—too few screens. Only about 15 percent of U.S. screens can show 3-D. To address the issue, Katzenberg has persuaded studio and movie-chain executives to share costs for installing more 3-D-enabled projectors. In 2011 about 500 more projectors were being installed a month. With 39,000 screens in the United States, there remains a ways to go.

Another obstacle: Many critics see 3-D as a gimmicky detraction. Influential reviewer Roger Ebert is unequivocal: "I Hate 3-D." Indeed, the glasses aren't fun. Too, it can be argued that the dazzle of the technology intrudes into the movie-viewing experience. Katzenberg dismisses the critics: "With 3-D, we give them the feeling of being immersed in the stories and characters." Katzenberg says that 3-D isn't going to go away and that critics can't ignore the phenomenon and DreamWorks' own run of 3-D successes—*Shrek Forever After, How to Train Your Dragon* and *Megamind,* all 2010 blockbusters. About Ebert, Katzenberg is mocking: "He can see *Megamind* in 2-D."

Another obstacle is consumer resistance. Tickets for 3-D run $3.25 higher.

Also, in a post-*Avatar* rush to 3-D, some producers slapped movies into 3-D after they had been filmed. Characters looked like cardboard cutouts—no dazzle, just distraction.

The post-*Avatar* enthusiasm also saw 3-D home televisions and games introduced. There wasn't enough 3-D content available to drive these sales beyond $1.2 billion in 2010. But, says Katzenberg, just wait.

What Do You Think?

In your experience, are moviegoers sufficiently attracted to 3-D to pay more for tickets and put up with the annoyance of special eyeglasses?

What are the prospects for Katzenberg's enthusiasm for 3-D movies to take root in other delivery systems, like television?

Over the next half-century, technology developed for reproducing photographs on printing presses. Brady's legacy was issued in book form. Emotional advertisements stirred sales, promising lifelike images of "soldiers dashing and flags flying and horses leaping all over." Hundreds of thousands of copies were sold to a generation of Civil War veterans and their families. By the time World War I began, however, the market was saturated. Also, people had new gruesome photographs from the European front. New grisliness replaced the old.

Movies

The motion picture, a late-1800s development, was rooted in chemistry too. The new media linked the lessons of photography to the recognition of a phenomenon called **persistence of vision**. It had come to be recognized in the late 1800s that the human eye retains an image for a fraction of a second. If a series of photographs captures motion at split-second intervals, those images, if flipped quickly, will trick the eye into perceiving continuous motion. For most people the illusion of motion begins with 14 photos per second.

Cameras.   At the research labs of prolific inventor and entrepreneur Thomas Edison, **William Dickson** developed a camera that captured 16 images per second. It was the first workable motion picture camera. Dickson used celluloid film perfected by **George Eastman**, who had popularized amateur photography with his Kodak camera. By 1891 Edison had begun producing movies.

Projectors.   Edison's movies were viewed by looking into a box. In France the **Lumière brothers**, Auguste and Louis, brought projectors to motion pictures. By running the film in front of a specially aimed, powerful light bulb, the Lumières projected movie images onto a wall. In 1895 they opened an exhibition hall in Paris—the first movie house. Edison recognized the commercial advantage in projection and patented a projector that he put on the market the next year.

APPLYING YOUR MEDIA LITERACY

- **Explain this assertion: Photography and words are not mass media but are essential for the media to exploit their potential.**
- **How does persistence of vision work in movies? How about in 3-D movies?**

Laurens Hammond
First 3-D movie *Radio-Man* 1922

stereoscopy
Early 3-D technology that flashed two slightly offset images simultaneously, one for the right eye, one for the left.

persistence of vision
Fast-changing still photos create the illusion of movement

William Dickson
Developed first movie camera

George Eastman
Developed celluloid film

Lumière brothers
Opened first motion picture exhibition hall

Electrical Technology

STUDY PREVIEW Electricity transformed people's lives beginning in the late 1800s with dazzling applications to all kinds of activities. The modern music industry sprang up around these new systems for recording and playing back sound. Radio and television, both rooted in electricity, were among the technologies around which new industries were created.

Electricity as Transformational

The harnessing of electricity had a profound impact on American life beginning in the late 1800s. The infrastructure for an electricity-based lifestyle was wholly in place half a century later when, in the 1930s, the government launched a massive project to extend electricity-distribution networks to every end-of-the-road farmhouse. During this

▲ **Granville Woods.** *New possibilities for communication were suggested in his invention of railway telegraphy in 1887. The invention allowed train conductors to communicate with each other in transit and with dispatchers.*

phonograph
First sound recording and playback machine

Thomas Edison
Inventor of phonograph

Emile Berliner
Inventor of process for mass production of recorded music

Joseph Maxfield
Introduced electrical sound recording in 1920s

telegraph
Electricity-enabled long-distance communication, used mostly from Point A to Point B

Samuel Morse
Inventor of telegraph 1844

period, inventors and tinkerers came up with entirely new media of mass communication that went beyond books, newspapers and magazines. In the span of a generation, people found themselves marveling at a dizzying parade of inventions ranging from the light bulb to streetcars. Among the new delights were phonographs, radio and then television.

Consider how much these new media transformed lifestyles. A person who as a child had read into the night by kerosene lantern could in adulthood be watching television.

Recordings

Sound recording did not begin as an electronic medium. The first recording machine, the **phonograph** invented by **Thomas Edison** in 1877, was a cylinder wrapped in tinfoil that was rotated as a singer shouted into a large metal funnel. The funnel channeled the vibrations against a diaphragm, which fluttered and thus cut grooves into the rotating tin. When the cylinder was rotated in a playback machine, a stylus picked up sound from the varying depths of the groove. To hear the sound, a person placed his or her ear next to a megaphone-like horn and rotated the cylinder.

Inherent in Edison's system, however, was a major impediment for commercial success: A recording could not be duplicated, let alone mass-produced. In 1887 **Emile Berliner** introduced a sturdy metal disk to replace Edison's foil-wrapped cylinder. From the metal disk Berliner made a model and then poured thermoplastic material into the mold. When the material hardened, Berliner had a near perfect copy of the original disk—and he could make hundreds of them. The process was primitive by today's standards—entirely mechanical, nothing electronic about it. But it was a marvel at the time.

Those early machines eventually incorporated electrical microphones and electrical amplification for reproducing sound. These innovations, mostly by **Joseph Maxfield** of Bell Laboratories in the 1920s, had superior sensitivity. To listen, it was no longer a matter of putting an ear to a mechanical amplifying horn that had only narrow frequency responses. Instead, loudspeakers amplified the sound electromagnetically.

Electromagnetic Spectrum

The introduction of electricity into mass communication occurred with the **telegraph.** After experimenting with sending electrical impulses by wire for more than a decade, **Samuel Morse** talked Congress into spending $30,000 to string electricity-conducting wires 41 miles from Washington to Baltimore. In 1844, using his code of dots and dashes, Morse sent the famous message "What hath God wrought." The demonstration's high visibility showed that real-time communication was possible over great distances. Morse's instantaneous-communication gizmo overcame an impediment of the printed word—the inherent delay of producing and delivering a physical product.

The possibilities of the Morse invention electrified people—and investors. Within only four years, by 1848, promoters had rounded up the money to construct a system that linked the most populous parts of the United States, up and down the eastern seaboard and inland as far as Chicago and Milwaukee. By 1866 a cable had been laid on the floor of the Atlantic Ocean to connect North America with Europe for telegraphic communication.

Although telegraph messages basically were Point A to Point B communication, not mass communication, the way was opened for applying electricity for communication to broad audiences—perhaps even without wires.

Wireless. The suggestion of wireless communication was inherent in a discovery by **Granville Woods** in 1887 of a way to send messages to and from moving trains. Railway telegraphy, as it was called, allowed dispatchers to communicate in real-time with trains and prevent collisions. Although the invention was intended for electric trains, which drew their power from overhead lines and on-ground rails, Woods' work also posed the question: Could communication be untethered?

For hundreds of years scientists had had a sense that lightning emitted invisible but powerful electrical waves. The word *radi,* from the Latin *radius,* was used because these waves rippled out from the lightning. A German scientist, **Heinrich Hertz**, confirmed the existence of these waves in 1887 by constructing two separate coils of wire several feet apart. When electricity was applied to one coil, it electrified the other. Thus, electricity indeed could be sent through the air on what soon were called Hertzian waves.

The scientific journals, full of theories about Hertzian waves, intrigued a young nobleman in Italy, **Guglielmo Marconi**. Whether he realized it or not, Marconi's reading was educating him as an engineer. Obsessed, refusing to take time even for food, he locked himself in an upstairs room at his father's estate near Bologna and contemplated and fiddled. By grounding Hertz's coils to the earth, Marconi discovered in 1895 that he could send messages farther and farther. Soon he was ringing a bell across the room by remote control, then downstairs, then 300 feet away—the first wireless messages.

Marconi suddenly was hopeful that he was disproving the notion among scientists at the time that Hertzian waves could not penetrate solid objects, let alone Earth. He devised an antenna, which further extended transmission range. Also, he hooked up a Morse telegraph key, which already was widely used to tap out dots and dashes for transmission on telegraph lines. Marconi had his brother go three miles away over a hill with instructions to fire a rifle if the Morse letter *s*, dot-dot-dot, came through a receiver. Metaphorically, it was a shot heard around the world.

Heinrich Hertz
Demonstrated existence of radio waves 1887

Guglielmo Marconi
Transmitted first wireless message 1895

Philo Farnsworth

Philo Farnsworth was 11 when his family loaded three covered wagons and moved to a farm near Rigby in eastern Idaho. Cresting a ridge, young Farnsworth, at the reins of one wagon, surveyed the homestead below and saw wires linking the buildings. "This place has electricity!" he exclaimed. Philo obsessed about the electricity, and soon he was an expert at fixing anything electrical that went wrong.

The day when his family settled near Rigby in 1919 was a pivotal moment in young Farnsworth's life that led to technology on which television is based.

The next pivotal moment came two years later when Philo Farnsworth was 13. By happenstance he ran across a magazine article saying that scientists were working on ways to add pictures to radio but they couldn't figure out how. He then went out to hitch the horses to a harvesting machine to bring in the potatoes. As he guided the horses back and forth across the field, up one row, down the next, he visualized how moving pictures could be captured live and transmitted to a faraway place. If the light that enables people to see could be converted to electrons and then transmitted one at a time, but very quickly as a beam, back and forth on a surface, then, perhaps, transmitting pictures over the airwaves could work.

The ideas simmered a few months and then, when he was 14, Farnsworth chalked a complicated diagram for "electronic television" on his chemistry teacher's blackboard.

Farnsworth's native intelligence, earnestness and charm helped to win over the people around him. When he was 19, working in Salt Lake City, Farnsworth found a man with connections to San Francisco

Television Inventor. *Thirteen-year-old Philo Farnsworth came up with the concept of live transmission of moving images by zipping electrons back and forth on a screen—just as he was doing, back and forth, in harvesting a potato field. Barely in his 20s, Farnsworth moved from theory to practice with what he called an image dissector.*

investors. With the investors' backing, the third pivotal moment in Farnsworth's work occurred, he set up a lab in Los Angeles, and later in San Francisco, and put his drawings and theories to work. In 1927, with handblown tubes and hand-soldered connections, Farnsworth had a gizmo he called the image dissector. It picked up the image of a glass slide and transmitted it. The Idaho farm boy had invented television.

Although Marconi didn't realize it at the time, the hill separating him from his brother did, in fact, impede radio waves. But the hill blocked only straight-line waves. Other waves emanated upward and ricocheted off the ionosphere back to Earth. Thus radio transmissions go far, far beyond the horizon. Marconi didn't understand the phenomenon at the time, but he saw immediate business potential for establishing communication with ships at sea. Hitherto, ships had been limited to semaphore flags and flashing mirrors which, of course, meant that ships were incommunicado with anything over the horizon. Marconi made a fortune.

Television. After radio, television seemed a logical next step in media technology. There was agreement that television signals could be transmitted on the airwaves somewhat like radio. The trick, though, was to capture movement visually for transmission. Physicists and engineers at major universities research labs toyed for years to create "radio with pictures," as early television was called.

MEDIAtimeline

TECHNOLOGY MILESTONES

MOVABLE TYPE
Mass communication began with the Gutenberg printing process (1446)

PRINTING
Printing presses with Gutenberg technology in every European city (1500)

PIVOTAL EVENTS

- Columbus discovered Americas (1492)
- First African slaves arrived in Americas (1502)
- Michelangelo completed Statue of David (1504)
- Copernicus proposed sun as center of solar system (1512)
- Machiavelli wrote The Prince (1513)
- Luther sparked Protestant Reformation (1517)
- William Shakespeare (1564–1616)

Gutenberg

TECHNOLOGY MILESTONES

BOOKS
Cambridge Press issued first book in British North American colonies (1640)
Cambridge Press also issued religious pamphlets, materials

NEWSPAPERS
Ben Harris printed *Publick Occurrences*, first newspaper in the English colonies (1690)

PIVOTAL EVENTS

- Rembrandt van Rijn (1606–1669)
- Pilgrims established colony (1620)
- First English dictionary (1623)
- John Milton wrote Areopagitica (1644)
- Isaac Newton built telescope (1669)
- French and Indian wars (1689–1763)

Rotary press

TECHNOLOGY MILESTONES

MAGAZINES
Andrew Bradford and Benjamin Franklin introduced competing magazines in British colonies (1741)
Meanwhile, weekly newspapers existed in larger colonial cities, reprinting items from Europe and each other

PIVOTAL EVENTS

- Johann Sebastian Bach (1685–1750)
- French found New Orleans (1718)
- Daniel Defoe wrote Robinson Crusoe (1719)
- Peak of Little Ice Age (1750)
- Industrial Revolution began (1760s)
- Revolutionary War (1775–1781)
- Washington presidency (1789–1797)

Early 3-D audience

1400s/1500s

1600s

1700s

But it was a south Idaho farm boy, **Philo Farnsworth**, who, at age 13 while out plowing the field, came up with a concept that led to his invention of television. Plowing the fields, back and forth in furrows, the young Farnsworth had an epiphany. Applying what he knew about electricity from science magazines and his own tinkering, he envisioned a camera-like device that would pick up light reflected off a scene, with the image being sent radio-like to a receiver that would convert the varying degrees of light in the image and zap them one at a time across stacked horizontal lines on a screen, back and forth so rapidly that the image on the screen would appear to the human eye as real as a photograph. And then another electron would be zapped across the screen in, so to speak, "furrows," to replace the first image—with images coming so quickly that the eye would perceive them as motion. Farnsworth called his device an **image dissector**, which literally was what it did.

Philo Farnsworth
Inventor of television

image dissector
First device in early television technology

TECHNOLOGY MILESTONES

RECORDING
Thomas Edison introduced phonograph, which could record and play back sound (1877)
Meanwhile, the book, newspaper and magazine industries flourished

MOVIES
William Dickson devised motion picture camera (1888)
Meanwhile, newspapers were in their heyday as dominant medium

PIVOTAL EVENTS

- Size of United States doubled with Louisiana Purchase (1803)
- Morse invented telegraph (1844)
- U.S. Civil War (1861–1865)
- U.S. coasts linked by rail (1869)

Battle scene photography.

1800s

TECHNOLOGY MILESTONES

RADIO
Guglielmo Marconi transmitted first message by radio waves (1895)
Meanwhile, sensationalism and muckraking attracted growing newspaper and magazine audiences

TELEVISION
Philo Farnsworth discovered how to pick up moving images electronically for live transmission (1927)
Meanwhile, radio networks created national audiences unprecedented in their reach

INTERNET
U.S. military established computer network that became the Internet (1969)
Television firmly dominated as an entertainment medium and was maturing as a news medium

PIVOTAL EVENTS

- Right to vote extended to women (1920)
- Great Depression (1930s)
- World War II (1941–1945)
- Russian-Western rivalry triggered Cold War (1945)
- Humans reached moon (1969)
- Soviet empire imploded (1989)

Orbiting satellite

1900s

TECHNOLOGY MILESTONES

CONVERGENCE
Delivery of mass messages fragmented into a growing number of digital mechanisms. By and large, the historic media industries remained in place producing content

CLOUD COMPUTING
On-demand mini-programs, called apps, catch on, add function to mobile devices (2010)

TABLET COMPUTER
Apple introduced iPad (2010)

PIVOTAL EVENTS

- 9/11 terrorist attacks (2001)
- Iraq War (2003–2011)
- Hurricane Katrina (2005)
- Tōhoku, Japan earthquake and tsunami (2011)
- World population passed 7 billion (2011)
- George W. Bush presidency (2001–2009)
- Great Recession (1007–1009)
- Obama presidency (2009–)

Digital conception

2000s

Like motion picture technology invented 40 years earlier, television froze movements at fraction-of-a-second intervals and played them in fast sequence to create an illusion that, like movies, capitalized on the persistence of vision phenomenon. Unlike movies, Farnsworth did not do this with photographic technology. Television uses electronics, not chemicals. Also unlike movie technology, images recorded by a television camera are transmitted instantly to a receiving device, called a *picture tube*, or to a recording device for later transmission.

Although Farnsworth had sent the first television picture from one room in his San Francisco apartment to another in 1927, the complexities of television technology delayed its immediate development. So did national survival while Americans focused on winning World War II. By the 1950s, however, a radio-like delivery infrastructure for television was in place.

CHECKING YOUR MEDIA LITERACY

- **How does the impact of Emile Berliner's invention of the metal recording disk compare with Gutenberg's printing press?**
- **What impact did the discovery of wireless communication have on society and globalization?**
- **How is persistence of vision employed differently in television and movies?**

Current Technologies

STUDY PREVIEW | Satellite and fiber-optic technologies in the late 1900s improved the speed and reliability of delivering mass messages. These were backshop developments that were largely invisible to media consumers. Plainly visible, though, was the related advent of the internet as a new mass medium.

Orbiting Satellites

More than 50 years ago the Russians sent Sputnik into orbit, the first human-made satellite. The accomplishment ignited a rush to explore space near Earth. Technology surged. Weather forecasting became less intuitive, more scientific and many times more accurate. With geopositioning signals from satellites, maps had new, everyday applications that only Spock could have imagined. Communication was transformed too, with signals being bounced off satellites for a straight-line range that far exceeded anything possible with the existing network of ground-based relay towers located every 10 or so miles apart.

For communication, the key to utilizing satellites was the **geosynchronous orbit.** It was a concept of sci-fi author **Arthur C. Clarke,** who also was a serious scientist. Clarke figured out in 1945 that a satellite 22,300 miles above the equator would be orbiting at the same speed as Earth's rotation, thus always being above the same point below on Earth—an ideal platform for continuous service to pick up signals from Earth stations and retransmit them to other Earth stations. It was like a 22,300-mile-high relay tower. With only one relay, not hundreds, signals would move faster and with more reliability. The **Telstar** communication satellite, launched in 1960, took the first telephone signals from **uplink** stations on Earth, amplified them, and returned them to **downlink** stations. Television networks also used Telstar.

Satellite technology, however, did not change the fundamental structures of the industries that had built up around print, chemical and electronic technology. Rather, satellites were an efficient alternative for delivering traditional media products. Prime-time

geosynchronous orbit
A satellite's period of rotation that coincides perfectly with Earth's rotation

Arthur C. Clarke
Devised the concept of satellites in geosynchronous orbits for communication

Telstar
First communication satellite

uplink
A ground station that beams a signal to an orbiting communication satellite

downlink
A ground station that receives a relayed signal from a communication satellite

network programming still came from the networks. Major newspapers including *USA Today*, the *Wall Street Journal* and the New York *Times* were sending pages by satellite to remote printing plants around the country, with far-away readers picking up fresh copies as if they had just come from a press within driving distance. In short, satellite technology was important for enabling media companies to improve delivery of their products but was largely invisible to consumers.

Back to Wires

Even as possibilities with satellites were dazzling scientists, the old reliable of mass communication—the wire, sometimes called a **landline**—was in revival. A radio repair-shop owner in Astoria, Oregon, **Ed Parsons,** wired the town in 1949 to receive television signals from Seattle, which was too far away for signals to be received unless they were intercepted by a very tall antenna. From an antenna atop a hotel, Parsons sent television signals around town by copper wires strung up and down Astoria alleys. In mountainous West Virginia, entrepreneurs also were stringing up local cable systems to distribute television signals that were blocked by terrain. **Cable television,** as it was called, was a small-town success. On the television industry's radar, however, cable was merely a blip. Local cable operators only passed on signals from elsewhere. Hardly any of these cable systems created any content of their own.

The role of the cable industry changed in 1975 when the Time Inc. media empire put HBO on satellite as a programming service for local cable companies. With exclusive programming available to subscribers, cable suddenly was hot. More cable programming services, all delivered by satellite, came online. Wall Street investors poured billions of dollars into wiring major cities, where huge population masses were eager for HBO, CNN and other new programming available only through cable operators. No longer was cable merely small-town enterprise that merely relayed signals from over-air stations.

landline
A conventional telecommunications connection by cable laid across land, typically buried or on poles

Ed Parsons
Built first community-antenna television system

cable television
A television transmission system using cable rather than an over-air broadcast signal

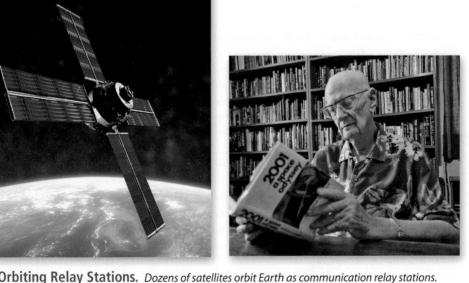

◀ Arthur C. Clarke.

▲ **Orbiting Relay Stations.** *Dozens of satellites orbit Earth as communication relay stations. The concept dates to 1945 when Arthur C. Clarke, known mostly as a science fiction writer but also a serious scientist, conceived of satellites remaining stationary above a point on Earth if their speed matched the planet's rotation. Fifteen years later, in 1960, the first communication satellite Telstar proved Clarke right.*

fiber-optic
Thin, flexible fibers of glass capable
of transmitting light signals

In the 1960s, meanwhile, Corning Glass had developed a cable that was capable of carrying light at incredible speeds—theoretically, 186,000 miles per second. The potential of these new **fiber-optic cables**, each strand carrying 60,000 messages simultaneously, was not lost on the telephone industry. So fast was the fiber-optic network that the entire *Oxford English Dictionary* could be sent in just seconds. Soon hundreds of crews with backhoes were laying fiber-optic cable to replace those copper wires that had been the backbone of landline communication. Coupled with other new technologies, notably digitization of data, the new satellite-based and fiber-optic landline communication systems enabled the introduction of the internet.

APPLYING YOUR MEDIA LITERACY

- Satellite television companies advertise they are available to homeowners anywhere in the United States as long as they have unrestricted access to the southern sky. Why south?
- What technologies transformed the sleepy small-town cable television industry beginning in the 1970s?

Digital Integration

STUDY PREVIEW

Digital technology has brought efficiency to almost every aspect of human lifestyles, including products from traditional mass media companies. A wholly new medium, the internet, is built entirely on binary digital signals. This newest media technology is melding the once-distinctive delivery systems of many products from old-line media companies.

Semiconductor

Researchers at AT&T's Bell Labs knew they were on to something important for telephone communication in 1947. Engineers Jack Bardeen, Walter Brittain and William Shockley had devised glasslike silicon chips—pieces of sand, really—that could be used to respond to a negative or a positive electrical charge. The tiny chips, called **semiconductors**, functioned very rapidly as on/off switches. With chips, the human voice could be reduced to a stream of digits—1 for on, 0 for off—and then transmitted as rapid-fire pulses and reconstructed so quickly at the other end of the line that the sound was like the real thing. Bardeen, Brittain and Shockley won a Nobel Prize.

Little did they realize that they had laid the groundwork for revolutionizing not just telephonic communication but also mass communication.

Bell Labs then took digital on-off binary signals to a new level. By breaking messages into pieces and transmitting them in spurts, Bell suddenly, in 1965, could send multiple messages simultaneously. People marveled that 51 calls could be carried at the same time on a single line. The capacity of telephone systems was dramatically increased without a single new mile of wire being laid.

The potential of the evolving technology was no less than revolutionary. Not only could the human voice be reduced to binary digits for transmission but so could text and even images. Futurologists asked: "Who needs paper?" Might digitization even replace the still newfangled technology of television that had flowed from Philo Farnsworth's pioneering work?

Digitization, alas, did not replace Gutenberg-based print media. The core media industries are still pigeonholed easily into their traditional categories—books, newspapers, magazines, movies, sound recordings, radio and television. The technology did, however, spawn new media industries built around the new technologies. America Online was in the first generation. Now Google, YouTube and Twitter are leaders. Tomorrow? Stay tuned.

◀ Jack Bardeen, Walter Brittain and William Shockley.

▲ **Nobel Winners.** *The 1956 Nobel Prize went to the inventors of the semiconductor. They had devised tiny, low-cost crystals that could be used as switches to transmit data that had been converted to binary codes of 0s and 1s. Digital communication followed, with innovations that led to today's global communication networks.*

Internet Origins

Another building block for digitized communication was the **internet**. It originated with the military, which saw potential in digitized communication for a non-centralized network. Without a central hub, the military figured that a non-centralized system could sustain itself in a nuclear attack. The system, called ARPAnet, short for Advanced Research Projects Agency Network, was up and running in 1969. At first, the network linked military contractors and universities so that researchers could exchange information. In 1983 the National Science Foundation, whose mandate is to promote science, took over and involved more universities, which tied their own internal computer-based communication systems into the larger network. As a backbone system that interconnected networks, the term *internet* fit.

internet
High-capacity global telephone network that links computers

Media Convergence

The construction of a high-capacity network in the 1990s, which we call the internet, is emerging as the delivery vehicle of choice for any and all media products. The technological basis, called **digital**, is distinctive. Messages, whether text, audio, image or a combination, are broken into millions of bits of data. The bits are transmitted one at a time over the internet, which has incredibly high capacity and speed, then reassembled for reception at the other end. The process is almost instantaneous for text, whose digital bits of data are small and easily accommodated. Audio and visual messages can take longer because far more data bits are required to reconstruct a message at the reception point.

A digitization revolution, called **media convergence**, is in progress.

digital
Technology through which media messages are coded into 1s and 0s for delivery transmission and then decoded into their original appearance

media convergence
Melding of print, electronic and photographic media into digitized form

Distribution. The internet has unmatchable efficiency in delivering messages. In contrast, a newspaper company needs a fleet of trucks and drivers for predawn runs from the production point to intermediate distribution points. There, individual carriers pick up papers for delivery to individual customers. Magazine companies rely on the postal system, which takes at least a day and countless gallons of fuel for delivery. Traditional book publishers have massive inventories, which require expensive warehousing, and then high shipping costs. Although books, newspapers and magazines have not vanished from the media landscape, these companies are shifting to delivering their content over the internet.

Tim Berners-Lee

Original Webmaster. *Tim Berners-Lee and his associates at a Swiss research facility created new internet coding in 1989, dubbing it the World Wide Web. Today the coding is the heart of global computer communication.*

Single-handedly, **Tim Berners-Lee** invented the World Wide Web. Then, unlike many entrepreneurs who have used the internet to amass quick fortunes, Berners-Lee devoted his life to refining the web as a medium of communication open to everyone for free. Berners-Lee, an Oxford engineer, came up with the web concept because he couldn't keep track of all his notes on various computers in various places. It was 1989. Working at CERN, a physics lab in Switzerland, he proposed a system to facilitate scientific research by letting scientists' computers tap into each other.

In a way, the software worked like the brain. In fact, Berners-Lee said that the idea was to keep "track of all the random associations one comes across in real life and brains are supposed to be so good at remembering, but sometimes mine wouldn't."

Working with three software engineers, Berners-Lee had a demonstration up and running within three months. As Berners-Lee traveled the globe to introduce the web at scientific conferences, the potential of what he had devised became clear. The web was a system that could connect all information with all other information.

The key was a relatively simple computer language known as HTML, short for "hypertext markup language," which, although it has evolved over the years, remains the core of the web. Berners-Lee also developed the addressing system that allows computers to find each other. Every web-connected computer has a unique address, a universal resource locator (URL). For it all to work, Berners-Lee also created a protocol that actually links computers: HTTP, short for "hypertext transfer protocol."

It's hard to overstate Berners-Lee's accomplishment. The internet is the information infrastructure that likely will, given time, eclipse other media. Some liken Berners-Lee to Johannes Gutenberg, who 400 years earlier had launched the Age of Mass Communication with the movable type that made mass production of the written word possible.

Tim Berners-Lee
Created hypertext markup language and World Wide Web

Devices. With a single device, consumers can pick up media content whatever its origin. The device can be a cell phone, an electronic notepad, or a desktop or laptop computer. What the devices have in common is an internet connection.

Distinctions. Digitization is breaking down old distinctions. Newspaper people increasingly talk about being in the news business, not the newspaper business. Radio people do likewise, talking about being in the music business, not the radio business. Publishers talk of intellectual property, not books. The new emphasis is on content—not the medium. Consumers acknowledge this underlying shift. Instead of reading a newspaper, for example, more people talk about reading news. Instead of watching television, as they said in the old days, people today say they watch a sitcom. This makes sense as digital devices supplant Gutenberg print technology and combine radio, television, movie and recording reception appliances into single devices.

Production. For almost a century, print media publishers have recognized their inherent disadvantage in production costs. Presses for a big-city daily require millions of dollars in investment. In contrast, as publishers have seen it, albeit simplistically, their broadcast counterparts merely flick a switch. But with digitized delivery, the broadcast equivalent of a printing press, even transmitter and tower maintenance seem hopelessly expensive. Production costs for newspaper content also can be cut drastically with internet delivery.

Democratization. The relatively low cost of internet production and delivery may have its greatest impact in broadening the sources of media content. Almost anybody can afford to create messages for internet delivery and, theoretically anyway, reach everyone on the planet who has a reception device. In contrast to a generation ago, the price of entry into the mass media no longer requires millions of dollars for production facilities and millions more for

■ "Technologizing" The Written Word

Walter Ong. *The Jesuit scholar Walter Ong saw the internet as a modern-day "technologizing" of the written word. Reading online, as an emerging norm, could render Gutenberg-based print media as obsolete.*

Great drama with high stakes is playing out in mass media. Will any of the established media industries, some with technology going back 550 years to Gutenberg, survive into this new age of internet delivery? The question applies not only to ink-on-paper media but also to the television industry and all the post-Gutenberg technologies that staked their claim on the media landscape in the 20th century.

When these newcomers arrived, each seemed a serious challenger to ink-on-paper industries. But print media held their own. Entering the 21st century, seven identifiable industries—books, newspapers, magazines, audio recording, movies, radio and television—had pretty much settled into a comfy coexistence. With distinct products, each industry was economically sustainable, indeed highly profitable.

With Marc Andreessen's Netscape browser in the mid-1990s, the internet burst into the media mix. History would suggest that this new kid on the block would find a niche amid existing media industries, as had television and all the other 20th century newcomers.

Everything changed with the internet. Word-centric ink-on-paper media lost their monopoly on the written word. As literary and cultural historian Walter Ong put it, the printed word suddenly was "technologized in a new way." With the internet, people are reading onscreen as easily as on paper if not easier.

Too, the internet lends itself to delivery of sound, visuals and video. Watch out television, movies, CDs and radio.

Today the seven traditional media industries have less need for traditional production mechanisms like printing presses and broadcast transmitters. Perhaps too late, perhaps not, these traditional media are moving to internet delivery. This process is called media convergence, with the old media companies turning to the internet as a common one-size-fits-all delivery platform.

The problem of this media convergence is proving two-fold for traditional media industries:

- Old distinctions that identified media platforms fade online. Old niches are gone. Magazines don't compete only with other magazines anymore. Or newspapers with other newspapers. Online, every media product is equally accessible with a click.
- Products of the traditional media industries are in an endless online sea of competing products. Although there is room for all, the market is finite. There are only 7 billion pairs of eyeballs on the planet, all limited to 24 hours, no more, for media consumption. And people do need time to sleep, eat and earn a living.

While doomsayers doubt whether traditional mass media industries will survive the convergence to the internet, at least not as we know them, it may be too early to write epitaphs. We've had old media written off prematurely before:

1920s: "In this age of cinema, who will read novels anymore?" "Why pick up a newspaper when radio can deliver news quicker?"

1950s: "Radio will die now that all the good shows have moved to television." "Now that most national advertising has gone to television, magazines cannot survive." "Television will render movies so passé."

Those dire forecasts proved wrong. The doom-and-gloom forecasters had missed the fact that all the media, new and old, were being buoyed by four cultural, social and economic phenomena that marked the 20th century:

- Population grew significantly, enlarging the market for media products.
- Work weeks shrank to a standard 40 hours, creating more discretionary time for people to spend with media.
- Public interest swelled in a broad range of political and social issues, as well as in sports and other diversions that mass media were uniquely suited to satisfy.
- Explosive growth of the consumer economy vastly strengthened the financial base of media industries that carried advertising.

In the fog of the moment, the long-term positive effects of these phenomena were missed by the analysts. Their doubts were misplaced. The question today is whether we are missing something, as did those earlier media prognosticators. Will media convergence indeed not be the end of mass media as we know them?

Technological convergence is upending media infrastructures. The end is near for media industries that once had secure niches but which are now in direct competition with each other on the internet.

POINT COUNTER POINT

Media industries have always adapted to new technology and survived, indeed thrived. This adaptation process probably is occurring now, although hard to perceive.

DEEPENING YOUR MEDIA LITERACY

EXPLORE THE ISSUE: Search for the Tribune Company bankruptcy and for current information on the difficulties of the parent company of the Chicago *Tribune*, Los Angeles *Times*, superstation WGN and other media entities.

DIG DEEPER: Search for explanations on what went wrong at one of the historically strongest U.S. media companies.

WHAT DO YOU THINK? How much of the Tribune Company's woes are due to the internet? What steps has the company taken to counter the internet's drain on its audiences and advertising revenue? What are the prospects ahead?

startup costs, including costs for personnel. Ask any blogger or garage band. Media moguls are struggling to identify ways to maintain their dominance. We are in a turbulent environment of change that's still playing out but that has been described, perhaps with prescience, perhaps prematurely, as the democratization of mass communication.

Cloud Computing

Computing devices for everyday people have proliferated. Desktop computers have been joined by laptops with plenty of storage capacity and at less than five pounds very portable. Tablets like iPads are even lighter and more portable. Smartphones perform many functions of a computer cradled in your palm.

The Cloud. The miniaturization of devices, some only a few ounces, has been facilitated by cloud computing. These devices draw data as it's needed from an external source—a cloud, as it's called. So rather than 10,000 music files stored in your computer, your songs are available on-demand for instant downloading one at a time.

Cloud computing is like an electrical grid. When you flick on a light switch, you don't much care whether the electricity originated at the Grand Coulee Dam on the Columbia River or any of thousands of other interlinked power-generating sites. Your electricity is delivered seamlessly. For most people, similarly, it doesn't matter whether their favorite music is stored inside their three-ounce smartphone or delivered from a cloud somewhere whenever they want to listen. With cloud computing, devices themselves can be even lighter. The size of the internal hard drive, once the holy grail in measuring a computer's data-storage capacity, is becoming less relevant. And the less gadgetry inside a device, the less it weighs.

Apps. **Cloud computing** has spurred an avalanche of software applications designed for users to accomplish a singular task. An App, as these small programs are known, deliver only one service, like a calorie-counter or a single game. Thousands of Apps are free. But you can find several solitaire games downloadable at no cost, some at 99 cents and some super-duper models at $4.99. And Apps also are facilitating subscriptions. *The Wired* magazine App, for example, costs $20 for a year. A New York *Times* App is free for top news and up to $35 a month for full access,

Apps have become a huge software enterprise. The Apple iStore had 500,000 available for iPhones in 2012. More than 200,000 were available for devices using Android software.

In some ways, Apps are eclipsing the World Wide Web. The web offered universal access to any and everything that was posted online. In fact, so much was available that you needed a search engine like Google, to sort through it all. With Apps, you choose what you want.

APPLYING YOUR MEDIA LITERACY

- **How has the semiconductor transformed modern life? And mass media too?**
- **Is Tim Berners-Lee in the same league as Gutenberg? Edison? Marconi? Farnsworth?**

Technology and Mass Communication

STUDY PREVIEW | Theorists have devised models to help understand and explain the complex and mysterious technology-dependent process of mass communication. But many models, now more than 50 years old, have been outdated by rapid changes in technology. These changes have added more complexity and mystery to how mass communication works.

App
Small software program, usually for mobile devices, for a narrowly defined use

cloud computing
Providing access to databases through seamless on-demand downloading rather than storing them on a personal computer.

Lasswell Model

In the 20th century, scholars got serious about trying to understand how mass communication works. Theories came and went. One of the most useful explanations, elegant in its simplicity as an overview, was articulated in the 1950s by Yale professor **Harold Lasswell**. It is a narrative model that poses four questions: Who says what? In which **channel**? To whom? With what **effect**?

With his reference to *channel*, Lasswell clearly differentiated his model as not just another model for human communication. His channel component clearly made his model one of mass communication technology. Lasswell's channel was a technology-defined mass medium—a book, a movie, television.

The Lasswell model is easy to apply. Pick any media message, say former Vice President Al Gore's documentary *An Inconvenient Truth:*

- **Who says what?** Gore told a story based on expert testimony and recorded evidence about global warming. His message was that global warming is a human-accelerated phenomenon that threatens Earth as a habitat for life as we know it.

- **In which channel?** The documentary itself was a movie. Also, it was distributed widely in video form for home and group audiences. There also was a book bearing the same title.

- **To whom?** Although unfriendly critics tried to dismiss the work as intended for penguins, the movie's video and book quickly became best-sellers.

- **With what effect?** Public attention quickly embraced the notion that it was possible for human beings, acting quickly, to counter the deterioration of Earth as a habitable planet. Under former Governor Arnold Schwarzenegger, California shifted into high gear with new public policies to reduce greenhouse emissions. The U.S. Supreme Court upheld tougher emission standards that big industries had resisted. These were effects.

Values and Limitations of Models

For all their usefulness, models of mass communication fall short, way short, of capturing the complexities occurring in our media systems. The volume of messages is incalculable. The word *zillions* comes to mind. What we do know about the volume is that it's increasing rapidly. Nobody has come up with a model to portray the overlays and interplay of all the content moving through the mass media.

All models, whether of ships, planes, automobiles, have the same deficiency. By definition, a model is a facsimile that helps us see and understand the real thing. But no model shows everything. An aircraft engineer, for example, can create a model of an airplane's propulsion system. Although essential to illustrating how the plane will be powered, a model of its propulsion system doesn't illustrate the plane's aesthetic features, nor its ventilation system, nor its electrical system, nor any of hundreds of other important features. Engineers are able to overlay various models to show connections and interrelations—which itself is a major challenge—but far short of what it would take to illustrate all that is going on. It's the same with communication: Too much is occurring at any given nanosecond. So, like all models, mass communication models are useful illustrations but limited because there is far, far more to what's happening than can be reduced to a schematic.

Different models illustrate different aspects of the process. That the process is too complex for a single model to convey it all is clear from the Lasswell model. Sweeping as it is, the Lasswell model is far less than a detailed framework for understanding how mass communication works; but it is a starting point.

Concentric Circle Model

One of the most useful models from the late 20th century was conceived by scholars Ray Hiebert, Donald Ungurait and Thomas Bohn. It is a series of concentric rings with the source of the message at the center. The source encodes information or an idea, which then ripples outward to the outermost ring, which is the receiving audience. In between are several elements unique to the mass communication—including gatekeepers, a technologically-based

Harold Lasswell
Devised the narrative communication model

channel
The medium through which a message is sent to a mass audience

effect
The consequence of a message

medium, regulators and amplification. The model creates a framework for tracking the difficult course of a message through the mass communication process. In effect, the model portrays mass communication as an obstacle course.

Medium.   Hiebert, Ungurait and Bohn, aware that media affect messages, put the label *mass media* on one of their rings. Media make a difference. A message that lends itself to visual portrayal, like a comedian's sight gag, will fall flat on radio. The medium is indeed critical in ensuring that an outward-rippling message makes its way to the goal—an effect, which Hiebert, Ungurait and Bohn place at the outermost ring.

Amplification.   Important in understanding mass communication is knowing how a mass medium boosts a message's chance of reaching an audience and having an effect. Radio exponentially increases a commentator's audience. A printing press amplifies a message the same way. Indeed, it's the **amplification** made possible by media technology that sets *mass* communication apart from chatting with a neighbor or making a class presentation.

amplification
Giving a message a larger audience

Message Controls.   Most mass communication involves a team, usually dozens of people, sometimes hundreds. Consider video of a terrorist attack shot by an AP photographer in Afghanistan. The video passes through a complex gatekeeping process, with editors, packagers, producers and others making decisions on how much of the rough footage ends up in distribution to television stations—or whether the images will make the cut at all. **Gatekeepers** are media people who make judgments on what most merits inclusion in what is sent to networks, stations and web site operators.

gatekeepers
Media people who influence messages en route

Gatekeeping is an unavoidable function in mass communication because there is neither time nor space for all the messages that might be passed through the process. Gatekeepers are editors who decide what makes it through their gates and in what form.

Like gatekeepers, **regulators** can affect a communicator's messages substantially, but regulators are not media people. A military censor who stops a combat story is a regulator. Some regulators function more subtly than a censor but nonetheless powerfully affect messages. The Federal Communications is an example. The FCC, which regulates U.S. broadcasting, is a mighty force in its authority to grant and deny licenses to over-air stations. In 2006 FCC fines for vaguely defined indecency prompted broadcasters to rein in scriptwriters and producers who had been pushing the envelope. The regulation process can be heavy-handed. China, for example, has insisted that U.S. and other countries' media companies comply with vaguely defined but stridently enforced bans on subjects the government sees as challenges to its authority. Censorship, yes, but Google, Yahoo, StarTV and other transnational media companies eager to profit from access to potentially huge Chinese audiences have chosen to comply.

regulators
Nonmedia people who influence messages

In-Process Impediments.   If speakers slur their words, the effectiveness of their messages is jeopardized. Slurring and other impediments to the communication process before a message reaches the audience are called **noise**. In mass communication, based as it is on complex mechanical and electronic equipment, the opportunities for noise interference are countless because so many things can go wrong.

Mass communicators themselves can interfere with the success of their own messages by being sloppy. This is called semantic noise. Sloppy wording is an example. So is slurring. Channel noise is something that interferes with message transmission, such as static on the radio. Or smudged ink on a magazine page. Or a faulty microphone on a television anchor's lapel. An intrusion that occurs at the reception site is environmental noise. This includes a doorbell interrupting someone reading an article, which distracts from decoding. So would shouting kids who distract a television viewer.

noise
Impediment to communication before a message reaches a receiver, can take multiple forms: semantic, channel, environmental

Deciphering Impediments.   Unwittingly, people who tune in to mass messages may themselves interfere with the success of the mass communication process. Such interference is known as a **filter.**

If someone doesn't understand the language or symbols that a communicator uses, the communication process becomes flawed. It is a matter of an individual lacking enough

filter
Receiver factor that impedes communication in various types, informational, physical, psychological

information to decipher a message. This deficiency is called an informational filter. This filter can be partly the responsibility of the communicator, whose vocabulary may not be in tune with the audience. More often, though, filters are a deficiency in the audience.

There are also physical filters. When a receiver's mind is dimmed with fatigue, a physical filter may interfere with the communication process. A drunk whose focus fades in and out suffers from a physical filter. Mass communicators have little control over physical filters.

Psychological filters also interfere with communication. Conservative evangelist James Dobson and Parkinson's patient Michael J. Fox, for example, likely would decode a message on stem cell research far differently.

The Hiebert, Ungurait and Bohn model has been incredibly useful in diagramming the process of mass communication—until new technologies ushered in the internet and transformed a lot of mass communication. Twentieth-century models quickly became, well, so old.

21st Century Models

Scholars again are at work on devising models to help explain the new mass communication. Clearly, the coding of internet messages has become largely automated. There are no typesetters or press operators. Nor are there broadcast control room engineers. Gatekeeping

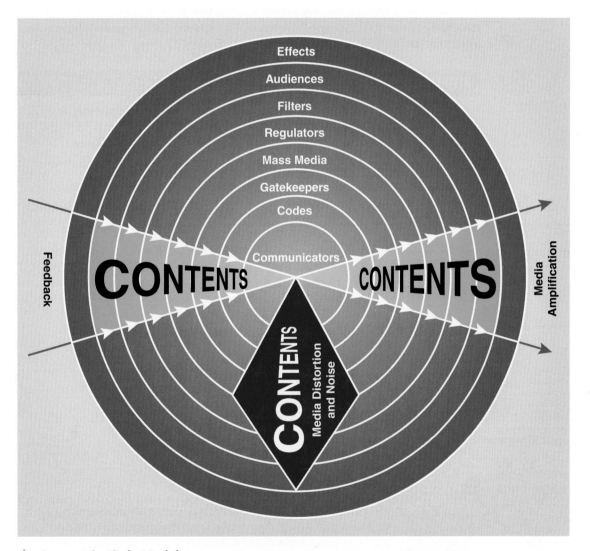

▲ **Concentric Circle Model.** *The concentric circle model illustrates a great number of obstacles for a mass-communicated message to reach an audience. These include obstacles in the technology, including coding for transmission. It's a detailed model that acknowledges that the media amplify messages, which can compound their effects. Feedback is shown, too. In mass communication, feedback usually is muted and almost always is delayed.*

is minimal. Bloggers blog unfettered. Camera phones and YouTube have changed the game. Gatekeeping is more difficult now that the ability to transmit messages to mass audiences is so easy. The closest that Facebook comes to editing are anonymous monitors whose controls are so light-fingered as to be almost nonexistent. Regulators? Governments have scratched the surface on transnational copyright issues, but largely the governments of Western countries have dallied in trying to apply old regulation models to the internet.

In part the problem is that the heart of the technology for the internet is decentralized. There are no central sources that can be regulated—no newsroom, no production centers, no presses. In some ways it's a free-for-all. One useful way to envision the internet is to think of old telegraph communication in the 1800s, in which messages went from Point A to Point B. In the 1900s, technology ushered in an explosion of mass communication. Radio, for example, picked up on the mass communication model of print media. Messages went from a single Point A to many, many recipients—magazine readers by the millions, radio listeners by the millions and television viewers by the millions. That was the process that Hiebert, Ungurait and Bohn's concentric circle model captured so well.

In the 21st century with the internet, every Point A is theoretically reached by every Point B and C and also Points X, Y and Z. It's not a linear Point A to Point B. Nor is it a message emanating from Point A to multiple points. It's a web of interactive messages reaching an incalculable number of points, which in part is why the term *World Wide Web* came to be. Think the Egyptian revolution of 2011 and the impact camera-phone images had on the stability of the government.

APPLYING YOUR MEDIA LITERACY

- How does the Lasswell model of mass communication differ from models for interpersonal communication?
- Can complex phenomenon like mass communication be reduced to a model?
- How has the technology underlying the internet rendered early mass communication models obsolete?

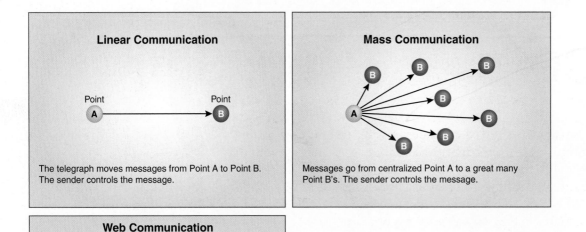

Linear Communication

The telegraph moves messages from Point A to Point B. The sender controls the message.

Mass Communication

Messages go from centralized Point A to a great many Point B's. The sender controls the message.

Web Communication

Every point in the network can send and receive messages. The recipient has access to every transmission point and controls what is received.

◀ **Points Model.** *Web communication shifts much of the control of the communication through the mass media to the recipient, turning the traditional process of mass communication on its head. Receivers are no longer hobbled to sequential presentation of messages, as on a network television newscast. Receivers can switch almost instantly to dozens, hundreds even, of alternatives through a weblike network that, at least theoretically, can interconnect every recipient and sender on the planet.*

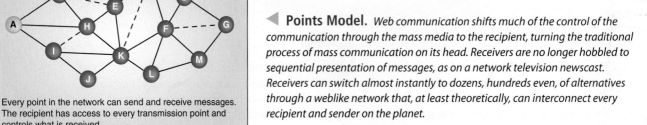

■ Media Technology (Pages 27–28)

Mass communication is unique among various forms of human communication because it cannot occur without technology. These technologies include modern printing. Books, newspapers and magazines are rooted in printing technology. Motion pictures are rooted in chemical technology. Sound recording, radio and television are called electronic media for a reason. The latest media technology is binary digital signals.

■ Printing Technology (Pages 28–33)

The importance of Johannes Gutenberg in human civilization cannot be overstated. In the 1440s Gutenberg invented movable metal type, which permitted mass production of the written word. Hitherto difficult communication between far-distant people became possible. Human communication multiplied exponentially. Especially important were exchanges among scientists and other scholars who were pressing the bounds of human knowledge. Pivotal movements in human history began, including the Age of Reason and the Age of Science and quantum leaps in literacy. These all could be called part of the Age of Mass Communication, now about 550 years old.

■ Chemistry Technology (Pages 33–35)

Photography was discovered through chemistry. With the invention of the halftone, photography became an important component of the printed media, notably newspapers and magazines. This dramatically increased the powerful effects of printed media messages. Movies also drew on chemical technology but evolved in a separate path.

■ Electrical Technology (Pages 35–40)

Electricity and the mastery of electromagnetic waves brought us whole new delivery mechanisms for mass messages. Most notably these were radio, which established itself in the early 1900s, and later television. The electronic media transmitted messages invisibly through the air by shaping and warping electromagnetic waves that are omnipresent in the physical universe. Latter-day variations include cable delivery, but even the cable industry is dependent on over-air signals from program suppliers. Electronic media of a different sort include sound recording, which although not electronic to begin with has become so.

■ Current Technologies (Pages 40–42)

Speed and reliability in delivering mass messages increased dramatically with satellite and fiber-optic technologies in the late 1900s. The improvements were mostly invisible to media consumers, except that everyone recognized that the inventory of media products was increasing and creating more choices. People who once could receive only a handful of television signals suddenly, with new satellite and cable services, could receive dozens of channels, even hundreds. The volume of media content, including news coverage, grew exponentially.

CHAPTER WRAP UP

■ Digital Integration   (Pages 42–46)

In merely 40 years the internet has grown from a concept into a major mass medium. Built entirely to transmit binary digital signals, the internet is melding the once-distinctive delivery systems for many products from old-line media companies. In addition, entire new media products and content forms have been invented. A generation ago nobody would have any idea what tweeting meant. Or what it meant to *like* something on Facebook.

■ Technology and Mass Communication
(Pages 46–50)

The mass communication process is complex and mysterious. In attempts to understand the process, scholars have devised a broad range of models and schematics and invented terminology to explain some of the phenomena they observed when they dissected the process. Although useful in limited ways, modeling the mass communication process leaves many questions and issues open to further inquiry. If we had all the answers to how the process works, every advertising campaign would be a success, every book a best-seller, and every television pilot the next *American Idol.*

■ Thinking Critically

1. **What were early effects of Gutenberg's movable type on civilization? Can you speculate on what our culture would be like without Gutenberg's invention?**

2. **Photography and movies are both rooted in chemical technology, but one is a mass medium and one is not. Please explain this distinction with this paradigm: A photograph is to a book what a script is to a movie.**

3. **How did the introduction of systems for delivering mass messages with electricity and electronic technology affect society?**

4. **Describe components that led to the creation and refinement of our latest mass medium, the internet.**

5. **The digital technology underlying the internet changed industries that were built around older mass media. What must traditional media companies do to survive as we know them?**

■ Media Vocabulary

amplification (Page 48)

App (Page 46)

Arthur C. Clarke (Page 40)

cable television (Page 41)

channel (Page 47)

cloud computing (Page 46)

digital (Page 43)

downlink (Page 40)

Ed Parsons (Page 41)

effect (Page 47)

Emile Berliner (Page 36))

fiber-optic (Page 42)

filters (Page 48)

Frederick Ives (Page 32)

gatekeeping (Page 48)

George Eastman (Page 35)

geosynchronous orbit (Page 40)

Guglielmo Marconi (Page 37)

Media Sources

■ Ken Auletta. *Googled: The End of the World as We Know It.* Penguin, 2009. Auletta, media critic for the *New Yorker,* tracks Google from humble origins into an online powerhouse that displaced traditional media, then deals with its profit-driven quest to dominate media delivery and become a major advertising vehicle.

■ Linda Gordon. *Dorothea Lange: A Life Beyond Limits.* Norton, 2009. Gordon, a historian, glimpses with convincing insight into the psychology of Lange to explain her as a person and as a pre-eminent Depression photographer.

■ Steve Knopper. *Appetite for Self-Destruction: The Spectacular Crash of the Record Industry in the Digital Age.* Free Press, 2009. Knopper, a writer for *Rolling Stone,* blames a lack of foresight and imagination, and, yes, also arrogance and stupidity, for the record industry's brush with death as the internet came of age.

■ Greg Milner. *Perfecting Sound Forever: An Aural History of Recorded Music.* Faber & Faber, 2009. Milner, an arts critic and historian, enthusiastically tracks sound recording technology in a definitive treatment.

■ Stephen W. Littlejohn. *Theories of Human Communication,* eighth edition. Wadsworth, 2004. In this classic treatment, Littlejohn traces developments in communication theory and synthesizes the research. One chapter focuses on mass communication.

■ Linda Simon. *Dark Light: Electricity and Anxiety from the Telegraph to the X-Ray.* Harcourt, 2004. Simon, a literary scholar, finds both excitement and fear in 19th century novels and short stories about the transforming effect of electricity on life and values.

■ Lev Manovich. *The Language of New Media.* MIT Press, 2001. Manovich, a media art theorist, offers a seminal and rigorous exploration of the concept of *new media* in a cultural context.

■ Denis McQuail and Sven Windahl. *Communication Models for the Study of Mass Communication,* second edition. Longman, 1993. McQuail and Windahl include dozens of models from the first 30 years of mass communication research with explanatory comments. Included in the discussion are Shannon-Weaver and helix models.

A Thematic Chapter Summary

MEDIA TECHNOLOGY

To further deepen your media literacy here are ways to look at this chapter from the perspective of themes that recur throughout the book:

MEDIA TECHNOLOGY

Gutenberg's movable type a transformational event in human communication.

Mass communication is technology-assisted communication. In fact, the defining difference between mass communication and other human communication is the role of technology. The basic technologies are printing, chemistry and electronics. Entire industries have grown from each of the technologies. These are the book, newspaper and magazine industries from printing; the recording, radio and television industries from electronics; and the movie industry from chemistry. Digital technology has made the internet possible. Some blurring of distinctions among traditional media products is occurring.

MEDIA ECONOMICS

Unanticipated technologies have changed media economics and wrought new regulation.

The economic underpinnings of modern business and industry, including the economics of media industries, were set in place during the Industrial Revolution. Media companies in most countries need to make a profit to survive. As a result, these companies are highly sensitive to legal requirements established by governments for their operation, including restrictions of the content of messages. Scholars who have modeled the mass communication process call the forces responsible for these restrictions regulators. The role of regulators is most apparent in U.S. mass media in the over-air broadcast industry, whose operations are licensed by the Federal Communications Commission, a government agency.

MEDIA FUTURE

Among evolving media technologies is almost everything in 3-D.

Futurologists have an uneven record foreseeing applications of new media technologies. Sometimes they're right, as was science thinker Arthur C. Clarke about possibilities for geosynchronous satellites in 1945. So was cartoonist Chester Gould, who gave his Dick Tracy a two-way wrist radio in 1946 and a two-way wrist TV in 1964. Vannevar Bush foresaw Wikipedia with his 1945 idea for a machine he called Memex, short of *memory* and *index*. Too, fortunes have been squandered on applying new technologies. Who remembers Betamax anymore? Or the gramophone? Today there are those who see 3-D as how we will see almost all media messages in the future. Time will tell. It's a technology that's been refining slowly after lots of failed attempts.

MEDIA AND DEMOCRACY

How do powerful profit-oriented media enterprises mesh with a democratic society?

The major mass media companies have humble origins, but now are so established and entrenched—and huge and powerful—that they are called "empires." As control of mass media became concentrated in relatively few corporate hands, ordinary folks found very limited access to outlets for their voice. This isn't how democracy is supposed to work. Newer technology, however, is reducing the price of entry for mass communication. Low-cost recording equipment and digital file-sharing have given garage bands the ability to produce and distribute music of a quality earlier possible only with costly studios controlled by major recording companies. Similarly, low-power radio and television has enabled mass communication with narrow niches within society. Blogging is another example of this democratization of mass communication. Just about anybody can blog.

MEDIA AND CULTURE

What was the impact of mass distribution information and ideas, including visuals?

Human existence has been profoundly changed by the technology that has made mass communication possible. The power of the printing press was obvious early on. For the first time scientists could share their theories and findings not with just handwritten correspondence but with printed articles. The wide distribution of these scientific articles was key to the quantum increases in scientific knowledge that have been transforming our existence since Gutenberg. Structures that define society have been in transition too. Printing helped facilitate the Reformation that shook traditional religious structures beginning in the 1500s. Values have shifted over the decades with mass-produced and mass-distributed literature, in printed and other forms, including movies. The spread of values expressed in music and theater isn't limited any more to drama troupes and traveling balladeers. The argument can be made that the explosion of decentralized digital communication will have a cultural impact of the same magnitude as Gutenberg. Indeed, that impact is already occurring.

CHAPTER 3

MEDIA ECONOMICS

■ As Others Played, He Built

When Mark Zuckerberg was in his early teens, his dad, a dentist whose hobby was dabbling in software, taught him how to program for Atari home computers. Atari was the rage in the 1990s. His dad saw Mark's excitement and hired a tutor. Next thing, in 1995, the kid had networked the house and his father's home-based dental practice. ZuckNet, Mark called it. Every computer could ping every other computer—a kind of instant-messenger. That was a year before AOL introduced instant messaging. Mr. and Mrs. Zuckerberg had a prodigy on their hands.

By the time Zuckerberg was a Harvard sophomore, he was writing software for students to choose courses based on ratings by other students. Other software helped students form study groups. Then there was his sophomoric Facemash, a software program that invited students to rank each other's looks using

◀ **Internet Entrepreneur.** *The computer programming whiz who's best known for the social networking site Facebook.*

CHAPTER INSIGHTS

● Economics explains most mass media companies' behavior.

● Conglomerates dominate mass communication, although not necessarily for the better.

● Alternatives to traditional mass media business models are being implemented.

● Government policy has shaped U.S. media development and industry infrastructure.

● Hybrid revenue structures are emerging for mass media.

● Media follow predictable business patterns from innovative to mature stages.

photos he lifted from dorm directories. Like wildfire, Facemash caught on. Zuckerberg and friends expanded to other campuses. Refined and renamed, the site became Facebook.

Today Facebook hosts 700 million users and is the world's leading social networking service. The revolution in human communication that Facebook introduced prompted *Time* magazine to name Zuckerberg its 2010 Person of the Year. Zuckerberg, by age 26, had become the world's youngest billionaire. His net worth, all based on Facebook's global success, had passed $19 billion.

Although Facebook has made Zuckerberg incredibly wealthy, a theme in his life is that money isn't a primary motivation. His mission, he says is "making the world more open." Responding to one of the first offers to sell Facebook, Zuckerberg explained the goal was not profit but to "create an open information flow for people." Too, experts agree that Facebook has potential to create a far larger revenue stream from advertising—even though ad revenues topped a whopping $2 billion in 2011. So what's the potential? Characteristically Zuckerberg says: "We make enough money."

Zuckerberg has exhibited generosity. In 2010 he gave $100 million to the strapped school system in Newark, New Jersey. He had wanted to be an anonymous donor but was persuaded by the governor to go public to draw publicity to Newark's budget plight. Among other public donations has been money to Diaspora, an anti-Facebook project started by four New York University students. A counterintuitive gift? No, said Zuckerberg: "It's a cool idea."

Lesson: Zuckerberg both affirms and contradicts a fundamental lesson in this chapter: Media aren't free. Someone has to pay the bills, whether advertisers, subscribers, investors, government, philanthropists. Zuckerberg's Facebook became an online juggernaut because investors poured in the cash that fueled its growth. Sustaining the company is advertising revenue. Ads now comprise about 10 percent of screen space. Facebook undoubtedly could carry more advertising, probably more than the 20 percent average of all other web sites. But Zuckerberg, who has kept control of the company, is truer to his passion for the potential of his creation than to typical obsession of media moguls on profits. In that, Zuckerberg is the notable anomaly. ■

Financial Foundations

STUDY PREVIEW

Most media behavior can be explained by economics. Who pays the bills? Advertising generates most of the revenue for newspapers, magazines, radio and television. More and more, advertising also drives online media. On the other hand, books, music and movies rely largely on direct sales to consumers. Investors can also create revenue streams in hopes that self-sustaining revenue streams will come along. Today the mix of revenue streams is in a major upheaval that is reshaping media companies and their products.

Capitalism

Most mass media products are from companies that operate in the profit-driven system of **capitalism.** Companies that don't make money can't meet their expenses and pay their bills. They dissolve, some in bankruptcy. This is just as true for media companies as for widget factories and mall chains.

Media owners put people in charge of their companies with a mandate to deliver profits. These people have titles like president, publisher and general manager. The expectation is that the executives will manage the owner's enterprises to generate revenue. Depending on the medium, revenue-generation takes different forms. Building readership works in newspapers and magazines. Publishing bestsellers works in the book industry, filming blockbusters in movies. Leading the ratings works in broadcasting. Put bluntly, the spoils go to whoever creates media products that attract the most eyeballs—or ears, in the case of radio.

capitalism
An economic system with private owners operating trade and industry for profit

The pressure for profits is intense. If profits lag, the owners look for a new executive who will deliver. By and large, media executives are a transient bunch. Job security depends on their profit performance. A series of sitcom flops won't bode well for a network president. Plummeting circulation will be telling a career-savvy magazine publisher to start mailing out resumés.

Revenue Streams

The best-known media companies have become economic behemoths through one of two ways: advertising and direct sales to consumers.

Advertising.   Advertising involves selling space or time to advertisers that need access to the audience that a media product delivers. Commercial television and radio, which dominate the U.S. broadcasting industry, depend solely on advertising.

Sales to Media Consumers.   Almost all the income of the book, recorded music and movie industries is from selling their products directly to consumers. Sales usually are through the mail or downloads or through intermediaries like bookshops and box offices.

Typical newspapers and magazines are a hybrid. They depend mostly on advertising but also on subscriptions and so-called street or news rack sales.

In recent years the dependence of media companies on this narrow range of revenue sources has resulted in major changes in the media landscape. Readership losses, largely to the internet, eroded confidence among advertisers in whether their ad budgets were being spent wisely in newspapers and magazines. Advertisers also were rethinking how they were spending in broadcasting. Television weathered advertising losses by de-emphasizing the traditional infrastructure of the network-affiliate over-air delivery system, moving into cable and satellite and, yes, to the internet. Radio has had a harder time maintaining ad revenue.

Investors

Some new enterprises with prospects for success are jumpstarted by investors who pour money into them with the hope of a return on their investment. Early investors can do well if an enterprise takes off and generates its own revenues. Early investors can make a real killing

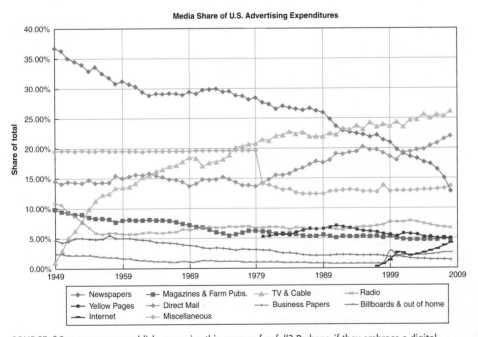

◀ **Wavering Advertising Revenue.** *The newspaper share of U.S. advertising spending has shrunk nearly 50 percent since 1933. This chart is based on data compiled by media marketing consultant Martin Langeveld in Nieman Media Lab and it shows that newer media have grown their share over the decades. Also, since 1998 the internet has been taking a growing share of the revenue. Langeveld notes that the advertising spending pie has grown in dollars over 50 years but has held steady at 2 percent of the nation's economy.*

SOURCE: "Can newspaper publishers survive this revenue freefall? Perhaps, if they embrace a digital future," by Martin Langeveld from Nieman Journalism Lab, August 31, 2009. Copyright © 2009 by Martin Langeveld. Reprinted by permission.

if an enterprise attracts enough additional investors who, in effect, bid up the value of the enterprise. Some investors cash out when they're ahead. Others stay aboard in hope of profits or in hope that further investor demand for a share of the enterprise will drive up its value. Investing is risky. When an enterprise fails, investors can lose everything they've put into it.

Most investing in major media companies is institutionalized in ownership shares that are bought and sold either among investors or through the issuance of ownership shares to the public. The New York Stock Exchange is one venue for trading stocks. When the U.S. cable television industry was called a "Wall Street darling" in the 1980s, for example, investors were driving up the value of cable companies and creating mounds of cash for the industry to expand.

When Jeff Bezos, founder of Amazon.com, issued stock, he found himself with so much cash to fuel expansion that he didn't need to worry about turning a profit. To the dismay of some investors, Amazon didn't make any money for the first five years that Bezos made shares of the company available to investors.

Investors also buy into established media companies. Some investors seek a steady long-term return in their investment. Others anticipate a spurt in revenue and move their money in and out quickly.

Venture Capital. Besides publicly traded stock, media companies can raise money from **venture capitalists,** who buy a stake in a company. This was the route that Mark Zuckerberg went with Facebook. Entrepreneur Sean Parker, whom Zuckerberg installed as president, stirred up investor interest and brought in an investment in 2004 from Peter Thiel, the cash-rich co-founder of PayPal. Other investors followed, driving up the value of the company, their purchases of shares providing the cash needed to relieve the pressure for the company to generate profits. Not until five years later, in fact, did Facebook replace red ink with black.

venture capitalists
Investors who take substantial risk, typically in a new or expanding business

Dot-Com Bust. Upstart internet-based enterprises were hot among investors in the 1980s. In fact, overspeculation drove the value of upstarts to unrealistic levels. It was called the Dot-Com Bubble, which eventually burst, just like other bubbles in history. The **Dot-Com Bubble** ranked right up there with the Dutch Tulip mania that wiped out fortunes in 1637 and the U.S. Housing Bubble of 2008 that shook the whole economy. While Amazon and Google eventually paid off handsomely for those who invested towards the end of the Dot-Com Bubble, some truly dubious concepts flopped. The mass of failures in 2000, the so-called **Dot-Com Bust,** saw billions of dollars in investments wiped out. Among hundreds of enterprises littering the dot-com landscape:

Dot-Com Bubble
Highly speculative investments in internet companies 1995-2000

Dot-Com Bust
Sudden collapse of value in internet companies 2005

- The Broadband Sports network raised more than $60 million before going bust.
- CyberRebate promised customers a 100 percent rebate on products priced 10 times the retail cost. Go figure.
- Perhaps ahead of its time, Kibu.com was an online community for teen-age girls that burned through $22 million in venture capital.
- DigiScent tried to transmit smells over the internet.

APPLYING YOUR MEDIA LITERACY

- **Why is profit a necessity for mass media in a capitalistic system?**
- **What's happening with the historically primary revenue streams of U.S. mass media?**
- **What drives investors to risk money in unproven media ventures?**

Ownership Structures

STUDY PREVIEW | One dynamic for media literacy is knowing the corporate structure within which media products exist. Knowing the entities comprising News Corporation, for example, explains a lot about the content issued by corporate stablemates Fox television and HarperCollins books.

Conglomerate Dominance

Frank Gannett
Founder of Gannett media corporation

Frank Gannett started small. In 1906 Gannett and a few associates pooled enough money to buy a half interest in the Elmira, New York, *Gazette.* Things went well. Soon they added nearby small-town papers. Eventually they created the Empire State group of dailies and moved the headquarters to Rochester. Gradually more papers were added. Today Gannett owns 81 daily newspapers coast-to-coast, including *USA Today.* The company also owns 17 dailies in Britain. Holdings also include 23 television stations. Along the way Gannett has been in and out of radio, billboards, magazines, polling, job placement and other related enterprises.

conglomeration
Process of companies being brought into common ownership but remaining distinct entities

The Gannett story is also that of Big Business—**conglomeration.** Somebody began with a concept and a willingness to take on risk. Success begat growth: A single entity became two, then three. In Gannett's case, the Elmira *Gazette* grew into a newspaper chain, then a full-blown media conglomerate with dozens of subsidiaries.

Giant media operations don't just burst full-blown in the marketplace. To many Americans, Rupert Murdoch's News Corporation may have seemed to have become a major player suddenly. There he was, hitherto a relatively obscure Australian, in control of Fox television, movie studios, newspapers, books, magazines and home-delivery satellite television. But Murdoch began with a relatively small inheritance, a single newspaper in Adelaide, Australia.

Conglomerates are giant. The largest came into being in 2011 when giant cable-television systems operator Comcast acquired control of General Electric's NBCUniversal. These are the largest U.S. media conglomerates, all with stakes in multiple media enterprises, ranked by domestic revenue:

Comcast/NBCUniversal	$ 51.2 billion
Disney/ABC	38.0 billion
News Corp.	30.4 billion
Time Warner	26.9 billion
Viacom	13.6 billion
Cox	7.1 billion
Clear Channel	6.8 billion
Tribune Company	5.7 billion
Gannett	5.6 billion
New York Times Company	2.4 billion

These are the largest media companies, ranked by domestic revenue, that have had a narrower focus than conglomerates but that nonetheless have grown by acquiring other companies:

Google	$ 23.6 billion
DirecTV	17.3 billion
Yahoo	6.5 billion
Echo Star	11.6 billion
Facebook	800 million

The reality that a few major corporations own the major media does not sit well with everyone.

▶ CASE STUDY: The Franken Crusade

Al Franken wasn't laughing. When the former *Saturday Night Live* skit-meister was elected to the U.S. Senate, he made opposition to media mega-mergers his signature issue. Franken said he had seen too much in his six-year *SNL* stint at the NBC television network. In the Senate, Franken repeatedly warned government regulators against the proposed merger of

NBC with the giant cable-system operator, Comcast. Franken argued that the American people stood to lose if fewer companies controlled the major pipelines of information. Historically in the United States there had been companies that created content, like NBC, and companies that owned distribution systems, like AT&T and Comcast.

Franken saw a Comcast-NBC merger paving the way for other big telecom companies to gobble up other big broadcast networks—like an AT&T-CBS hookup or a Verizon-ABC-Disney. Said Franken: "Now is the time to decide if we want four or five companies owning and delivering all of our information and entertainment." Franken's answer was clear: No.

Franken knew the lore of the corporate culture that discouraged certain content—like news stories critical of network business interests and also of corporate parents:

- There was an affiliate-provided story on faulty GE jet engines, for example, that never made NBC's *Today* show. At the time General Electric owned NBC.

- At Disney-owned ABC, there was a record of top-down orders from Disney to ABC not to report child molestation at Disney theme parks.

- The partisanship of Fox News, dictated as corporate policy, put news coverage over the line on political issues.

- In 2011, Comcast executives were uncomfortable with MSNBC political commentator Keith Olbermann's strident arguments against Big Business hypocrisy. Stories were widespread that NBC had indeed promised Comcast that Olbermann would be gone before the Comcast-NBC merger was consummated. Olbermann's departure happened.

Franken himself has never quite gotten over what happened after his *SNL* skit, "A Limo for the Lame-O" in 1980. Franken had mocked NBC's president Fred Silverman as "a total unequivocal failure." Silverman, he said, didn't deserve a limousine. Furious, Silverman squelched an in-process promotion of Franken to become *SNL's* head producer. Angry, Franken left the network.

Years later, as a U.S. senator, Franken caught Comcast in duplicitous testimony. Comcast had been asking government regulators to support the merger with NBC. At one point in Congressional testimony, Comcast President Brian Roberts stated that consumers need not fear a Comcast-NBC merger because Federal Communications Commission rules required Comcast to carry programs from NBC's rivals to all 23.9 million Comcast-served households. Franken then confronted Roberts with an attempt by Comcast attorneys to have those same FCC rules voided as unconstitutional. Referring to an earlier meeting, Franken said: "In other words, looking to get approval for this merger, you sat there in my office and told me to my face that these rules would protect consumers, but your lawyers had just finished arguing in front of the Commission that it would be unconstitutional to apply these rules." Befuddled, Roberts mumbled something about Comcast's reputation. Then he said he was confused when speaking with Franken earlier. It was not a good moment for Comcast, which Franken took to characterizing as *Comcatastrophe*.

Even so, the NBC-Comcast merger won federal approval. The approval, said critics who sided with Franken, was an example of corporate influence-peddling. Indeed, the media industry spends $15 to $20 million a year on lobbying Congress and federal agencies for public policy that serves industry purposes. Only the pharmaceutical industry spends more. In one year, Comcast alone put $5.5 million into political campaigns.

Distrust of the NBC-Comcast deal is rooted in the reality that the core purposes of corporations and of government are different:

- Businesses exist to serve their owners. This means expanding profits, which can include mergers.

- Government, on the other hand, exists to serve the citizens. This includes protection from businesses whose mandate for profits can run counter to the public interest.

In the NBC-Comcast saga, the score is 1-0 against Al Franken. Just ask Franken.

Conglomerate Behavior

Most companies, including conglomerates, have a board of directors that chooses executives to achieve their profit goals. These executives appoint subordinates to do the job. In a hierarchical business structure, decisions by the board determine the shape of their subsidiary

▲ **Al Franken.** *The comedian-cum-U.S. senator argues that media consumers are disadvantaged by media mega-mergers. Despite Franken's opposition, the proposed 2011 merger of NBCUniversal and Comcast gained federal approval. Franken was more successful in opposing the merger proposed by telecommunication heavyweights AT&T and T-Mobile, which fell apart when the government cited unfair market domination as a possible result.*

media companies. At giant Time Warner, this includes the big decisions—whether to buy or sell AOL, to enter a partnership with Getty Images to repurpose the images from *Life* magazine as Life.com, or to make the majority of their TV content available online and on mobile devices. These are decisions, made in board rooms, that are off the radar of all but the most savvy and media-literate.

Most conglomerates leave day-to-day decision-making to the appointed managers of their subsidiary media products. Most boards don't micromanage. It's a performance-based system that regards subsidiary managers as expendable. Those who don't deliver are replaced.

Divestiture

Media companies have a long history of jockeying their properties for new advantage. But in the recession that began in 2007, and leading up to it, divestiture became panic-driven. There were no buyers. The most obvious major crack in the conglomeration pattern of the previous 30 years, even going back longer by some measures, began in 2005. The landmark newspaper chain Knight Ridder exemplifies what happened. Knight Ridder, the second largest chain in the United States and a consistent Pulitzer Prize winner, wasn't making enough money in its shareholders' eyes. The decision was made to sell the company. Another chain, McClatchy, bought most of the Knight Ridder properties. Overextended, McClatchy's capitalized value plummeted. The company ended up with no choice but to sell assets and to put some of its newspapers into bankruptcy in an attempt to survive.

Fast-changing economic realities have bred unexpected alliances. The struggling AOL internet content company somehow came up with $315 million in 2011 to buy the *Huffington Post* news site. *Newsweek* magazine, hemorrhaging money, became part of the company that owned the *Daily Beast* news site. The New York *Times* Company similarly fell short of cash. Facing momentous advertising losses, the *Times* borrowed $250 million from Mexican telecommunications titan Carlos Slim Helú at a subprime rate of 14 percent. The *Times* repaid the loan early, but had the newspaper defaulted, Slim could have taken control of 17 percent of the Times Company and become the third-largest shareholder.

In an austere economic environment and internet-generated fluxes, media ownership no longer is a sure avenue, so to speak, to print money. There are bright spots, to be sure, but few. But the media landscape is fast changing.

APPLYING YOUR MEDIA LITERACY

- **How do you explain the pluses of media conglomeration for mass audiences? Any downsides?**
- **How have ownership changes affected the performance of your local newspapers and television and radio stations?**
- **What do media companies do when profitability flounders?**

Alternative Media Ownership

STUDY PREVIEW | Some media operate outside the usual capitalistic structure. The *Christian Science Monitor* has been a model of sponsored media since 1908. Other ownership models have emerged more recently, including those with funding from community foundations, philanthropies and government.

Institutional Sponsorship

Sponsored media are not always visible. Many listeners of the historically powerful Chicago radio station WCFL had no idea that the call letters stood for the Chicago Federation of Labor. Yes, labor unions owned and operated the station. Going back to the 1920s, many churches have been in and out of station ownership.

■ The Complexity of a Media Mogul

Journalists shuddered the day that Rupert Murdoch offered a phenomenal $5 billion to buy the *Wall Street Journal.* Media watchers were dumbfounded. Murdoch was the immensely rich Australia-born media baron whose empire included Fox television, HarperCollins books and an array mostly of low-brow media ventures, indeed some sleaze. What would Murdoch want with the *Wall Street Journal,* one of the world's prestige newspapers? The question was all the more poignant because at that moment, in 2007, the newspaper industry, its heyday decades earlier, seemed to be approaching its deathbed.

Murdoch, some say, is hard to figure out, his success hard to explain.

Indeed, Murdoch, now in his 80s, is a complex person. But two themes have marked his career. First, he latches onto goals, sometimes impetuously, and pursues them no-holds-barred. Second, in the end he acts in his economic self-interest. This means correcting, even reversing impetuous decisions when it's clear the financial payoff is unlikely or too distant. Murdoch thus epitomizes a recurrent theme in media behavior—economic self-interest.

And Murdoch does OK himself, thank you very much. His company, News Corp., pays him $33 million a year.

With the *Wall Street Journal,* as conventional wisdom has it, Murdoch saw a way to vindicate his reputation as a media sleaze king. Yes, the low-budget tabloid New York *Post* is his. With the *Wall Street Journal,* Murdoch was explicit that he wanted to compete directly against the gold standard in world journalism, the New York *Times.* Obsessed, he offered the Bancroft family more for Dow Jones, parent company of the *Journal,* than what every expert calculation said was its worth.

After the deal was consummated, financial realities quickly caught up with Murdoch's dream for the *Journal.* To rein in costs, he ordered shorter stories and less-researched reporting. He trimmed page width, which cut postage expenses. Staff was reduced. Ad space was sold on the once-sacrosanct front page.

In earlier ventures Murdoch bailed when financial expectations turned bleak. He dumped his control-ling interest in the DirecTV satellite delivery service in 2006 when, for example, he saw that the potential had peaked. He had controlled DirecTV three years. What lesson is there in Murdoch's short term invest-ment in DirecTV? In the end, the bottom line for Rupert Murdoch is the bottom line. He said as much at a Congressional hearing. To critics that his Fox News is biased to the conservative right politically, Murdoch didn't deny the charge in his testimony and

characterized himself as apolitical: "Conservative talk is more popular." His point: Money drives content. If liberalism would draw audience cost-effectively, then Fox, he was saying, would be liberal. In fact, in the 2008 presidential campaign, with the conservative-backed Republican candidate John McCain lagging badly, Murdoch endorsed Barack Obama, who was building a progressive, liberal coalition. Yet two years late he contributed $2.2 million to organizations that were bankrolling conservative candidates.

The overarching principle in Murdoch's behav-ior, say critics, is opportunism in pursuit of profits.

In the 1980s, for example, Murdoch ran into an obstacle to building his network of Fox television stations because stations in the United States are licensed by the government only to U.S. citizens. So Murdoch applied for U.S. citizenship and took the exam. Problem solved. For Murdoch, citizenship was a means to an end.

When he needed friends in Congress on a broadcast regulation issue, Murdoch's book sub-sidiary, HarperCollins, offered House Speaker Newt Gingrich an extraordinarily sweet $4.5 million advance for an autobiography. Gingrich hadn't even started the book. When word about the deal leaked out, the book industry was aghast. There was no way a Gingrich book could ever earn back such an advance. In the glare of the negative publicity, the deal exposed, Murdoch denied he was trying to buy influence. His problems on the Hill and the book deal, he said, were an unfortunate coincidence.

Murdoch has no problem backpedaling. In one speech, waxing on the future of democracy, Murdoch predicted that advanced communication technology would spell the end of totalitarian regimes. He hadn't reckoned that the totalitarian leadership in China might hear the speech. They did. When the Chinese then threatened to deny permission for Murdoch's StarTV satellite to transmit into China, he moved quickly to placate the Chinese totalitarians. He signed a deal for HarperCollins to publish a book by the daughter of head of state Deng Xiaoping. Also, he can-celed another book that probably would have provoked the Chinese. Knowing that the Chinese were wary of the BBC's independent news broadcasts, he discontin-ued BBC from his StarTV satcast service to Asia.

Murdoch has become synonymous with media power. Former CBS executive Howard Stringer once called him "the leader of a new Napoleonic era of communications." Critics claim that his emphasis on corporate profits has undermined the notion that the mass media have a primary responsibility to serve the public.

▲ Rupert Murdoch.

Global media mogul Rupert Murdoch, here in the set of his Fox News network Bill O'Reilly talk show, is upfront that he's driven not by politics but profits. Money explains the content of Murdoch's diverse media empire. In fact, economics explains most media behavior.

What Do You Think?

Would you be attracted as an investor to a Rupert Murdoch enterprise? Explain the plusses and minuses you see.

Would you value Murdoch as a friend? As a neighbor? Or is he someone from whom you would keep your distance? Explain.

By some measures, there are more sponsored media than financially stand-alone media. Of roughly 12, 000 magazines in the United States, most are issued by organizations to select audiences. These include corporate magazines for employees, shareholders, customers and other audiences. Every college has publications for alumni.

▶ CASE STUDY: Christian Science Monitor

Mary Baker Eddy, the influential founder of the Christian Science faith, was aghast at turn-of-the-century Boston newspapers. The Boston dailies, like papers in other major U.S. cities, were sensationalistic, overplaying crime and gore in hyperbolic battles to steal readers from each other. Entering the fray, Eddy introduced a newspaper with a different mission. Her ***Christian Science Monitor***, founded in 1908, sought to deal with issues and problems on a higher plane and to help the world come up with solutions. The *Monitor* was a sponsored paper, produced by an institution as part of a larger purpose. Unlike many church-sponsored media, the *Monitor* has never been preachy either as a newspaper or today in its new online format. As for all sponsored media, the church as the sponsor has underwritten expenses when subscriptions, newsstand sales and advertising revenue fell short.

▲ **Sponsored News.** *Since its founding in 1908, the Christian Science Monitor has offered global news coverage from a solution-oriented perspective advocated by the Christian Science church. The goal of church founder Mary Baker Eddy was accurate and truthful reporting to help people address serious problems facing humankind. In 2009, short of funds to maintain the newspaper, the Monitor went to a slick weekly format and also online delivery.*

▲ **Mary Baker Eddy.**

Community Foundations

With the asset value of newspapers plunging after the 2007 financial collapse, concern rose about the possibility of a void in important local forums for news and ideas. Some media analysts suggested that newspaper owners donate their papers to charities that could operate them tax-free. Freed of paying taxes, otherwise financially marginal newspapers could remain in publication. Ben Shute, director of the Rockefeller Brothers Fund for grants to encourage democratic practices, says community foundations, which are set up as charities, could identify informational and other voids that a newspaper's demise would leave and then take over the newspaper to meet those needs. **Community foundations,** common throughout the United States, are funded with donations. Their purpose is to support worthy community causes.

Skeptics are wary, however, whether all community foundations could provide the detached and neutral coverage that newspapers had offered under private ownership. Many foundations are community boosters, whose agenda would hardly countenance courageous investigative reporting. The concern is that many community foundations, with their boosterism instincts, would wield a newspaper as a publicity machine and not a vehicle for public service through unbridled truth-seeking.

The jury remains out on how community foundations may fit into the future of economic support systems for mass media.

Nonprofits

Another possibility is wider use of the **cooperative** model. In news, the largest model is the global news-gathering organization the **Associated Press.** The AP began in 1848 as a joint effort of several New York newspapers to pick up bundles of mail from Europe by sending boats out to transoceanic ships at anchor off Sandy Point and not yet docked. Rather than all the papers hiring their own newsboats to fetch the mail bundles, the papers agreed to share a single fleet to eliminate redundant costs. The Harbor News Association, as the co-op was known, evolved and grew into the AP. Then as now, member newspapers control the AP and share the coverage as well as the costs of operation. The member newspapers also share the costs of operating bureaus in every state in the United States as well as 243 abroad. To meet expenses, the AP also sells its coverage to broadcasters, investment firms, government agencies and other customers.

The cooperative model precludes profits as essential, which gives the AP an advantage over profit-driven enterprises. Over the years the AP's nonprofit status has given it a financial edge over competing for-profit news agencies, which have mostly disappeared. Does anybody hear about United Press anymore? Or International News Service? The major players in international coverage are merely two—the AP and the British agency Reuters.

That nonprofits can work is clear from the AP model. An estimated 3 billion people a day see or hear news from the Associated Press. National Public Radio, another nonprofit although not a cooperative, reaches 24 million listeners a week in the United States.

In local news, a possible AP equivalent could be a consolidated newsroom serving newspaper, broadcast and web outlets. As with the Harbor News Association, duplicate costs could be eliminated. Alas, so would be the competition that historically has contributed to vibrant coverage.

Nonprofits and Investigative Reporting. Nonprofits, many organized by journalists from the shrinking newspaper industry, are filling voids left by for-profit news organizations. Worldwide, about 40 investigative reporting nonprofits are operating. These organizations are engaging in the most expensive and riskiest form of news reporting, the investigative story, which has been abandoned by many budget-strapped traditional media companies.

These nonprofits take different forms. In Boston, the Global News Enterprises operates as a newsroom. To get Global News going, Philip Balboni, who earlier founded New England Cable News, and Charles Senott, a Boston *Globe* reporter, raised close to $8 million. Global News has a network of 70 reporters, all freelancers. Another nonprofit, the Center for Public Integrity, has a specific mission, to promote honesty in government and other powerful institutions. The center, in Washington, was founded by Charles Lewis, a frustrated producer of the CBS news program *60 Minutes.* With an annual budget of $5 million, the center's 40 reporters have issued more than 400 reports. The center also has freelance contracts with hundreds of reporters around the world. Another nonprofit, ProPublica, also in Washington, is run by a former managing editor of the *Wall Street Journal,* Paul Steiger. He had a startup budget of $10 million a year. With a news staff of 30, ProPublica focuses on "important stories with moral force."

Nonprofit Sustainability. Not everyone sees nonprofits as viable. Business economists are wary of switching a for-profit enterprise into a nonprofit because of the baggage that can come with the acquisition. Even if a nonprofit can generate sufficient revenue to underwrite operations, itself a challenge, the entity still accumulates expenses to maintain its own infrastructure. With a newspaper, for example, printing presses have a useful life of 30 years. And most newspapers have put off purchasing replacement presses. Eventually the presses will fall apart and need replacing. Other deferred capital expenses include maintaining facilities, replacing vehicles, upgrading software. A nonprofit may keep a media operation going for a period, but the longer-term issue is sustainability. Robert Picard, a media economist, casts the prospects bleakly in calling for a "sustainable model," rather than something that gets up and running for two or three years, maybe longer, and then fails because underlying financial problems don't go away.

University Media Generators

Charles Lewis of the Center for Public Integrity separately established a student investigative reporting unit at American University in Washington in 2009. Such university-based incubators of investigative reporting gained attention earlier when David Protess at Northwestern University created the Medill Innocence Project. Protess' students uncovered judicial lapses that sent 11 innocent men and women to prison, five to death row. At Brandeis University, former Washington *Post* reporter Florence Graves founded the Schuster Institute for Investigative Journalism. Lowell Bergman, formerly of the New York *Times* and PBS' *Frontline*, heads the Investigative Reporting Program at the University of California at Berkeley, which provides salaries, benefits and editorial guidance for journalists pursuing careers in in-depth public-service reporting.

Campus-based generators of media content may be a long-term part of the emerging patchwork of new media organizations. The fact, however, is that not all universities, whatever their claims for academic freedom, have top-level administrators with the courage to support investigative journalism that tackles wrong-doing and abuses in powerful political and social institutions.

Family Ownership

A nostalgia-driven alternative is a return to family ownership of media. Almost all media companies began as sole proprietorships. The usual pattern was for the founders to bequeath their companies to their heirs. Some families maintained ownership for subsequent generations, although federal inheritance tax laws in the latter 1900s forced most media families to sell outside the family, usually to chains that were eager to expand. Two factors figure into revised interest in family ownership, including a yearning for old ways:

Personality-Driven Media.   Historically there were great contributions to media content during the era of individual and family ownership. Generally this family ownership has acquired an aura, perhaps rose-tinted, of a commitment to public service and commonweal. Certainly, media products bore the stamp of their founders and family owners more than in the successor phase of media ownership. The chains and conglomerates that acquired the family-run operations made policies that emphasized profits and, as the lore has it, a risk-averse blandness set in. Here are examples of the pattern:

	Media Unit	**Early Proprietor**	**Later Ownership**
Books	Scribner	Charles Scribner	CBS
Newspapers	*Wall Street Journal*	Bancroft family	News Corp.
Magazines	*Time*	Henry Luce	Time Warner
Recordings	Motown	Berry Gordy	Universal Music
Movies	Paramount	Adolph Zukor	Viacom
Radio	NBC	David Sarnoff	NBCUniversal
Television	NBC	David Sarnoff	Comcast & General Electric
Internet	*Huffington Post*	Arianna Huffington	AOL

This pattern toward chain ownership has been repeated throughout the United States in local newspaper, radio, book publishing and television ownership. The often colorful characters associated with the earlier periods have been subsumed by a bland corporate mindset focused myopically on the bottom line.

Pride of Ownership.   Whether the proverbial good ol' days were better can be debated. But there is a nostalgia that pride-of-ownership in the family media era made for better content. Indeed, a local family's reputation was inherent in the product. Jay Hamilton of the Louisiana State University journalism school has suggested that family owners may be willing to trade off maximum profits for doing the right thing for their community. Hamilton's point is that chain ownership put profits above community good, families less so.

■ News-Gathering Gone Too Far?

▲ Hacked Off.

When actor Hugh Grant was tipped that his voice-mail exchanges with woman-friend Jemina Khan may have been hacked by News of the World, *he went to court. A judge ordered police to share what they knew so Grant could decide what to do next legally. Grant is among celebrities involved with the Hacked Off lobby group that is campaigning for a rigorous inquiry into eavesdropping by British newspapers.*

After 13-year-old Milly Dowler was kidnapped on her way home from school in southern England, her parents made desperate and tearful pleas for her safe return. The disappearance and the parents' anguish made headlines throughout British media. Six months later Milly's body was found dumped in the woods. Years later a nightclub bouncer was convicted of the murder.

From the beginning, the horrific crime ranked high for newsworthiness. In 2011, nine years after the disappearance, it became clear exactly how aggressively one newspaper, *News of the World*, had pursued the story. It turned out that reporters at *News of the World* had hacked into Milly Dowler's voicemail for information and tips. The revelation, even all those years later, incensed the British public.

But the revelations about the newspaper's aggressive news-gathering went beyond tasteless invasions of privacy. The newspaper hackers, when they realized that Milly Dowler's voicemail box was full, secretly deleted messages from their remote site. This was during the months that police, desperate for clues, were checking Millie Dowler's incoming calls. In their quest for more headlines, the hackers wanted more messages. Indeed, there were calls, all hoaxes as it turned out, from weirdos pretending to be the kidnapper.

The phone-hacking scandal deepened with allegations that *News of the World* had also hacked into the phones of families of soldiers killed in Iraq and Afghanistan as well as members of the royal family, including Prince William. Politicians and celebrities were hacked. Actor Hugh Grant claimed phone messages with a woman friend were intercepted. Within months of the revelations, 7,000 people had contacted attorneys with claims that their phones had been hacked by *News of the World*.

For years the newspaper's titillating and shocking headlines screamed for reader attention. *News of the World*, at 2.4 million circulation, was among Britain's most profitable tabloids. But people were unaware of how the stories came to be. The presumption was that it all was good old-fashioned news-gathering, aggressive to be sure, but hardly to the extent of interfering with police investigations. Or violating privacy laws. Strict free press advocates argue that the media should have no limits in pursuing information.

The idea has roots with 17th century thinker John Milton who argued for uninhibited inquiry: "Let truth and falsehood grapple, whoever knew truth put to the worse in a free and open encounter." Traditional libertarianism, strictly applied, trusts good things to come eventually if not immediately from the fullest array of information being available through mass media.

But what of decency? What of mucking up a police investigation? What of pressing political leaders into favorable policy by suggesting that embarrassing information gathered by the newspaper would be kept out of print? It was all tawdry, to say the least.

Under intense pressure from Parliament, Rupert Murdoch acknowledged that his *News of the World* had gone too far. The admission surprised many people because Murdoch had made his fortune, estimated at $7.6 billion, with no-holds-barred tabloid newspapers and television for decades. Others thought the admission was typical Murdoch, who has a history of elasticity to preserve his media empire. In fact, so threatened was the empire in Britain that Murdoch fired executives at the newspaper left and right, some of whom went to jail. Then, under continuing pressure, including the withdrawal of millions of dollars in advertising accounts, he shut down *News of the World*. All the while, Murdoch claimed he had no idea about the hacking,

POINT **You can't have a free press without the press being free. This means uninhibited inquiry.**

COUNTER POINT **Decency should trump news-gathering that invades privacy, interferes with criminal investigations, and has nothing to do with serving a public good.**

DEEPENING YOUR MEDIA LITERACY

EXPLORE THE ISSUE: Check online for news about the demise of the *News of the World*.

DIG DEEPER: Check online for commentary on the scandal.

WHAT DO YOU THINK? How would John Milton respond to the *News of the World* hacking scandal? How about an absolutist on free press issues? How about you?

The same kind of concern prompted a 2009 proposal in Congress to allow newspaper companies to restructure as nonprofits, with advertising and subscription revenue being tax-exempt. The Newspaper Revitalization Bill, proposed by Senator Benjamin Cardin of Maryland, would have classified newspapers as educational institutions, somewhat like public broadcasting stations. Cardin explained his proposal this way: "The business model for newspapers, based on circulation and advertising revenue, is broken, and that is a real tragedy for communities across the nation and for our democracy." Cardin said his plan would not bring any government influence in news coverage, but newspapers would be barred from their traditional role in endorsing political candidates. The bill was referred to the Committee on Finance. It never went any further.

APPLYING YOUR MEDIA LITERACY

- Are government postal subsidies for print media still justified? Were they ever?
- What arguments, if any, remain viable for government regulation of broadcasting?
- How relevant is the FCC in light of the rapid changes in communications technology?
- If the Newspaper Revitalization Bill of 2009 had passed, how different do you think the news media industry would be today?

New Media Funding

STUDY PREVIEW | Advertising and subscription revenue are weakening as a revenue source for traditional mass media but they won't disappear entirely. What will pick up the slack? A patchwork, possibly of more government funding and charity support, seems likely. Also, media consumers themselves may pay for media access through new mechanisms.

Advertising and Subscriptions

New patchworks of revenue, some traditional, some not, are emerging to finance mass media. For some media, the role of advertising will diminish as advertisers find new ways on the internet to connect directly with potential customers, rather than through traditional media. Also, subscription revenue will dry up for most periodicals. Already people are finding much of their information and other media needs can be met free on the internet. Only a chump would pay for what can be had for nothing. Unless what they're getting is less than what they want.

Numerous media are instituting ways to generate revenue through online delivery via tablets, smart phones and computers. The New York *Times* instituted a new approach: You can view 20 articles a month free of charge, but you need a subscription to access anything beyond that. Listen to Pandora free of charge for 320 hours a month with advertisements. Or if you don't want ads, you can pay a fee and sign up for uninterrupted music via your computer using Pandora One.

Hybrid Mix

In niches in the mass media, alternative funding mechanisms have been at work for decades. Every public broadcasting listener knows about on-air fund drives exhorting viewers and listeners to pony up. Until now, the legacy media ignored such alternatives. Not any more.

Government Funding.   As the newspaper industry crumbled, Congress in 2009 launched hearings on what might be done. Senator John Kerry, who chaired subcommittee hearings, put the focus on newspapers even though the issue was broader: "The history of our republic is inextricably linked to the narrative of free and independent press," Kerry said. "Whatever the model for the future, we must do all we can to ensure a diverse and independent news media endures." Options included expanded government funding on the model of U.S. public television and radio.

A similar model is for state and municipal government funding. Several cities and states already subsidize noncommercial radio. Among them are Minnesota and New Mexico, whose appropriations are essential to the budgets of state networks and stations. Other states and municipalities, however, have divested themselves from media ownership. New York City sold the license for WNYC radio in 1995, and New Jersey sold its NJN network to WNET in 2011.

At the federal level there is a perennial battle on whether to continue funding to noncommercial stations through the quasi-government Corporation for Public Broadcasting. At one point 20 percent of revenue for these public television and radio stations was through Congressional appropriations. The argument to cut or eliminate financial support from government is that a wide range of programming is available through commercial stations in the so-called 500-channel universe. Unlike 50 channels a half-century ago when Congress created CPB, a need no longer exists for subsidies for alternatives to commercial stations. Or so goes one side of the argument.

Government support of media can be indirect for ostensibly unrelated reasons rather than a direct subsidy. At the behest of state newspaper associations, state legislators require counties and municipalities to designate an "official newspaper" to carry legal notices, usually called **legals**. These legals are detailed budget and other documents, usually from government agencies. The stated purpose is to provide the public with information on government policy and spending. The newspapers charge government agencies by the inch for the space these legals take, usually pages and pages annually. For some weeklies, legals are significant revenue sources. Competing papers engage in spirited bidding to win the "official" designation.

In some states, certain companies are required by law to publish periodic reports in the official local press. It's a condition of doing business, aimed mostly at out-of-state insurance companies. In effect, insurance policyholders are being taxed to subsidize local newspapers.

Similarly, the federal government requires some product manufacturers, including drug makers, to publish great detail about their product and its dangers in magazines. Too, federal and state governments buy lots of advertising time and space. Consider the Marines recruiting ads. Or, have you been exhorted recently to vacation in Arkansas?

Philanthropy. Significant gifts to support media organizations in recent years demonstrate untapped potential for philanthropy in the revenue mix for media into the future. The $200 million bequest to National Public Radio from Joan Kroc, from the McDonald's fast-food fortune, in 2003 established a new mark for media **philanthropy**. Herbert Sandler, who built Golden Financial West into a mortgage giant and then sold it to the larger Wachovia banking empire, gave $10 million to create the ProPublica investigative reporting organization. Large charitable donations to media upstarts are becoming more common.

philanthropy
Generous donation for good causes

Loosely related to philanthropy is corporate **underwriting**. Major oil companies, as an example, already underwrite costs of some programs, ostensibly from a civic-minded instinct. The supporters, however, are acknowledged on-air, which gives the companies a public association with the sponsored program. In reality, it's low-key advertising, although nobody wants to call it advertising because noncommercial station licenses issued by the federal government forbid advertising. The term *underwriting* is used to sidestep the federal rules against advertising and yet allow on-air acknowledgments that include product descriptions.

underwriting
On-air acknowledgments of non-commercial broadcast sponsors

Fund Drives. Nonprofit media organizations are not bashful about asking for gifts. Public broadcasting has made an art form of periodic fund drives. The 42-station Minnesota Public Radio Network, as an example, raises 11 percent of its $70 million budget from listener memberships and donations. Local public television stations are no less successful in raising money from their viewers. WNET in New York has an annual fund-raising goal of $90 million. Many donations are less than $100 a year but an occasional $1 million or $2 million pledge comes in. Online sites have their palms out too. The Center for Public Integrity, which produces investigative journalism, asks readers for $5 a month with prestige donor recognitions for $500 or more.

Micropayments.   Telephone companies mastered how to bill for tiny bits of long-distance time years ago. It is a **micropayment** system that newspapers and magazines have contemplated with the disintegration of their old model of a single charge for a bundle of content—like $1 a copy or a $150-a-year subscription. The unbundled model would charge per item, like 4 cents for a news story, and keep a running tab for periodic billing. The system would have efficiencies for many consumers. A sports fan with no other interests in life would not have to pay for unwanted political news or advice to the lovelorn. This system is already being used by online services like iTunes and Google for its sales of music and publishers' content.

micropayment
A small sum generally billed with related charges, often on a credit card

   Auxiliary Enterprises. Rather than originating content, which is costly, many media organizations have taken to regurgitating more and more material from other sources. The diminishing quantity of original content has been widely decried, but the upside for media companies that continue to generate fresh content is that they can derive revenue from selling it for reuse. ProPublica, for example, peddles its investigative reporting to newspapers and other media companies. **Auxiliary enterprises** take many forms. PBS issues regular catalogs with DVDs of programs and spin-off products as wide-ranging as Sesame Street paraphernalia and PBS logo t-shirts.

auxiliary enterprise
A business sideline that generates revenue

APPLYING YOUR MEDIA LITERACY

- **What is the future of advertising as a media revenue stream?**
- **Which hybrid mix of revenue can be expected to dominate mass media business models in the future and why?**

Media Economic Patterns

STUDY PREVIEW | Media technology is the product of inventive genius, but the application of technology to create a medium that in fact reaches a mass audience is a trial-and-error process. Eventually some entrepreneur gets it right, which spawns imitators. It's an evolutionary process. Major media industries inevitably fall into a trap of their success and either fade in the face of new competition or radically reinvent themselves.

Phase 1: Invention

Invention is the first phase in a predictable pattern of mass media evolution through a cycle into maturity and, then, past prime. The origins of each mass media industry are easily identified. Everyone agrees that today's print media have roots in technology invented by Johannes Gutenberg in the 1440s. Gutenberg had no idea at the time that his movable metal type would enable the creation of massive industries in book, newspaper and magazine publishing. Newspapers? Magazines? Gutenberg could never have envisioned such things. Inventors frequently focus mostly on their tinkering.

Phase 2: Entrepreneurship

The transition from invention to commercial viability generally involves costly false starts. Consider the internet, whose history as a business enterprise is littered with upstarts, some with big-buck financing and names that flashed into prominence and quickly dimmed. Remember General Electric's GEnie portal? Nobody else does much either. How about such other forgottens as Napster file sharing? Time Warner's Pathfinder magazine megasite?

The entrepreneurial phase of media evolution is a marriage of vision, capital and risk. Most initiatives flop. Finally, though, someone gets it right. An application of the technology finds an audience, and an industry is born.

Radio illustrates the point. Guglielmo Marconi's discovery in 1898 that messages could be carried through the air entirely missed radio's potential as a mass medium. His focus was on point-to-point communication modeled on the telegraph. In fact, he called his invention *radiotelegraphy*. It was a Marconi employee, David Sarnoff, who had the vision for radio as a mass medium. In 1916 Sarnoff wrote a memo to his boss: "I have in mind a plan of development, which would make radio a 'household utility' in the same sense as the piano or phonograph. The idea is to bring music into the house by wireless...The receiver can be designed in the form of a simple Radio Music Box." Sarnoff also proposed advertising to fund his vision for radio as a mass medium. The boss didn't share the young Sarnoff's enthusiasm for reinventing radio. On his other merits, however, Sarnoff rose quickly in a spinoff Marconi company, Radio Corporation of America. Then Sarnoff redefined radio as a new mass media industry under the banner of RCA subsidiary NBC.

A few inventors see commercial potential in their inventions. Thomas Edison, for example, forged his way into sound recording and movies as business enterprises. Generally, however, the entrepreneurial phase isn't dominated by inventors. It can be argued, for example, that Edison did less inventing as time went on. Instead, he left research and innovation to the people who ran his labs. George Eastman of Kodak camera was an Edison-like exception too. He also created labs where others did the later inventing under his name.

Failures in the entrepreneurial phase can be gigantic. In the 1990s, investors poured billions of dollars into internet and other digital-medium enterprises. Most flopped. In the annals of business history, the collapse of hundreds of these companies, called the Dot-Com Bust of 2000, triggered a severe economic recession. In the ashes, though, were companies whose visions were economically viable. The late Steve Jobs of the resurgent Apple computer company typifies entrepreneurial success.

Phase 3: An Industry

Success breeds imitators. In radio, NBC was followed by CBS, then ABC. Television took the same course. As soon as one book publisher in the 1800s began a magazine to promote its books, others soon followed. There was *Harper's, Scribner's, Collier's*. Adolph Zukor created a new model for movie-making with his Paramount Studios in 1912. So quickly did others follow that Hollywood became known for the studio system. Even within an industry, imitation is inevitable. *Time* was a significant innovation in 1923. Then came *Newsweek* and *U.S. News*.

Although competitors, successful upstarts and their imitators come together to comprise a rising industry. This has been the pattern in all of the enterprises rooted in media technology. The first attempts at radio stations in the 1910s hardly comprised an industry, but by the 1920s with a few hundred stations on the air, clearly an identifiable new business segment was functioning. This earlier was true with books, newspapers and magazines. At some point a critical mass of sound recording companies was a recognizable industry. The same with Hollywood. Later, television.

Within an industry, consolidation almost always occurs over time. Situations evolve that encourage competing companies to merge. Or blatant expansion can lead to buyouts. The result, played out in industries within the mass media and beyond, is an **oligopoly,** in which a few companies dominate an industry. Consider the monikers the *Big Four* in the recording industry, the *Big Six* in movies, *Big Four* in network television, and the *Big Five* in trade book publishing.

Oligopolies fall short of **monopolies,** in which one company dominates production and distribution nationally or locally. In the United States, where there is a cultural preference for competition, monopolies have been illegal since 1890. Despite the cultural predilection, public policy has allowed consolidations into oligopolies. When he was president, Bill Clinton made the point that corporate bigness was essential for the United States to compete globally with international giants. Later presidents have been likewise accepting of corporate mergers and acquisitions that create bigger and bigger U.S. companies as global players. Indeed, the largest media players are global, many based abroad.

oligopoly
An industry in which a few companies dominate production, distribution

monopoly
Single company dominates production, distribution in an industry, either nationally or locally

Consider the recorded music industry, ranked by U.S. market share:

Parent Company	Labels	
Sony-BMG (Japan-Germany)	Arista, BMG, Columbia, Epic, RCA	30%
Universal (France)	MCA, Interscope, Geffen	27%
Warner (United States)	Atlantic, Elektra	15%
EMI (Britain-Netherlands)	Capitol, Virgin	10%

Or trade book publishing:

Parent Company	Subsidiary	
Pearson (England)	Penguin	40%
CBS (United States)	Simon & Schuster	21%
Bertelsmann (Germany)	Random House	21%
News Corp. (United States)	HarperCollins	12%

Today everyone recognizes that something is coming together with technological roots in digitization, but the outline of a new industry is still too blurry for a firm label. Attempts include the *software* industry, the *new media* industry, the *internet* industry. Maybe what's happening will shake out into several distinctive industries. Or maybe we'll devise a new umbrella term drawn from what they all have in common. Stay tuned. These are exciting times to watch a new media industry, or perhaps industries, in formative stages.

The fact, though, is that consolidation is occurring, sometimes in bits and spurts, always unevenly. The proposed Yahoo-Microsoft merger in 2008 fell apart but illustrates that an urge to merge is instinctive at the industry stage of the business maturation cycle. Consider the consolidated corporate names—NBCUniversal, Disney-ABC and Sony-BMG. And also the myriad of contrived corporate names that camouflage a rich history of predecessor companies—Cumulus, Entercom, Viacom and Comcast itself.

Phase 4: Maturation

One mark in the evolution of media companies into something bigger than individual entities is the recognition of common issues that need to be addressed collectively. This point is when **trade groups** are formed. Some of the most powerful U.S. trade groups represent media industries, almost all with headquarters in Washington to influence government policies to their advantage.

trade groups
An organization created by related endeavors, sometimes competitors, to pursue mutual goals

Trade groups also sponsor research, much of it on technology, to benefit their members. This includes developing industry-wide technical specifications. These include:

- A single standard for television transmission to avoid incompatible systems, like vying technologies for color television in the 1950s and more recently the orderly shift from analog to digital transmission.
- Common newspaper column widths and page sizes so advertisers don't have confusing, multiple dimensions to sort through.
- Standard dimensions for magazines, which facilitates news rack display.

Phase 5: Defending Infrastructures

Once solidly established, mass media industries risk complacency, gentrification and failure. **Andy Grove**, the fabled leader of computer-chip manufacturer Intel, later a scholar on business strategy at Stanford University, says that the final phases of an aging industry follow a predictable three-stage course.

Andy Grove
Theorist on gentrification in industries

Ignore New Challenges.   Complacent in their companies' long-term rise and success, executives first minimize threats from cross-industry innovations. In short, they just don't get it. We see Grove's point over and over. The recording industry, slavishly committed to its traditional distribution channels, turned a blind eye to the internet as a new technology for music. The recording business has been limping since, a shadow of its former self. Similarly, the newspaper industry, after riding high for 140 years, deluded itself about slippages in readership until, wham, advertising as the industry's economic foundation began a free-fall plummet in 2001.

Resist Change.   When crisis can no longer be dismissed, Grove says, industry executives move into a resistance mode. This can involve consolidations to create economies. Usually

■ Will The Internet Slow Revolving Doors?

Political lobbying has been fraught with controversy since it first appeared.

The problem is called the Washington turnstile—a buddy system with well-positioned people moving back and forth between public service jobs in government and private service jobs for industry. The problem has hounded broadcasting since the Federal Radio Commission was created as a regulatory agency in 1927. Should President Calvin Coolidge have appointed broadcasters to the commission because they understood the nascent industry's issues? Or should Coolidge have chosen ordinary citizens to represent the public good even though virgin to the issues and unknowledgeable?

Examples of the revolving door in media lobbyists include:

- **Motion Picture Association ofAmerica.** Chris Dodd is chief executive, capping 20 years as a U.S.senator, succeeding Dan Glickman, a former member of Congress, who succeeded Jack Valenti, who had White House connections back into the 1960s.

- **Recording Industry Association of America.** Mitch Bainwol became RIAA chair after 25 years in federal policy-making and policy.

- **Newspaper Association of America.** Paul Boyle, chief NAA lobbyist, previously worked for a five-term congressman.

▲ **Gordon H. Smith.** *The former U.S. senator now works out of the broadcast industry trade association's steel-and-glass headquarters on N Street as president— and as chief lobbyist.*

- **National Association of Broadcasters.** Gordon H. Smith became NAB's president after 12 years in the U.S. Senate.

- **Association of American Publishers.** Tom Allen became president of AAP, the book industry trade organization, after six terms in Congress. Before Allen, the AAP's president was Pat Schroeder. Earlier she served 12 terms in Congress.

- **Association of Magazine Media.** In an exception to the revolving career door between special interest groups and government, Nina Link joined AMM in 1999 after a media career in publishing.

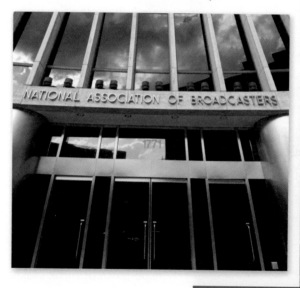

The cozy relationship of lobbyists and their former colleagues in public service jobs has grown as a policy issue: Are these lobbyists taking an unfair advantage of their relationships with government policy-makers that shuts out the public's interest? If so, what can be done?

Lobbyists often work using one of two strategies, according to Koen Droste, writing for the *Financial Times*.

- **Iceberg Strategy.** Lobbying is done a tiny bit in public, like the top of an iceberg, with the rest being done below the surface where it's safe from the often unpredictable public debate.

- **Buoy Strategy.** Lobbyists put a topic on the agenda publicly, where it is clearly visible above water, then plan some specific actions under the surface for the delicate points.

So enter the internet, which inevitably can make lobbying more transparent. "The iceberg strategy is becoming much riskier," says Droste. He believes the rise of digital media gives the more transparent buoy strategy an advantage. An organization with an engaged online fan base can employ its fans to get a topic on the public agenda. The world's largest online marketplace eBay used this strategy when it collected nearly a million signatures for its policy proposal to end unfair online trading practices. Although this method of marshaling grassroots support is often called **astroturfing** by companies and government entities that are targets of organized campaigns, it has become an effective tool in public debate about public policy. And is sure to become more so.

What Do You Think?

Will companies need old-fashioned lobbyists like Valenti in the future? Or will they be more likely to hire digital media experts?

What form of lobbying best serves the public's interest?

astroturfing
Political activism designed to appear as "grassroots" but actually part of an organized campaign

these mergers and acquisitions are heralded as steps toward a stronger future. That, says Grove, is delusional. The reality is that the disparate deal-making is merely staving off the inevitable.

Resistance can take other forms, like enlisting Congress and government agencies to adjust public policy to protect existing media infrastructures. The traditional television industry, based on locally licensed stations, spent three decades pressing the federal government to impede the natural growth of cable and satellite delivery alternatives. In the end, however, the customer appeal of cable and satellite reception eroded the lobbying effectiveness of local stations' trade groups and lobbyists.

Radical Reforms.   Usually too late, an ailing industry launches heroic but doomed reforms for survival. How, for example, can local radio stations that have built themselves as music sources compete with iPods? Can daily newspapers ever again claim a monopoly as a news medium? Drastic overhauls and reinventions may work in some cases, but Grove is dubious: "Your doctor says you are going to die, but if you don't smoke you'll live a little longer."

APPLYING YOUR MEDIA LITERACY

- **Why do you think innovators don't always have a vision for their inventions?**
- **What marks the transition of media businesses into an industry?**
- **Why do rival media companies join together to form trade groups?**
- **Select a troubled media conglomerate and apply Andy Grove's stages of an industry's decline. Is there hope for a company turnaround?**

CHAPTER WRAP UP

■ Financial Foundations   (Pages 57–59)

Mass media fit well into the profit-driven capitalistic system until two major revenue streams began drying up. Advertising revenue has fallen dramatically, dooming most daily newspapers and many magazines. The broadcast industry also faces new challenges with declines in advertising. A second significant U.S. media revenue source historically has been sales. This revenue too has declined for companies that have been losing audience. Might there be lessons from how other countries finance their media? Or from the experience of niche players in the U.S. media landscape?

■ Ownership Structures   (Pages 59–62)

The structure of the mass media in the United States has followed a common business pattern. Most companies began with a hard-working entrepreneur, often a visionary whose media products bore a personal, sometimes quirky imprint. Ownership then moved into chains or conglomerates. In general, the result was a blander product with the corporate imperative being to enhance profits and less on distinctive products to serve the commonweal. The chain and conglomerate structure hit rough sledding in some media industries, especially newspapers and magazines, when profits vaporized in the early 2000s. No longer financially viable, some chains broke up. Others were auctioned off, then broken up by new owners. It is unclear what new ownership structures will emerge from current uncertainties.

■ Alternative Media Ownership (Pages 62–67)

Tremendous energy is going into rethinking how the mass media need to be restructured to survive economically. The first to be hit hard in the internet age was the recorded music industry. After significant downsizing and painful adjustments, an equilibrium has been found for the radio industry to, it seems, sustain itself. More radical changes may be necessary for the withering newspaper industry and magazines. Brainstorming is as far-ranging as heavier government funding, as foundations taking on publications as charity cases, and as positing universities as news-gathering institutions. Nobody has come up with a panacea.

■ Government Role (Pages 67–72)

An ideal of government-press separation dates at least to democratic political philosopher John Locke in the late 1600s and still has many followers. Democracies have found ways, however, to channel public funding into the media and both serve the common good and avoid government control. If government is to have a greater role in supporting the mass media financially, the challenge is to assure that the media retain the ability to be a watchdog on government for the people.

■ New Media Funding (Pages 72–74)

Losses in the twin traditional sources of U.S. mass media income—advertising and subscription revenue—have been substantial. One new model is for products like newspapers to give up their bundled content. The bundling concept, going back to the 1830s, was to create an affordable package with something for everyone. That model now is failing. One proposal is charging the audience by the item—a micropayment, perhaps just pennies for, as an example, a sports story. Customers would pay a monthly bill for content they choose. Such a system already works in pay-per-view television and iTunes downloads. More government funding and charity support is a possibility in a new patchwork of media revenue streams.

■ Media Economic Patterns (Pages 74–78)

Some mass media are in a mature stage of their development. After a history dating to the 1830s, the daily newspaper industry probably is on its last legs, eclipsed by technology and unable to reinvent itself in time to save itself. These patterns of business are predictable, with industries moving through phases of innovation, entrepreneurship and maturation. The process is evolutionary. Major media industries are not exempt from the process and inevitably fall into a trap of their success and either fade in the face of new competition or radically reinvent themselves.

CHAPTER WRAP UP

Thinking Critically

1. How have mass media fit historically into the capitalist economic system?

2. What are problems inherent in conglomerate ownership of mass communication?

3. Describe alternative business models for new revenue streams for mass media.

4. What lessons do you see for us today from the U.S. experience of government-aided communication?

5. What are downsides and upsides of alternatives being discussed for historic mass media business models?

6. Project out and apply Andy Grove's maturation business model to the developing social media industry. Where do you see it ending up?

Media Vocabulary

Associated Press (Page 65)

astroturfing (Page 78)

auxiliary enterprise (Page 74)

capitalism (Page 57)

Christian Science Monitor (Page 64)

community foundations (Page 64)

conglomeration (Page 60)

cooperative (Page 65)

death tax (Page 67)

Dot-Com Bubble (Page 59)

Dot-Com Bust (Page 59)

joint operating agreements (Page 70)

legals (Page 73)

marketplace model (Page 70)

micropayment (Page 74)

monopoly (Page 75)

Newspaper Preservation Act (Page 70)

1927 Federal Radio Act (Page 70)

oligopoly (Page 75)

philanthropy (Page 73)

scarcity model (Page 70)

1789 Postal Act (Page 67)

trade groups (Page 76)

underwriting (Page 73)

venture capitalist (Page 59)

Media Sources

■ John Allen Hendricks, editor. *The Twenty-First Century Media Industry: Economic and Managerial Implications in the Age of New Media.* Lexington Books, 2010. Hendricks, whose scholarship has examined social media, looks at how managers of news and entertainment media are adapting to technologies and innovations.

■ Jeff Kaye and Stephen Quinn. *Funding Journalism in the Digital Age: Models, Strategies, Issues and Trends.* Peter Lang, 2010. Kaye and Quinn, both with international journalism experience, review business models and strategies that might help journalism survive the disruptions caused by changing technologies, social trends, and economics.

■ Nicole LaPorte. *The Men Who Would Be King*. Houghton Mifflin Harcourt, 2010. LaPorte, an entertainment industry reporter, blames the fall of Dreamworks on its conflicting goals of promoting artistic expression and of breaking even in the unpredictable pursuit of blockbusters to pay the bills.

■ Daniel Lyons. "Arianna's Answer," *Newsweek* (August 2, 2010), Pages 44–47. Lyons, a reporter on media and technology, looks at *Huffington Post* in assessing the financial vicissitudes of breaking even with web sites.

■ Ken Auletta. *Googled: The End of the World as We Know It.* Penguin, 2009. Auletta, media critic for the *New Yorker,* tracks Google from humble origins into an online powerhouse that displaced traditional media, then deals with its profit-driven quest to dominate media delivery and become a major advertising vehicle.

■ Jim Cox. *American Radio Networks: A History.* McFarland, 2009. Cox is leading historian on radio programming.

■ Robert Burgelman, Andrew Grove and Philip Meza. *Strategic Dynamics: Concepts and Cases*. McGraw-Hill/Irwin, 2005.

■ Ben Bagdikian. *New Media Monopoly*, fifth edition. Beacon, 2004. Bagdikian, perhaps the best-known critic of media conglomeration, includes data on the digital revolution in this classic work.

■ David Croteau and William Hoynes. *Media/Society: Industries, Images, and Audiences,* third edition. Pine Forge Press, 2003, 3–30. The authors, both sociologists, construct a model of how news media play a crucial unifying role within a well-delineated social system that includes government, economic activities and conditions, and citizenry.

■ Benjamin M. Compaine and Douglas Gomery. *Who Owns the Media? Competition and Concentration in the Mass Media Industry*, third edition. Erlbaum, 2000. The authors update the 1979 and 1992 editions with details on further concentration, more attention to the cable and home video business and discussion of the effect of technological convergence.

■ Ben Bagdikian. *The Media Monopoly*, fifth edition. Beacon, 1997. Bagdikian, perhaps the best-known critic of media conglomeration, includes data on the digital revolution in this update of his classic work.

A Thematic Chapter Summary

MEDIA ECONOMICS

To further deepen your media literacy here are ways to look at this chapter from the perspective of themes that recur throughout the book:

MEDIA ECONOMICS

Declining readership and advertising is sending dailies online.

The mass media are part of a capitalistic economic system in the United States, dependent almost entirely on finding consumers willing to buy media products. If no one wants to see a movie, the studio behind it will be in big trouble, maybe flop. It is the same for book publishers and music marketers that invest in new products. For some media, a more complex revenue stream is from advertising. Companies pay newspaper, magazine, radio, television and online companies for space and time for advertisements. In effect, advertisers are buying access through mass media to reach potential customers.

MEDIA TECHNOLOGY

Major media companies like the Murdoch empire are positioned to exploit technology to expand.

Technology and advances, some incremental, some incredibly transforming, vastly increased the reach of mass media to larger audiences and created giant industries beginning in the 1800s. Since then, media companies, ranging from local newspapers to national magazines and broadcast networks, became major employers and significant components in the economy.

MEDIA AND DEMOCRACY

Government hands off the press.

The concept that mass media must be independent from government for democracy to work is being rethought. Why? Because newspapers, magazines, radio and television today are vulnerable with advertising diminishied as their financial engine. The concept of media independence from government is mythical at least to some extent. Government policy from the earliest days of the nation has favored mass media in ways both small and significant. History has numerous models for using tax-generated government policy and revenue to maintain mass media as we know them. These models include the BBC broadcast empire in Britain and the public broadcasting infrastructure in the United States.

AUDIENCE FRAGMENTATION

Audience demassification may be at its ultimate with wireless delivery of digitized messages.

The economic dislocations that are reshaping mass media are due largely to continuing shifts in audience habits and preferences. Every moment that someone spends on a web site is a minute less that could be spent with a book, for example, or a magazine. Modern life also has other alternatives for people. Do the math: Nobody has more than 24/7 available. People have unprecedented choices on how to spend their time. Consider television alone: Fifty years ago, three U.S. television networks dominated the nation's television programming. Today there are dozens and dozens of networks that gear programming to narrow audience segments. This kind of audience fragmentation is rewriting the economics of mass media industries.

MEDIA FUTURE

Media serve their own interests through organizations that lobby for favorable public policy.

An unresolved issue is the lobbying practices of mass media industry groups going too far in lobbying government for their special interests, which are mostly economic, which can run contrary to the media's responsibilities for public service. Can media be a watchdog against government abuses of power and misdeeds when the media are dependent on the government for tax breaks and regulatory favors and other special favors? The question: Watchdog or lapdog? The question has special poignancy because the media have followed the model of other industries and made lobbying a standard practice. Further, also like other industries, mass media trade groups routinely hire powerful public office-holders as lobbyists when they retire from government positions but retain old and newly useful contacts in Congress and government agencies and departments.

MEDIA AND CULTURE

Critics warn of cultural impact of media conglomeration.

The shift from individual and family ownership of mass media has been consistent with the move to a corporate-created culture. A pattern for financially successful media companies has been to acquire other media companies. This trend is the result of inheritance taxes that make it almost impossible for heirs of media companies to keep them. The heirs have no choice but to sell the inheritance to pay the taxes. What happens goes by many terms, among them chain ownership and conglomeration. One result has been the rise of diverse shareholders controlling media companies. The primary focus of these shareholders is on improving profits. Often profitability has trumped community service, investigative journalism and cultural enrichment as values to which media can contribute.

4 INK ON PAPER

■ The Wikipedia Breakthrough

Sometime in the 1960s Jimmy Wales' folks purchased a set of the *World Book Encyclopedia* from a door-to-door salesman. Jimmy got hooked on information. In college he became committed to the notion that people can best acquire wisdom by pooling what they know. He calls himself "an Enlightenment kind of guy."

Wales put his idea on the web in 2000 with an ambitious project for an online reference book. Nupedia, he called it. Like dozens of ink-on-paper encyclopedias before, Nupedia solicited experts to write articles. Wales also ran the articles by a traditional review panel. Things went slowly. A year later, Nupedia had only 21 entries.

Then, secondhand from an assistant, **Jimmy Wales** heard about a simple software tool called *wiki*. The software enabled several people to collaborate on writing and editing. Why not thousands? Millions? By 2001 Wales had modified Nupedia to accept online contributions directly from, well, anyone—with anyone able to edit entries online and do so instantly. It was a process called **open editing**.

◀ **Wikipedia Founder.** *Only a few employees led by Jimmy Wales keep Wikipedia humming. The entries, almost all from volunteers, are growing to many multiples of those in traditional encyclopedias.*

CHAPTER INSIGHTS

- Mass media functioned at a minor scale the first 400 years after Gutenberg.

- Newspapers flowered with the Industrial Revolution, as did other ink-on-paper media.

- The New York *Times'* reputation dates to unearthing the Boss Tweed scandal.

- Advertisers liked early magazines to promote mass-produced products.

- Magazines and newspapers are vulnerable to advertiser defections, with survival at stake.

- For better or worse, transnational ownership has altered the book industry's historic values.

- Online sites have decimated reference books, but other book genres are less in jeopardy.

- Printed media have helped move democracy and culture ahead, which poses doubts about a post-print future.

An e-notice went out to 2,000 people on Nupedia's mailing list: "Wikipedia is up! Humor me. Go there and add a little article. It will take all of five or 10 minutes."

Only five years later **Wikipedia,** as the project was renamed, carried 1 million articles, compared to 120,000 in *Encyclopaedia Britannica*, the printed encyclopedia against which all others are judged. Today the total is pressing 3.8 million in the English version alone, more than over 6.2 million in other languages. Being on the web, Wikipedia has no physical limit on its size. The site has become the seventh-most visited on the internet. There are 30,000 hits per second. It is ranked fourth in web globalization with versions in more than 35 languages.

In many ways, Wikipedia represents much of the free-for-all that is the internet. Among Wikipedia's few rules are these: First, articles must be from a neutral point of view. Second, content must be verifiable and previously published. Contributors must be anonymous.

Despite these rules, nonsense does get posted. Too, there are vandals who take perverse joy in messing up entries. Wales has robots that roam entries for disruptive submissions. When accuracy is an issue, administrators make judgment calls. When contributors differ on facts, Wales runs the facts by a mediation committee and an arbitration committee.

How accurate is Wikipedia? Stories are legion about members of Congress cleaning up entries posted about themselves. Voting records have been tampered with in self-serving ways. On several occasions every member of Congress has been barred from posting changes while Wikipedia administrators sorted out the facts and the truth.

To address questions about accuracy, the journal *Nature* tested 43 entries in Wikipedia and in the *Encyclopaedia Britannica* and found both amazingly accurate. Wikipedia did, however, have four errors for every three in *Britannica*, but errors were rare both places. A 2010 study of toxicology, cancer research and drug entries found that Wikipedia's depth and coverage were comparable with physician databases.

Whatever the pros and cons of Wikipedia, it represents the techno-driven environment in which printed media, whether the book, the newspaper or the magazine industry, will survive or fail. For many companies solidly wedded to ink-on-paper technologies, the prospects are not good. A media revolution is in progress. ■

Wikipedia
User-created and
-edited online encyclopedia

Print Media Industries

STUDY PREVIEW

As an industry, the mass media didn't take form until the 1830s with the introduction of newspapers that were affordable to most people and edited for mass readership. Key factors in the development of mass audiences at the time were intertwined economic and social changes—growing industrialization, urbanization, immigration and literacy.

Discovery of Mass Audiences

Gutenberg printing technology in the mid-1440s made mass media possible, but for almost four centuries there was nothing resembling media industries as we know them. Magazines were irregular and mostly short-lived. Newspapers were weekly sidelines of printers struggling to make a living. Newspaper content was largely a hodgepodge of whatever a printer fancied or had handy to fill space. There were no reporting staffs. The concept of a newspaper as a comprehensive package of the day's events had yet to take form. Book production was modest by current measures.

The 1830s wrought major changes in the social order in the United States that gave birth to modern mass media. Were there a pivotal moment, it would be September 3, 1833.

▲ Benjamin Day.

▲ **Mass Media Pioneer.** *When Benjamin Day launched the New York* Sun *in 1833 and sold it for one cent a copy, he ushered in an era of cheap newspapers that common people could afford. Mass media today have many of the* Sun *'s pioneering concepts. These include content of interest to a great number of people, a financial base in advertising, and easy access.*

Benjamin Day
Published the New York *Sun*

On that day a 22-year-old New York printer, **Ben Day,** launched the **New York *Sun*** at a penny a copy. Affordable by just about anyone, the *Sun* was an instant success. Until then, papers had been expensive. An annual subscription cost as much as a full week's wages. The penny *Sun* quickly had imitators. The new-style papers exploded into a significant industry. Day had, indeed, discovered mass audiences. Day's motto for the *Sun*, "It Shines for All," was a pun fully intended. In media history the era came to be called the Penny Press Period.

Incubating Context

Several social and economic factors, all upshots of the Industrial Revolution, made the penny press possible:

- **Industrialization.** With new steam-powered presses, hundreds of copies an hour could be printed. Earlier presses had been hand-operated.

- **Urbanization.** Workers flocked to cities to work in new factories, creating a great pool of potential newspaper readers for easy same-day delivery. Until the urbanization of the 1820s and 1830s, the U.S. population had been almost wholly agricultural and scattered across the countryside.

- **Immigration.** Waves of immigrants arrived from impoverished parts of Europe. Most were eager to learn English and found that penny papers not only were affordable but also were good tutors with their simple, direct writing style.

- **Literacy.** In general, literacy was increasing, which contributed to the rise of mass-circulation newspapers and magazines.

These were powerful and inexorable forces that transformed human existence. Indeed, had Day not started the New York *Sun*, somebody else would undoubtedly have put the pieces together to jumpstart the modern mass media. Even so, Day was first.

penny papers
Affordable newspapers introduced in 1833 created unprecedented mass audience

Financial Framework

Merchants saw the unprecedented circulation of the **penny papers** as a way to reach great numbers of potential customers. Advertising revenue meant bigger papers, which

Differentiating Print Media

Major ink-on-paper media have distinctive characteristics, albeit with some blurring crossovers.

	Books	Magazines	Newspapers
Binding	Stitched or glued	Stapled	Unbound
Regularity	Single Issue	At least quarterly	At least weekly
Content	Single Topic	Diverse topics	Diverse topics
Timeliness	Generally not timely	Generally timely	Timeliness important

attracted more readers, which attracted more advertisers. A snowballing momentum continued, with more and more advertising being carried by the mass media. A significant result was a shift in newspaper revenues from subscriptions to advertisers. As a matter of fact, Day did not meet expenses by selling the *Sun* for a penny a copy. He counted on advertisers to pick up a good part of his production cost. In effect, advertisers subsidized readers, just as they do today.

Magazine also grew into an advertising-dependent mass medium. For almost 200 years mags have been a major component of the mass media. The book industry also grew rapidly. But in contrast to newspaper and magazines, books rely on readers alone for revenue. And without advertising as a subsidizing revenue stream, books have remained relatively expensive.

APPLYING YOUR MEDIA LITERACY

- **How was the New York *Sun* pivotal in the growth of mass media?**
- **From your studies in U.S. history, what can you add to the list of mid-century changes in the 1830s and later that helped drive the explosive growth of print media?**
- **What impact are e-readers and online versions of newspapers, magazines, and books have on the traditional revenue model?**

Newspaper Industry

STUDY PREVIEW

With the success of penny papers, newspapers grew into the first major media industry. The newspaper business model endured for decades for all news media. The dominance of newspapers among media products has been shaken by internet-triggered alternatives for readers and advertisers.

Newspaper Business Model

The success of Ben Day's New York *Sun* and other penny papers marked a transition of newspapers to a significant industry. These newspapers created a **business model** that remains the core today of news enterprises, print and otherwise. In this business model, newspapers had creative staffs that specialized in designing and creating the product. This creative core was mostly editors and writers in newsrooms with reporters in the field. Other staff specialized in production, including operation of complicated and sophisticated new presses. Another staff specialized in selling space to advertisers.

business model
A design operating a business, identifying revenue sources, customer base, products, financing

publisher
Magazine or newspaper's proprietor

news-editorial
A newspaper staff component that produces news, amusement and opinion content

editor
A manager who is responsible for news media content

The organizational structure is headed by a **publisher**, who is either the owner or someone appointed by the ownership. These are the subordinate organizational units:

- **News-Editorial.** Headed by an **editor**, who has a staff of assistants at all but the smallest papers. The news-editorial unit produces content in a bifurcated structure. The news side focuses on covering events and issues and generating amusement and other content. At its peak the New York *Times* had one of the largest news-editorial staffs, about 1,200 editors, reporters and writers. The editorial side produces opinion sections separately and apart from the news side.

- **Production.** In the early days, typesetters and other technicians performed the mechanical assembly of the product. Typesetters have been displaced by technology. But other specialized technicians remain required to maintain and operate the presses, which are gigantic, complex machines that rival anything else from the Industrial Age.

- **Advertising.** The huge expenses of the news-editorial and production functions are underwritten mostly by revenue from advertisers. The content of ads is not created by newspapers but by advertisers that buy space to reach a newspaper's audience with their spiels.

- **Circulation.** A separate department works at promoting sales of a newspaper. The core idea is that the greater the readership the more attractive a paper is to advertisers.

- **Business.** The immensity of a newspaper's operations requires bookkeepers, accountants, lawyers and other standard business apparatus.

With modest refinements, the structure has remained viable more than 150 years.

Media Dominance

The long-running dominance of newspapers among mass media was built on a model of bundling news, information and entertainment in an affordable package. For a penny a copy, later a nickel, then a quarter, nothing provided the package of essentials like news and diversions like sports and comics, not to mention horoscopes, advice for the lovelorn and even serialized light fiction. The other print media, books and magazines, had niches but never approached the financial might of the newspaper industry.

Newspaper Influence.   Newspapers were influential in the lives of generations of readers. What was reported was what people talked about. What wasn't reported generally didn't have alternate avenues into public dialogue.

Less clear is whether newspapers could dictate public opinion. Conventional wisdom was that a newspaper's editorial support was essential for political candidates. The conventional wisdom came into doubt in the 1930s and 1940s when a majority of newspapers wrote editorials supporting Republican candidates for the presidency, but the Democrat Franklin Roosevelt won four elections in a row by landslides. Of course, no candidate would spurn an editorial endorsement, but the maxim that newspapers could deliver elections was flawed. Still, a campaign ritual is for candidates to call on the editorial boards at newspapers to explain their positions, take questions and curry support.

Benjamin Franklin
In the U.S. colonial era, he created first newspaper chain

chain newspaper
Owned by a company that owns other newspapers elsewhere

William Randolph Hearst
Publisher of New York *Journal, other major dailies in the yellow period*

Newspaper Chains.   The first printer to get rich from owning a newspaper was **Benjamin Franklin**. By age 25, he was wealthy with his *Pennsylvania Gazette*. With his typical pragmatism, Franklin reasoned that if he could make money with one newspaper, he could make more money with more. Franklin financed former apprentices to start newspapers elsewhere in the colonies, which made him the first **chain newspaper** owner. He set up printers in Antigua, New York, Rhode Island and South Carolina. The former apprentices shared the profits with Franklin as their grubstake investor.

Franklin's chain was a piker compared to what came later. By the late 1800s, with newspapers in their heyday, publishers like **William Randolph Hearst** had multiple metropolitan dailies that created some of the largest personal fortunes in the nation. The phenomenon of chain ownership hit a new stride in the 1970s. Newspapers' profitability was skyrocketing, which prompted chains to buy up locally owned

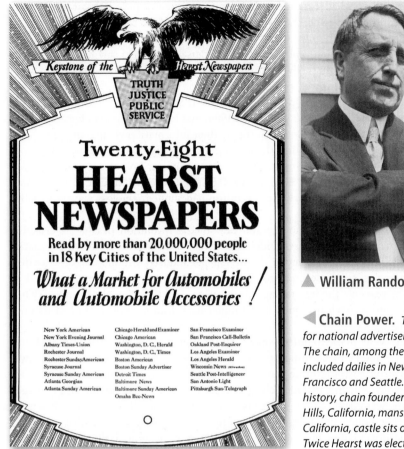

Keystone of the Hearst Newspapers

TRUTH
JUSTICE
PUBLIC
SERVICE

Twenty-Eight HEARST NEWSPAPERS

Read by more than 20,000,000 people in 18 Key Cities of the United States...

What a Market for Automobiles and Automobile Accessories !

New York American	Chicago Herald and Examiner	San Francisco Examiner
New York Evening Journal	Chicago American	San Francisco Call-Bulletin
Albany Times-Union	Washington, D. C., Herald	Oakland Post-Enquirer
Rochester Journal	Washington, D. C., Times	Los Angeles Examiner
Rochester Sunday American	Boston American	Los Angeles Herald
Syracuse Journal	Boston Sunday Advertiser	Wisconsin News (Milwaukee)
Syracuse Sunday American	Detroit Times	Seattle Post-Intelligencer
Atlanta Georgian	Baltimore News	San Antonio Light
Atlanta Sunday American	Baltimore Sunday American	Pittsburgh Sun-Telegraph
	Omaha Bee-News	

▲ William Randolph Hearst.

◀ **Chain Power.** *The Hearst newspaper chain offered discounts for national advertisers that bought space in multiple newspapers. The chain, among the most profitable through the 20th century, included dailies in New York, Chicago, Los Angeles, Boston, San Francisco and Seattle. With his fortune, one of the largest in U.S. history, chain founder William Randolph Hearst lived well. His Beverly Hills, California, mansion had 29 bedrooms. His San Simeon, California, castle sits on a 240,000-acre site that today awes tourists. Twice Hearst was elected to Congress.*

newspapers, sometimes in bidding frenzies. Chains bought up other chains. From 1983 to 1988 eight newspaper companies tracked by the business magazine *Forbes* earned the equivalent to 23.9 percent interest on your checking account. Only Coke and Pepsi did better.

The U.S. newspaper industry became concentrated in fewer and fewer companies in the late 1900s. At one point, four of five U.S. local newspapers were in absentee chain ownership. The largest of the chains, Gannett, owned almost 100 dailies and corporate policies emanated from the company's skyscraper headquarters overlooking the Potomac. In the same sense, the Los Angeles *Times* may have looked local with *Los Angeles* prominent atop the front page, but business strategy and practices were dictated from chain bosses at the Tribune Company in Chicago.

The new industry mavens, in the corporate offices of the chains, rewrote the book on running newspapers. The new orientation was geared to the bottom line. Quality journalism became not a value for its own sake but merely a vehicle for sustaining and pushing profits. Despite platitudes about an ongoing commitment to public service, the chains—indeed, most of the industry—were myopically focused on the bottom line and saw journalistic content as a burdensome cost center.

Hidden Implosion

The profits, however, masked an industry already in a slow implosion. Readership was largely stagnant or slipping. People had less time in their lives to spend with a newspaper. Television, then the internet, competed for eyeballs. More family members were spending more hours outside the home in full-time jobs. With more people in 9-to-5 office jobs, in contrast to factory shifts that dominated earlier times, typically starting at 6 a.m. and ending in mid-afternoon, people had less time in the evenings for newspapers. PMs, as newspapers issued in the afternoon were called, had once outnumbered AMs but virtually disappeared in the 1980s. PMs either shut down or were absorbed into their morning competition. This goosed profits at the surviving morning papers because advertisers saw little alternative, but the upshot in revenue eventually dissipated. A traditional balance between producing a quality journalistic product as well as making money was lost.

For decades, historians will ponder when the U.S. newspaper industry began its decline. Circulation peaked at 63.3 million in 1984, just before computers became a part of everyday life. Newspapers continued to supply their information via ink on paper. They were slow, even resistant, to moving their content to the internet. By 2009 newspaper circulation was 45.6 million, off almost one-third and slipping 7 percent a year. The drop over a quarter century occurred even as the U.S. population continued to grow. As a financial analyst would put it, **market penetration** had slipped. The loss was undeniable. There was no way to gloss it over.

In the last decade the technology and new media revolution has had a crushing impact on the newspaper business model. The establishment and explosive popularity of free resources like Craigslist ended the newspaper industry's monopoly on classified advertising—a major source of income. In late 2009 advertising revenue seemed in free-fall, off 23.7 percent. The free-fall appeared easing in 2010, although the industry had already moved into a survival mode and trimmed itself into a mere shadow of its once mighty dominance.

The losses were masked during most of the decline because the industry had maintained profitability by slashing operating expenses. Pages were trimmed narrower to reduce newsprint costs. Trimmer products weighed less, which reduced fuel costs for distribution. Penny-pinching included cheaper grades of paper. Cost-cutting also damaged content. Staffing was cut at outlying bureaus, as in state capitals. The result was less news coverage of public policy and a dramatic drop in labor-intensive investigative reporting. The nation's leading dailies cut back on Washington bureaus and shut down foreign bureaus. These kinds of measures, which came about gradually, maintained profits and masked underlying problems for the industry.

Generally the cuts went unnoticed outside the industry. By 2010, however, there was no way to disguise the continuing erosions in readership and the concomitant loss in advertising revenue. Owners took increasingly drastic steps to stay afloat, including further staff cutbacks that visibly diminished the product. The U.S. Labor Department estimated that 20,000 newspaper jobs were eliminated in 2008. In one swoop, not the first, the giant Los Angeles *Times* cut back 300 jobs. In 2008, the *Rocky Mountain News*, a Denver fixture for 150 years, shut down. Up until then, the *Rocky Mountain News* was the largest newspaper to fail in the industry's implosion. Also shutting down were the *Christian Science Monitor* and Seattle *Post-Intelligencer*, although both maintained an online presence. The shift from "ink on paper" to "words on a page" was well underway. Or, more precisely, to "word on an on-screen page."

Scramble Online

Some newspapers had an early sense of the potential for internet delivery. In 1992, the Albuquerque *Tribune* created the first newspaper site for postings. These early news sites, however, were half-hearted. Their nickname, applied derisively, was *shovelware* because print-edition content was shoveled almost mindlessly online. There wasn't any sense that the web was read differently than a newspaper. By and large, the graphics potential of the web was missed entirely.

Gradually newspapers beefed up their online presence with presentations that were better adapted to onscreen viewing. While online viewership grew, advertising revenue didn't. Experiments to charge subscriptions didn't work.

In 2011 the New York *Times* set up a **paywall** for its nytimes.com. People who read more than 20 online articles a month were blocked unless they subscribed. The *Times'* goal was 300,000 paying subscribers within a year. In the first three weeks, the company was

market penetration
Sales per capita

paywall
Block access to a website content unless a payment is made

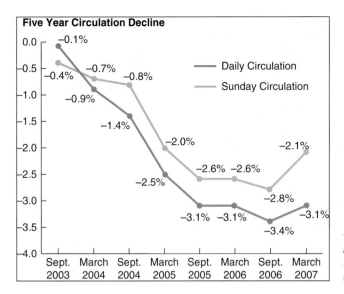

Five Year Circulation Decline

◀ **Newspaper Circulation.** *No matter how you slice the numbers, daily newspaper circulation is in trouble in the United States. Using 1984 as a base, the Audit Bureau of Circulations has found consistent drops in its six-month tabulations, albeit an uptick in the period ending in March 2007. Even so, daily circulation had dropped more than 2 percent over five years and Sunday circulation had dropped more than 3 percent.*

pleased with 100,000 subscribers for packages varying from $15 to $35 a month. Other newspapers followed with paywalls.

Among all news sites, newspaper companies rank among leaders. In the United States these were the unique visits per months in early 2011 with the sites of companies mostly in the newspaper business highlighted:

Yahoo News	86.6 million
CNN	80.2 million
MSNBC	54.2 million
AOL	47.2 million
New York *Times*	**38.0 million**
Huffington Post	31.0 million
Tribune Company	**26.8 million**
Fox News	27.0 million
ABC News	22.4 million
USA *Today*	**21.3 million**
Advance Internet	18.3 million
Washington *Post*	**17.9 million**
CBS News	17.4 million
Mail Online	16.6 million
Wall Street Journal	**15.5 million**
BBC News	15.0 million

APPLYING YOUR MEDIA LITERACY

- Compare and contrast the newspaper business model with the structure of another business or industry—retailing, higher education, fast food. How does the newspaper business model stack up?
- What unseated newspapers as the dominant U.S. media industry?
- How did the newspaper industry disguise its vulnerability after its heyday and miss its own deteriorating financial fundamentals?

Leading Newspapers

STUDY PREVIEW

Although not the largest U.S. daily, the New York *Times* is the most influential. The T*imes* is known for comprehensive news coverage and journalistic enterprise and courage. The largest U.S. dailies are the *Wall Street Journal* and *USA Today* followed by the New York *Times*.

New York *Times*

Despite being buffeted financially as part of the beleaguered U.S. newspaper industry, the New York *Times* remains the standard-bearer of journalistic excellence. Even critics of the *Times* are hard-pressed to name a better newspaper.

A Paper of Record. Since its founding in 1851, the *Times* has had a reputation for fair and thorough coverage of foreign news. Also, it is a newspaper of record, for decades printing the president's annual State of the Union address and other important documents in their entirety. Recently the *Times* began offering interactive video, the transcript and reactions to the speech via its web site. The *Times* is an important research source, in part because of a monthly and an annual index that lists every story. More than 150 years of the *Times* pages are available online and in many libraries in bound volumes.

In an attempt to attract younger readers, the *Times* has followed the lead of other newspapers by adding some lighter fare to the serious coverage. A Thursday style section includes more lifestyle-oriented advertising. For most of its history, the *Times* scorned comics but now has a 10-page "Funny Pages" section at the front of its glitzy Sunday magazine. The magazine, edited for a high-brow audience, includes work by graphic artists, serialized genre fiction and a venue for humor writers called "True-Life Tales." A serious book review magazine and one of the world's most popular crossword puzzles remain weekly fixtures.

Times Heritage. The New York *Times'* journalistic reputation was cemented in the 1870s when courageous reporting brought down the city government.

William Tweed
Corrupt politician exposed by
New York *Times*

- **Tweed Scandal.** City Council member **William Tweed** had built a fortune with fraudulent streetcar franchises, sales of nonexistent buildings to the city and double billing. In 1868 Tweed and like-minded crooks and scoundrels were swept into city offices in a

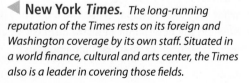

◀ **New York *Times*.** *The long-running reputation of the Times rests on its foreign and Washington coverage by its own staff. Situated in a world finance, cultural and arts center, the Times also is a leader in covering those fields.*

landslide election, and more fraud grew like a spider web. The *Times* launched an exposé in 1870, which prompted Tweed to press the *Times'* largest advertisers to withdraw their advertising. Neither the management of the *Times* nor the main reporter on the story, **George Jones,** was deterred. With documents leaked from a disgruntled city employee, the *Times* reported that the Tweed Gang had robbed the city of as much as $200 million. Desperate, Tweed sent an underling to offer Jones $5 million in hush money—a bribe to back off. Jones refused and sent the underling packing.

- **Sullivan Libel Case.** In 1960, in the heat of U.S. racial desegregation tensions, the Montgomery, Alabama, police commissioner was incensed at criticism in an advertisement in the New York *Times* that promoted racial integration. He sued for libel and won in Alabama courts. The *Times* could have settled but chose an expensive appeal to the U.S. Supreme Court to prove a First Amendment principle about free expression. The **Sullivan decision** came in 1964, establishing new rules on libel and untethering the U.S. news media in reporting public issues.

- *Pentagon Papers.* After being leaked a copy of a secret government study on U.S. policy in the Vietnam war, the *Times* conducted an exhaustive examination of the documents and decided to run a series of articles based on them. The government ordered the *Times* to halt the series, creating a showdown between the free press and the secretive Nixon administration. Not to be intimidated, the *Times* took the so-called **Pentagon Papers** case to the U.S. Supreme Court, arguing that the people in a democracy need information to make intelligent decisions on essential issues like war and peace. The Supreme Court sided with the *Times,* adding new legal obstacles to government censorship.

Wall Street Journal

The *Wall Street Journal,* the nation's largest newspaper, began humbly in 1882 as a newsletter that circulated in the New York financial district. As more information-hungry investors signed up, the service was expanded into a newspaper. By 1900 circulation had reached 10,000, miniscule in the rapid-growth newspaper industry.

Kilgore Formula. The *Wall Street Journal* might have remained a relatively small albeit successful business paper had it not been for the legendary **Barney Kilgore**, who joined the newspaper's San Francisco bureau in 1929. Within two years Kilgore was the *Journal's* news editor and in a position to shift the newspaper's journalistic direction. Kilgore's formula was threefold:

- Simplify the *Journal's* business coverage into plain English without sacrificing thoroughness.

- Provide detailed coverage of government but without the jargon that plagued most Washington reporting at the time.

- Expand the definition of the *Journal's* field of coverage from "business" to "everything that somehow relates to earning a living."

The last part of the formula, expanded coverage, was a risk. Critics told Kilgore that the newspaper's existing readers might switch to other financial papers if they thought the *Journal* was slighting business. Kilgore's vision, however, was not to reduce business coverage but to seek business angles in other fields and cover them too. It worked. Today, with circulation at 2.1 million, the *Journal* is the largest U.S. daily.

For advertisers, the *Journal's* attraction is more than circulation totals. The median household income of *Journal* readers is $124,600. That's a lot of discretionary income and exceeds even that of the readers of the New York *Times,* which is high at $95,400.

The *Journal* puts significant resources into reporting. It was not unusual in the paper's heyday for a reporter to be given six weeks and an open-end expenses budget to collect research for a major story. This digging gave the *Journal* big breaks on significant stories.

The *Wall Street Journal* has 500 editors and reporters, but not all are at the newspaper's Manhattan headquarters. The Journal has 37 foreign and 14 domestic bureaus, and its European and Asian editions have their own staffs.

Murdoch Focus. In 2007 the heirs of the *Journal's* founders sold the newspaper to media baron **Rupert Murdoch**. As critics expected, Murdoch, known mostly for low-brow media operations, ordered shifts in emphasis—noticeably shorter stories, more visuals, snappier headlines and jazzier presentation. Murdoch explained he sought to widen the *Journal's* appeal to compete more directly with the New York *Times.* Murdoch's

George Jones
New York *Times* reporter who pursued Tammany Hall scandal

Sullivan decision
Landmark libel case in which New York *Times* argued for unfettered reporting of public officials

Pentagon Papers
Secret government-generated Vietnam war military documents revealed by New York *Times*

Barney Kilgore
Revamped concept of *Wall Street Journal* 1940s

Rupert Murdoch
Founder of global media conglomerate News Corporation

remake rankled many *Journal* aficionados. The revamped *Journal* was both less than the old *Journal* and anemic compared to the *Times.* The changes, however, were a work in progress, and Murdoch, ever a keen business operator, had a long history of shifting course if his changes didn't work out rather than jeopardize an investment. Also, Murdoch was cautious not to dabble too much with the *Journal*'s historic appeal for its finance and business coverage.

As in the Kilgore era, the challenge for the *Journal* remains finding a balance between its original forte—covering business—and its expanding coverage of broader issues. It is a precarious balance. Numerous business media, ranging from the magazine *Bloomberg Businessweek* to the cable television network CNBC and uncountable online sources, vie for the same readers and advertisers. So far, the *Journal* has succeeded with a gradual broadening of general coverage without losing its business readers.

USA Today

A strict format, snappy visuals and crisp writing give *USA Today* an air of confidence and the trappings of success. Indeed, the newspaper has strengths. In less than a decade of its founding in 1982 by the giant Gannett chain. *USA Today*'s circulation reached 1.6 million. By 2007 *USA Today* was the largest circulation U.S. newspaper at 2.3 million, passing the *Wall Street Journal,* although it since has dropped behind.

From the start, *USA Today* was distinctive. Historically the United States had been a nation of provincial newspapers. Aside from the *Wall Street Journal* there never had been a significant national daily. With Gannett chain's massive profitability, chief executive Allen Neuharth took a big-bucks risk into untried waters with a general-interest national daily.

Neuharth Concept.   Unlike most U.S. dailies, *USA Today* built its circulation mostly on single-copy sales and bulk sales—not individual subscriptions. Neuharth targeted business travelers who wanted a quick fix on the news. Many sales were at airport newsracks. Deep discounts were given to upscale hotels to buy the papers in bulk and slip them under guests' doors free as a morning courtesy.

Stories strained to be lively and upbeat to make the experience of reading the paper a positive one. Most stories were short, diverting little of a reader's time from pressing business. The brevity and crispness of *USA Today,* combined with the enticing graphics and the razzle-dazzle compendium of blurbs, earned the newspaper the derisive nickname *McPaper.*

Adjusting the Concept to Online Delivery.   Facing declines in circulation and advertising revenue steams, like the newspaper industry overall, publisher Dave Hunke reorganized the paper going into 2011 to de-emphasize the print edition and ramp up online delivery. Hunke's focus remained *USA Today*'s traditional strength—business travelers, even though recession-beleaguered corporations had cut their travel budgets drastically and put fewer people on the road. Hunke's idea, however, was to reach business travelers on mobile devices like smartphones and iPads and hang on for an upturn in business travel: "This gets us ready for our next quarter century," he said. The question is how advertisers will see the revamp. In the latest quarter before Hunke launched the reorganization, which included 120 layoffs, advertising pages were down to 580 from 1,098 two years earlier.

***USA Today* Impact.**   Whatever its financial prospects, *USA Today* has been influential in American journalism. When *USA Today* was launched, most newspapers were trying to distinguish themselves from television news with longer, exploratory and interpretive stories. While some major newspapers such as the New York *Times* and the Los Angeles *Times* have been unswayed by *USA Today*'s snappy, quick-to-read format, many other newspapers moved to shorter, easily digested stories, infographics and more data lists. *USA Today* has influenced today's newspaper style and format. Color became standard.

■ A Subscription Digital News Gamble

The crown jewels in Rupert Murdoch's media empire are his lucrative Fox television franchise, HarperCollins books and major newspapers including the *Wall Street Journal*. But Murdoch has had failures too. The question now is whether his digital-only newspaper the *Daily*, launched in 2011, will make it as an app for Apple's iPad. Murdoch says he has the right numbers for the *Daily* to usher in the digital newsstand of the future.

Murdoch's start-up costs for the *Daily* were relative pocket change, $30 million. Production costs he projected at $26 million a year—low by daily newspaper standards because the *Daily*, being digital-only, requires neither expensive presses nor fuel-consuming delivery trucks or costly postage. There were 15 million iPad devices at the time, each capable of receiving the *Daily*. With subscriptions at 99 cents a week and the iPad audience growing, Murdoch foresaw a profitable revenue stream, albeit only a fraction of iPad users would sign on.

At a roll-out ceremony for the new iPad-specific product, Murdoch acknowledged fading prospects for ink-on-paper newspapers and magazines: "We can and we must make the business of newsgathering and editing viable again." He called the *Daily* "a new journalism," but it was more a slick packaging of traditional content.

To be sure, there were twists, including video and stories packaged as in a newscast, as well as interactive features, all wedded in a seamless presentation with iPad users able to skip easily to what most interested them individually.

Mostly what was new was digital delivery. Media consultant Mike Vorhaus called the *Daily* "about as close as you're going to get to the first big test of content on the iPad."

No Daily Planet. *What Rupert wants Rupert doesn't always get. Rupert Murdoch initially planned to give his digital-only newspaper a Superman aura by naming it the* Daily Planet. *But DC Comics exercised its claim to the name of the fictional newspaper and said no. So is the* Daily, *launched in 2011, the right publication at the right time? Will a generation of readers who have picked up the habits of free news on the internet prove the* Daily's *kryptonite?*

Actually the *Wall Street Journal*, another Murdoch product, was available months earlier as an iPad app. But the *Journal* app was a sideline to the print newspaper—not a digital-only product. There had been a few other newspapers as iPad apps, but for sale only an issue at a time—not a continuing subscription.

Murdoch talks euphorically about the *Daily* being geared to a new generation of readers looking for "content tailored to their specific interests to be available anytime anywhere." Murdoch's optimism was not universally shared. Indeed, for a generation readers had moved away for pay-for-access news and custom-assembled their understanding of world events and issues from the panoply of free sources on the internet. The *Daily*-Apple business model was subscriber-supported, although the model was open to advertising as a revenue stream. Early issues carried ads from the HBO cable television network, Virgin Atlantic airline and auto-maker Range Rover.

So is the *Daily* a preface to the future for newspaper and magazines companies? Media analysts hedged their predictions, at least about a quick success. Sarah Rotman Epps said the success of any pay-for-news product will be in "small numbers." longer term, she said Murdoch needs to take a long view.

What Do You Think?

Visit the *Daily* web site and check out the content. How does the *Daily* compare with traditional newspapers?

Is the *Daily* making the best use of the iPad technology?

- Look for clues in the online editions of the New York *Times, Wall Street Journal* and *USA Today* for their ongoing and distinctive contributions to covering news.
- Explain how you would rank the importance of Ben Day, George Jones, Barney Kilgore and Allen Neuharth for their impact on the newspaper industry.
- What impact do you see mobile devices, e-readers and online subscriptions having on the way the New York *Times, Wall Street Journal* and *USA Today* report the news of the day?

Magazine Industry

STUDY PREVIEW

Advances in printing and in transportation, as well as postal discounts, propelled magazines into a major media industry in the 1800s. Content innovations like long-form journalism and photojournalism drew massive readerships. In recent times, competing media have eroded magazines' province on the innovations. Digital technology has cut into the audience and also advertising revenue.

Scope of Magazine Industry

Early magazines were minor enterprises. The content was geared to classically educated and well-to-do elites. After the Civil War, however, several developments precipitated huge circulation growth, and an identifiable magazine industry took form. What happened?

- New rotary presses from R. Hoe & Co. made possible larger press runs.
- The growing national railroad system enabled wide distribution.
- Congress created second-class postage rates that cut distribution costs dramatically.

With the economy of scale from larger press runs, the per-unit production costs fell. In 1883, S. S. McClure dropped the price of his general-interest *McClure's* to only 15 cents. Rival publisher Frank Munsey then lowered the price of his *Munsey's* to 10 cents. Magazines became a mass medium, the leading titles offering an array of articles to appeal to broad spectrums of readers. An identifiable magazine industry soon took form.

Today about 17,800 magazines are published in the United Sates, although only 400 have circulations exceeding 100,000. Most have modest and tightly focused circulations, like employee magazines, college alumni magazines, and aficionado magazines. Even so, the industry is large with revenue of $40 billion a year.

The industry is concentrated. Fifty companies generate 70 percent of the revenue. Here are leading U.S. magazine publishing companies with some of their titles:

- **Condé Nast:** *Allure, Architectural Digest, Bon Appetité, Bridal, Details, Glamour, Golf Digest, GQ, House & Garden, Lucky, New Yorker, Self, Vanity Fair, Vogue, W, Wired.*
- **Hachette Filapacchi:** *Car & Driver, Cycle World, Elle, Road & Track, Women's Day.*
- **Hearst:** *Cosmopolitan, Country Living, Esquire, Good Housekeeping, House Beautiful, Marie Claire, Popular Mechanics, Redbook, Seventeen, Town & Country,* and *O, the Oprah Magazine.*
- **Meredith:** *American Baby, Better Homes & Gardens, Family Circle, Fitness, Ladies' Home Journal, Midwest Living, Parents, Traditional Home.*
- **Primedia:** *Automobile, Car Craft, Home Theater, Horse & Rider, Hot Bike, Motor Trend, Motorcyclist, Power & Motoryacht, Sail, Snowboarder, Skateboarder, Soap Opera Digest, Stereophile.*
- **Time Inc.:** *AllYou, Cooking Light, Entertainment, Essence, Fortune, Golf, Health, Inside People, Life, Money, People, Real Simple, Southern Living, Sports Illustrated, Sunset, This Old House, Time.*

Magazine Innovations

Through their history, magazines have been innovators in media content. Other media then picked up on the innovations, which included long-form journalism.

▲ **Daniel Defoe.** *The British novelist and pamphleteer had his quill in many ink pots. Defoe's* Weekly Review, *in publication from 1704 to 1713, created a legacy for magazines as a vehicle for essays and thought-provoking commentary.*

Essays.   Although many flashy magazines these days have shifted toward infotainment tidbits and treat serious issues only briefly, an enduring magazine tradition is articles of length and depth that cannot be boiled down to a few sentences. This tradition dates to **Daniel Defoe**. Although remembered mostly for his adventure tale *Robinson Crusoe*, Defoe was also a magazine pioneer. In 1704 he established an influential journal in London, *Weekly Review*, which carried essays. Defoe's *Review* had a nine-year run, establishing a role for magazines as a bridge between society's book-reading intelligentsia and a broad audience.

The Defoe tradition carries on in what are called **highbrow slicks**. These magazines, of which *Atlantic* and *Harper's* are examples, work at being at the cutting edge of thinking on political economic, social, artistic and cultural issues. The *New Yorker* prides itself on breaking ground on significant issues in articles that run as long as editors think necessary, some the length of a small book. Ideological magazines like the *New Republic, Nation* and *National Review* frequently are both partisan and cerebral. Like the highbrow slicks, they are edited for **literati**.

Investigative Reporting.   In the early 1900s, magazines honed **muckraking**, usually called *investigative reporting* today. Magazines ran lengthy explorations of abusive practices in government, business and other institutions in society. It was Theodore Roosevelt, the reform president, who coined the term *muckraking*. Roosevelt generally enjoyed investigative journalism, but one day in 1906, when the digging got too close to home, he likened it to the work of a character in a 17th century novel who focused so much on raking muck that he missed the good news. The president meant the term derisively, but it became a badge of honor among journalists.

Muckraking established magazines as a powerful medium in shaping public policy. In 1902 **Ida Tarbell** wrote a 19-part series on the Standard Oil monopoly for *McClure's*. As a result of Tarbell's reporting, the government broke up the monopoly. **Lincoln Steffens** detailed municipal corruption. Reforms followed. Other magazines picked up on the investigative thrusts. *Collier's* took on patent medicine frauds. *Cosmopolitan*, a leading muckraking journal of the period, tackled dishonesty in the U.S. Senate. Muckraking expanded into books with **Upton Sinclair's** *The Jungle*. In the novel, which only slightly veiled reality, Sinclair shocked the nation about filth in meat-packing plants. Federal inspection laws followed.

Personality Profiles.   The in-depth **personality profile** was a magazine invention in the 1920s. **Harold Ross** of the *New Yorker* began pushing writers to a thoroughness that was new in journalism. In the 1950s the conversational Q & A was refined by **Hugh Hefner** at *Playboy*, adding cogent authenticity to long-form profiles. The exhaustive nature of lengthy Q & As like *Playboy's* can draw out people in ways that other journalistic forms do not. Most *Playboy* interviews are drawn from weeks, sometimes months, of face time, all recorded and then spliced into a coherent article running 7,000 words or more. Many political and religious leaders, scientists and other thinkers, celebrities too, covet the opportunity that long Q & As give them to expand and elaborate on what they have to say.

Photojournalism.   Perhaps the most enduring innovation from the magazine industry is visuals. *Brother Jonathan* was a pioneer in the mid-1800s, but the illustrations were meager.

Daniel Defoe
His 1704 *Weekly Review* established magazines as forum for ideas

highbrow slicks
Magazines whose content has intellectual appeal

literati
Well-educated people interested in literature and cerebral issues

muckraking
Early 1990s term for investigative reporting

Ida Tarbell
Exposed Standard Oil monopolistic practices in 1902 magazine series

Lincoln Steffens
Exposed municipal corruption

Upton Sinclair
Exposed bad meat-packing practices

personality profile
In-depth, balanced biographical article

Hugh Hefner
Playboy editor who created modern Q-A

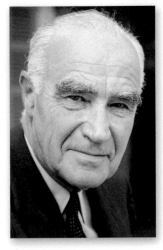

▲ Henry Luce.

ELIZABETH
TAYLOR

JULY 14, 1947 **15** CENTS
YEARLY SUBSCRIPTION $5.50

◀ **Oversize and Visual.** *With Luce's* Life *magazine, launched in 1936, photojournalism came of age. On slick paper for good resolution, closely cropped photos jumped off the page at readers for maximum impact. Some photos we bled into the margins and off the page to be even more potent.* Life *was a powerful weekly look, literally, at the world.*

Henry Luce
His magazine empire included *Time, Life, Sports Illustrated, Fortune*

Otherwise magazines were entirely word-driven. A breakthrough came in the Civil War when *Harper's Weekly* sent artists to draw battles, leading the way to journalism that goes beyond words. Today visuals are a core element in all mass media except radio. This will not change in the digital age: Visuals pixelate well.

A whole new world of documentary coverage was opened in 1936 when magazine entrepreneur **Henry Luce** launched *Life* and propelled photojournalism into new importance. The oversized weekly demonstrated that newsworthy events could be covered consistently by camera. *Life* captured the spirit of the times photographically and demonstrated that the whole range of humane experience could be recorded visually. Both real life and *Life* could be shocking. A 1938 *Life* photo essay on human birth was so shocking for the time that censors succeeded in banning the issue in 33 cities.

Challenges For Magazines

The U.S. magazine industry prospered in the 20th century. The number of magazines grew six-fold from 3,000 to 17,800, far faster than the population. Industry historian David Sumner has noted that although *Time* magazine co-founder Henry Luce coined the term *The American Century,* it could also be called *The Magazine Century.* Americans averaged less than half a magazine per month in 1920. By the end of the century, the average had tripled to 1.35. The U.S. magazine industry publishes three times as many magazines as any other country.

This was despite setbacks. Network television, for example, stole major advertisers from leading national magazines in the 1950s. Advertisers found the new networks more efficient at reaching potential customers. A case in point: A full-page in *Life* magazine ran $65,000 in 1970. In advertising lingo, that was $7.75 CPM, shorthand for cost per thousand, the *M* for the Roman numeral thousand. The network CPM was $3.60 for the same number of eyeballs. *Life* and other leading general-interest magazines like the *Saturday Evening Post, Look* and *Collier's* were soon out of business. Exceptions among general interests title were weekly newsmagazines like *Time* and *Newsweek,* which continued to prosper. So did shelter magazines, like *Ladies' Home Journal* and *Better Homes & Gardens.* And so did niche magazine, which offered special-interest readerships to advertisers for products with narrower appeals.

These days *Life* shows up only on news racks as an occasional photo-strong, commemorative, thematic edition. There also is a Life partnership with Getty Images at Life.com, making use of the millions of images from their combined collections available on the internet. Of course, the site is filled with advertisements as well as opportunities to make purchases from the Life Store. Not quite a magazine anymore, the site takes a new approach to photojournalism, using the latest technology to do so.

The magazine industry's shift toward niche audiences was called **demassification.** The niche audiences, although significant, were really submass audiences—not the broader audiences that magazines like *Life,* with something for everyone, had cultivated. Some niches grew rapidly, especially new-breed celebrity and human-interest magazines like *People.* Launched in 1974, *People* today is the largest circulation U.S. weekly at 3.6 million.

APPLYING YOUR MEDIA LITERACY

- **How has technology been both the bedrock and the nemesis of the magazine industry?**
- **Compare the innovations of *Brother Jonathan, Harper's Weekly, National Geographic* and *Life* in media visuals.**
- **What has become of word-driven magazine innovations like investigative journalism personality profiles that have identified magazines historically?**

Reinventing Magazines

STUDY PREVIEW | The twin revenue streams for the magazine industry, advertising and direct sales to readers, are in rapid decline. Newsmagazines are a case study in survival strategies with no course guaranteeing success. Even so, some magazines continue to hold their own, particularly shelter and niche titles.

Declining Magazine Circulation

When Jon Meacham, the editor at *Newsweek,* was invited to drop in at Columbia University to discuss magazines with a group of 100 grad students one day in 2008, he started by asking for a show of hands on how many read *Newsweek.* Nobody did. It was a telling moment. Two years later, with *Newsweek* losses passing $71 million, the magazine's long-time owner, the Washington Post Company, put the magazine up for sale. Finding no serious bidders, the magazine went for a token $1 to stereo-equipment tycoon Sidney Harman, who agreed to pick up the magazine's debts. What had happened at the once high-riding *Newsweek?* Meacham's explanation: The magazine had been caught in the same problems as almost all historically print-based periodicals—advertising declines, competition from digital media, and an increasingly fragmented audience. "The task before us now is to find the right economic and digital means to meet our traditional ends while trying to discover a sustainable business model," he said.

A tally of almost 500 leading U.S. magazines found that newsstand sales fell 9 percent leading into 2010, after a 24 percent decline the year before. A slight uptick in 2011, propelled by subscription sales, was not exactly bright news: Subscriptions are less profitable because of heavy discounting. Worse, the magazine industry's primary revenue stream—advertising—was down about 26 percent as measured by ad pages.

The question is whether the magazine industry can survive with ink-on-paper products. One survival strategy has become: If you can't beat 'em, join 'em. Many traditional magazines have extended their presence online. The online environment however is already crowded, and these traditional magazines are trying to find a place in the frenzied internet array of sources for all kinds of information, amusement and enlightenment. The traditional strengths and distinguishing characteristic of magazines as a mass medium are no longer their exclusive province. The web is far more competitive than a newsstand.

Like newspapers, magazines historically have had two revenue streams—direct sales to readers and advertising. While single-sale and subscription revenue make a dent in fixed business costs, it is advertising revenue that drives profits. Now, with circulation dropping, advertisers have shifted to alternate vehicles to carry their messages. With broader media choices for readers and advertisers than ever before, the magazine industry is in a shakeout. The bottom line: At what point do circulation and advertising revenue drop magazines below a level of sustainability?

MEDIApeople

■ Ritzy, Risky, Rescue Plan

▲ Richard Beckman.

He sees life left in the print media. Beckman is adding glitz to old trade journals, like Hollywood Reporter, *in hopes of attracting upscale outside-the-trade readers. If Beckman's plan works, advertisers for high-end consumer products will flock to his publications.*

With the magazine industry flailing frantically to re-invent itself, Richard Beckman's B-to-I idea is at least as promising as any. *B-to-I* is shorthand for **business-to-influentials.** Beckman has taken a handful of dowdy trade journals, edited for small professional audiences, with the idea of building them into glitzy advertising-laden magazines. He's trying to do this without losing the trade journals' solid base.

Might B-to-I be the future of magazines?

Beckman, a former executive in the tony Condé Nast magazine empire, points to the trade journal *Hollywood Reporter.* Beckman's Prometheus Global Media bought the *Reporter* in 2009, the magazine had 12,000 circulation among movie-industry insiders. That was peanuts compared to Condé Nast's glossy flagships like tony *GQ, Vanity Fair* and *Vogue.* But *Hollywood Reporter,* like many trade journals, was relatively recession-proof. Movie studios place their big-buck ads to sway members of the Academy of Motion Pictures to vote for their Oscar nominees. Oscars, of course, translate exponentially into box office and video sales.

Hollywood Reporter's readership was comprised of what Beckman calls *influentials.* Their influence far outdistances their numbers.

Beckman's vision goes further. In *Hollywood Reporter,* he sees potential to expand the audience by editing for not only Hollywood insiders but a broader audience of movie enthusiasts. The *Reporter* could become not just an advertising vehicle for reaching industry outsiders buy all for reaching general consumer advertising as well.

In his 24 years as a Condé Nast executive, Beckman learned the flashy side of the magazine and advertising businesses. In his last assignment with Condé Nast, he headed a company unit that included *Footwear News, Women's Wear Daily* and a handful of trade journals. He knows both the glitzy, high-visibility side of the magazine industry and the often-overlooked trade journal side.

The question is whether Beckman can parlay his experience and contacts into his B-to-I model.

For Beckman personally, a lot is at stake. In founding Prometheus, he convinced investors to pony up $70 million to buy a polyglot assortment of trade journals that included not only *Hollywood Reporter* but also *Adweek,* circulation 47,000, mostly in U.S. advertising agencies, and *Billboard,* widely recognized for its music charts but not much read beyond 16,000 music-industry insiders. In magazine industry circles, Beckman was called

crazy for paying $70 million. Too much, way too much, the critics said. Beckman's response: It's time to forget the conventional wisdom that magazines should be measured quantitatively by circulation. Instead, he said, look at circulation qualitatively and ask whether the readership has influence that can drive consumer demand.

Time will tell. The critics have difficulty envisioning a trade journal being more than a trade journal. Consider, for example, *Footwear News,* which focuses on news on shoe-making companies, retail shoe strategies and international regulations on footwear. The advertising in Footwear News is directed at shoe manufacturers, designers and retailers—everything from novel fabrics, new display rack designs, and manufacturing equipment. It's a classic **business-to-business** trade journal, B-to-B for short. The question: Can trade journals become a home for the high-fashion products of the sort on which the Condé Nast empire had polished its **advertiser-to-consumer** business model—Vuitton handbags, Armani suits, exotic travel, Rolex watches.

Some signs are positive for Beckman. In the first 15 months after relaunching *Hollywood Reporter,* advertising grew 50 percent. One 156-page issue carried 67 pages of advertising including ads from beauty, fashion, liquor and consumer electronic products. Traffic at hollywoodreporter.com was up nine-fold. Pounding the drum for his B-to-I model, Beckman proclaimed that the magazine gives access for advertisers to "the most influential constituency in the entertainment space." The entertainment magazine field, though, is littered with casualties— *V Life, Premiere, American Film Monthly.*

Also, doubters are leery of mixing media business models. Although tricky, it has been done. In the 1940s Barney Kilgore took the *Wall Street Journal,* a narrowly focused newspaper for investors, and broadened the audience and the advertising base to build the largest-circulation newspaper in the United States. Today the *Journal* is home for B-to-B advertising and also business-to-consumer advertising for the likes of high-end handbags and luxury vacations.

At *Billboard* too, Beckman is looking for striking up new endeavors to move into the B-To-I model. *Billboard* has partnered with MySpace Music to lend its brand name to unsigned bands. Beckman revived the annual Billboard Music Awards in Las Vegas to enhance the brand beyond that of a little-read B-to-B trade journal.

What Do You Think?

How do you rate Richard Beckman's chances for success in shifting trade journals into high-end consumer magazines?

What possibilities do you see for slowing the slippage of the magazine industry?

▲ Michael Kinsley.

▲ **Online Upstart.** *Backed by giant software developer Microsoft,* Slate *was a pioneer as a web-only magazine.* Slate *specializes in politics, arts and culture, sports, and news.*

Web-Only Magazines

For most of the 1980s and 1990s the worst kept secret in Washington was who wrote the must-read column "TRB" in the leftist magazine the *New Republic.* The column was witty, insightful, thought-provoking—and all **Michael Kinsley**. Although mostly associated with the *New Republic,* Kinsley was a magazine gadfly with editorships also at *Harper's, Washington Monthly,* the *Economist,* as well as editing the Los Angeles *Times* opinion section for a while and dueling intellectually with conservative columnist Pat Buchanan on the CNN political program *Crossfire.* He also took parts in three movies in the 1990s.

Slate.   As home as Kinsley was with traditional media, he took an online plunge in 1996 with the Microsoft-funded Slate.com. **Slate** had been launched two years earlier, the first major online upstart of a magazine that didn't have ownership roots in the ink-on-paper magazine industry.

Under Kinsley, the Seattle-based *Slate* became known for the mini-columns "Explainer," "Chatterbox" and "Dear Prudence" as well as long-form journalism, usually an essay or project per week. In 1999 Kinsley was named Editor of the Year by *Columbia Journalism Review* for his work at *Slate.*

Although *Slate* made media history as a web-only magazine, its finances have been wobbly. From 1998 to 1999 it tried charging $20 for an annual subscription. When that didn't work, *Slate* went free again with an explanation that advertising revenue was improving. In the meantime, Microsoft sold the magazine to a Washington Post Company subsidiary that specializes in web-only magazines.

Salon.   A rival to *Slate* is *Salon,* founded in 1995 in San Francisco—also far from the U.S. magazine hub in New York City. Like *Slate, Salon* updates content daily with a focus on politics and current affairs and coverage and reviews on music, books and films. There is a leering, sassy tone. Editor David Talbot once described *Salon* as "a smart tabloid."

The *Salon* formula has attracted a following, but, like *Slate,* its finances have been iffy. In 2001, almost broke, *Salon* introduced pay-to-view "premium content" but continued free

business-to-influentials (B-to-I)
A business model with advertising aimed at creating sales indirectly by reaching influential audiences.

Michael Kinsley
Founding editor of *Slate* magazine as well as editor for the *New Republic* and numerous other publications

Slate
Online magazine of news, politics and culture

access to most of the site. The magazine picked up 130,000 subscribers at $45 a year. But financial difficulties have been an ongoing issue, prompting ongoing pleas for donations.

Sponsored Web Magazines. Patrons keep some online magazines afloat. These sugar daddy-sponsored sites usually have a narrow bent, some ideological, which limits their broad appeal. Also, some sponsored online magazines are from zealots without deep pockets but who can create an internet presence without much investment.

Among the sponsored web magazines, appearing in 2010 was the shadowy *Inspire* that claims to be from the terrorist organization Al-Qaeda on the Arabian Peninsula. An early issue reprinted messages from Osama bin Laden and other terrorist leaders. One article, "Make a Bomb in the Kitchen of Your Mom," called for terror attacks in Britain and the United States. Suggestions included opening fire at a Washington, D.C. restaurant and using a pickup truck to mow down pedestrians.

Although in English, *Inspire* wasn't geared for a large mass audience. British and U.S. intelligence authorities saw *Inspire* as an attempt to recruit English-speaking Muslims into the Al-Qaeda cause.

The base of *Inspire* was Yemen. Intelligence experts believed the magazine to be mostly the work of Samir Khan, an American blogger who distributed terrorist propaganda online before moving to Yemen. He signed one article, "I Am Proud to be a Traitor to America," in the 74-page second issue of *Inspire*.

MEDIAtimeline

PRINT MEDIA MILESTONES

PRINT MEDIA
Gutenberg invented movable metal type (1446)

PROLIFERATION
Gutenberg printing technology in use throughout Europe (1500)

PIVOTAL EVENTS

- Joan of arc burned at stake (1431)
- First Christopher Columbus voyage to Americas (1492)
- Martin Luther posted his 95 Thesis, launching Protestant Reformation (1521)
- Spanish Inquisition began (1481)
- Leonardo da Vinci, artist, thinker (1452–1519)
- Copernicus posited that sun center of solar system (1512)
- Henry VIII established break-away Church of England (1532)

Ink-on-paper begins a long run

1400–1500s

PRINT MEDIA MILESTONES

FIRST PRESS
Puritans established Cambridge Press (1638)

PIVOTAL EVENTS

- Age of Science, Age of Reason began (1600s)
- Pilgrims founded Plymouth colony (1620)
- Isaac Newton discovered natural laws (1687)

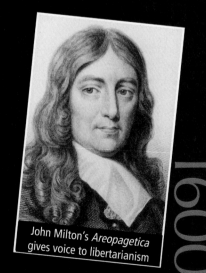

John Milton's Areopagetica gives voice to libertarianism

1600s

PRINT MEDIA MILESTONES

RISE OF BOOK INDUSTRY
J.B. Lippincott established as major publishing house (1792)

PIVOTAL EVENTS

- Industrial Revolution (1760s–)
- Revolutionary War (1776–1781)
- Thomas Newcomen invented steam engine (1712)
- Johann Sebastian Bach, composer (1685–1750)
- Jonathan Swift, satirist (1667–1745)
- Daily Courant, London, first daily newspaper (1702)
- Little Ice Age peaked (1750)
- French and Indian War (1754–1763)
- Antonio Vivaldi, composer (1648–1741)

Daniel Defoe creates essay tradition for magazines

1700s

Online Hate. *The slick web-only magazine* Inspire, *in English, appeared to be the work of disaffected American blogger Samir Khan. From Yemen, Khan operated the low-cost site to recruit young U.S. and British Muslims to jihad militancy and terrorism. The sponsors of* Inspire *measure the site's success not in advertising revenue but in blood.*

Late in 2011 Khan was killed in a U.S. drone strike along with al-Qaeda leader Anwar al-Awlaki. Because both were U.S. citizens, the targeted killings raised questions about Constitutional guarantees of free expression for American citizens and the right to a trial. Even so, the deaths were a major blow to the al-Qaeda brand and to the organization al-Qaeda in the Arabian Peninsula.

PRINT MEDIA MILESTONES

PENNY PRESS
New York *Sun,* first penny newspaper (1833)
New York *Times* founded as serious alternative to penny papers (1851)

MEGA-CHAINS
Hearst aquired San Francisco *Examiner,* which became flagship for major chain (1887)

PIVOTAL EVENTS

- Public education took root as social value (1820s)
- Machine-made paper widely available (1830s)
- Civil War (1861–1865)
- Public education spurs quantum growth in literacy (1880s)
- World population passed 1 billion (1804)
- Charles Darwin wrote On Origin of Species (1859)
- Heinreich Hertz produced radio waves (1886)

Industrialization fueled huge circulations

PRINT MEDIA MILESTONES

MUCKRAKING
Ida Tarbell magazine exposé on Standard Oil (1902)
Upton Sinclair's *The Jungle* (1906)

MAGAZINE INNOVATION
The compendium *Reader's Digest* founded (1922), newsmagazine *Time* (1923), *New Yorker* (1924)

PHOTOJOURNALISM
Henry Luce founded *Life,* coined term *photo essay* (1936)

DIGITAL BOOKS
E-book introduced (1998)

Henry Luce creates magazine empire for his American Century

PRINT MEDIA MILESTONES

WIKIPEDIA
Wikipedia launched as reader-edited online reference tool (2001)

NEWSPAPER CHAINS FALTER
Historic chain Knight-Ridder fumbles financially, sold (2006)

READERSHIP SHIFT
More people get news online than from newspapers, magazines (2008)

FAILURES
Rocky Mountain News, Denver, shut down, largest newspaper to fold; others follow (2009)

PIVOTAL EVENTS

- Dot-Com Bubble burst (2000)
- Great Recession (2007–2009)

Wiki founder Jimmy Wales

1800S

1900S

2000S

The cost of producing online magazines is relatively low if the content, as with *Inspire*, is from volunteers and is mostly regurgitated from elsewhere. The operating budget of *Inspire* was estimated at less than $5,000 an issue. Costs rise rapidly when content is original, as with *Slate* and *Salon*. The services of experienced journalists and commentators are not free.

Book Industry

STUDY PREVIEW

The book industry held its own more than media companies with ink-on-paper products after the economic recession that began in 2007. Niche publishers were especially strong. One factor in the book industry's state of affairs is the mergers and acquisitions of publishing companies, many on a global scale, which put more emphasis on the bottom line. A downside is the disappearance of quirks that once gave publishing houses their distinctive characters. A negative component of the U.S. book industry is retailing, with bookstores losing to online vendors.

Scope of Book Industry

The U.S. book publishing industry has weathered the internet-triggered downturn of other traditional ink-on-paper media. Estimates peg the future growth of the 10 largest publishers of mass-market books at 3.5 percent. This is especially noteworthy considering the ongoing negative impact of the 2008 recession on the economy. In 2010 sales were growing 11.3 percent at HarperCollins and 10.7 percent at Penguin. Wiley, whose offerings include the *For Dummies* series, racked up a 6.7 percent advance. Combined revenues at the 10 largest publishers topped $7.9 billion.

But there are soft spots. Sales of $23.9 billion in 2009 overall were off 1.8 percent, hurt largely by budget-strapped schools that delayed replacing textbooks for their students. Also, sales of highly visible trade books, which include best-selling novels, were down 5 percent. On the upside, college textbook sales, about one-fifth of industry sales, grew almost 13 percent. College sales were propelled in part by the expansion of online courses in which textbooks carry a heavy role in instruction.

The industry produces about 289,000 titles a year in the United States. The largest growth, offsetting declines in traditional books, has been from reprint houses that specialize in public domain works and use digital technology to produce small batches that were not economically feasible before.

Publishing Houses

Major publishing houses are widely recognized brand names: Simon & Schuster, Knopf, Doubleday, HarperCollins, Penguin. To most people, though, a book is a book is a book, no matter the publisher—although there are exceptions, such as Harlequin, which is almost a household word for pulp romances. Scholars are exceptions. Their vocabularies are peppered with publishers' names, perhaps because of all the footnotes and bibliographies that are essential in academics.

Major publishing houses once had distinctive personalities that flowed from the literary bent of the people in charge. Scribner's, for example, was the nurturing home of Tom Wolfe, Ernest Hemingway and F. Scott Fitzgerald from the 1920s into the 1950s. The house very much bore the stamp of Charles Scribner and his famous editor Maxwell Perkins. Typical of the era, book publishing was a male-dominated business, everybody wearing tweed coats and smoking pipes. Today the distinctive cultures have blurred as corporate priorities have shifted more to the bottom line.

Globzalization and Consolidation

As with other mass media industries, book publishing has undergone consolidation, with companies merging with each other, acquiring one another, and buying lists from one another. Some imprints that you still see are no longer stand-alone companies but a part of international media conglomerates. Random House, a proud name in U.S. book publishing, is part of the German company Bertelsmann. The company also owns the Bantam, Dell Knopf and Doubleday imprints, among other media subsidiaries, including numerous magazines. Harcourt has passed through Anglo-Dutch hands in a dizzying series of deals, finally landing with the U.S.-based Houghton Mifflin Company. Half of Simon & Schuster, once the world's largest book publisher is part of the British conglomerate Pearson. St. Martin's Press is part of Holtzbrinck of Germany. HarperCollins is in the hands of Rupert Murdoch, whose flagship News Corp. has roots in Australia. Warner Books is part of French publishing giant Lagardére. In short, fewer and fewer companies are dominating more and more of the world's book output. And many once-U.S. companies now have their headquarters abroad.

Book Retailing

The retailing component of the U.S. book industry has been in transition for decades. Beginning in the 1960s B.Dalton and other chains with mall stores decimated independent bookstores. The few remaining indies, once the mainstay of book sales, are struggling. The mall chains, however, had their own comeuppance when venerable New York book dealer Barnes & Noble built superstores, some as large as 70,000 square feet with 160,000 titles. This dwarfed the typical B.Dalton of 4,000 to 7,000 square feet and 20,000 titles.

◄ **Jeff Bezos.** *As Jeff Bezos saw it back in 1994, the web had great potential for e-commerce. But what to sell? Figuring that products that lent themselves to direct mail would also work well on the web, Bezos settled on books. He founded Amazon.com in the garage of his Seattle home, pioneering book retailing on the web. By 2000 sales topped $1 billion.*

More recently, the surviving indies and superstores alike have been under siege from internet booksellers led by the remarkable **Jeff Bezos** and his Amazon.com. Starting in 1994, Amazon's stunningly successful online retail model has changed the way that people browse and buy books and inaugurated a dramatic shift away from the bricks-and-mortar model that dates to the 17th century.

Bookstores are in crisis. Sales at the major chains have dropped precipitously. Barnes and Noble has undergone major restructuring. The Borders chain, teetering on bankruptcy, closed 250 of its 650 stores. Internet competition like Amazon, with no costly storefronts, has wounded the big retailers. So has the surge in e-reader sales. The introduction of Apple iTunes books and Google eBooks has created a whole reading population that is internet-savvy and buys online.

APPLYING YOUR MEDIA LITERACY

- **If you were an investor, in what kind of publishing houses would you invest your money today?**
- **Can we expect the modern book publishing industry to nurture the talents and genius of the likes of F. Scott Fitzgerald, Ernest Hemingway and Tom Wolfe? Does it need to?**
- **Is the consolidation of the book industry into fewer houses reducing the diversity of new fiction in our society? How about nonfiction?**
- **Will internet purchasing force brick-and-mortar bookstores completely out of existence?**

Book Genres

STUDY PREVIEW | Reference works are vulnerable in this age of the internet. Do you know anybody who's bought a set of encyclopedias lately? Wikipedia is the new norm. Textbooks are less vulnerable. Textbooks each have a perspective that dovetails into how an adopting professor or school board sees how a course should be taught. Yet the demand for lower priced books and e-reader versions is rising. Trade books can adapt easily to e-reading devices.

Reference Books

reference books
Compilations, including encyclopedias, dictionaries, atlases

Publishing houses that produce **reference works** are vulnerable to internet competition. An analysis by Comscore found that for every page viewed on Britannica.com, 184 pages were viewed on the user-authored and user-edited Wikipedia. The numbers are staggering: 3.8 billion page views per month for Wiki, 21 million for the online Britannica, which is drawn from the legendary ink-on-paper multi-volume encyclopedia. Sales of all traditional encyclopedias have plummeted. Why? In short, online reference works are free, easily accessible and frequently updated.

Although the user-authored Wikipedia and other online reference sites are redefining the reference publishing industry, the wiki authoring concept is hardly new. The Oxford English Dictionary, which dates to 1857 and is one of the greatest reference works in the English language, had its origins long ago in a wiki-style model. Scholars put out the word to English speakers far and wide that they would welcome hard evidence of the earliest appearances of English words. So many submissions were mailed in that the Britannica building began to sink under the weight of all the paper.

Even reference books that have been essential professional tools for generations, like the classic *Physician's Desk Reference* in medicine or the Associated Press stylebook in journalism, are at risk. The information in the compilations is readily available online, mostly free, with a quick search. The best hope for many reference publishers is to create subscription sites that aggregate the latest, reliable information that is scattered all around the globe on servers available at a click.

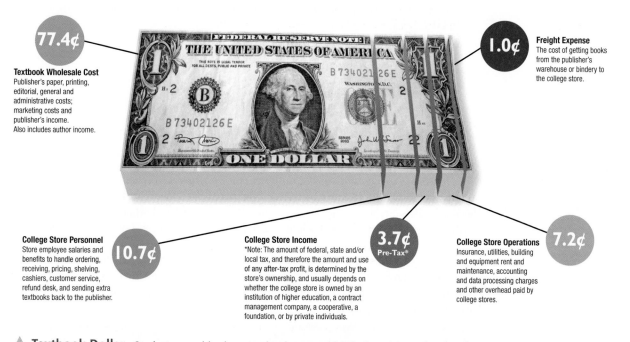

77.4¢

Textbook Wholesale Cost
Publisher's paper, printing, editorial, general and administrative costs; marketing costs and publisher's income. Also includes author income.

1.0¢

Freight Expense
The cost of getting books from the publisher's warehouse or bindery to the college store.

College Store Personnel
Store employee salaries and benefits to handle ordering, receiving, pricing, shelving, cashiers, customer service, refund desk, and sending extra textbooks back to the publisher.

10.7¢

College Store Income
*Note: The amount of federal, state and/or local tax, and therefore the amount and use of any after-tax profit, is determined by the store's ownership, and usually depends on whether the college store is owned by an institution of higher education, a contract management company, a cooperative, a foundation, or by private individuals.

3.7¢
Pre-Tax*

College Store Operations
Insurance, utilities, building and equipment rent and maintenance, accounting and data processing charges and other overhead paid by college stores.

7.2¢

▲ **Textbook Dollar.** *Students grumble about textbook costs, which fuel suspicions about profiteering. By most business and retail standards, however, profits are slim. The National Association of College Stores says pre-tax profits on new textbooks average 3.7 percent for retailers. For used books, however, the breakdown is drastically different. College stores often have twice the markup. On used books, there are no expenses for manufacturing, publishing house overhead, author royalties or marketing.*

Textbooks

Wikipedia cofounder Larry Sanger proposed in 2006 that **textbooks** be written and edited anonymously online. Sanger's proposed Citizendium would invite anybody and everybody to contribute and update online, wiki-like, and to correct and adjust content from fellow contributors. Sanger's initial focus was K-12 school books. This idea evolved into *Wikibooks*. With the tag line "Open books for an open world," open-content textbooks are offered for children, post-secondary students. Even cookbooks are on the site.

But textbook publishers are hardly quaking in their boots over this competition. Sanger's doubters point out that textbooks, unlike reference compilations, have the advantage of a perspective from a single author or a few coauthors. A textbook has thematic coherence. Also, textbook publishers are quick to note the convenience of their products. In one place, students have a well-organized presentation of what they need to know and understand. In other words, a textbook is a highly efficient learning tool—vastly more so than the "open" internet. Students don't need to wander hither and thither online in their learning quest and then end up with uneven jumbles of information, ideas and perspectives. What about Sanger's Citizendium? There are doubts.

In the meantime, textbook publishers are moving into online delivery. Several major college publishers, including McGraw-Hill, Pearson and Wiley, are using CourseSmart.com to download textbooks to students. The books aren't sold but licensed. Students, in effect, rent the textbooks for the duration of the license, typically a semester, at about half the cost of a print copy.

textbooks
Curriculum-related titles for learning and understanding

Trade Books

The most visible book industry product is the **trade book**. These are general-interest titles, including fiction and nonfiction, that people usually think of when they think about books. A 2008 Harris poll asked Americans to name their favorite books. The leaders:

The Bible
Gone With the Wind by Margaret Mitchell

trade books
General-interest titles, including fiction and nonfiction

The *Lord of the Rings* series by J. R. R. Tolkien
The *Harry Potter* series by J. K. Rowling
The Stand by Stephen King
The Da Vinci Code by Dan Brown
To Kill a Mockingbird by Harper Lee
Angels and Demons by Dan Brown
Atlas Shrugged by Ayn Rand
Catcher in the Rye by J. D. Salinger

All are trade books, except the Christian Bible. Most Bibles are sold to churches or other groups or specialty retailers—not through the usual "book trade," as it's called.

Trade books can be incredible best-sellers. Since it was introduced in 1937, Tolkien's *The Hobbit* has sold more than 100 million copies. Margaret Mitchell's 1936 *Gone with the Wind* has passed 30 million. Most trade books, however, have shorter lives. To stay atop best-seller lists, Stephen King, Dean Koontz, Danielle Steel and other authors have to keep writing. Steel, known for her discipline at the keyboard, produces a new novel about every six months.

Although publishing trade books can be extremely profitable when a book takes off, trade books have always been a high-risk proposition. One estimate is that 60 percent of them lose money, 36 percent break even, and 4 percent turn a good profit. Only a few become best-sellers and make spectacular money.

APPLYING YOUR MEDIA LITERACY

- **What are the next steps for reference publishing in the digital age?**
- **What percentage of the market do you predict will move to electronic textbooks, eliminating the use of printed materials?**
- **How many current or recent best-selling trade books can you name? Authors?**

Book Industry Prospects

STUDY PREVIEW | In general, the book industry is well positioned to continue shifting successfully to digital formats. The book industry doesn't rely on advertising, which has proven fickle as a revenue stream for newspapers and magazines. Also, book publishers, unlike newspapers, have no costly investment in printing presses.

Prospects for Publishing Houses

The U.S. book industry, particularly retailers, took a battering from the economic disaster that struck in 2007. High-visibility retailers began 2009 after horrible December holiday sales. Revenue at the largest chain retailer, Barnes & Noble, was off 7.7 percent from a year earlier, Borders off 14.4 percent, Books a Million off 5.6 percent. Online retailer Amazon.com held its own, although it trimmed expenses by shuttering four warehouses. Publishing houses have fared better by laying off employees, consolidating imprints, and other economizing—and, not incidentally, moving further into paperless e-book editions that are delivered digitally.

The book publishing industry seems more likely to recover over the long term than the other major ink-on-paper media of mass communication—newspapers and magazines. Consider these differences:

Negligible capital investment. Unlike newspapers, book publishers have no huge capital investment in presses. The printing of almost all books is contracted out to companies that specialize in printing only. It is these printing companies, not the publishing houses, that will take the hit from the transition to paperless books that is ahead.

Sales-based revenue. The decimation of the newspaper and magazine industries followed the flight of advertising to online alternatives. The book industry, however, has no dependence on advertising. Almost all publishing house revenue comes from customer purchases. There is nothing akin to the advertising subsidy that underwrote the rise of the newspaper and magazines industries into media powerhouses. When the advertising base on which newspapers and magazines had relied for more than a century fell apart as a business model, newspapers and magazines went into a free-fall.

The challenges for book publishers are two-fold: First is a need to create well-edited, high-quality works that people will be willing to pay for. Second, there needs to be a compensation model that sustains profitability through e-book distribution. Publishers continue to negotiate e-book prices with distributors with e-readers: Amazon—Kindle, Apple's iPad and iPhone, and Barnes & Noble's Nook. The tables have turned from the original pricing policy where publishers set the prices and profitability for retailers. As is already happening, traditional brick-and-mortar book retailers are losing out in the transition to online delivery. Even Barnes & Noble with its online ordering and e-reader is struggling to stay viable.

Dominance of online products.   Most book publishers have no existing online competition. For newspapers and magazines, on the other hand, their type of content had been widely available from thousands of online sources before their business structures collapsed. But for novels, biographies, long-form journalism and textbooks, there is a dearth of serious online competition—except what's being created already by book publishers themselves.

E-books

Like the other ink-on-paper media, the book publishing industry is migrating to digital ways of doing business, from scanning, archiving and searching on Google to print-on-demand technology to online bookselling. Two of the most talked about digital apps in publishing are e-books and e-readers. An **e-book** is usually a digital version of a print book formatted to be readable on computers or, increasingly, on digital devices called **e-readers**.

Most of these devices, like the Amazon Kindle and Sony Reader, are the size of a paperback book and intended for downloading word-centric material for reading. Among e-readers are tablets, including the Apple iPad, which have broader capabilities. Also, smartphone updates of the traditional cell phone can be used for reading, although, because of limited screen size, usually only for brief snippets. The hottest sector of the Japanese book industry, for example, is the cell-phone novel. These are mini-novels composed of short sentences delivered a few at a time. The serial delivery has a following among on-the-go Japanese teens and young adults who aren't in the habit of sitting down with a full volume.

Although e-book technology is relatively simple, a significant impediment delayed early e-book success in the marketplace. There were too many incompatible platforms. In part the problem was self-induced by companies that chose to amass titles for exclusive distribution to their devices. Apple, for example, sold books through its iStore only for its iPad device. Apple-like attempts to create monopolies took a major blow in 2010 with the launch of Google eBooks. Titles from Google could be displayed on a wide range of devices, including the widely used Android platform, Apple's iOperating System, and the Adobe eBook platform that was used by the earlier Barnes & Noble Nook and Sony devices.

Google eBooks offered a record 3 million titles, most of them from a company project to digitize every book ever published. These included classics that were available free for digitizing because their copyrights had expired. At its outset Google eBooks also offered 400,000 more recent titles acquired from publishing houses that had still held copyrights and were already selling books to other e-book retailers like Amazon, Barnes & Noble and Apple's iStore. Suddenly Google was a major e-book player, with not only trade books like its competition but also scientific, technical, medical, scholarly and professional works with smaller followings. Google also offered versions in multiple languages. In addition Google allowed authors an avenue to sell individual books from their web sites, bypassing traditional publishing houses.

e-books
Digital files of book content that are stored, searched, sampled, downloaded and paid for online for use on computer, dedicated reader or cell phone

e-reader
Portable electronic device for on-screen reading of books

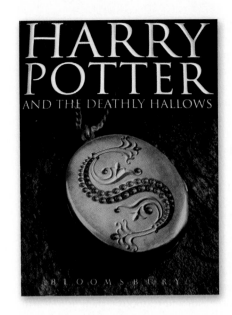

◀ **Harry Potter.** *The popularity of the Harry Potter series engaged a new generation in the old-fashioned appeal of serial fiction. Young readership grew 20 to 75 percent in the period that the Potter series began.*

E-book sales in the United States passed 169 million in 2010, double the year before and about 10 percent of U.S. book sales. Amazon's e-book sales passed hard copies.

The Habits of Young Readers

A troubling aspect of the book industry's fundamentals is whether young people are reading as much as earlier generations. These are future book buyers. Studies come to contradictory conclusions. In the early 2000s, bookstores reported increases of 20 to 75 percent in young buyers. Some called it the **Harry Potter Effect**, which indeed prompted a swelling of new titles for 10- to 14-year-olds. Established authors including Isabel Allende, Clive Barker, Michael Crichton and Carl Hiaasen all turned to writing books for the juvenile market. Some observers noted that teenagers, spurred earlier than ever to do well on college admissions tests, worked harder at getting a sense of a larger world beyond their own experience. Too, the book industry became increasingly clever with marketing lures, including Hollywood and celebrity tie-ins and book readings at teen clubs.

Harry Potter effect
Impact of a single best-selling book

Even so, concern is growing that young people are drifting away from books. A landmark study by the National Endowment for the Arts, called *Reading at Risk*, found that fewer than half of American adults read literature, loosely defined as fiction or poetry. That was a 10 percent decline over 20 years. For young adults, the drop was 28 percent. It's not that people can't read, which would be illiteracy. Instead, people are increasingly **aliterate**, which means they can read but don't.

aliterate
A nonreader who can read but doesn't

The findings of the National Endowment study, although alarming, may be overstated. As book industry spokesperson Patricia Schroeder once noted, the book industry has ups and downs that reflect the times. Schroeder says that in serious eras, like wartime and economic depression, people spend less time with fiction and more time with biography, history, current events and other nonfiction. Even so, more time now is being spent on alternatives to books, like on-screen news and blogs.

APPLYING YOUR MEDIA LITERACY

- **How might major publishing houses use new technologies to parlay their unique intellectual property into viable revenue streams?**
- **Do you see Jeff Bezos as a genius? Or just lucky?**
- **If it's true that young people are less inclined to read books than their parents, is this for better or worse? Will the transition to e-readers adjust the balance for the publishing industry?**

Post-Print Culture

STUDY PREVIEW For nearly 300 years, newspapers have contributed importantly to making democracy work with news coverage. Both newspapers and magazines, also, have been at the forefront promoting openness in government and rooting out corruption. What will happen if periodicals vanish?

Print-less Democracy

One disparaging joke about newspapers is that they make good wrappers for day-old fish. The loss of newspapers, however, is more worrisome than not having something for wrapping kitchen scraps. Magazines too. The question is whether essential social and political functions served by these behemoth industries of the ink-on-paper media era can be sufficiently replaced by other media.

News Coverage. For day-to-day news, broadcast stations have never matched the staffing that newspapers put into coverage of public policy and governance. Too, no television network has ever approached global staffing on the scale of the New York *Times.* Most internet news organizations are thinly staffed too. This raises troublesome questions about the prospects for democracy in a post-newspaper world. No one can argue that a less informed populace is better equipped for self-governance. What will pick up the information void if newspapers continue in their decline?

Investigative Reporting. Besides a core chronicling of events, newspapers in their heyday had the financial resources to dig for truths on political and governance abuses that would not otherwise be uncovered. A mark of great magazines also has been muckraking. Consider these landmarks in investigative reporting:

- Intrepid reporting by the New York *Times* sent crooked city leaders to prison in the 1870s, with the *Times* standing up to big-time crooks who tried wielding their power, money and muscle to silence the paper. Municipal reforms followed.

- Magazine muckraking in the early 1900s exposed graft and corruption, like David Graham Phillip's "Treason of the Senate" in *Cosmopolitan.*

- The Watergate scandal of the early 1970s was uncovered by the dogged reporting of the Washington *Post.* President Nixon resigned amid *Post* revelations of arrogance of power and contempt not only for democratic processes but also contempt for openness, honesty and decency for the people.

Regional and local newspapers also have carried the torch for tough, enterprise reporting. More than non-print media, newspapers and magazines have exercised the historic watchdog function of the media against wrongdoing in government, and also in business and other institutions.

Without newspapers and magazines, a void would be left in investigative reporting. Muckraking has been part of a newspaper and magazine culture of public responsibility that never took such firm roots in broadcasting nor has become a significant thrust of internet content except on newspaper and magazine sites. It is telling that of 42 finalists for 2011 Pulitzer prizes for journalism, the only online honoree was ProPublica. So, as a political cynic once put it, "Who will keep the rascals honest?" With weakened newspapers and magazines, or in an entirely post-print culture, might an important check be in jeopardy against dishonesty among those in positions of public trust?

Government Openness. More than other media, newspaper companies have fought expensive battles to go after truths hidden in government meetings and documents. Yes, laws require these documents to be open to the public to assure that government conducts the public's business with transparency. The idea behind the laws: no closed-door deals for fat contracts to the mayor's brother-in-law, no short-circuiting of the civil rights of impoverished groups who don't have a voice, no pay-to-play political

MEDIAcounterpoints

■ Newsmagazine Crisis

As editor at *Newsweek,* Jon Meacham cannot be faulted for lack of innovation as the magazine's fortunes wavered. He recognized early that internet-delivered news had pre-empted his magazine's forte of recapping the week's events. He shifted to commentary and analysis. Although superbly done and intellectually provocative and stimulating, the new thrust didn't stem reader and advertiser defections. It was the same at the other leading newsmagazines, which once were a crown of the magazine industry. Here's what's happened next:

Hoping for synergies, *Newsweek* and the *Daily Beast* online news site merged in 2010. The *Daily Beast* had been a creation of Tina Brown, who had joined the *Daily Beast* after a long record of successes at *Vanity Fair* and the *New Yorker.* In the new arrangement, Brown became editor of both the *Newsweek* and *Daily Beast* enterprises. It was high-risk linkup to rescue a wavering print product and a not-yet financially secure online product. Indeed, the *Daily Beast,* only two years old, was gobbling up cash as it moved from 20 percent original content, the rest regurgitated from elsewhere, to 80 percent original content. One of *Newsweek's* lures for the *Daily Beast* was that the ink-on-paper magazine, although losing money and down to as few as 56 pages, was still drawing $65 million a year in advertising revenue.

Tina Brown saw her job as stabilizing *Newsweek's* losses with a formula she had mastered at earlier magazines—not *Newsweek*-style news as much as what was called low-high journalism and splashy graphics and design. In the magazine industry, Brown had star power that it was hoped would cause *Newsweek's* remaining advertisers to stick with the magazine and also buy space on the *Daily Beast.* Newsstand sales of the first *Newsweek* issue with Brown's redesign, with Hillary Rodham Clinton on the cover, were up 19 percent from the magazine's average. Whether the gains can be sustained remained to be seen. And clouding the good sales was that advertising revenue was sagging 25 percent.

Meanwhile, *U.S. News & World Report* attempted another survival model. The magazine had abandoned its weekly print issues and went biweekly in 2008 and hoped readers would shift to a weekly online edition. The plan didn't work. The magazine cut back to monthly issues and in 2011 shut down both the print magazine and an online digital replica entirely. Editor Brian Kelly declared ink-on-paper, after a 77-year run was "no longer sustainable."

The owner, U.S. News Media Group, kept its usnews.com web site with the magazine's well-known rankings of the best colleges, hospitals and mutual funds. Also, single-topic print issues, like annual college ranking, continued to be produced for newsstands.

Pushing the Envelope. *Tina Brown's record of revamping a string of magazines, including* **Vanity Fair,** *made her a media celebrity herself. Looking for new challenges, she took over the* **Daily Beast** *news site and then, when the* **Beast** *bought* **Newsweek,** *became editor of both. Is Brown deluding herself with a bipolar tactic that only forestalls the end to magazines as a printed product?*

Print magazines have a strong chance of survival if they parlay their historic strengths and bridge the digital divide between their ink-on-paper heritage and the realties of the digital age.

POINT

COUNTER POINT

The print magazine is a dinosaur in the final throes of extinction in the 21st century. Nothing will sustain it. Better to shut the presses and migrate completely online.

DEEPENING YOUR MEDIA LITERACY

EXPLORE THE ISSUE: Visit the website for *U.S. News & World Report* and learn about subscriptions for *U.S. News & World Report Weekly.* What are the incentives for ordering this digital magazine?

DIG DEEPER: With a search engine, locate other digital magazines providing online news coverage. Compare their approach to *U.S. News & World Report.* Focus on: content, applications, timeliness, length of articles, breadth of sources, interactiveness with blogs and reader posts.

WHAT DO YOU THINK? Imagine that you are a magazine media owner of a traditional ink-on-paper weekly. How could you establish an effective online presence that would generate revenue?

appointments. But with newspapers less aggressive in pursuing news in general, a danger in a post-newspaper era is that more misfeasance, even criminal malfeasance, will go unnoticed.

Print-less Culture

Without newspapers and magazines, the book industry may be hobbled as a torch-bearer for the revelations and insights of long-form journalism and fiction.

Cultural Incubator.   Periodicals have been spawning beds of great literary figures who made lasting impressions on the culture. Ernest Hemingway started at the Kansas City *Star*. Jack London cut his teeth in magazine fiction. The list is endless: Bruce Catton, Stephen Crane, Theodore Drieser, Sinclair Lewis, Margaret Mitchell, Hunter S. Thompson, Mark Twain. Even though books as long-form journalism and fiction appear well positioned to make the transition into a post-print culture, a question is whether the periodical publications can be replaced as a springboard for important literary careers.

Free Expression.   With their financial might as well as their self-interest, newspapers have been crusaders for free speech as a citizen right. In the pivotal 1964 legal case *New York Times v. Sullivan*, the *Times* fought for the right for people to comment on the performance of public figures. It was a case in which the *Times* had been accused of libeling a bullying Alabama police commissioner. The *Times* could have settled out of court for a fraction of the legal fees for an appeal to the U.S. Supreme Court. Instead the *Times* went the costly route to do the right thing, not the easy thing—and prevailed in a landmark ruling.

In their heydays, newspapers and magazines sided with unpopular causes that forced Americans and the courts to come to grips with difficult but nonetheless important free-expression issues:

- The Chicago *Tribune* financed the landmark *Near v. Minnesota* appeal. It was a case on behalf of a small Minneapolis newspaper that had displeased local authorities and been padlocked by the sheriff. The U.S. Supreme Court ruled in 1931 that the local government was acting unconstitutionally in banning controversial, even obnoxious expression.

- With wide support in the newspaper and magazine industry, the *Progressive* magazine battled for a right to publish a 1979 article on how to make an H-bomb in your basement. The upshot was a further lid on censorious government impulses.

- At media fringes have been magazines that have defended their erotica and poor taste. *Hustler* magazine, as an example, spent five years battling the televangelist Jerry Falwell over a 1983 *Hustler* magazine spoof. The costly court fight ended with wide latitudes being confirmed for humor. Although the value of *Hustler's* taste can be debated, the magazine had further loosened yokes that impede artistic creativity and expression.

Not all newspapers historically have chosen to crusade for First Amendment rights, but newspapers and magazines and their trade associations have a far longer and stronger record on free expression than other media. Civil libertarians, indeed all citizens, are right to be concerned about who will replace newspapers and magazines in fighting the good fight?

APPLYING YOUR MEDIA LITERACY

- **What can internet-based media do as well as newspapers? And as well as magazines? And how do internet-based media fall short?**
- **Of novelists and authors to whom you've been introduced in literature classes, how many have early newspaper and magazine backgrounds?**
- **Why have newspaper and magazines pursued free expression in the courts more than broadcasters? More than internet-based media?**

CHAPTER WRAP UP

■ Print Media Industries (Pages 85–87)

Although ink-on-paper mass media are rooted in Gutenberg technology from the 1440s, it took almost 400 years for media industries to take form. A pivotal event was the introduction of one-cent newspapers in the United States in the 1830s. Suddenly, masses of people could afford printed media. The transformation was facilitated by a confluence of factors. These included faster presses that could mass-produce printed products. Also a factor was a growing audience in rapid-growth urban areas. The growth itself was a result of new factory jobs and an influx of immigrants to work the factories. Literacy improved, especially with non-English speaking immigrants looking to the new mass media as vehicles for learning the language.

■ Newspaper Industry (Pages 87–91)

Newspapers grew into an identifiable industry in the mid-1800s, as did magazines and books. Newspapers dominated. The heyday of newspapers continued into the 1940s. Within 20 years the media newcomers—first radio, then television and the internet—eroded newspaper circulation and took away advertisers. Major declines in sales and advertising, exacerbated by the 2008 world economic recession, forced a major downsizing throughout the newspaper industry.

■ Leading Newspapers (Pages 92–96)

The New York *Times,* founded in 1851, has an illustrious record for thoroughness in reporting, public service, and investigative revelations. Today it remains the most prestigious and respected newspaper in the world. Under the new ownership of Rupert Murdoch, the *Wall Street Journal* moved from a nationally distributed paper with a forte in business coverage to challenge the *Times* in the New York area. The national newspaper *USA Today* was founded in 1982.

■ Magazine Industry (Pages 96–99)

Magazines became a national advertising medium beginning in the mid-1800s when railroad networks provided ways for mass-produced products to widen their distribution. Railroads also distributed magazines nationally to potential customers for the new products. Magazines had an advantage over books as a mass medium because they cost less. Magazine innovations distinguished them from newspapers. These innovations included long-form journalism and photojournalism, which drew massive readerships. The internet, however, has significantly cut into print magazine readership and advertising in recent years.

■ Reinventing Magazines (Pages 99–104)

As an industry, magazines proved resilient when the new national television networks siphoned off advertising in the 1950s. Magazines retrofitted themselves for niches within the mass audience in a process called demassification. The current challenge for the industry is from the internet, which, like television half a century earlier, offers more for readers and usually less expensively if not free. Advertisers have followed readers to the internet. Traditional magazines are trying with uneven success to make a transition to digital delivery, but the online universe has many competitors. Despite difficulties, the magazine industry has bright spots that include that shelter and niche titles.

■ Book Industry (Pages 104–106)

Under ownership of mega-transnational corporations, the book publishing industry has shifted more into myopically profit-driven enterprises. In the process, books have lost some of the traditional claim as a nurturer of cultural growth. The bottom-line focus, however, has helped the industry weather the economic recession that began in 2008. An industry component that seems less able to cope with changing times is book retailing. The major retailers, like Barnes & Noble, are under pressure from online competition and decreased book sales.

■ Book Genres (Pages 106–108)

The internet has displaced traditional reference works like printed and bound encyclopedias. The user-driven Wikipedia typifies the online standard for reference. Remaining major genres of the book industry are trade books, which include bestsellers, and textbooks, which are useful compendiums designed to facilitate learning and understanding.

■ Book Industry Prospects (Pages 108–110)

Unlike newspapers and magazines, the book industry is not dependent on advertising. Readers are the single revenue stream. It's a very straightforward business model that has positioned the book industry to shift successfully from ink-on-paper to digital products. The book industry's prospects are strong too because there is no competition offering long-form reading products.

■ Post-Print Culture (Pages 111–113)

With newspapers and magazines diminishing in American life, there are questions about what will replace their traditional role. Newspapers have financed significant legal recognition for civil liberties, notably a right to free expression. Newspapers and magazines have been significant forums on public issues. Newspapers and magazines also have been at the forefront promoting openness in government and rooting out corruption. What will happen if periodicals vanish? Are there negative implications for democracy? For the culture?

■ Thinking Critically

1. **Explain the historical context that gave rise to ink-on-paper media industries in the mid-1800s.**

2. **Why did newspapers dominate so long among mass media?**

3. How will the transition of newspapers to digital format change the way stories are researched and written?

4. What made magazines a major and financially viable industry in the mid-1800s?

5. How did magazines survive the advent of network television? Can magazines survive now as an ink-on-paper industry?

6. Which genres produced by the book industry are most vulnerable to internet competition? Why?

7. What long-range impact will digitization of book content have on the book industry? On the way audiences read and relate to books?

8. Explain how the changes to the operating models of the ink-on-paper mass media will affect the quality of democracy and culture in the United States and elsewhere.

■ Media Vocabulary

aliterate (Page 110)

business model (Page 87)

chain newspaper (Page 88)

demassification (Page 98)

e-book (Page 109)

e-reader (Page 109)

editor (Page 88)

Harry Potter effect (Page 110)

highbrow slicks (Page 97)

intellectual property (Page 110)

literati (Page 97)

market penetration (Page 90)

muckraking (Page 97)

news-editorial (Page 88)

open editing (Page 84)

penny papers (Page 86)

personality profile (Page 97)

publisher (Page 88)

reference works (Page 106)

textbooks (Page 106)

trade books (Page 107)

wiki (Page 84)

Wikipedia (Page 85)

■ Media Sources

■ David E. Sumner. *The Magazine Century: American Magazines Since 1900.* Peter Lang, 2010. Sumner, a scholar on the magazine industry, examines the rapid growth of magazines and their role in U.S. culture. Sumner traces demassification to the early 1900s.

■ Mike Farrell and Mary Carmen Cupito. *Newspapers: A Complete Guide to the Industry.* Peter Lang, 2010. Farrell and Cupito, both scholars with journalism backgrounds, see a future for newspapers in this overview that includes the industry's history.

■ John Thompson. *Merchants of Culture.* Polity, 2010. Thompson, a sociologist, draws on extensive interviews with book industry leaders and concludes that the industry's future has been determined by incessant pressure for growth and profits, by the rise of powerful author agents, by the rise of a few giant retailers, and to a lesser degree by e-books.

■ Sarah Ellison. *War at the Wall Street Journal: Inside the Struggle to Control an American Business Empire.* Houghton Mifflin Harcourt, 2010. Ellison, once a *Journal* reporter, portrays Rupert Murdoch variously as crafty and resistant in adding *Dow Jones* to his global media empire. The Bancroft family is portrayed as hapless and mired in squabbles and dark secrets that doomed their rebuffs to Murdoch's persistent offers to buy them out.

■ Alan Brinkley. *The Publisher: Henry Luce and His American Century.* Knopf, 2010. Brinkley, a New Deal historian, uses Luce's essay, "The American Century," in his title to capture the inspiring role of the *Time* publisher in American life. Luce's idea was to remake the world on the American model.

■ Norberto Angeletti and Alberto Oliva. *Time: The Illustrated History of the World's Most Influential Magazine.* Rizzoli, 2010. The authors, both journalists, track the evolution of *Time* and decisions on innovations, including Man of the Year.

■ Naomi Rosenblum. *A History of Women Photographers*, third edition. Abbeville, 2010. Rosenblum, a historian of photography, updates her pioneer biographical work, this time with photographers born after 1950.

■ Jan Goggans. *California on the Breadlines: Dorothea Lange, Paul Taylor, and the Making of a New Deal Narrative.* University of California Press, 2010. Goggans, a professor of literature, offers a text-based analysis of the impact of Depression photographer Dorothea Lange and her labor-economist husband Paul Taylor on American attitudes toward the disadvantaged.

■ Bertrand Lavédrine with Jean-Paul Gandolfo, John McElhone and Sibylle Monod; John McElhone, translator. *Photographs of the Past: Process and Preservation.* Getty Conservation Institute, 2009. This is an encyclopedic illustrated review of photographic processes back to the early 1800s.

■ Ken Auletta. *Googled: The End of the World as We Know It.* Penguin, 2009. Auletta, media critic for the *New Yorker,* tracks Google from its humble origins into an online powerhouse that displaced traditional media, then deals with its profit-driven quest to dominate media delivery to become a major advertising vehicle.

■ Chris Anderson. *The Long Tail: Why the Future of Business Is Selling Less of More.* Hyperion, 2006. Anderson, editor of *Wired*, says blockbusters are becoming less important with the advent of technology that has expanded the marketplace into microniches.

■ Diane Cole. "Publish or Panic," *U.S. News & World Report* (March 13, 2006), Pages 46–53. Cole, a reporter, offers an overview of book industry issues with special focus on prospects for small publishers.

■ John Thompson *Books in the Digital Age: The Transformation of Academic and Higher Education Publishing in Britain and the United States.* Polity, 2005. A comprehensive analysis of university presses and academic publishing.

■ Charles Brownstein. *Eisner/Miller: A One-on-One Interview.* Dark Horse, 2005. Graphic novelists Will Eisner and Frank Miller, both with roots in comic books, discuss their craft with rich detail on issues and personalities.

■ Arthur Klebanoff. *The Agent: Personalities, Publishing and Politics.* Texere, 2002. Klebanoff, owner of the Scott Meredith agency, offers insights into the literary agent business in an anecdote-laden account of working with celebrity authors.

■ John P. Dessauer. *Book Publishing: What It Is, What It Does.* second edition. Bowker, 1981. Dessauer, a veteran book publisher, is especially good on the organization of the book industry.

A Thematic Chapter Summary

INK ON PAPER

To further deepen your media literacy here are ways to look at this chapter from the perspective of themes that recur throughout the book:

MEDIA TECHNOLOGY

Presses with less and less to print. Bye, bye newspapers.

Printing technology begat the book, newspaper and magazine industries, which grew into giant influences in society. For newspapers, printing machinery clearly had become an albatross early in the 21st century. The whole business model for the newspaper industry was wedded to in-house presses, which constituted multi-million capital investments for even mid-size dailies. Then two essential revenue streams in the business model disappeared. Readership slipped, then advertising revenue. These presses had increasingly unused capacity. Magazine and book companies were less affected because they farmed out their printing.

MEDIA ECONOMICS

Ink-on-print media evacuating online.

With advertising revenue drastically off, newspapers and magazines have scrambled to the internet as a low-cost way to reach readers and win back advertising. By and large, it isn't working. Thousands of other companies were already entrenched online with the same kind of content as newspapers and magazines. Big-name publications, once the only place people could find news and sports, were suddenly just another player in a crowded, competitive field. The book industry, never dependent on advertising, was better situated. The internet had little quality book-length competition for the book industry, which has shifted adroitly into online delivery.

MEDIA AND DEMOCRACY

Woodward and Bernstein dig up stuff on the Watergate break-in with the noble goal of exposing political abuses of power and real threats to the democratic process.

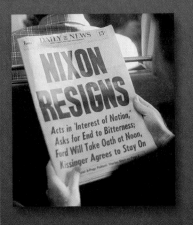

Mass media have played an essential role in democracy. Since the 1870s at least, newspaper, magazines and books exposed corruption and abuse in government and business that worked against the public's interest. A newspaper tradition has been to hammer away daily for prosecution and reform. What institutions of society will fill the void if newspapers and magazines aren't around? No online company has the advertising base to fund costly investigative reporting. In the 21st century, a new Tammany Hall gang might be running New York City without a press watchdog. Would a new Watergate coverup go unchecked?

ELITISM AND POPULISM

The debate whether block-busters are good literature goes back to Harriet Beecher Stowe's Uncle Tom's Cabin.

Newspapers created in the Penny Press era built unprecedented circulation with stories that pandered to large audiences. These newspapers created the modern concept of mass audiences and mass communication. Although the audience has fragmented with a plethora of competition, there remains a strong populist strain in media content. The book industry, for example, has obsessed about bestsellers since *Uncle Tom's Cabin* in 1852. A book industry commentator, Alvin Kernan, makes a case that our culture has paid a heavy price for the obsession. Kernan believes that major publishing houses, in their quest for profits, are using resources for projects with mass appeal rather than for books that could contribute to moving the culture forward. Keman is making an elitist argument. By pandering to mass tastes, he says, the book industry is abdicating its responsibility to do good things—not merely popular things.

MEDIA FUTURE

Who says young people don't read?

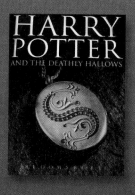

Young people have glommed onto digital media that are less word-driven than ink-on-paper media. Does reading have a future? This generational shift has been a factor in the decline of newspapers. At the same time, studies go both directions on reading. Book publishers cite their survey that nonfiction is on the rebound. Indeed, until the recession beginning in 2007, book sales were growing 3 to 5 percent a year. And the incredible sales of the Harry Potter series demonstrate that the new generation is hardly averse to reading.

MEDIA AND CULTURE

The New York Sun motto of 1833, "It Shines for All," wouldn't resonate as well in today's fragmented media environment.

At their strongest points in history, newspapers helped create communities by providing people with a common source of information and entertainment. Magazines and books did the same at national levels. Figuratively, everybody read *Uncle Tom's Cabin* and Ida Tarbell. Even if some content was contentious, everyone was on the same agenda on what constituted the pressing cultural, political and social values of the day. As ink-on-paper media lost their monopolies, first a little to broadcasting, then massively to the internet, the mass media became less a binding force for local communities and the nation but a vehicle through which social fragmentation occurred. People had choices for media that catered to their individual interests rather than common interests.

CHAPTER 5 SOUND MEDIA

▲ **Exclusively Yours.** *Tim Westergren's Pandora Genome Project slices and dices the DNA of music, then with algorithms finds patterns in an individual music-lover's preferences. Subscribers, who pay nothing, are streamed a unique playlist. It could be called a "radio station for one"—you.*

CHAPTER INSIGHTS

- The success of the recording and music industries is based on an inextricable linkage.
- File-sharing on the internet derailed the recording industry's business model.
- Government regulation has been a major shaper of the radio industry.
- U.S. radio has local and national tiers, both financed mostly by advertising.
- Music dominates radio amid a rich mix of news and information.
- Traditional terrestrial commercial radio is under siege from alternative delivery methods.

Tim Westergren's Pandora

For sure, Tim Westergren is an entrepreneur. But exactly what business is he in: Music? Radio? Internet? The answer: All of them. Westergren has found a way to integrate his passion for music and old-style technology into a new media form that might be called do-it-yourself DJ-ing.

At Stanford, Westergren studied computers, acoustics and recording technology. He is a piano player who later learned drums, bassoon and clarinet. He played in bands and produced music.

In 2000, like so many others in the early heyday of the internet, Westergren saw potential for a new online business. It would combine his love and knowledge of music with a bold and clever new idea—create a product with an appeal to a core audience, and deliver it over the internet. He cofounded the new company with a partner and pitched it successfully to venture capitalists.

The idea was simple: to develop a technology that would define and collect different attributes of music and organize them in such a way as to be maximally useful to people. The new company's first model, licensed to retailers such as Best Buy, helped music buyers find bands they liked. Westergren's classification and organization technology remains the heart of the business today.

The company is called Pandora. With about 80 million users, it is one of the top internet radio sites in the world. By some measures, Pandora is the number one free iPad application and number two for the iPhone.

Internet radio is not a new or unique idea. Radio stations have been streaming their signals online since the mid-1990s and many services, including Apple's iTunes, offer listeners a variety of free music channels by genre.

Pandora's innovation is to change the basic model of one-way communication common to all radio. Pandora transforms listeners from passive recipients into active partners in determining what they hear. It asks listeners to interact with its music classification algorithm by voting—thumbs up or down—on songs. This classification is called the Music Genome Project. It is a dizzyingly ambitious attempt to unpack and classify the hundreds of possible essential attributes of any song—to decode its musical DNA. All 800,000 songs in the growing Pandora database are analyzed by a professional musician. In a process that takes 20 to 30 minutes, each song is assigned a list of "genes" that mirror particular attributes of a song, like the, gender of lead vocalist, acoustic or electric bass, and distortion of rhythm guitar. Rock and pop songs have 150 genes, rap 350, jazz 400.

A Pandora user creates a radio station by naming a performer or individual song. Pandora plays a song that it calculates to share the genetic attributes of the song or artist named, not necessarily the song itself or a particular performer. Pandora asks whether you like it. Based on your responses, Pandora continues to play new songs on your "station," getting continually smarter about what it plays as it learns more about what you want to hear.

Although a complex process, the idea is simple. It's the original innovation of classifying music that Westergren started with. ■

Long-Term Symbiosis

STUDY PREVIEW

The music industry relies on radio airplay as a free promotional vehicle for selling recorded music. The radio industry also is reliant on recordings as a low-cost and audience-pleasing source of programming. This symbiosis, almost a century old, is firmly established and so important that pay-to-play bribery occasionally raises itself as a legal issue.

Airplay Marketing

The shape of the music industry, including recorded music, reflects a convenient relationship with the radio industry. The relationship goes back almost a century. Sound recording attained quick popularity in the early 1900s, fueling a dance craze that further enhanced sales of **phonographs** and records. In the mid-1920s, however, the bottom fell out of the

phonographs
Early devices for playing recorded disks

record business. Floundering in the downturn, the Victor Talking Machine Company began courting the fledgling NBC radio network. Both Victor and NBC became parts of the giant Radio Corporation of America. Similarly, the Columbia Phonograph Company acquired a radio network, which later became CBS.

In those days the recorded music and radio technologies were very different, but in common was that the products of both industries were the mass-marketing of sound. In that relationship, the recording industry found an outlet to promote its wares—**airplay**. It was free advertising. People who liked a song on the radio might go out and buy the record. By the 1940s, when the record-radio symbiosis was firmly established, it was clear that on-air performances by performers like Bing Crosby and Ella Fitzgerald could send record sales soaring.

When radio shifted almost entirely to record music in the 1950s, airplay clearly was essential for a new recording to succeed. Today recording companies are pleased to provide free copies of their latest music to radio stations in hope they get played.

airplay
Radio time devoted to a particular recording

Programming Efficiency

Just as the music and recording industries have relied historically on radio, so has radio relied on them. Recorded music is cheap programming. It costs a lot less to play Adele from a recording than to book her into a station's studio. This radio reliance on recorded music became a radio programming mainstay in the 1950s, when television robbed radio of its audience and, also, of advertisers. Neither radio stations nor networks could afford live performances any more. Live radio drama, comedy, concerts and variety shows were displaced almost overnight and almost entirely by canned music. For radio, low-cost recorded music was necessary for survival with the evaporation of national advertising.

Cultural Fallout. The shift to recorded music programming undermined radio as a medium that promoted local culture. A piano as a standard fixture at local stations became a thing of the past. So did well-miked performance studios for bands and combos. Local drama and poetry readings disappeared. For better or worse, you decide, local culture over the radio was displaced by homogenous cultural content from national recording companies based in New York, Los Angeles and Nashville.

Payola. The competition among music promoters for airplay led to a practice of paying radio station music directors and influential disc jockeys to put certain music on the air. The practice, called **payola**, led to prosecutions in 1959. It was against federal law to play music without an on-air acknowledgment that there had been an exchange of money. Lots of money was involved. A popular Chicago disc jockey, Phil Lind, told investigators he had accepted $22,000 to play a single record. A Congressional committee found 335 disc jockeys admitted to receiving $263,000 in "consulting fees." In response, the ABC network, which owned several stations, began requiring disc jockeys to sign statements that they weren't on the take or be fired. Some signed. Some left town quietly.

payola
A bribe to promote a product, like airplay for a music

But payola didn't go away. Airplay was too important to the recording industry. Some companies hired independent promoters in an attempt to buffer themselves from bribery. These latter-day promoters didn't always deal in cash. An Albany, New York, station program director, Donnie Michaels, took a Manhattan hotel room and Yankees baseball tickets in 2004 to put songs by Brian McKnight and Nick Lachey on his station's **playlist**. In other cases, the payola was laptop computers, even drugs.

playlist
A list of songs that a radio station plays

Under threat of a new wave of prosecutions, major recording companies were shamed by the then-New York state attorney general, Eliot Spitzer, into huge settlements to atone for payola. In 2005 the world's biggest recording company, Universal Music, paid $12 million to settle accusations that executives were involved in pay-to-play activities. BMG paid $10 million, Warner $5 million. Spitzer also went after radio companies. Spitzer said that the understanding in the industry was that radio play is the best way to motivate sales: "Folks would do what needed to be done to get the airtime."

- What is the financial interdependence of the music and radio industries?
- How do you evaluate the cultural implications of the symbiosis of the music and radio industries? How about the cultural implications of payola?

Recording Industry

STUDY PREVIEW

The music industry is dominated by four major recording companies—Universal, EMI, Warner and Sony. Fast-changing, often fickle public tastes make it a risky business. The greatest upset—nobody had seen anything like it—came when Napster file-swapping was introduced on the internet in 1998 Music sales fell precipitously. Apple's iTunes helped stem the declines, but the industry remains a shadow of its former self.

Big Four

The global recording industry is concentrated in a handful of companies. The so-called Big Four hold 84 percent of the U.S. market, 75 percent of the global market. Each of these companies is part of a larger media conglomerate:

	Annual Revenue	Parent Company	Headquarters
Universal Music	$6.1 billion	Vivendi	France Among labels: Decca, Def Jam, Geffen, Interscope, Island, MCA, Motown, Verve
EMI	1.6 billion	Citigroup	United States Bluenote, Capitol, EMI, Liberty, Venture, Virgin
Warner Music	3.0 billion	Access Industries	United States Asylum, Atlantic, Bad Boy, Elektra, Lava, Nonesuch, Rhino, Warner
Sony Music (BMG)	1.1 billion	Sony	Japan Columbia, Epic, Legacy, Odyssey, Provident, RCA, Sony

Revenue is dependent on hot songs and is volatile, but the Big Four all together generally hold about three-quarters of the global market. Lesser companies, called indies, have small markets segments. When an indie hits it big, as Motown did with its Detroit Sound in the 1960s, inevitably it is purchased by a major. After a 31-year run Motown founder Berry Gordy sold Motown for $61 million in 1988 to MCA, a major at the time. Now both MCA and Motown are part of Universal.

File-Swapping Blow

Conditioned by decades of success, the record industry, especially the major companies, had become smug in their formulas for manufacturing and marketing high-profit pop culture. Then along came an 18-year-old college kid, **Shawn Fanning**. Single-handedly, Fanning almost brought down the whole industry. Over Christmas break his freshman year, Fanning put together peer-to-peer software so his dorm buddies could swap audio files among themselves. With this P2P there was no central infrastructure and no cost. Fanning called his free-wheeling system **Napster**, after his nickname as a toddler. At first it all seemed kind of cute. Young people, who comprise the main market for recorded music, saw it as a friendly application of technology. Instead of forking over $15 for a CD, they could exchange music worldwide free. They loved Napster.

Recording companies were slow to pick up on Napster's ominous potential to wipe out the retailing structure for the music industry. Soon Napster had 25 million users who had 80 million songs on their hard drives. Instead of buying music, they were swapping it for free. Customer traffic slowed to a trickle at music retailers. Best Buy shut down its Sam Goody's, Musicland and other music outlets that had been steady money-makers. The recorded music industry went into freefall. From a pre-Napster peak of $14.6 billion, recorded music sales in the United States plummeted to $6.9 billion in 10 years—a loss of more than half its revenue.

The Recording Industry Association of America, which represents the recorded music companies, was late to act but finally slowed the decline by going to court against Napster. In 2005 the U.S. Supreme Court bought the RIAA argument that Napster was participating in copyright infringement by facilitating illicit copying of protected intellectual property. Napster was toast. So were other file-swapping services that had cropped up.

iTunes Recovery

Besides the anti-Napster intervention of the U.S. Supreme Court, the record industry owes its survival also to Apple mastermind **Steve Jobs**. In 2001 Jobs opened **iTunes** to sell songs by downloading them to Apple's popular handheld iPod playback device. ITunes was convenient. Unlike Napster's unpredictable sound, iTunes had consistent fidelity. People could sample songs with a single click and then download with another click at 99 cents a song. In iTunes' first week, more than 1 million songs were downloaded, juicing a 27 percent spike in Apple stock. By 2008 iTunes was the largest U.S. music retailer in the United States. In all, iTunes has sold 16 billion songs since its inception.

Unlike download-swapping, iTunes wasn't free. But it had advantages. The sound quality was exceptional. Apple used a new format that compressed music efficiently, downloaded faster and consumed less disk space. It was a clean system, without the annoying viruses that affected swap systems like Kazaa, Morpheus and Grokster. Apple benefited too from the guilt trip that RIAA was trying to lay on illegal downloaders.

Jobs began iTunes with huge repertoires from some major labels. Other labels begged to sign on as soon as the iPod–iTunes success was clear. By 2005, 62 percent of all music downloads were from iTunes. To be sure, copycat services spawned quickly.

▲ **Napster Guy.** *Shawn Fanning introduced free-for-all online music-swapping technology that he dubbed Napster. The incredible popularity of swapping threatened the recording industry's traditional profit model. Why pay $15 for a CD? The industry went to court claiming that swap services were facilitating copyright infringements and won.*

Shawn Fanning
Pioneered music file-swapping through original Napster

▲ **Download Solution.** *Steve Jobs of Apple Computer gave the recording industry an online retailing outlet with his iTunes store, from which music could be downloaded into incredibly popular Apple iPod listening devices at 99 cents a song. Downloaders could feel good that they weren't violating the intellectual property rights of recording companies or performers, lyricists or composers. And recording companies, desperate to stem revenue losses from illegal but free downloading, could derive income from the sales.*

APPLYING YOUR MEDIA LITERACY

- If you were a Big Four executive, where would you look to grow your company?
- To what extent do you regard Shawn Fanning as a folk hero? Or a criminal who facilitated the theft of legitimate income from composers, lyrics, performers and recording companies?
- How would you rate iTunes 99-cent-a-download charge for a song? High? Optimal? Low?

Radio Industry

STUDY PREVIEW

A government role in radio was based on a premise that the public owned the airwaves and could regulate them in the public interest. This so-called trusteeship model has shaped the radio industry. Today 11,000 commercial stations, after rebounding from a major slump, generate $17.3 billion in revenue annually.

Government Licensing

Broadcasters are wont to grumble about government regulation. But press them. You'll learn they wouldn't have it any other way. Before 1927 broadcasters had made such a mess of the airwaves that they couldn't straighten it out. They went to Congress begging for regulation to assign frequencies and otherwise manage the airwaves. Congress responded with regulations and a licensing system. To be on the air under the new systems, stations needed a government license to comply with technical and other government regulations.

The 1927 **Federal Radio Act** made the government a stakeholder in the system that the government itself created. As a stakeholder, the Federal Radio Commission saw stability as essential to assure the orderly growth of the medium's potential for public service. With stability as a goal, the FRC and its successor, the Federal Communications Commission, have protected the industry's status quo. This status quo mindset was not without problems. The FRC and FCC, have stalled changes in the industry's infrastructure that threatened tried-and-familiar business models and even thwarted new technologies. No better example exists than the lengthy delays in authorizing satellite radio through the 1990s. Owners of terrestrial stations, acting through their National Association of Broadcasters, opposed satellite competition. The FCC dallied on approving satellite radio to protect existing station owners who feared a new rival for advertising revenue.

Here is the infrastructure of regulation that the 1927 Radio Act and the 1934 Communications Act created:

Ownership Limits. The law allowed stations to be licensed only to a locality. The idea was to encourage local ownership and community service enforced informally though the dynamics of local accountability.

The idea was also to prevent more stations than could be supported financially through advertising and sponsorship. With this cap on the number available licenses, competition was limited. Critics of the system note that, considering the profitability of radio that was coming into being, licensees were being issued government licenses to make money.

The system also precluded national stations, unlike the systems of many other countries that have national stations.

Technical Restrictions. Stations were assigned frequencies with their signal strength capped so their signals wouldn't overlap. The caps solved the pre-1927 problem of stations amping up their signals to reach larger audiences and drowning each other out.

Content Requirements. In an attempt to keep favoritism out of the licensing process, the government established quality criteria. License applicants were told to broadcast "in the **public interest, convenience and necessity**." It was a high-minded although vague standard. The upshot has been, among other things, to keep stations taking political favoritism in elections and to maintain decorum in language.

Trusteeship Concept

Government regulation of radio may seem contradictory to the U.S. Constitution's prohibition of government interference with mass media. But the cacophony of 732 stations trying to broadcast on a spectrum of 568 available frequencies in 1927 was a

Steve Jobs
The driving force behind the Apple Computer revival, iPod and iTunes

ITunes
Apple-owned online retail site for recorded music

Federal Radio Act
1927 law establishing government regulation of radio

public interest, convenience and necessity
Standard by which the U.S. government grants and renews local radio and television station licenses

MEDIAcounterpoints

■ Unviable Business Model?

The global recorded music industry is divided on its future. The question: Is there much of a future?

Global sales have been slipping 8 to 9 percent a year for a decade. During the decline, a glimmer of hope had been that sales of digital music would offset declining CD sales. It hasn't happened. For 2010, the industry's sales of music in digital formats, mostly downloads, were indeed up 6 percent. But that was hardly enough to offset worsening sales overall. Worse, there are indications that digital sales have peaked while the non-digital sales, mostly CDs, dwindle. Analyst Mark Mulligan of Forrester Research says it's not unreasonable to conclude that the recording industry's hopes for digital music have failed. Mulligan told the New York *Times*: "Music's first digital decade is behind us and what do we have? Not a lot of progress."

Are people listening less to music? No. But instead of buying music many are downloading music free from the internet. By its nature, the leakage cannot be measured, but estimates at the high end say that 95 percent of downloaded music worldwide is acquired outside of revenue-generating channels.

The situation is not as bleak in the United States as elsewhere. In the United States, the industry went to court against peer-to-peer internet services that had facilitated free music-swapping. The recording industry also sued individual music downloaders in showcase suits to discourage the practice. In Duluth, Minnesota, a federal jury fined Jammie Thompson $1.9 million for copyright violations for downloading 24 songs. In addition, the industry pressed colleges to close student access to illegal music downloading through campus servers. In effect, the industry said to colleges: "If you don't, we'll sue you too."

Even though the U.S. government sided with recording companies against downloading cheats, the companies got serious too late. By the time the companies went to court, their retailing business model was in ruins. Desperate for a new business model, the companies turned to Apple's iTunes as a download retailer—even though Apple took the top 30 cents off every 99-cent sale. But the issue was survival. It worked. Americans turned to iTunes, which was technically reliable, easy to use,

▲ Kesha Doing OK.
The recording industry does well from big-name performers. Kesha's "OK to ToK" sold $12.8 million in downloads alone in 2010. But for the recorded music industry, the looming issue is how much is less how much Kesha earned than how much was lost to download piracy.

inexpensive and legal. Although still grumbling about Apple's 30-cent cut, the U.S. industry has stabilized—although smaller than at its peak.

No matter how shaken the recording industry was in the United States, in Europe the situation was worse. The iTunes model for music retailing hasn't caught on.

Also, European governments were slow to crack down on unauthorized downloads. Not until 2009 did France, pressured by the recording industry, create a law requiring internet service providers to disconnect repeat offenders. But several warnings were required, and internet providers balked at enforcing. Although hundreds of thousands of e-mail warnings were sent to suspected violators, nobody was cut off in the first year.

Despite problems, the French law is being modeled elsewhere. If enforced, these laws may stall, perhaps even stem the recording industry's decline.

The record industry has only itself to blame for declining prospects. It was too cozy, too smug, too long with an outdated business model. Stop griping. Adjust to the new reality.

POINT

COUNTER POINT

Music is at the heart of a vibrant modern culture. The recording industry's survival is essential. Its financial well-being must be protected.

DEEPENING YOUR MEDIA LITERACY

EXPLORE THE ISSUE: Look for data from the Recording Industry Association of America and the Motion Picture Association of America on how much their members lose annually to piracy?

DIG DEEPER: How successful have these trade associations been in curbing piracy?

WHAT DO YOU THINK? In your experience, do young people have a sense that the creators of music and also movies are denied a financial incentive when their property is downloaded free?

reality. Something had to be done or the potential of radio as a medium would be lost. Indeed, when the FRC denied some stations licenses to clear the air, so to speak, the stations waged battle in the courts. The stations argued that the **First Amendment** of the Constitution literally says: "Congress shall make no law abridging . . . freedom of the press." The courts sidestepped the issue, stating simply that the FRC was within its authority.

The theoretical justification for government regulation was the **trusteeship concept.** A premise of the concept was that the airwaves are the public's property and cannot be subject to ownership. Ever heard the phrase "free as the air"? That's the idea. Because the air waves belong to the public, the theory says, the government, as trustee for the public, is uniquely qualified to regulate the use of the airwaves for the public's good.

Underlying the trusteeship concept is that the public was being poorly served with more stations trying to squeeze into the electromagnetic spectrum than could fit. There was a scarcity of frequencies.

The trusteeship concept has survived even though scarcity is hardly an issue any more. Technology has eliminated the scarcity. In fact, more than 14,000 stations are on the air in the United States. In some respects, government regulation has eased with the emergence of a **marketplace concept**. Today the government protects license-holders less from competition than it once did. Increasingly the industry is left to marketplace forces to decide what stations survive. The public is more directly the regulator, rather than through the government as a trustee or some kind of middleman. Under the marketplace concept, stations that survive and thrive are those that the most people listen to and for which advertising pays the bills. It's a survival-of-the-fittest model as determined by listenership directly.

First Amendment
Provision in U.S. Constitution against government interference with free citizen expression, including media content

trusteeship concept
Government serves as a trustee for the public's interest in regulating broadcasting

marketplace concept
Listeners through marketplace mechanisms determine the fate of a business.

APPLYING YOUR MEDIA LITERACY

- **How do you regard the argument that government regulation of the U.S. radio industry came about for common-sense reasons?**
- **Do you favor marketplace forces as the sole regulator of radio? Or is government better positioned as a regulator? Or do you favor a marketplace-government hybrid?**

Characteristics of U.S. Radio

STUDY PREVIEW
The financial base of the U.S. radio system is mostly advertising revenue to stations that are licensed to operate in a defined locality or in some cases a region. A second tier of radio is comprised of network and programming sources that lend a national character to programming.

Radio Infrastructure

When government began regulating the U.S. radio industry in 1927, many existing practices were accepted. These included selling airtime to advertisers to generate revenue. Government also introduced other new policies that shaped the industry.

Advertising. Early government regulators accepted the emerging financial model at the time that the financial foundation of the industry would be advertising. Advertising already had long been the financial foundation of the newspaper and magazine industries.

The government also provided for noncommercial stations, mostly for education. These noncommercial stations comprised a miniscule part of the industry until much later when public radio took hold.

◀ **Radio as a New Medium.** *The commercial and cultural potential of radio were recognized clearly in the 1920s. But the potential was threatened by too many stations elbowing their way into a limited number of channels. Congress addressed the issue in 1927 with a system of strict licensing and regulations. With stations no longer drowning out each other's signals, the industry flowered.*

The radio industry today remains largely dependent on advertising. This is unlike some countries, which see radio programming as a national service meriting government financing.

Ownership Limits. Wary about powerful newspaper chains in the 1920s, Congress capped the number of stations that a single person or corporation could own The goal: No radio chains.

For most of its history, there was a cap of seven stations in a single ownership. When the FM part of the electromagnetic spectrum was opened up, stations were allowed to add a sister FM station. Further relaxations followed on the limits. The 1996 **Telecommunications Act**, the first major revision of radio regulation since 1927, eliminated most other restrictions marking a widened acceptance of the marketplace concept over the trusteeship model. The new reality was far from the long-standing limit of seven stations in a market.

For most intents and purposes, there are no ownership limits anymore. The large Clear Channel chain owned more than 1,200 stations at its peak in 2005, including seven stations in some markets.

Localism. The 1927 ownership limits were intended to give radio a local flavor: Local personalities as on-air hosts with local talent and playing back local culture to the community. The ideal of **localism** has faded. Music, which comprises most radio programming today, is from the nation's centers of pop-culture manufacturing. Local announcers still exist, but many stations import programming from far-away central studios and programmers who have never set foot in most of the communities that carry the programming. Radio has a coast-to-coast homogeneity albeit exceptions.

Even at the time that government regulation began, the NBC and CBS networks were linking major stations. This worked against the ideal of localism. But the networks escaped

Telecommunications Act
1996 law overhauling federal regulation. Ended most limits on chain ownership.

localism
Issuing broadcast licenses for service to a specified community and its environs

the FRC's purview. As program suppliers, the networks didn't use the public's airwaves directly and were exempt from regulation. From the 1930s on, the networks provided more and more programming and clearly diminished localism as a key characteristic that Congress originally envisioned for the U.S. radio industry.

Two-tier infrastructure. The U.S. radio industry today operates at two tiers. At one tier, stations remain licensed in local communities—although ownership generally is far-away and not community-connected. At the second tier, networks, programming suppliers and recording companies give radio a national identity. You hear the same network news coast-to-coast, and Katy Perry, Kelly Rowland and Blake Shelton play in every market, the same everywhere.

Scope of Radio Industry

After slippage for a decade, the revenue of U.S. commercial radio stations grew 6 percent in 2010 to $17.3 billion. The news was welcome to the industry, after a decade of slippage and an 18 percent drop the year before. The revenues were shared by 11,000 stations.

Two Technologies. Stations broadcast with one of two technologies. Stations licensed as FMs, short for **frequency modulation**, have strong signals within line-of-sight of a transmission tower and some fringe areas. FM signals go out in a straight line. In contrast, signals from AM stations with **amplitude modulation** technology ricochet off the ionosphere. In effect, AM signals follow the curvature of the planet and reach much more distant points than FM, although with less fidelity. FM lends itself to music because of superior sound. AM stations are more for information and talk.

frequency modulation (FM)
Radio technology with superior fidelity. Signals travel in straight lines

amplitude modulation (AM)
Radio technology with great range. Signals follow curvature of Earth.

Public Radio. Besides commercial radio, the Federal Communications Commission licenses an additional 2,500 stations that are prohibited from selling advertising. The legacy of these stations, in radio's early days, was the idea that some of the radio spectrum should be preserved for educational purposes. Most were operated by colleges and school districts but some by churches and labor unions. The concept expanded in the 1960s into public radio as an alternative to formats that might be hard to sustain commercially, like classical music, cultural programming and public affairs. These stations derive revenue from donations from well-wishers, including listeners and philanthropic and corporate sponsors. They also receive from the federally funded Corporation for Public Broadcasting and state governments.

Radio Chains. Although stations are licensed to serve an FCC-designated area, generally local, few stations remain locally owned. In its heyday in 2005, the conglomerate Clear Channel owned more than 1,200 stations with revenues of $3.5 billion. But financially overextended, Clear Channel began a sell-off and trimmed its radio holdings to 850 and laid off 1,800 employees. In second place, Cumulus Media operates 570 stations, followed by Citadel with 240, and CBS with 130. Rare is the locally owned independent station anymore.

Formats. Stations broadcast in a wide range formats, mostly defined by music but also news and information. Religious, foreign language and ethnic stations are enduring format segments. Formats largely are a marketing tool to attract a defined audience that advertisers want to reach and are continually being refined to lure listeners from competitors.

Because of the flux, and also the ever-changing subcategories of formats, the number of stations using formats is impossible to track precisely. But this is a recent snapshot of major formats:

Country	2,041 stations
News/talk/sports	1,579 stations
Adult contemporary	1,213 stations
Religious	1,019 stations
Golden oldies	822 stations
Classic rock	639 stations
Top 40	444 stations
Alternative/modern rock	334 stations
Urban contemporary	312 stations

- What changes do you see occurring in the shape of U.S. radio industry?
- How do you differentiate radio networks from radio chains?

Influence of Radio

STUDY PREVIEW | Radio has become a ubiquitous mass medium, available everywhere, anytime. As an industry, however, there are troubling signs. Radio's primary programming is music, news and talk. Radio has lost its one-time monopoly on music, which has become available through other devices.

Radio Ubiquity

Radio is everywhere. The signals are carried on the electromagnetic spectrum to almost every nook and cranny. There are 6.6 radio receivers on average in U.S. households. Almost

MEDIAtimeline

SOUND MEDIA MILESTONES

PHONOGRAPH
Thomas Edison introduced a recording-playback device (1877)

MASS PRODUCTION
Multiple copies of recordings possible with Emile Berliner's invention (1887)

RADIO
Marconi transmitted first message (1895)

PIVOTAL EVENTS

- Emergence of a middle class in U.S., with new leisure time, discretionary income (1870s)
- Congress created first regulatory agency, Interstate Commerce Commission (1887)

SOUND MEDIA MILESTONES

VOICE
Audion tube for voice transmission (1906)

TITANIC
News from the mid-Atlantic tragedy established radio in public mind (1912)

Radio as a new mass medium

COMMERCIAL RADIO
KDKA, Pittsburgh, became first licensed commercial station (1920)

REGULATION
Congress created Federal Radio Commission (1927)

BUZZ
Electricity added to recording, playback technology (1920s)

PIVOTAL EVENTS

- Recorded music added to movies (1927)
- Amos 'n' Andy radio show (1928–1943)

SOUND MEDIA MILESTONES

FM RADIO
Edwin Armstrong patented FM (1933)

RADIO NETWORKS
Mutual Radio formed to serve non-CBS, non-NBC stations (1934)

TELEVISION
TV networks drew audiences from radio (1950s)

PIVOTAL EVENTS:

- Great Depression (1930s)
- Franklin Roosevelt presidency (1933–1945)
- Federal Communications Commission replaced Federal Radio Commission (1934)
- Orson Welles' War of the Worlds radio drama (1938)
- Superman radio series (1941–1951)
- World War II (1941–1945)

1800s

1900–1929

1930–1949

all automobiles come with radios. People wake up with clock radios and commute with car radios. People listen to sports events on the radio even if they're in the stadium. Thousands of people build their day around commentators like Rush Limbaugh. Millions rely on hourly newscasts to keep up-to-date. People develop personal attachments to their favorite announcers and disc jockeys.

Statistics abound about radio's importance:

- **Arbitron**, a company that surveys radio listenership, says that teenagers and adults average 22 hours a week listening to radio.

- People in the United States own 520 million radio sets. Looked at another way, radios outnumber people 2 to 1.

- More people, many of them commuting in their cars, receive their morning news from radio than from any other medium.

Although radio is important, cracks are developing in the medium's reach. The audience is slipping from the traditional, federally licensed local stations to iPods, direct-to-listener satellite services, webcasts and smart phones. Yes, 200 million people, a sizable number, still tune in at least once a week, but the audience is shifting.

Arbitron
Radio listener survey company

SOUND MEDIA MILESTONES

ROCKABILLY
Hybrid musical form became rock 'n' roll (1950s)

MUSIC RADIO
Radio shifted to niche audience segments, mostly recorded music (1950s)

WHAT A&R?
Record companies lost tight control of pop music (1960s)

PUBLIC BROADCASTING
Congress established national noncommercial system (1967)

PIVOTAL EVENTS

- Rise of network television (1950s)
- Korean war (1950–1953)
- Eisenhower presidency (1953–1961)
- Supreme Court banned segregation in public schools, *Brown* v. *Board of Education* (1954)
- Gordon McLendon created Top 40 radio format (1954)
- Elvis Presley brings rock 'n' roll to white audiences, transforms pop music (1956)
- Elvis Presley recorded "Heartbreak Hotel" (1956)
- Construction of U.S. interstate highway system (1956–1991)
- Soviet Union orbited Sputnik (1957)
- Kennedy presidency (1961–1963)
- Beatles recorded "Love Me Do" (1962)
- Escalating war in Vietnam leads to protests, cultural upheaval (1965–1975)
- Astronaut Neil Armstrong set foot on moon (1969)
- Nixon presidency (1969–1974)

1950–1969

SOUND MEDIA MILESTONES

DIGITIZATION
Introduction of compact discs (1982)

DEREGULATION
Congress relaxed broadcast regulations, including caps on ownership (1996)

PIVOTAL EVENTS

- Gloria Steinhem co-founded Ms. magazine (1972)
- United States withdrew from Vietnam (1973)
- Reagan presidency (1981–1989)
- Andrew Lloyd Weber composed Phantom of Opera (1986)
- Soviet Union collapses, end of Cold War (1989)
- Rise of rap as major commercial force (1990s)
- Rise of internet as major commercial medium (late 1990s)
- Clinton presidency (1993–2001)

1970–1999

SOUND MEDIA MILESTONES

INTERNET RADIO
Pandora streams customized medleys (2000)

MP3
Handheld iPod on market (2001)

SIRIUS AND XM
Digital signal delivery to listeners via satellites (2001)

PODCASTING
Adam Curry invented podcasting (2004)

GROKSTER
Online music-swap services outlawed (2005)

PIVOTAL EVENTS

- 9/11 terrorist attacks (2001)
- iPod introduced (2002)
- Iraq war (2003–2011)

2000s

Adam Curry: Dooming radio as we know it?

MEDIApeople

■ Rallying Listeners for Social Causes

▲ **Tom Joyner.**
They called him the "fly jock" for his daily Dallas-Chicago commute to host radio shows.

Tom Joyner grew up during the Civil Rights movement. He remembers well the 1960s when Montgomery, Alabama, blacks boycotted merchants in an early display of collective economic power. In his native Tuskegee, 50 miles away, he remembers the weekly unity marches. Joyner got his first peek inside radio while protesting against a white-owned station that refused to play "black music." Joyner prevailed. The station manager left.

After college, majoring in sociology, Joyner landed a radio job in Montgomery. He moved from station to station in the 1960s in the burgeoning of black radio. By then there were 800-plus black stations nationwide. Joyner honed his mix of

music, guests and goofy comedy and appeals for donations to worthy causes. Even on incendiary issues with which he dealt, Joyner maintained his dulcet cool.

By 1985 Joyner was in demand. When KKDA in Dallas offered him a morning slot and WGCI in Chicago offered him an afternoon slot, he took both. The daily commute made Joyner the first frequent-flyer disc jockey. They called him the Fly Jock. In 1994 he went into syndication on the ABC network and was eventually piped through 95 stations and stayed home more.

Joyner knows the power of radio. When Christie's auction house in New York decided to auction off items from the slave trade, Joyner and buddy Tavis Smiley were quick to note that Christie's had a policy against trafficking in Holocaust items. So why traffic in items from the slave trade? Day after day, Joyner and Smiley called on listeners to jam Christie's phone lines in protest. Christie's canceled the auction.

Joyner has courage. For weeks he urged listeners to jam the lines at CompUSA, which didn't advertise on black radio. The company complained to ABC, which carried Joyner's show. In a decision that the network later regretted, ABC lawyers ordered Joyner to lay off. Joyner read the corporate ultimatum on the air, sparking a massive listener protest to the network. ABC backed off. So did CompUSA, which dispatched a representative for a guest appearance on the Joyner show to make nice.

When Hurricane Katrina devastated New Orleans, Joyner canvassed stations still on the air for the earliest comprehensive accounts of the damage. It was he who coined the catchy term *black folks' tsunami*. Joyner raised $1.5 million to provide housing for the displaced.

In the tradition of black radio generating money for social causes, Joyner has created a foundation to help students who have run out of money at historically black colleges. To his listeners, Joyner says, these students are our future.

Radio Content

Radio Entertainment. The comedies, dramas, variety shows and quiz shows that dominated network-provided radio programming in the 1930s and 1940s moved to television in the 1950s. So did the huge audience that radio had cultivated. The radio networks, losing advertisers to television, scaled back what they offered to **affiliates**. As the number of listeners dropped, local stations switched to more recorded music, which was far cheaper than producing concerts, dramas and comedies. Thus, radio reinvented itself, survived and prospered.

The industry found itself shaken again in the 1970s when the listeners flocked to new FM stations. Because FM technology offered superior sound fidelity, these became the stations of choice for music. AM listenership seemed destined to tank until, in another reinvention, most AM stations converted to nonmusic formats.

Radio News. Radio news preceded radio stations. In November 1916, Lee De Forest arranged with a New York newspaper, the *American,* to broadcast election returns. With home-built receivers, hundreds of people tuned in to hear an experimental transmission and heard De Forest proclaim: "Charles Evans Hughes will be the next president of the United States." It was an inauspicious beginning. De Forest had it wrong. Actually, Woodrow Wilson was re-elected. In 1920 KDKA signed on as the nation's first licensed commercial station and began by reporting the Harding-Cox presidential race as returns were being counted at the Pittsburgh *Post.* This time, radio had the winner right.

Radio news today has diverse forms, some taken from the De Forest notion of drawing listeners to reports on breaking events as they happen, some more focused on depth and understanding. Mostly, though, radio news became known for being on top of events as they happen. Unlike newspapers, radio had immediacy. There are none of the inherent print media delays of going to press and delivery. Radio could be on the scene and live.

- **Breaking News.** Radio news came into its own in World War II, when the networks sent correspondents abroad. Americans, eager for news from Europe, developed the habit of listening to the likes of **Edward R. Murrow** and other giants of mid-20th-century journalism, including **Walter Cronkite**. As a medium of instantaneous reporting, radio offered news on breakthrough events even before newspapers could issue special extra editions. The term **breaking news** emerged to describe something to which radio was uniquely suited.

- **Headline Service.** In the relatively tranquil period after World War II, with people less intent on news, the radio industry recognized that listeners tuned away from lengthy stories. News formats shifted to shorter stories, making radio a **headline service**. Details and depth were left to newspapers. **Gordon McLendon**'s influential rock 'n' roll format, which he introduced in the 1960s, epitomized the headline service, generally with three-minute newscasts dropped every 20 minutes amid a running stream of three-minute songs. Rare was a story more than 20 seconds, most only two sentences.

- **All-News.** As contradictory as it may seem, considering that Gordon McLendon is the father of Top 40 music formats that trivialized news, he also invented **all-news radio**, also in the 1960s. For the Los Angeles market, McLendon set up a skeletal staff at XTRA across the border in Tijuana to read wire copy nonstop. When XTRA turned profitable, McLendon took over a Chicago station, renamed it WNUS, and converted it to all-news. This was a dramatic departure

affiliates
Locally licensed stations that have an affiliation with a network to carry network programming

Edward R. Murrow
War correspondent who helped establish radio as a news medium

Walter Cronkite
Part of renowned CBS World War II radio news crew. Later prominent television anchor

breaking news
Reports, often live, on events as they are occurring

headline service
Brief news stories

Gordon McLendon
Reinvented radio with narrow formats in the 1950s

all-news radio
A niche format that delivers only news and related informational content and commentary

▲ **Radio News Icon.** *Edward R. Murrow's World War II coverage from Europe, with bombs in the background during his reports, gave CBS listeners the feeling of being there.*

from the idea of radio as a mass medium with each station trying for the largest possible audience. McLendon's WNUS and later all-news stations sought niche listenership, finding profitability in a narrow part of the larger mosaic of the whole radio market. Today all news stations prosper in many large cities, some going far beyond McLendon's low-cost rip-and-read XTRA with large reporting staffs that provide on-scene competitive coverage that goes beyond a headline service.

National Public Radio
Network for noncommercial stations

All Things Considered
Pioneer NPR afternoon news-magazine

news packages
Carefully produced, long-form radio stories that offer depth; the hallmark of NPR

- **News Packages.** When **National Public Radio** went on the air in 1970, its flagship program *All Things Considered* set itself apart with long-form stories that ignored two premises that had become traditional in radio. First, these were stories didn't necessarily fit the news peg of breaking news. Second, the stories ran as long as the reporter or producer felt necessary to tell the story, ignoring the premise that radio listeners had extremely short attention spans. The stories, called **news packages**, were slickly produced and reflected a commitment of time and energy in reporting that other radio news formats lacked. Many personified issues. News packages typically are full of sounds and recorded interviews and are often marked by poignant examples and anecdotes and powerful writing.

Decline of Radio News. Despite the ascendancy of all-news radio and National Public Radio, news is hardly a core element of radio programming anymore. By the 1990s, after the Federal Communications Commission dropped public service as a condition for license renewal, many stations eliminated their expensive news departments. Instead, these stations emphasized low-cost programming based on playing recorded music. Many metropolitan stations, once major players in news, have cut to just one or two people who anchor brief newscasts during commuting hours. Global and national headlines are piped in from a network, if at all. Some stations don't even commit one full-time person to news.

Talk Radio

Talk formats that feature live listener telephone calls emerged as a major genre in U.S. radio in the 1980s. Many AM stations, unable to compete with FM's superior sound quality for music, realized that they were better suited to talk, which doesn't require high fidelity. Call-in formats were greeted enthusiastically at first because of their potential as forums for discussion of the great public issues. Some stations, including WCCO in Minneapolis and WHO in Des Moines, were models whose long-running talk shows established high standards and expectations. So did *Talk of the Nation* on NPR. However, many talk shows went in other directions, focusing less on issues than on wacky, often vitriolic personalities.

Much of the format degenerated into advice programs on hemorrhoids, psoriasis, face-lifts and psychoses. Sports trivia went over big. So did pet care. Talk shows gave an illusion of news but in reality were lowbrow entertainment.

talkers
Talk shows

Rush Limbaugh
Conservative radio talk-show host

Whatever the downside of **talkers**, as they're known in the trade, they have huge followings. **Rush Limbaugh** was syndicated to 660 stations at his peak but has since slipped to 600, The size of Limbaugh's audience is hard to calculate because not all stations carry all three hours a day and stations in his patchwork "network" air it at different times of day. Limbaugh, ever a self-promoter, has claimed 26 million listeners a week, but there are no ratings or a statistical basis for the number. Michael Harrison of radio trade journal *Talkers*, estimates 14.3 million for Limbaugh in a typical week, which itself is a sizeable number. Harrison has this rank for other talkers, all conservatives: Sean Hannity, 13.3 million; Michael Savage, 8.3 million; and Laura Ingraham, 5.5 million.

Liberals are also talking. The alternatives to conservative talkers, however, have never attracted as many listeners. The most aggressive left-wing effort, the network Air America, floundered financially and went dark in 2010.

The influence of talkers can be overrated. A 1996 Media Studies Center survey of people who listen to political talk shows found that they are hardly representative of mainstream Americans. The political talk-show audience is largely white, male, Republican and financially well-off. It is much more politically engaged than the general population but on the right wing. Also, these people distrust the mainstream media, which they perceive as biased to the left.

Many stations with music-based formats used the advent of news and talk stations to reduce their news programming. In effect, many music stations were saying: "Let those guys do news and talk, and we'll do music." The rationale really was a profit-motivated guise to get out of news and public affairs, which are expensive. Playing recorded music is cheap. The result was fewer stations offering serious news and public affairs programming.

To many people, talk formats leave the perception that there is more news and public affairs on radio than ever. The fact is that fewer stations offer news today. Outside of major markets with all-news stations, stations that promote themselves as news-talk are really more talk than news, with much of the talk no more than thinly veiled entertainment that trivializes the format's potential.

Public Radio

For 40 years the noncommercial component of the U.S. radio industry, called *public radio*, has grown steadily with distinctive programming. A 1967 law provided federal funding—a response to a vision that radio could do better in serving the public good. A major gift from Joan Kroc, the widow of McDonald's founder, has secured the future for the backbone of the system, the network National Public Radio.

From its beginnings in the 1920s, the U.S. radio industry was built around government licenses assigned to local communities and a financial advertising structure. In the backwaters were noncommercial stations, conceived originally as testbeds for experimentation. Many were licensed to universities, many to the physics departments.

There also were noncommercial licenses for educational purposes. These stations, barred from raising revenue through advertising, were merely a blip in the radio landscape until the privately funded blue-ribbon Carnegie Commission for Educational Television began rethinking noncommercial broadcasting. The influential commission concluded that noncommercial broadcasting was an undeveloped national resource.

Congress followed through on the Carnegie recommendations for a government funded television and radio system to meet "the full needs of the American public." The enabling legislation, the 1967 Public Broadcasting Act, was a slap at commercial broadcasting, whose content was mostly entertaining at a low and vapid level. The idea was for broadcasting to do better. Only a few years earlier, in 1961, FCC Chair Newton Minow had chastised broadcast executives at a convention as responsible for a "vast wasteland." The term stuck. So did the sting. But nothing changed in content.

The new law established the **Corporation for Public Broadcasting**, a quasi-government agency to channel federal funds into noncommercial radio and television. Right away, National Public Radio, which had been founded in 1970, created *All Things Considered*, a 90-minute newsmagazine for evening drive time. Many noncommercial stations offered *ATC*, as it's called in the trade, as an alternative to the headline services on commercial stations. The program picked up an enthusiastic albeit small following but grew steadily. In 1979 NPR created an early drive-time companion program,

Corporation for Public Broadcasting
Quasi-government agency that administers federal funds for non-commercial radio and television

◀ **WNYC's** *Takeaway.* John Hockenbery, long a fixture in public radio, commands the mike on the New York public radio program Takeaway. Like many noncommercial stations WNYC has found a growing audience for intelligent discussion on serious subjects—and also just plain interesting subjects. Takeaway *was launched in 2008.*

Morning Edition
NPR morning newsmagazine

The Takeaway
WNYC-originated morning show
for public stations

Morning Edition. In 2008 a new type of conversation and personality-driven morning program, *The Takeaway*, was launched by a subsidiary of American Public Media and WNYC in New York. The program integrated social media and included partnerships with the BBC News Service and the New York *Times* and was seen as a possible challenger to *Morning Edition* among public stations.

Although NPR is the most visible component of U.S. noncommercial radio, its programs constitute only about one-quarter of the content on its affiliate stations. These stations originate 49 percent of their own programming. Stations also buy about 19 percent of their programming from a competing program service, **American Public Media**. APM, a creation of the Minnesota Public Radio network, has the folksy Garrison Keillor live-audience variety show *A Prairie Home Companion,* which dates to 1974.

National Public Radio and its local affiliates have skimmed off the listenership whose demographics, including educational attainments and income, are coveted by advertisers. Although public stations cannot carry advertising, they are allowed to acknowledge supporters on the air, including purveyors of high-end products and services. These acknowledgments can sound like advertising as long as they don't exhort listeners to action.

APPLYING YOUR MEDIA LITERACY

- **How has radio lost its competitive edge as a source for music?**
- **Where can you find radio news these days?**
- **How is talk radio different from news radio?**
- **How is public radio a formidable and growing component of the U.S. radio industry?**

Radio Industry Directions

STUDY PREVIEW | Satellite radio, transmitting directly from national networks to individual listeners, is squeezing traditional locally licensed stations. The SiriusXM satellite network offers 140-plus channels, some commercial-free, some duplicating what's available on over-air stations.

Satellite Radio

satellite radio
Method to deliver radio from an orbiting satellite directly to end users

Two **satellite radio** operations, the first national U.S. radio stations, went on the air in 2001. Both Sirius and XM beamed multiple programs from multiple satellites, providing digital-quality sound, much of it commercial-free, for a monthly fee ranging between $10 and $13. In 2007 the companies merged. Expanding their market beyond traditional radios was a key to their growth. Buy a new car lately? SiriusXM is often part of the package.

terrestrial radio
The industry based on audio transmission from land-based towers, as opposed to transmission via satellite

A battle between satellite radio and what's come to be called **terrestrial radio** has been waging for over a decade now. The term identifies the traditional radio industry built around local stations that transmit from towers, in contrast to SiriusXM's satellite transmission. Every listener whom local commercial stations lose to SiriusXM makes these stations less attractive to advertisers. The exodus has been major. SiriusXM has more than 18.5 million subscribers.

New Technologies

Other technologies also are working against the traditional radio industry:

iPod. Handheld MP3 players, epitomized by the Apple iPod, have been siphoning listeners from over-air local radio for years. With these devices and music downloaded

■ Podcast Revolution

Podcasting had lots of creators. But MTV video jock **Adam Curry**'s knack for self-promotion earned him the title "podfather." In 2005 Curry had founded Podshow. Available at the Podshow site were audio files created by would-be disk jockeys for downloading. Curry likened himself to a media revolutionary. Indeed, podcasting was the start of a revolution.

Curry described the new application of internet technology as liberating. "Mainstream media," he said, "are so diluted, so packaged, so predictable. There is very little that is new or interesting."

Curry was right. Traditional commercial radio had homogenized itself in a quest for larger audiences. Although stations featured music in a couple handfuls of genres, the genres had become constricted and narrow and duplicative. One country station's playlist sounded pretty much like every other country station. Big radio chains even centralized programming decisions at their headquarters. Innovation was not on the corporate agenda.

Podcasts, in contrast, tended to be highly individualistic. The appeal was to niches of music aficionados whose interests didn't fit the narrow genres of commercial radio.

Within a year 4,700 podcasters were offering their individual programs through Curry's Podshow—an alternative to mainstream radio's vanilla-bland music package. Today the directory Podcast Alley lists 94,000 podcasts.

Podcasts are but one part of a fragmenting universe of music sources.

The Pandora innovation was custom music playlists for listening at any time that a user found convenient. It was music on demand. This was a departure from commercial radio, which required listeners to wait through music that didn't interest them much to hear what did.

The on-demand radio concept went a further direction with the 2008 introduction of Stitcher. With Stitcher; listeners could download news and talk radio programs whenever they wanted. Once a listener chose a program, Stitcher used algorithms to rank every program in its inventory by each user's preference. If a user downloaded the Michael Savage talk show, Stitcher would suggest the listener might also want fellow conservative talker Laura Ingraham. In other words, listeners "stitch" together a personalized list of favorite shows.

Stitcher has been likened to doing for radio news what Pandora did for music. The fact, however, is that Stitcher is more than news. Programs include talk, sports, news and comedy.

The proliferation of sources for what traditionally had been radio entered a new dimension in 2011 when retailer Hammacher Schlemmer added a 45,000-station car radio to its catalog. The $99 device, which plugged into a car's 12-volt power socket, could download thousands of local, global and internet-only radio stations live through the car's radio speakers. An iPhone app facilitated quick searches by genre.

Meanwhile, Ford, General Motors and automakers had launched partnerships with Stitcher and Pandora for built-in internet radio units in their cars.

Radio modes into the future include:

- Over-air stations that download live programming to internet-connected devices like smartphones and computer tablets.

- Playlists customized to your tastes by services like Pandora for listening on-demand.

- Public affairs, news, sports and other talk-based radio programs through services like Stitcher for listening on-demand.

Adam Curry. *The inventor of podcasting found thousands of bands connecting with podcasters and listeners: "What we're building here is a social media network." Curry calls it "a do-it-yourself digital revolution in music."*

What Do You Think?

How do you see the effect of podcasting on the retailing of recorded music?

What do you think of Stitcher as a metaphor for the process of downloading a variety of selected radio programming for on-demand listening?

Adam Curry
Pioneer in podcasting technolog-yartists' free expression

from the internet or ripped from their own CDs, people are able to create their own playlists—no inane disc jockey patter, no commercials, no waiting through less-than-favorite tunes for the good stuff. But the emergence of radio apps are changing this dynamic. Now listeners can listen to live radio via their smartphones and wirelessly enabled tablets and computers. This application of new technologies may just resurrect over-air local radio. Now you can be in Dubuque, Iowa, and listen to a San Francisco jazz station.

Podcasting.   Almost anybody who wants to create a show can prerecord a batch of favorite music, complete with narration, as an audio file on a personal computer or smartphone or MP3 player. Then, by adding a hyperlink on a web server, these self-anointed disc jockeys can let the world download the show for playback. Whenever the listener links to the server again, a new show from the same source will be downloaded automatically. **Podcasting** has the potential to make everybody a disc jockey. This too has cut into the audience of traditional radio.

On-Demand Radio.   Like the earlier TiVo device for television, **on-demand radio** devices are available for recording programs for later playback. The leading service, TuneIn Radio, offers a real-time database of 50,000 stations from 140 countries without a subscription. Some TuneIn models include an AM-FM tuner to grab local shows that aren't webcast.

APPLYING YOUR MEDIA LITERACY

- **What might revitalize locally licensed terrestrial commercial radio?**
- **What are your music habits? MP3 devices like iPods? Or over-air stations? How about podcasts? How about on-demand radio? What attracts you to one more than the other?**

■ Long-Term Symbiosis (Pages 121–123)

The music and radio industries rely on each other. Recording companies encourage radio stations to play their music, knowing that airplay promotes sales. Stations receive recorded music free, which gives them low-cost programming that is popular with audiences. The symbiosis dates to radio's early history in the 1920s and continues today. A downside has been the occasional practice of music promoters to bribe radio people to play certain music. This practice, called *payola,* distorts the genuineness of popularity for heavily promoted music.

■ Recording Industry (Pages 123–124)

Four companies hold 75 to 85 percent of the market for recorded music. A business model fashioned in the early 1900s proved highly profitable, even with ups and downs that reflected ever-changing and fickle public tastes. The business model fell apart when Napster software in 1998 enabled people to share music in their hard drives for free, rather than buy music. The Supreme Court ruled eventually that Napster violated copyright protection for music owners, which eased but didn't solve the recording industry's problems. Apple's iTunes also helped but largely displaced traditional brick-and-mortar retail outlets for recorded music.

■ Radio Industry (Pages 125–127)

The trusteeship model was a useful justification for early government regulation of radio. At the time there were too few frequencies for everyone who wanted to build a station. As a trustee for the public's interest in making radio useful, government decided who could broadcast. Over time, technology diluted the trusteeship rationale. Today there being room for 13,000 radio stations, compared to a few hundred in the beginning.

■ Characteristics of U.S. Radio (Pages 127–130)

Although government-regulated, most of the U.S. radio industry has advertising as its financial base. The financial structure, however, is within the government-defined structure of licensing that limits each station to operate within a geographic locality. Functioning outside direct government control are the networks and programming sources that lend a national character to programming. Even so, the licensed stations are answerable to government for network and other outside programming they carry.

■ Influence of Radio (Pages 130–136)

Most radio programming is entertainment, primarily recorded music. There is not much indigenous creative programming. Although news once was a major component of radio programming, it's now been replaced with piped-in music. Talk programs are a significant programming mainstay at many stations but are mostly imported from faraway network sources and are not local.

■ Radio Industry Directions (Pages 136–138)

The recording industry has been technologically challenged. Focused on its traditional distribution channels, the industry missed the impact of the internet for people to swap music until it was almost too late. In desperation, the recording industry attempted numerous online distribution mechanisms to combat unauthorized downloading. None worked. Then Apple introduced the iPod device and the iTunes music store, which gave recording companies a 21st century distribution system through which they could draw revenue.

■ Thinking Critically

1. What do you see as pluses of the symbiotic relationship of the recording and radio industries? The minuses?

2. How would you address the contradiction of government regulation of broadcasting and the First Amendment's guarantee of a free press?

3. Why do radio networks need to meet government rules and regulations even though the networks themselves are not regulated?

4. Do you see changes ahead in the characteristics of the U.S. radio industry that go back the 1927 regulatory legislation?

5. Pretend you were a knight in shining armor assigned to save traditional terrestrial commercial radio. What would you do?

6. Which new technology delivery methods do you see as most enduring for the radio industry?

■ Media Vocabulary

Media Sources

- The biweekly *Rolling Stone* is the leading periodical for fans who want to track the music business. So is the magazine *Billboard*.

- Ethan Brown. *Queens Reigns Supreme*. Anchor, 2005. Brown traces the roots of many big-name rappers to the 1988 shooting death of rookie cop Edward Byrne, which spurred a police crackdown on Queens drug barons. Many left the drug trade, turning to creating music about what they knew best. Although writing in a detached, neutral journalistic tone, Brown is unsympathetic.

- Barry Truax. *Acoustic Communication*, second edition. Greenwood, 2001. Truax, a Canadian scholar, draws on interdisciplinary studies to create a model for understanding acoustic and aural experiences.

- James Miller. *Flowers in the Dustbin: The Rise of Rock 'n' Roll, 1947–1977*. Simon & Schuster, 1999. Miller, an academic who also is a book and music critic, traces rock to earlier origins than most scholars.

- Charles H. Tillinghast. *American Broadcast Regulation and the First Amendment: Another Look*. Iowa State University Press, 2000. Tillinghast, an entertainment industry lawyer, reviews the history of government regulation and the difficulty it poses for First Amendment advocates.

- Donna Harper. *Invisible Stars: A Social History of Women in American Broadcasting*. Sharpe, 2001.Harper, a historian, bases this work on interviews with pioneer women broadcasters and their survivors. She also draws on letters and newspaper and magazine articles.

- Marc Fisher. "Resurgent Radio," *American Journalism Review* (December 2000), Pages 32-37. Fisher, a Washington Post writer on the media, surveys new radio technologies, including satellite and internet delivery and digital transmission.

- Gerald Eskenazi. *I Hid It Under the Sheets: Growing Up with Radio*. University of Missouri, 2006. Eskenazi, a New York Times sports reporter, reminisces about the so-called Golden Era of Radio. His focus is the comedies, quiz shows, soap operas, dramas, mysteries, Westerns and thrillers and of the1930s and 1940s, as well as early radio sports.

- Thomas Doherty. "Return With Us Now to Those Thrilling Days of Yesteryear: Radio Studies Rise Again," *Chronicle of Higher Education* (May 21, 2004), Pages B12-B13. Doherty, a broadcast scholar, sees new interest in radio as social phenomenon, in this report on the state of recent scholarship.

- Robert L. Hilliard and Michael C. Keith. *Dirty Dscourse: Sex and Indecency in American Radio*. Iowa State Press, 2003. Hilliard and Keith, both communication scholars, trace the course of radio deregulation and changes in FCC decency standards.

- Gerd Horten. *Radio Goes to War: The Cultural Politics of Propaganda During World War II*. 2002.

- Kevin G. Wilson. Deregulating Telecommunications: U.S. and Canadian Telecommunications, 1840-1997. Rowman & Littlefield, 2000. Wilson, a Canadian communication scholar, reviews evolving regulatory policies historically into the era of converging technologies.

- James C. Foust. Big Voices of the Air: The Battle Over Clear Channel Radio. Iowa State University Press, 2000. Foust, a journalism professor, offers a history and analysis of federal licensing for 40 superstations to reach rural audiences.

A Thematic Chapter Summary

SOUND MEDIA

To further deepen your media literacy here are ways to look at this chapter from the perspective of themes that recur throughout the book:

MEDIA TECHNOLOGY

For a flicker in the span of recorded music's history, the Napster Kid, a.k.a. Shawn Fanning, threatened to bring down the entire music industry. Such wasn't Fanning's intent with his Napster peer-to-peer music-sharing software but an unanticipated and near-devastating consequence.

A pattern among established mass media companies is to miss transformational opportunities from new technology until it's almost too late. The recording industry, as an example, was caught unawares by Napster, which allowed fans to swap music free. Rather than embrace the fact that the new technology wouldn't go away, the industry resisted it and began filing lawsuits against fans. Now, a slightly different retailing model, Apple's iTunes, has been widely accepted.

MEDIA FUTURE

Tottering precariously in moving into the future, the recorded music and radio industries have little margin for error.

Lulled by decades of success with decades-old business models, the sound media industries missed opportunities to adapt to new times. Radio failed to upgrade to digital transmission technology in the 1990s. As a result, satellite radio companies like SiriusXM, which could deliver signals directly to listeners, have siphoned listeners away from terrestrial radio. The technology of terrestrial radio, beaming signals from towers on high points in the landscape, has been refined over the past century but fundamentally is unchanged. Terrestrial radio is attempting to regain its lost listeners. By 2008, about 2,000 radio stations were sending digital signals with improved clarity.

MEDIA ECONOMICS

The hopes of the recording industry to offset fast-declining CD sales with downloaded music haven't quite worked out that way. Download sales are rising but not fast enough.

When the bottom fell out of the record business in the mid-1920s, record companies looked to advantageous partnerships with radio. Radio stations found that music was their biggest draw and also their biggest draw for advertising dollars after deregulation in the late 1900s. As the Federal Communications Commission eased license requirements on radio stations for public affairs and news, stations found that music was less costly to produce than maintaining staffs of news reporters and public affairs producers. The shift away from news to music was dramatic evidence of the fact that media companies are capitalistic enterprises that seek the least expensive routes to the greatest financial return.

MEDIA AND DEMOCRACY

Over a career in radio, Tom Joyner has mobilized listeners to join his causes, often to speak Truth to Power. In one Joyner campaign, listeners donated $1.5 million to help victims of Hurricane Katrina. He coined the term black folks' tsunami for the devastation and the government malfeasance to address it.

The potential of radio as a medium for news has a long history. Returns in the 1916 presidential election were reported by radio. Television took over much of this role in the latter 20th century, but parts of the radio industry have continued the medium's role as a forum for discussion of public issues. Today this role is mostly played by talk stations, although much of the content is more showmanship and bluster than enlightenment. Noncommercial public stations, meanwhile, grew as a contributor to public affairs dialogue.

ELITISM AND POPULISM

There is no better way to see the contrasts in cultural tastes offered by mass media than to flick through your radio frequencies for music stations. Bubble-gummer or high-brow, it's all there. But what dominates?

Neuroscience is teaching us that brain development is not entirely under our control as individuals. There is no lock-step progression. Mental capacities are acquired at different rates. So are capacities for understanding and appreciation. This makes a case for diversity in media content. We need kid-rock radio stations for kids and others whose appreciation hasn't grown much beyond that. The question is whether the media, in seeking huge audiences, are failing in their potential to elevate tastes and appreciations: Is kid stuff displacing better stuff.

MEDIA AND CULTURE

The syndicated WNYC show The Takeaway typifies programming in a smart, sophisticated conversational style that has marked the rise of public radio in the United States. NPR led the way with All Things Considered.

Government also has had a hand in the growing audience for news, public affairs and reporting on culture on noncommercial radio stations. After Congress channeled major funding into the noncommercial system starting in 1967, spawning the National Public Radio network and programs like *All Things Considered* with a focus on political, social, economic and cultural affairs, often in a conversational and friendly environment. The programming attracted listeners who were hungry for more than a bland and repetitive diet of pop music that had become the core of commercial radio. It's a type and style of programming that unlikely would have found sufficient traction to get going on advertising-supported stations. The approach has been picked up on many state-level noncommercial networks.

CHAPTER 6 MOTION MEDIA

■ Tyler Perry's Convergence

Born to working-class parents in a poor neighborhood of New Orleans, a high-school dropout at 16, a self-taught playwright and actor, Tyler Perry seems an unlikely personification of the "new Hollywood." But he is all that and more: Tyler Perry just may be the thin end of the wedge—the next phase in the evolution of media content, platforms and channels. He is a new media *auteur* who creates, owns, brands, produces and distributes his creations across platforms completely without regard for the old lines that have traditionally divided movies, television, the stage, print and digital channels. Before he was 40 Perry was media's "new man."

In his early 20s, Perry began writing and producing plays in his Atlanta, often for audiences of just 20 to 30 people. His actors were young, talented unknowns from the African-American community. Perry often played a part as well, sometimes appearing in wig and housedress as the formidable matriarch Madea, modeled on his grandmother. Perry did audience research after every

▲ **Convergence Personified.** *Tyler Perry is the media's "new man." He sees seamless possibilities for developing content on multiple platforms. You may know his character, Madea, from the movies. It's also his stage play. He writes books. He produces television series. He acts. He directs. Print media? Sound media? Motion media? It doesn't matter. What matters to Perry is communicating content to mass audiences whatever the medium.*

CHAPTER INSIGHTS

- The movie and television industries are distinct in many ways but also increasingly integrated.

- The fast-growing early movie industry lost momentum after a government break-up and the advent of television.

- U.S. television industry originally was a federally licensed two-tier system that now competes with cable systems and direct-to-consumer satellite delivery.

- The movie industry is dominated by a handful of major studios, but essential too are companies that distribute and exhibit movies.

- Motion media industries are melding, but their products retain some distinctions amid overlapping genres.

- The exhibition component of the movie industry is in rapid transition.

performance, standing on stage, talking with the audience, finding out what they liked and what they wanted to see. What Perry says he learned from the experience was that it is the women in African-American families who are key to building an audience: "The women bring the men and the children and everybody to everything." He realized then that his focus needed to be the women.

Perry's third play, *Diary of a Mad Black Woman,* centered on the character of Madea. It became his first movie, produced on a shoestring budget of $5.5 million. Distributed by indie LionsGate, it opened in 2005 and eventually grossed over $50 million. *Diary* was panned by critics, but it seemed to fill a gap with audiences who felt ignored by Hollywood, and it set a pattern for Perry's highly energetic output in the next several years, in which he wrote, produced and toured six more plays, a total of nine motion pictures, two television series, and a book.

All Perry's works regardless of medium are branded with the possessive, "Tyler Perry's . . ." His 2009 film *Tyler Perry's Madea Goes to Jail,* based on his play, had an opening weekend gross of $41 million, proving, as if further proof were needed, that a large and underserved market exists for middlebrow, middle-class comedies aimed at an African-American audience.

Perry to date has had two hit sitcoms running on the TBS network: *Tyler Perry's House of Payne* debuted in 2006, ran successfully for seven seasons and is in syndication. *Tyler Perry's Meet the Browns* debuted in 2009. It is, like many of his creations, a perfect example of content driving the convergence of media: *Meet the Browns* began life as a stage play; became a movie in 2008, opening at Number 2 with a $21 million weekend gross; and was quickly adapted to series television. For the 2012 season Perry launched his third television sitcom, *For Better or Worse,* also on the TBS network, adapted from his two successful movies, *Why Did I Get Married?* and *Why Did I Get Married Two?*

Perry once told a gathering of network and advertising executives that audiences crave shows like *Meet the Browns.* These shows, he said, tell people that someone is paying attention to them. Like on a playback machine, people see themselves in the stories and portrayals.

In addition to branding his own creative output, Perry has now turned to producing other artists' work, with the establishment of Tyler Perry Studios, an enormous studio, soundstage and office complex in Atlanta that guides the work of other filmmakers.

It may just also give him a base for his next dream: owning his own cable network. He's ambitious—always looking to spread out more, as he puts it. He characterizes *House of Payne* and *Meet the Browns* as endeavors that have helped him "sharpen the anchor" for his next big thing. ◼

Movie-Television Meld

STUDY PREVIEW After early distrust between them, the television and movie industries have largely melded. Many major corporations are planted in both industries. Synergies have been found between both traditional television and Hollywood products.

Divergent Legacies

Despite their current coziness, Hollywood and the television industries once were rivals that saw each other as Darth Vaders. The rivalry dated to the 1950s when television grabbed eyeballs from the Big Screen by the millions. Until then, Hollywood had been entrenched as the sole media purveyor of screen sound-and-motion for half a century.

The two motion media came from different corporate and artistic cultures. Fueled by huge popularity and profitability, a distinctive Hollywood culture and lifestyle had evolved—celebrity-obsessed, gilded and flashy. Suddenly, there came the insurgent television with entirely different cultural roots in the relatively buttoned-down New York-based radio industry. Even the technologies were different. Movies were created through photographic chemistry in those days. Television was electronic.

Actors made strong distinctions between the warring media. In the era before videotape technology in television, some stage actors would consider appearing on television, which was broadcast live, but never in a movie. In those days, television, had the spontaneity of live performance. Then there were actors who preferred movies. They liked the control that filming and editing gave in exorcising slip-ups, and providing alternate takes for creating the perfect filmic moment.

Synergies

The rivalry is hard to understand today. Actors are platform-neutral and easily dance back and forth between stage, movies and television. The television and film industries have subsumed each other as content-generators. In fact, the melding is evident in corporate titles that draw on both legacies: NBCUniversal; Disney-ABC; and Fox television and 20th Century Fox.

So what happened? And what distinctions remain in the blurring of these important media industries?

synergy
An interaction that produces a combined effect greater than the sum of separate effects

In 1954, an alliance between the ABC television network and the Disney studio, the Sunday night series *Disneyland*, showed potential **synergies.** Then popular movies begat television series, and popular television series begat movies. Another breakthrough occurred in the mid-1960s when television networks began offering Hollywood blockbusters, like *Bridge over the River Kwai*, and then regularized them in a prime-time *Movie of the Week* series. Financially these were a win-win for the networks and the movie studios, which suddenly discovered additional income in recycling their products. To be sure, local stations earlier had filled time with hand-me-down movies from Hollywood, but these mostly were from B-lists and shown at obscure times of the day.

The television-movie divide further crumbled with the television comedy series *I Love Lucy*. The show, launched in 1951, was filmed with three cameras, which moved television away from live shows and nearer to the conventions of Hollywood production. *Lucy* editors chose from three sets of film, each from a different angle, for the greatest impact. Important too, actors Desi Arnaz and Lucille Ball, whose success gave them plenty of clout with the CBS network, insisted that they be allowed to produce the show in Hollywood. Up until that point the television industry was New York-centric. Desi and Lucy preferred West Coast sunshine and glamour.

◀ **Lloyd and Levitan.**
Television Producers

◀ **Modern Mockumentary.** *Christopher Lloyd and Steven Levitan have their* Modern Family *characters take asides and talk directly into the camera. The mockumentary style, as it's called, sets the sitcom apart. The Colombian trophy wife, played by Sofia Vergara, reminds some viewers of the whacky Latin element that Desi Arnaz created in the long-running screwball* I Love Lucy *series starting in 1951.*

Digitization later facilitated the shift of technicians from producing movies to television and back to movies. Distinctions blurred. And in corporate offices, executives were focused not on their old rival medium for eyeballs but on how to maximize profits by adapting products to any and all delivery vehicles.

Although these once bitterly rival industries have found an easy and profitable peace with each other, there remain differences that are deeply rooted in their distinctive pasts.

APPLYING YOUR MEDIA LITERACY

- **What dynamic do you see as the single most significant explanation of the post-World War II battle between Hollywood and the television industry: Economics? Technology? Corporate culture? Acting styles? Or something else?**
- **From your own experience, create a list of actors and of television producers and movie directors who have succeeded in both movies and television. What do they have in common?**

Movie Industry

STUDY PREVIEW

As a visual medium portraying motion, movies quickly became major industry in the early 1900s. With innovations by Adolph Zukor, Hollywood became associated with glamour and glitz. The arrival of television as a competing medium in the 1940s, as well as an antitrust court decision against major studios, forced Hollywood to downsize. Although excesses of Hollywood's heyday receded, the movie industry remains a major mass medium but in a larger universe of competing media.

Formative Era

A U.S. inventor, Thomas Edison, pioneered the movie industry. With a projector to display images on a wall, his early exhibition halls amazed audiences. His shots of ocean waves rolling toward a camera on a beach scared audiences. People covered their heads. Instinctively they expected to be soaked. Such was their **suspension of disbelief.** Natural human skepticism gets lost in the darkened cocoon of a movie-house auditorium, compounding the impact of what's on-screen.

suspension of disbelief
Occurs when you surrender doubts about the reality of a story and become caught up in the story

Although moviegoers are insulated in a dark auditorium, the experience is communal. You're not the only one sobbing or terrified or joyous. Among your fellow viewers is a reinforcement of emotions that other media can't match. A newspaper article, for example, may be read by thousands, but the experience is individual and apart. The emotional impact is less. Television, watched at home, often alone, is similarly disadvantaged, even though television has most of the accoutrements of movies—visuals, motion and sound.

Movies have come a long way since Edison. With wide screens, sophisticated amplified sound and other effects, movies are a more potent medium than ever. Consider the fuss over Dan Brown's thriller *The Da Vinci Code*, which attracted reproach as a megaselling book for its account of Catholic church history. The book was a big deal—but nothing compared to the fury that occurred when Sony moved Ron Howard's movie adaptation toward release. The full crescendo came when the movie premiered. The unprecedented fury in the dialogue demonstrates the impact of movies as a storytelling and myth-making medium, which for mass audiences can far exceed the impact of other media for at least short windows of time.

In the same way, Al Gore's documentary movie *An Inconvenient Truth* gave new urgency to finding solutions for global warming. Michael Moore and other docu-ganda producers have stirred significant issues far beyond what magazine and newspaper articles had been doing for years. *Guess Who's Coming to Dinner?*, with a theme that was interracially edgy for the 1960s, moved the public toward broader acceptance of interracial relationships.

The movie industry has impact because of delivery to audiences in the cocoon of a theater. In a darkened auditorium there are no distractions. The movie industry, however, has moved far beyond movie houses to other forums, which although less potent have spread the influence of the movie industry— on television, on DVDs at home, through downloads to a computer or smartphone.

Adolph Zukor's Paramount

Adolph Zukor
Innovative creator of Paramount as a major movie studio

Early moviemakers kept their actors' names secret. The idea was to discourage formation of a fan base that might give actors a star complex and demands for better pay. Fifteen dollars a day was tops then. But in 1912 a Hungarian immigrant, **Adolph Zukor,** started a studio, Famous Players, with a different idea. Zukor tracked fan letters to identify the most-mentioned actors, whom he signed to exclusive contracts. So to speak, Zukor put their names in lights. It cost him. Mary Pickford was soon at $15,000 a week. The payoff for Zukor was that Mary Pickford's name attracted repeat customers just to see her, even in lackluster movies. Zukor's **star system** became widely imitated.

star system
Making actors into celebrities to increase the size of movie audiences

Mass-Production Movies.   The star system brought mass production to moviemaking. Zukor needed a great number of projects to keep his stars productive, as well as other contract employees, including hundreds of directors, writers, editors and technicians. By the time that Zukor changed the name of his studio from Famous Players to Paramount, movies had become factory-like products. On tight mass-production schedules, Paramount eventually was issuing a movie a week.

studio system
When major studios controlled all aspects of the movie industry

block booking
A rental agreement through which a movie house accepts a batch of movies

Federal Break-Up.   By the mid-1930s, the big movie companies owned acre upon acre of studios and sets, which were money machines. Awash with profits, these movie-making companies went beyond making movies and entered the movie distribution and movie-exhibition business, squeezing out independent operators. The business model that emerged, the **studio system,** was an integrated structure that controlled everything from the conceptual to the production stages to the end-consumer stage. The control of the whole system led to abuses. Paramount and other major movie studios went into **block booking,** allowing the remaining independent movie houses to play major movies from a studio's repertoire only if

▲ **Hollywood Survivor.** *Most studios sold their huge sound lots to real estate developers for cash to see them through revenue slumps after big-budget flops. Today only Paramount has retained its facilities in Hollywood.*

▲ **Adolph Zukor.**

they also took the clunkers. This coercive practice brought further riches to the major studios, funding opulent lifestyles and other excesses that gave Hollywood its gilded reputation.

This all came to an end in an antitrust case decided by the U.S. Supreme Court in 1948 in the so-called the **Paramount decision.** The court told the studios to divest. The studios responded by selling their movie houses. It was a setback for the studio system. Suddenly the major movie companies had to compete for screen time in movie houses. Without a guaranteed outlet for movies, including proverbial B movies, the studios had no choice but to scale back on payrolls and facilities. The lavish excesses of Hollywood's gilded age were over.

Paramount decision
U.S. Supreme Court breakup of movie industry oligarchy in 1948

Television as a Rival

While the Paramount decision was a sudden strike at the big movie companies' business model, an even larger threat was looming. An emerging rival medium, television, had stalled in the early 1940s when the nation's resources were consumed by World War II. But after the war the NBC and CBS radio networks resumed projects for national television networks. Families by the millions made budget decisions over the kitchen table to buy a television set, often a hefty $500 at the time, and amortize the cost by staying home rather than going to the neighborhood Bijou for entertainment. Movie attendance, which peaked in 1946 at 90 million tickets a week, began eroding. To Hollywood, with its survival in jeopardy, television was the enemy.

The original technologies underlying movies and television bore little in common. Movies were on film, a chemistry-based medium. Performances were filmed in bits and pieces over weeks or months, then painstakingly assembled, and audiences saw the product later. With early television, viewers saw events and performances live. In one sense, early television had the live tension and excitement of the stage. Movies, on the other hand, were edited, the final presentation slicker. For sure, television programs could be recorded on film, but for broadcast to an audience in the early days the transmission needed to be live.

Too, the mindset for early television and movies were different. The network television industry was modeled on New York-centric network radio. Television technicians and producers came from radio. In contrast, the modes and traditions of the movie industry had been evolving in their own directions for more than half a century a continent away in Hollywood.

APPLYING YOUR MEDIA LITERACY

- **Besides the novelty of media-depicted motion, what made movies a powerful new medium?**
- **Who would you consider the Adolph Zukor of today's movie industry? Why?**
- **How would you as a media consumer have viewed the Paramount decision at the time? In retrospect?**
- **How did the traditions and practices of the movie and television industry work against early compatibility?**

Television Industry Structure

STUDY PREVIEW

The regulatory mechanism created by Congress for television in the 1930s resulted in a two-tier U.S. television system. Corporate entities that entered the television business comported with the regulatory infrastructure. The original television industry comprised local stations, generally with the most successful carrying programs from national networks. Today those terrestrial stations, with local earth-bound transmission towers, are in competition with cable and satellite delivery.

Two-Tier Infrastructure

Just as government policy shaped the movie industry with the 1948 Paramont antitrust action, so did government policy shape television. In the 1930s, with television on the horizon, Congress looked at how its regulation of radio had worked. Congress was pleased with

Federal Radio Act
Original law in 1927 for government
regulation of U.S. broadcasting

Federal Communications Act
Revision of Federal Radio Act in 1934
to include television

two-tier system
Original U.S. broadcast infrastructure
had two tiers, one of locally licensed
stations, the other of national networks

Big Three
ABC, CBS, NBC

Newton Minow
FCC chair who called television a "vast
wasteland"

Corporation for Public
Broadcasting (CPB)
Quasi-government agency that channels tax-generated funds into the U.S.
noncommercial television and radio
system

Public Broadcasting Service (PBS)
Television network for noncommercial
over-air stations

its **Federal Radio Act** of 1927. If the regulatory system worked for radio, why wouldn't it work for television? With the **Federal Communications Act** of 1934, Congress tidied up the 1927 law and expanded the scope to television.

The backbone of the national television system was local stations that were licensed by the Federal Communications Commission, just as with radio. There were no national stations because the government didn't want to encourage powerful centralized media. But just like radio, these new television stations looked to national networks with budgets for programming that local stations couldn't afford to produce on their own. No surprise, these networks were NBC, CBS and later ABC, which were already established in radio. Larger cities also had unaffiliated, independent stations, but they were mostly secondary players. Even less prominent were noncommercial stations tyat were licensed for educational programming, mostly operated by school districts.

Thus the infrastructure of the early television industry matched radio's **two-tier system.** Stations, licensed for local communities by the government, were one one of the tiers. The networks provided a national tier of infrastructure. The networks were not licensed but comported with FCC expectations for local stations by avoiding programming that could jeopardize the local affiliates' licenses to broadcast.

The **Big Three,** as ABC, CBS and NBC were called, came to be evenly matched with about 300 affiliates each. Network programs reached the whole country, with the exception of remote and mountainous areas unreachable by signals from transmission towers in the cities that had licensed stations. In 1986, Australian media mogul Rupert Murdoch launched Fox, modeled on the success of the other networks, making it the Big Four.

Besides the U.S. commercial television system, whose financial base is advertising revenue, the Federal Communications licenses noncommercial stations. Originally these mostly were operated by universities and school districts as part of their mission to broaden their educational reach. In 1967, responding to FCC Chairman **Newton Minow's** still-quoted criticism that television programming was a "vast wasteland" of lowbrow content, Congress set up the **Corporation for Public Broadcasting** to develop a national noncommercial broadcasting system. The goal was high-quality programming distinct from that of the commercial networks, which, by their nature, pandered to mass audiences. Thus was born the network known as the **Public Broadcasting Service.**

To pay the bills, public television stations cobble together motley sources of revenue, including donations from public-spirited corporations and also viewers themselves. Until recent years, congressional appropriations, buffered from political control through a quasi-government agency known as the Corporation for Public Broadcasting, were essential to keep public television operating. As federal funding has declined, the public television system has significantly stepped up its drive for donations from philanthropic and corporate sponsors that are briefly acknowledged on the air, as well as regular viewers.

Fragmented Television Industry

When Congress created the Federal Communications Commission in 1934, nobody envisioned any other way to deliver television signals than from ground-based transmitters. Back then, cable delivery through the low-capacity telephone lines wasn't practical. And transmission from orbiting satellites? Pipedream stuff.

Terrestrial Television. Early television stations mounted their transmitters on ridges, mountaintops or skyscrapers or built tall towers to extend their signals as far as possible. A station in North Dakota's very flat Red River Valley, mounted its transmitters 2,063 feet up a guy wire-supported mast. When hoisted in 1963, the tower was the tallest structures in the world. The station chose the call letters KTHI—short for Tower High.

Because television signals move in straight lines and don't follow the curvature of the earth, height is essential for earth-based transmission of more than a few miles. Signals from the North Dakota tower, midway between the cities of Fargo and Grand Forks, go 55.6 miles. Such are the limits of terrestrial television.

Cable Television. Entrepreneurs in mountainous sections of Oregon, West Virginia and western Pennsylvania figured out how to bring television to their communities in the late 1940s even though mountains blocked the signals. At the time the only stations were in

Largest U.S. Television Markets

NETWORK-OWNED AND AFFILIATED.

Television stations attract advertisers by how many viewers they deliver. Translation: Each viewer is a potential customer. These are the largest television markets in the United States, ranked by the number of households with television in the city's television broadcast range. All television markets have federally licensed local stations carrying network programs, and the networks themselves are well-positioned in major markets with their own owned-and-operated stations. In cities without a network's o-&-o station, an affiliate carries network programs.

New York City 7.5 million households
WABC (ABC), WCBS (CBS), WNYW (Fox), WNBC (NBC),

Los Angeles 5.7 million
KABC (ABC), KCBS (CBS), KTTV (Fox), KNBC (NBC)

Chicago 3.5 million
WLS (ABC), WBBM (CBS), WFLD (Fox), WMAQ (NBC)

Philadelphia 3.0 million
WPVI (ABC), KYW (CBS), KTFX (Fox), WCAU (NBC)

Dallas 2.6 million
KTVT (CBS), KDFW (Fox), KXAS (NBC)

San Francisco 2.5 million
KGO (ABC), KPIX (CBS), KNTV (NBC)

Boston 2.5 million
WVZ (CBS), WFXT (Fox), WVIT (NBC)

Atlanta 2.4 million
WAGA (Fox)

Washington 2.4 million
WTTG (Fox), WRC (NBC)

Houston 2.1 million
KTRK (ABC), KRIV (Fox)

Detroit 1.9 million
WWJ (CBS), WJBK (Fox)

Phoenix 1.9 million
KSAZ (Fox)

Seattle 1.9 million
No o-&-o

Tampa 1.8 million
WOGX (Fox), WTVT (Fox)

Minneapolis 1.8 million
WCCO (CBS), KMSP (Fox)

Miami 1.6 million
WFOR (CBS), WTVJ (NBC)

Denver 1.6 million
KCNC (CBS) ·

Cleveland 1.6 million
No o-&-o

Orlando 1.5 million
WOFL (Fox)

Sacramento 1.4 million
KOVR (CBS)

big cities. Putting a reception tower on nearby mountaintops, these entrepreneurs caught the faraway signals and strung a cable down to town, and from there to every house. Voila, places like Astoria, Oregon, had television. Gradually every small town beyond the reach of over-air television signals had a local **Community Antenna Television,** known as CATV. Small-town America saw mainstream entertainment nightly—Milton Berle, Jack Benny and *The Honeymooners.* Hardly any cable systems offered local-origination programming, however.

Cable Networks.   By the 1970s, with orbiting satellites in use for telephone relays, a young executive at Time Inc. in New York, **Gerald Levin,** put two and two together and came up with a new direction for television. Levin's idea was to create a network exclusively for local cable systems to augment what they were picking up from over-air stations. The network, built on a floundering Time entity called Home Box Office, **HBO** for short, would send programming via orbiting satellites.

A year later, Atlanta station owner **Ted Turner** put his WTBS on satellite as mostly a movie channel for local cable systems. Turner called WTBS a "superstation." Overnight the station became a money machine. Leveraging the revenue, Turner then created **CNN,** the first 24-hour cable news network.

These networks avoided most government regulations because their programming was delivered to viewers by cable, bypassing FCC-regulated airwaves that terrestrial stations used. National programming for local cable systems siphoned viewers from over-air television and shook up the industry.

The potential of the cable television industry did not go unnoticed on Wall Street. For investors, cable suddenly was hot. CATV systems were gobbled up in hundreds of acquisitions. What emerged were **multisystem operators,** called MSOs in the industry. These companies, many of them subsidiaries of larger media companies, simultaneously were raising money from investors to wire big cities so that cable programming could be offered for a monthly subscription. Today, more than 90 percent of U.S. households have access to cable, although only about two-thirds of them subscribe.

The company Comcast catapulted into becoming the largest multisystem operator in 2002 by buying AT&T Broadband and claiming, with earlier acquisitions, more than 21 million subscribers. Comcast continued acquisitions until in 2011 it bought the television and movie giant NBCUniversal. Meanwhile, the consolidation of cable systems into large ownerships has reduced the number of MSOs nationwide to 25—a far cry from the individual local systems that began in the late 1940s.

Satellite Delivery.   Next came a third program delivery service that bypassed both local terrestrial stations and cable systems— satellite-direct transmission to individual earth stations, usually a rooftop dish the size of a large pizza pan. The cost of entry for satellite-direct delivery has limited the number of U.S. satcom operators to two. **DirecTV,** the larger, has 19.2 million subscribers. **Dish Network** has 14.3 million subscribers. Dish has a fleet of 16 satellites, DirecTV 13.

Both DirecTV and Dish have taken subscribers away from cable. In 2003 Dallas became the first major city with more satellite than cable customers. Cable, however, easily leads with 42.2 million subscribers to the satcoms' 33.5 million. Terrestrial stations, free and available almost everywhere, typically attract 27.7 million prime-time viewers.

The multiple delivery systems have rendered the idea of a television industry somewhat dated. So competitive are the companies in the different delivery methods that each can be considered an industry in of itself, although there is growing cross-ownership. As one example, the NBC network, once a service to local terrestrial stations, now owns the A&E, Bravo, Syfy, Chiller, CNBC, MSNBC, Telemundo, Weather Channel and USA networks. And NBC itself is part of the larger NBCUniversal, which itself is a subsidiary of the even larger Comcast media conglomerate.

CATV
Early local cable television systems; short for *community antenna television*

Gerald Levin
Used orbiting satellite to relay exclusive programs to local cable systems in 1975

CNN
First 24-hour television news service

multisystem operator (MSO)
A company that owns several local cable television delivery units in different, usually far-flung, communities

DirecTV
Larger of two U.S. satellite-direct companies

Dish Network
Satellite-direct company

APPLYING YOUR MEDIA LITERACY

- **What do you say to people who argue that tight regulation of terrestrial television doesn't make sense anymore if the cable and satcom television industries are exempt?**
- **What future role do you see for traditional television networks that have historically served local terrestrial affiliates?**

Movie Industry Structure

STUDY PREVIEW

Hollywood is dominated by six movie studios, all engaged in both producing and distributing movies. These studios, each part of a conglomerate, are enmeshed with the television industry through corporate connections. Meanwhile there continues to be a place for independent movie producers.

Post-Paramount Decision

The big Hollywood companies didn't take kindly to the U.S. Justice Department's order to break up their oligopoly. But after the 1948 Paramount decision, in which the U.S. Supreme Court sided with the Justice Department, the movie companies had no choice but to retreat and do business differently. Paramount and the other big studios each decided to stay in the movie-making business, the industry's production component. The studios gave up their ownership in distribution and exhibition. This triad of movie industry components—production, distribution and exhibition—each under its own ownerships, remains the structure of the industry.

Production. The movie industry's creative heart is production. This includes marquee names like Angelina Jolie, Tom Hanks, Denzel Washington and Meryl Streep, and big-name directors like Tom Hooper, Kathryn Bigelow, Martin Scorsese and John Ford. Less visible are producers, who organize projects and raise money to produce them, and screenwriters, composers and lyricists, costumers, technicians and thousands of support people.

Distribution. Although their names appear briefly on-screen, the companies that book movies into theaters and negotiate releases in other venues are mostly unknown to audiences. These distribution companies produce trailers and place advertising. Distribution companies are major players in the complex financial arrangements that confound most mortals about the inside workings of the movie industry. In fact, some distribution companies have close relationships with widely recognized studios and bear similar names, which blur the different corporate and functional role of distribution. Buena Vista, for example, once was the distributor for Disney films, although now does only video DVD releases, with replacement companies like Walt Disney Distribution and others bearing variations on the Disney name.

Exhibition. The movie exhibition business took a major hit in the 1950s when families by the millions bought a television set and stayed home rather than going to the movies. Attendance had peaked in 1946 at 90 million tickets a week, at a time when the nation's population, 141 million, was less than half of today. Exhibitors have frantically tried to stem their box-office decline with multiple but smaller auditoriums, some spartan, some elegant. Movie-makers have tried to help with technical innovations—like Cinemascope and 3-D—from time to time. Digital cinema is coming on stream, promising to replace the physical distribution of film in clunky 85-pound canisters. To offset box-office losses, exhibitors have put popcorn at ridiculous prices, buttered or not, and moved aggressively into selling on-screen advertising ahead of the main feature.

The fact is that 1946 won't come back. People have manifold more diversions, including television's small screen and the even smaller online screens of smartphones and tablets.

Major Studios

A few major movie companies, all part of larger media companies, dominate Hollywood—Disney, Columbia, Paramount, 20th Century Fox, Universal and Warner. Ranking studios is tricky because one megahit or one clunker can upset a listing. But Disney is perennially among the leaders.

Disney. Although not realizing it, illustrator **Walt Disney** created the Disney franchise with Mickey Mouse in a synch-sound cartoon in 1928. In 1937 Disney risked it all with a full-feature animated film, *Snow White and the Seven Dwarfs*. Audiences wanted more. Disney responded with *Pinocchio*, *Dumbo* and *Bambi*.

Walt Disney
Pioneer in animated films

With animated movies, nature documentaries and pre-teen television shows like the *Mickey Mouse Club,* Disney's reputation was for family-oriented entertainment by the mid-1950s. Theme parks cemented the reputation. For the next 20 years the mandate at Disney was to cultivate the brand. In 1995 Disney moved beyond family fare with cutting-edge and niche movies like *Powder* and *Dangerous Minds,* but buffered many of the projects under subsidiary units and partnerships to shield the wholesome Disney aura. Films were produced through Touchstone, Caravan, Hollywood Pictures and Miramax. Meanwhile, Disney's distribution unit at the time, Buena Vista, the largest in the world, branched out into producing Broadway plays.

The Lion King, under the Disney imprimatur, was a great success in 1995, but during that same time the company experienced a run of animated feature flops. After a messy management fight, the company's directors offered $7.4 billion to Steve Jobs, the genius behind Apple's resurgence, for his Pixar animation studio. It was Pixar that had stolen Disney's animation pre-eminence with blockbusters like *Toy Story, Finding Nemo* and *The Incredibles.* The deal, in 2006, made Jobs the largest Disney shareholder and put him on the Disney board of directors.

Disney has lots of signature products, most recently *Pirates of the Caribbean* and, in partnership with Jobs' Pixar, *Cars.*

Columbia. Founded in 1919, Columbia has moved through high-visibility ownership, including Coca-Cola and the Japanese electronics company Sony. Movies are produced and distributed under brand names Columbia and TriStar. Major recent films include *Battle Los*

MEDIAtimeline

MOTION MEDIA MILESTONES

JOSEPH NIÉPCE'S PROCESS
Photographic technology discovered, essential for early movies (1727)

PIVOTAL EVENTS

- Benjamin Franklin (1706–1790)
- Death of influential scientist Isaac Newton, whose work included a theory of universal gravitation (1727)
- French and Indian War (1754–1763)
- Revolutionary War (1775–1783)

Edmund Burke coined "Fourth Estate" (1787)

1700s

MOTION MEDIA MILESTONES

THOMAS EDISON
Edison lab invented movie cameras, projectors (1888)

PIVOTAL EVENTS

- U.S.industrialization, urbanization accelerating (1830s)
- Charles Darwin, *On Evolution* (1859)
- Civil War (1861–1865)
- Professional baseball takes hold (1870s)
- U.S. middle class with discretionary time for amusement emerged (1870s–)
- Spanish-American War (1898)

Civil War photography

1800s

MOTION MEDIA MILESTONES

STRAND
First of the opulent movie palaces (1912)

PARAMOUNT
Hollywood studio system took form (1912–1948)

POPULARITY
U.S. movie box office peaked at 90 million a week (1946)

BREAKUP
U.S. Supreme Court broke up Hollywood's vertical integration (1948)

TELEVISION
Philo Farnsworth invented a tube to capture and transmit moving images (1927)
First television network feeds (1948)
Cable television introduced (1949)

PIVOTAL EVENTS

- Fox introduced sound in newsreels (1922)
- *Black Pirate,* first color movie (1927)
- Warner distributed first talkie, *The Jazz Singer* (1927)

1900–1949

Angeles, Green Hornet and *The Social Network*. The company is also in television production and distribution, including the venerable game show *Jeopardy*.

Paramount. Founded in 1912 and the oldest existing movie studio, Paramount has the distinction of being the only major studio with headquarters still in Hollywood proper. The company's franchises includes *Indiana Jones, Mission Impossible, Star Trek* and *Transformers*. Since 1994 Paramount has been part of the Viacom media empire, which also includes CBS and the MTV and BET cable television channels.

20th Century Fox. With roots dating to 1915, this studio is now part of the global media empire of Rupert Murdoch's News Corporatuion, whose roots are in Australia. Corporate siblings include the Fox television network. James Cameron's blockbuster *Avatar* was co-produced by a consortium of three studios, including 20th Century Fox, to share the risk of the high-budget project. Cameron's earlier film *Titanic* was a partnership between Paramount and 20th Century Fox, also to share the risk.

Universal. The cable television giant Comcast acquired the controlling share of Universal from General Electric in 2011, along with the NBC television network and other media properties.

Warner. Founded in 1918, Warner Bros. became part of the Time Inc. media empire in a 1989 acquisition, prompting the parent company to rename itself Time Warner. The company produces and distributes movies and television programs mostly through units carrying the Warner name but also the names Castle Rock, New Line and Lorimar.

MOTION MEDIA MILESTONES

TELEVISION
Network television hurt movie attendance (1950s)

PUBLIC TELEVISION
Congress established Corporation for Public Broadcasting (1967)

DISNEY
Disney produced weekly television show (1954)

MULTIPLEX
Multiscreen theaters attempted to recover movie audience (1970s)

PIVOTAL EVENTS

• FCC chair Newton Minow characterized television as "vast wasteland" (1961)
• Telstar in orbit (1961)

Farnworth's television invention took off in 1950s

1950–1975

MOTION MEDIA MILESTONES

VHS
Home movie rentals hurt home theater attendance (1990s)

Backbone of U.S. television: Network affiliates

HBO
First satellite-delivered programming to cable systems (1975)

DISHES
Satellite-direct programming began (1994)

DIGITAL
FCC adopted digital standards for gradual phase-in (1996)

PIVOTAL EVENTS

• First AIDS case reported in United States (1981)
• Microsoft introduced Windows operating system (1985)
• Internet emerged as commercial medium (late 1990s)
• British pop group Spice Girls formed (1994)
• AIDS drug HAART introduced (1996)
• Clinton presidency (1992–2001)

1976–1999

MOTION MEDIA MILESTONES

MOVIE-HOUSE MAKE-OVER
Webcasting for content distribution over internet (2000s)

HIGHER RESOLUTION
10-year conversion to digital projection began (2006)

PIVOTAL EVENTS

• Iraq War (2003–2011)
• Apple introduced video iPod (2005)
• Great Recession (2007–2009)
• James Cameron's 3-D epic Avatar (2009)
• Obama presidency (2009–)
• BP oil spill in Gulf (2010)
• Arab Spring revolutions (2010)
• World population passed 7 billion (2011)

Television anywhere, any time

2000s

◀ **Reducing the Risk.** *For the 2011 movie The Help, with Viola Davis and Octavia Spencer, five studios shared the costs and made money. The $25 million investment generated $175 million revenue. Not all movies do so well. It's because movie-making is high risk endeavor that studios team up.*

Independents

indies
Minor movie studies; not among Big Five

Besides the major studios that dominate Hollywood, independent studios and producers come and go—often with a single breakthrough film, then not much that attracts attention. The term *independent* is misleading in a sense because these **indies** frequently lean on majors for financing. Also, there are no suitable options for distribution other than through the corporate siblings and subsidiaries of the major studios. The history of independents is that those that establish a track record end up being acquired by a major studio. A notable exception is United Artists.

United Artists. Unhappy with profit-obsessed studios limiting their creativity, friends Charlie Chaplin, Douglas Fairbanks, D. W. Griffith and Mary Pickford broke away in 1919. They created United Artists. With full creative control, they produced movies that scored well among critics and attracted huge audiences. United Artists has been among only a few insurgent movie companies to make a long-term mark on Hollywood after the giants established themselves early on.

Despite box office successes, United Artists has had its share of movies in red ink. After Michael Cimino's costly *Heaven's Gate* in 1980, United needed a white knight. The Transamerica insurance company bought the studio, then unloaded it on MGM. The new company, MGM/UA, produced one box office disaster after another.

Dreamworks. In the United Artists spirit, three Hollywood legends—David Geffen, Jeff Katzenberg and Steven Spielberg—founded a new studio, Dreamworks, in 1994. The three founders were well-connected and seasoned Hollywood people, each with a fortune from successful entertainment industry careers. They were called the Hollywood dream team. Spielberg's *Saving Private Ryan* in 1998 established an early Dreamworks benchmark for film excellence. Then came *Gladiator*, named 2000's best picture at the Academy Awards. Like most upstarts, even the most successful ones, Dreamworks has disappeared. Geffen, Katzenberg and Spielberg sold the enterprise in 2005 to Paramount for $1.6 billion.

Miramax. Brothers Bob and Harvey Weinstein blew into Hollywood in 1979, introducing themselves as concert promoters from Buffalo, New York. They set up a movie distribution company, Miramax, with a simple premise: Find low-budget, independently produced movies and buy them cheap, then promote them lavishly.

After 10 years of struggling, the Weinsteins hit gold with the bio-pic *My Left Foot*, on Irish writer-painter Christy Brown. An Academy Award nomination for best picture stirred the box office. So did Daniel Day-Lewis' winning the Oscar for best actor. In the same year the Weinsteins released the indie favorite, *Sex, Lies and Videotape* Other hits followed, prompting Disney to buy into Miramax in 1993. The deal left creative control with the hands-on Weinsteins, who seemed to have a deft touch for cultural edginess that Disney lacked. The arrangement produced Quentin Tarantino's *Pulp Fiction* in 1994, a a film that cost $8 million to make and grossed $200 million worldwide and earned an Oscar.

More financial and critical successes followed, including *The English Patient, Good Will Hunting, Shakespeare in Love, Kill Bill*, and the *Scary Movie* and *Spy Kids* franchises. Like any studio the Weinsteins had their failures, including *Cold Mountain* and *Gangs of New York*, which never earned back their $100 million production budgets.

Lions Gate.   Founded in 1997 by a Canadian investor, Lions Gate found early financial success in acquiring and producing tight-budget movies and then promoting them aggressively and imaginatively. Typical was *Crash*. Production cost $3.3 million, and marketing sextupled that—to $21 million. The U.S. and global box office generated $254 million. To create buzz for the Academy Awards, Lions Gate sent 110,000 DVDs to members of the Screen Actors Guild. The movie subsequently won the 2005 Academy Award for best picture. That generated the predictable bump for *Crash* in movie attendance and rentals. Alongside critical favorites like *Crash*, Lions Gate has made big money with the slasher franchise of *Saw* films—the seventh and final installment *Saw3-D* released in 2010.

Lions Gate releases fewer than 20 pictures in a typical year. In 2011 the studio announced it would release up to 10 low-budget films a year. To see itself through slumps, Lions Gate invested in film libraries and gradually amassed an archive of 8,000 titles that generate continuing revenue through domestic and overseas licensing. The catalog includes *Basic Instinct, Total Recall, Dirty Dancing* and the lucrative *Leprechaun* horror series.

APPLYING YOUR MEDIA LITERACY

- How can it be argued Hollywood has regained dominance as a producer of motion-media products?
- Has the absorption of major movie studios into conglomerates been a good thing for movies?
- Who are the newest entries into the independent film market? What are the chances they will soon be acquired by established studios?

Motion Media Products

STUDY PREVIEW

The products of motion media industries include genres that overlap but also include significant distinctions. The lesson: What works on big screens, like in a movie theater, doesn't necessarily work on small screens, like television and handheld devices. Or at least work differently. One factor is the impossible-to-duplicate impact of larger screens. Another is ergonomics. Nobody has the patience to hold a smartphone 14 inches from your face and watch feature-length movies in a single sitting.

Movie Genres

Ask someone what a movie is. You'll likely hear a description of what's called feature films that tell stories. Their impact is partly from the overwhelming images on a huge screen. The impact also is from being sealed inside the darkened cocoon of an auditorium. No distractions.

Narrative Films.   Movies that tell stories, much in the tradition of stage plays, are **narrative films.** These features films are promoted heavily, their titles and actors on marquees. Most are in the 100-minute range. A French magician and inventor, Georges Méliès, pioneered narrative films with fairy tales and science-fiction stories to show in his movie house in 1896. Méliès' *Little Red Riding Hood* and *Cinderella* ran less than 10 minutes—short stories, if you will.

Notable innovations in narrative films since the earliest films have been sound, color and computer generated imagery.

Talkies.   Earlier audiences were so mesmerized by moving visuals that they didn't mind that the movies were silent. Four upstart moviemakers, the **Warner brothers,** Albert, Harry, Jack and Sam Warner, changed that in 1927. The Warners' ***The Jazz Singer*** starring

narrative films
Movies that tell a story

Warner Brothers
A movie studio that introduced the first successful sound movie

The Jazz Singer
The first feature sound movie

The Singing Fool
The first full-length sound movie

Gone with the Wind
Pioneer color film

The Black Pirate
The first feature movie in color

computer-generated imagery (CGI)
The application of three-dimensional computer graphics for special effects, particularly in movies and television

animated film
Narrative films with drawn scenes and characters

Steamboat Willie
Animated cartoon character that became Mickey Mouse

Snow White and the Seven Dwarfs
First full-length animated film

Robert Flaherty
First documentary filmmaker

documentary
A video examination of a historical or current event or a natural or social phenomenon

Frank Capra
Hollywood movie director who produced powerful propaganda movies for the U.S. war effort in World War II

Why We Fight
Frank Capra's war mobilization documentary series

Al Jolson included sound in two segments, 354 words total. Soon theaters everywhere were equipped with loudspeakers. The next year, 1928, the Warners issued *The Singing Fool,* also with Jolson, this time with a full-length soundtrack. The Warners earned 25 times their investment. For 10 years no other movie attracted more people to the box office.

Color. Overtaking *The Singing Fool* in 1939 was a narrative movie with another technological breakthrough, **Gone with the Wind** with color. Although *Gone with the Wind* is often referred to as the first color movie, the technology had been devised in the 1920s, and **The Black Pirate** with Douglas Fairbanks was far earlier, in 1925. But *GWTW*, as it's called by buffs, was a far more significant film. *GWTW* marked the start of Hollywood's quest for ever-more-spectacular stories and effects to attract audiences—the blockbuster.

Computer-Generated Imagery. You can imagine why early moviemaker Alfred Clark used a special effect for his 1895 movie *The Execution of Mary Queen of Scots.* "Illusion" was what special effects were called then. Although audiences were amazed, the effects were nothing like today's *CGI*, the shoptalk abbreviation that movie people use for three-dimensional **computer-generated imagery.** There were CGI scenes in *Star Wars* in 1977, but the technology remained mostly an experimental novelty until 1989 when the pseudopod sea creature created by Industrial Light & Magic for *The Abyss* won an Academy Award.

Computer-generated imagery soon became the dominant form of special effect. For stunts, CGI characters began replacing doubles that were nearly indistinguishable from the actors. Crowd scenes were easily created without hiring hundreds of extras. This raised the question of whether movie actors themselves might be replaced by pixels.

Movie commentator Neil Petkus worries that some filmmakers may overuse their toy. "CGI effects can be abused and mishandled," Petkus says. "Directors sometimes allow the visual feasts that computers offer to undermine any real content a movie may have had." Petkus faults director George Lucas for going too far in later *Star Wars* movies: "Any interesting character developments that could have occurred in these movies were overwhelmed by constant CGI action sequences."

Animated Films. The 1920s were pivotal in defining genres of narrative films. In his early 20s, Walt Disney arrived in Los Angeles from Missouri in 1923 with $40 in his pocket. Walt moved in with his brother Roy, and they rounded up $500 and went into the **animated film** business. In 1928 **Steamboat Willie** debuted in a short film to accompany feature films. The character Willie eventually morphed into Mickey Mouse. Disney took animation to full length with **Snow White and the Seven Dwarfs** in 1937, cementing animation as a subspecies of narrative films.

Animated films were labor-intensive, requiring an illustrator to create 1,000-plus sequential drawings for a minute of screen time. Computers changed all that in the 1990s, first with digital effects for movies that otherwise had scenes and actors, notably the *Star Wars* series by George Lucas, then animated features. Disney's *Toy Story* in 1995 was the first movie produced entirely by computers. This new technology led to the resurgence of animated films and re-established them as a box office staple.

Documentaries. Nonfiction film explorations of historical or current events and natural and social phenomena go back to 1922 and **Robert Flaherty**'s look into Eskimo life. With their informational thrust, early **documentaries** had great credibility. Soon, though, propagandists were exploiting the credibility of documentaries with point-of-view nonfiction. Propagandist films found large audiences in World War II, including **Frank Capra**'s seven 50-minute films in the **Why We Fight** series.

Little Movies. New structures have evolved for moviemaking newcomers to interest the distribution units of major studios in their work. A model for these so-called little movies is the Sundance Film Festival in Park City, Utah. Every January, Hollywood dispatches teams to audition films by independent filmmakers at the event. These are low-budget projects that sometimes bring substantial returns on investment. *The Blair Witch Project*, by a team of University of Central Florida grads, is classic. The movie cost $35,000 to produce. The young colleagues on the project made a killing when scouts from Artisan Entertainment

■ A Movie-Maker's Sense of Wonderment

Although born in 1946, Steven Spielberg couldn't have made films like *Jaws, E.T.* and *Indiana Jones* if he weren't still a kid himself. At the dinner table when his seven kids were growing up, Spielberg used to start with a few lines from a story that popped into his head, then each of the kids would add a few lines. Where it would go, nobody knew, but everybody kept the story moving.

Spielberg loves stories, especially with ordinary characters meeting extraordinary beings or finding themselves in extraordinary circumstances. Another theme is that of lost innocence and coming-of-age. A persistent theme is parent-child tensions, which has been attributed to Spielberg's own distress as a child at his parents divorcing.

Critics, however, see unrealistic optimism and sentimentalism in Spielberg films although they admit exceptions. Certainly Indiana Jones is not all that has earned Spielberg his reputation as one of history's great moviemakers. One ranking has him number one. Twice he has won Academy Awards as best director, for *Schindler's List* and *Saving Private Ryan*, both gritty films set in wartime misery. Schindler took an Oscar for best picture.

As a kid, Spielberg was infected with a love for making movies. At 12 he put two Lionel toy trains on a collision course, turned up the juice to both engines and made a home movie of the crash. By that time he already had shot dozens of short films. For one of them, he coaxed his mother into donning a pith helmet and an Army surplus uniform, and then rolled the film as she bounced the family Jeep through backhill potholes near Phoenix. That was his first war movie.

Later, on a family trip to Los Angeles he lined up an unpaid summer job on the Universal Studios lot. He enrolled at California State University in Long Beach in 1965 but interrupted his studies to take a television director job at Universal before finishing his degree. Ironically, Spielberg tried three times for admission to the prestigious film program at the University of Southern California and failed—although in 1994 he was awarded an honorary USC degree.

Most Spielberg films, although wide-ranging in subject matter, have family-friendly themes with a childlike wonderment. There also are strong emotions, as in the Schindler depiction of the horrors of the Holocaust, social and sexual injustice in *The Color Purple,* slavery in *Amistad* and terrorism in *Munich.* But amid the heavy-duty treatments he mixes in rollicking adventures, like yet another in the *Indiana Jones* series or a *Jurassic Park* sequel.

Spielberg's financial success, $250 million alone for the first *Jurassic Park,* has given him the wherewithal to make whatever movie he wants. In 1994 he teamed with Hollywood legendaries David Geffen and Jeffrey Katzenberg to create Dreamworks, a stand-alone movie studio outside of Hollywood's Big Six. *Amistad* and *Saving Private Ryan* set a benchmark for achievement for the enterprise, which produced acclaimed movies although not in huge numbers. Twelve years later, Geffen, Katzenberg and Spielberg sold Dreamworks to Paramount for $1.6 billion.

The sale of Dreamworks, however, didn't mean an end to Spielberg's moviemaking. A fourth in the *Indiana Jones* series was finished in 2007. An Abraham Lincoln bio-pic is coming along. Might we meet the thoroughly ugly but oh-so-lovable E.T., the extraterrestrial, at least one more time?

▲ Steven Spielberg.
Down and dirty, Spielberg does what it takes as director of Indiana Jones and the Kingdom of the Crystal Ball *to get it right. Since his break-out blockbuster* Jaws *in 1975 Spielberg has directed a wide range of movies, many on issues that kids deal with bit also on a wide range of subjects including science, war and history. Oh, yes,* E.T. *was his creation too.*

AMONG FILMS
- *Close Encounters* (1977)
- *Raiders of the Lost Ark* (1981)
- *Back to the Future* (1984)
- *The Color Purple* (1985)
- *Who Framed Roger Rabbit* (1988)
- *Jurassic Park* (1991)
- *Shindler's List* (1993)
- *Saving Private Ryan* (1997)
- *Munich* (2005)
- *War Horse* (2010)
- *Lincoln* (2012)

watched a Sundance screening of it in 1998 and paid $1.1 million for distribution rights. For Artisan, the movie generated $141 million at the box office.

Television Genres

Television has moved through waves of programming that rise into sudden popularity, then fade. Prime-time once was dominated by variety performance shows, then cowboy Westerns, then family dramas, then detective shows. A perennial has been situation comedies, called *sitcoms* in industry lingo.

Sitcoms. Many programs that early television adapted from radio were series with continuing characters in a new, usually dilemmatic situation every week and lots of laugh lines. Soon television was creating original sitcoms, most notably *I Love Lucy*, which ran 197 episodes over nine seasons starting in 1951 followed by special programs through 1960. *Lucy* replays even today. Since 2003 the CBS sitcom *Two and a Half Men* has been a ratings leader with 15 million viewers a week, although there have been questions about whether the numbers can be sustained with Ashton Kutcher replacing Charlie Sheen in the lead for the 2012 season.

Dramatic Series. The series *CSI* was a ratings smash for CBS beginning with gruesome leave-nothing-to-the-imagination high-tech investigations into grisly murders. Other series followed, many like *NCIS* finding large and continuing audiences. Before pathology-themed crime series, there have been other rages in dramatic series. The longest running were Westerns. *Gunmoke* ran 635 episodes from 1955 to 1975, *Bonanza* 431 episodes from 1959 to 1973. Another genre wave was criminal dramas, led by *Law & Order*, which started a 20-plus season run in 1990.

Reality Shows. Mark Burnett likes telling the story of parlaying his early life experiences as a British Army parachutist, beach T-shirt hawker, Hollywood chauffeur, and nanny into the pioneer prime-time reality show *Survivor*. The key was spotting a 2001 newspaper article about a French adventure contest. With four other members, he created a team, American Pride. Quickly he saw a business opportunity and created a similar race that he called *Eco-Challenge*. That led to *Survivor*, which premiered in 2000 and ushered in a wave of reality programs with contestants in continuing elimination tests and trials. Burnett has created dozens of other shows, including *The Apprentice*.

In all, Burnett produced 1,100 hours of television in the decade beginning with the first *Survivor* season. Success begat imitators. Reality-based shows became a major television genre. Dozens of shows followed in the same grain, many with the

◀ **Flak Jacket Reporting.** *Although most U.S.news operations have trimmed their international staffs substantially, the tradition of the roving foreign correspondent has not been lost. NBC's Richard Engel hops from crisis to crisis in the Middle East. He keeps a video journal, turning a mini-camera on himself and reflecting on his thoughts. The journal became the documentary* War Zone Diary.

◀ **Docu-ganda.** *Movie-maker Michael Moore has proven that documentaries with points of view can do well in the marketplace. Although fact-based, Moore's work carries slants and uses rhetorical techniques that short-circuit what could be honest persuasion. The techniques leave Moore an easy target for those whose values and behaviors he attacks. He revels in their discomfort.*

money-making magic of being relatively low-budget audience-builders that attract big-bucks advertisers. These shows, each with a twist, many on cable networks, included *Storage Wars, Top Chef, Pawn Stars, Deadliest Catch*, and *Ice Road Truckers*. Many combined attractions of the quiz-show genre.

News. When television emerged as a major medium, people already were watching newsreels at movie houses. These audiovisual features, typically 10 minutes, played with the previews and cartoons before the featured attraction. Network newscasts on television displaced newsreels in the 1950s. Walter Cronkite's evening newscast on CBS was a staple in the lives of Americans from 1962 to 1981.

The legacy networks still carry evening newscasts but also have nurtured news-entertainment hybrids like NBC's *Today*, with affiliates piggybacking local programs that mix their own coverage with soft news and fluff.

But people no longer need to wait for scheduled newscasts. Since 1980 Cable News Network, CNN for short, has offered around-the-clock news. MSNBC and Fox News Channel came along in 1996. The future of network evening newscasts on the legacy networks may be in question with their aging viewerships and diminishing ratings.

Television Documentaries. Film documentaries during World War II were propagandist. After the war, however, television journalists sought to bring balance and fairness to documentaries in the 1950s. In part it was that journalists of the just-the-facts mold were doing the documentaries. Also, it was the television networks that underwrote the budgets of these documentaries. Their purpose was to build corporate prestige, not

▲ **Ken Burns.** *Documentary producer Ken Burns drew more viewers to PBS with his 1990 Civil War series than any other program the network's history. He casts his net wide for subjects—baseball, jazz, wars—and consistently delivers definitive treatments. His piece on U.S. national parks debuted in 2009 followed by works on Prohibition, the Dust Bowl, and the Central Park Five murder convictions.*

Fairness Doctrine
A U.S. government requirement from 1949 to 1987 that broadcast presentations had to include both sides on competing public issues

docu-ganda
Documentaries that seek to influence their viewers

Michael Moore
Producer–director of point-of-view documentaries

webisode
A short episode of story line created for downloading to internet television or hand-held devices, The word is a contrivance of *web* and *episode*.

propagandize. A factor in the neutral thrust of most of these documentaries also was the Federal Communications Commission's **Fairness Doctrine,** a licensing dictate to stations for balance in treating contentious issues.

The FCC withdrew its **Fairness Doctrine** in 1987, setting in motion a new rationale for documentaries that, in many cases, seeks not so much to inform as to influence the audience. What emerged was a new-form genre that critics call **docu-ganda.** Independent filmmaker **Michael Moore** has epitomized the new generation of documentary-makers in movies, first with *Roger and Me*, a brutal attack on General Motors. Moore's 2004 *Fahrenheit 9/11*, aimed at President Bush's motivations for the Iraq war, was the largest-grossing documentary in history—a demonstration of the economic viability of documentaries.

Television largely has followed the tradition of the Fairness Doctrine, but the detached, neutral tone has given way to some single point-of-view documentaries. For better or worse? To critics, new-style documentary producer David Zieger says, "Guilty as charged." Zieger raised eyebrows with his *Sir! No Sir!* on the anti-war movement within the military during the Vietnam war and acknowledged his lopsidedness: "If you make a film with both sides, you're going to make a boring film." Film is not journalism, Zieger says.

The point-of-view documentaries, whether in movies or television, require viewers to have a high level of media literacy. Competing viewpoints aren't always presented within a single package. Some critics say that the contemporary documentaries that make the biggest splash are, in fact, dangerous because they can dupe viewers into accepting them as the whole truth.

Small-Screen Genres

Smartphones and other small-screen devices have been problems for media companies trying to recycle existing products to squeeze out more revenue. Cinemascope doesn't translate well to a laptop, never mind a smartphone. Besides technical issues, there also are very human issues. Rare is the person who will sit through 92 minutes of Jake Kasden's *Bad Teacher*, let alone Paul Johannson's 102-minute screen adaptation of Ayn Rand's 414-page *Atlas Shrugged*. Bad ergonomics doesn't attract audiences.,

Video Games. The most successful genre of small-screen content has been the video games designed for-small screen playing. Finnish game maker Rovio sold 12 million copies of Angry Bird in 2010 for Apple iPhones and quickly added versions for Android phones and other touch screen systems.

Quick Drama. Television networks have tried bridging the attention-span issue of small devices with **webisodes**—short segments from full-length programs or completely new material, some only three minutes. The webisode concept can be traced to filmmaker Scott Zarakin and his interactive fiction website program *The Spot* in 1995. Zakarin claimed more than 100,000 hits a day, impressive at its time, for his 20s-somethings cast and their beach house dramas. The *Spot* was original drama, in contrast to the later network television attempts to adapt produced-for-television material for small screens.

When initiated, the relatively short network webisodes addressed slow internet downloads. Improved technology has since made television-length programs available for internet TV fulfills the need for on-demand watching.

Live TV. The universal love affair with small-screen devices made the availability of live television for smartphone and tablet users a no brainer. Subscription-based applications like Netflix, AT&T U-verse Live TV and Hulu Plus offer instant access to television shows and movies.

Product and Advertising Quality. Technically and often artistically, the best small-screen motion visuals are produced exclusively for small screens, not adapted from other platforms. This includes videos on products—and also advertising. Just as the advertising industry has long had variations on campaigns for television, radio and print presentation, ad agencies now work to assure a campaign also lends itself to small-screen viewing.

Do-it-yourself Quality. The weakest small-screen genre technically and artistically comprises post-your-own videos on sites like the original YouTube. By their nature, these are mostly amateur offerings that, when they go viral, are often for the attractions of funny, odd or bizarre content rather than for quality.

APPLYING YOUR MEDIA LITERACY

- How is it that movies on television fall short of the experience of the experience of viewing the same movie in a theater?
- Programming for the expanding cable television market continues. What might be the next genre for television programming and why?
- What kind of moving-image content works well on smartphones and other small-screen devices? Why?

Platform Flux

STUDY PREVIEW

The 90 million-tickets-a-week heyday of U.S. movie houses in 1946 is ancient history. It's been a bumpy road since. The exhibition business has problems with the continuing erosion of box office revenue. Attempts to address the declines include spiffier theaters, enforced audience conduct codes and new technology—like d-cinema.

Box Office

While the production components of the competing movie and television industries have moved into peaceful coexistence— it could be called a melding— much remains unsettled in distribution and exhibition. Nothing is more unsettled as the movie exhibition business, whose past has been full of booms and busts.

The movie exhibition beginnings, early in the 1900s, were modest. Images were projected onto a white sheet spread across a wall in low-rent storefronts and onto white-washed plywood hoisted upright in circus tents. By 1912, there was a new standard—the Strand in New York, an opulent 3,300-seat theater that rivaled the world's best opera houses. Nattily groomed and uniformed doormen and ushers made movie-going an experience. So did expansive lobbies, lavish promenades, columns and colonnades and plush velvet wall upholstery. The first air-conditioning was in theaters, using technology invented at Chicago meatpacking plants. Downtown movie palaces were built throughout the land.

Attendance Peak. To capitalize on the popularity of movies, and to keep access affordable, less ostentatious movie houses were built in neighborhoods and small towns. Although neither as large nor as lavish as the downtown palaces, the neighborhood movie houses were the heart of movie-going when U.S. attendance peaked in 1946 at 90 million tickets a week. People even watched movies from automobiles parked row upon row in front of huge outdoor screens with clunky loudspeakers hooked into car windows. Movies were handy and affordable. For many people they were a habit two or three times a week The advent of network television in the 1950s cut into movie attendance. A lot of marquees went dark, some permanently, some at least a few nights a week.

Multiplexes. The exhibition business adapted. Beginning in the 1970s, moviehouse chains followed their customers to the suburbs and built a new form of movie house—the multiscreen **multiplex.** Attendance revived, although far short of the 1946 peak and also dependent on what was showing. People, newly discriminating, turned out mostly for movies that had received good reviews—unlike in the heyday of the Strands and the neighborhood theaters, when even weak movies drew crowds. Also, by the 1970s, people had many alternatives for entertainment.

multiplex
Movie theater with multiple screens

MEDIAcounterpoints

■ Artistry Versus Accountancy

Avatar Pointer. *On a set of his mega-budget sci-fi epic* Avatar, *movie director Kames Cameron lays out his vision for a scene for actor Sam Worthington. Nearby, as always, were agents for the film's financial backers. Their job: Avoid costs that could ruin the investment.*

Early movie directors, including **D. W. Griffith,** tested the storytelling potential of their new medium. Growing public enthusiasm was the proof of what worked. Griffith's 1915 Civil War epic *Birth of a Nation* was cinematically innovative and a commercial success. By the standards of the time, it was a **blockbuster**.

The movie fueled Griffith's imagination to push the envelope further in a more complex project, *Intolerance.* In the new movie Griffith wanted to examine social justice through all of human history. He built huge sets and hired hundreds of actors. In all, he spent an unprecedented $2 million. In 1916, when *Intolerance* debuted, the critics were ecstatic at Griffith's audacity and artistry as a director. With audiences, however, the movie bombed. People were baffled by the movie's disparate settings, including ancient Babylon, Renaissance France and the Holy Land at the time of Christ.

Broke, Griffith had to obtain outside financing to make further movies. This meant that bankers and financiers sent agents to look over Griffith's shoulders to control expenses., always with a pencil and balance sheet in hand, Not infrequently the money guys overruled Griffith's creative impulses. The second-guessing involved not only cost issues. Sometimes the on-site agents of the bankrollers imposed their assessment of what would work with audiences. In effect, accountants gained a pivotal role in storytelling.

The *Intolerance* experience demonstrated a dynamic that continues to play out in Hollywood—the tension that erupts not infrequently between financiers and directors. The tension is all the greater as production costs have soared. James Cameron's *Avatar* in 2009 was budgeted at $237 million. Some say costs passed $300 million. Considering the investment, there was lots of nail-biting at the three studios that co-produced *Avatar*—Lightstorm, Dune and Ingenious Film Partners. But the investment paid off. Handsomely. Not all do. A blockbuster disaster can haunt a studio or production company for years. MGM, once a reigning studio, slipped with miscalculations and never recovered. United Artists almost went under with the costs of Michael Cimino's obsession with historical detail in *Heaven's Gate* in 1980.

The lure of spectacular profits from blockbuster successes drives studios into increasingly expensive projects. It's a quest to outdo the latest blockbuster. However, with great expectations can come great risk.

To balance the risk of blockbusters, studios look for safe bets. There can be profits if production costs can be contained. The result is a preponderance of formulaic movies that offer little in creative storytelling and don't advance the art of moviemaking but that turn a profit. Called **B-movies,** these include sequels, remakes and franchises that, although hardly great movies, are almost sure to out-earn their expenses.

Fast action films which don't require fine acting and are cheap to produce have figured heavily into low-budget and mid-budget movies. So too have violence and sex. Dialogue is minimal in many of these movies, which makes them easily adaptable for distribution to non-English-speaking audiences abroad.

Besides the risky quest for blockbusters, huge budget movies can suck money out of a studio budget for less costly yet worthy projects. The result is a vast distance between blockbusters, some of which are aristically excellent, some less so, and the great number of second-rate B-movies that flood the market.

Bean-counters are the enemy of creative enterprise. They put limits on artistry that prevent movies and television from attaining their potential.

POINT  **COUNTERPOINT**

A company in the media business must be a business first. This means making money or at least breaking even. It's silliness to think that media products exist outside the reality of profit as an imperative.

DEEPENING YOUR MEDIA LITERACY

EXPLORE THE ISSUE: Read what you can find about a critically acclaimed movie that flopped at the box office. Possibilities: *Intolerance* (1916), *Cleopatra* (1963), *Heaven's Gate* (1980), *Tetro* (2009).

DIG DEEPER: For the movie you choose, compare the production budget and the gross domestic and foreign revenue. Why were production costs as high as they were? How could costs have been kept down without diminishing artistic quality? How do you explain the weak audience reception?

WHAT DO YOU THINK? Should this movie have been made at all?

The multiplexes addressed the unevenness in attendance. With multiple auditoriums, each with different seating capacity, movies could be switched among auditoriums to coincide with demand. Wildly popular films could be shown simultaneously in several auditoriums. With multiplexes the new measure of a movie's success was not in how many theaters it was booked in but onto how many screens it was projected.

Exhibition Constriction   In the 1990s, sensing better days ahead, major movie-house chains went on a spending spree to expand and spiff up theaters. Attendance was strong at multiplexes, some with as many as 30 screens. State-of-the-art sound systems were installed. Some auditoriums were outfitted with plush stadium seating. In recent years, the box office has fluctuated from 1.2 to 1.4 billion tickets a year.

The expansion and upgrades, however, overextended some chains financially. Bankruptcies followed. Then came a wave of consolidations that eliminated some chains and left Regal dominant with 5,800 screens, followed by Carmike at 3,700 and AMC at 3,300. The situation worsened with continued box office slippage, further reflecting competition from DVD sales and rentals for home viewing on television sets. Pay-per-view home satellite and cable options also hurt. So did video games, which particularly attracted young men who had been core movie-house patrons.

The movie-house crisis is no better illustrated than in these 2010 figures:
- Box office revenue: $10.9 billion
- Home entertainment revenue: 18.8 billion

Video on Demand

Devices that allow people to watch what they want when they want, **video on demand,** date to Betamax videotape players introduced by Sony in 1976.

Time Shifting.   Betamax and later devices, like **TiVo** and other digital recording devices, provide other options for what's called **time shifting.** People don't have to schedule their activities around a broadcaster's schedule. They don't even have to be home to set programming. It's possible to program a DVR to record shows and then watch them whenever. Time shifting has dramatically reduced the tyranny that network and station programmers once had over people's lives. Also, with the increasing migration of television content online, it is possible to watch a lot of television without actually even owning a television set. Many shows are archived online and deliverable free through a variety of official and unofficial portals. Many are partially uploaded before they actually air, and fully uploaded immediately upon airing.

A troubling upshot of the technology for television networks and stations is that they are losing their power to amass great numbers of people in front of the screen at the same time. That had been a selling point to advertisers. An advertiser for time-of-day products like Subway sandwiches wants to reach viewers at mealtime—not whenever viewers decide to watch a show. What good is an advertisement designed to stir excitement for the weekend introduction of the new Fiat 500 or Chevy Volt if viewers don't see the spot until a week later? Also, those DVR devices allow viewers to skip commercials entirely.

Portable Devices.   In 2005 a video-playing internet device introduced by Apple fully liberated viewers from planting themselves before large and stationary television sets. The Apple video iPod suddenly splintered television as an industry. By 2012 handheld iPods could play seven hours of video and display the images on a $3\frac{1}{2}$-inch color screen. People could watch television shows on the road or wherever—and whenever. It was true video on demand, with people downloading programs from the internet to watch any time they wanted. Apple iPads and other tablets with larger screens compounded the problem for traditional means of delivery for motion media.

VOD continues to influence the future of television and movies. On demand services like Netflix are racing to keep up with the evolving media habits of their consumers while Apple and others continue to produce ever more portable and convenient digital devices to record and play whatever the viewer desires. Other networks and studios are jockeying to market their products in these new venues. Video on demand is no longer a revolution, but a force of nature with which all motion media must contend.

MEDIAtomorrow

■ D-cinema Amid The Streaming

With a financial boost from Hollywood, , the motion picture exhibition business is outfitting theaters with digital projectors. Theater owners first resisted because of the cost, at least $100,000 minimum per screen. But they finally decided, with box-office slippage in the face of DVDs and other competing exhibition platforms, there was no choice. The Hollywood subsidies were a sweetening incentive. By 2012, more than half the screens in North American had been converted.

So-called d-cinema is not new. Mark Cuban began converting theaters in his 270-screen Landmark chain in 2005. Once people saw their first digital movie on a big screen, Cuban figured they would settle for nothing less. Digital projection is not the same as HDTV technology, but its clarity and impact are similar. With d-cinema, colors are more vivid. Graininess is gone. Projection-room goofs, like reels out of sequence, are no more. Nor is there any more distracting focus adjustments or scratchy reels that have been pulled over the sprockets too many times.

Despite its attributes, d-cinema is hardly alone as an enticing new way to deliver motion-media products. There's lots of competition—and lots of experimenting and floundering. Setbacks and failures too.

Streaming, as an example, is a booming business. Amazon Prime offered more than 5,000 streaming television shows and movies to customers in 2011. But in one aborted scheme to remain competitive, Netflix chief executive Reed Hastings tried to shift from its slipping DVD-by-mail business into streaming movies from a new company website cleverly called Qwikster. Quicker than mail, get it?

Netflix claimed that DVD shipments had likely peaked—that it needed to wind that business down and bet everything on streaming. Part of the scheme was hiking DVD rental rates to encourage Netflix's mail customers to switch over to streaming. Faithful Netflix customers, although dwindling in number, were outraged. Netflix scrapped the plan.

Hastings' explanation for the mess was revealing about companies trying to maneuver through the fast-changing technology of motion media: "My greatest fear at Netflix has been that we wouldn't make the leap from success in DVDs to success in streaming."

Just like Netflix, cable and satellite television companies are worried about the impact of streaming services on their networks. In 2010, streaming media accounted for 43 percent of peak time traffic in the United States—nearly half during prime cable and satellite network watching periods between 8 and 10 p.m.

Another new motion-media competitor is Hollywood itself. Motion picture companies have experimented with streaming their own movies directly to consumers. The goal was to make up for plunging DVD sales. Paramount's 2011 blockbuster *Transformers: Dark of the Moon* was streamed online directly from a studio-owned website. Customers paid $4 or $5 to for movies ton be streamed to their laptop or computer. They then had 48 hours to watch the film. The obvious benefit of this direct-to-consumer streaming for Paramount was cutting out the middleman. No longer would the studio need a Netflix, a Hulu, an HBO or movie houses to distribute films. The studio could stop providing films to the middlemen and keep all the profits.

Theater owners haven't been happy at being cut out. Several chains, representing 4,680 screens, protested vociferously when DirecTV wanted to make some movies available for video on demand 60 days after their movie-house premieres—a much shorter window than usual between movie-house debuts and post-cinema releases.

Meanwhile, Netflix and Hulu are looking at another way to make money in the shifting streaming market and have started creating their own content for streaming. The HBO and AMC cable networks have become their own production powerhouses too. Why pay for content rights when you can create it yourself and keep 100 percent of the revenue?

Reed Hastings. *Can he keep Netflix riding high amid fast-changing media delivery methods? Netflix made its mark with mail-delivery of movie DVDs, but the challenge for Hastings now is to catch the wave of download delivery. One Netflix attempt, called Qwikster, backfired. What next?*

What Do You Think?

Is there any value left in the big-screen, movie-theater experience? Does d-cinema technology make a difference?

Will online streaming video overtake movie theaters, DVDs, broadcast television, or cable television, or all of them?

How can broadcast television change to remain competitive in the future? How will that affect people who rely on broadcast television's free content?

- How many more tricks-up-the-sleeve does the movie exhibition business have to address audience losses to television and new platforms? Or is the day of the moviehouse doomed?
- What is being lost with the miniaturization of devices for viewing movie motion?

■ Movie-Television Meld   (Pages 145–147)

In the 1950s, television encroached on the movie industry's dominance as a motion medium. Both industries saw themselves locked in a battle for the same audience. Common ground gradually developed, beginning a meld of the once-rival industries. Although the movie and television industry share corporate owners, content and stars today, they also maintain many distinctions.

■ Movie Industry   (Pages 147–149)

Early movies fascinated people. They had never seen anything like it—pictures in motion. Such a thrilling experience. Soon a major new media industry was in business to serve an insatiable demand. Adolph Zukor introduced mass production. Soon a few major movie companies not only were producing movies but also controlling distribution and exhibition. Coercive monopolistic practices led to a government break-up of the industry in 1948. About the same time, television began siphoning off the movie audience. Could the industry recover?

■ Television Industry Structure   (Pages 149–152)

The television industry has three components, each defined by distinctive delivery technology. The original structure had government-licensed local stations that transmitted programming on airwaves. The rationale for government regulation is that the airwaves are the public's property and must be government-managed as a public resource. Although the United States has no national stations, many local stations are networked to national programming provided by companies like ABC, CBS, Fox and NBC. Since the 1930s, when this dual-tier system was created, technology has led to two new delivery program-delivery systems. Local cable systems send programming to subscribers by wire. Not using the public airwaves, cable companies are exempt from the tight regulation. A more recent technology is satellite-delivered programming direct to consumers, not going through either a local affiliates or cable systems, is also unregulated.

■ Movie Industry Structure   (Pages 153–157)

Six studios, all parts of conglomerates, dominate Hollywood movie production and distribution. These studios are enmeshed with the television

CHAPTER WRAP UP

industry through corporate connections. A growing component in movie distribution channels is independent films, which originate outside the Hollywood structure but often with financing and other support for major studios.

■ Motion Media Products   (Pages 157–163)

Motion-media productions have distinctions rooted in their original movie and television technologies and the cultures and business models that grew out of these technologies. Motion pictures as viewed in a theater have potency that cannot be matched on small screens. In the same sense, handheld media don't lend themselves across-the-board to movie and television content. The distinctions can be parsed by the impact of screen size and the ergonomics of viewing. Huge movie screens have powerful effects unmatched by smaller screens.

■ Platform Flux   (Pages 163–167)

Although U.S. movie house attendance has recovered from dramatic losses, it's a wobbly business. Box office revenue is a far lesser percentage of the market with the rise of television in the 1950s and today with devices that offer video on demand. The movie industry needs to reconfigure itself because of VOD devices as does the television industry.

■ Thinking Critically

1. How have the movie and television industries patched up their bitter rivalry from the early 1950s?

2. How does the Hollywood you know today differ from the industry that was based on the star system and the studio system in the era before the Paramount court decision?

3. How does government regulation differ for over-air stations, cable systems and satcoms? Why?

4. How are delivery structures different in the movie, television and online industries?

5. What are the similarities in genres in the movie, television and online industries?

6. What does the future hold for the movie exhibition industry?

Media Vocabulary

animated film (Page 158)

b-movies (Page 164)

Big Three (Page 150)

block booking (Page 149)

blockbuster (Page 164)

Community Antenna Television (CATV) (Page 151)

computer-generated imagery (CGI) (Page 158)

Corporation for Public Broadcasting (CPB) (Page 150)

docu-ganda (Page 161)

documentary (Page 158)

Fairness Doctrine (Page 161)

Federal Communications Act (Page 150)

indies (Page 156)

multisystem operator (MSO) (Page 152)

narrative films (Page 157)

Paramount decision (Page 149)

star system (Page 148)

studio system (Page 148)

suspension of disbelief (Page 147)

time shifting (Page 165)

two-tier system (Page 150)

video on demand (Page 165)

webisode (Page 162)

Media Sources

■ Steven Bingen, Stephen X. Sylvester and Michael Troyan. *M-G-M: Hollywood's Greatest Backlot.* Santa Monica Press, 2011. The authors draw on film historians for this map of the MGM studios in the heyday and explanation on all that went wrong.

■ Ken Auletta. *Googled: The End of the World as We Know It.* Penguin, 2009. Auletta, media critic for *The New Yorker*, tracks Google from humble origins into an online powerhouse that displaced traditional media, then deals with its profit-driven quest to dominate media delivery and become a major advertising vehicle.

■ Bill Carter. *Desperate Networks.* Doubleday, 2006. Carter, a television reporter for the New York *Times*, tracks network television programming for a season.

■ Colin McGinn. *The Power of Movies.* Pantheon, 2006. McGinn, a philosopher, builds an easy-to-follow case for the long-analyzed Dream Theory of Cinema to explain the compelling nature of the medium.

■ J.D. Lasica. *Darknet: Hollywood's War Against the Digital Generation.* Wiley, 2005. Lasica draws on a wide range of interviews in making a case that the framework for U.S. broadcasting is outdated for the digital age.

■ Peter Biskind. *Down and Dirty Pictures: Miramax, Sundance and the Rise of Independent Film.* Simon & Schuster, 2004. Biskind, once editor of *Premiere* magazine, casts Sundance and Miramax as makers of a new Hollywood mold, each with very different motivations.

■ David L. Robb. *Operation Hollywood: How the Pentagon Shapes and Censors Movies.* Prometheus, 2004. Robb, a veteran Hollywood reporter, chronicles the coerciveness of the government in providing and denying technical support for war movies.

■ Gary R. Edgerton. *Ken Burns' America: Packaging the Past for Television.* Palgrave, 2002. Edgerton, a communications professor, is enthusiastic and detailed in examining Burns' documentaries.

A Thematic Chapter Summary

MOTION MEDIA

To further deepen your media literacy here are ways to look at this chapter from the perspective of themes that recur throughout the book:

MEDIA TECHNOLOGY

Is programming delivered directly to viewers the future of television?

Movies were the first medium with visual motion. It was a technology that marveled people. Then came television, a fast-growth industry built on a new technology that also marveled people. "Radio with pictures," it was called. Networks supplied programming to local affiliates for relay to anyone within a signal's reach. Now that's all old technology. The new technology, digital and internet-based, delivers video any time, anywhere. One result is a challenge to the traditional U.S. television infrastructure and the program forms built around it—30-second spots and 30-minute and 60-minute scheduled programs.

MEDIA EFFECTS

Too gritty? Too real? With the Civil war, photographers put the reality of war in everyone's hands. Television put Vietnam everyone's living room. Reporters today can be 24/7 from war zones in real time.

While some researchers focus on whether movies, television and other media affect public attitude and opinion, cultural sociologists focus on lifestyle effects that lend themselves to firmer conclusions. The effect of early television was obvious. Wednesday-night boxing, an early program fixture, kept people home and dented the attendance at older venues for out-of-home activities. And who in America in the 1950s would have missed the *$64,000 Question*? Today, devices that enable time shifting and on-the-go video pickups are putting the audience in charge.

MEDIA ECONOMICS

Movie studios once buffered themselves from financial risk with now-outlawed practices like blockbooking. Today moviemakers reduce risk with joint projects. Five studios divided the revenue from The Help, which returned $175 million on a $25 million investment.

The economics of the movie industry became bumpy with the rise of television. In the early years of television, the networks and their affiliates were in money-making bliss. Advertisers lined up to buy every spot available, particularly in prime time. The whole industry was built on charging advertisers what the market would bear, which was on a roll with double-digit annual growth. Today the economic structure is fracturing. Advertisers have options galore in which to make visual appeals to consumers, not only on cable and satcom channels but also via internet venues and a dizzying array of digital-based alternative media. Where the unraveling of the traditional economic infrastructure will end is for clairvoyants to predict.

ELITISM AND POPULISM

A little good history, anyone? Documentary producer Ken Burns has drawn large audiences for series on war, poverty, jazz and baseball. Is there a place for serious-minded works on television?

The new medium of television, quickly engaging millions of viewers in the 1950s, seemed to have great potential as a force for cultural enlightenment and for encouraging public participation in the great issues. A decade later FCC chair Newton Minow had, in effect, given up on this potential. He called television a "vast wasteland," a label that has stuck ever since. Minow was bothered that the networks were pandering to low tastes with programming that neither excited the mind nor motivated political engagement. In the main, television was narcoticizing, lowbrow stuff—comedy geared to momentary chuckles, drama with predictable outcomes, and superficial takes on news. Whether television overall is less a wasteland today can be debated, but at least public stations are in existence as an alternative, as are subscription-based cable networks that produce dramas and documentaries on a grand scale, along with a lot of junk.

AUDIENCE FRAGMENTATION

The television industry now has outlets for programming besides local terrestrial-footed, over-air affiliates. But handheld and other reception devices also connect to the internet for all kinds of competing content. The mass audience is fragmenting as never before.

The explosion of television as a new medium ruined the magazine, radio and movie industries, at least for a while, and took away time that people had spent with books. The consolidation of audiences around the new medium was phenomenal. Magazines and radio demassified to survive, seeking segments of their former audiences. No question about it, the magazine and radio industries surrendered large segments of their audiences to television. In a comeuppance, the television audience itself now is fragmenting. The core network-affiliate over-air system has lost audience to hundreds of channels available on cable systems and by satcom delivery as well as to direct-to-consumer access via the internet.

MEDIA AND DEMOCRACY

Portable video viewing is freeing people from half a century of lifestyle tyranny by television network executives who schedule when programs will air.

Video-on-demand technology has liberated people from being tied down to a television set. The control that networks once had over lifestyles with their tantalizing prime-time and other fare is breaking down. People can watch television at their convenience with recording and playback devices. Portable devices enable people to choose not only when to watch but where. This has been called the democratization of television, the power shifting from national network program schedulers at corporate offices in New York to individual viewers surfing the internet.

7 NEW MEDIA LANDSCAPE

■ Architect of a New Order

Everybody knew in the 1990s that computer technology would transform the mass media. Some sensed it earlier. But it was the late **Steve Jobs** who most clearly saw the future. Jobs, the driving force behind the computer giant Apple, reinvented three floundering media industries. Incredible as it seems, the corporate leaders of the music, movie and mobile telephone industries were so tradition-bound and comfy that they had allowed themselves to be blindsided. The recorded music industry was reeling in a downward spiral. The movie industry seemed destined for the same.

Jobs, however, was unencumbered by the blinders of old ways of doing things. To Jobs, the future was a new media-centric digital lifestyle. His Apple inventions included the handheld **iPod** music player and the online **iTunes** music retail site, introduced in 2001 and 2002. The iPod-iTunes combo slowed the recorded music industry's

▲ **Hub in a Digital Lifestyle.** *Apple visionary Steve Jobs saw a single device as a hub for accessing the whole media landscape. His giant stride toward this digital future was the iPad tablet—light, portable and capable of tapping into news, music, video—everything the traditional media did separately but all in one device.*

CHAPTER INSIGHTS

- The Digital Lifestyle is the third transformation of mass media since 1980.

- Browsers were key in rewriting the history of the internet.

- Search engines are essential in the new media landscape.

- Messaging via texting or email is an essential component of the Digital Lifestyle.

- Sites built on user-based content are revolutionizing mass media communication and international commerce.

- Commerce has come to drive internet growth.

- Google gave us a map for the internet, just as Facebook maps us users.

- Online games have surpassed the music in sales and are gaining on movies and books.

- Digitization is rewriting how data are stored.

decline. Then came new iPod models with new capabilities, including video. In 2007 came the **iPhone,** which integrated a mobile telephone, an audio and video player and an internet browser in a single device,

People loved Apple's "iDevices," which propelled Apple, which itself had been floundering, into a magnet for investors. The business magazine *Fortune* tabbed Jobs as the top chief executive for the first decade of the 21st century.

So who was this Steve Jobs?

Jobs and chum Steve Wozniak, barely in their 20s, were there in the early days of personal computers. In a garage, literally, they created a revolutionary personal computer. They founded Apple in 1976. Despite the success, the road was rocky. Some products backfired. Wozniak left the enterprise. Jobs himself was fired by investors who had taken over the company. In 1997, a dozen years after being fired, the investors begged Jobs back. He took drastic steps to get the company back on its feet after a dizzying series of unfocused missteps in his absence.

Then Jobs was on a roll. Within a few months, in 2001, Apple rolled out the iTunes software, a new operating system called Mac OS X, the first Apple retail store and the first iPod. These all were building blocks, but only Jobs and

confidants within the company knew where it was headed. He did drop a hint, though. In a 2002 interview with *Time* magazine, Jobs said: "We're the only company that owns the whole widget—the hardware, the software and the operating system." Jobs talked about having "full responsibility for the user experience."

One endearing asset of Apple products for consumers was a magical aura flowing from Jobs' obsession with detail and design. In 2010 Apple launched the iPad, a 1-1/2-pound tablet as a platform for audio and visual media such as books, periodicals, movies, music, and games, as well as web content. The iPad was nearing Apple to becoming the hub of a digital lifestyle.

What does all this mean? Apple products don't just give people access to powerful technology; the pre-Apple personal computers did that. The Jobs' genius is that Apple products have enabled people to integrate the access to powerful technology into their ordinary lives. Jobs called it the "digital hub" concept—a digital lifestyle. No longer is it easy to delineate the music industry and the movie industry and the book industry and the news industry. It's all becoming one —with Jobs' Apple stamp on the leading products. ■

Jobs' Historical Model

STUDY PREVIEW

The genius architect of mass media's new landscape, Steve Jobs of Apple, saw a revolution that has moved through three stages. The Computer Revolution, as he called it, ran roughly from 1980 to 1994. The main change: Vastly faster productivity. From 1994 to 2000 came the Internet Revolution with unprecedented human interconnectivity worldwide. Jobs saw a digital lifestyle dawning. Personal computers are the hub.

Steve Jobs
Leader of Apple computer who engineered the "digital hub"

iPod
Handheld Apple digital music player

iTunes
Online Apple music download site

iPhone
Handheld Apple smart phone

iPad
Ultralight Apple tablet computer with e-book, video, music functions

Computer Revolution
Vast increases in human productivity, roughly 1980–1994

Jobs' Model
Three-step developmental model for stages of a new media-centric lifestyle—Computer Revolution, Internet Revolution, Digital Lifestyle

Stage 1: Computer Revolution

Just about everybody is struggling still to make sense of the gigantic transforming influence of computers dating back roughly to 1980. Every new theory on what's happening and where it's all going is eclipsed almost immediately in a dizzying accumulation of innovation and adaptation. Before he died in 2011, Apple wunderkind Steve Jobs devised a useful model for understanding new media landscape. Job said it all began roughly in 1980 with what's commonly called the **Computer Revolution**.

The **Jobs' Model** is a three-stage map. In the first stage, the Computer Revolution, computers exponentially increased productivity. Although nothing compared to what came later. The economic, social and technological impact was overwhelming. Sometimes the post-1980 period is characterized as the **Information Revolution**, which captures the transcendental changes that were afloat—something as far-reaching as the Industrial Revolution two centuries earlier.

Stage 2: Internet Revolution

From 1994 to 2000, the role of personal computers shifted into universal interconnectivity. All it took was a modem to hook up low-cost computers to connect to anyone with the same equipment just about anywhere on the planet. Because of technical limitations, communication was mostly by text, but soon there were graphic, still-video, audio and moving-visual capabilities.

With the **Internet Revolution**, as Jobs called this period, computers became a vehicle for consumer transactions. The internet, indeed, created a marketplace of commerce. The Internet Revolution, although itself a major transformation, was a mere precursor of what lay ahead.

Stage 3: Digital Lifestyle

If anyone had the stature to define the latest era in the digital transformation dating to the 1980s, it was Steve Jobs. He was an innovator from the first Apple computer models in

MEDIAtimeline

NEW MEDIA LANDSCAPE MILESTONES

ARPANET
U.S. military linked computers of contractors, researchers (1969)

PIVOTAL EVENTS

- Telstar in orbit (1961)
- Vietnam war (1964–1975)
- Nixon presidency (1969–1974)
- Humans on moon (1969)

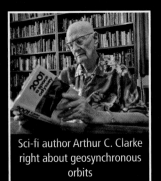

Sci-fi author Arthur C. Clarke right about geosynchronous orbits

NEW MEDIA LANDSCAPE MILESTONES

APPLE, INC.
Steve Jobs, Steve Wozniak create Apple Computer Inc. (1976)

The easier-to-use Apple

NEW MEDIA LANDSCAPE MILESTONES

SIMULATION GAME
Will Wright created simulation game (1984)

"WALLED GARDEN"
AOL founded (1989)

Pivotal Events

- Reagan presidency (1981–1989)
- Soviet empire imploded (1989)
- Tiananmen Square protests (1989)

1960-1969

1970-1979

1980-1989

the 1970s. To Apple aficionados in 2001 Jobs declared that the personal computer would become "the digital hub for the digital lifestyle." The term **Digital Lifestyle** stuck. The personal computer, Apple's iBooks and MacBooks most of all, had capabilities to connect a wide range of products—digital cameras, digital books and other once ink-on-paper products, retail music libraries and, in Jobs' vision, smartphones. This was a whole new integration of music, film and video, as well as interpersonal voice communication. People were living their lives differently, even differently than in the so-called Internet Revolution and the predecessor Computer Revolution.

Jobs had a way with putting his vision into words. In introducing the iPhone in 2007, Jobs described the multi-tasking hand-held device as the culmination of the new era. The iPhone is "like having your life in your pocket." He called it "the ultimate digital device."

Harvard University business historian Nancy Koehn paints the significance of the Jobs' Digital Lifestyle even more broadly: "We have much more opportunity for people to get into the marketplace—not just the marketplace of commerce but the marketplace of ideas, the marketplace of publications, the marketplace of public policy, you name it."

Digital Lifestyle
Personal and hand-held computers become a centerpiece of outgoing and incoming communication; roughly 2000 on

NEW MEDIA LANDSCAPE MILESTONES

COMPUTER REVOLUTION
Personal computers improve productivity (1980–1994)

INTERNET REVOLUTION
Human communication is a new age of interconnectivity (1994–2000)

BROWSER
Netscape introduced (1994)

SOCIAL NETWORKING
Facebook predecessor Facemash (1993)

SEARCH ENGINE
Yahoo created (1994); Google created (1996)

FIRST BLOG
Rob Marta created slazhdot.org (1997)

PIVOTAL EVENTS

• George H. W. Bush presidency (1989–1993)
• Persian Gulf war (1990–1991)
• Investor exuberance in dot-coms (1990s)
• Clinton presidency (1993–2001)
• Legislation fuels rapid fiber-optic network growth (1996)

1990-1999

NEW MEDIA LANDSCAPE MILESTONES

WIKIPEDIA
Collaboratively edited online encyclopedia (2001)

IPOD-ITUNES
Apple device and download store save recording industry (2001–2002)

FACEBOOK
Social media network founded (2004)

GOOGLE BOOK PROJECT
To digitize all books ever published (2005)

GAME GROWTH
Video game sales twice the music industry's (2008)

NANOTUBE
U.S. and Chinese research perfected mass production (2009)

PIVOTAL EVENTS

• Dot-com bust (2000)
• 9/11 terrorist attacks (2001)

2000-2009

NEW MEDIA LANDSCAPE MILESTONES

TABLET DEVICES
Apple launched iPad (2010)

PIVOTAL EVENTS

• Environmentalism intensifies as public policy issue (2010)

iPad a hub in Digital Lifestyle?

2010-

walled garden
Early business model for online portals with access limited mostly to proprietary content

America Online (AOL)
Once-dominant internet service provider

Steve Case
Built AOL into media giant with walled-garden model

browser
Software to navigate the internet to countless web sites

Marc Andreessen
Software wunderkind who designed pioneer browser Netscape

Silicon Valley
Area near San Francisco noted for computing and electronics industries

Netscape
First of browsers

APPLYING YOUR MEDIA LITERACY

- **How did the Computer Revolution, which was Stage One in Steve Jobs' framework for a digital history, pave the way for the new media landscape?**
- **How did Jobs' Stage Two, the Internet Revolution, affect our everyday life?**
- **What does the Stage Three Digital Lifestyle mean to you?**

Portals

STUDY PREVIEW
Early attempts to draw mass audiences to the internet with "walled gardens" of services, such as America Online offered, were successful but short-lived. The AOL concept was doomed by the invention of browsers. With browsers, even first-time computer owners at home found access to the whole internet. There is a lot beyond the garden wall.

Walled Gardens

Visionaries recognized in the 1990s that the internet had potential to transform the mass media. But the visions were blurred. The first concept to take root was the **walled garden**. A one-time online games company redubbed itself **America Online** and set out to offer an encyclopedic array of features by subscription. For $20 a month, people could buy access to news, games, email and whatever AOL posted inside the "garden."

AOL executive **Steve Case** became legendary with an audacious marketing scheme. He mailed millions of CDs, unsolicited, that gave non-technical people quick and easy access to AOL. Case's savvy marketing ploy gave AOL 30 million subscribers.

With the "walled garden" business model, AOL provided limited interfaces with the internet as a whole. But non-subscribers were not allowed inside the garden walls.

Things changed fast. People were learning to use newly invented **browsers**. With browsers, first Netscape, then Explorer and others, there was free and direct access to more content than any walled garden could provide. And what's better than free?

Gradually AOL lowered or dismantled the "wall" and began frenzied attempts to re-invent itself. But its moment in the sun was over in the rapidly changing media landscape.

Browsers

While AOL was in its formative ascendency, **Marc Andreessen** and some grad-school buddies at the University of Illinois were designing software to connect disparate computer operating systems with the internet and each other. Their invention was the browser.

When Andreessen graduated in 1993 he headed to **Silicon Valley**, the high-tech capital of the world with some grad-school friends. They created **Netscape**—a product for navigating the web. With Netscape, computer newbies could uncrate their first home computer and point-and-click their way to just about anything on the internet. Well, maybe not quite that easily but almost. No matter how nontechnical, anyone with a computer could unlock more content than ever before possible in human history. At first Andreesseen charged modestly for the software but, unlike AOL, there was no subscription fees. The Netscape advertising line said it all: "The web is for everyone."

▲ **Marc Andreessen.** *His browser Netscape sealed the fate of subscription-only walled-garden access to the Internet. Netscape and copycat products offered free access to just about anything posted by anyone anywhere.*

In 1996 Andreessen was on the cover of *Time* magazine, age 25, barefoot and a multimillionaire.

With the advent of browsers, the question then became: What to do once you got to the vast, seemingly infinite territory of unsorted content on the internet? The orderly walled garden of AOL had been replaced with uncharted wilderness. With hundreds of thousands of sites, updated daily if not more often, how could anyone figure out where to go? True, browsers had bookmarking capability that allowed users to create a list of personally useful sites, but what about all those hundreds and thousands of sites that could be useful but that nobody in a lifetime could conceivably run across by random trips through the aptly named web?

APPLYING YOUR MEDIA LITERACY

- **Why did the walled garden online business model peak and then flounder?**
- **Browsers were a quantum leap in online technology but still fell short. How so?**

Search Engines

STUDY PREVIEW | Search engines are an essential tool in the new media landscape for access to countless sites on the internet. Google and Yahoo are the major search engines. Each is a multimillion-dollar player. And both seek are growing into other internet-related activities.

Google

Just as important as browsers for making the internet useful to most people are **search engines**. Using elaborate software, search engines dispatch **crawlers** through the internet to take snapshots of web pages and key words. The search engines amass huge reference files, update them continuously, and organize them by the frequency in which certain words appear in the text. If someone searches with the term *webTV*, the search engine produces a list of sites, probably hundreds. The terms *webTV Canada* will narrow the list, *webTV Canada news* even more.

Today's most used search engine, **Google**, was the brainstorm of two Stanford University doctoral students **Sergey Brin** and **Larry Page**. In 1996 Brin and Page developed an idea to improve internet searches with algorithms that ranked web pages by the number of links to them from other relevant web pages. They chose the term *google* for what they were doing. It was catchy with a cachet of geekiness. Actually the word is a common misspelling among mathematicians of the *word googol,* which means 1 to the power of 1 followed by 100 zeroes. In one sense, the word overstates what Google delivers. Only 1,000 results are provided max for any specific search query. But who's complaining? Or counting?

Company lore at Google is loaded with mottos and slogans. One googlism that captures what search engines are about: "To organize the world's information and make it universally accessible and useful."

Search engines were not only incredibly useful but also were free to users, adding another nail to the coffin of subscription sites whose walled gardens were hardly as extensive. But if Google was free, how was it, then, that Brin and Page became multimillionaires within a couple years? Most of Google's revenue, 99 percent now, is from advertising.

Google has expanded into other services with its Gmail brand email and also mobile media delivery. In the fourth-quarter of 2010 its smart phone platform **Android** became the world leader. The advertising revenue gained from mobile advertising significantly increased the company's profits. Its core, though, remains its search engine. Among search engines Google clearly leads by global market share:

Google	85 percent
Yahoo	6 percent
Baidu	3 percent

search engine
Tool to identify and rank web sites by key terms

crawler
Computer program that scours the web to create an index of sites

Google
Dominant search engine

Sergey Brin, Larry Page
Creators of Google search engine

Android
Google operating system for smartphones

MEDIApeople

■ Saga of The Google Guys

▲ Google Guys.

Google headquarters in Silicon Valley is an unorthodox place designed to inspire creative thinking. In a playful creativity cove, Google founders Sergey Brin and Larry Page take a break in sinking into bean-bag pillows. Maybe they need a break. In amassing their huge fortune, one of the largest in internet history, they've been pushing the company in seemingly countless new directions, including a project to digitize all the books ever published into a giant reference source.

What Do You Think?

Nobody can begrudge Brin and Page's success with Google, but can the company become too big? With Google's corporate acquisitions and by expanding as it is into new fields, should the U.S. Justice Department be watchful of monopolistic and anti-trust possibilities?

Google founders Sergey Brin and Larry Page met in 1995 on a tour arranged for incoming Stanford University grad students. They found each other obnoxious. Page was an engineering major from the University of Michigan, and Brin was a graduate student in computer science. Both opinionated, they argued about everything. In retrospect, they call it "bantering."

A few months later, Page was searching for a topic for his doctoral thesis. He was attracted to the new World Wide Web and decided to investigate its mathematical characteristics. At the time, an estimated 10 million documents resided on the web, all linked in numerous ways, but there was no way to know about links from one web page back to another. Page thought being able to know who was linking to whom could be useful and started a project he called BackRub. His premise was that a link should be treated like a footnote in scholarly works.

The complexity of Page's idea appealed to Brin, who was looking for a new project. Brin had emigrated to the United States from Russia at age 6, the son of a NASA scientist and a University of Maryland math professor. A math prodigy, he left high school a year early to attend the University of Michigan. After graduation, he enrolled at Stanford, where he basically goofed off. He once told a reporter that the weather was so good he loaded up on classes like sailing and scuba diving and spent his intellectual energy on interesting projects instead of the classroom. But after Brin joined Page's project, the two decided to create a ranking system for links based on the importance of their sources.

Page and Brin soon realized their project could have implications for internet searches. BackRub's results already were better than those from existing search engines, which didn't rank the results they returned. With ranking, the BackRub project could grow naturally as the internet expanded. In fact, the bigger the web, the better the engine would be.

They named their new search engine Google, after googol, the term for the numeral 1 followed by 100 zeroes. The first version of Google was released on the Stanford web site in August of 1996, just one year after they first met.

Unfortunately for Brin and Page, search engines use a huge amount of computing resources. The students were too broke to buy new computers, so they begged and borrowed—and Page's dorm room soon filled with computers made from spare parts. Brin's dorm room became their office and programming center. They ran their search engine through Stanford's broadband campus network. The search engine crawled every page on the web and then ranked the results. The quantity of data regularly crashed Stanford's internet connection.

As the Google project became better known, the question became what to do next. Page and Brin weren't sure they wanted to run a company. Page wanted to finish his doctorate as a tribute to his father, who had died during his first year at Stanford. Brin also didn't want to leave the program. Eventually they decided to set up a company, figuring that if it didn't work out, they could always go back to school.

They incorporated Google in September 1998, moved to a friend's garage, and hired an employee. Since then, Google has become an international powerhouse with more than 20,000 employees worldwide. Today the company is much more than a search engine. It has expanded to include Gmail, Google Earth, and smartphones.

In 2000, Google began selling advertisements associated with search keywords. Page and Brin had been opposed to advertising as a commercial contaminant of their creation, but ads eventually found a place on Google, although only as text to maintain an uncluttered page design and not to slow down searches. Google's advertising revenue passed $29.3billion in 2010.

Advertising on Google has made its founders billionaires. In 2011 Brin and Page had a personal wealth of $16.7 billion each, and Google surpassed the 1 billion mark for unique visitors for the first time.

Yahoo

Before Google there was **Yahoo**, also created by two Stanford grad students. **David Filo** and **Jerry Yang** created their search engine in 1994 and chose the name Yahoo, to which they attached an exclamation mark affectation—Yahoo! An odd name, true. But catchy. In a playful, sophomoric spirit, Filo and Yang saw Yahoo as an acronym for "Yet Another Hierarchical Officious Oracle." The inspiration actually came from Jonathan Swift's name for a bumpkin in his 1726 novel *Gulliver's Travels*. Yahoo, whatever its name, was something new and incredibly useful—a web directory. Within a year Yahoo had 1 million hits.

Yahoo became an instant magnet for venture capital in the heady overinvestment of the 1990s for computer-related companies. The value of Yahoo plummeted in the burst of the bubble—the so-called **dot-com bust** of 2000. But by then the company was already diversified and substantial enough to survive. Today Yahoo is worldwide with internet businesses in 20 languages on a wide range of subjects, together averaging 8.7 billion visits a day.

The scope of Yahoo is a dream-come-true for marketing. A 2007 study concluded that Yahoo could collect far more information on individual consumers for advertisers than any other data-aggregation agency. On average Yahoo could build a profile of 2,500 records per month about each of its visitors.

Indeed, Yahoo has become an advertising powerhouse by delivering the relatively precise segments of potential customers that advertisers covet. Eighty-eight percent of Yahoo revenue comes from selling screen space to advertisers. Advertisers pay 2.5 to 3 cents for every click-through from a notice on Yahoo. The company also sells advertising space on Yahoo News, Yahoo Movies, Yahoo Finance, Yahoo Sports and other sites. Advertising revenue was projected at $3.5 billion for 2012, roughly half of the company's total income and second only to Facebook among online companies. The company, however, has recent revenue problems with slacking income from its search engine.

One measure of the significance of search engines has been the wealth created for their founders. The business magazine *Forbes* lists Google's Larry Page and Sergey Brin tied at the 11th richest Americans at $15.3 billion each. Yahoo's David Filo is 240th at $2.9 billion, and Jerry Yang 317th at $2.4 billion.

Yahoo
A major search engine and internet services company

David Filo, Jerry Yang
Founders of Yahoo

dot-com bust
Economic collapse of most investments in internet commerce in 2000

APPLYING YOUR MEDIA LITERACY

- **How would the internet and web be different today without browsers and search engines?**
- **How do search engines earn money without charging their users? What do you see as their long-term revenue streams?**

Messaging

STUDY PREVIEW | A core element of today's media landscape is e-mail and related text-based messaging. E-mail is a computer-based system whose history dates to a military communication network launched in 1969. A similar but more limited variation for mobile phones is texting, generally with a maximum of 140 characters per message.

E-Mail

One of the first mass uses of the internet was **e-mail**, a shortened form of the term *electronic mail*. The history of e-mail goes back to 1969 when the U.S. military created a computer network, called **ARPAnet**, which stood for Advanced Research Projects Agency Network. The Pentagon built the network for military contractors and universities doing military research to exchange information. In 1983 the National Science Foundation, whose mandate is to promote science, took over. New software coding evolved that enabled disparate computer systems to talk with each other.

e-mail
A system for computer users to exchange messages through a network

Advanced Research Projects Agency Network (ARPAnet)
Military network that preceded internet

Today anyone with a computer and a modem can exchange e-mail messages with anyone on the planet who is similarly equipped. E-mail has become a nearly universal communication tool. Most users prefer e-mail to letters, now derisively called *snail mail*.

The unadorned text of e-mail messages is quick to compose, straightforward and can be left in the in-boxes of busy and away-from-the-desk recipients. Endless telephone tag became less an irritant to everyday business and social transactions.

Despite all its roots in new and dazzling technology, e-mail generally is not mass communication. People use e-messages mostly one-to-one. True, multiple parties can be coded into a message. Also true, hucksters have devised **spams** that blanket thousands, indeed millions of people with pitches and pleas. In one sense spams meet the definition of mass communication because of the size, heterogeneity and distance of the audience. In another sense, e-mail spams are mostly unpolished and amateurish with few of the marks of carefully and professionally crafted mass-communication messages.

E-mail did take on more earmarks of mass communication when new software integrated plain vanilla text with hypertext, which is the underlying World Wide Web coding, and with graphics. Even then, however, organizations seeking slick presentations for mass audiences generally use web sites.

spam
E-mail message sent indiscriminately to large numbers of recipients

Texting

A variation on e-mail is **texting**, which uses a mobile telephone keypad to tap messages that a recipient with a mobile phone can read on a tiny phone screen, either live or later. Text messages usually are brief and text-only. In fact, the cellular networks that carry texting have a 140-character limit per message, about 30 words.

Texting originally was an idea for telephone-like point-to-point communication, not mass communication. But businesses and organizations have come to use newer software to send notices to select groups, like a reminder for a club meeting or an upcoming real deal. Some news services sell premium services and flash blurbs on breaking news, sports scores and market ups and downs. After several campus massacres, including Virginia Tech in 2007 and Northern Illinois in 2008, many colleges set up systems to alert students, faculty and staff by texting their cell phones.

The proliferation of cell phones and enthusiasm for texting, especially among young people, has had a wide range of impact. It's not all idle chit-chat. Police know, for example, that raiding a college kegger is more difficult because one person who spots officers congregating in a neighborhood can get the word down the street by texting silently and undetected. Imagine this late-night party scene: The only illumination is from hand-held telephone screens.

Texting also can work for police. In the Netherlands, police were the first to issue text alerts routinely for citizens to be vigilant if something is awry—like a kidnapping or a robbery in progress.

Political organizers—yes, including rabble-rousers—have found texting a superior 21st century substitute for bullhorns. It is thought, too, that texting campaigns have turned elections in several countries. Backers of Philippines President Joseph Estrada blamed his ouster in 2001 on what was called a "smart mob."

The United States is hardly the leader among nations in the rise of texting, but the U.S. data nonetheless are staggering. The Nielsen media-audience tracking service says text users passed 100 million in 2010, almost one-third of the total population, Four of five mobile-phone users in the United States use texting. Among teenagers and young adults, it's 87 percent. One estimate puts the U.S. average at 17 texts a day per user.

Texting in the United States got a publicity boost when the telephone company AT&T opened up its texting network to viewers of the run-away successful television program *American Idol* to vote on their favorite talent. In 2009, fans sent 178 million text messages to the show, more than double the year before. Do the math: U.S. population, 306 million; *American Idol* texts, 178 million. True, many viewers sent multiple messages over the season.

Texting
Brief typed messagge over internet between portable devices

APPLYING YOUR MEDIA LITERACY

- **When is e-mail mass communication and when not?**
- **How has texting affected how people live their lives?**
- **What do you see as political implications of texting?**

■ Complicity with Chinese Censorship

When Chinese authorities asked the U.S.-based internet service provider Yahoo for information on Wang Xiaoning's Chinese e-mail account, Yahoo gave it to them. Promptly Wang Xiaoning, an engineer, was arrested. Why? In anonymous posts to an internet mailing list he had called for democratic reforms in China

Such is life in authoritarian China, which presents a dilemma for companies like Yahoo with roots in democratic ideals that value free expression as a human right.

The case of Wang Xiaoning is not isolated. Journalist Shi Tao was sentenced to 10 years in prison for "providing state secrets to foreign entities." The "state secrets"? The government had had sent an e-mail warning to Chinese journalists, including Shi Tao, not to cover the 15th anniversary of the Tiananmen Square massacre. When the warning appeared online in places the government had not intended, authorities asked Yahoo about who held the anonymous email account used to spread the message. Yahoo complied. Police went straight to Shi Tao's office and picked him up.

In at least four cases Yahoo has handed over user information from its China-based e-mail service to Chinese authorities, according to Human Rights Watch. As a result four Chinese dissidents were locked up.

So why would Chinese citizens risk their freedom to swap information and thoughts on the internet? Should they have to? What can U.S. internet companies do in defense of human liberties like free expression and the open exchange of ideas?

▲ Policing Internet Users.

Inspectors make the rounds at an internet cafe inYangzhouCityas part of the Chinese government apparatchik to keep reins on traffic deemed unacceptable. These senior volunteer supervisors look for visits to dissident sites and traffic with suspect e-mail addresses.

Major U.S.-based internet companies like Yahoo and Google argue that the Chinese people are better off having internet access even though they are censored and spied on. Sergey Brin, one of Google's founders, notes that political searches are not that big a fraction of the searches coming out of China: "You want to look at the total value." **POINT** Also, internet companies cannot be unmindful of profits. With 253 million users, China is the world's biggest internet market. And advertising in China is in explosive growth. Estimates peg online advertising is growing 60 to 70 percent a year. No wonder Yahoo and other internet companies want to cash in.

COUNTER POINT

But internet access and profits should never carry a price tag of human liberties. Human Rights Watch, which monitors the Chinese situation closely, has called for U.S. internet companies "to act more ethically." Rebecca MacKinnon, a consultant to Human Rights Watch, says these companies can be more ethical and still operate in China. As she puts it: "It is time for internet companies to decide whether they want to be part of the problem or part of the solution."

DEEPENING YOUR MEDIA LITERACY

EXPLORE THE ISSUE: To comply with laws in Germany, France and Switzerland, Google has blocked access to sites with material likely to be judged racist or inflammatory. Can you find other evidence of internet intervention?

DIG DEEPER: Human Rights Watch has compiled a list of principles that it thinks should be included in legislation on corporate responsibility to uphold human rights. What would be on your list for internet companies?

WHAT DO YOU THINK? What role should ethics play when internet companies do business in other cultures? Should the companies consider the bottom line or other users when making ethical decisions?

MEDIAtomorrow
■ Cell Phone Novels

Yoshi-inspired. *Under the pen name Yoshi, a Japanese teacher invented a new genre of book—the cell phone novel, delivered in 160-character chunks. Eighty-six percent of Japanese high school girls have read a cell phone novel, most of them light romances. The genre is spreading to Europe and the United States.*

A Japanese prep-school tutor in his mid-30s had plenty of interaction with young people. The school was rich fodder for a novel. Yoshi, which the tutor chose as a pen name, started a novel, a romance filled with detailed love scenes. Aimed for teen-age girls, the novel, *Deep Love*, details the struggles of a 17-year-old prostitute in Tokyo. She works to pay for a heart operation for her boyfriend. Tragically, the money never reaches him, and she dies of AIDS contracted from a client. The writing is concise and fast-paced. The language is conversational, simple, often erotic.

What set *Deep Love* apart was that it was for people to read on cell phones. In effect, Yoshi turned the limitations of texting on a cell phone, 160 characters at a time, into a sensation.

In a sense *Deep Love* was collaborative. In 2000, Yoshi had set up a web site with an investment of $900 and started posting his novel a segment at a time. To promote the novel, he printed 2,000 business cards and gave them out to high school girls in front of Tokyo's busy Shibuya Station. Within three years Yoshi's site had received 20 million hits. As Yoshi wrote, readers emailed him with their feedback. He incorporated some of their ideas into the story. When finished, the cell phone book sold 100,000 copies.

While Yoshi had invented the cell phone novel, the book also caught the attention of a traditional publisher, which issued it in print. *Deep Love* was also made into manga, a Japanese comic book genre; a television drama; a film; and a series of novels that sold 2.7 million copies.

Yoshi reads dozens of e-mail messages daily from his teen fans. He uses some of their material for story ideas and plot twists. Since his books are interactive, he knows immediately when readers are getting bored. "It's like playing live music at a club," he said. "You know right away if the audience isn't responding, and you can change what you're doing right then and there."

In Japan, 86 percent of high school girls and 75 percent of middle school girls read *keitai shosetsu*, as cell phone novels are known. In recent years five of the 10 best-selling novels in Japan were originally cell phone novels. The top three spots on the best-selling list were first-time cell phone novelists.

Today sites abound for aspiring cell phone novelists, most of whom are young women and teenagers who follow Yoshi's example of a one-word pen name. Traditional book publishers use the sites to find work that will sell also in printed form. Bookstores in Japan now have entire sections devoted to the new genre.

The market for the cell phone novel appears to be stabilizing in Japan, but in Europe and the United States it is just beginning to take off. Sites such as textnovel.com and quillpill.com cater to new writers and readers. Many books on these sites are in progress, and readers are asked for their input as writers continue to send in their sentences from their cell phones, 160 characters per chunk.

What Do You Think?

Will cell phone novels become the new book industry?

What could be the effect of cell phone novels on American culture if they become as popular here as in Japan?

User-Generated Sites

STUDY PREVIEW

Bloggers have made a potent presence in the mass media landscape. Blogs may be uneven in quality, but they have demonstrated that they can be watchdogs for the public. Important, too, is that blogging demonstrated potential for additional new and important mass communication vehicles, including social networking sites.

Blogs

The ease with which individuals can create a personal media presence has been made possible by software from internet service providers to create simple web pages. Because these pages were like personal journals or logs, they were called *web logs*, or **blogs** for short. Some bloggers developed followings and added software features that allowed visitors to chime in. A running narrative became a running dialogue.

Blogs have become a distinct and influential mass medium. Blogger Joshua Marshall, for example, reported on his talkingpointsmemo.com in 2002 that the most powerful member of the U.S. Senate, Trent Lott, had made comments in a speech that were, depending on your point of view, either racist or racially insensitive. Lott had uttered his comments at the 100th birthday party of Senator Strom Thurmond, once a strong segregationist. Mainstream media missed the implications of Lott's comments. Not Joshua Marshall. On his blog, Marshall hammered away at Lott day after day. Other bloggers, also outraged at Lott's comment, joined in. Three days later the story hit NBC. Four days later Lott apologized. Two weeks later, his Senate colleagues voted him out as majority leader.

As a blogger who made a difference, Joshua Marshall is hardly alone. Best known is Matt Drudge, whose revelations propelled the Bill Clinton-Monica Lewinsky dalliances in the Oval Office into a national scandal. Another blogger, college student Russ Kirk, at his computer in Arizona, looked for information on government refusals to release photographs of caskets of fallen U.S. soldiers in Iraq and Afghanistan, which he regarded as documents to which the public, himself included, had legal access. Kirk filed a request for the documents under the Freedom of Information Act. Once he had the photos in hand, Kirk on his web site thememoryhole.org, he posted the photographs of the flag-draped coffins and also of the astronauts who had died in the *Columbia* disaster. The photos became front-page news. At one point, Kirk's blog was receiving 4 million hits a day—more than twice the circulation of *USA Today*.

Blogging not only is important in the new media landscape but for spawning a wide range of **user-generated** internet content. The effect has been transformational on the mass media. Just about anybody can create and distribute content—in contrast to the traditional model with monumentally high costs of entry, like starting a newspaper or putting a television station on the air. With user-generated content, the internet has democratized the mass media by enabling anyone with a computer and web access to become a mass communicator.

Social Networking

The giant social networking site **Facebook** had dubious beginnings. In 2003 when Mark Zuckerberg was a sophomore at Harvard, he raided sorority house membership rosters for photos of members. He posted the pictures in pairs on his blog, then invited his visitors to vote for the "hotter" of the paired women. Zuckerberg's Facemash didn't last long. The university shut it down for a host of issues, including privacy.

However, the reception for Facemash among students—some anyway—was enthusiastic, and Zuckerberg figured he was onto something. He re-mounted the site on a non-university server as Facebook, named for those photo pamphlets that small colleges once issued for freshman orientation to help new students get to know each other. First it was Harvard mugs, then Stanford, Columbia and Yale. Zuckerberg kept tweaking the concept.

blog
A journal-like web site with continuing narrative, generally personal in nature, on a narrow subject. Short for *web log*

user-generated content
Internet messages that originate with an individual to communicate directly with a mass audience

Facebook
Social networking service

▲ **Mark Zuckerberg.** *He spent weeks of all-nighters his sophomore year at Harvard writing code that became the Facebook social networking site. At 26, Zuckerberg became the world's youngest billionaire. His net worth was listed at $6.9 billion, 35th on the Forbes magazine list of richest Americans.*

Myspace
Social entertainment networking service

Flikr
Image and video hosting website

YouTube
Video-sharing website

Twitter
Platform for 140-or-fewer-character communications among computer and cell phone users

▲ **Jack Dorsey.** *At 14 Dorsey was intrigued with designing software to improve the dispatching of taxis. By 23 he was making a living with his inventions for dispatching couriers, taxis and emergency services from the web. Then he became interested in instant messaging and came up with the concept for Twitter. It was a blend of IMing and blogging that gave new dimension to social networking–and opened significant new potential for human communication.*

Today Facebook is not only the granddaddy of social networking sites but the largest. People post their own photos and choose friends with whom they want to keep in touch and exchange messages easily. On their pages, people can update their personal profiles to notify friends about themselves through written posts, photos and videos. Facebook users identify their "likes" and Facebook uses this information to alert friends of other's interest in products and services.

The success of Facebook has been phenomenal. One tracking service says Facebook is the second most visited site worldwide. Daily traffic averages 115 million visitors a day. Members total 500 million, about one-seventh of the population on the planet. They have uploaded 50 billion photos.

Facebook's early reputation was strong among college students. One study concluded that only beer outranked Facebook among collegians' favorite things. Since then, Facebook has broadened its appeal to other demographic groups. In 2010 a rival site in the Fox media family, **Myspace**, gave up competing with Facebook to reinvent itself as an entertainment news site.

As a user-generated site, Facebook's content originates with users—in contrast with the early AOL concept of a walled garden. Other major players include **Flickr,** for posting photos, and **YouTube**, for videos. The usual revenue model is on-screen advertising that directs ads to users based on lifestyle profiles.

The impact of social networking sites on traditional media has been twofold. The sites are one more competitor for advertising revenue, which has been slipping away from traditional media. Also, the sites are an additional competitor for audience time: every minute on Facebook is one less minute for something else—like reading a magazine or watching a sitcom.

Twitter

Who knows what whimsy captured actor Ashton Kutcher in April 2009. What we do know is that Kutcher set a goal of becoming the first user of **Twitter**, then a four-year-old social networking site, to have 1 million followers. It may seem a dubious distinction to have 1 million people tracking your daily commentary, like whether you chose sandals or flipflops for the beach, but such statistics are why the *Guinness Book of World Records* sells in the millions.

Although Twitter was a distant third among social networking platforms at the time of Kucher's record, its growth has been phenomenal—up 14-fold globally in one recent year and now past 175 million. In the United States alone, Twitter averages 54 million unique visitors a month.

What made Twitter different? Similar to texting, **tweets**, as they are called, are limited to 140 characters. Unlike texting, Twitter integrates communication among cell phones and computers. It's all seamless. And it's not limited to one-to-one communication. If you decide to become an Ashton Kutcher follower, for example, you sign on and then receive all the latest postings from Kutcher and fellow followers, each posted sequentially with the latest at the top.

tweets
Messages on the Twitter platform

▶ CASE STUDY: Twitter-dee and Twitter-dum

Twitter took a lot of early ribbing: How much depth is there in a message limited to 140 characters? Who cares whether Ashton Kutcher chose Wheaties or Lucky Charms for breakfast? Or to tool the L.A. freeways in a Ferrari or Hummer? Indeed, is Twitter a messaging form for an attention-deficit-disordered society?

To that question, technology author Steven Johnson, who assessed the Twitter phenomenon for *Time* magazine, has answered resoundingly: No. Johnson cited a conference for 40 invited educators, entrepreneurs, philanthropists and venture capitalists on the future of education. Everyone was encouraged to post tweets of live commentary during the presentations and discussions for display on a screen everyone could see. Distracting? Johnson recapped the six-hour experience by describing a "shadow conversation." There were summaries of discussion, occasional jokes, suggested links for further reading. "At one point a brief argument flared up between two participants in the room—a tense back-and-forth that transpired silently as the rest of us conversed in friendly tones." Yes, Johnson's lesson is that people indeed can multitask. Those 140-character tweets can be enriching.

passed links
References to web sources shared among computer users

Then, to Johnson's surprise, outsiders got wind of the interesting dialogue inside the conference and joined in. The interloping followers of the Twitter thread were adding their observations and ideas, which the participants inside the conference room integrated into their thinking and face-to-face conversation. Said Johnson: "Integrating Twitter into that conversation fundamentally changed the rules of engagement. It added a second layer of discussion and brought a wider audience into what would have been a private exchange."

Important too, Johnson said, was that a public record of hundreds of Tweets, none more than 140 characters, had been created. The whole was far more than the sum of the parts. And then, the record continued for weeks with follow-up twitters. The conference has "an afterlife" on the web.

These points can be made to counter frequent claims that tweets constitute an alarming dumbing-down of the culture:

- Brevity is not necessarily without profundity.
- Individual tweets are part of a thread of dialogue and thought that should be considered in its entirety.
- Tweets inform of world events taking place in real time. The raid on Osama Bin Laden was tweeted live by a technology consultant staying in northern Pakistan. The elections in Iran and the political change in Egypt were both fueled by the flow of information transmitted via Twitter accounts.
- Twitter discussions include links to additional materials, like supporting data elsewhere on the internet or a fresh perspective in *Atlantic Monthly*. These are called **passed links**.

▲ **King Tweeter.** *Actor Ashton Kutcher is the first user of Twitter to have 1 million followers. Why? Ask them. In a contest to reach the million mark, Kutcher's main rival, CNN's breaking news feed, came in a half an hour later.*

The possibilities for passed links could be a next step in the new media landscape. Johnson sees shared links as "a fantastic solution for finding high-quality needles in the immense spam-plagued haystack that is the contemporary web."

Video Sharing

Measures of the social impact of user-generated sites are as elusive as measuring media effects in general. Since its creation in 2005, however, the video-sharing site YouTube has shown the significant effect of user-generated media. Users can upload videos and do so 5.4 million times a day. Most are amateur videos, but other media, including television networks and consumer advertisers, post snippets to draw attention to their programming and their wares. The site is a major media stopping point in the lives of many people.

YouTube is ingrained in the internet culture. The impact goes further: Two of the presidential debates for the 2008 U.S. elections, carried on the CNN television network, were built around questions on video from YouTube users. The debates extended YouTube's visibility beyond its core younger viewers. One of the debates had an unusually high viewership of 2.6 million. In the early run-up for the 2012 election, Fox teamed with Google and NBC with Facebook.

Authoritarian governments have found YouTube vexatious in tense times. During the 2009 Iranian election crisis, the government tried to block access to YouTube and other sites to prevent the upload of video footage of mass demonstrations and police violence against citizens. Iran and other regimes, including the democratic government of Turkey, have cut off access to YouTube on grounds of morality and decency.

APPLYING YOUR MEDIA LITERACY

- **How can it be said that bloggers have democratized mass communication?**
- **What is the immense attraction of Facebook?**
- **Twitter has been characterized as a tool for people with short attention spans and contributes to a decline in culture. What is your view?**
- **How do social networking sites make money to stay in business?**

Online Commerce

STUDY PREVIEW | The internet was conceived as a commercial-free communication network. The concept evaporated as the internet's potential for e-commerce became evident. Commercial sites are often catalog-like, offering products that can be shipped to customers or downloaded or they provide services for a fee.

Sales Sites

domain name
An identification label for a web site, each with a suffix like .com, .org, .gov.

Corporation for Assigned Names and Numbers
Internet's chief oversight agency

As the internet was coming together under National Science Foundation auspices in the 1980s, the creators were of one mind about keeping the system commercial-free. The goal was a serious medium of mass communication uncontaminated by a free-for-all in quest of filthy lucre. Early users policed the system to keep it pristine, sending sharp rebukes to offenders. The "police" gave up as the commercial potential of the medium burst into everyone's consciousness, When it came time to organize the internet into useful segments with **domain names**, the suffixes approved by the **Corporation for Assigned Names and Numbers**, the chief internet oversight agency, included the telling .com and later .biz. Now even some sites with the suffix .edu, reserved for educational institutions, carry commercial messages.

Auction Sites

Pierre Omidyar
Creator of eBay online auction site

eBay
Pioneer online auction site

No story better illustrates the transformation of the Internet into a commercial medium than the rise of the auction site **eBay**. In 1995 a computer programmer, **Pierre Omidyar** of San Jose, California, added an auction function on his personal site. Somebody posted a broken laser pointer, which sold, to Omidyar's amazement, for $14.83. Omidyar figured he was onto something, and found investors, and the company grew exponentially. When ownership shares were offered to the public in 1998, three years after the launch, Omidyar was an instant billionaire.

Today eBay operates globally with 97 million active users. In 2010 the total value of goods sold through eBay was almost $62 billion. As an auction site, eBay is not alone. Some are narrowly focused, like diecast.com, which specializes in scale automobile models.

Mail Order

The internet has transformed retailing, with many brick-and-mortar stores losing sales, some even going out of business. In response, retailers across the spectrum from giant Walmart to mom-and-pop shops have created an online presence to, at minimum, steer customers to their physical stores or to make online sales for shipping to customers.

The pioneer in rewriting the rules of retailing on a large scale was **Amazon.com**. It was the concept of **Jeff Bezos**, who saw great potential in the internet for e-commerce but didn't know what to sell. Figuring that products that lent themselves to mail delivery would work well on the internet, Bezos settled on books. He founded Amazon.com in the garage of his Seattle home and went live in 1995, pioneering online book retailing. Amazon sales topped $1 billion by 2000. Today Amazon is a department store with a wide range of products, like the Sears Roebuck catalogs of earlier times, with everything delivered directly to buyers through the Postal Service or other carriers.

Amazon.com
Electronic commerce company that upended traditional book retailing

Jeff Bezos
Created Amazon online site, originally for selling books

The book retailer Barnes & Noble responded with its own internet sales site, but Amazon had a head start. Many local independent book retailers failed to get with the new retailing model. Their market share shrank. Many closed down.

Product Downloads

The computer manufacturer Apple took e-commerce in a new direction with their **iTunes Store**, which, unlike Amazon, delivered an intangible product—music. Digitized music was downloaded to customers' computers. The delivery was non-physical. Like Amazon, the Apple iStore quickly won customers and hurt traditional music retailing through stores and mail order. As download technology improved to allow video downloading in reasonable times, the iStore inventory grew to include television episodes and movies.

iTunes Store
Online digital media for consumer downloads, originally music

At Amazon, Bezos picked up on the Apple iTunes model. In 2008 Amazon introduced an e-book, **Kindle**, and offered books by download for reading on the device. Not to be outdone, Apple's iPad functions as a slick e-reader. Clearly, the internet had certainly become a major medium for commerce.

Kindle
Amazon e-book to which books and periodicals can be downloaded

APPLYING YOUR MEDIA LITERACY

- Why the early disdain for commercial content on the internet?
- Can a case be made that eBay forced the commercialization of the internet?
- Why did Jeff Bezos choose books for online commerce? What was the effect on traditional book retailing?
- How does Kindle move Amazon nearer the iTunes model? How does its impact on e-commerce compare to that of the iPad?

Online Domination

STUDY PREVIEW

The search engine Google dominates the internet with intuitive and focused search algorithms. Advertising revenue has grown because commercial messages can be targeted to likely customers. The social networking site Facebook is in a position to offer even more precisely targeted information to advertisers because so much personal information is stored on its servers.

Amassing Target Audiences

The new media landscape is being shaped by traditional media economics. The company that dominates will be the company that attracts the largest audiences, or, in today's parlance, the most eyeballs. Advertisers want eyeballs and are willing to pay for the access. The potential of the internet for commerce remains largely untapped. Of an estimated $500 billion a year spent on brand advertising globally, only about 15.2 percent is projected to go the internet by 2013.

Easily dominating the search engine market, Google has so many visits every day, every hour, every second, that advertisers pay handsomely for on-screen advertising space on pages with search results. It's **targeted marketing**. Someone searching for information on, say, mosquitoes, is a more likely customer for an anti-itch spray than someone searching for spaghetti sauce recipes or Nordic vacations. Google's search algorithms offer an unrivaled linkage of products and potential customers—a marketing dream. Although Google has created revenue streams besides advertising, much of its $23.6 billion income a year is from advertising.

In effect, Google slices and dices the mass audience in ways that give advertisers unusual efficiency in reaching the people they seek. In advertising lingo, there is less *wastage*. Why, for example, should a marinara company buy space in a food magazine whose readers include people with tomato allergies when Google offers a targeted audience of people looking for spaghetti sauce recipes with nary a one among them who's allergic to tomatoes?

targeted marketing
Matching advertisers with potential customers with relative precision

Behavioral Targeting

The social networking site Facebook has positioned itself to outdo Google for delivering audience segments to advertisers. Unlike Google, whose algorithms build an atlas of the online universe, Facebook amasses personal information on its users—the people who make purchases. The users' personal data, when organized and sorted, can be a gold mine for marketing goods and services with new precision. Consider these facts: Every month the 200 million individuals with Facebook accounts post 4 billion bits of information, 850 million photos and 8 million videos. All this is held exclusively on Facebook's 40,000 servers.

Facebook has incredible potential to deliver customers to advertisers based on information that members submit themselves, albeit unwittingly, when they communicate with friends, identify their "likes" on anything from coffee vendors to department stores to cola products and share their interests. The **Like button**, introduced in 2010, allows advertisers to shower anyone who clicks it, as well as their Facebook friends, with messages. Within a year the button was on 2 million websites. The button is a vehicle for what's called *referral traffic*. Advertisers and other sites reported huge increase in traffic. Sports News was up six-fold, Gawker tripled, ABC News 190 percent, Facebook had become NBA.com's second largest referral source.

Like button
A thumbs-up Facebook widget to identify cohorts of potential customers

Like buttons have not been without controversy. In the German state of Schleswig-Holstein, the data protection commissioner shut down Facebook fan pages to remove Like buttons as a violation of German and European law. Thilo Weichert, the commissioner, didn't like that Facebook servers were passing personal data all over the place: "Whoever visits facebook.com or uses a plug-in must expect that he or she will be tracked by the company for two years," His concern was that Facebook was building broad individual and personalized profiles of users.

Some people share the German concern. Some don't. In the technology magazine *Wired*, business writer Fred Vogelstein noted that people behave differently on Facebook than anywhere else online: They use their real names, connect with real friends, link to their real e-mail addresses and share their real thoughts, tastes and news. In contrast, Vogelstein notes, Google knows little about its users except their search histories and some browsing activity.

That Facebook is positioned to become the central component in the new media landscape has not been lost on investors. Microsoft bought a chunk of Facebook stock in 2007 at a price that suggested the company was worth $15 billion. Three years later, analysts put Facebook's assets at $53 billion to $64 billion. Vogelstein explains the Facebook-Google contrast colorfully with the example of a friend whose Facebook profile has the usual stuff— birthday, address, resume and pictures of his wife and kids. Plus, Vogelstein notes, his friend explained that he likes to make beer, ate at one of Vogelstein's favorite restaurants the week before, and likes to watch cartoons. The friend pondered in a Facebook message to a friend whether his son's Little League game might be rained out. Also, he asked friends for help figuring out how the impeller in his central heating unit works. In contrast, a search of the name of Vogelstein's friend on Google yielded that he holds a doctorate in computer science on a dated personal web site with links, most of them expired, and a list of scholarly papers he had written over the years.

The future of the internet may well be the **behavioral targeting** that Facebook and other social networking sources can offer advertisers. There are hurdles. Users objected loudly in 2007 when Facebook began injecting advertising into news feeds. Users were concerned about privacy. Accused of betraying users' privacy expectations through data mining for commercial purposes, Facebook backed off. Then in 2009 Facebook quietly modified its terms of service, to which users must agree or leave, so anything posted on the site gives ownership of the material to Facebook in perpetuity. The small print read: "We may share your information with third parties, including responsible companies with which we have a relationship." To a new batch of criticism, the company denied an intention to provide information to third parties. Even so, the language remained in the terms of service. In late 2010 Facebook again modified its terms of service.

Even so, Facebook is explicit that it doesn't share information on users with advertisers without users' permission, but the company does use its aggregated information about users to deliver paid advertising. In the fine print of a legal agreement to which users must agree, Facebook explains: "We serve the ad to people who meet the criteria the advertiser selected, but we do not tell the advertiser who any of those people are. So, for example, if a person clicks on the ad, the advertiser might infer that the person is an 18-to-35-year-old woman who lives in the US and likes basketball. But we would not tell the advertiser who that person is.

"After the ad runs, we provide advertisers with reports on how their ads performed. For example we give advertisers reports telling them how many users saw or clicked on their ads. But these reports are anonymous. We do not tell advertisers who saw or clicked on their ads.

"Sometimes we allow advertisers to target a category of user, like a 'moviegoer' or a 'sci-fi fan.' We do this by bundling characteristics that we believe are related to the category. For example, if a person "likes" the 'Star Trek' page and mentions 'Star Wars' when they check into a movie theater, we may conclude that this person is likely to be a "'sci-fi fan."

behavioral targeting
Using personal information and patterns in activities to match advertisements with potential customers

APPLYING YOUR MEDIA LITERACY

- **What is the advantage of social-networking sites to target customers for advertisers?**
- **What obstacles does Facebook have as a behavioral targeting service?**

Games

STUDY PREVIEW | With growing sophistication in software, new broadband capacity and interactivity, games have acquired qualities akin to mass communication. This includes expanding acceptability as an advertising medium.

Online Game Audience

Firmly established in the internet universe is online video gaming. Gaming has grown from the simple games added to software packages with the first generation of home computers even before people had heard of the internet. Today, the top online role-playing games such as *Call of Duty: Black* Ops, *Madden* NFL, and *Halo: Reach* boast tens of thousands of players worldwide at any given time.

With their huge and growing following, video games have become a natural target for advertising. It's an attractive audience. The Entertainment Software Association says that players average 6.5 hours a week at their games. Players include a broad range of people, and 39 percent earn $50,000 a year or more—an attractive demographic that advertisers have a hard time tapping with other media.

Game Advertising

Advertisers came to recognize games as a platform to reach a significant and growing audience—58 percent of them men and most age 18 to 49—an elusive audience for advertisers. The trade analyst group Screen Digest projects in-game advertising will reach $1 billion globally in 2014, up $300 million over five years.

APPLYING YOUR MEDIA LITERACY

- **How do your game habits compare with the 6 1/2 hour-a-week average reported by the entertainment software association? What impact does your playing have on your daily schedule?**
- **What do advertisers find attractive about buying space in game messages?**

Archives

STUDY PREVIEW

The capacity to store digitized data seems infinite. The impact is at its most obvious with library collections. Who needs miles of shelf space? The online encyclopedia Wiki and specialized banks of data and information have revolutionized the reference book industry. On-call digitized data has profound social and political effects.

Digital Storage

The seemingly endless capacity for digital storage has eliminated the scarcity of space for moving and storing text, images, sound and video. Theoretically, librarians no longer need to shred the least-used parts of their collections for want of shelf space. Encyclopedia editors no longer have arbitrary limits, whether 10 volumes or 20, to encapsulate all human knowledge. Archivists, rejoice! There's plenty of room for anything that can be digitized.

Google Book Search

Google Books Library Project
Project to put all books in human history online

In terms of previous human experience, a proposal by the search engine company Google to digitize every book ever produced is boggling. Google's collection will far surpass the holdings of any library. That includes Harvard University, whose collection of 15 million volumes is the largest academic library in the world. The **Google Books Library Project** will also exceed the Library of Congress' 42.3 million volumes and the British Library' 25 million. With the project's expansion to additional languages, the collection will dwarf French Bibliothéque's 13 million volumes in French.

The new challenge is organizing the digitized material to facilitate access. Good-bye to the Dewey decimal and other indexing systems. Digitized materials can be searched in infinite ways—not just titles and authors and subjects but even passages. Book retailer Amazon.com has dabbled with searches for passages and phrases in books in its inventory.

The Google project has raised issues about who owns published works. With Shakespeare and Aristotle, the core works have long been in the public domain and, in effect, belong to everyone. For more recent works, old-line media companies have resisted Google's digitizing. The companies claim that they hold exclusive rights to control their dissemination—and to charge for it. The issue is a core one involving copyright protection, which involves almost all media products. A fundamental question is whether the concept of encouraging creative production by offering creators the incentive of profiting from their work has been rendered obsolete.

Wikipedia

The archival potential of digitization has been demonstrated by Wikipedia, an online encyclopedia whose users volunteer the articles, which then go through a free-wheeling editing process by fellow users. In its first eight years the collaborative process generated 2.9 million articles in English and almost five times that many in additional languages. The scope of the endeavor, and also the process, could not have been fathomed as practicable even a few years before.

The impact: Bound encyclopedias like the Britannica, currently at 32 volumes, have become the digital era's horse-and-buggy. Traditional encyclopedia companies are in crisis. How can Britannica, with overhead that includes 100 full-time and 4,000 expert contributors, compete against Wiki? Even a DVD edition drawn from various Britannica versions has but 120,000 entries—impressive by earlier standards but a pale one-25th of Wiki's total in English alone.

The collaborative model is not without its critics. While many—perhaps the majority—of Wikipedia entries are generally accurate, mistakes, inaccuracies and even deliberate falsehoods can flourish unchecked in the online environment. For that reason, Wikipedia is not yet considered an acceptable source of information for most school or college papers, much less professional research.

The effect of a 2009 decision at Wiki to add professional staff editors is unclear. The goal is to improve entries in general.

News Record

School teachers once lectured students that a knowledgeable citizen read several newspapers a day to be well-informed. While once good advice, every student today has easy access online to dozens of news sources—and to digitized archives of earlier news. Yesterday's newspaper is now in a digital version and archived for reference in perpetuity. It's the same with magazines.

Internet-only news services may tout their latest coverage, but posterity will value the archives. A paperless age for news is upon us.

APPLYING YOUR MEDIA LITERACY

- **What is digital storage replacing?**
- **Why are many book publishers and authors concerned over the Google Print Library project?**
- **Contrast the Wiki collaborative process with how the Britannica is edited.**
- **What advantage do digital archives of news have over traditional news archives?**

■ Jobs' Historical Model (Pages 173–176)

When Steve Jobs tried to make sense of the new media landscape, people listened. He was there almost since the beginning. Indeed, he had a remarkable record of success in keeping Apple products ahead of the curve. Jobs saw the digital media revolution in three stages: The Computer Revolution, 1980–1994, marked by quantum leaps in productivity; the Internet Revolution, 1994–2000, marked by interconnectivity; and the Digital Lifestyle, now underway, with personal computers as the hub.

■ Portals (Pages 176–177)

Desktop computers became a standard household appliance in the late 1980s. A gateway to the internet opened for millions of people. Everybody sensed a new media landscape was being formed. One popular idea, epitomized by America Online, was modeled loosely on subscribing to a newspaper or magazine. With a subscription, people would buy access to a rich array of online material from AOL or a competing "walled garden" of content. That concept disintegrated with the introduction of browsers like Netscape, which gave everybody—geeky and otherwise—access beyond walled gardens.

■ Search Engines (Pages 177–179)

Almost from the beginning the internet was so vast—and also growing—that it was easy to get lost. Search engines were the answer. Software tracked the internet and clumped websites by subjects. Computer users could type in a search term and their search engine would rank hundreds of relevant sites. Google became dominant, listing as many as 1,000 possible sites every search and making the new media landscape navigable.

■ Messaging (Pages 179–182)

The internet became a major artery for interpersonal communication. E-mail exceeds the reach of the Postal Service and the telephone for communicating from Point A to Point B and also for mass communication. A variant, texting with portable telephones, added mobility to communication.

■ User-Generated Sites (Pages 183–186)

Software that allowed anyone with a computer and a modem to upload content was the last nail in the coffin of the "walled garden" concept. No longer did media companies have a monopoly on content. Blogging became a national, indeed global, pastime. Facebook facilitated an online presence for millions of people. YouTube made everybody a movie producer or, gee whiz, a star. Twittering stands to transform participatory communication profoundly.

■ Online Commerce (Pages 186–187)

The founders of the internet had a typically American disdain for filthy lucre. They didn't want commerce to taint their wonderful new medium for communication. Another American value, capitalism, emerged as dominant, however. Today the internet is a primary vehicle for commerce with online catalogues and ordering, auctions, product downloads. Rare is a company without an online presence to, at minimum, promote itself.

■ Online Domination (Pages 187–189)

The Google search engine mapped the internet and made it functional for everyday use. By selling on-screen advertising space, Google became a media juggernaut financially. But the social networking site Facebook has a potential and huge advantage in attracting advertisers. Facebook maps the internet and internet users and has amassed incredible quantities of data to help advertisers target potential customers with unprecedented precision. Facebook users keep pumping personal data in to Facebook servers, updating it regularly and identifing and sharing their "likes" for all things from products to charities.

■ Games (Pages 189–190)

The gaming industry has surpassed the music industry in sales and is gaining on movies and books. Interactivity among players has created a huge audience and online usage continues to grow.

■ Archives (Pages 190–191)

Digitization enables the storage of incredible quantities of data. Would you believe every word published in human history? Who needs bricks-and-mortar libraries with miles of shelf space? Every breaking news story, including text, image, audio and video, can be archived for posterity and almost instant retrieval. The effect of digital archiving on traditional media is enriching new content with readily available background. One example: Consider how illuminating an interview can be when a journalist plays back a politician's words from last week, last month, last year or the last campaign: "Yes, senator, how do you square what you said today with what you said last January? Take a listen."

CHAPTER WRAP UP

■ Critical Thinking Questions

1. What vulnerabilities do you see that future historians may find in Steve Jobs' history of media digitization?

2. How did former media business models beget the walled-garden business model for the internet and then fail?

3. Why are search engines essential for making full use of the internet?

4. How are e-mailing and texting different? And similar?

5. What new dimension has user-based content added to the new media landscape?

6. Should commerce have been allowed to become the economic driver of the internet?

7. Contrast the potential of Google and Facebook in attracting advertising.

8. How much more growth possibilities do you see for the online game industry?

9. How is digitized data storage enriching mass communication and society and culture?

■ Media Vocabulary

ARPAnet (Page 179)

behavioral targeting (Page 189)

blog (Page 183)

browser (Page 176)

Computer Revolution (Page 173)

Corporation for Assigned Names and Numbers (Page 186)

crawlers (Page 177)

digital lifestyle (Page 175)

domain names (Page 186)

dot-com bust (Page 179)

e-mail (Page 179)

Internet Revolution (Page 174)

Jobs' Model (Page 173)

like button (Page 188)

passed links (Page 185)

search engine (Page 177)

spam (Page 180)

targeted marketing (Page 188)

texting (Page 180)

user-generated content (Page 183)

walled garden (Page 176)

■ Media Sources

■ Juliann Sivulka. *Soap, Sex and Cigarettes: A Cultural History of American Advertising*, Second Edition. Wadsworth, 2012. Sivulka, a scholar in American studies, examines the two-way interplay of cultural trends and advertising.

■ Walter Isaacson. *Steve Jobs*. Simon & Schuster, 2011. Isaacson, chosen by Apple genius Steve Jobs for this biography, draws on extensive interviews for what's considered the definitive work on Jobs.

■ Douglas Edwards. *I'm Feeling Lucky: The Confessions of Google Employee Number 59*. Houghton Mifflin, 2011. This first-person account by an early Google marketing manager has insights into the company's attempt to define itself.

■ Steven Levy, In *the Plex: How Google Thinks, Works, and Shapes Our Lives*, Simon & Schuster, 2011. Levy, a journalist focused on technology, draws on extensive interviews with Google insiders.

■ Chris Berry, Soyoung Kim and Lynn Spigel, editors. *Electronic Elsewheres: Media, Technology and the Experience of Social Space*. Minnesota, 2010. The editors have collected thinking by leading scholars on the confluence of sociology, anthropology, politics and mass media.

■ Jessica Clark and Tracy Van Slyke. *Beyond the Echo Chamber: Reshaping Politics through Networked Progressive Media*. New Press, 2010. Scholars Clark and Van Slyke argue that social media lend themselves to making progressive arguments and prevailing over conservative voices that mastered techniques of traditional media in the 1980s and 1990s. Listen up, Rush Limbaugh.

■ Tim Wu. *The Master Switch: The Rise and Fall of Information Empires.* Knopf, 2010. Wu, a scholar, worries that the internet may move from a relatively open sector of the economy to an oligopoly with few players. It's happened before, he warns, in radio, television, telecommunication and other information industries.

■ Ken Auletta. *Googled: The End of the World as We Know It.* Penguin, 2009.

■ Auletta, media critic, for the *New Yorker*, tracks Google from humble origins into an online powerhouse that displaced traditional media, then deals with its profit-driven quest to dominate media delivery and become a major advertising vehicle.

■ Leah A. Lievrouw and Sonia Livingstone, editors. *New Media.* Sage, 2009. Lievrouw, a U.S. scholar, and Livingstone, a British scholar, have gathered a rich collection of interdisciplinary thinking on historical, economic, social and behavioral issues in four volumes. Their perspective is international.

■ Ben Mezrich. *The Accidental Billionaires: The Founding of Facebook: A Tale of Sex, Money, Genius and Betrayal.* Doubleday, 2009. This tell-all biography on Facebook founder Mark Zuckerberg draws on interviews with Eduardo Saverin, who was pushed out of the company after a falling out.

■ Uta Kohl. *Jurisdiction and the Internet: Regulatory Competence over Online Activity.* Cambridge, 2007. Kohl, a British scholar, examines issues of transnational regulation through defamation or contract law, obscenity standards, gambling or banking regulation, pharmaceutical licensing requirements or hate speech.

■ Jack Goldsmith and Tim Wu. *Who Controls the Internet?: Illusions of a Borderless World.* Oxford University Press, 2006. Goldsmith and Wu see cracks in the widespread notion that governments are powerless at controlling internet content.

■ Bruce Abramson. *Digital Phoenix: Why the Information Economy Collapsed and How It Will Rise Again.* MIT Press, 2005. Abramson, a computer scientist and lawyer, attributes the Dot.Com Bust to network theorists who didn't know classical economics, and giddy investors, who missed that competition would wipe out most start-up companies. Future innovation, he says, can be furled by relaxed rules on protecting intellectual property.

Thematic Chapter Summary

NEW MEDIA LANDSCAPE

To further deepen your media literacy here are ways to look at this chapter from the perspective of themes that recur throughout the book:

MEDIA TECHNOLOGY

Expect more speed, capacity, applications.

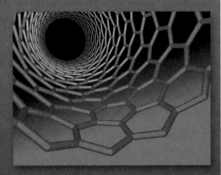

Change arrives rapidly with each new development in the underlying technologies of computers and the internet. Portals grew few walled gardens. They became public parks where everyone was invited to play on new laptops with internet access. Starting with the World Wide Web protocols of Tim Berners-Lee and Marc Andreessen's revolutionary Netscape browser, the Internet began its domination of new media. E-mail, search engines, social networking, texting, blogging, printing books on-demand, on-call digital storage in online archives, gaming and real-life simulations—each new advancement has been revolutionary. Who knows what will be next?

MEDIA ECONOMICS

Perennial battles among media for revenue streams are marking new digital media too.

The early walled garden business model for the internet was drawn from traditional media products that tried to be all things to all people, to serve mass audiences. The model fell apart when Marc Andreessen 's Netscape browser and Sergey Brin and Larry Page's Google came along. The Netscape-Google combo gave people free access to the whole universe of internet content. What the companies built in digital media have in common with their predecessors in a new to find revenue streams. The answer: Advertising. Just like the old days.

MEDIA AND DEMOCRACY

Social media including YouTube are new political tools.

In the 2008 elections, YouTube users could pose questions during presidential debates. Candidates put their messages out to voters through e-mail, YouTube, Facebook and Twitter. Just about anyone can create and distribute content on the internet. Individuals can open their own blogging sites, or they can send content to social networking sites like Facebook, Twitter, YouTube or Flickr. Unlike traditional media, which relied on trained reporters, anyone with a cell phone or a computer can become a citizen journalist. This has become problematic for authoritarian governments around the world, which regularly try to block access to YouTube and other sites. The advent of user-generated content has had the effect of democratizing the mass media.

MEDIA AND CULTURE

What message do kids pick up from media that make homework shortcuts so easy?

New media have had profound effects on our culture. Hardly anyone still writes letters and sends them through the U.S. mail. E-mail and texting have become the dominant forms of communication. We do business, send party invitations, birthday cards and pictures via e-mail and texts. Facebook and other social networking sites keep us in touch with our friends and colleagues. Even when someone lives across the globe, we can know what they're having for lunch, who they're dating, and how they're doing in school—and we know almost instantly. We no longer need to look at bulky catalogs for mail-order shopping—we can shop and order online. Researching school papers and finding obscure information is only a few key taps away thanks to powerful search engines and faster connections to the internet. Online games consume major parts of many people's lives. All of these innovations are not without controversy. Since almost everything we do on the internet is trackable, advertisers and marketers are anxious to tap that information in spite of the inherent privacy issues.

MEDIA FUTURE

China looms as huge market for internet companies to nurture revenue streams.

Internet companies have smelled profits in nascent capitalism in China. The Chinese economy, the fastest growing on the planet, is well on its way to being driven by consumer products. That means manufacturers and retailers will be seeking platforms to hawk their products. U.S.-based internet companies, including Google and Yahoo, are building their presence in China and positioning themselves for future profits. This is creating occasional crises, in which these companies find themselves compromising American principles like free expression when pressed to cooperate with authoritarian crackdowns and other repressive actions by the Chinese government.

AUDIENCE FRAGMENTATION

There was a time when people drew on only a few media regularly—a local newspaper, a few magazines, a favorite radio station, and three, maybe four local television stations. What a difference a few inventions made in the late 20th century, culminating in the access-to-everything-everywhere internet. The huge audiences of the legacy media have dispersed. The in-on-paper New York Times, for example, competes for the eyes of newshounds with Salon, Slate, Politico, Talking Points Memo, Drudge and Huffington among dozens more—plus against itself with nytimes.com. There are even sites that facilitate wandering into unexplored media territory, like Stitcher for radio. The media landscape is changing even as you read this. And widening.

CHAPTER 8 NEWS

■ Missing Real News

In a massive study of news coverage on global warming, brothers Maxwell Boykoff, an environmental geographer, and Jules Boykoff, a political scientist, reviewed four leading U.S. newspapers—the New York *Times, Wall Street Journal,* Washington *Post* and Los Angeles *Times.* Over 14 years they identified 3,542 news items, editorials and other articles on global warming. Randomly they chose 636 articles for analysis. Fifty-three percent, more than half, gave equal weight to the opposing views. The Boykoffs said that readers could conclude only that the scientific community

was "embroiled in a rip-roaring debate on whether or not humans were contributing to global warming." The fact, however, was scientists generally agreed that global warming was an alarming species-threatening phenomenon.

How could news media in their reporting of science be so out of sync with scientists? It's a question at the heart of this chapter on news, which examines the process of gathering and telling news. This chapter also examines how news media, no matter how well intentioned, can get big stories wrong. Yes, like global warming. Most important: How can media-literate consumers decide which reporting to trust?

The original Boykoff scholarship, in 2004, received little attention from news media. Since then, larger studies have gone beyond prestigious U.S. newspapers to include 50 papers in 20 countries. News coverage of pending climatic catastrophe remained wanting. Environmental sociologist Robert Brulle, who looked at major newscasts on U.S. television networks, has come to similar conclusions.

The Boykoffs have a theory about what's wrong: In a sense, as counterintuitive as it seems, journalists try too hard to be fair. "The professional canon of journalistic fairness requires reporters who write about a controversy to present competing points of view," the Boykoffs explained. "Presenting the most compelling arguments of

◀ **Glacier Calving Disaster.** *A landmark study by scholars Jules and Maxwell Boykoff found journalists getting trapped in their desire for balance. For too long, journalists gave equal play to sources lined up by big energy companies to downplay the seriousness of global warming. This "balance" diminished the alarming evidence, like disappearing ice caps, that warming was being accelerated by environmentally reckless human activity. Follow-up studies have found no improvement in the reporting of science.*

CHAPTER INSIGHTS

- The term *news* can be understood only by also understanding *newsworthiness.*
- The publisher James Gordon Bennett established the idea of news in the 1830s.
- The Hutchins Commission drastically revised the concept of news in the mid-1900s.
- Hybrid news models are melding fact-centric news and informed perspective.

- Journalists bring personal, social and political values to their work.
- What ends up reported as news is the result of the convergence of multiple variables.
- Mechanisms for quality have been eroded by the growing number of news sources.
- Journalistic trends include exploratory news, soft news and 24/7 coverage.

both sides with equal weight is a fundamental check on biased reporting. But this canon causes problems when it is applied to issues of science. It seems to demand that journalists present competing points of view on a scientific question as if they had equal scientific weight, when actually they do not."

The fairness chink in journalistic armor has given special interests an opportunity to manipulate news by making misleading and even false information easily available to reporters who, dutifully if not mindlessly, apply the principle of fairness. A legion of spokespersons, many funded by special interests, end up with roles in journalists' stories. The Boykoffs cite many examples, one being the New York *Times* quoting a global warming skeptic that carbon dioxide emissions aren't a threat to the climate but "a wonderful and unexpected gift from the Industrial Revolution."

Who are these special interests? Former Vice President Al Gore, himself a journalist early in his career, has been blunt. He blames "a relatively small cadre of special interests including Exxon Mobil and a few other oil, coal and utilities companies." Why? "These companies want to prevent any new policies that would interfere with their profit plans that rely on the massive, unrestrained dumping of global-warming pollution of the Earth's atmosphere every hour of every day."

The Boykoffs put it this way: "Balanced reporting has allowed a small group of global-warming skeptics to have their views amplified." Balanced coverage, according to the Boykoffs, has not translated into accurate coverage.

Are journalists dishonest? Jules Boykoff doesn't blame the journalists themselves. Boykoff notes that giant media companies, intent on improving profits, have cut back on newsroom staffs and labor-intensive investigative reporting. The result: More and more reporters are called upon to be generalists and are being denied time to build expertise on a complex subject such as climate change.

The implications are serious because public policy in democracies is derived, theoretically, from public perceptions. The Boykoffs note that news media, by devaluing scientific evidence, give "real political space for the U.S. government to shirk responsibility and delay action regarding global warming."

The Boykoffs and other media scholars have additional explanations for weak—or should we say *bad*—news coverage of global warming.

- News media have slashed their science reporting in a shift toward celebrity and flashy news. More than ever, news judgments are driven by what draws an immediate audience: "If it bleeds, it leads." Global warming, on the other hand, doesn't have cinematic moments. It's a process.

- Environmental scholar William Freudenburg also blames the widespread assumption that science comes to black-and-white conclusions. That assumption is wrong. Science actually is a cumulative process. It is true that years ago there wasn't much concern among scientists about global warming, but the consensus has shifted dramatically, in fact to an alarm level. A consensus that develops over time is much more difficult for journalists to cover and for people to get excited about than smack-wham revelations of something entirely new and earthshaking.

To be sure, the news media can be too easily blamed for not headlining global warming every day. Wars, elections and policy debates on issues like health care and education also compete for coverage in ever-smaller news holes and cannot be ignored. ■

Concept of News

STUDY PREVIEW

News is a report on change that survives the competition for reporting other change that is occurring. What ends up being reported is the result of news judgments by reporters, editors and producers who package their regular updates on what they believe their audiences need and want to know.

News as Change

Ask anybody: "What's news?" Everybody thinks they know, but press them and you'll hear a lot of fumbling. So why is consensus elusive about something as much a part of everyday life as news? In part it's because the U.S. Constitution forbids government from interfering with almost anything that the media report. This freedom has led to diverse presentations under the label of news. Compare the outrageous tabloid website *News Bizarre* and the New York *Times,* the pillar of U.S. daily journalism. Not even mainstream media report events and issues in lockstep.

news
A report on change

A useful definition of news involves two concepts—news and newsworthiness.

In short, **news** is a report on change. This is most apparent in traditional newspaper headlines, which contain a verb—the vehicle in a language to denote change:

> Earthquake rattles Chilean coast
> Roadside Afghan bomb kills four soldiers
> New York Legislature sanctions gay marriage

Newsworthiness

newsworthiness
A ranking of news that helps decide
what makes it into news packages

Not all change can fit into the limited time in a newscast or the limited space in a newspaper or on a web page. Nor does all change warrant audience time online. So what change makes the news? Journalists apply the concept of **newsworthiness** to rank change. When Barack Obama sniffles, it's change—and the whole world cares. A lot is at stake. For most of us, when we sniffle, only Mom cares. Applying a newsworthiness test to a series of events that might be reported requires judgment. No two people will assign all priorities the same. See for yourself: Rank the following hypothetical events by newsworthiness and ask a friend to do the same:

> Yankees win World Series
> Congress votes to remove Mexico fence
> Navy launches new aircraft carrier
> Bin Laden successor killed in drone attack
> Scientology founder returns from dead
> Airline crash kills 220 in Kenya

A lot of factors go into determining newsworthiness: proximity to audience, prominence of people involved, timeliness, impact on society, even the so-called "gee-whiz" factor. But there is no clinical formula for newsworthiness. A subjective element flowing from journalists' values, and sense of the world and sense of audience is at the heart of what is reported and how it's reported.

APPLYING YOUR MEDIA LITERACY

- **How are the concepts of news as change and the concept of newsworthiness inextricably linked?**
- **Compare the leading stories in competing newspapers, newscasts or online sites and explain the role that judgment makes in deciding what makes the news.**

Bennett News Model

STUDY PREVIEW | Penny newspaper publisher James Gordon Bennett recognized fresh information as a commercial commodity in the 1830s. The fresher the news, the more eager the audience is to buy. Timeliness was Bennett's mantra. The result was a body of premises and practices that dominated the concept of news in the United States for 100-plus years and remains a strong influence in the way news is reported today.

James Gordon Bennett

James Gordon Bennett
Early Penny Press publisher; founder
of New York *Herald* 1835

The concept of news as we know is less than 200 years old. A struggling New York printer, **James Gordon Bennett,** seeing the success of fellow printer Ben Day with a one-cent newspaper, decided to start his own. With a plank laid across two flour barrels for a desk, a dilapidated press and barely enough type, Bennett produced his own humble penny sheet, the New York *Herald,* in 1835. An early Bennett story, shocking but irresistible for readers, was a front-page interview with the fashionable Madame Rosina Townsend after one of her prostitutes was slain. Bennett was there as police investigated. He packed juicy detail into a story loaded with quotations. It was the first published news interview in history. More important, it showed Bennett's knack for identifying details to put in the *Herald* to draw readers. He intuited what people wanted to know.

Bennett quickly recognized that being first with news gave him an advantage over competitors. His obsession with getting news to readers quickly brought an emphasis on timeliness as an important element in the concept of news. It also contributed to the fact-oriented telling of news because reporters rushing to get a dispatch together are too pressed to be analytical.

Bennett made a fetish of timeliness. He used small, fast boats to sail out to Sandy Point, on the coast beyond New York, to pick up parcels of newspapers and letters from arriving oceanic ships and then sail back to the city before the ships themselves could arrive and dock. He beat other papers by hours with fresh news.

In one case Bennett himself went to Halifax, Nova Scotia, where many European vessels landed before continuing down the coast. With a news packet in hand he hired a locomotive to take him back to Boston, Worcester and New London, where he took a ferry to Long Island, and then another locomotive to New York. That news was days ahead.

The *Herald* was a quick success, surpassing the circulation of Ben Day's *Sun.* Bennett never relented in his quest for quick news. After Samuel Morse invented the telegraph in 1844, Bennett instructed reporters to use the infant network that was being built around the country to send back their dispatches without delay.

Bennett organized the modern newsroom, applying the division of labor principle. Reporters were assigned subjects to cover and were responsible for being first with news on their subjects. These **news beats**, as they were called, included the police, the courts and other fertile subjects for news. New York, then 150,000 people, was large and complex enough that nothing short of a beat system could come close to comprehensive coverage. Bennett's system recognized that finding a broad audience meant covering a wide range of subjects and issues.

In short, Bennett's sense of his audience's interests and his innovations established a foundation for news-gathering practices and for techniques for packaging news. The **Bennett Model** has become a baseline understanding of what comprises news.

news beats
A specific subject or field that a news reporter covers as a specialty, like a police beat, a science beat

Bennett Model
An enduring concept of news that emphasizes event-based reporting on deadline

Bennett Model Components

No surprise: James Gordon Bennett's techniques were imitated quickly, finding larger and larger audiences.

Compelling Events.   Reporting on events became an art form, transforming newspapers into a major industry through the 1900s. The basic human hunger for information was being satisfied as never before in history. At the same time, the emerging role of consumers in the economy drew advertisers to newspapers. The purchase of advertising space made for

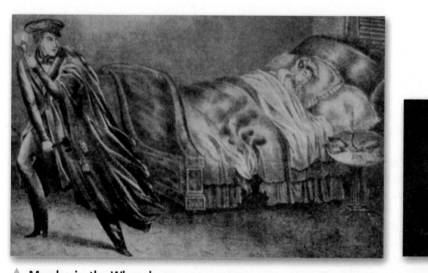

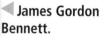 James Gordon Bennett.

▲ **Murder in the Whorehouse.** *The murderer steals away in this artist's reconstruction of the 1836 murder scene of Helen Jewett in a New York brothel. Public interest in the murder had first been fanned by journalistic innovator James Gordon Bennett who listened in while detectives quizzed the brothel's madame after Jewett was found dead in her burning bed. Bennett's account made a compelling story and prompted who-dun-it interest for decades.*

Stunt Journalism. *New York World publisher Joseph Pulitzer sent Nellie Bly, his star reporter, on an around-the-world trip in 1890 to try to outdo the fictional Phineas Fogg's 80-day trip. Her feat took 72 days. Pulitzer was good at creating compelling stories, some frivolous, some not. In a major serious endeavor, Bly faked insanity to get checked into an asylum and then exposed the dreadful conditions in a Page 1 series in the* World. *Reforms resulted.*

lightning news
Delivered by telegraph

objectivity
A concept in journalism that news should be gathered and told value-free

byline
A line identifying the reporter or writer, usually atop an article

thicker dailies from the 1830s on. Demand then led to both morning and evening editions, and then to multiple editions in both the morning and evening news cycles. Like hungry lions, newspapers were always in need of fresh meat to fill the paper. To feed the lions, reporters leaped from one unfolding event to the next. Competition for big stories was keen. The news business was an adrenaline rush for reporters and a vicarious rush for readers.

Deadline-Driven.   Bennett's focus on beating other penny papers grew heated. Pressure to get the latest developments in the soonest possible edition became intense, indeed frenzied. Readers were dazzled at getting reports faster than they'd ever imagined. In 1844 came the telegraph. Within only four years, all the major cities were linked by wire—even Chicago and Milwaukee, locations considered to be in the distant west.

Public fascination with local breaking news expanded into an obsession with far-away events. The term **lightning news** evolved, reflecting that telegraph delivery was not only instantaneous but also electrical. In the late 1800s, electricity was lighting cities for the first time and powering factories and transforming human existence. It was awe-inspiring stuff. Among all the new technologies, lightning news was a prominent product.

In the 1920s with radio emerging as a news medium, public interest in breaking news was fueled as never before. A radio reporter could be on the scene, at an event, and people could listen live. Wow.

Objectivity.   A dispassionate presentation evolved as a major tenet of the Bennett Model, displacing the opinionated content of earlier partisan papers. Chasing the largest possible audiences, penny papers like Bennett's New York *Herald* chose to avoid slants that might offend major audience segments. Opinion was out, storytelling in.

A detached tone became a norm with the early Associated Press as a model. Several cost-conscious New York newspapers created the AP in 1848 as a joint venture to cover distant news and split the costs. The newspapers, no longer needing to each field reporters for far-away coverage, saved a lot of money. An upshot of the shared-staff concept was that AP stories needed to be non-partisan to be useable in all AP papers. The result: an emphasis on fact-driven reporting devoid of any hint of partisanship.

Another fundamental shift cemented the detached, neutral AP tone, often characterized as **objectivity,** into the Bennett Model. As news became more profitable, newspapers matured into financial engines. By the 1880s major publishers—Pulitzer, Hearst, Scripps and others—saw their newspapers as money machines. With the bottom line gaining more weight, the safest route to continue building their audiences and enhancing revenue was to avoid antagonizing readers and advertisers. There was money to be made in neutral presentations. Picking up a lesson from the AP, profit-driven publishers opted for information-driven news.

True, most newspapers ran opinions, but they were fenced off in editorial sections. The coverage of events, which became the definition of daily journalism, was presented as neutrally as possible.

Veiling the Reporter.   The Bennett Model's neutral tone resulted in impersonal journalism. The role of the reporter was so suppressed that news came across as almost robotic. Until the latter 1900s, **bylines** were a rarity. The first-person *I* or *me* was forbidden. The idea was to keep the reporter's role in the story as invisible as possible. The deliberate obscuration of a journalist in the telling of news denied the reality that news work is a highly cerebral process.

In contrast, news models elsewhere have been far different. In London, the *Manchester Guardian,* founded in 1821, its name now shortened to the *Guardian,* has a long tradition of encouraging reporters to apply their expertise and observations overtly in their work. Truth-seeking at the *Guardian* is fact-based, to be sure, but there is no cloak of impartiality. The same is true at the *Daily Telegraph,* founded in 1855, and at other leading British and European papers.

Sourcing.   News in the Bennett Model is largely reactive. The role of the journalist is to cover events as they unfold. Bennett did not emphasize investigative reporting in which reporters set out proactively to unearth news. The thrust of American journalism under the Bennett Model has been reactive: Wait for events to happen, then report them.

Problems in Bennett Model

The Bennett Model for chronicling events remains a valid way to think about what is news. Although enduring, the Bennett Model is not without flaws. The focus on events can mean missing significant truths that merit reporting. Too, the fixation on events has proved inadequate for spotting trends until too late to head off major societal problems and crisis. Also, the model leaves the news media vulnerable to partisanship and other manipulation.

Superficiality.   With the Bennett Model, reporting was frequently superficial. Reporters opted for easy stories with facts that were readily available. What about story possibilities that required more time and digging? Too often these harder stories lost out in deadline-driven priorities.

Imagine a hard-to-ignore event like an oil refinery fire. A fire is relatively easy to cover. Harder to get at can be the safety record of the company that operates the refinery. A safety record story could be more important than a story on the fire itself, especially if the company has several refineries. But a story on the safety record would require lots of extra time to go after, especially if the company erects obstacles intentionally to get at the information. For journalists it's easier to win prominent display of their work by racing after the next breaking event. And news packagers— the people who assemble front pages, newscasts and internet news pages—reward photogenic stories like fires and play them big, rather than less visually gripping issues like follow-up studies on safety.

Also contributing to the Bennett Model's passivity is that reporters wait for events. Waiting for a company to unveil its safety records can be a long wait. Very long. An important story that needs telling goes untold.

Deadline Haste.   Mass production, with all its incredible complexities, was the hallmark of the Industrial Age in which James Gordon Bennett and newspapers flourished. For mass production to work there needed to be a military-like confluence of raw materials, human labor and management genius. And deadlines. When it all worked, factories turned out things that had only been imagined before, but deadline pressure inevitably undermines quality whether the product is widgets or news. Ask Toyota after its massive 2009 and 2011 safety recalls. Or ask the Chicago *Tribune*, which has yet to outlive mockery for its Page 1 banner in 1948 that Thomas Dewey had been elected president of the United States. Yes, deadlines were met at *Tribune* that night, but indeed haste made waste: Truman won, Dewey lost.

Dullness.   At its most severe, the Bennett Model was spartan, shorn of any hints of reporters as anything more than mindless aggregators of facts that somehow, magically, spoke for themselves. Making sense of the facts was for the readers to do—no matter how slight the background a reader might possess to put the facts in any meaningful perspective. The premise that readers could be sufficiently knowledgeable on a broad range of subjects and issues was no longer valid, if ever it had been, in a world of growing complexities.

Also, the facts-only style was incredibly bland. Journalism scholar Dan Gillmor has made the point that culling a point-of-view out of news coverage had resulted in writing "some of the dullest prose on the planet."

Missed Trends.   The massive migration of black people out of the American South was one of the 20th century's most important and, alas, unreported stories. The immigration was historic and transforming, but even after decades the immigration was not reducible to an easily identifiable event. Operating with the Bennett Model's focus on events, the story of social injustice among the new generations of Northern black people went untold. For decades, outrage simmered somewhere outside the media's radar—until the 1960s, that is, when urban race riots erupted with horrible death tolls and destruction. The riots, of course, were impossible to miss. The riots were events, and they were reported. But the riots themselves represented years of journalistic failure.

What if reporters had seen beyond the superficiality of the Bennett Model and caught the social changes triggered by the black migration? What if reporters had examined the implications earlier? Had the nation been apprised of what was going on, there would have been opportunities to create public policy solutions to right the wrongs and ease tensions before the horrific blowups.

Questions Unasked.   An upshot of the Bennett Model was a slant toward authorities in news coverage. In covering a robbery, for example, reporters go to police for information. The cops are accessible, which means reporters can get a story together quickly. But why not also interview witnesses? Why not victims? That would mean a broader-based story. And when there's an arrest, why not try to interview the accused or the family, friends and acquaintances of the accused for a balance, a depth and a richness that doesn't come across from police and court sources. In short, the deadline pressure on reporters for fresh stories with a detached, neutral tone encourages authority-centric coverage that is one-sided and superficial.

On a national scale, superficial reporting in 1846 led to war against Mexico on a flimsy pretext. Bennett-style reporters told President Polk's official line to which reporters had easy access and didn't pursue anything more than the official sources. This can be said, too, about the U.S. government's false claim before the 2002 invasion that Iraq had weapons of mass destruction.

Manipulation.   When he was president from 1901 to 1909, Theodore Roosevelt joshed that he had "discovered Mondays." Recognizing that Sundays were what's called a "slow news day," with reporters having little new stuff to write for Monday morning editions, Roosevelt took to issuing statements to the press on Sundays. He knew his chances for front-page coverage were stronger on Mondays than any other day. Roosevelt understood the dynamics of the news business. The Bennett Model, which demanded fresh meat for the lions all the time, was vulnerable to manipulation by people who understood it. Roosevelt had figured out the processes of news in the Bennett Model, although his manipulation was quaint compared to what came later.

▶ CASE STUDY: The McCarthy Lessons

In 1950, a previously obscure U.S. senator from Wisconsin warned a Republican gathering in West Virginia about a communist spy ring inside the State Department. **Joseph McCarthy** suddenly was Page 1 news. How could it be otherwise: To most Americans at the time, communism was the sinister ideology behind aggressive and scary Soviet policies. The United States and the Soviet Union were engaged in jingoist rivalry as world powers. Considering the importance of a U.S. senator in national policy-making, reporters could hardly ignore McCarthy's words. By definition the West Virginia speech was newsworthy.

McCarthy reveled in the news coverage. A few days later in a Utah speech he repeated his charge, again hitting the headlines. In subsequent weeks McCarthy continued hammering away with his theme. Newspapers, movie newsreels and radio glommed onto McCarthy's every word. Applying deadline-driven journalistic practices, reporters got all the facts right. They quoted and paraphrased McCarthy accurately. But reporters failed to tell the truth—that McCarthy was a liar. To do so would have seemed opinionated and partisan—a violation of the idea, from the Bennett era, that news should be reported in an objective tone. The problem was that the truth would have appeared less than neutral and dispassionate.

There were clues aplenty that McCarthy was spinning fiction. His "list" of communists in the government fluctuated—205 one day, 81 another day, then 108. He mixed labels: Somebody was a communist one day and "inclined towards communism" on another. Reporters failed to press McCarthy in his slippery terminology. Was a communist necessarily a Soviet spy? McCarthy used labels like *communist, CPUSA member* and *loyalty risk*. News reporters focused on McCarthy's words with a penchant for verbatim accuracy. But they failed to examine McCarthy's discrepancies. Deadlines didn't allow time for fact-checking. Nor did reporters include background, including that McCarthy had fabricated his military record. No time to check on that. Nor did they report that McCarthy was a hopeless drunk whose thinking processes were increasingly muddled.

Question: Which would have been more truthful?

SALT LAKE CITY, Utah—Sen. Joseph McCarthy, R-Wis., declared 81 security risks are on the U.S. State Department payroll

SALT LAKE CITY, Utah—Sen. Joseph McCarthy, R-Wis., a drunk who falsified his war record in campaigning for the U.S. senate, repeated his charge that security risks are on the U.S. State

Joseph McCarthy
U.S. senator from Wisconsin; fueled anti-communist hysteria 1950-1954

▲ **Joseph McCarthy.** *The U.S. senator's fabrications about communist and Soviet infiltrations of government were reported accurately. McCarthy indeed said what he said. But he was lying. In retrospect, the issue for journalists is how to distinguish truth from falsity in what sources tell them, while also maintaining the detached neutral stance that news audiences expect.*

Joseph Pulitzer.

William
Randolph
Hearst.

▲ **Journalistic Sensationalism.**
Rival New York newspaper publishers Joseph Pulitzer and William Randolph Hearst tried to outdo each other daily with anti-Spanish atrocity stories from Cuba, many of them trumped up. Some historians say the public hysteria fueled by Pulitzer and Hearst helped to precipitate the Spanish-American War, especially after the U.S. battleship Maine exploded in Havana harbor. Both Pulitzer and Hearst claimed that it was a Spanish attack on an American vessel, although a case can be made that the explosion was accidental.

Department payroll, this time changing his figures to 81 persons and, as before, citing no specific sources or evidence.

These are extreme possibilities, but they illustrate that a barebones presentation of facts can be accurate but miss the truth. The fact is that McCarthy's inconsistencies and questionable behavior were left unexplored journalistically until **Edward R. Murrow** at the CBS television network exposed McCarthy for what he was—but that was in 1954, more than four years after McCarthy grabbed his first national headlines. And four years too late.

In the meantime, McCarthy had distracted the nation's attention from legitimate and pressing issues. The State Department, running scared at McCarthy's charges, barred works by leading U.S. literati from its overseas information libraries. The "suspect" authors included John Dewey, Edna Ferber, Dashiell Hammett and Theodore White. Inside the State Department, careers in the U.S. diplomatic corps were ruined. The smear tarnished a generation of aspiring public servants. Years later, reporter E.J. Kahn of the *New Yorker* magazine blamed McCarthy for the fumbling U.S. involvement in Vietnam. Kahn made a case that the State Department had been so decimated 15 years earlier by McCarthy's recklessness that the "China Hands," diplomats with knowledge of China and Asia, were mostly gone. The State Department had a vacuum of expert knowledge of Asian languages, cultures and peoples.

Indeed, there had been a journalistic failure. The Bennett Model for news, whatever its virtues, had shown flaws with its emphasis on superficial facts and deadlines and an obsession for appearances of objectivity.

Edward R. Murrow
CBS television reporter who confronted
McCarthy on demagoguery

APPLYING YOUR MEDIA LITERACY

- **What would James Gordon Bennett say about news practices today?**
- **How did economics factor into the dominance of the Bennett Model for so long in U.S. journalism?**
- **How can a mindless pursuit of the objective tone lead to journalistic failure? Cite examples.**

Journalism Traditions

Several periods in U.S. media history have contributed to the evolving concept of news, each adding refinements.

Colonial Press. In Boston in 1690 **Benjamin Harris** published the first newspaper, *Publick Occurrences*. He was in hot water right away. Harris scandalized Puritan sensitivities by alleging that the king of France had dallied with his son's wife. Other stories irritated the royal governor who shut the paper down. The stories amused readers, however. Although not surviving more than a single issue, *Publick Occurrences* was precursor to the idea that news is defined by reader interest, not government decree.

Printers of later colonial papers relied on subscriptions to stay in business, putting news into a capitalistic system. Although government-subsidized papers came and went, they never had the following of reader-supported papers.

The news business has been grounded through most of U.S. history in a for-profit environment. A lot of media behaviors—some say almost all—can be explained by the economic self-interests of the media owners.

Penny Press. A struggling printer, **Benjamin Day**, started the New York *Sun* in 1833 and sold copies at a penny apiece. Just about anybody could afford the *Sun*. More successful in drawing readers than any other paper, Day had a commercial success on his hands. Indeed, it can be said that Day discovered the mass audience. It didn't matter that Day lost money selling papers at a penny a copy because the *Sun's* circulation drew advertisers. They paid handsomely for space in the *Sun*, firmly establishing the financial structure of the U.S. news business as dependent on advertising revenue.

Mass Circulation. *The New York* **Sun** *was first to find a mass audience as we understand it today.*

Yellow Press. The quest to sell more copies led to excesses that are illustrated by the Pulitzer-Hearst circulation war in New York in the 1890s. **Joseph Pulitzer**, a poor immigrant, had made the St. Louis *Post-Dispatch* into a finance success. In 1883 Pulitzer decided to try a big city. He bought the New York *World*. He emphasized human interest, crusaded for reforms and worthy causes, and ran lots of promotional hoopla. Two year later a successful young San Francisco publisher, **William Randolph Hearst**, bought the New York *Journal* and vowed to out-Pulitzer Pulitzer. The inevitable resulted. Pulitzer and Hearst launched crazier and crazier stunts. Not even the comic pages escaped the competitive frenzy. Pulitzer ran the *Yellow Kid*, then Heart hired the cartoonist away, giving rise to the term **yellow journalism** as a derisive reference to sensationalistic excesses in news coverage that also marked both the Pulitzer and Hearst papers.

Yellow Journalism's Namesake. *The Yellow Kid, a popular cartoon character in New York newspapers in the 1890s, became the namesake for sensationalistic "yellow journalism."*

The excesses reached a feverish peak when Pulitzer and Hearst covered growing tension between Spain and the United States. Fueled by hyped atrocity stories, the tension exploded into war. One story, probably apocryphal, epitomizes the no-holds-barred competition between Pulitzer and Hearst: Although Spain had consented to all demands by the United Sates, Hearst sent artist Frederic Remington to Cuba to illustrate the situation, Remington cabled back: "Everything is quiet. There is no trouble here. There will be no war. Wish to return." Hearst replied: "Please remain. You furnish the pictures, I'll furnish the war." Whether Hearst wielded such power can be debated, but the power of news to effect history could not be denied.

As for sensationalism, the yellow tradition still lives as an element in news, especially in celebrity coverage.

Hutchins News Model

Robert Hutchins
Philosopher whose interests included news practices

Hutchins Commission
Recommended reforms in news practices to emphasize social responsibility

Benjamin Harris
Published *Publick Occurrences*

Publick Occurrences
First colonial newspaper, Boston, 1690

Benjamin Day
Printed first successful penny paper, New York *Sun*, 1833

STUDY PREVIEW

In 1947 the Hutchins Commission, a group of leading scholars, recommended updating the century-old Bennett Model to fit a changing media landscape and to correct flaws. A major change was to go beyond the facts in news coverage and put them in a meaningful context.

Hutchins Commission

In 1947, before Joseph McCarthy had been elected to the U.S. Senate, a group of scholars headed by one of the era's leading intellectual, **Robert Hutchins,** issued a report that called for news media to be socially responsible. The Commission on Freedom of the Press, more commonly called the **Hutchins Commission,** added dimension to the Bennett Model for news. The commission said that news needed to be presented in a meaningful context. The commission was less impressed with the superficial deadline-driven, fact-obsessed journalistic practices that had prevailed since Bennett's time than with "a truthful, comprehensive account of the day's events in a context which gives them meaning." This was significant reform. The Hutchins Commission's new emphasis was on truthfulness and understanding. Facts? Accuracy remained essential, but facts didn't count for much unless they contributed to understanding.

Mixed Reception

Old practices die hard. The Hutchins recommendations were disavowed by *Life* and *Time* magazine publisher Henry Luce, who had funded the commission over the four years that the commissioners, all academics, spent thinking through long-held premises for journalistic practice. Other critics criticized the commission members as out-of-touch eggheads. The influential publisher Robert McCormick of the Chicago *Tribune* commissioned one of his reporters to write a book rebutting the commission. Gradually, however, a post-Bennett sensitivity took root—in no small part because of the journalism-enabled McCarthy travesties that began in 1950.

Also, a 1948 textbook by **Curtis McDougal,** *Interpretative Reporting,* was building traction in journalism schools with its thrust on reporting that sought not just to relay information but to make sense of it.

Critics railed against **editorializing** if news reporters ventured into putting information in a perspective. On the other side, as media scholar Dan Gillmor has put it more recently, there need be no conflict between "having a worldview and doing great journalism."

Changing News Dynamics

New platforms for news opened cracks in the Bennett Model, first with radio, then, more significantly, with television. In the 1920s when radio was emerging as a news medium, people heard human voices delivering the news. News suddenly was connected with personality. This was unlike the anonymity of unsigned stories in the newspapers of the time.

Television.   When news became a television staple in the 1950s, people not only heard but saw reporters. This gave television news an additional personal dimension. The anonymity of news, a component of the Bennett Model, was broken.

Television formats also undermined the Bennett Model of delivering news as fact devoid of interpretation. Television formats favored brief stories, typically with reporters having 60 seconds to work with roughly 140 words. That's six or seven sentences—hardly enough, except for the simplest stories, for audience members to make any sense of the facts. Of necessity, television reporters developed techniques, mostly in wrapping up their brief stories that provided what the Hutchins Commission called "meaningful context." Consider these:

> That's what the defense attorneys claim. And they don't square at all with the police reports. Now it's up to the jurors to decide who is telling the truth.

> The Jurgen political ads are incendiary to say the least. The question now: How will Rodriguez respond?

Those kinds of context-creating comments were unthinkable in pre-television news practices. They helped open the door beyond a just-the-facts style of reporting.

Internet.   In the 1990s the internet opened access to large audiences to just about anybody who had something to say. You didn't need a journalism degree or any indoctrination in age-old journalistic practices to blog. Unlike the Bennett Model, blogging was full of contextualized facts. The result was further audience acceptance of contextualized information.

Media Literacy.   The growth in audience sophistication also contributed to a broadened sense of shortcomings in the Bennett Model. The sophistication also signaled a new onus on audiences to sort through not only facts and but also a multiplicity of contexts in which different reporters cast coverage.

APPLYING YOUR MEDIA LITERACY

- **What are the distinctions between interpretive reporting and editorializing and how can audiences determine one from the other?**
- **What helped overcome the initial kneejerk negativism to the Hutchins recommendations?**

Joseph Pulitzer
Emphasized human interest in newspapers; later moved sensationalism to greater heights

William Randolph Hearst
Built circulation with sensationalism

yellow journalism
Sensationalized news accounts

Curtis McDougal
His journalism textbook advocated interpretation

editorializing
Opinionated comments that go beyond just stating the straightforward reporting

▲ **Robert Hutchins and Meaningful Context.** *The Hutchins Commission called on news media in 1947 to adjust their definition of news. The commission called for a "truthful, comprehensive, and intelligent account of the day's events in a context which gives them meaning."*

Rethinking News Models

STUDY PREVIEW

Earlier paradigms for news have become obsolete by technology-generated changes in mass media. Among the changes has been as explosion of news sources and approaches and concurrent audience fragmentation. A hybrid news model is evolving to meld perspective with straightforward coverage. A hybrid model from the New York *Times* uses a complex labeling system to alert readers to stories with perspective.

Transforming News Environments

The environments in which news businesses functioned were very different in the eras when the Bennett Model dominated and later when the Hutchins Model gained traction. Although no year clearly delineates the two eras, a useful dividing point is 1947 when the Hutchins Commission called for reforms.

Abundant Newspaper Dailies. In Bennett's time, pre-1947 and also before broadcasting, most people had access to news from several local or nearby newspapers. The idea was that

MEDIAtimeline

NEWS MILESTONES

JAIL TIME
Colonial printers to jail for irking authorities: William Bradford (1692), James Franklin (1722), John Peter Zenger (1733)

ZENGER TRIUMPH
Jury freed John Peter Zenger despite his newspaper's criticism of royal governor (1735)

POLITICAL SPONSORSHIP
Party Press Period reflected newspaper sponsorship by political partisanship (1791–1932)

PIVOTAL EVENTS

- Lexington skirmish started Revolutionary War (1775)
- Congress passed laws to suppress criticism of government (1798)
- Jefferson presidency (1801–1809)
- Jackson presidency (1829–1837)

NEWS MILESTONES

MASS AUDIENCE
Ben Day founded New York *Sun* at a penny a copy (1833)

Bennett Model for news begins long run

MODERN NEWS
James Gordon Bennett established systematic news coverage, emphasizing speed (1840s)

TELEGRAPH
Samuel Morse invented telegraph, leading to *lightning news* (1844)

ASSOCIATED PRESS
AP predecessor formed as news cooperative (1848)

PIVOTAL EVENTS

- Public education took root as a social value (1820s)
- Factory jobs fueled urban growth (1830s–)
- Waves of immigration added to urbanization (1830s–)
- Harriet Beecher Stowe wrote Uncle Tom's Cabin (1852)
- Charles Darwin wrote On Species (1859)
- Civil War (1861–1865)
- Trans-Atlantic cable operable (1866)
- Transcontinental railroad (1969)

NEWS MILESTONES

NEWS INDUSTRY
Newspaper clearly firm as a major profit-driven industry (1880s)

YELLOW PRESS
Sensationalistic excesses (1880s)

HEARST-PULITZER WAR
Joseph Pulitzer arrived in New Yorkjournalism (1883); William Randolph Hearst arrived (1895)

OCHS FAMILY
Adolph Ochs bought New York Times (1896

PIVOTAL EVENTS

- Populism widened effective political participation (1880s–)
- Samuel Gompers founded American Federation of Labor predecessor (1881)
- Spanish-American War (1898)

Yellow Kid, cartoon namesake for an era

1800–1832

1833–1869

1870–1899

these papers would be driven to improve their coverage by competing for readers. It was a marketplace model typical of the period, with robust and unfettered competition fully seen as capable of serving the public good.

One-Paper Towns.   By the mid-1900s, the number of competing dailies had diminished. An era of one-paper towns was on the horizon. This new environment worried the Hutchins Commission scholars. Competition was less an incentive for newspapers to better service the information needs of the public. Although radio was gaining a role in the news arena by 1947, when the Hutchins Commission issued its recommendations, newspapers remained the dominant news medium by far. Television news was yet to be invented.

Responding toward one-paper towns, the Hutchins Commission called on newspapers to shift their focus from free-market competition to being self-inspired to be socially responsible. It was undeniable that competition was waning as a dynamic to fuel a high quality of public service. Gradually, the idea of social responsibility as a driving force in news took hold, albeit unevenly.

Audience Fragmentation.   Today the Hutchins Model premise about a shrinking universe of news sources is no longer valid. Television networks long ago became a significant rival to newspapers for national news. The establishment of the 500-plus channel television universe with

NEWS MILESTONES

MUCKRAKING
Ida Tarbell and journalism aimed at reform (1902–)

RADIO
Presidential returns broadcast (1916)

HUTCHINS COMMISSION
Recommendation to re-orient to promote understanding (1947)

INTERPRETIVE REPORTING
Curtis McDougall's textbook urged reporting news in a context (1948)

PIVOTAL EVENTS

- World War I (1914–1918)
- 18th Amendment ended prohibition (1919)
- 19th Amendment allowed women to vote (1920)
- Radio emerged as commercial medium (late 1920s)
- Great Depression (1930s)
- World War II (1941–1945)
- Russian-Western Cold War (1945–1989)

New York *Daily News* reporting Watergate

1900–1949

NEWS MILESTONES

MCCARTHYISM
Senator Joseph McCarthy began feeding false information to press (1950)

NEWSPAPERPEAK
Newspaper circulation at 63.3 million (1964)

HOT-COOL MEDIA
Marshall McLuhan wrote *Gutenberg Galaxy* (1962), *Medium Is the Massage* (cq) (1967), *War and Peace in the Global Village* (1968)

WATERGATE
Confidential sources key in covering scandal (1972)

TELEVISION
CNN introduced 24-hour news cycle (1980)

PARTISAN NEWS
Fox News launched, skewing coverage to right (1996)

PIVOTAL EVENTS

- Television emerged as commercial medium (early 1950s)
- Vietnam War (1964–1973)
- Race riots follow Martin Luther King Jr. assassination (1968)
- Internet emerged as commercial medium (late 1990s)

1950–1999

NEWS MILESTONES

REFINING INTERNET LANGUAGE
HTML5 introduced (2007)

INDUSTRY REALIGNMENT
Newspapers, magazines falter with rise of Iinternet as news platform (2008–)

PARSING COVERAGE
New York *Times* introduced fine-tune labeling for news (2010)

PIVOTAL EVENTS

- 9/11 terrorist attacks (2001)
- Iraq War (2003–2010)
- Afghan War (2001–)
- Economic recession (2007–2009)
- BP oil spill in the Gulf of Mexico (2010)
- World population passed 7 billion (2011)

Rachel Maddow, news from a left perspective

2000s

cable and satellite delivery further strengthened television's hold on the news. Audiences fragmented into niches that met narrower interests, including news geared to sub-audiences within the mass audience. By 1996, when media mogul Rupert Murdoch launched Fox News, there was a clear audience for ideologically spun programming. The audience fragmentation then accelerated exponentially with the internet. A whole new news environment has shaken the premises underlying both the Bennett and Hutchins models.

Hybrid News Models

The transition into yet another new model for news is not easy. Significant parts of the news audience take comfort in the fact-centric Bennett Model. Other parts of the audience want information in a meaningful context. At no place more than the New York *Times*, the premiere newspaper in the United States, is this tension more evident. The *Times* has restated its commitment to the tradition in the fact-centric event coverage extolled in the Bennett Model, but acknowledges that other journalistic forms, including the meaningful context prescribed by the Hutchins Commission, can add important perspective.

The result at the *Times* is a hybrid form of reporting, generally with labels on articles that go beyond straightforward news reporting. The *Times'* detailed categorization of articles with perspective both in print and online may seem strained if not tedious, but it is an attempt to navigate the wide range of reader expectations that flow from the Bennett and Hutchins periods. These are some of the major categories that the *Times* has devised:

News Analysis: Under this label, thorough reporting draws heavily on the expertise of the reporter. The goal: To help readers understand underlying cases or possible consequences without reflecting the writer's personal opinion.

Appraisal: These usually accompany an obituary, with a critic or specialized writer offering a broad evaluation of the career or work or a major figure.

Reporter's Notebook: These are behind-the-scene glimpses, usually anecdotes or brief reports from an on-scene reporter, to flesh out the reader's sense of a major story.

Memo: These are reflective articles, often informal and conversational, offering a behind-the-scenes look that connects several events. An example was Memo from Paris by Steven Erlanger headlined: "Films Open French Wounds from Algeria."

News Column: A regularly scheduled essay on the news with original insight or perspective and a distinct point of view.

Journal: These are sharply focused and stylishly written articles that rely on the writer's observations to give readers a vivid sense of a place, an event or a time.

Man in the News: This label, or, as appropriate, Woman in the News, is for articles offering portraits of a central figure in a news situation, featuring background and career details that shed light on a current event while being analytical.

Review: These are evaluations of movies, books, restaurants and fashion and other creative works from specialized critics who are expected to render their opinions.

The Caucus: These online articles on politics and government encourage bloggers to add their two cents' worth.

The *Times*, meanwhile, has retained its opinion section, which itself is labeled as such. A distinction the *Times* makes is that news coverage is not opinion but rather observational detail and perspective that reflects a reporter's expertise and judgment without treading into persuasion. The home for persuasion is the opinion section.

APPLYING YOUR MEDIA LITERACY

- How does traditional U.S. news reporting that stops short of perspective and context affect audience interest?
- What has been the most influential factor in broadening the concept of news in the United States?
- Should people be wary of hybrid news models like that being used by the New York *Times*?

Personal Values in News

STUDY PREVIEW | Journalists make important decisions on which events, phenomena and issues are reported and which are not. The personal values journalists bring to their work and that therefore determine which stories are told, and also how they are told, generally coincide with mainstream American values.

Role of the Journalist

Even with Bennett Model's values-free pretext under which most mainstream U.S. journalism functions, values cannot be wished out of existence. The fact is that journalists make choices. NBC newscaster Chet Huntley, after years of trying to come up with a definition of news, threw up his hands and declared: "News is what I decide is news." Huntley wasn't being arrogant. Rather, he was pointing out that there are no clinical criteria for news that sidestep human judgment about which stories to tell and how to tell them. Even if an event has intrinsic qualities as news, such as the prominence of the people involved and the event's consequence and drama, it becomes news only when it's reported. Huntley's point was that the journalist's judgment is indispensable in deciding what is news.

Huntley's conclusion underscores the high degree of autonomy that individual journalists have in shaping what is reported. The First Amendment of the U.S. Constitution guarantee of a free press, which prohibits government regulation, also contributes to the independence and autonomy. Constitutionally, journalists cannot be licensed. The news practices embodied in the Bennett Model, including a commitment to accuracy, served informally as a check against abuses. Those checks, however, are less effective with the opening of an impossible-to-track number of sources of information in our age of 24-hour cable and internet news.

Objectivity

Despite the high quotient of judgment in deciding what changes to report, a lot of people use the term *objectivity* to describe news. By this they mean a value-free process in making choices about what to tell and how to tell it. It's a self-contradictory concept: Choice, by definition, is never value-free. So how did we end up with this idea that news should be objective when it cannot be? History has the answer.

- **Penny Press.** Part of the answer goes back to the era of Ben Day and his New York *Sun*, the first of the penny papers with a mass audience. Day looked for stories with mass appeal. Suddenly, what made the paper was not the opinionated ramblings of the preceding partisan press but stories chosen to appeal to the largest possible audience. Opinion was out, storytelling in. The writer became subordinate to the tale, even to the point of near-invisibility. No more first person. Facts carried the story.

- **Associated Press.** Several cost-conscious New York newspaper publishers agreed in 1848 to a joint venture to cover distant news. The Associated Press, as they called the venture, saved a lot of money. It also transformed U.S. journalism in a way that was never anticipated. Inherent in the AP concept was that its stories needed to be nonpartisan to be usable by all of its member newspapers, whose political persuasions spanned the spectrum. The result was an emphasis, some say fetish, on fact-driven journalism devoid of even a hint of partisanship.

- **Newspaper Economics.** Another fundamental shift cemented the detached, neutral AP tone, often characterized as objective. News became profitable—highly so. The fortune that Benjamin Day made with the New York *Sun* in the mid-1830s was puny compared with the Pulitzer, Hearst and other news empires that came within 50 years. These super-publishers saw their newspapers as money machines as much as political tools. The bottom line gradually and inevitably gained more weight. The safest route to continue building their mass audiences and enhancing revenue was to avoid antagonizing readers and advertisers. There was money to be made in presenting news in as neutral a tone as possible. Picking up a lesson from the AP, but with a different motivation—to make money rather than save money—profit-driven publishers came to favor information-driven news.

By the early 20th century, when news practices became institutionalized in the first journalism textbooks and in the formation of professional journalistic organizations, the notion of a detached, neutral presentation was firmly ensconced. Ethics codes, new at the time, dismissed other approaches as unacceptable and unethical, even though they had been dominant only three generations earlier. The word *objectivity* became a newsroom mantra.

To be sure, there are exceptions to the detached, neutral presentation, but traditionalists are quick to criticize the departures. The goal is to keep the reporter, even the reporter's inherently necessary judgment, as invisible in the presentation as possible.

Journalists' Personal Values

The traditional journalistic ideal, an unbiased seeking of truth and an unvarnished telling of it, remains a core value with mainstream media. Yet as human beings, journalists have values that influence all that they do, including their work. What do we know about these values among mainstream journalists.

As a sociologist who studied stories in the American news media for 20 years, **Herbert Gans** concluded that journalists have a typical American values system. Gans identified primary values, all in the American mainstream, that journalists use in making their news judgments:

Herbert Gans
Concluded that journalists have mainstream values

Ethnocentrism. American journalists see things through American eyes, which colors news coverage. In the 1960s and 1970s, Gans noted, North Vietnam was consistently characterized as "the enemy." U.S. reporters took the view of the U.S. government and military, which was hardly detached or neutral. This **ethnocentrism** was clear at the end of the war, which U.S. media headlined as "the *fall* of South Vietnam." By other values, Gans said, the communist takeover of Saigon could be considered a *liberation.* In neutral terms, it was a *change in government.*

ethnocentrism
Seeing things on the basis of personal experience and values

This ethnocentrism has created problems as news media have become more global. Is it not ethnocentric and less than neutral for a reporter embedded with a U.S. infantry unit to use the term *enemy.* Imagine the challenge for a diplomatic reporter for a global news agency in Tehran or in Washington. In reports on the Iraq and Afghanistan wars, this has been an issue for Atlanta-based CNN and Doha-based Al-Jazeera.

Democracy and Capitalism. Gans found that U.S. journalists favor U.S.-style democracy. Coverage of other governmental forms dwells on corruption, conflict, protest and bureaucratic malfunction. The unstated idea of most U.S. journalists, said Gans, is that other societies do best when they follow the American ideal of serving the public interest.

Gans also found that U.S. journalists are committed to the capitalist economic system. Even in the economic crisis that began in 2008, news coverage remained committed to capitalism as an economic system. Greed, corruption, misbehavior and bad business practices were treated as aberrations that required corrections. The underlying posture of the news coverage of the U.S. economy, as Gans observed, is "an optimistic faith" that businesspeople refrain from unreasonable profits and gross exploitation of workers or customers while competing to create increased prosperity for all. In covering controlled foreign economies, U.S. journalists emphasize the downside.

It may seem only natural to most Americans that democracy and capitalism should be core values of any reasonable human being. This sense itself is an ethnocentric value, which many people do not even think about but which nonetheless shapes how they conduct their lives. Knowing that U.S. journalists by and large share this value explains a lot about the news coverage they create.

Tempered Individualism. Gans found that U.S. journalists love stories about rugged individuals who overcome adversity and defeat powerful forces. Although journalists like to turn individuals into heroes, there are limits. Rebels and deviates are portrayed as extremists who go beyond another value: moderation. To illustrate this bias toward moderation Gans noted that "the news treats atheists as extremists and uses the same approach, if more gingerly, with religious fanatics. People who consume conspicuously are criticized, but so are people such as hippies who turn their backs on consumer goods. The news is scornful both of the overly academic scholar and the oversimplifying popularizer. It is kind neither to highbrows nor to lowbrows, to users of jargon or users of slang. College students who play when they should study receive disapproval, but so do 'grinds.' Lack of moderation is wrong, whether it involves excesses or abstention."

Social Order. Journalists cover disorders—earthquakes, hurricanes, industrial catastrophes, protest marches, the disintegrating nuclear family and transgressions of laws and mores. This coverage, noted Gans, is concerned not with glamorizing disorder but with finding ways to restore order. Coverage of an oil spill and the recovery goes on for days, even weeks as in the case of the BP oil spill in the Gulf of Mexico. The media focus is far more on restoring order than on covering death and destruction.

The journalistic commitment to social order also is evident in how heavily reporters rely on people in leadership roles as primary sources of information. These leaders, largely representing the Establishment and the status quo, are the people in the best position to maintain social order and to restore it if there's disruption. This means government representatives often shape news media reports and thus their audiences' understanding of what is important, "true" or meaningful. No one receives more media attention than the president of the United States, who is seen, said Gans, "as the ultimate protector of order."

Watchdog Function. The idea that the news media serve a **watchdog function** in American life is implicit in the First Amendment to the U.S. Constitution, which bars the government from interfering with the press. Since the nation was founded, journalists have been expected to keep the people holding positions of public trust honest and responsible to the electorate by reporting on government activities, including shortcomings.

watchdog function
The news media role to monitor the performance of government and other institutions of society

In performing their watchdog function, reporters often find themselves accused of partisan bias. Generally, the truth is that journalists are handy whipping boys when news is less than positive. The classic case was in 1968 when the White House had been beset with unfavorable news. Vice President Spiro Agnew, addicted as he was to alliteration, called the press "nattering nabobs of negativism." Successive presidential administrations, Democratic and Republican alike, have been no less gentle in charging the media with bias whenever news isn't what they want told.

This is not to suggest that journalists are perfect or always accurate, especially in reporting confusing situations against deadline. Nor is it to suggest that there are no partisans peppered among reporters in the press corps. But critics, usually themselves partisans, too often are reflexive with a cheap charge of bias when reporters are, as one wag put it, doing their job to keep the rascals in power honest. In the process of doing their work, journalists sometimes indeed become facilitators of change—but as reporters, not advocates.

APPLYING YOUR MEDIA LITERACY

- **How did so many people come to the vexatious opinion that news should be objective?**
- **How would you propose the licensing or certifying of journalists be accomplished?**
- **Find examples of journalistic ethnocentricity in current news, or partiality to U.S.-style democracy and capitalism, or lionizing of individualism, or reporters serving a watchdog function. What do all of these reports have in common?**

Variables Affecting News

STUDY PREVIEW

The variables that determine what is reported include things beyond a journalist's control, such as how much space or time is available to tell stories. Also, a story that might receive top billing on a slow news day might not even appear on a day when an overwhelming number of major stories are breaking.

MEDIApeople

■ Clever, Smart, Dorky?

▲ **Rachel Maddow.** *Rachel Maddow broke into the old boys' club of cable television, dominated by Bill O'Reilly at Fox, Larry King at CNN and Keith Olbermann at MSNBC, with a distinctive take on political news.*

What Do You Think?

Do you see room on television for the news and perspective hybrid that Rachel Maddow epitomizes? Or would you prefer your news straight and perhaps even bland if not dull?

How many Maddow-like approaches to political news can you find on network television? On network radio? On local television and radio?

Rachel Maddow was no ordinary kid. At 4, her mother remembers, little Rachel would perch on a kitchen stool as her mom fixed breakfast and, still in pajamas, read the newspaper. At 7, during the 1980 presidential campaign, Maddow remembers an intense repulsion to Ronald Reagan on television.

Maddow, now a leading political commentator on the political left, can't explain her Reagan-loathing as a grade-schooler. Noting Reagan's political conservatism, Maddow quips that some kind of "reverse engineering" must have set in. It's a self-deprecating line typical of Maddow's quick humor that draws audience chuckles and then double takes as the irony settles in.

The fact is that Maddow is hardly a slouch intellectually. She roots what she says on premises, not on whatever instinctive gut reactions may have been playing on her when she was 7. Maddow holds a degree from Stanford University in public policy. Then she won a Rhodes scholarship for an Oxford doctorate in political science.

Maddow has a common touch that goes beyond her trademark 501 baggy jeans and sneakers. Yes, that's how Maddow showed up for work at the radio network Air America, where she started a talk show in 2004. Maddow didn't change her style when, at age 35, the MSNBC television network gave her a show during the 2008 heated presidential campaign. The button-down MSNBC culture in Manhattan hasn't affected Maddow. She says she's still comfortable dressing like a 13-year-old boy. Before going on the air nightly at MSNBC, however, she pulls a pantsuit from a closet of identical suits. She calls her style "butch dyke."

The common touch is more than wardrobe. Maddow earned money in college heavy-lifting. For a while she unloaded trucks. She also did yard-clearing for a landscaper. Then there was a job putting stamps on coffee packets. For reading she's as at home with Malthus and Machiavelli as with graphic novels.

At MSNBC in the intensive 2008 presidential campaign Maddow quickly doubled the 9 p.m. Eastern audience to 1.9 million. Among viewers 25 to 54, she outdrew the CNN icon Larry King 27 of 44 nights in her first two months.

Her work ethic from college has carried into her career. Her days run 16 hours. She admits to getting only a couple hours of "drunk sleep" some nights.

Maddow's drive is contagious. Her crew at MSNBC, political junkies in their 20s and 30s, uses the same term "drunk sleep" and concedes to crankiness as they show up at mid-afternoon to brainstorm themes with Maddow for the night's show. The sessions harken to those all-night free-form college dorm jams on imponderables.

Maddow, lanky and 6 foot, flops on the floor however she's comfortable at the moment. Bubbling through the give-and-take is a rich mixture of optimism for the future and skepticism about politicians—and bedrock patriotism. The session is heavy on the day's events and questions that need to be asked and on guests to line up to address the issues. Maddow twirls and lobs a foam basketball. Shifting her body on the floor, she scribbles ideas in a notebook.

The loosely structured planning is all rehearsal for Maddow—a kind of free-form cerebral internalizing. On air there is focus, although an informal feel that has attracted the young audience that the major television networks covet. There's a practiced sneering, her sarcasm punctuated with a trademark "Duh." Cliches, none. There is no doubt of Maddow being bright, authentic and original.

To be sure, Maddow has detractors. Her innuendos and nudge-nudge, wink-wink comments have been called theatrical and biased. Others see Maddow as finding a flavorful balance that is substantive and distinctly refreshing. For sure, Maddow resonates with a mass audience that finds the old boys' club that has dominated cable television suddenly stuffy.

News Hole

A variable affecting what ends up being reported as news is called the **news hole.** In newspapers the news hole is the space left after the advertising department has placed all the ads it has sold in the paper. The volume of advertising determines the number of total pages, and generally, the bigger the issue, the more room for news. Newspaper editors can squeeze fewer stories into a thin Monday issue than a fat Wednesday issue.

In broadcasting, the news hole tends to be more consistent. A 30-minute television newscast may have room for only 23 minutes of news, but the format doesn't vary. When the advertising department doesn't sell all seven minutes available for advertising, it usually is public-service announcements, promotional messages and program notes—not news—that pick up the slack. Even so, the news hole can vary in broadcasting. A 10-minute newscast can accommodate more stories than a five-minute newscast, and, as with newspapers, it is the judgment of journalists that determines which events make it.

News hole, of course, is a non-issue on the internet.

news hole
Space for news in a newspaper after ads are inserted; time in a newscast for news after ads

News Flow

Besides the news hole, the **news flow** varies from day to day. A story that might be displayed prominently on a slow news day can be passed over entirely in the competition for space on a heavy news day.

On one of the heaviest news days of all time—June 4, 1989—death claimed Iran's Ayatollah Khomeini, a central figure in U.S. foreign policy; Chinese young people and the government were locked in a showdown in Tiananmen Square; the Polish people were voting to reject their one-party communist political system; and a revolt was under way in the Soviet republic of Uzbekistan. That flow of major nation-rattling events pre-empted many stories that otherwise would have been considered news.

Heavy news days cannot be predicted. One would have occurred if there had been a confluence on a single day of these events: Hurricane Katrina, the BP Deepwater Horizon oil platform explosion, the death of Osama bin Laden, the conviction of Michael Jackson's physician, the Japanese tsunami nuclear disaster, the shooting of Congresswoman Gabby Gifford, and the 3,000th U.S. combat death in Afghanistan.

In a broader sense, an issue like global warming with the future of the planet at stake can end up neglected. In 2012, for example, coverage of health-care reforms, war in Afghanistan and the presidential election squeezed out climate change as an issue in U.S. news media.

news flow
Significance of events worth covering varies from day to day

News Staffing

Another variable affecting news is **staffing.** News coverage is affected by whether reporters are in the right place at the right time. A newsworthy event in Nigeria will receive short shrift on U.S. television if the network correspondents for Africa are occupied with a natural disaster in next-door Cameroon. A radio station's city government coverage will slip when the city hall reporter is on vacation or if the station can't afford a substitute reporter at city hall.

staffing
Available staff resources to cover news

Perceptions About Audience

How a news organization perceives its audience affects news coverage. The *National Enquirer* lavishes attention on unproven cancer cures that the New York *Times* treats briefly if at all. The *Wall Street Journal* sees its purpose as news for readers who have special interests in finance, the economy and business. The Bloomberg cable network was established to serve an audience more interested in quick market updates, brief analysis and trendy consumer news than the kind of depth offered by the *Journal.*

The perception that a news organization has of its audience is evident in a comparison of stories on different networks' newscasts. CNN may lead newscasts with a coup d'état in another country, while Bloomberg leads with a new government economic forecast and Comedy Central with the announcement of a comedian's tour.

Competition

Two triggers of adrenaline for journalists are landing a scoop and, conversely, being scooped. Journalism is a competitive business, and the drive to outdo other news organizations keeps news publications and newscasts fresh with new material. Competition has an unglamorous side. Journalists constantly monitor each other to identify events that they missed and need to catch up on to be competitive. This catch-up aspect of the news business contributes to similarities in coverage, which scholar Leon Sigal calls the **consensible nature of news.** It also is called "pack" and "herd" journalism.

In the final analysis, news is the result of journalists scanning their environment and making decisions, first on whether to cover certain events and then on how to cover them. The decisions are made against a backdrop of countless variables, many of them changing during the reporting, writing and editing processes.

consensible nature of news
News organization second-guessing competition in deciding coverage

---

APPLYING YOUR MEDIA LITERACY

- **Why does the news hole variable affect media platforms differently?**
- **How is news coverage affected by the number of reporters available to cover a story and their varying expertise levels on all issues?**
- **How is audience a factor in determining news coverage?**
- **What evidence of herd journalism can you spot in current coverage? How can it be avoided? Should it?**

Quality of News

STUDY PREVIEW

The advent of internet news has eroded some standard operating practices in newsrooms that historically had given readers a high level of expectation for accuracy and judgment. One standard is firm, that news is non-fiction. A reality remains, however, that news is a function of judgment by reporters and others in the information-gathering and information-packing process. The multiple contributors and varying levels of human intelligence, values and judgment involved in the process makes gatekeeping a complex enterprise.

News as Non-Fiction

Everyone accepts accuracy as bedrock in news. This penchant for accuracy can be traced to the first criticisms of falsity and distortions in news. This became explicit in the outrage over the Great Moon Hoax, a series of items in Benjamin Day's New York *Sun* in 1835. Writer Richard Locke described bird-like creatures spotted on the moon through a new powerful telescope. Readers gobbled up the story. Whether competing newspaper publishers were outraged more at the fantasy-as-news or at losing readers to the *Sun* can be debated. The fact, however, is that a chorus erupted for accuracy and truthfulness in news.

A penchant for accuracy became institutionalized in codes of ethics, first with a code from the American Society of Newspaper Editors in 1923.

As 'tis often said, to err is human. And mistakes creep into news, which is regrettable but usually forgiven. Serial sloppiness with facts, however, has become a near-cardinal sin in traditional newsrooms, and fabrication a cause of immediate dismissal. Take the case of Jayson Blair and the New York *Times*. Blair resigned after both plagiarism and fabrication were found in his news stories and the *Times* did major damage control to salvage its reputation. Now anyone can create a one-person news operation online. The widely held standard for accuracy has become less, well, less a standard. Many of these self-styled and self-proclaimed journalists are untrained in post-Moon Hoax news ethics and practices and unsteeped in traditional newsroom traditions.

▲ Richard Locke.

▲ **Great Moon Hoax.** *As a lark, Richard Locke penned a brief news item for the New York* Sun *in 1835 that a South Africa telescope had spotted winged humanlike creatures flitting from crater to crater on the moon. Locke offered further embellishment for several days and goosed* Sun *readership. But then Locke was found out and he resigned. The upshot was a firm focus on accuracy in news reporting, albeit with notable lapses and, of course, human error.*

Gatekeeping as Creative

More complex than accuracy is the newsroom function of gatekeeping, which also is less at work in small-staff upstart newsrooms. So what is gatekeeping? Not everything can be reported because of practicalities—not enough room in the paper, not enough time in a newscast, not enough staff to pursue all stories. Decisions need to be made on what to tell. These decisions are made by **gatekeepers.** Their job is to exercise news judgment, deciding what most deserves to be told and how.

Gatekeeping can be a creative force. Trimming a news story can add potency. A news producer can enhance a reporter's field report with file footage. An editor can call a public relations person for additional detail to illuminate a point in a reporter's story. A news-magazine's editor can consolidate related stories and add context that makes an important interpretive point. Most gatekeepers are invisible to the news audience, working behind the scenes and making crucial decisions in near anonymity on how the world will be portrayed in the evening newscast, the latest blog posting and frequent web site updates. With the smaller staffs of many web newsrooms, some of them one-person shops, fewer hands and eyes and minds process and sort incoming information and material.

Also, so many voices are out there that it becomes more difficult for civic-minded citizens to find the kind of journalistic leadership that marked an earlier era. Jill Edy, a communication scholar at the University of Oklahoma, says that the "collective memory" created for the public by professional news people is at risk: "It's likely instead that 'the media' will continue to multiply and morph into a thousand different voices and versions and visions. Under such conditions, how will a collective memory be formed? Will it be observed? Where, in the future, will we find collective memory?"

Aggregation Sites

The incredibly low cost of entry into web news has spawned thousands of news sites. Matt Drudge had merely a primitive 286 computer and a modem. Today, with his site generating advertising revenue, Drudge is a millionaire. Like many news sites, the *Drudge Report* offers less original reporting than aggregated news from elsewhere, including core Associated Press coverage and links to many sources, plus a bevy of opinion writers. These **aggregation sites** serve largely as portals to comprehensive coverage.

gatekeepers
Media people influencing messages en route

aggregation sites
News sites that regurgitate news compiled from elsewhere or that offer pass-through links to other sources

MEDIAtomorrow

■ The One-foot Media Experience

Although the Canadian thinker Marshall McLuhan did most of his works in the 1960s, his ideas still shape how many scholars see the interplay of people and media. It was McLuhan who identified media experiences as hot or cool or in between, depending on how thoroughly the audience was engaged. Although McLuhan refined and reworked his media concepts over a career of writing, firm in his legacy is the idea that media can be understood on a hot-cool continuum.

So what's hot? What's cool? Ink-on-paper media are hot. A reader has to choose to engage. Picking up a book, for example, is a deliberate act. Reading then requires focus and concentration to derive the message. The engagement is intimate and all-consuming, or in a word, hot. Even casual reading requires engagement, although not as intense as Faulkner, Shakespeare, Tolstoy or a textbook.

Media that don't require near-total engagement are cool. Elevator music is about as cool as you can get. Nobody thinks twice about exiting the elevator when the door opens. Disengagement is easy.

In contrast, viewing a movie in a theatre can be a total experience. Being cocooned without distractions in a darkened auditorium is highly experiential. Suspending disbelief comes as easily as being absorbed in a compelling novel. Movie-going is a hot media experience. A

Updating McLuhan. *The idea of pigeonholing media along a hot-cool continuum dates to the Canadian thinker Marshall McLuhan in the mid-20th century. But technology kike HTML5 is facilitating the delivery of media content both to cool devices, like television screens viewed from several feet away, and to held-held devices that require hot user engagement that's as focused and intent as reading a book.*

movie on your iPad, smart phone or portable DVD player? Not so much. You can talk to someone in the next chair, car seat, or on the checkout line while watching a movie on a hand-held device.

McLuhan, who died in 1980, never saw a smartphone or an iPad. But McLuhan's insights are playing out in new paradigms that compare media by eyeball-to-screen measures:

- TEN-FOOT MEDIA. Typically a television set is viewed from 10 feet, which somehow allows people to feel at ease disengaging. You converse with people in the room. You get up and do some other things, either disengaging yourself from the content for a while or multitasking.

- TWO-FOOT MEDIA. With a desktop computer, people sit roughly two feet from the screen. People are more engaged than with 10-foot media, partly because the internet offers countless more choices than today's over-air, cable and satellite television delivery systems. Also, focusing on the screen narrows peripheral vision.

- ONE-FOOT MEDIA. McLuhan would say that mobile devices—handheld with screens up close and personal, require the same engagement as a book. With handheld devices, people don't multitask. They're holding the device in their hands and staring into it. There's not that much else they can really be doing. The former digital president of MSNBC, Charles Tillinghast, put it this way: "They're very intentional in terms that they're selecting themselves. They have control of that clip. They're going to watch it as long as they want and no longer. The comprehension of that content will be higher. A higher level of engagement is what we're seeing on a mobile." In other words, using McLuhan's continuum, one-foot media are hot.

- DISTANT MEDIA. The engagement "temperature" of media viewed from more than a television set's 10 feet depends on other factors. A billboard, designed to be read at 60 miles an hour, has such quick engagement that it's cool, very cool, on McLuhan's engagement continuum. Motorists have too much going on to obsess on a billboard. A movie screen, although certainly a distant medium, can be a hot media experience if distractions are walled off.

What Do You Think?

How have the new one-foot media changed the way of defining different media as hot or cool or in between?

Next From W3C

Tim Berners-Lee.

The British engineer who created the internet coding for the World Wide Web in 1989, Tim Berners-Lee, followed up by creating the World Wide Web Consortium to "lead the web to its full potential." The current major project of W3C, as consortium insiders call it, is HTML5 internet technology that automatically detects the kind of device a user has and adapts transmission formats for rapid and seamless presentation. HTML5 precludes the need for users to acquire a welter of device-specific and source-specific applications, which is problematic because most apps for iPads and Android-equipped and other devices are largely incompatible.

Although launched in 2007, HTML5's commercial value wasn't much embraced until three years later when Steve Jobs of Apple proclaimed it the new standard for video on the web. Among early proponents has been Charles Tillinghast, Former digital president for the MSNBC television network. Tillinghast saw HTLM5 as a way to grow the network's audience among people who weren't in the habit of watching news. Television programming that once went to devices for 10-foot viewing now can be transmitted simultaneously to two-foot and one-foot devices, no app required. MSNBC is streaming 150 million news programs and items a month to hotter-than-television devices.

A miniscule staff, sometimes one person, can operate an aggregation site—just as Drudge did at the outset.

Some aggregation sites have had a jump start. The well-connected **Arianna Huffington,** wealthy almost beyond imagination from a flashy divorce settlement, launched her *Huffington Post* in 2005 as a liberal alternative to the *Drudge Report.* Huffington put up $11 million. Huffington started by aggregating news and gossip mostly from print and television sources or somebody's cell phone or video camera. In 2011 the *Huffington Post* had 88 full-time employees—miniscule compared to the 1,200 newsroom employees at the New York *Times* at its peak—and received 22 million clicks a day from different computers. Revenue topped $30 million a year and is doubling every year. The *Huffington* Post was sold to the floundering media-tech company AOL for $315 million as part of America Online's attempt to reinvent itself. The deal put Huffington in charge of runningAOL's expanding online media operations. Quite a return on her investment.

Arianna Huffington
Founder of online news site
Huffington Post

Custom News Portals

The aggregation concept has been taken to perhaps an ultimate step with **news alerts** triggered by search engines like Google. With internet access, anyone can ask a search engine to send an e-message whenever a news story appears anywhere containing search terms. At Google, you could enter *Marco Rubio U.S. Senate hurricane.* You would receive a link whenever stories appear with all those search terms in the text.

news alerts
Email links to news from search engines on subjects that users request with key search terms

Social-networking sites perform a similar function. People alert friends to things they spot online that seem to be of mutual interest. In one sense, Twitter is a headline service among friends.

APPLYING YOUR MEDIA LITERACY

- **Hoaxes still plague the media, but today it's the media that are conned. Identify a recent hoax widely reported by the media as non-fiction news.**
- **What are the hazards in the gatekeeping process in news?**
- **What impact does aggregating have on delivery of the news?**
- **How might the aggregation of news via new alerts impact the way a story is evaluated by the reader?**

Journalism Trends

STUDY PREVIEW

The explosion of 24/7 news on television, the internet and mobile devices is transforming news gathering and redefining news practices and audience expectations. Traditional avenues for news, sometimes called mainstream media, were shaken in the 2004 political campaign by individuals, mostly without journalistic training, generally operating alone, who created hundreds of blog sites. Bloggers offer an interconnected web of fascinating reading. Sometimes they score scoops.

Newsrooms in Transition

Two dynamics are reshaping newsrooms. One is the transition into internet delivery of news, which is pushing editors to find ways to stretch their staffs to produce their traditional products—plus offer competitive web sites. The other dynamic is financial, primarily at newspapers where recent years have seen drastic staff reductions. Newspaper industry reporter Joe Strupp, writing in the trade journal *Editor & Publisher*, put it this way: "So with newsrooms shrinking and corporate demands growing, the question inevitably may be asked: 'What gives?'" Most television newsrooms face the same issue. How can the extra duty of a 24/7 web site or perhaps multiple sites, some interactive, be absorbed by existing staff?

Among the new realities:

Less Comprehensive Coverage.   Newsrooms once put lots of energy into catching up on their competitors' scoops and taking the coverage further. Less so now. Ken Paulson, editor of *USA Today*, said he now applauds the New York *Times* and Washington *Post* when they break an exclusive story. Applauds—and forgets it. Said Paulson: "We have to make judgment calls on what our priorities are."

The new *USA Today* practice, common in all financially strapped newsrooms, doesn't speak well for the kind of excellence that competition has generated historically in U.S. journalism. The coverage of historically significant stories, like the Pentagon Papers and Watergate in the 1970s, was marked by intense competition. Independent coverage by competing newsrooms led to revelations that no one news organization could have managed single-handedly. Every breakthrough from competing newsrooms in Watergate, for example, further peeled away at the truth and became a stepping stone for new rounds of pursuit.

Less Enterprise.   With smaller, stretched staffs, newsrooms are opting for easier stories. This has meant a greater quotient of stories that chronicle events and fewer stories that require labor-intensive digging. This further means fewer reporters being freed for what David Boardman, executive editor at the Seattle *Times*, calls "two- and three-day stories." There was a time in the lore of the *Wall Street Journal* that editors would work up a promising story possibility with a veteran reporter, give the reporter an American Express card, and say "Come back with a story in six months." Although the *Journal* still features exhaustive journalistic examinations, they are becoming less common in American journalism and even in the *Journal* too.

Less Outlying and International News.   Many newsrooms have trimmed or shuttered bureaus in outlying areas and abroad. Typical is the Memphis, Tennessee, *Commercial Appeal*. The bureaus in Jackson, Mississippi, and Little Rock, Arkansas, have been shut down. The state capital bureau in Nashville, once with three reporters, has been trimmed to one.

Foreign bureaus are fewer every year. ABC and CBS, for example, had long shuttered their Cairo bureaus when the Egyptian revolution erupted in 2011. Fox never had one. That dearth of U.S. journalists on the ground explains in part why Americans were so unaware when the hundreds of thousands of people brought down the government. The over-air networks had to rush in reporters. So did cable network CNN, although CNN did have a small continuing presence in Cairo. The pan-Arabic network Al Jazeera, on the other hand, offered stronger coverage from its staff stationed in Egypt. Al Jazeera, in fact, became a source for the U.S. networks and also for the White House and U.S. State Department.

Fewer Beats.   Reporters assigned to cover specialized areas are being given broader beats. Some police beat reporters, for example, now also cover the courts. To cover some beats, editors in some newsrooms have shuffled reporters from general assignment duties to beats, which means there are fewer resources for day-to-day coverage of breaking news that doesn't fall in the bailiwick of one of the surviving beats.

Less Independent Reporting.   Newsrooms are sharing stories among corporate siblings, which fills space cheaply but reduces the traditional value of competitive reporting yielding better coverage overall. Many newspapers and newscasts fill up with a growing percentage of faraway content from the Associated Press, which is far less costly per story than staff-generated local coverage. One upshot is less diversity in content when AP stories, appearing word for word in news packages statewide, even nationwide, displace local coverage.

The trend toward shared stories is most obvious with so-called multimedia newsrooms. One of the first was the integrated newsroom of the Tampa, Florida, *Tribune,* television station WFLA and TBO.com. Some local television stations are sparing themselves the cost of operating a newsroom and contracting with crosstown stations to provide the newscasts. Efficient? Yes. That repackaging is better than fresh content, however, is hard to argue.

Nonstop Coverage

Reporters for the Associated Press and other news agencies were a breed apart through most of the 20th century. In contrast to most newspaper reporters, who had one deadline a day, agency reporters sent dispatches to hundreds of news organizations, each with its own deadlines. Agency reporters literally had a deadline every minute.

◀ **More Is Less.** *Chuck Todd of NBC News, like reporters everywhere, recognizes that the economic pressure to generate more content takes a toll on original, substantive reporting. Todd leans on his Blackberry for quick questions to his White House sources and quick stories than he would like. Nothing wrong with quickness and efficiency, but there is a toll on thoughtful, reflective reporting, which is hard to do when reporters are on the run, run, run.*

The advent of all-news radio and then CNN expanded nonstop coverage beyond the news agencies. Network reporters at the White House, for example, once concentrated on a piece for the evening newscast. They had time to think through issues, line up sources, and frame questions. Today correspondents seem always in a frantic race, over and over and often breathless, to Pebble Beach, as they call a camera area with a White House backdrop.

Consider a day in the in the life of NBC reporter Chuck Todd:

First, Todd scans newspapers and other competitors to orient himself. Then he writes an item for the NBC blog "First Read." Next is an appearance live on NBC "Today" or MSNBC "Morning Joe." On a heavy news day he makes more than a dozen stand-up reports from Pebble Beach, never fewer than six. In addition, he adds three to five blog entries during the day and posts as many as a dozen tweets or Facebook updates. Too, Todd has the one-hour newscast "The Daily Run-Down."

The work is important, the adrenaline rush exciting. But Todd, like reporters everywhere, acknowledges that the pressure to produce quantity diminishes the opportunity for fresh reporting, for turning up news angles, for developing good stories that end up untold. He uses his Blackberry to scour sources for tidbits, knowing, as all reporters do, that texting is hardly a substitute for a substantive sit-down interview.

Not only are reporters pressed to produce more stories for 24/7 news cycles, tighter news budgets in recent years mean that fewer news reporters are doing the work.

Quality erosion shows up in small ways. Reporters shudder at their typos making it online because fewer editors are assigned to check copy. At the Baltimore *Sun*, Bill Salganik, the president of the Newspaper Guild, which represents reporters as a collective-bargaining agent, says the pressures make more mistakes inevitable: "How do we maintain ethical and journalistic standards?"

In short, nonstop coverage, whatever the advantage of keeping people on top of breaking events, has shortcomings. The pressure for new angles tends to elevate the trivial. Also, context and understanding are sacrificed.

Live News

Over the past 150 years in the United States, elsewhere too, standard and accepted practices have evolved in news. These practices, taught in journalism schools and institutionalized in codes of ethics, guide reporters and editors in preparing their summaries and wrap-ups. In general the traditional practices worked well when newspapers were the dominant news medium, and they worked well in broadcasting too—until the advent of highly portable, lightweight equipment that enabled broadcasters to report news events live, bypassing the traditional editing process.

Diminished Gatekeeping. With television cameras focused on the towers of the World Trade Center as they turned into infernos in the 2001 terrorist attack, trapped people began jumping from windows hundreds of feet above ground. The plunges were desperate and fatal, and audiences viewing the scene live were shocked and horrified. Neither the video nor still photographs were included in most later newscasts. Whatever the virtues of live coverage, a significant downside is that the coverage is raw. Nobody is exercising judgment in deciding what to organize and how to present the material. There is no gatekeeper.

Live coverage, of course, can be interrupted by reporters and anchors to insert background and context and it can be turned off. Even so, for better or worse, the role for news media as gatekeepers is lessened.

Lost Time for Audience. Following live coverage is time-consuming for the audience. Compare, for example, the efficiency of reading or listening to a 60-second report on a congressional hearing or watching the whole four-hour session live. With high drama exceptions like Super Bowl games and sensational murder trials, news audiences prefer to have news boiled down and packaged.

■ When Journalists Are Afraid

▲ Chilling Effect.

Journalist Rocio Gonzalez was found slain gruesomely in a park in Mexico City, among thousands of victims of ongoing drug gang violence in Mexico. Although news reporters are a small fraction of the violence, they are targeted for unflattering news reports on gang activities.

It would be news anywhere—a gun battle between drug gangs and authorities that shut down a neighborhood for five hours. Twelve people were dead, 20 wounded. But in the Mexican city of Nuevo Laredo, population 300,000, across the Rio Grande from Texas, the battle went unreported in the city's five daily newspapers and five television stations. Silent too were Nuevo Laredo's 21 radio stations.

News media in many Mexican cities have been bullied into silence. Among 29,000 people killed in the drug wars over four years have been 30 journalists. For many newsrooms, the risk of reporting the drug wars is too high.

In the southern Gulf city of Villahermosa, population 550,000, the publisher of *Tabasco Hoy* received threats after unflattering coverage of drug cartels: "Stop writing shit. We know where your son works. Next time we won't warn you." There already had been one journalist murdered after a story on drug traffickers, or *narcotiendas,* as they're called. After the new threats, publisher

Roberto Cuitláhuac added locks on his house, varied his routes to work every day, and kept colleagues posted on his whereabouts all the time. Also, *Hoy* went silent on the cartels.

In one border city across from El Paso, Texas, the newspaper *Diario de Juarez* addressed an editorial to drug lords: So more of our journalists are not killed, *Diario* pleaded, "tell us what we should try to publish or not publish." In Juarez, population 1.4 million, drug lords had killed more than 3,000 people over two years. The toll included a *Diario* photographer and reporter.

The news blackouts, which can be called *media self-censorship,* are journalistic failures.

Into the news vacuum has emerged an internet site, blogdelnarco. com. A college student put up the site and passes along drug-war information that comes his way. Blog Del Narco has become essential reading, with 3 million hits a week. With the blog maintaining anonymity, angry drug lords don't know whom to send their gun-toting and machete-swinging thugs to attack.

After a bloody day in Nuevo Laredo, for example, Blog del Narco listed streets that were unsafe, essential information for people planning their daily lives. For people worried about family and friends, the site listed places where wounded people were being treated. None of this was in Nuevo Laredo newspapers or on television. Blog del Norte was alone in reporting that the U.S. Embassy was urging people to stay indoors.

With information pouring in from all kinds of sources, probably including cops and low-level soldiers, Blog del Narco reported army arrests of several members of the brutal Zetas gang. Posted too were videos, some gory with decapitated heads, with machete-chopped and bullet-riddled bodies oozing innards and brain matter, and with corpses in nooses from back-shed rafters. The worst probably originated with gang members themselves, apparently a perverse bravado to intimidate rivals.

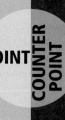

POINT In difficult times, blogs are important alternative sources of essential information. At Blog del Narco, the webmaster is a college student who collects information in his bedroom for posting. For his own protection he posts anonymously and shields the identity of his sources.

COUNTER POINT Anonymous blogging is a weak substitute for traditional journalism. Anonymity undermines the accountability that makes journalism credible. Who is the publisher? Who are the reporters? Anybody can submit unsigned information and photos. Anonymous blogging can't substitute for journalistic courage.

DEEPENING YOUR MEDIA LITERACY

EXPLORE THE ISSUE: Visit blogdelnarco.com. Even if you don't know Spanish, the flavor of the site will be plain.

DIG DEEPER: With a search engine, look for online news coverage of the Mexican drug wars by foreign correspondents.

WHAT DO YOU THINK? Imagine that you are a news media owner, editor or reporter in a major Mexican city being ravaged by drug wars. How could you do your journalistic duty to provide essential and robust coverage?

▲ **Investigative Journalism.**
Dogged pursuit of meticulous factual detail became a new wrinkle in 20th century journalism after Washington Post reporters Carl Bernstein and Bob Woodward unearthed the Watergate scandal. For months they pursued tips that a break-in at the Democratic Party national headquarters in the Watergate hotel, office and apartment complex in Washington, D.C., had been authorized high in the Republican White House and that the White House then had tried to cover it up. In the end, for the first time in U.S. history, a president, Richard Nixon, resigned.

◀ **Carl Bernstein and Bob Woodward.**

Bob Woodward
Carl Bernstein's colleague in the Watergate revelations

Carl Bernstein
Washington *Post* reporter who dug up Watergate

Watergate
Nixon administration scandal

investigative reporting
Enterprise reporting that reveals new information, often startling; most often these are stories that official sources would rather not have told

muckraking
Fanciful term for digging up dirt but that usually is used in a laudatory way for investigative journalism; aimed at public policy reform

Ida Tarbell
Muckraker remembered for her series on monopolistic corruption at Standard Oil

News-Gathering Unveiled. Before live coverage, journalists did their interviewing and observing and then sat down and organized their material. Live coverage has changed the old practices. Today, the audience can see, as they say, how the sausage is made. An interviewer, for example, is as on-stage as an interviewee. Fumbled questions are on display too.

Exploratory Reporting

Although in-depth reporting has deep roots, the thrust of U.S. journalism until the 1960s was a chronicling of events: meetings, speeches, crimes, deaths and catastrophes. That changed dramatically in 1972. Two persistent Washington *Post* reporters, **Bob Woodward** and **Carl Bernstein,** not only covered a break-in at the Democratic national headquarters, at a building called the Watergate, but also linked the crime to the White House of Republican President Richard Nixon. The morality questions inherent in the reporting forced Nixon to resign. Twenty-five aides went to jail. The **Watergate** scandal created an enthusiasm for **investigative reporting** and in-depth approaches to news that went far beyond mere chronicling, which is relatively easy to do and, alas, relatively superficial.

The roots of investigatory reporting extend back to the **muckraking** period in U.S. history. **Ida Tarbell,** a leading muckraker, uncovered abusive corporate practices at Standard Oil in 1902, triggering government reforms that broke up the Rockefeller oil monopoly and paved the way for antitrust legislation. Today's newspapers continue this tradition. But is anybody listening? The New Orleans, Louisiana, *Times-Picayune* won a fistful of awards for John McQuaid and Mark Schleifstein's 2002 series "Washing Away," a chilling prediction of the Hurricane Katrina disaster that came true three years later. Government didn't do anything at the federal, state or local level.

Because all reporting is investigative in the sense that it seeks truth through inquiry, the term *investigative reporting* is tricky. Here is a useful definition:

- A story that would not have been revealed without the enterprise of a reporter.
- A story that is pieced together from diverse and often obscure sources.
- A story that may be contrary to the version from officials, who might have tried to conceal the truth.

Some examples:

Barbara Laker and Wendy Ruderman Philadelphia *Daily News* — Exposed a rogue police narcotics squad, resulting in a review of hundreds of criminal cases.

Sheri Fink ProPublica	Chronicled urgent life-and-death decisions by one hospital's exhausted doctors cut off by Hurricane Katrina floodwaters.
David Barstow New York *Times*	Tracked how some retired generals, working as television analysts, had been co-opted by the Pentagon to make its case for the Iraq. Also exposed the generals' hidden ties to companies that profited from the war.
Brett Blackledge Birmingham, Alabama, *News*	Exposed cronyism and corruption in Alabama's two-year college system, resulting in the chancellor being fired and in reforms.
Michael Kirk Public Broadcasting System	Explored failure of the government to heed warnings of the pending economic meltdown from Brooksley Born, chief of the U.S. Commodity Futures Trading Commission.

Soft News

In contrast to hard investigative reporting came a simultaneous trend toward **soft news.** This includes consumer-help stories, lifestyle tips, entertainment news and offbeat gee-whiz items often of a sensational sort. The celebrity-oriented *National Enquirer,* whose circulation skyrocketed in the 1960s, was the progenitor of the trend. Time-Life launched *People* magazine. The staid New York *Times* created *Us.* Newspaper research found that readers like soft stuff. Soon many dailies added "People" columns. The television show *TMZ* focuses on glamour and glitz, usually as a lead-in to the evening news on many local stations. The show was an outgrowth of the original operation, *TMZ*.com, a news web site for celebrity gossip. Traditionalists decry the space that soft news takes in many news products today, but hard news does remain part of the product mix in traditional media.

Some of the public appetite for soft news is being met by web sites and Twitter and also by apps for smart phones. Uncertain is whether these digital sources for soft news will relieve the pressure on traditional media to compete for soft news or to give it up and return to their strength in hard news.

soft news
Geared to satisfying audience's *information wants, not needs*

APPLYING YOUR MEDIA LITERACY

- How are tighter finances at media companies affecting news?
- Nonstop news coverage is well established. What impact does it have on the way people interpret the facts and truth of news stories?
- All reporting results from inquiry. What sets investigative reporting apart?
- Rank half a dozen news sources from all media in the quotient of soft news in their content mix. Then evaluate them for how well they attract eyeballs for advertisers.

■ Concept of News   (Pages 199–200)

News is a report on change that journalists deem most worth their audience's attention. In the United States there is a high premium on a detached, neutral presentation in which reporters keep their presence as much in the background as they can. The emphasis generally is on the story, not the storyteller, even though the reporter's role in seeking and organizing stories requires judgments that are subjective and flow from personal values.

■ Bennett News Model   (Pages 200–206)

Modern news practices draw heavily on values identified by James Gordon Bennett after founding the New York *Herald* in 1835. Bennett recognized information as a perishable commodity. When Bennett obtained information first, his competitors were left with a stale product. Also Bennett established a network of reporters with assigned specialties. This beat system, as it's called, assures comprehensive coverage. Although Bennett's ideas have dominated the concept of news for more than a century, flaws are showing.

■ Hutchins News Model   (Pages 206–207)

A blue ribbon panel of scholars, the Hutchins Commission, concluded in 1947 that democracy was best served by news that went beyond the Bennett Model's facts-only presentations. The upshot was a distinction between facts and truth. It was not enough just to amass facts. Instead, the Hutchins Commission said that facts need to be presented in a context that gives them meaning. The Hutchins recommendations slowly took hold in redefining news practices.

■ Rethinking News Models   (Pages 208–210)

News media have proliferated with the cable television and the internet. Almost anybody can blog, no journalism degree needed. In this new media universe, Mainstream news organizations have struggled to adapt, as demonstrated with the ascendency of the ideologically driven Fox News dethroning of CNN from cable news dominance with its tradition of straightforward reporting. The internet is loaded with ideologically slanted reports. The New York *Times* and other traditional news sources are struggling to develop a new model for news, a hybrid, to remain commercially viable.

■ Personal Values in News   (Pages 211–213)

Since news cannot be values-free, the question is what values do journalists bring to their work? Values include those that prevail in society. In the United States these include broad values often taken for granted, like family, education and health. Studies have found other values that flavor American journalism. These include a rural ethnocentrism, a commitment to democracy and capitalism, a favoring of individualism about rural and small-town lifestyles, tempered by moderation, and a commitment to social order.

■ Variables Affecting News   (Pages 213–216)

Practical matters shape much of what appears in the news. How much space is there in an edition? Never enough to tell all that journalists would like to tell. Time on a newscast? Never enough either. Nor does the audience have the time to be engaged in everything that gets reported. Also, more stories are worth telling than any news organization has the staff and resources to pursue.

■ Quality of News   (Pages 216–219)

Lots of journalism professors begin courses by telling students what they need to master: "Accuracy. Accuracy. Accuracy." To be sure, the prof's point is overstated. Nonetheless, accuracy is a core element in news as a non-fiction literary form. Accuracy is relatively easy to measure, compared to essential elements of judgment in news. The complexity of judgment is no better illustrated than in the gatekeeping process, with stories being processed by many hands in moving from reporter to delivery to an audience. Judgment also is a factor in deciding what most merits coverage.

■ Journalism Trends   (Pages 220–225)

Journalism is going in many directions. Lengthily treated, typical television network documentaries, are long-form journalism—labor-intensive to produce but often with breakthrough revelations. At another extreme are snippets sometimes only a couple lines long that are packaged in radio newscasts. The advent of 24/7 news on television and the web has stretched the resources of many newsrooms. With a limited number of reporters being asked to repackage stories for multiple outlets, there has been a shift to stories that are quicker to report. The result: a decline in significant enterprise reporting that takes major commitments of newsroom time and resources.

■ Thinking Critically

1. Why is it unavoidable that journalists disagree among themselves on what merits being reported on a given day?

2. What did James Gordon Bennett bring together to create his enduring concepts of news and journalistic practices?

3. How can the Hutchins model be seen as overturning the Bennett model? Or is the Hutchins model more a refinement?

4. Is the hybrid news model as laid out by the New York *Times* too complicated for news audiences? Are there alternatives? Explain your assessment.

5. How are journalists captives of the personal values they bring to their work?

6. What variables about news-gathering and news-packaging are beyond the control of reporters and editors but nonetheless affect what people read, hear and see?

7. How would you explain the necessity of judgment as a component in news to someone who is committed to a fact-centric and judgment-free news model?

8. What are the best ways to evaluate the divergent trends in news reporting over the long term?

Media Vocabulary

aggregation sites (Page 217)

bylines (Page 202)

consensible nature of news (Page 216)

editorializing (Page 207)

ethnocentrism (Page 212)

gatekeepers (Page 217)

Hutchins Commission (Page 206)

investigative reporting (Page 224)

lightning news (Page 202)

muckraking (Page 224)

news (Page 200)

news alerts (Page 219)

news flow (Page 215)

news hole (Page 215)

newsworthiness (Page 200)

objectivity (Page 202)

staffing (Page 215)

soft news (Page 207)

watchdog function (Page 213)

Watergate (Page 224)

yellow journalism (Page 207)

Media Sources

Jodi Enda. "Retreating from the World," *American Journalism Review* (December-January 2011). Enda, a veteran journalist, documents the decline of resources that U.S. news organizations put into foreign coverage.

Jon Marshall. *The Investigative Impulse: Watergate's Legacy and the Press.* Northwestern University Press, 2011. Marshall, a news reporter-turned scholar, sees the scandal that ruined the Nixon presidency as shaping how investigative reporting has come to be practiced and how political leaders and the public respond to journalists.

Kimberly Meltzer. *TV News Anchors and Journalistic Traditions: How Journalists Adapt to Technology.* Peter Lang, 2010. Meltzer, herself a veteran of network news, examines the effect of television on traditional journalistic standards and practices.

Bonnie Brenen and Hanno Hardt. *American Journalism History Reader.* Routledge, 2010. Brennen and Hardt have gathered primary texts, news articles, and core works by media historians and critics through the span of U.S. history.

Sean Tunney and Garrett Monaghan, editors. *Web Journalism: A New Form of Citizenship?* Sussex Academic, 2010. This wide-ranging collection includes essays on the internet expanding political participation globally into societal segments that have lacked effective voices.

■ Robert W. McChesney and John Nichols. *The Death and Life of American Journalism: The Media Revolution that Will Begin the World Again.* Nation Books, 2010. McChesney and Nichols, both historians, explain 20th century U.S. journalism traditions and practices as self-serving news industry rationales to protect their business from government interference. They call for reorienting journalistic traditions more to produce a public good than to enrich media owners.

■ Geoffrey Baym. *From Cronkite to Colbert: The Evolution of Broadcast News.* Paradigm, 2010. Baym, a scholar, argues that the "fake" news of the Colbert sort should be understood as a new style contributor to robust citizen dialogue on important issues.

■ Mike Conway. *The Origins of Television News in America: The Visualizers of CBS in the 1940s.* Peter Lang, 2009. Conway, a media scholar, examines the precursor years to television network news with illuminating anecdote and detail.

■ William David Sloan, editor. *The Media in America,* seventh edition. Vision Press, 2009. This textbook is the standard for U.S. media history.

■ David Wallis, editor. *Killed: Great Journalism Too Hot to Print.* Nation, 2004. Wallis has compiled great magazine articles that never made it to print, mostly to avoid litigation or not to offend advertisers or the editors' sensitivities. Among the stricken are works by Betty Friedan, George Orwell and Terry Southern.

■ Bob Woodward and Carl Bernstein. *All the President's Men.* Simon & Schuster, 1974. The reporters' own chronicle of the obstacles they overcame in the classic unfolding series of investigative reports in the Nixon Watergate scandal.

A Thematic Chapter Summary

News | To further deepen your media literacy here are ways to look at this chapter from the perspective of themes that recur throughout the book:

MEDIA TECHNOLOGY

James Gordon Bennett and other among Penny Press publishers capitalized on new technologies.

News as we know it today did not exist before the 1830s and 1840s, when presses were invented that could produce thousands of copies an hour. The question became: What content will sell all this product? Stories on current events displaced the opinion thrust that had marked earlier papers. In the 1920s when broadcasting was introduced, stories became briefer. Internet technology is now changing the rules again, with many mainstream news media conventions being ignored in the shaping and exchanging of information. Whether these changes are merely amateur-hour bloggers breaking rules they never knew is unclear. Some changes may have long futures.

MEDIA ECONOMICS

How to attract audiences? Cover the antics of Charlie Sheen? Or processes like the creation of public policy? Or global warming?

Because news companies cannot survive without audiences, the quest to deliver content that attracts audiences is never-ending—and also competitive. Recent years have seen a rise in celebrity news, mostly inconsequential but followed avidly. This is an example of news following the dollar. Economics also shapes news in other ways. To varying degrees, news companies are cautious about reporting events and issues that might offend their advertisers. The issue is whether serving the audience or serving advertisers comes first. In some newsrooms, it's an easy call. In others, advertisers usually win out.

MEDIA AND DEMOCRACY

One function of news is "keeping the rascals honest."

An independent streak has been present in American news media going back to Ben Harris. Government banned Harris' *Publick Occurrences* in 1690 after one issue. Although Ben Harris' paper hardly contributed to the making of public policy, the independence of the news media became an enduring and important element in U.S. democracy. News media convey information, ideas and opinions that enable the people to participate in the creation of public policy. The mechanisms of participation are uneven, but without them the people would be woefully lacking in what they need to know to participate in governance. Democracy needs an independent media.

MEDIA EFFECTS

Richard Nixon did himself in, but news media were catalytic.

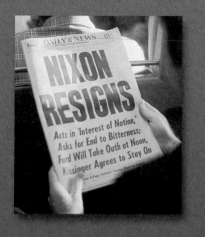

The news media can have powerful effects. The resignation of Alberto Gonzales as attorney general in 2007 was fueled by the news coverage in which he demonstrated continuing ineptness. In 2008 New York Governor Eliot Spitzer resigned after the New York *Times* identified him as a client of a call-girl ring. The 1972 Watergate scandal that sent Richard Nixon packing midterm was the result of news coverage of dirty tricks and deceits that he and his lieutenants committed. Today, news coverage of the pending global-warming disaster is mobilizing public alarm, which is translating into public policy reform.

ELITISM AND POPULISM

Ben Day's motto for his New York Sun, "It Shines for All," said it all–a newspaper for everyone, a true mass audience. This meant a new thrust in content: Stories that made people say: "Gee whiz." Even hoaxes like Richard Locke's moon creatures.

Publications in the early days of the Republic were too expensive for most people. Articles were narrowly focused. These publications were forums where the thinkers and ideologues of the time shared their views. The political, economic and not uncommonly philosophical thrust was elitist. The commercialization of newspapers, with the mass audience beginning in the 1830s, sparked a shift to news of interest to all strata of society. Ben Day's motto for his New York *Sun* in 1833 said it all: "It Shines for All." The beginning of marketing that relied on advertising, which changed the financial base of newspapers from subscriptions to advertisers, made it essential economically that news be found to attract and keep as many readers as possible. Advertisers went with papers with the largest circulations.

MEDIA FUTURE

Rachel Maddow at MSNBC slides easily from news to commentary.

No media maven has all the answers on where the news media are headed. Trends point in no single direction. Faster-pace lifestyles and spare-time diversions are robbing people of time once spent tracking news. The upshot is briefer coverage that's often superficial. At the same time, news junkies abound. Long-form journalism thrives on national and specialized subjects, albeit not so much in local daily coverage. A major change involves the around-the-clock news cycle, particularly with CNN and other cable channels and the Internet. The competition to be first is changing reporting conventions. Not long ago reporters had time, albeit not much, to think and assess their reportage before telling their stories. Today more and more reporting is going live—now.

CHAPTER 9

ENTERTAINMENT

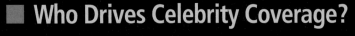

■ Who Drives Celebrity Coverage?

As long as there have been celebrities, there has been someone to bring them to the public eye. Once the role was filled mostly by celebrity magazines. But today's media universe is much more vast with television, cable, print and electronic tabloids and social media. Competition is fierce. Stakes are high to land an original celebrity story or photograph.

Sad to say, some media solve the problem of a finite amount of available celebrity news by running stories filled with rumors, half-truths and falsities. What if the story's wrong? "Well, we can retract it later. No big deal." Sadly, so goes tabloid thinking.

Another tool for celebrity coverage is spying. In the old days this could mean climbing a tree to snap pictures of a celebrity at home. The latest tool to slake the thirst for celebrity coverage is phone hacking.

▲ **Not All So Glitzy.** *Detail-craving fans can't get enough of celebrities and their lives. And profit-craving celebrity media know what sells. At a premiere for a new movie, Mila Kunis turned testy at a reporter who asked co-star Justin Timberlake why he was acting more and singing less, Kunis intervened: "What kind of question is that? Why are you here?"*

CHAPTER INSIGHTS

- Mass media technology has magnified the audience for storytelling and entertainment.

- Pure performance and mediated performance are different.

- Mass media powerfully extend the reach of literature.

- Technology has accelerated music as a social unifier.

- Mass media feed an insatiable demand for sports.

- Gaming has become a mass medium with advertisers pursuing gamers.

- Mass media have championed the right of adult access to sexual content.

- Mass media entertainment quality is compromised by factory-style production.

- Mass media often fall short in elevating cultural sensitivity.

Ironically, the most notable victim of phone hacking so far has been international media tycoon Rupert Murdoch, who built his fortune on tabloid tawdriness. In 2011 Murdoch was forced to shut down his 168-year-old *News of the World,* Britain's biggest newspaper, after it was learned that reporters had been routinely hacking into voice mail messages for years. Thousands of people have claimed they were hacked. In some cases, like those of actresses Scarlett Johansson and Mila Kunis, pictures and texts were taken from their phones.

Generally celebrities just grumble at the excesses and put up with them silently. Sometimes they speak out, as did Kunis: "I've been engaged, I think I've already been married. And I'm sure I have a child somewhere. No, I'm not married. And, no, I'm not engaged. And, no, I do not have a child. Half the time you can say they misconstrued the facts. But, more often than not, they just make stuff up."

Would tabloid television shows, paparazzi, or even phone hackers exist without our star-hungry society? It's one of those chicken-or-egg questions. A Pew Research Center poll found that the vast majority of us feel coverage of celebrity scandals has gone overboard. The poll found that most people blame the media for the attention to the stars' trials and tribulations. Many think there is too little coverage in the media of good things that are happening in the world.

On the other side of the chicken-egg teeter-totter, the media blame the audience. It is a fact that scandal and gossip sell. Some in the media claim they are only giving the public what it wants. The audience for this stuff is huge and seemingly insatiable. Directly or indirectly, the audience finances media content.

Mila Kunis got fed up with celebrity-media irrelevancies at a Moscow news conference with Justin Timberlake to promote their romantic comedy *Friends with Benefits.* A reporter wanted to know why Timberlake was acting instead of making more music. The Ukraine-born Kunis replied hotly in Russian, "Why movies? Why not? What kind of question is that? Why are you here?" Testy perhaps, but, yes:

Why, indeed? ■

Entertainment in History

STUDY PREVIEW | Mass media, during their 550-year existence, have magnified the audience for entertainment. Technology has wrought many refinements, but the core categories of media entertainment remain storytelling and music.

Pre-Mass Media Roots

Entertainment predates the written history of the human species. Around the prehistoric campfire there was music. We know this from Neolithic animal hide drums that archaeologists have unearthed. Certainly, the cave dwellers must have told stories. Who knows when the visual arts began? The record goes back to paintings on cave walls. Through the eons, entertainment became higher and higher art. Archaeologists know that the elites of ancient civilizations enjoyed lavish banquets that included performing entertainers—acrobats, musicians and dancers. Sports and athletics became institutionalized entertainment by the time of ancient Greece with the Olympic games. Then came the Circus Maximus in ancient Rome that could hold 170,000 spectators for chariot races and gladiator games.

Entertainment that has survived the ages includes music, literature, sports and sex. Other breakdowns can be made, like performing arts and visual arts. Some people distinguish entertainment from art, relegating entertainment to a somehow less worthy category. On close examination, however, these distinctions blur. Art is in the eye of the beholder, a highly personal and subjective issue.

Technology-Driven Entertainment

What distinguished the Age of Mass Communication, which began with Gutenberg's movable type in the 1440s, was that messages could be mass-produced to reach audiences of unprecedented size. The post-Gutenberg press gave literature wider and wider audiences. For example, even 200 years after Gutenberg, the audience for John Milton's *Paradise Lost* was remarkable for the time but minuscule compared to the audience for every book now on the New York *Times* weekly best sellers list. Today, literature has taken on diverse forms from academic tomes to pulp romances and Westerns—and it's not all in printed form.

As media technology leapfrogged into photographic and electronic forms, literature adapted to the new media. Movies extended the reach of the artistic form of books. So did radio and then television. Music, a rare treat in people's lives before audio recording was invented, is everywhere today. Indeed, the impact of the entertainment content of today's mass media is hard to measure. With television turned on seven hours a day in U.S. homes on average, most of it tuned to entertainment content, it's obvious that people are being entertained more than ever before in history.

genres
Broad thematic categories of media content

Entertainment Genres

To make sense of the gigantic and growing landscape of entertainment in the mass media, people have devised **genres** that are, in effect, subdivisions of the major categories of storytelling and music.

▲ **Perennial Cop Shows.** *The police story is an enduring genre that spikes periodically in popularity. The latest generation is led by the prime-time CBS series CSI and its spin-offs. Here, true to the series' title, characters played by Ted Danson and Marg Helgenberger are at a crime scene investigation.*

Storytelling. Whether novels, short stories, television drama or movies, literature can be divided into genres. Popular genres include suspense, romance, horror, Westerns, fantasy, history and biography. There are also subgenres, such as detective stories. Some subgenres cut across two or more genres, such as sci-fi Westerns: Remember the 2011 movie *Cowboys & Aliens?* Some genres are short-lived. In the 1960s a movie genre dubbed *blaxploitation* emerged, for better or worse, with a black racist appeal to black audiences. The genre culminated in the *Shaft* series, which, although updated in 2003, had been eclipsed by the ongoing racial integration of society.

Music. A lot of crossover makes for genre confusion in music. Wanting to define their tastes, aficionados keep reinventing thematic trends. The array of subgenres is dizzying. How is acid rock different from hard rock, from solid rock, from progressive rock, from alternative rock, from power rock, from metal rock? Don't ask. Categorizing is not a neat, clinical task.

Sports. Genres are clearest in sports because the rules, although not set in granite, have been agreed on, as have the procedures for revising the rules. Nobody confuses baseball with soccer or the shot put with Formula One auto racing. Attempts at crossover genres, like Vince McMahon's wrestling-inspired XFL football experiment in 2001, don't do well. The league lasted one less-than-memorabe season.

APPLYING YOUR MEDIA LITERACY

- **What is the role of media technology in entertainment?**
- **What are major genres of media-delivered entertainment?**

■ She Is Her Art

At 18, she told everyone that she was going to be a superstar. Her friends scoffed, thinking her an egomaniac. But Lady Gaga's success has been nothing short of phenomenal. She's made the cover of *Time's* 100 Most Influential People in the World alongside Barack Obama and Sonja Sotomayor, and she topped the artists category. *Forbes* put her on its Most Powerful Celebrity list, ahead of Oprah Winfrey, Justin Bieber, Tiger Woods and LeBron James. She was the youngest woman to make the magazine's list of the 100 Most Influential Females in the world at Number 11.

Lady Gaga is the queen of social media and interacting with her fans. She calls them "monsters." She became the first Twitter user to attract 12 million followers. By 2011, she had more than 33 million Facebook fans. She made $90 million in 2010, and the sales of lipstick and lip gloss that she endorsed raised more than $202 million to fight HIV and AIDS. She is a staunch supporter of gay rights.

By 2011 she had won five Grammy Awards and 12 nominations. She had sold 15 million albums. All of that before her 26th birthday.

Lady Gaga's performances are outlandish. Also unique and trend-setting: "Some artists are working to buy the mansion or whatever the element of fame must bear, but I spend all my money on my show." She appeared at the Grammys inside a semi-transparent egg that was carried by four men and one woman down the red carpet. She didn't "hatch" until the moment she sang her new song, "Born This Way."

At a concert, the diminutive artist is likely to appear in an outfit that features sparks spraying from metal breasts. Her meat dress is now on display at the Rock and Roll Hall of Fame. In a tribute in *Time* magazine, actress-songwriter Cyndi Lauper said: "She isn't a pop act, she is a performance artist. She herself is the art."

Gaga was born Stefani Joanne Angelina Germanotta in 1986 in Manhattan. She taught herself to play piano by ear at age 4. By 14 she was performing in clubs.

She always knew she was different from her classmates—eccentric, talkative, audacious and theatrical—and she got "picked on." She was thrown in a trash can by some boys when she was 14, and says it made her feel mortified and worthless. "I got profanity written all over my locker at school. I got pinched in the hallways and called a slut." She wrote her hit single "Born This Way" as a response to being bullied. And she has thrown

◄ **Lady Gaga.**

Outrageous and fun, she has mastered an unpredictable media persona and parlayed her talent and celebrity into causes that she believes will leave the world a better place. Among her causes is campaigning against bullying.

much of her considerable clout behind programs aimed at eradicating bullying. "Born This Way" was hailed as an anthem for America's disenfranchised. The song set a music industry record—the fastest single in history to sell one million copies within five days.

At 17, she was one of 20 people to gain early admission to the New York University's Tisch School of the Arts, but she didn't last long and dropped out. She moved out on her parents, got her own place, and survived on her own. "I made music and worked my way from the bottom up. I didn't know somebody who knew somebody who knew somebody."

She never let anyone change her style: "I truly believe in the glamorous lifestyle that I present to the outside world. I love glamour. I love the crazy, more eccentric stuff. For years I was practically broke, but I was still vain and glamorous."

Gaga says she doesn't want to look pretty on stage and sing about the same things everyone else does. She would rather write songs about betrayal and forgiveness and feeling misunderstood. As Cyndi Lauper put it: "Gaga's lyrics are incredibly literary." Gaga says she wants her lyrics to talk to her fans, to help figure out what it is society needs. "If you were to ask me what I want to do—I don't want to be a celebrity, I want to make a difference."

What Do You Think?

Does Lady Gaga's notoriety help or hinder the causes she backs? Does her act make her hard to take seriously?

Is she elevating cultural sensitivity or is she unintentionally engendering cultural insensitivity?

Mediated Performance

STUDY PREVIEW | Media's entertainment content is performance, but it's not pure performer-to-audience. Media change the performance. Authentic performance is live and eyeball-to-eyeball with the audience. Mediated performance is adapted for an unseen and distant audience.

Authentic Performance

Before Al Franken was elected to the U.S. Senate, he was a liberal commentator on radio. Before that he was a stand-up comic. On stage before a live audience, Franken was uproariously funny. Sometimes his comic bite hit raw ideological nerves. That's why conservatives avoided his shows. But in 2004, when Franken took his humor to radio in a talk show on the new Air America network, his humor and bite didn't translate well. On radio he was flat. The fact is that the media change performance. There are many reasons:

Audience. At a play, whether on Broadway or in a high school auditorium, the audience is assembled for one purpose. It's **authentic performance**, live with the audience on-site. Everyone is attentive to the performance. Nuances are hard to miss.

Feedback. Performers on stage are in tune with their audience's reactions. There can be reaction and interplay. For the same performance through a mass medium, performers guess—some better than others—at how they are coming across. The fact is, taking television as an example, what resonates in one living room does not necessarily resonate in another. A performer can be great at maximizing impact on stage and live, but to reach the massive, scattered, heterogeneous mass audience requires pandering to some extent to common denominators. There is less edge.

Technology. The equipment that makes mass communication possible is what sets it apart from interpersonal and group communication. Technology imposes its own requirements on performance. The aural beauty of operatic trills in an acoustically optimal concert hall cannot be duplicated by a home stereo, no matter how many woofers. Andrew Lloyd Webber's stage musical *Starlight Express,* with roller-skating singers on ramps in front of, behind and above the audience, would be a different audience experience in a movie or on television. Media transform a performance. In ways large and small, it becomes **mediated performance**.

By definition purists prefer pure, unmediated performance. There will always be a following for Broadway, live concerts and ghost stories around the campfire.

Mediated Performance

In ways we don't always realize, media technology affects and sometimes shapes the messages the media disseminate. The changes necessary to make a **mediated message** work are a function of the technology that makes it possible to reach a mass audience.

Music. Edison's mechanical recording technology, which captured acoustic waves in a huge horn, picked up no subtleties. Brass bands and loud voices recorded best. Scratchy background noise drowned out soft sounds. It's no wonder that the late 1800s and early 1900s were marked by the popularity of martial music and marching bands. High-pitched voices came through best, which also shaped the popular music of the period.

When Joseph Maxfield's electrical technology was refined in the 1920s, subtle sounds that could survive the recording and playback processes came into vogue. Rudy Vallee and Bing Crosby were in. John Philip Sousa was out. Improvements in fidelity beginning in the 1950s meant that music could be played louder and louder without unsettling dissonance— and many rockers took to louder renditions, some very loud.

Movies. Media technology profoundly affects art. When audio and film technology were merged to create talkies, moviemakers suddenly had all kinds of new creative options for their storytelling. Directors had more new possibilities when wide screens replaced squarish screens in movie houses. When technology changes the experience for the moviemaker, it also changes the experience for moviegoers.

authentic performance
A live performance with an on-site audience

mediated performance
A performance modified and adjusted for delivery to an audience by mass media

mediated message
Adjusted to be effective when carried by the mass media

▲ **Flash Mobs.** *The idea of street theater has taken new meaning with flash mobs. If media can catch them, flash mobs represent both authentic and mediated entertainment. A group of people who have been secretly coached, usually through social media, assemble unannounced in a public place and perform a pointless act for a few seconds. Then, poof, they disperse and vanish. For Worldwide Pillow Fight Day, an estimated 5,000 people gathered in two dozen cities as flash mobs for momentary shows that left unsuspecting witnesses agasp in wonderment and confusion but in the end amused.*

Sports. Technology has dazzled sports fans. Instant replays on television, tried first during an Army-Navy football game in the early 1960s, added a dimension that in-stadium fans could not see. Then came miniature cameras that allow viewers to see what referees see on the field. Putting microphones on referees, coaches and players lets the mass audience eavesdrop on the sounds of the playing field that no one in the stands or sidelines can pick up—unless they're toting a media device in order to, ironically, see the game better.

Some digital cable channels allow viewers to select various static camera angles during a game. Viewers, in effect, can participate in creating the media coverage they see. This is a profound development. Watching television, once a largely passive activity, now can involve the viewer at least to some degree.

APPLYING YOUR MEDIA LITERACY

- **What are advantages of mediated performances over live performances?**
- **Conversely, what are advantages of live performances over mediated performances?**

Storytelling

STUDY PREVIEW | The media are powerful vehicles for exponentially extending the reach of literature. The most enduring genres include romances and mysteries, but variations and hybrids come and go in popularity.

Genres of Literature

Some of literature's storytelling genres have lasted through the centuries. Shakespeare was not the first to do romances and mysteries. Nor the last. Genres help us make sense of literature, giving us a basis for comparison and contrast. Literature can be categorized in many ways, one as basic as fiction and nonfiction, another being prose and poetry. There are periods: medieval, antebellum, postmodern. There are breakdowns into geographic, ethnic and cultural traditions: Russian, Hispanic and Catholic. Ideologies comprise genres: Marxist, fascist and libertarian. Bookstores use thematic genres to sort their inventory, including mysteries, romances, sports, biographies and hobbies.

Media-Defined Trends

Genres rise and fall in popularity. Early television was awash with variety shows, which featured a range of comedy, song and dance, and other acts. Then came the wave of 1950s quiz shows, then Westerns, then police shows. Going into the 21st century, the television programming fads were talk shows in the style pioneered by Phil Donahue and sustained by Oprah Winfrey, reality shows epitomized by the unending CBS *Survivor* series, and yet another rush of whodunit police shows, which this time around, were obsessed with forensic science.

Some categories are short-lived. A wave of buddy movies was ushered in by *Butch Cassidy and the Sundance Kid* in 1969. Later *Thelma and Louise* spawned girlfriend movies.

Genre trends are audience-driven. People flock to a particular book, song, film or television show and then to the thematic sequels until they tire of it all. Although a lot of genre content is derivative rather than original art, new twists and refinements can reflect artistic fine-tuning by authors, scriptwriters and other creators. People may quibble about whether Francis Ford Coppola's *The Godfather* or *The Godfather Part II* was the better, but almost everyone, including the critics, concurs that both were filmic masterpieces. At the same time, nobody serious about creative media content is looking forward to Sylvester Stallone in *Rocky XXXIII*. At some point the possibilities for fresh treatments within a theme are exhausted.

APPLYING YOUR MEDIA LITERACY

- **What genres of media content can you identify besides those mentioned here?**
- **What genres of media content have you seen come and go?**

Music

STUDY PREVIEW	Audio technology accelerated the effect of music as a social unifier. This is no better illustrated than by the integration of traditional black music and white hillbilly music into rock 'n' roll, a precursor to the furthering of racial integration of U.S. society. The potency of music has been enhanced by its growing role in other media forms, including movies and television.

Rockabilly Revolution

Most music historians trace contemporary popular music to roots in two distinctive types of American folk music. There was the black music emanating from the enslaved black culture. Another form was hillbilly music, also from the South but with roots in rural Appalachia.

Black Music. Africans who were brought to the colonies as slaves used music to soothe their difficult lives. Much of the music reflected their oppression and hopeless poverty. Known as **black music**, it was distinctive in that it carried strains of slaves' African roots and at the same time reflected the black American experience. This music also included strong religious themes, expressing the slaves' indefatigable faith in a glorious afterlife. Flowing from the heart and the soul, this was folk music of the most authentic sort.

After the Civil War, black musicians found a white audience on riverboats and in saloons and pleasure palaces of various sorts. That introduced a commercial component into black music and fueled numerous variations, including jazz. Even with the growing white following, the creation of these latter-day forms of black music remained almost entirely with African-American musicians. White musicians who picked up on the growing popularity of black music drew heavily on black songwriters. Much of Benny Goodman's swing music, for example, came from black arranger Fletcher Henderson.

In the 1930s and 1940s a distinctive new form of black music, **rhythm and blues**, emerged. The people who enjoyed R&B were all over the country, and these fans included both blacks and whites. Mainstream American music had come to include a firm African-American presence.

black music
Folk genre from American black slave experience

rhythm and blues
Distinctive style of black music that took form in 1930s

Hillbilly Music. Another authentic American folk music form, **hillbilly music**, flowed from the lives of Appalachian and Southern whites. Early hillbilly music had a strong colonial heritage in English ballads and ditties, but over time hillbilly music evolved into a genre in its own right. Fiddle playing and twangy lyrics reflected the poverty and hopelessness of rural folk, "hillbillies" as they called themselves. Also like black music, hillbilly music reflected the joys, frustrations and sorrows of love and family. However, hillbilly music failed to develop more than a regional following—that is, until the 1950s, when a great confluence of the black and hillbilly traditions occurred. This distinctive new form of American music, called **rockabilly** early on, became rock 'n' roll.

hillbilly music
Folk genre from rural Appalachia, Southern white experience

rockabilly
A splicing of rock 'n' roll and hillbilly, used for early rock music

Rock 'N' Roll

If **rock 'n' roll** as a musical genre has a single progenitor, it may be Memphis disc jockey and promoter **Sam Phillips**. In 1951 Phillips recorded a cars and girls song, *Rocket 88,* an ode to a new Oldsmobile. The recording itself was technically flawed. Willie Kizart's guitar had a cracked amp, but, folded into a boogie-woogie piano, a blues sax and Jackie Brenston's rhythm and blues vocals, the fuzzy guitar sounds seemed to fit. Right away, *Rocket 88* was atop the R&B charts.

rock 'n' roll
A popular dance music characterized by a heavy beat, simple melodies, and guitar, bass and drum instrumentation, usually on a 12-bar structure

Sam Phillips
A Memphis music producer who recorded and promoted early rock music

Rock 'n' roll was hardly calculated. *Rocket 88* had come from four buddies, Ike Turner and His Kings of Rhythm. Infatuated with the new Oldsmobile and driving to a recording session in Memphis, they scribbled rhymes about the Oldsmobile. A blown tire, a rainstorm and a night in jail later, they were in Sam Phillips' recording studio and jamming impromptu—Turner boogie-woogieing his piano, Raymond Hill blowing his blues sax, Willie Kizart hitting fuzzy chords on his failing guitar, and Jackie Brentson intoning those on-the-fly lyrics from the trip.

Sam Phillips was pleased that *Rocket 88,* from a black group, caught on with white as well as black teenagers. But Phillips realized that this emerging hybrid musical genre needed a white face in order to find an enduring place in mainstream pop. In 1954 a white crooner, Elvis Presley, was in the studio recording ballads. During a break Presley belted out a variation of black composer Arthur Crudup's *That's All Right.* Phillips knew he had found what he called, at least apocryphally, his "white boy who sang colored."

Elvis wasn't the first rocker, but he put a white face on rock 'n' roll. A cultural race barrier was transcended on an unprecedented scale. It can be argued that the racial integration of music paved the way for the accelerated civil rights movement in the 1960s that profoundly changed U.S. society.

Music of Dissent

Entertainment can be political, potently so. A folk revival was a centerpiece of the anti-Vietnam war movement of the late 1960s into the 1970s. There were countersingers too, who sold lots of vinyl. *The Ballad of the Green Berets* cast soldiers in a heroic vein. *An Okie from Muskogee* glorified blind patriotism.

This was nothing new. Stephen Foster's *Nothing but a Plain Old Soldier* in 1863 kept the legend of George Washington going. *The Battle Hymn of the Republic* still moves people. The Civil War generated a spate of patriotic music. The catchy *Over There* did the same in World War I.

It was an offhand remark, not their music, that made the sassy Dixie Chicks the bad girls among George W. Bush loyalists. In 2003 at the height of public enthusiasm for the Iraq war, lead singer Natalie Maines, a Texas native, told a London audience that she was "ashamed" that the president, who had launched the war, was from Texas. Despite the popularity of their music, the Chicks were banned by many radio stations

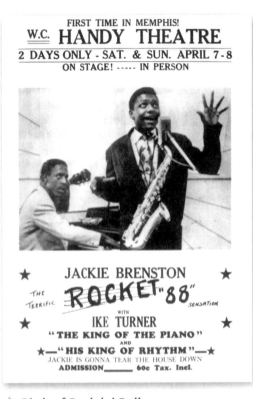

▲ **Birth of Rock 'n' Roll.** *A strong claim can be made that a two-minute ode to a powerful new Oldsmobile, the Rocket 88 model, with a firm backbeat, launched rock 'n' roll as a musical genre in 1951. Other claimants: Louis Jordan's* Caledonia, *Fats Domino's* Fat Man, *and Lloyd Price's* Lawdy Miss *Clawdy.*

▲ **Rage Lives.** *The rapper Zack de la Rocha of the on-again off-again group Rage Against the Machine seldom pulls punches in lyrics or on-stage diatribes. His antiestablishment views can be fierce and uncompromising. He's been known to call American presidents war criminals, quoting linguist-philosopher Noam Chomsky's argument that the U.S. principles in the post-World War II Nuremburg war trials need to be applied anew. Who says protest music is dead?*

rap
Dance music with intense bass, rhyming riffs, the lyrics often with anti-establishment defiance

whose managements were cowed by the volume of listener outrage. The Chicks had the last word, however. In 2006, with public sentiment shifted against the war, the group rebuffed the angry reaction with *Not Ready to Make Nice* on a CD that opened at Number 28 on *Billboard*'s Hot 100.

Classic rockers Pearl Jam added to the anti-war revival with an album that included *World Wide Suicide,* which opened with a newspaper casualty report. The new anti-Iraq war repertoire was perhaps most strident with Neil Young's track *Let's Impeach the President,* in which he sings "flip" and "flop" amid Bush quotes. Paul Simon, whose popularity, like Young's, dated to the Vietnam period, entered the anti-war revival in 2006 with the politically tinged album *Surprise.*

Political leaders know the power of incorporating popular music into their campaign personas. Can you imagine a documentary on Franklin Roosevelt without Jack Yellen and Milton Ager's *Happy Days Are Here Again*? The first President Bush paraphrased the Nitty Gritty Dirt Band on the campaign trail, then borrowed from Paul Simon's *Boy in the Bubble* to make a point about the economy: "If this age of miracles has taught us anything, it's that if we can change the world, we can change America."

In short, music has tremendous effects on human beings, and the technology of sound recording amplifies these effects. The bugle boy was essential to World War II's Company B, but today reveille is digitized to wake the troops. Mothers still sing Brahms' *Lullaby,* but more babies are lulled to sleep by Brahms on an MP3 download. For romance, lovers today rely more on recorded music than on their own vocal cords. The technology of sound recording gives composers, lyricists and performers far larger audiences than would ever be possible through live performances.

Rap

As transforming as rock was, so too 40 years later was **rap**. Born in the impoverished Bronx section of New York, this new style of music had an intense bass for dancing and rhyming riffs, often with a strong and rapid-fire attitude overlaid on the music. Slowly rap spread to other black urban areas. *Run-DMC* and *King of Rock,* both from small independent studios, were the first black rap albums to break into the U.S. music mainstream. Major record companies soon were signing up rap acts. Controversial groups Public Enemy and N.W.A., with violence and racism as themes of their songs, made rap a public issue in the 1990s, which only fanned diehard enthusiasm.

Like rock 'n' roll, major labels missed the significance of early rap, scrambling to catch up only after the catchy lyrics were siphoning sales from older pop genres. A maxim in media studies is that large media business enterprises become mired in tradition with an aversion for risk taking.

Music as Multimedia Content

Although music often is studied as the content issued by the recording industry, music is hardly a one-dimensional form of media message. Even in pre-mass media eras, going back to prehistoric times, music was integrated with dance and theater. When movies were establishing themselves, music was an important component. Even before movie sound tracks were introduced with the "talkies," many movie houses hired a piano player who kept one eye on the screen and hammered out supportive music. D. W. Griffith's

The Birth of a Nation of 1915 had an accompanying score for a 70-piece orchestra.

Some movies are little more than musical vehicles for popular performers, going back to Bing Crosby and continuing through Elvis Presley and the Beatles. Rare is the modern movie without a significant musical bed. Just count the number of songs in the copyright credits at the end of today's movies.

Early radio recognized the value of music. Jingles and ditties proved key to establishing many brand names. Today many composers and lyricists derive significant income from their work being built into advertisements for television, radio and online. Think about the Intel and NBC tones or the grating "Nationwide Is on Your Side."

▲ **"I Love College."** *White rappers are rare, but performer Asher Roth has given the genre a white suburban spin. His rhymes and riffs make no apology for his non-dysfunctional upbringing in the Philadelphia suburb of Morrisville. His style has been called by critics amateurish and uneven, but his music reflects a coming-of-age experience laced with Nintendo, Ford Tauruses and getting high on marijuana. Roth calls it "yoga and yogurt covered in fruit." And he's built a college following.*

APPLYING YOUR MEDIA LITERACY

- What distinctive American musical genres melded in rockabilly?
- How did Elvis Presley personify the music traditions that fused into rock 'n' roll?
- Historically what has been the role of protest music?
- Why were significant renovations, like rock 'n' roll and rap, such difficult adjustments for major media companies?
- What is the difficulty of separating music from other forms of entertainment?

Sports as Media Entertainment

STUDY PREVIEW

Early on, mass media people sensed the potential of sports to build their audiences, first through newspapers, then through magazines, radio and television. The media feed what seems an insatiable demand for more sports. Why the huge public intrigue with sports? One expert suggests it's the mix of suspense, heroes, villains, pageantry and ritual.

Mass Audience for Sports

The brilliant newspaper publisher **James Gordon Bennett** sensed how a public interest in sports could build circulation for his New York *Herald* in the 1830s. Bennett assigned reporters to cover sports regularly. Fifty years later, with growing interest in horse racing, prizefighting, yacht racing and baseball, **Joseph Pulitzer** organized the first separate sports department at his New York *World*. Sportswriters began specializing in different sports.

Audience appetite for sports was insatiable. For the 1897 Corbett-Fitzsimmons heavyweight title fight in remote Nevada, dozens of writers showed up. The New York *Times* introduced celebrity coverage in 1910 when it hired retired prizefighter John L. Sullivan to cover the Jeffries-Johnson title bout in Reno.

Sports historians call the 1920s the Golden Era of Sports, with newspapers glorifying athletes. Heroes, some with enduring fame, included Jack Dempsey in boxing, Knute Rockne and Jim Thorpe in football, and Babe Ruth in baseball. The 1920s also marked radio as a medium for sports. In 1921 **KDKA** of Pittsburgh carried the first play-by-play baseball game, the Davis Cup tennis matches and, blow-by-blow, the Johnny Ray versus John Dundee fight. Sportswriter Grantland Rice, the pre-eminent sportswriter of the time, covered the entire World Series live from New York for KDKA, also in 1921.

James Gordon Bennett
New York newspaper publisher in 1830s; first to assign reporters to sports regularly

Joseph Pulitzer
New York newspaper publisher in 1880s; organized the first newspaper sports department

KDKA
Pittsburgh radio station that pioneered sports broadcasting in 1920s

Sports magazines have their roots in *American Turf Register,* which began a 15-year run in Baltimore in 1829. The *American Bicycling Journal* rode a bicycling craze from 1877 to 1879. Nothing matched the breadth and scope of *Sports Illustrated,* founded in 1954 by magazine magnate **Henry Luce**. The magazine, launched with 350,000 charter subscribers, now boasts a circulation of 3.2 million a week.

Henry Luce
Magazine publisher known for *Time, Life, Sports Illustrated* and others

Roone Arledge
ABC television executive responsible for *Wide World of Sports* in 1961

Although television dabbled in sports from its early days, the introduction of *Wide World of Sports* in 1961 established that television was made for sports and, conversely, that sports was made for television. The show, the brainchild of ABC programming wizard **Roone Arledge**, covered an unpredictable diversity of sports, from ping-pong to skiing. In this period, professional athletic leagues agreed to modify their rules to accommodate television for commercial breaks and, eventually, to make the games more exciting for television audiences.

Television commentator Les Brown explains sports as the perfect program form for television: "At once topical and entertaining, performed live and suspensefully without a script, peopled with heroes and villains, full of action and human interest and laced with pageantry and ritual."

The launching of ESPN as an all-sports network for cable television systems prompted millions of households to subscribe to cable. The success of ESPN spawned sibling networks. Regional sports networks have also emerged, including many created by Fox as major revenue centers.

Audience and Advertiser Confluence

The television networks and national advertisers found a happy confluence of interest in the huge audience for televised sports. This goes back at least to *Friday Night Fights,* sponsored by Gillette razors, and *Wednesday Night Fights,* sponsored by Pabst beer, in the 1950s. Today, sports and television are almost synonymous. Not only does the Super Bowl pack a stadium, but in 2011 some 111 million U.S. households, a record, tuned in. The World Cup soccer tournament draws the largest worldwide television audiences.

In part to keep their names on screen, some firms have bought the rights to put their name on sports stadiums. The value of brand-name exposure at places like the Target Center in Minneapolis, the Bank One Ballpark in Phoenix and Coors Field in Denver is impossible to measure.

Advertiser interest flows and ebbs, as do audiences. The 1950s audience for Wednesday night fights, for example, grew fickle. The phenomenal success of the World Wrestling Federation lost steam after the September 11 terrorist attacks in 2001. Too, there seems to be a saturation point. The WWF's colorful promoter, Vince McMahon, bombed with his new XFL professional football league in 2001. Even with its own rules, designed to add excitement for television audiences, and even with tireless promotion by NBC, it seemed that football fans already had their plates full.

Cost of Sports Broadcasting

Sports attract huge audiences to television. For the 2010 Vancouver Olympics, which spanned 17 days, NBC averaged 24.4 million prime-time viewers. The Super Bowl has become the most-watched television program ever. Advertisers pay millions of dollars for commercial time to reach these audiences. AT&T and Anheuser-Busch each spent $366 million on sports advertising in 2010.

With the exception of the 2008 Beijing Olympics, for which NBC budgeted $1 billion, the networks seldom generate enough revenue to offset fees negotiated by sports leagues. Together CBS and Fox pay the NFL $1.3 billion a year for broadcast rights. The NCCA men's basketball tournament cost CBS and Turner $771 million. For ESPN, Fox and TNT, broadcast rights exceed $570 million a year for NASCAR auto races.

Considering the economics, the networks occasionally retreat from the bidding frenzy for broadcast rights. NBC opted out of bidding to renew its four-year $1.6 billion National Basketball Association contract after losing $100 million in 2003. What happened? ESPN won the rights for $2.4 billion.

Madness, you say? Maybe not. Consider the experience of CBS, which was the leading sports network in 1994. CBS, trying to make the numbers work to continue its National

Football League coverage, was outbid by Fox. Six local CBS affiliates switched to Fox. CBS fell to fourth among the networks with male viewers, an important demographic group for advertisers. Smarting at the setbacks, CBS was not to be outdone. When CBS regained NFL rights again in 1998, the network resumed leadership in terms both of total viewers and of men 18 and older. CBS and Fox then bid $8 billion for NFL games from 2007 to 2010, 25 percent more than the previous deal. And through 2013 CBS, Fox and NBC agreed to $603 million to $720 million each for NFL games.

The networks have adjusted their business model from seeing sports as a profit center. Instead, sports has become recognized as a **loss leader**. The goal now is to use sports programs to promote other network programming, to enhance the network as a brand, and to deny coverage to competing networks—and at the same time generate enough in advertising and in some cases subscription revenue to minimize the loss. Les Moonves, president of CBS, explained the new thinking this way: "Broadcast networks must look at sports as a piece of a much larger puzzle and not focus on the specific profits and losses of sports divisions."

Culturally the Moonves mindset has negative effects. The sports drain has forced CBS and other networks to emphasize more low-cost programming, like reality shows, for the rest of their schedules. The idea is to tell audiences what's worth watching after the game. It's worth noting too, as critics point out, the huge licensing fees paid for broadcast rights make possible the mega-salaries of top athletes.

loss leader
A product sold at a loss to attract customers

APPLYING YOUR MEDIA LITERACY

- **What have been landmarks in the growth of media sports for amusement?**
- **Why are advertisers attracted to sports?**
- **Why do broadcast companies compete to air sports even though the programming generally is a money loser?**

Sex as Media Content

STUDY PREVIEW | Despite the risk of offending some people's sensitivities, the media have long trafficked in sexual content. Undeniably, there is a market. The media have fought in the U.S. courts for their right to carry sexually explicit content and for the right of adults to have access to it.

Adult Entertainment

Sexually oriented content has bedeviled the mass media in the United States for longer than anyone can remember. Clearly, there is a demand for it. Sales of banned books soared as soon as the courts overruled government restrictions, no better illustrated than by the Irish classic **Ulysses** by James Joyce in 1930. Firm data on the profitability of sexual content are hard to come by, partly because definitions are elusive. *Ulysses*, as an example, is hardly a sex book to most people, yet its sexual content is what once prompted a federal import ban. The difficulty of a definition gives partisans the opportunity to issue exaggerated estimates of the scope of the sexual media content.

Ulysses
James Joyce novel banned in the United States until 1930 court decision

Even so, there is no denying that sex sells. Although revenues are difficult to peg precisely, most estimates are in the range of $8 billion to $10 billion annually for the entire U.S. sex industry, a major part of which is media content. About 8,000 adult movie titles a year are released. Pay-per-view adult movies on satellite and cable television generate almost $600 million in revenue a year.

It was no sleazy outfit that first imported *Ulysses* but the venerable publisher Random House. Today the major purveyors of adult content include Time Warner's HBO and Cinemax, which pipe late-night adult content to multiple-system cable operators including Time Warner. Satellite providers DirecTV and Dish Network offer porn to their subscribers. Big-name hotel chains pipe adult movies into rooms. Not unsurprisingly, moralists periodically picket Barnes & Noble and other mainstream

obscenity
Sexually explicit media depictions that the government can ban

pornography
Sexually explicit depictions that are protected from government bans

Miller Standard
Current U.S. Supreme Court definition of sexually explicit depictions that are protected by the First Amendment from government bans

Sam Ginsberg
Figure in U.S. Supreme Court decision to bar sales of pornography to children

George Carlin
Comedian whose satires on vulgarities prompted rules on radio programming to shield children

Pacifica case
U.S. Supreme Court ruling to keep indecency off over-air broadcast stations at times when children are likely to be listening or watching

bookstores to protest the books and magazines they stock. There is an online roster of "clean hotels" for people who don't want to stay in a room where pay-per-view porn is available on television.

Decency Requirements

Most media companies have found comfort in the definition of sexually acceptable content that has evolved in free expression cases in the U.S. courts. Today the courts make a distinction between **obscenity**, which is not allowed, and **pornography**, which the courts find to be protected by the First Amendment guarantee not only of free expression but also of adult access to other people's expressions.

How are obscenity and pornography different? Since 1973, when the U.S. Supreme Court decided the case *Miller* v. *California*, the courts have followed the **Miller Standard**. In effect, sexual content is protected from government bans unless the material fails all of these tests:

- Would a typical person applying local standards see the material as appealing mainly for its sexually arousing effect?
- Is the material devoid of serious literary, artistic, political or scientific value?
- Is the sexual activity depicted offensively, in a way that violates a state law that explicitly defines offensiveness?

The Miller Standard protects a vast range of sexual content. Only material for which the answer is "yes" to all three Miller questions can be censored by government agencies.

The Miller Standard notwithstanding, the Federal Communications Commission fined CBS $550,000 for the Janet Jackson breast flash during the 2004 Super Bowl halftime show. The producer, CBS's Viacom cousin MTV, called the incident a "wardrobe malfunction." About 89 million people were tuned in. Some complained.

Sexual Content and Children

Although government limits on sexual content gradually eased in the late 20th century, there remain restrictions on media content for children. The U.S. Supreme Court established the childhood exception in 1968 in a case involving a Bellmore, New York, sandwich shop owner, **Sam Ginsberg**, who had sold girlie magazines to a 16-year-old. The local prosecutor went after Ginsberg using a state law that prohibited selling depictions of nudity to anyone under age 17. The U.S. Supreme Court upheld the constitutionality of the state law.

In broadcasting, the U.S. Supreme Court has upheld restrictions aimed at shielding children. After New York radio station WBAI aired a comedy routine by **George Carlin** with four-letter anatomical words and vulgarities, the Federal Communications Commission, which can yank a station's license to broadcast, took action against the station's owner, the Pacifica Foundation. In the **Pacifica case**, as it came to be known, the U.S. Supreme Court upheld the FCC's limits on indecency during times of the day when children are likely to be listening. Carlin's monologue, *Filthy Words*, had aired at 2 p.m. In response, stations now are careful to keep the raunchiest stuff off the air until late night.

The courts also have upheld laws against sexual depictions of juveniles as exploitative. Many prosecutors come down hard even for the possession of such materials. Child pornography is one of society's last taboos.

▲ **Filthy Words.** *After Pacifica radio station WBAI in New York aired a 12-minute recorded George Carlin monologue, the U.S. Supreme Court authorized government restrictions on indecency at times of the day when children might be listening.*

APPLYING YOUR MEDIA LITERACY

- Why is government regulation of media sexual content difficult?
- How is the Miller standard helpful in distinguishing pornography from obscenity?
- Describe attempts by the government to create a double standard, one for adults and one for children, on sexual media content.

The Future of Gaming

Bouquet depth of field? Subsurface scattering? Sounds like some sort of statistical analysis. Actually these are some of the new techniques programmers and artists are using to advance video games to the next level.

With a bouquet depth of field, you see a bright spot that is out of focus and then replaced with another image. With the subsurface scattering effect, light on a human face penetrates the layers of skin and makes the skin glow.

When Epic Games first showed off these effects in a short demo at the Game Developers Conference in 2011, its 3D graphics represented a new high point in realism. The fight scene in the demo played out against a gritty city with effects such as a glowing blow torch, detailed face close-ups, and skin morphing. The graphics were real-time computer graphics, not a video of pre-fabricated computer graphics that was the norm at the time. The demo was assembled in three months by 12 programmers and artists.

In the future, real-time computer graphics, like all new software, will require leaps in hardware too. Engineers are working on creating chips for mobile computing, driven by the demand for smartphones and tablets, that could force changes in the PC design and performance to keep up with the gaming features on new mobile devices. Nvidia, the company that invented the graphics processing unit that drives the computer graphics in video games, is upping the number of cores in a single chip. The company expects its Tegra mobile computing chips will go from the standard of eight cores in 2011 to 100 in a single chip by 2015.

The company's Project Denver is expected to be able to run Windows using its mobile chips. Jen-Hsun Huang, chief executive of Nvidia, said it took PCs about 25 years to disrupt the minicomputer and main-frame business. He thinks mobile computing is changing the world faster and will likely disrupt the PC and server markets in a much shorter time. "The mobile computing revolution is a seismic shift."

What else does the future hold for gaming? Some of the other intriguing predictions made by to-day's developers for gaming's future include:

- Games will be designed to accommodate micro-transactions. Game-makers will be able to sell virtual goods such as clothing for a few cents to a few dollars.
- Evolving control methods will translate into the entire home entertainment system. A console will be everything, if you need a console at all.
- Gaming will continue to become more interactive, with social media, user-generated content, and cooperative play playing central roles.
- The audience for gaming will continue to grow and age, and gaming will become more mainstream.
- Online and multiplayer gaming will continue to grow. More casual games will be developed to be played on the browser.
- Reality TV shows will merge viewing and gaming seamlessly.

Experts all agree on is that the future of gaming will be become more integrated with other forms of entertainment, perhaps to the point that games will be far less a distinctive media entity than today. Like other entertainment, games will be available on all kinds of devices—everywhere and whenever. Chris Pickford, associate producer at video game development studio Bizarre Creations, believes that video games will become an important extension of all visual entertainment. "There will be lots more crossover between media formats—films, games, websites, and even theme parks." Pickford says that games will be a full encompassing experience: "In terms of worldwide respect, video games will be side by side with Hollywood—they may even overtake it at points."

End of Desktops?

The ever-sharper graphics of video games, as demonstrated by developer Epic Games, are spectacular for their visual effects. But what's under the hood, not on-screen, that foretells the future of personal computers. The technology that makes tablets and phones ideal for gaming is set to displace the personal computer architecture that's been around 25 years.

What Do You Think?

Does the future of gaming depend on the future of mobile computing?

Will Hollywood and gaming developers do battle or will they work together?

What other possibilities do you see for the future of gaming?

Gaming as Media Content

STUDY PREVIEW | Gaming has grown as a form of mass entertainment. Some games outdraw television. As typical with new media content, gaming has become a whipping boy for society's ills with calls for restriction. The courts have not found compelling reasons to go along with restrictions.

Growing Entertainment Form

Nobody could doubt the significance of video games as a media form after 2001. For the first time, sales of games in the United States outpaced movies. When popular games are issued, retailers open their doors at midnight on the release date. One of the first times this happened, in 2004 when Microsoft introduced its *Halo2,* it was a news event. Thousands of gamers at 6,800 stores nationwide waited in line as long as 14 hours. Within 24 hours, sales surpassed $125 million—way ahead of the $70 million opening-weekend box office for the year's leading film, *The Incredibles.*

That same year, players of *Madden NFL* spent an estimated average of 100 hours on the game. With 4 million players, that was 400 million hours. The full season of *The Sopranos,* then at its heyday, was claiming 143 million viewing hours. Do the math: *The Sopranos* averaged 11 million viewers for 13 episodes that year.

To catch consumers who spend less time with television and more time with video games, advertisers have shifted chunks of their budgets to gaming. The potential is incredible. Half of Americans 6 and older play games, and that elusive target for advertisers, men 18 and older, makes up 26 percent of the gamers.

Censorship and Gaming

Like other entertainment forms, gaming is a lightning rod of concern about the effects of explicit violence and sex on children. The industry devised a voluntary rating system with EC for "early childhood" to AO for "adults only," but critics have called the system a joke among retailers. Three high-visibility U.S. senators once went so far as to propose $5,000 fines for every time a retailer violates the code for kids under 17.

In 2011 the U.S. Supreme Court threw out a California law banning the sale of violent video game to children. In response, the Court ruled that the game industry's own voluntary rating system was sufficient. Justice Antonin Scalia wrote that the law abridged the First Amendment rights of young people by superseding the judgment of parents and aunts and uncles who view violent video games as a harmless pastime.

APPLYING YOUR MEDIA LITERACY

- **Why is gaming shedding its status as a niche medium?**
- **How have gaming companies responded to calls to censor violence and sex?**

Artistic Values

STUDY PREVIEW | The mass media are inextricably linked with culture because it is through the media that creative people have their strongest sway. Although the media have the potential to disseminate the best creative work of the human mind and soul, some critics say the media are obsessive about trendy, often silly subjects. These critics find serious fault with the media's concern for pop culture, claiming it squeezes out things of significance.

Media Content as High Art

Mass media messages can be art of a high order, as was perhaps no better illustrated than by early filmmaker D. W. Griffith. In the 1910s Griffith proved himself a filmmaking genius whose

■ When Artistry Irks Totalitarianism

Iranian Filmmaker. *Jafar Panahi is home in Tehran, under house arrest, after more than two months in custody and after paying $200,000 bail. The thin-skinned Iranian government leadership doesn't much appreciate his films. At the world's leading film festivals, however, Panahi has been honored for the very stories and themes that have landed him in jail in his homeland.*

At 51 and at a pinnacle in his career, Iranian filmmaker Jafar Panahi found himself under house arrest. At least he was home—after another stay in a Tehran jailhouse. Most of Panahi's films, although highly regarded internationally, are banned in his home country. His film *The White Balloon* holds the Camera d'Or from Cannes. Panahi won the Golden Lion at Venice. But the Islamic regime in Iran doesn't approve of Panahi's satires on life in Iran or his views. They keep trying to silence him.

Panahi was arrested in 2009 when he supported protesters killed following Iran's disputed presidential election. He was soon released. But in 2010 he was again arrested with his family and colleagues and taken to Tehran's Evin prison. His "crime"? Making an anti-government film without permission and inciting opposition protests after the presidential election. The film in question, *The Accordion*, was based

on Article 18 of the Universal Declaration of Human Rights: "Everyone has the right to freedom of thought, conscience and religion."

Panahi was sentenced to six years in prison and banned from making films, travelling abroad or speaking to the news media for 20 years. While in prison Panahi carried out a hunger strike to protest his demeaning treatment, including being forced to stand outside in the cold with no clothing. He was later released to house arrest after paying $200,000 bail.

His documentary *This Is Not A Film*, about a day in his life as he waited under house arrest to hear about his appeal, was shown at the Cannes film festival. It was smuggled out of Iran on a USB stick hidden in a cake. Panahi received the Golden Coach prize at the festival, a lifetime achievement award previously given to legendary filmmakers including Clint Eastwood and Agnes Varda. A festival statement said that honoring Panahi was to honor all Iranian filmmakers who continue to make films whether in exile or in their own country. Panahi was invited to judge at Cannes but was in detention in Iran and couldn't attend. An empty chair was kept prominently on stage during the festival to recognize his absence.

Panahi isn't the only artist in the entertainment business in Iran to face government censure. In 2011 an Iranian court sentenced actress Marzieh Vafamehr to a year in jail and 90 lashes for acting in the film *My Tehran for Sale*, a film about how artists are not allowed to speak their minds in Iran. Ironically, it's about an Iranian actress who is jailed and beaten for acting immodestly.

Filmmaker Mohammad Rasoulof, who was arrested at the same time as Panahi in 2010, also received a six-year sentence, but it was reduced to one year. Panahi's co-director Mojtaba Mirtahmasb was arrested and charged with espionage for working for the BBC in 2011. Three other filmmakers also were arrested and charged with espionage, their fates unannounced. In the unpredictable artistic atmosphere of Iran, two other directors who had been arrested were released. And Panahi's latest appeal was denied. Panahi's attorney, who learned about the court's ruling through the media, promised to appeal to Iran's supreme court.

Meanwhile, the Writers Guild of America has urged the Iranian government to remember that artists have the right to hold and express opinions, as do all free people. "We urge the government of Iran to remember that their work is the most powerful ambassador of understanding between the people of Iran and the people of the world."

A government-backed Iranian newspaper said Panahi was being punished for acting against national security and creating anti-regime propaganda.

POINT

COUNTER POINT

In a statement of support for Panahi, the Writers Guild urged the government of Iran to remember that these are artists, not political enemies.

DEEPENING YOUR MEDIA LITERACY

EXPLORE THE ISSUE: What other countries have banned films for political reasons?

DIG DEEPER: What type of government rules these countries? Do they share the same policies? Do they have anything else in common?

WHAT DO YOU THINK? Why do artists continue to produce films under the threat of arrest and imprisonment? What can be done to help them? Should they be helped, even if what they do is critical of their government?

contribution to the culture, for better or worse, was original in scale, content and style. Griffith had something to say, and the new mass medium of film was the vehicle for his message.

In the 1950s, when French New Wave directors were offering distinctive stories and messages, film critic **Andre Bazin** devised the term **auteur** to denote significant and original cinematic contributions. European auteurs included Jean Luc Godard, who made *Breathless,* and François Truffaut, who made *The 400 Blows.* Their work was marked by distinctive cinematic techniques—freeze-frames, handheld cameras and novel angles, all common in movies now. Perhaps the most famous of these highbrow filmmakers who developed a global following was the Swedish director Ingmar Bergman, with 2 *The Seventh Seal* and other dark, moody and autobiographical works.

American filmmakers have also contributed to the auteur movement. The original auteurs were those Hollywood directors working within the constraints of the studio system who nevertheless imparted their unique artistic vision across their body of work. John Ford, John Huston, Howard Hawks and Elia Kazan all left their distinctive mark on otherwise homogenous Hollywood products of that era. More recent auteurs include Stanley Kubrick, who directed *2001: A Space Odyssey;* Martin Scorsese, whose films include *Taxi Driver* and *Goodfellas;* David Lynch, who made *Blue Velvet;* and Spike Lee, who focuses on African-American life.

Culturally significant media content is hardly limited to movies. Older media forms, including novels and short stories, have long been home for creative people whose work adds insight to our lives and deepens our understandings and appreciations.

Andre Bazin
French film critic who devised the term *auteur* for significant cutting-edge filmmakers

auteur
A filmmaker recognized for significant and original treatments

MEDIAtimeline

MEDIATED ENTERTAINMENT MILESTONES

PRINTED MUSIC
First printed music, *Harmonice Musices Odhecaton* (1501)

AMERICAN MAGAZINE
Colonial printer Andrew Bradford issued American Magazine (1729)

PIVOTAL EVENTS

- Stories, music as part of human communication (Prehistory-)
- Olympic games in Greece (776 B.C.)
- Gutenberg's moveable type (1446)
- Shakespeare, *Two Gentlemen of Verona* (1589)
- United States founded (1776)

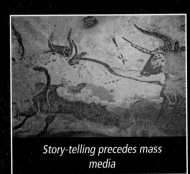
Story-telling precedes mass media

Prehistory–1700s

MEDIATED ENTERTAINMENT MILESTONES

SPORTING NEWS
American Turf Register magazine (1829–1844)

SONGBOOKS
Stephen Foster published songbook Ethiopian Melodies (1849)

BEST-SELLING BOOKS
Harriet Beecher Stowe best-seller *Uncle Tom's Cabin* (1852)

CELEBRRITY SPORTS
Celebrity sports coverage with John L. Sullivan covering prize fight (1910)

PIVOTAL EVENTS

- Civil War (1861–1865)
- Thomas Edison phonograph (1877)
- News coverage of prize fights, bicycling (1880s)
- First Army-Navy football game (1890)
- Thomas Edison premiered 10 short films (1894)

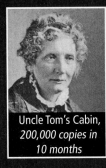
Uncle Tom's Cabin, 200,000 copies in 10 months

1800s

The impact of great composers from eras before the mass media has been exponentially extended through recording, film and television. The printing press greatly expanded the audience for religious scriptures, whose messages go back to prehistoric times.

Lesser Art

To be sure, not all media content is high art.

Production-Line Entertainment. A television soap opera, whatever its entertainment value, lacks the creative genius of Shakespeare's enduring *Romeo and Juliet*. Why can't all media content rank high on an artistic scale? Besides the obvious explanation that not everyone is born a Shakespeare, the modern mass media are commercial enterprises that must produce vast quantities of material. In the 1920s, for example, an insatiable public demand for movies led to the creation of the Hollywood **studio system**, in effect turning moviemaking into a factory process. Production quotas drove movie production. The studios, awash in money, hired leading authors of the day, including F. Scott Fitzgerald and William Faulkner, for creative story lines and scripts, but inexorable demands for material drained them. It has been said that Hollywood had some of the most gifted writers of the time doing their weakest work.

The factory model, a product of the Industrial Age, extends throughout the media. The Canadian book publisher **Harlequin** grinds out romance novels with their bodice-busting covers. Nobody confuses Harlequins with high art. Imagine, also, filling a

studio system
A production-line movie system devised by Hollywood in the 1920s

Harlequin
Canadian publisher known for romances with clichéd characters, settings and themes; the term is applied generically to pulp romances

MEDIATED ENTERTAINMENT MILESTONES

MOVIE EPICS
D. W. Griffith film *Birth of a Nation* (1915)

SEX DEPICTIONS
James Joyce novel *Ulysses* (1930)

BROADCAST SPORTS
World Series play-by-play on radio (1921)

PIVOTAL EVENTS
- First baseball World Series (1903)
- World War I (1914–1918)
- Crooners, dance music (1920s–)
- Joseph Maxfield invented electrical recording (1925)
- Great Depression (1929–1940s)
- First soccer World Cup (1930)
- Federal licensing of radio (1927)
- Rhythm and blues (1940s–)
- World War II (1941–1945)

Rock 'n' roll from black, hillbilly roots

1900-1949

MEDIATED ENTERTAINMENT MILESTONES

LOOSENING MORES
Hugh Hefner founded *Playboy* magazine (1953)

GLOSSY SPORTS
Henry Luce founded *Sports Illustrated* (1954)

TELEVISION SPORTS
ABC television Wide World of Sports (1961)

Growing tolerance for vulgarity

VIDEO GAMES
John Madden football video game (1988)

PIVOTAL EVENTS
- Rock 'n' roll (1950s–)
- Gulf of Tonkin incident escalated Vietnam war (1964)
- Protest songs (late 1960s–)
- First football Super Bowl (1967)
- *Pacifica* case on broadcast decency (1968)
- Miller Standard on sexual explicitness (1973)
- Rap (1990s –)

1950-1999

MEDIATED ENTERTAINMENT MILESTONES

PORNOGRAPHY
U.S. sexually explicit video sales at $3.3 billion (2006)

3-D
James Cameron's Avatar a CGI and 3-D epic (2009)

TABLETS
Apple introduced iPad as multi-media device (2010)

PIVOTAL EVENTS
- Downloaded music sales fail to offset declining CD sales (2001)
- Video games emerge as industry (2001)
- Iraq war (2003–2011)
- Great Recession (2007–2009)
- Obama presidency (2009–)
- BP Gulf oil spill (2010)
- Borders bookstore chain shuts down (2011)
- Court decision allowing violence in video games (2011)

2000S

Sports big as mediated amusement and diversion

television network's prime-time obligation, 42 half-hour slots a week. It can't all be great stuff, despite the promotional claims in preseason ramp-ups. Also, many in the mass audience don't want great art anyway.

Copycat Content.   Significant amounts of media content are imitative. Copycat sounds abound in material from the recording industry. In network television a sudden success, like ABC's *Who Wants to Be a Millionaire* in 2001, spawned other, albeit less successful, quiz shows. Alas, even *Millionaire* was hardly original. The concept was licensed from an already-running show in Britain.

Cross-Media Adaptations.   The demand for content creates a vacuum that sucks up material from other media. Movie studios draw heavily on written literature, from best-selling novels to comic books like *Spider-Man* and *The X-Men*. Conversely, fresh movies sometimes are adapted into book form.

Cross-media adaptations don't always work well. Movie versions of books often disappoint readers. Scenes change. So do characters. Inevitably, a lot is left out. Some of the criticism is unfair because it fails to recognize that movies are a distinct medium. How, for example, could a screenwriter pack everything in a 100,000-word novel into a 100-minute script? These are different media. Passages that work brilliantly in a word-driven medium, like a magazine or short story, can fall flat in a medium with visual enhancements. Conversely, the nuances compactly portrayed by a master actor, like Meryl Streep or Jack Nicholson, could take pages and pages in a book and not work as well. Also, movie studio producers, almost always needing to appeal to the widest possible audience, will alter plots, scenes and characters and sometimes even reverse a story line's climactic events.

Some cross-media adaptations are commercial disasters. With limited success, movie studios have tried to cash in on the popularity of video games. Despite high expectations, *Super Mario Bros.* flopped in 1993. The explanation? Some critics cite the same difficulties that occur in transferring messages from books to movies. With video games the audience member plays an active role by exercising some control over the story line. Watching a movie, however, is relatively passive.

Unpretentious Media Content

pulp fiction
Quickly and inexpensively produced easy-to-read short novels

Although critics pan a lot of media content as unworthy, the fact is that lowbrow art and middlebrow art find audiences, sometimes large audiences, and have a firm place in the mix that mass media offer. There is nothing artistically pretentious in **pulp fiction**, including the Harlequin romances, nor their soap-opera equivalents on television. The lack of pretension, however, can have its own campy charm.

▲ **Surviving Movie House.** *Pashto movies were hardly great film-making, but they built an audience over the years in the remote Khyber Pass region of Pakistan and Afghanistan. Today, after vigilante fire-bombings and intimidation by religious extremists, the Pashto movie industry has largely vanished. The Shabistan Cinema in Peshawar is among the few remaining movie houses. Go at your own risk.*

▶ **CASE STUDY:** When Extremism Trumps Entertainment

Perhaps nowhere on earth is entertainment as suspect, even loathed, as in regions with a strong presence of Taliban religious fundamentalism. Through intimidation, the fundamentalists have shut down the movie industry in northwest Pakistan. *Time* magazine reporter Aryn Bakers tells the story of Aziz ul-Haq, a shopkeeper in the frontier city of Peshawar. One day a Taliban devotee visited the shop and accused Haq of selling pornography. The Taliban jabbed a finger at a DVD cover depicting a man and woman about to kiss. "These movies are destroying the character of our children," the Talib declared. Haq defended the movie: "This is a family drama, a romance, nothing more."

Next: Haq's shop was destroyed in a pre-dawn firebombing. Over several months, vigilantes also left messages with their bombs at other shops. Afraid not only for their livelihoods but also for their lives, shopkeepers one by one stopped stocking videos. Some, like Haq, went out of business.

Peshawar once had a small, thriving movie industry. Although never known for great films, the studios issued movies that depicted values of Pashto-speaking people in north-west Pakistan and southeast Afghanistan. Today, what's left of the Pashto movie business is underground. Movies are produced secretly. DVDs are distributed through anonymous channels. Most Pashtun movie-makers have moved to safer cities to avoid the wrath of zealous Tailiban mullahs and their adherents.

The Peshawar music industry has been decimated too. Without distribution channels, there is no market. A Peshawar professor explained: "These entertainers are stealing an audience away from the mullahs, so the musicians have become their enemies."

Elitist Versus Populist Values

The mass media can enrich society by disseminating the best of human creativity, including great literature, music and art. The media also carry a lot of lesser things that reflect the culture and, for better or worse, contribute to it. Over time, a continuum has been devised that covers this vast range of artistic production. At one extreme is artistic material that requires sophisticated and cultivated tastes to appreciate. This is called **high art**. At the other extreme is **low art,** which requires little sophistication to enjoy.

One strain of traditional media criticism has been that the media underplay great works and concentrate on low art. This **elitist** view argues that the mass media do society a disservice by pandering to low tastes. To describe low art, elitists sometimes use the German word **kitsch,** which translates roughly as "garish" or "trashy." The word captures their disdain. In contrast, the **populist** view is that there is nothing unbecoming in the mass media's catering to mass tastes in a democratic, capitalistic society.

In a 1960 essay still widely cited, "Masscult and Midcult," social commentator **Dwight Macdonald** made a virulent case that all popular art is kitsch. The mass media, which depend on finding large audiences for their economic base, can hardly ever come out at the higher reaches of Macdonald's spectrum.

This kind of elitist analysis was given a larger framework in 1976 when sociologist **Herbert Gans** categorized cultural work along socioeconomic and intellectual lines. Gans said that classical music, as an example, appealed by and large to people of academic and professional accomplishments and higher incomes. These were **high-culture audiences**, which enjoyed complexities and subtleties in their art and entertainment. Next in Gans' breakdown came **middle-culture audiences**. These audiences, less abstract in their interests, liked Norman Rockwell paintings and prime-time television. To Gans, **low-culture audiences** were factory and service workers whose interests were more basic; whose educational accomplishments, incomes and social status were lower; and whose media tastes leaned toward kung fu movies, comic books and supermarket tabloids.

Gans was applying his contemporary observations to flesh out the distinctions that had been taking form in art criticism for centuries—the distinctions between high art and low art.

Highbrow. The high art favored by elitists generally can be identified by its technical and thematic complexity and originality. High art is often highly individualistic because the creator, perhaps a novelist, perhaps a television producer, has explored issues in fresh ways, often with new and different methods. Even when it's a collaborative effort, a piece of high art is distinctive. High art requires a sophisticated audience to appreciate it fully. Often it has enduring value, surviving time's test as to its significance and worth.

The sophistication that permits an opera aficionado to appreciate the intricacies of a composer's score, the poetry of the lyricist and the excellence of the performance sometimes is called **highbrow**. The label has grim origins in the idea that a person must have great intelligence to have refined tastes, and a high brow is necessary to accommodate such a big brain. Generally, the term is used by people who disdain those who have not developed the sophistication to enjoy, for example, the abstractions of a Fellini film, a Matisse sculpture or a Picasso painting. Highbrows generally are people who, as Gans noted, are interested in issues by which society is defining itself and look to literature and drama for stories on conflicts inherent in the human condition and between the individual and society.

Middlebrow. **Middlebrow** tastes recognize some artistic merit but don't have a high level of sophistication. There is more interest in action than abstractions—as in Captain

high art
Requires sophisticated taste
to be appreciated

low art
Can be appreciated by almost
everybody

elitist
Mass media should gear to
sophisticated audiences

kitsch
Pejorative word for trendy,
trashy, low art

populist
Mass media should seek largest
possible audiences

Dwight Macdonald
Said all pop art is kitsch

Herbert Gans
Said social, economic and intellectual
levels of audience coincide

*high-, middle- and low-culture
audiences*
Continuum identified by Herbert Gans

*highbrow, middlebrow and
lowbrow*
Levels of media content sophistication
that coincide with audience tastes

Kirk aboard the starship *Enterprise*, for example, than in the childhood struggles of Ingmar Bergman that shaped his films. In socioeconomic terms, middlebrow appeals to people who take comfort in media portrayals that support their status-quo orientation and values.

Lowbrow. Someone once made this often-repeated distinction: Highbrows talk about ideas, middlebrows talk about things, and **lowbrows** talk about people. Judging from the circulation success of the *National Enquirer* and celebrity tabloid television, there must be a lot of lowbrows in contemporary life. Hardly any sophistication is needed to recognize the machismo of Rambo, the villainy of Darth Vader, the heroism of Superman or the sexiness of Lara Croft.

Case Against Pop Art

Pop art is of the moment, including things like body piercings and hip-hop garb—and trendy media fare. Even elitists may have fun with pop, but they traditionally have drawn the line at anyone who mistakes it as having serious artistic merit. Pop art is low art that has immense although generally short-lived popularity.

Elitists see pop art as contrived and artificial. In their view, the people who create **popular art** are masters at identifying what will succeed in the marketplace and then providing it. Pop art, according to this view, succeeds by conning people into liking it. When capri pants were the fashion rage, it was not because they were superior in comfort, utility or aesthetics but because promoters sensed that profits could be made by touting them through the mass media as new and cashing in on easily manipulated mass tastes. It was the same with pet rocks, Tickle Me Elmo and countless other faddish products.

The mass media, according to the critics, are obsessed with pop art. This is partly because the media are the carriers of the promotional campaigns that create popular followings but also because competition within the media creates pressure to be first, to be ahead, to be on top of things. The result, say elitists, is that junk takes precedence over quality.

Much is to be said for this criticism of pop art. The promotion by CBS of the screwball 1960s sitcom *Beverly Hillbillies*, as an example, created an eager audience that otherwise might have been reading Steinbeck's critically respected *Grapes of Wrath*. An elitist might chortle, even laugh, at the unbelievable antics and travails of the Beverly Hillbillies, who had their own charm, but an elitist would be concerned all the while that low art was displacing high art in the marketplace and that society was the poorer for it.

Pop Art Revisionism

Pop art has always had a few champions among intellectuals, although the voices of **pop art revisionism** often have been drowned out in the din of elitist pooh-poohing. In 1965, however, essayist **Susan Sontag** wrote an influential piece, "On Culture and the New Sensibility," that prompted many elitists to take a fresh look at pop art.

Pop Art as Evocative. Sontag made the case that pop art could raise serious issues, just as high art could. She wrote: "The feeling given off by a Rauschenberg painting might be like that of a song by the Supremes." Sontag soon was being called the High Priestess of Pop Intellectualism. More significantly, the Supremes were being taken more seriously, as were a great number of Sontag's avant-garde and obscure pop artist friends.

Pop Art as a Societal Unifier. In effect, Sontag encouraged people not to look at art on the traditional divisive, class-conscious, elitist-populist continuum. Artistic value, she said, could be found almost anywhere. The word *camp* gained circulation among 1960s elitists who were influenced by Sontag. These highbrows began finding a perversely sophisticated appeal in pop art as diverse as Andy Warhol's banal soup cans and ABC's outrageous *Batman*.

popular art
Art that tries to succeed in the marketplace

pop art revisionism
The view that pop art has inherent value

Susan Sontag
Saw cultural, social value in pop art

▲ **Susan Sontag.** *Her defense of less-than-highbrow art earned Susan Sontag the title of High Priestess of Pop Art. Sontag, a thinker on cultural issues, said paintings, music and other art with wide, popular appeal can evoke significant insights and sensitivities for some people.*

High Art as Popular. While kitsch may be prominent in media programming, it hardly elbows out all substantive content. In 1991, for example, Ken Burns' public television documentary *The Civil War* outdrew low-art prime-time programs on ABC, CBS and NBC five nights in a row. It was a glaring example that high art can appeal to people across almost the whole range of socioeconomic levels and is not necessarily driven out by low art. Burns' documentary was hardly a lone example. Another, also from 1991, was Franco Zeffirelli's movie *Hamlet,* starring pop movie star Mel Gibson, which was marketed to a mass audience yet could hardly be dismissed by elitists as kitsch. In radio, public broadcasting stations, marked by highbrow programming, have become major players for ratings.

APPLYING YOUR MEDIA LITERACY

- **Which media content easily ranks as worthy art?**
- **What mass media dynamics work against consistent delivery of quality content?**
- **What kinds of scales can be used to rank creative content?**
- **How do pop art revisionists defend pop art?**

■ Entertainment in History (Pages 233–235)

Entertainment far predates its modern eminence as a mass media enterprise. People always have loved stories and music. Media technology, beginning with printing, dramatically changed entertainment. Master storytellers and musicians, for example, could have audiences whose size could never have been anticipated in earlier times. Entertainment of a high caliber became available widely. People gradually took less responsibility for creating their own entertainment, becoming consumers of entertainment.

■ Performance as Media Entertainment
(Pages 236–237)

Mass media affect performance. A stage product transferred to television, for example, needs to be adapted to camera possibilities such as close-ups. The relationship to the audience is far different. So are cutaway possibilities to multiple additional scenes. Audio technology has brought dramatic changes to music. Early acoustic technology was crude, which put a premium on loud if not blaring martial music. Amplification technology brought the crooners. Changes are not entirely wrought by technology, however. Economics can affect performance. The NFL, for example, has changed football rules to accommodate television's requirement for commercial breaks.

■ Storytelling (Pages 237–238)

Mass media companies have made storytelling in its various forms a commodity. Always looking for a competitive edge, companies shift in their promoting of different genres of literature programming. A book

CHAPTER WRAP UP

or program that catches the public's fancy becomes hot and spawns imitators. The public inevitably grows weary of a genre. Having run their course, genres are displaced by what's newly hot.

■ Music (Pages 238–241)

The impact of music is impossible to measure. Think about Scottish pipes at a funeral, a love ballad in a romantic tragedy, a patriotic march in a Fourth of July parade. Then there's *Here Comes the Bride.* In a broader sense, music can help society adjust its attitudes, especially when performance is broadened to audiences of millions of people by the mass media. The genius of independent record-maker Sam Phillips in the 1950s was apparent when, so goes the story, he recognized Elvis Presley as a "white boy who sang colored." The result was a breakdown in racial divisions in U.S. music. The impact reverberated in the civil rights movement of the 1960s and new laws to end racial segregation.

■ Sports as Media Entertainment (Pages 241–243)

Mass media have taken sports beyond the amphitheater, exponentially compounding the audience. The huge fan base created by the mass media is an attractive target for advertisers, especially because male consumers are hard to reach as a demographic cluster. But guys come together for sports, by the millions in front of television receivers for some events. Sports has shaped the media in ways not always recognized. What percentage of the pages of your daily newspaper is devoted to sports? It's easy to argue that sports coverage panders disproportionately to an audience mania. The media also shape sports. Time-outs and period lengths have been adjusted in the rules to accommodate broadcast and advertiser priorities.

■ Sex as Media Content (Pages 243–244)

The presence of sexual content in mass media products has been largely settled by the U.S. Supreme Court. Adults, according to the Court, have constitutional rights to sexual depictions. 'Twasn't always so. The federal government once banned James Joyce's *Ulysses* through import regulations. Postal regulations were also used to stop distribution of other literary works, as well as some works of dubious literary merit. The issue has mostly been settled with the Court saying, in effect, that government should not be allowed to determine the material to which people can and cannot have access. Among major purveyors of sexually explicit material in recent years have been General Motors, when it controlled DirecTV, and Hilton hotels, which offer in-room pay-per-view porn. Among the last bastions of restrictions is over-air broadcasting. The Federal Communications Commission has statutory controls to maintain decency on the public airwaves, although defining *decency* remains contentious.

■ Gaming as Media Content (Page 246)

Advertisers have not missed the growing audience, largely male, for internet games. Advertising takes the form of billboards in game landscapes,

CHAPTER WRAP UP

scripted plugs and game sponsorship. The popularity of gaming has found critics who focus on violent and sexual elements. To blunt criticism, game makers have followed the lead of the recorded music and movie industries and incorporated product labeling.

◼ Artistic Values   (Pages 246–253)

Significant creative content can be found in the mass media. In movies there are auteurs. In literature there are Ernest Hemingways, Pearl Bucks and Toni Morrisons. Masterpieces, however, are exceptions in the huge ocean of media content. The economics of modern mass media pressures companies to produce quantities to meet huge demands. It's like zookeepers needing to keep the lions fed. Production lines for television series, romance novels and the latest hot genres are designed to produce quantities to meet low thresholds of audience acceptability.

◼ Thinking Critically

1. What categories of entertainment from prehistoric times to now reach people through mass media?

2. Do you prefer live or mediated performance? Why? In which do you partake more?

3. How do genres both clarify and cloud serious discussion of the quality of mass media content?

4. How has recorded music radically changed the social complexion of U.S. society?

5. How do you explain the exponential growth of sports as a form of entertainment?

6. What is driving gaming into its new status as a mass media vehicle?

7. What are the legal obstacles facing people who oppose sexual content in mass media?

8. What works against the presence of significant art and creativity in mass media content?

9. How well do mass media elevate cultural sensitivity? Explain.

◼ Media Vocabulary

auteur (Page 248)

genre (Page 234)

highbrow (Page 251)

kitsch (Page 251)

mediated performance (Page 236)

popular art (Page 252)

pornography (Page 244)

rhythm and blues (Page 238)

rockabilly (Page 239)

studio system (Page 249)

Media Sources

■ Dorian Lynskey. *33 Revolutions Per Minute: A History of Protest Songs, From Billie Holiday to Green Day.* HarperCollins, 2011. Lynskey, a music columnist, tracks radical songwriting and performance, mostly in folk music and jazz, including left-wing causes since the 1930s. He worries that the tradition has been subsumed into pop music with no edge sharper than "Give Peace a Chance."

■ Sigrid Nunez. *Sempre Susan.* Atlas, 2011. Nunez, a novelist, offers a brief memoir with a conclusion that, despite her brilliance as a social commentator, Sontag felt her intellectual legacy to have fallen short.

■ Jane McGonigal. *Reality is Broken: Why Games Make Us Better and How They Can Change the World.* Penguin, 2011. McGonigal, a videogame designer, argues that game-playing develops valuable skills that can be applied to solve real-world problems. McGonigal's own Urgent Evoke, a game for the World Bank Institute, encourages players to devise practical local solutions to global problems like food security and sustainable energy.

■ Chris Salter. *Entangled: Technology and the Transformation of Performance.* MIT, 2010. Salter, a Canadian scholar, examines effects of "machinic entanglements" on the creation and experience of performance, including theater scenography, audience perception of spaces, improvisation and interactive online games.

■ David Myers. *Play Redux: the Form of Computer Games.* University of Michigan Library, 2010. Myers, a mass communication scholar, argues that freedom is in jeopardy by applying social policy on computer games.

■ Nicole LaPorte. *The Men Who Would Be King.* Houghton Mifflin Harcourt, 2010. LaPorte, an entertainment industry reporter, blames the fall of Dreamworks on its conflicting goals of promoting artistic expression and of breaking even in the unpredictable pursuit of blockbusters to pay the bills.

■ Tom Chatfield. *Fun Inc. Why Gaming Will Dominate the 21st Century.* Pegasus, 2010. Chatfield, arts and books editor for *Prospect* magazine, offers an overview of the gaming industry from its 1972 origins, seeing a rapidly evolving art form.

■ Alex Ross. *Listen to This.* Straus and Giroux, 2010. Ross, music critic at the *New Yorker,* offers essays on music as a vehicle for understanding different cultures.

■ Howard Good and Sandra L. Borden, editors. *Ethics and Entertainment: Essays on Media Culture and Media Morality.* McFarland, 2010. A wide-ranging collection of scholarship and thinking on ethics in media entertainment.

■ Gail Dines. *Pornland: How Porn Has Hijacked Our Sexuality.* Beacon, 2010. Dines, an anti-porn activist, has reviewed narratives and visuals in concluding that pornography has de-humanizing results, but she draws only lightly on social-science research to support her thesis and relies on loose addiction terminology to make a case that critics say is simplistic and overdrawn.

■ Barbara Ching and Jennifer A. Wagner-Lawlor, editors. *The Scandal of Susan Sontag.* Columbia University, 2009. Scholars assess Sontag's contributions on a range of subjects, including the bridges she created between haute culture and middlebrow and lowbrow culture.

- Jonathan Pieslak. *Sound Targets: American Soldiers and Music in the Iraq War.* Indiana University Press, 2009. Pieslak, a scholar and himself a composer, examines the psychological impact of music, particularly in motivating soldiers into combat.

- Elijah Wald. *How the Beatles Destroyed Rock 'n' Roll: An Alternative History of American Popular Music.* Oxford University Press, 2009. Music historian Wald sees a demarcation in pop music with the Beatles. It was the Beatles' artier instincts as they matured, he says, that moved beyond the rhythmic, danceable qualities that set earlier rock apart.

- Steven Johnson. *Everything Bad Is Good for You.* Riverhead, 2005. Johnson, a thinker and essayist, draws on neuroscience, economics and media theory to present the contrarian perspective that media content that's often maligned as lowbrow, middlebrow at best, actually is intellectually enriching.

- Glenn C. Altschuler. *All Shook Up: How Rock 'n' Roll Changed America.* Oxford University Press, 2004. Altschuler, a writer specializing in the media, explores the social effects, including racial integration, of rock from the 1950s on.

- Guthrie P. Ramsey Jr. *Race Music: Black Culture from Bebop to Hip-Hop.* University of California Press, 2003. Ramsey, a scholar, sees popular music in the United States from the 1940s to the 1990s as a window into the diverse black American culture, society and politics.

- Steven L. Kent. *The Ultimate History of Video Games: From Pong to Pokemon— The Story Behind the Craze That Touched Our Lives and Changed the World.* Random House, 2001. Kent, drawing on hundreds of interviews, offers a comprehensive history of video games, starting from the first pinball machines.

- Dolf Zillmann and Peter Voderer. *Media Entertainment: The Psychology of Its Appeal.* Erlbaum, 2000.

A Thematic Chapter Summary

ENTERTAINMENT

To further deepen your media literacy here are ways to look at this chapter from the perspective of themes that recur throughout the book:

MEDIA TECHNOLOGY

The global sports industry is built on media coverage and attention. It's hard to imagine the World Cup or the NFL without the mass media. The Olympics? Sure, the Athenians had the Olympics, but how dull the ancient games must have been compared to today's sequenced quadrennial winter and summer games. Television, sports is a big draw. Sports is the second-largest section in most daily newspapers.

Entertainment's role has been amplified in human existence by media technology. Amusement and diversion are available any time, anywhere. Consider background music. How about 24/7 sports channels? Then there's handheld access to news and YouTube. Technology also shapes entertainment. Actors once needed strong voices that could carry to the back of the theater. Now audiences hear even hushed whispers from the lips of miked actors. With movies, screen tests are part of the audition process. Book publishers, too, want to know whether the author of a prospective book will look good during talk-show interviews.

ELITISM AND POPULISM

Quick, can you name the spin-offs of the successful CSI series plus copycat variations that have created a major primetime genre? As with all entertainment genres, the high-rolling crest of these dramas surely will peak and fade—only to be replaced by another genre that catches the ever-shifting fancy of mass audiences and advertisers.

The interplay between mass media content and public tastes may never be understood fully. Do media reflect public tastes and values? Or are media reshaping tastes and values? No one denies that mass media have the potential to put values to rigorous tests. Great authors have done this for centuries, posing and examining issues through fictional situations. Nonfiction can be just as influential. But lots of media content is not driven to help audiences seek understandings and appreciations. The goal instead is to attract audiences of sufficient size and variety to be platforms for advertisers to reach potential customers. This is true of books, magazines, radio, television and, more and more, the internet.

MEDIA AND CULTURE

Although lots of mass media content is easy to dismiss as second-rate, essayist Susan Sontag cautioned against being too quick to judge. An often-quoted line from a Sontag essay is: "The feeling given off by a Rauschenberg painting might be like that of a song by the Supremes." Also, Sontag made the point that pop art has social value in broadening the common experience of a society.

The elitist-populist tension is apparent in merit ratings of art. High art requires sophisticated and cultivated tastes to appreciate. Sergey Rachmaninoff was no rockabilly composer. This doesn't mean rockabilly is without value, but it falls into a category like pop art and folk art. Whether middlebrow or lowbrow on a merit rating, rockabilly is easy to appreciate. Anyone can get the message. One school of thought defends media on the lower rungs of rating scales if they bridge the gaps among the abilities of audience segments. Disney's *Fantasia* may be as close as some people get to a symphony hall. It's the same with Richard Strauss' or Wagner's prominence in sci-fi movie sound tracks.

MEDIA ECONOMICS

Can hardly wait for the low-budget reality show craze in television to pass? Like The Biggest Loser. It'll happen.

Factory-like production lines are among the techniques that mass media companies use to keep costs down. The factory model works well to increase profits for products that are imitative and attract audiences, which explains in part the rise of genres of media content. Imitative stuff lends itself to expanding a genre until it runs its course. In television, horse operas had their day in the 1960s *(Wagon Train)*. So have police dramas *(Cagney and Lacey)*, prime-time soaps *(Dallas)*, talk shows *(Donahue)* and reality shows *(Survivor)*. But audiences, ever fickle, tire of old stuff. Even the long-running sitcom genre seems in a fall from grace. If nobody's buying, further production is pointless, no matter the efficiency. Media companies then need to create a hot new genre or glom onto somebody else's next hot genre.

AUDIENCE FRAGMENTATION

Unthinkable in the mid-20th century would have been today's kid-centric culture today. Think pop music. Think mini-vans. Mass media content reflects the fragmentation just between generations but all kinds of other fragments of society.

Entertainment is easily dissected into genres, but the mass media have created such a massive audience that subgenres and sub-subgenres also are economically viable. Consider music formats in radio a half century ago. What once was country now is splintered into country rock, bluegrass, urban country, and a half-dozen others. Rock 'n' roll, once dominant in radio, is no less fragmented.

MEDIA AND DEMOCRACY

Slaps at the establishment have had historic roles on contentious issues in American life. Protest music had an especially high profile during the Vietnam war but remains alive with performers as diverse as the Dixie Chicks and Rage Against the Machine.

Mediated entertainment can give voice and feeling to ideas and build pressure for political and social change. Powerful sympathy for the mentally ill, as an example, has been generated in novels, movies and television in recent years, manifesting itself in growing pressure for public policy reforms. One all-time classic was Upton Sinclair's novel *The Jungle* in 1906, which led to government setting health standards for the meat-processing industry. Organized crime has been done no favors by Mario Puzo or Francis Ford Coppola. The debate over public policies is acted out through entertainment, no better illustrated than by Merle Haggard's *An Okie from Muskogee,* extolling blind patriotism, and the rising tide of anti-war music in the Vietnam war period.

10 PUBLIC RELATIONS

■ Blue Denim Revolution

Blue jeans hardly began as a fashion statement. The fabric, coarse, almost canvas-like, was both cheap and incredibly durable. For generations farmers and factory workers had liked denim's practicality. The U.S. Navy used denim as uniform work pants in World War II. Back from war, millions of sailors remained in love with denim. They continued their jeans habit. Sales soared—until 1953.

Then the movie *The Wild One,* with Marlon Brando leading a terroristic motorcycle gang, came out. Jeans suddenly carried an edgy antisocial connotation. The defiant image was cemented in 1955 by the surly jeans-wearing James Dean character in *Rebel Without a Cause.* That same year Hollywood further eroded the acceptability of jeans with *Blackboard Jungle,* drawn from Evan Hunter's book about inner-city juvenile delinquents. Jeans became a symbol of youthful defiance against adult authority.

No wonder that the Buffalo, New York, school board banned jeans in 1957. So did some restaurants and theaters. Then came James Leo Herihy's Broadway play *Blue Denim* about teen pregnancy and abortion, which 20th Century Fox made into a movie. Maybe worse, as absurd as it seems now, even sadly comic, jeans were targeted by the right-wing

◀ **Antisocial Fashion Statement.** *Movie directors found blue jeans, as well as tight leather jackets and boots, to be shortcuts in character development in edgy teen-culture flicks in the 1950s. The stereotypes torpedoed denim sales when parents put the foot down: "No jeans in this house." What happened since has been a case study in successful public relations.*

CHAPTER INSIGHTS

- Dialogue and ethical persuasion are essential elements for good public relations.
- Public relations works to win favor over time, while advertising seeks immediate action.
- The history of public relations teaches the value of populist support.
- Alternate labels like *strategic communication* and *integrated marketing* blur the lines between advertising and public relations.
- Effective public relations involves candid, proactive relations with mass media.
- Public relations organizations are working to improve the image of the craft.

hysteria-mongers of the era as a communist plot to corrupt young people.

For the jeans industry, none of this was a laughing matter. What to do? Manufacturers pooled their resources, created an organization called the Denim Council, hired public relations counselors, and launched a campaign in 1956 "to put school children back in blue jeans." The campaign, targeted at teenagers, failed to goose sales. Duh, it then dawned on the Denim Council that the perception problem was not with teens but their parents.

The Denim Council took a new tack, this time aimed at parents. One indirect tactic was to encourage the fashion industry to introduce new women's sportswear lines with denim. Denim also found a place in stylish haberdasher inventories. Fashion and business magazine editors were flooded with news releases and photos touting the "new look of durable denim." Jeans suddenly became studly in *Esquire*. Retail promotions touted a more casual dress ethic. The industry also kept an eye on the teen market with promotions like Jean Queen contests. Manufacturers also introduced new fashion touches in denim work clothes.

For the jeans industry, 1961 was a magical year. John Kennedy, new in the White House, had created the Peace Corps to wide acclaim. Volunteers, mostly college age, went around the world to help impoverished people learn basic skills like reading and to build simple infrastructures like wells for fresh water. The Denim Council outfitted early Peace Corps volunteers with blue jeans and was sure to photograph the young Americans, clean-cut, idealistic and energetic, doing their good deeds. New salvos of media kits were issued to magazines and newspapers. The Peace Corps became a clincher in the denim industry's long-term public relations project to counter the lingering image that associated jeans with juvenile delinquency and antisocial attitudes and tawdry behavior. By1963 denim sales were zooming.

The Denim Council was applying classic public relations techniques, using mass media as vehicles to sway public opinion. It worked, albeit the campaign had false starts, met some dead-ends, and took half a decade to implant jeans into the American psyche as not only a common-sense garment but a fun fashion statement without hardly any James Dean taint.

A new public relations triumph began for the jeans industry in 1996. The giant jeans marketer Lee found a way to proclaim itself as a socially responsible corporation with a worthwhile cause. People were encouraged on an assigned day in October, coinciding with National Breast Cancer Awareness Month, both to wear jeans to work and to donate $5 to fight breast cancer. Lee set a goal of $1 million the first year. The total collected ended up at $1.6 million. The event became the largest single-day fundraiser in the United States. By 2010 the total was averaging $5 million with 3,000 companies signed up to encourage employee participation.

The Denim Council campaign, running several years, was a classic in effective persuasion. The campaign relied heavily on mass media to achieve its strategic goal. ■

Public Relations Scope

STUDY PREVIEW

Public relations is a prolific generator of mass media messages. The public relations industry is large and growing. Despite its size, public relations functions mostly behind-the-scenes. Done well, public relations contributes to social consensus. Although sometimes confused with advertising and news, public relations is substantively different.

Public Relations Industry

To all but the most savvy-media consumers, the work of public relations is largely invisible. Even so, the industry is huge. According to government stats, more than 7,000 public relations firms operate in the United States with 64,000 employees. These numbers don't include thousands of people at in-house corporate, governmental, institutional and other public relations units, nor do they represent the global employees of multinational public relations firms.

A ranking of public relations companies is difficult because some are part of larger advertising companies that don't break out subsidiary revenue. These are the largest stand-alone agencies in the United States ranked by global revenue:

Edelman (New York)	$448 million	3,143 employees
Edelman (Chicago)	$349 million	2,300 employees
Fleischman Hillard (St. Louis)	335 million	1,400 employees
Waggener Edstrom (Bellevue)	94 million	628 employees
Ruder Finn (New York)	75 million	257 employees
APCO Worldwide (Washington)	100 million	507 employees
Ruder Finn (New York)	89 million	564 employees
Text 100 (San Francisco)	49 million	454 employees
Schwartz Comm'ns (Massachusetts)	25 million	177 employees

In addition global agencies include U.S. agencies. The largest, WPP, which includes Hill & Knowlton, Burson-Marsteller and Ogilvy, has global revenue of almost $1.4 billion. Omnicon is second at $1.1 billion.

In the United States, the Veronis research company projects that public relations spending would reach $4.4 billion by 2014. Veronis was seeing annual growth at 5.6 percent.

The Work of Public Relations

What does public relations do? The sophistication of the field makes quick definitions elusive. In short, public relations, practiced well, is an honest persuasive enterprise that contributes to social good by building consensus. This is done through communication, mostly through mass media. The communication is on behalf of institutions to build mutually beneficial *relationships* with their constituent groups, which are called *publics*. Hence the term **public relations**. This communication also can be on behalf of individuals. Think political candidates, think celebrities.

public relations
A management tool to establish beneficial relationships

Dialogic Theory.   Put another way, public relations tries to win people to a particular point of view or a favorable image. This is done through dialogue—two-way communication. Unlike most mass communication, this means communicating *with* people, not speaking *at* them or *to* them. Scholars call this **dialogic theory,** which draws on the idea that genuine dialogue leads to genuine consensus. Dialogic theory, which is rooted deeply in philosophy, psychology and rhetoric, sees persuasion as a two-way street—a true exchange without manipulation. There can be no shortcuts with evidence. Nor can there be fast-talk or fancy graphics or trickery. There must be an acknowledgment of a mutual search for answers and solutions and also a genuine give-and-take. The idea is to avoid manipulative or Machiavellian tricks.

dialogic theory
Dialogue-based approach to negotiating relationships

Scholars Michael Kent and Maureen Taylor have summarized five major features of dialogic theory in operation:

- **Mutuality.** A corporation or other institution engaged in public relations must recognize a responsibility to engage in communication on an even playing field. This means not taking advantage of financial might to talk down or push ideas without also listening.

- **Propinquity.** For communication to be genuine, interaction with publics must be spontaneous.

- **Empathy.** The institution must have a sincere sympathy in supporting and confirming public goals and interests.

- **Risk.** Dialogic theory can work only if there is a willingness to interact with individuals and publics on their own terms.

- **Commitment.** An institution must be willing to work at understanding its interactions with publics. This means that significant resources must be allocated not only to the dialogue but also to interpretation and understanding.

Dialogic theory offers a framework for a highly ethical form of public relations, but it is not without difficulties. As Kent and Taylor have noted, institutions have many publics, which makes dialogue a complex process. Participants in dialogic public relations put themselves in jeopardy. When publics engage in dialogue with organizations, they run the risk that their disclosures will be used to exploit or manipulate them.

Even so, discussion about dialogic theory is sensitizing many people in public relations to honesty and openness as ideals in the democratic tradition of giving voice to all. The theory is based on principles of honesty, trust and positive regard for the other rather than simply a conception of the public as a means to an end.

Public Relations and Commonweal.   Public relations has potential to make a democratic society robust and vibrant by encouraging the exchange of information and ideas on public issues. Public relations people going back to early theorist Edward Bernays have talked about seeking mutual understandings among constituent groups in society to sort through issues and reach decisions. More specifically, public relations practitioners, when doing their best work, do these things that contribute to the common good:

commonweal
The general welfare or public good

- Communicate the interests of an institution to the public, which broadens and enriches public dialogue.

- Seek mutual adjustments through dialogue between institutions in the society, which benefits the public.

- Create a safety valve for society by helping work out accommodations between competing interests, reducing the likelihood of coercion or arbitrary action.

- Activate the social conscience of organizations with which they work.

To be sure, some public relations activities are marginal on commonweal issues and fall far short of contributing to the common good. Even so, the industry likes to measure how well it can positively affect the functioning of society.

APPLYING YOUR MEDIA LITERACY

- **What differentiates the role of audience in public relations from most other mass communication?**
- **How could dialogic theory improve the practice of public relations?**

Public Relations in Context

STUDY PREVIEW #11

Public relations messages rely mostly on mass media to reach their target audiences. This means that the messages need to make sense to journalists, who decide whether to include them in their news products. Public relations is related to advertising but is different. One difference is that public relations tries to win minds and to build honest consensus, while advertising tries to make a sale.

Public Relations and Advertising

Public relations is at home in all the media of mass communication, whether with print, broadcast or digital delivery. Persuasion is platform-neutral. It's the message that counts and, of course, it is essential that it reaches audiences with which dialogue can be stirred.

Public relations and advertising often are viewed as synonymous and uttered in the same breath. At their core, however, public relations and advertising are different forms of mass communication. Although the differences sometimes are muddied in practice, neither advertising nor public relations can be understood without knowing their core differences.

Separate Purpose.   The purpose of public relations is to win favor, usually over time. The goal of advertising is sales as immediately as possible. Advertising's success is measurable relatively quickly in dollars and cents. Public relations, on the other hand, succeeds by creating and building on good will, which is not so easily measured but nonetheless important.

Different Means.   Properly done, public relations is a persuasive activity in the dialogic tradition. Advertising pitches are non-dialogic. Nobody, for example, expects an advertisement for a product to point out product disadvantages and flaws en route to making a reasoned case for a sale. Nor does anyone expect advertising to seek a dialogic exchange. Advertising's goal is commerce, not dialogue. In this sense, advertising messages are coercive in encouraging a decision by providing only enough information to close a deal. In contrast, public relations aspires to be persuasive with a full examination. Dialogics carries high standards for sharing the whole story, the bad as well as the good, to develop enduring commonality.

Management Role. In many well-run organizations, public relations is an upper-management function. Organizational policy-makers seek the counsel of public relations practitioners whose job is to be in tune with a wide range of constituents, or publics, and solicit their help in charting routes for mutual benefit. In contrast, advertising does not contribute to organizational policy. Rather, advertising practitioners do their work after policy decisions are made at the organizational levels of marketing or even higher echelons.

Media Time and Space. Both public relations and advertising use mainstream mass media to carry their messages, but each does it differently. Advertising appears in the media space or time that is purchased. Advertisers control the messages they place. After all, they've bought the time or space. Most public relations messages are issued to mass media organizations, like to newsrooms and bloggers, in hope the messages will make it through a screening on their merits and be passed on to mass audiences. Whether to carry the messages or not is up to the media. Public relations practitioners have limited control, sometimes none, over the eventual form that their messages take in reaching mass audiences.

The differences between public relations and advertising have exceptions. Nothing says advertising cannot be dialogic. The reality, though, is that word-heavy argumentation and exploration are rarities in advertising. There are quicker ways to make a sale. Another exception to the usual differences is in-house presentations, like a college's alumni magazine. For in-house presentations and publications like brochures, even for a Facebook page, public relations people have total control over the message their audience receives. Even so, these exceptions underscore that there are core differences between public relations and advertising.

Public Relations in News

A workhorse of the media relations component of public relations is the **news release.** These are statements issued to newsrooms ready-made for publication, posting or airing. The purpose can be informational or to promote a position, a product or a special interest. News releases go to all newsrooms that public relations people believe will be interested. Editors in newsrooms then generally recast the news releases to avoid the risk of running a piece that matches a competitor's piece word-for-word. News releases include announcements as routinely as calendar events. News releases also are used to attract reporter interest in hope of injecting a particular point of view in news stories.

News releases take a hybrid form in **media kits,** in which public relations people provide journalists not only news releases but also fact sheets, publicity photographs, videos, charts and graphs.

Significance of News Releases. Although public relations people have limited control over how and if their messages get into the media, news releases should not be underrated. Studies have found that 50 to 90 percent of news stories rely to some extent on information in news releases.

Ethics and News Releases. As television and the internet matured as news media, public relations people invented the **video news release.** Although not news, VNRs look like news stories, with an actor playing the part of a journalist doing a stand-up report. The actors conceal their true role, which serves the client's purposes, but is deceiving for viewers. The viewers have no sense that the report is from a public relations agent rather than from a real news reporter. Broadcast newsrooms that plug VNRs into newscasts leave a false impression that the report is the station's self-generated reporting. The practice has been targeted by ethicists for the deception, which has led to an investigation by the Federal Communications Commission. As a regulatory agency, the FCC could insist that stations cease being conduits for promotions that masquerade as news. The deception, however, is no less than the age-old practice of some newspapers and magazines that run news releases verbatim with no signal to the readers about their source.

news release
A tool in public relations to provide information or promotion in news media

media kit
A packet provided to news reporters to tell the story in an advantageous way

video news release
A television news story look-alike created by public relations people

- Look for examples of mass media messages that show how public relations and advertising seek to move people but do it differently and for different purposes. What similarities and differences do you observe? Evaluate the effectiveness of these two approaches and determine which is more effective at winning their audience.
- What ethics issues does the use of video news releases as straight news raise? How can media people revise these practices?

Roots of Public Relations

STUDY PREVIEW Many big companies found themselves in disfavor in the late 1800s for ignoring the public good to make profits. Feeling misunderstood, some moguls of industry turned to Ivy Lee, the founder of modern public relations, for counsel on gaining public support.

Social Darwinism

Nobody would be tempted to think of **William Henry Vanderbilt** as having been good at public relations. In 1882 when Vanderbilt was president of the New York Central Railroad he was asked about the effect of changing train schedules on people. He responded: "The public be damned." Vanderbilt's utterance so infuriated people that it became a banner in the populist crusade against robber barons and tycoons in the late 1800s. Under populist pressure, state governments set up agencies to regulate railroads. Then the federal government established the Interstate Commerce Commission to control freight and passenger rates. Government began insisting on safety standards. Labor unions formed in the industries with the worst working conditions, safety records and pay. Journalists added pressure with muckraking exposés on excesses in the railroad, coal and oil trusts; on meat-packing industry frauds; and on patent medicines.

The leaders of industry were slow to recognize the effect of populist objections on their practices. They were comfortable with **social Darwinism**, an adaptation of **Charles Darwin**'s survival-of-the-fittest theory. In fact, they thought themselves forward-thinking in applying Darwin's theory to business and social issues. It had been only a few decades earlier, in 1859, that Darwin had laid out his biological theory in *On the Origin of Species by Means of Natural Selection*. To cushion the harshness of social Darwinism, many tycoons espoused paternalism toward those whose "fitness" had not brought them fortune and power. No matter how carefully put, paternalism seemed arrogant to the "less fit."

George Baer, a railroad president, epitomized both social Darwinism and paternalism in commenting on a labor strike: "The rights and interests of the laboring man will be protected and cared for not by labor agitators but by the Christian men to whom God in His infinite wisdom has given the control of the property interests of the country." Baer was quoted widely, further fueling sentiment against big business. Baer may have been sincere, but his position was read as a cover for excessive business practices by barons who assumed superiority to everyone else.

Meanwhile, social Darwinism came under attack as circuitous reasoning: Economic success accomplished by abusive practices could be used to justify further abusive practices, which would lead to further success. Social Darwinism was a dog-eat-dog outlook that hardly jibed with democratic ideals, especially not as described in the preamble to the U.S. Constitution, which sought to "promote the

William Henry Vanderbilt
Embodied the bad corporate images of the 1880s, 1890s with "The public be damned"

social Darwinism
Application to society of Darwin's survival-of-the-fittest theory

Charles Darwin
Devised survival-of-the-fittest theory

▲ **Charles Darwin.** *His Survival of the Fittest theory found applications he never anticipated, like Social Darwinism.*

general welfare and secure the blessings of liberty" for everyone—not for only the chosen "fittest." Into these tensions at the turn of the century came public relations pioneer Ivy Lee.

Ivy Lee

Coal mine operators, like railroad magnates, were held in the public's contempt at the start of the 1900s. Obsessed with profits, caring little about public sentiment or even the well-being of their employees, mine operators were vulnerable to critics in the growing populist political movement. Mine workers organized, and 150,000 in Pennsylvania went on strike in 1902, shutting down the anthracite industry and disrupting coal-dependent industries, including the railroads. The mine owners snubbed reporters, which probably contributed to a pro-union slant in many news stories and worsened the owners' public image. Six months into the strike, President Theodore Roosevelt threatened to take over the mines with Army troops. The mine owners settled.

Shaken finally by Roosevelt's threat and recognizing Roosevelt's responsiveness to public opinion, the mine operators began reconsidering how they went about their business. In 1906, with another strike looming, one operator heard about **Ivy Lee,** a young publicist in New York who had new ideas about winning public support. He was hired. In a turnabout in press relations, Lee issued a news release that announced: "The anthracite coal operators, realizing the general public interest in conditions in the mining regions, have arranged to supply the press with all possible information." Then followed a series of releases with information attributed to the mine operators by name—the same people who

Ivy Lee
Laid out fundamentals of public relations

MEDIAtimeline

General Motors pioneered concept of "enlightened self-interest"

PUBLIC RELATIONS MILESTONES

FIRST NEWSPAPER OPINION SECTION
In Horace Greeley's New York *Tribune,* founded 1841

PROMOTIONAL EXCESSES
P. T. Barnum made huckster promotion a high art (1870s)

"THE PUBLIC BE DAMNED"
Yes, incredibly, railroad titan William Henry Vanderbilt said it (1882)

Darwinism took a twist into Social Darwinism

PUBLIC RELATIONS MILESTONES

IVY LEE
Founder of first public relations agency (1906)

GEORGE CREEL
Head of first government public relations agency (1917)

EDWARD BERNAYS
Wrote *Crystallizing Public Opinion* (1923)

ARTHUR PAGE
First corporate public relations vice president (1927)

PAUL GARRETT
Created term *enlightened self-interest* (1930s)

OFFICE OF WAR INFORMATION
Elmer Davis headed federal agency to generate war support (1942)

PIVOTAL EVENTS

- Public education took root as a social value (1820s)
- Charles Darwin wrote *Origin of Species* (1859)
- U.S. Civil War (1861–1865)
- Rise of banks, major corporations (1870s–)
- Populist political movement aimed against monopolies (1880s–)
- Samuel Gompers formed predecessor of American Federation of Labor (1881)
- Social Darwinism used to justify corporate excesses (1890s)

PIVOTAL EVENTS

- Labor crisis in coal industry (1902)
- Ludlow Massacre (1914)
- Right to vote extended to women (1920)
- Great Depression (1930s)
- World War II (1941–1945)

1800s

1900–1949

earlier had preferred anonymity and refused all interview requests. There were no more secret strike strategy meetings. When operators planned a meeting, reporters covering the impending strike were informed. Although reporters were not admitted into the meetings, summaries of the proceedings were given to them immediately afterward. This relative openness eased long-standing hostility toward the operators. A strike was averted.

Lee's success with the mine operators began a career that rewrote the rules on how corporations deal with their various publics. Among his accomplishments:

Institutional Openness.   Railroads had notoriously secretive policies not only about their business practices but even about accidents. When the Pennsylvania Railroad sought Ivy Lee's counsel, he advised against suppressing news—especially on things that inevitably would leak out anyway. When a train jumped the rails near Gap, Pennsylvania, Lee arranged for a special car to take reporters to the scene and even take pictures. The Pennsylvania line was applauded in the press for the openness. News coverage of the railroad, which had been negative for years, began changing. A "bad press" continued plaguing other railroads that persisted in their secretive habits.

Finding Upbeat Angles.   When the U.S. Senate proposed investigating International Harvester for monopolistic practices, Lee advised the giant farm implement manufacturer against reflexive obstructionism and silence. A statement went out announcing that the company, confident in its business practices, not only welcomed but also would facilitate an investigation. Then began

PUBLIC RELATIONS MILESTONES

ETHICS
Public Relations Society of America ethics code (1951)

ACCREDITATION
PRSA accreditation system (1965)

TYLENOL CRISIS
Classic campaign aided recovery from product-tampering crisis (1982)

INTEGRATED MARKETING
Attempt to subsume public relations into marketing (1990s–)

Tylenol scare, a model case study

PIVOTAL EVENTS

- Korean War (1950–1953)
- Vietnam War (1964–1973)
- Humans reached moon (1969)
- First Iraq War (1991)

1950–1999

PUBLIC RELATIONS MILESTONES

CONSOLIDATION
Advertising agencies bought up many public relations agencies to broaden client services (2002)

DIALOGICS
Scholars applied dialogic theory to public relations (2002)

IMAGE MAKE-OVER
BP campaign collapses amid oil rig disaster (2010)

PENN STATE
Sex abuse scandal poses questions public relations and college sports (2011)

PIVOTAL EVENTS

- 9/11 terrorist attacks (2001)
- Second Iraq War (2003–2011)
- Hurricane Katrina (2005)
- Great Recession (2007–2009)
- Obama presidency (2009–)
- BP oil disaster in Gulf of Mexico (2010)
- Supreme Court allowed wider corporate funding for political campaigns (2010)
- Congress widened health coverage (2011)
- Japanese tsunami and nuclear disaster (2011)
- World population passed 7 billion (2011)

Lobbyist bad boy Jack Abramoff gets prison time

2000s

a campaign that pointed out International Harvester's beneficence toward its employees. The campaign also emphasized other upbeat information about the company.

Giving Organizations a Face. In 1914, when workers at a Colorado mine went on strike, company guards fired machine guns and killed several men. More battling followed, during which two women and 11 children were killed. It was called the **Ludlow Massacre**, and **John D. Rockefeller Jr.**, the chief mine owner, was pilloried for what had happened. Rockefeller was an easy target. Like his father, widely despised for the earlier Standard Oil monopolistic practices, John Jr. tried to keep himself out of the spotlight, but suddenly mobs were protesting at his mansion in New York and calling out, "Shoot him down like a dog." Rockefeller asked Ivy Lee what he should do. Lee began whipping up articles about Rockefeller's human side, his family and his generosity. Then, on Lee's advice, Rockefeller announced that he would visit Colorado to see conditions himself. He spent two weeks talking with miners at work and in their homes and meeting their families. It was a news story that reporters could not resist, and it unveiled Rockefeller as a human being, not a far-removed, callous captain of industry. A myth-shattering episode occurred one evening when Rockefeller, after a brief address to miners and their wives, suggested that the floor be cleared for a dance. Before it was all over, John D. Rockefeller Jr. had danced with almost every miner's wife, and the news stories about the evening did a great deal to mitigate antagonism and distrust toward Rockefeller. Back in New York, with Lee's help, Rockefeller put together a proposal for a grievance procedure, which he asked the Colorado miners to approve. It was ratified overwhelmingly.

Straight Talk. Ivy Lee came on the scene at a time when many organizations were making extravagant claims about themselves and their products. Circus promoter **P. T. Barnum** had made this kind of **puffery** a fine art going back to the 1840s, and he had many imitators. It was an age of puffed-up advertising claims and fluffy rhetoric. Lee noted, however, that people soon saw through hyperbolic boasts and lost faith in those who made them. In launching his public relations agency in 1906, Lee vowed to be accurate in everything he said and to provide whatever verification anyone requested. This became part of the creed of good practice in public relations. And it remains so today.

Ludlow Massacre
Colorado tragedy that Ivy Lee converted into a public relations victory

John D. Rockefeller Jr.
Ivy Lee client who had been the target of public hatred

P. T. Barnum
Known for extravagant claims and hoaxes in publicity beginning in 1840s

puffery
Inflated claims

▲ **Ivy Lee.**

▲ **Ludlow Massacre.** *Colorado militiamen, called in to augment company guards, opened fire during a 1914 mine labor dispute and killed women and children. Overnight, John D. Rockefeller Jr. became the object of public hatred. It was a Rockefeller company that owned the mine. Even in New York, where Rockefeller lived, there were rallies demanding his head. Public relations pioneer Ivy Lee advised Rockefeller to tour the Ludlow area as soon as tempers cooled to show his sincere concern and to begin work on a labor contract to meet the concerns of miners.*

Public Relations on a Massive Scale

The potential of public relations to rally support for a cause was demonstrated on a gigantic scale during World War I and again during World War II.

Creel Committee.   In 1917 President Woodrow Wilson, concerned about widespread anti-war sentiment, asked **George Creel** to head a new government agency whose job was to make the war popular. The Committee on Public Information, better known as the Creel Committee, cranked out news releases, magazine pieces, posters, even movies. A list of 75,000 local speakers was put together to talk nationwide at school programs, church groups and civic organizations about making the world safe for democracy. More than 15,000 committee articles were printed. Never before had public relations been attempted on such a scale—and it worked. World War I became a popular cause even to the point of inspiring people to buy Liberty Bonds, putting up their own money to finance the war outside the usual taxation apparatus.

George Creel
Demonstrated that public relations works on a mammoth scale in World War I

Office of War Information.   When World War II began, an agency akin to the Creel Committee was formed. Veteran journalist **Elmer Davis** was put in charge. The new Office of War Information was public relations on a bigger scale than ever before. The Creel and Davis war operations employed hundreds of people. Davis had 250 employees handling news releases alone. These staff members, mostly young, carried new lessons about public relations into the private sector after the war. These were the people who shaped corporate public relations as we know it today.

Elmer Davis
Led Office of War Information in World War II

▲ George Creel.

▲ **War Bond Poster.** *World War I did not begin as a popular cause with Americans. There were anti draft riots in many cities. This prompted President Woodrow Wilson to ask journalist George Creel to launch a major campaign to persuade Americans that the war was important to make the world safe for democracy. Within months Americans were financing much of the war voluntarily by buying government bonds. This poster was only one aspect of Creel's work, which demonstrated that public relations principles could be applied on a massive scale.*

Corporate Public Relations

Arthur Page
Established the role of public relations as a top management tool

When giant AT&T needed somebody to take over public relations in 1927, the president of the company went to magazine editor **Arthur Page** and offered him a vice presidency. Before accepting, Page laid out several conditions. One was that he have a voice in AT&T policymaking. Page was hardly on an ego trip. Rather, he had seen too many corporations that regarded their public relations arm merely as an executor of policy. Page considered public relations itself as a management function. To be effective, Page knew that he must contribute to the making of high-level corporate decisions as well as executing them.

Today, experts on public relations agree with Arthur Page's concept: When institutions are making policy, they need to consider the effects on their many publics. That can be done best when the person in charge of public relations, ideally at the vice presidential level, is intimately involved in decision-making. The public relations executive advises the rest of the institution's leaders on public perceptions and the effects that policy options might have on perceptions. Also, the public relations vice president is in a better position to implement the institution's policy for having been a part of developing it.

No two institutions are organized in precisely the same way. At General Motors 200 people work in public relations. In smaller organizations PR may be one of several hats worn by a single person. Except in the smallest operations, the public relations department usually has three functional areas of responsibility:

External Public Relations.   Public relations helps organizations engage with groups and people outside the organization. These include customers, dealers, suppliers, and community leaders and policymakers.

Internal Public Relations.   Organizations need internal communication for optimal relations among employees, managers, unions, shareholders and other internal constituencies. In-house newsletters, magazines and brochures are common elements in internal public relations.

Media Relations.   For communication with large groups, organizations rely largely on mass media. It is media relations people who respond to news reporters' queries, arrange news conferences, issue statements to the news media and often serve as an organization's spokespersons.

APPLYING YOUR MEDIA LITERACY

- Why did public relations emerge during the application of social Darwinism to U.S. industry?
- What good business practices have endured from Ivy Lee's early rules on how corporations deal with their various publics?
- How did the media approaches during major 20th century wars lead to the emergence of corporate public relations?
- Why is public relations valuable at the policymaking level of an institution?

Public Relations as Strategy

STUDY PREVIEW The term *public relations* carries a stigma, but alternate names all have inadequacies at capturing the nature of the work. Concepts like *strategic communication* and *integrated marketing* blur public relations with advertising and miss the dialogic nature of good public relations.

strategic communication
Campaigns and messages to advance long-term goals, usually through mass media

Strategic Communication

As a field, public relations has evolved through dizzying reinventions. The reinventions have attempted to separate public relations from hucksterism and other dubious practices that have tarnished the image. Everybody has heard the term *PR* used skeptically and derisively: "That's just PR." To remake the field's troubled image, the public relations industry has passed through countless alternative names. These have included *public information*

Promotion also includes event planning—everything from staging to encouraging public participation and media coverage.

Image Management

Appearances make a difference. One function of public relations is creating, nurturing and rescuing images. Some agencies specialize in grooming clients for television interviews. It is at their own peril that rock stars, corporate executives and political candidates ignore these services. Image managers also offer services for corporations, industry trade groups and other organizations.

▶ CASE STUDY: British Petroleum

An explosion at a run-down British Petroleum oil refinery in Texas City, Texas, in 2005 killed 15 workers and injured 170. BP took a black eye when government investigators identified 700-plus safety violations, a record. The government imposed an $87 million fine, a record too. Even costlier in terms of BP's image were the stories that survivors and families told in the news media and in court. The company paid $1.6 billion to settle the claims. Meanwhile, the idea that British Petroleum had put aggressive production schedules and profits ahead of safety had taken root in the public mind. The company decided to change its image.

Hence was born an elaborate, costly and eventually failed attempt at an image make-over. In a multifaceted public relations campaign, British Petroleum portrayed itself as making big strides to improve safety worldwide. The campaign also drew on lessons in **image management** that had become a function of public relations. This included a decision to market the company by a new name, simply *BP*, with the letters standing not for British Petroleum but for Beyond Petroleum. The message was supplemented with

image management
A public relations function to create, groom and nurture client images

▲ **Demolition of an Image.** *For 87 days after an oil-rig explosion, an out-of-control oil well gushed contaminants into the Gulf of Mexico. The environmental disaster cast doubt on the sincerity of British Petroleum's public relations campaign to position itself in the public mindset as "beyond petroleum" and environmentally sensitive. Within months BP fell off the top 100 global brands in the marketing firm Omicom Group's annual ranking.*

advertising, mostly on television, to create the impression that BP was moving out of the oil business and into solar, wind and biofuel that were not only environmentally friendlier but also safer. In fact, however, the core of the company remained the same, with a long-term commitment to petroleum as its core product.

Image management has a strong record in shaping public images. For better or worse, the taboo on women smoking began crumbling in the 1920s after public relations pioneer **Edward Bernays** put a marching unit of young models in a New York parade. On signal, the women lit up their "torches of freedom." Photographers couldn't resist the staged stunt. Nor could almost every newspaper. Of course, campaigns 50 years later about the unhealthiness of tobacco eroded Bernays' image of smoking as stylish or liberating. So it can be said that the public can be malleable. But also there can be enduring image make-overs, like the Denim Council campaign to make jeans respectable in the 1960s. In the 1980s Mothers Against Drunk Driving rendered a major blow to any suave glamour attached to alcohol.

In truth, not all image campaigns succeed. BP's Beyond Petroleum campaign, which pitched lofty environmental ambitions, violated a fundamental rule for image-making. The idea that BP had switched its priorities away from oil wasn't true, which was apparent with continuing oil-related BP accidents and disasters. Further, BP's goal of distancing the company from the 2005 Texas City disaster failed with every new disaster in the news. In 2006, a year after the Texas City disaster, news broke about BP pipeline leaks in Alaska. Federal inspectors blamed cost-cutting and negligence. Then in 2007 a toxic spill went into the Prudhoe tundra, also in Alaska. In 2010 a leak at Texas City—yes, again at Texas City—pumped 265 tons of poison chemicals into the atmosphere. Two weeks later, the worst marine environmental disaster in history occurred. A BP deep-sea drilling rig 40 miles off the coast of Louisiana exploded, killing 11 and gushing 4.9 million barrels of raw petroleum uncontrolled into the Gulf of Mexico for 87 days. The spill extensively damaged marine and wildlife habitats as well as fishing and tourism industries.

BP went into **crisis management** to reduce damage to its carefully cultured *Beyond Petroleum* image, pouring a new $100 million into messages that acknowledged the

Edward Bernays
Early public relations practitioner whose practice and scholarship helped define the field

crisis management
A public relations function, ideally to devise plans to deal with possible crises ahead of time

▲ **Edward Bernays.**

◀ **Lucky Strike Girls.** *When a parade unit of models pulled out cigarettes and lit 'em up during a New York parade in 1929, news photographers lapped it up. The publicity stunt, outrageous at the time, carried the message that it was glamorous for women to smoke. The stunt was the work of public relations pioneer Edward Bernays. Unfortunately for Bernays' reputation, the stunt has overshadowed his other and more significant contributions. His seminal works in the field include* Crystallizing Public Opinion *in 1923 and* The Engineering of Consent *in 1955.*

undeniable safety lapses. The new BP messages also pledged that BP would clean up the mess and compensate Gulf Coast people whose fishing and tourism livelihoods were damaged. But the public, conditioned by the Beyond Petroleum image, saw only the gap between the image and the reality. It was a new example of the dismissive "It's just PR" burden that had plagued public relations for decades and that right-minded public relations people had been struggling to supersede by practicing their craft well. It was telling when John Kenney, an author of the Beyond Petroleum campaign, said he had been naïve. There had been no genuine attempt, Kenney said, to engage the public in dialogue or to change corporate practices. "Mere marketing," he called it. Put another way, sadly: "Just PR" in the worst sense of the phrase.

▶ CASE STUDY: Tylenol

Johnson & Johnson is best-known for Band-Aids and Tylenol. In business circles the company has a solid reputation for quality that dates to the 1940s when the legendary Woody Johnson was in charge. Johnson had a credo that J&J's first responsibility was to customers and then, in order, to employees, to management, to communities and to stockholders. When James Burke became president in 1976, he underscored the customer-first credo: "Whenever we cared for the customer in a profound—and spiritual—way, profits were never a problem." J&J spent millions of dollars to inspire public confidence in its products, the painkiller Tylenol among them. By 1982 Tylenol was the leader in a crowded field of headache remedies with 36 percent of the market.

Then disaster struck. Seven people in Chicago died after taking Tylenol capsules laced with cyanide. James Burke, president of Johnson & Johnson, and Lawrence Foster, vice president for public relations, moved quickly. Within hours, Johnson & Johnson:

- Halted the manufacture and distribution of Tylenol.
- Removed Tylenol products from retailers' shelves.
- Launched a massive advertising campaign requesting people to exchange Tylenol capsules for a safe replacement.
- Summoned 50 public relations employees from Johnson & Johnson and its subsidiary companies to staff a press center to answer media and consumer questions forthrightly.
- Ordered an internal company investigation of the Tylenol manufacturing and distribution process.
- Promised full cooperation with government investigators.
- Ordered the development of tamper-proof packaging for the reintroduction of Tylenol products after the contamination problem was resolved.

◀ **Product-Tampering Crisis.** *When cyanide-laced Tylenol capsules killed seven people in Chicago, the manufacturer Johnson & Johnson responded quickly. Company President James Burke immediately pulled the product off retailers' shelves and ordered company publicists to set up a press center to answer news media inquiries as fully as possible. Burke's action and candor helped to restore the public's shaken confidence in Tylenol, and the product resumed its significant market share after the crisis ended. It turned out that it probably was somebody outside Johnson & Johnson's production and distributing system who had contaminated the capsules rather than a manufacturing lapse.*

MEDIAtomorrow

■ Combating Bad News, BP-Style

Like many companies, British Petroleum had dabbled in **search advertising** for years. It had been paying the search engine company Google about $57,000 a year, relative peanuts, to put ads onscreen for anyone searching for indexed links to topics like *solar energy* or *environment*. When the BP oil rig Deepwater Horizon blew up in the Gulf of Mexico in April 2010, making the company the subject of massive negative news, BP upped its Google ad-search spending to $3.6 million a month—a 700-fold increase. Anyone searching Google for keywords like *oil spill, leak* and *top kill* was also presented onscreen with a paid-by-BP ad that linked to the company's own messages. It was a massive internet venture by BP to compete for clicks with news coverage of oiled and dying birds and marine life, indicting interviews with people in the devastated fishing and tourism industries, and, of course, plaintiff attorneys suggesting their services to sue BP.

In all, BP poured $100 million into post-disaster messages over a few months to counter unfavorable news accounts. Although search ads consumed only a fraction of the total, the BP commitment represented a hope that attracting eyeballs to corporate-centric messages online would influence public opinion. Search ads were not a new discovery, but BP's use of them in an attempt at crisis management was new territory. Of Google's top ad-search clients in one month in 2010, only BP was engaging in public relations persuasion, as opposed to companies advertising for sales:

- Expedia, $5.9 million
- Amazon, $5.8 million
- eBay, $4.2 million
- British Petroleum, $3.6 million

Damage-Control. *After British Petroleum's Gulf of Mexico oil catastrophe, the company countered the unfavorable news coverage with major purchases of time on network television but, more importantly, with search-ads on Google and other search engines and on social media sites like Facebook, YouTube and Twitter. Suddenly BP went from a minor Google client to its fourth largest.*

What Do You Think?

Do search ads level the playing field and invigorate public debate with a rich array of information, ideas and perspectives? Or do they provide a medium for countering unfavorable news coverage with company-generated propaganda?

Explain the future that you see for the use of search ads for public relations by people engaged in advocacy.

In fact, BP was on track to put as much annually into Google ad services as into its use of network, cable and local television media for image management.

Besides ad search messages, BP stepped up its presence on Facebook, YouTube, Twitter and other sites. Online social networking and video-sharing sites have become battlegrounds in the wars for public opinion. Chief executive Will Margiloff of the digital marketing agency Innovation Interactive made the point in an interview with the trade journal *Advertising Age* that online media have added impact because they actively involve people: "More than any other media, the messaging is requested. People are seeking out BP's answers as opposed to waiting to be told."

Companies like Google make their money from search ads and cookie-derived placements with a click-through charge. Online click-through mechanisms are unlike print and broadcast media, which charge for the space or time regardless of how many people respond to a message. Internet companies, instead, charge for eyeballs that actually click on a link, which gives a higher level of assurance to whoever is sponsoring the message that it was seen by someone interested in the content.

Investigators determined within days that an urban terrorist had poisoned the capsules. Although exonerated of negligence, Johnson & Johnson nonetheless had a tremendous problem: how to restore public confidence in Tylenol. Many former Tylenol users were reluctant to take a chance, and the Tylenol share of the analgesic market dropped to 6 percent.

To address the problem, Johnson & Johnson called in the Burson-Marsteller public relations agency. Burson-Marsteller recommended a media campaign to capitalize on the high marks the news media had given the company for openness during the crisis. Mailgrams went out inviting journalists to a 30-city video teleconference to hear James Burke announce the reintroduction of the product. Six hundred reporters turned out, and Johnson & Johnson officials took their questions live.

To stir even wider attention, 7,500 media kits had been sent to newsrooms the day before the teleconference. The kits included a news release and a bevy of supporting materials: photographs, charts and background information.

The resulting news coverage was extensive. On average, newspapers carried 32 column-inches of copy on the announcement. Network television and radio as well as local stations also offered heavy coverage. Meanwhile, Johnson & Johnson executives, who had attended a workshop on how to make favorable television appearances, made themselves available as guests on the network morning shows and talk shows. At the same time Johnson & Johnson distributed 80 million free coupons to encourage people to buy Tylenol again.

The massive media-based public relations campaign worked. Within a year, Tylenol had regained 80 percent of its former market share.

The Tylenol story has become a model for crisis management. When Toyota came under criticism for safety issues in 2009, the company took a page from the Tylenol playbook. So have hundreds of other companies, signaling that customers are first, even ahead of profits. Good deeds that flow from good policy trump short-term profit goals that are in the interest of doing the right thing and either build or rebuild long-term customer confidence.

Advocacy

From its roots as a promotional tool, public relations has grown into a tool for advocacy. This includes lobbying in public-policy debates with government leaders and also mobilizing public opinion.

Lobbying. Historians differ on the origins of **lobbying,** which is advocacy to influence public policy. But there is no doubt where the term lobbying came from. People who wanted to influence President Ulysses Grant, in office from 1869 to 1877, knew they could find him enjoying cigars and brandy in the lobby of the Willard Hotel two blocks from the White House. These "lobbyists" were not above offering gifts of appreciation to legislators and government functionaries.

To some extent the old-style lobbying remains, as we see in occasional scandals and prison time. Lobbying, however, has evolved into an essential and honorable component of the U.S. political system. Today lobbyists provide information and rationales to help government policy-makers choose the best course. This activity, which modern lobbyists prefer to call **government relations,** includes offering analysis, drafting position papers, ghosting speeches, and testifying to committees on behalf of clients. Lobbyists have personal contacts and know how government works. These are assets that are valuable, indeed essential, to clients. In a sense, lobbyists are expediters.

No doubt about it, lobbying is a growth industry. Every state capital has hundreds of public relations practitioners whose specialty is representing their clients to legislative bodies and government agencies. In North Dakota, hardly a populous state, more than 300 people are registered as lobbyists in the capital city of Bismarck. The number of registered lobbyists in Washington, D.C., exceeds 10,000 today. In addition, there are an estimated 20,000 other people in the nation's capital who have slipped through registration requirements but who nonetheless ply the halls of government to plead their clients' interests.

Despite high standards to which many lobbyists adhere, the derogatory term *influence-peddling* has retained its currency. It's easy to understand the negative connotations if you count the number of Congress members in jail for bribes and favors. In a particularly egregious case, Representative Duke Cunningham of California went to prison for eight years for accepting $2.4 million in bribes and favors, mostly from a defense contractor.

search advertising
Ads show up on-screen whenever you click a search term chosen by an advertiser

lobbying
Influencing public policy, usually legislation or regulation

government relations
Lobbying

MEDIAcounterpoints

■ What Role for Honest Advocacy

Advocacy for War. *Choking back tears, a 15-year-old Kuwaiti told a Congressional committee about witnessing invading Iraqi soldiers taking premature babies from hospital incubators and leaving them to die. The girl's testimony, which was false, had been arranged by the Hill & Knowlton public relations agency as part of its advocacy for the Kuwaiti government. The testimony helped launch a U.S.-led war to force Iraq out of Kuwait.*

For Ivy Lee, the founder of modern public relations, his last months of life were a tortured hell. In 1934 Lee had been summoned to Washington by the U.S. House Un-American Activities Committee. His Congressional inquisitors painted Lee as a publicity agent for the new Nazi regime in Germany. Lee responded that he provided counsel only to the German Dye Trust, not the Hitler government. Lee testified that the Trust wanted business advice for improving its image in the United States. Consistent with his creed as a public relations counselor, Lee had offered honest counsel.

Although cleared of the charge, the suggestion that Lee had been a Nazi publicity agent was a ruinous smear. Lee emerged from the investigation a broken man. Within months, at age 57, he was dead.

Not infrequently, criminal-defense attorneys are asked to explain how their consciences allow them to defend criminals. In effect, the critics are saying: "Just gas the serial killer." It's an understandable visceral repulsion. The legal profession's response, however, is rooted in the American tradition of justice for all. In short, everyone is entitled to an advocate to make the best case possible when the government brings a criminal charge.

Public relations people face similar questions when they take on questionable clients, some of them controversial, some despised. It's risky for defense attorneys to represent unpopular clients. Public relations work carries similar risk.

Many foreign interests, both governmental and corporate, covet favorable images among Americans. This means hiring experts on American culture for counsel on how to curry favor. That's what Ivy Lee did in the 1930s. Today, some public relations agencies go beyond offering counsel to foreign clients and offer advocacy services.

After Iraq invaded its tiny Persian Gulf neighbor in 1990, the government of Kuwait arranged through its U.S. embassy to hire the Hill & Knowlton agency to organize sympathy in the United States. It was a $10 million account. Hill & Knowlton flooded the U.S. news media with mailings, arranged hundreds of briefings and dispatched guests to talk shows. The book, *The Rape of Kuwait,* was propelled onto U.S. bestseller lists when the Kuwaiti embassy quietly purchased 200,000 copies.

For a Congressional hearing investigating the invasion, Hill & Knowlton arranged for a young Kuwaiti hospital volunteer to testify that she had seen invading Iraqi soldiers yank hundreds of premature babies from incubators in a hospital and leave them on the cold floor to die. Her tears were compelling. The atrocity story proved pivotal in making the case for a U.S. military invasion to rid Kuwait of the Iraqi invaders. What Hill & Knowlton had failed to note publicly, indeed concealed, was that the tearful testimony was from the 15-year-old daughter of Kuwait's U.S. ambassador. She was not an obscure hospital volunteer, as she had identified herself. Also, her story was a lie. But by the time the lie became apparent, the U.S. invasion was beyond the ability to call back its troop buildup. War followed.

The practice of public relations helps democracy function by providing expertise at crafting strategies and messages for anyone with a stake in public policy. This includes articulating client cases as expertly and strongly as possible. Sound public policy emerges from robust debate in the admittedly rough-and-tumble political discourse of free expression and a full exchange of views.

POINT / **COUNTER POINT**

In court, attorneys are accountable to the truth. A judge can sanction a lying attorney, who can then be disbarred. Public relations practitioners who lobby for their clients on public issues must be held to the same standard of accuracy and truth. Hill & Knowlton's record in arguing for the United States to go to war for Kuwait is sufficient evidence for regulation of public relations with sanctions for deliberate misrepresentations.

DEEPENING YOUR MEDIA LITERACY

EXPLORE THE ISSUE: Review the account of Hill & Knowlton's campaign for the Kuwaiti government for U.S. military intervention in John Stauber and Sheldon Rampton's book *Toxic Sludge Is Good for You* and also in other sources.

DIG DEEPER: Analyze the ethics code of the Public Relations Society of America and assess Hill & Knowlton's performance as an energetic advocate on behalf of a client.

WHAT DO YOU THINK? In the interest of the public good, should public relations advocacy be regulated and sanctioned for abuses? If not, why not? If you favor regulation, who should be the regulator?

▲ **Lobbyists Everywhere.** *Eager to bend the ears of legislators, public relations people lobby the halls of Congress and also of every state capitol. In North Dakota, a state with a small population, registered lobbyists outnumber legislators almost 30 to 1.*

Lobbyists get caught too. Jack Abramoff was an up-and-comer who had amassed the longest list of clients among Washington lobbyists by 2003. For the right ambiance to make pitches to members of Congress and top aides and also to acknowledge favors, Abramoff opened two posh restaurants down the street from the Capitol. He bought a fleet of casino boats. He leased four arena and stadium skyboxes. He sponsored golf outings to exclusive St. Andrews in Scotland and to the South Pacific.

The party began imploding with revelations by Susan Schmidt of the Washington *Post.* Schmidt tracked $45 million in lobbying fees from Indian tribes that were desperate to protect their casino revenue from possible taxation. There were irregularities galore, including massive overbilling. Abramoff told one aide, for example, to find some way to bill a Choctaw band $150,000 one month: "Be sure we hit the $150k minimum. If you need to add time for me, let me know." The aide responded: "You only had two hours." Abramoff fired back: "Add 60 hours for me."

An avalanche of other revelations followed in what became one of the biggest congressional corruption scandals in history. The scandal was a centerpiece issue in the 2006 elections. Abramoff went to jail. It was not only a few members of Congress and their aides who worried about subpoenas for accepting Abramoff's largesse. For lobbyists who conduct themselves honorably, it all was an embarrassing sullying of their craft.

Political Communication.   Every capital has political consultants whose work is mostly advising candidates for public office in **political communication.** Services include campaign management, survey research, publicity, media relations and image consulting. Political consultants also work on elections, referendums, recalls and other public policy issues.

The skills of political communication have widened to include so-called organizing front-organizations that masquerade as grassroots groups but actually represent big-spending special interests. Although presenting themselves as authentic citizen movements, these fronts are characterized more accurately as cash-rich and people-poor. The fronts, pretending to represent large constituencies of supporters, make impassioned cases in the mass media in a wide range of forums, including letters to newspaper opinion pages

political communication
Advising candidates and groups on public policy issues, usually in elections

and expensive network television ads. These fronts come and go as their usefulness to their corporate and ideological sponsors rises and wanes. Examples:

- **Center for Consumer Freedom**, a front group for the tobacco, restaurant and alcoholic beverage industries to defend the rights of consumers to choose to eat, drink and smoke as they please.

- **60-Plus Association**, funded by pharmaceutical manufacturer Pfizer to oppose prescription drug legislation.

- **Working Families for Wal-Mart**, organized by the giant retailer Wal-Mart although you had to look deeper than the group's public messages to learn the sponsorship.

- **Consumers for Cable Choice**, funded quietly by Verizon and AT&T.

- **National Smokers Alliance**, funded by the Phillip Morris tobacco company to oppose anti-smoking legislation.

- **Energy Citizen**, funded by ExxonMobil, ConocoPhillips, BP and other oil companies to organize rallies against legislation to slow climate change.

astroturfing
A pseudo-grassroots campaign, usually in politics; a take-off of the brand name for an artificial grass product

Such pseudo-grassroots organizations were derided as **astroturfing** by former Senator Lloyd Bentsen. His term, drawn from a widely known artificial grass product, in contrast to true grass, had been intended to discredit the practice. Although the term has stuck, it has not curtailed astroturfing. One Washington firm that specializes in astroturfing, Bonner & Associates, has a boiler-room phone bank with 300 lines with staffers. The staffers, assisted by robo-searching, make cold calls day and night around the country to encourage people to write their representatives in Congress on one side or another of pending legislation. Who pays the piper? Bonner clients include the Pharmaceutical Manufacturers Association, ExxonMobil, Dow Chemical, Citicorp, Ohio Bell, Miller Brewing, US Tobacco and the Chemical Manufacturers Association. It takes big budgets to lobby. How much? Stephen Engelberg, a New York *Times* reporter, found that one trade organization paid Bonner $3 million in one month to generate calls and letters to U.S. senators on one especially contentious bill.

Critics question whether Bonner and other such latter-day lobbying organizations are subverting democracy. Jack Bonner defends his firm's practices as a "triumph of democracy." The political system works better, he says, when more people are motivated to add their voices to the dialogue on public issues. All he does, says Bonner, is offer people information on who to call or write if they agree with his client's position.

Fund-Raising.   Fund-raising, an activity honed for decades by non-profit institutions and charities, has growing importance in political communication, especially with the advent of the internet. A 2004 presidential candidate, Howard Dean, democratized fund-raising by raising $25.4 million in the primary elections, almost all with appeals to people of ordinary means. Dean's average donation was only $80, far less than other candidates averaged by focusing on well-heeled donors with deep pockets. The modest donations, however, added together, represent a broader base of support.

The internet also has become a new tool for charities, like the Red Cross and American Cancer Society. They make mass appeals online, successfully tapping donors who make small donations but do so in great numbers.

APPLYING YOUR MEDIA LITERACY

- P.T. Barnum made a colorful career of outlandish claims in publicizing events. What current public relations campaigns employ Barnum's tactics?
- Evaluate BP's Beyond Petroleum campaign using Ivy Lee's rules. What could have been done differently before the Gulf oil-rig explosion? Might Lee's principles have salvaged BP's image after the explosion?
- How do you evaluate the point of Jack Bonner that front organizations for well-funded special interests enhance democracy?

Professionalization

STUDY PREVIEW | Sensitivity about ethics in public relations is being generated by theorists who favor open, honest dialogue with publics. Ethics discussions and accreditation aim to improve the practice of public relations.

Tarnished Image

Unsavory elements in the heritage of public relations remain a heavy burden. P. T. Barnum, whose name became synonymous with hype, attracted crowds to his stunts and shows beginning the mid-1800s with extravagant promises. Sad to say, some promoters still use Barnum's tactics. The claims for snake oil and elixirs from Barnum's era live on in commercials for pain relievers and cold remedies. The early response of tycoons to muckraking attacks, before Ivy Lee came along, was **whitewashing**—covering up the abuses but not correcting them. A more recent application of these principles is **greenwashing,** whereby companies hide their environmental abuses while touting their actions to be eco-friendly. It is no wonder that the term *PR* is sometimes used derisively. To say something is "all PR" means that it lacks substance. Of people whose apparent positive qualities are a mere façade, it may be said that they have "good PR."

whitewashing
Covering up

greenwashing
Hiding environmental abuses while claiming to be eco-friendly.

social media news release
Internet-based news releases with links to related material and interactive opportunities for news reporters

Ethics: Standards and Certification

The Public Relations Society of America, which has grown to 28,000 members in 114 chapters, has a different approach: improving the quality of public relations work, whatever the label. In 1951 the association adopted a code of professional standards. In a further professionalization step, PRSA established a credentialing process. Those who meet the criteria,which include significant professional experience, and who then pass exams, are allowed to place **APR,** which stands for "accredited in public relations," after their names. About 5,000 PRSA members hold APR status.

Since 1998 the APR program has been operated by the Universal Accreditation Board, which was created for that purpose by PRSA and a consortium of nine other public relations organizations.

■ Public Relations Scope (Pages 261–263)

In an era of media dominance in society, public relations is a growth industry with $4 billion a year in revenue. In terms of contributing to the common good, public relations has great potential in contributing to wide dialogue that leads to social consensus. The wider the public participation in the dialogue, the stronger the consensus and the more cohesive the society. In this sense, public relations is important for democracy to work well.

■ Public Relations in Context (Pages 263–265)

Messages are created for dissemination through mass media on behalf of institutions and clients that want to reach large audiences. Great effort goes into convincing news reporters and newsroom managers to carry the messages. Although public relations and advertising are frequently confused, there are essential differences. One difference is that public relations tries to win minds and, ideally, to build honest consensus, while advertising tries to make a sale.

■ Roots of Public Relations (Pages 265–270)

Modern public relations was the concept of Ivy Lee, who in 1906 began providing counsel to corporate clients that were under siege for a wide range of abusive practices. These practices included exploitation of labor and unfair monopolistic policies against consumers and competitors. Lee urged corporations to soften their closed-door and arrogant practices, to end cover-ups when things go badly and to face issues publicly, honestly and openly. Lee had disdain for misleading, circus-like publicity excesses of the P. T. Barnum variety. These not only were less than honest but also were wearing thin with the public. The industry grew, and public relations activities came to be identified as either external communication, which is aimed at external publics, or internal communication, which is aimed at employees, shareholders and other groups within the organization.

■ Public Relations as Strategy (Pages 270–271)

Hoaxes and misleading promotion have saddled public relations with a bad name. This is unfortunate because public relations can be practiced honorably—and is. Regardless, public relations people struggle with this negative image and over the years have concocted alternate names for their work. Terms like *strategic communication* and *integrated marketing* blur public relations with advertising and miss the dialogic nature of good public relations. Discussions on what to call themselves have sharpened an understanding among public relations people about their craft and ethical practices.

■ Public Relations Tactics (Pages 271–281)

Public relations is important for a democratic society because it can enable intelligent discussion by adding information, ideas and rationales to dialogue. Public relations goes beyond an informational role to provide articulate positions to influence both the public and public policy. This advocacy role, however, sometimes goes beyond principles of honest persuasion, which raises ethical questions about a worthy goal being used to justify the means. These ethics issues show themselves most prominently in the political communication branch of public relations. Lapses also show in public relations that focus on image-making.

■ Professionalization (Page 281)

Growing sensitivity about the ethics of persuasion, including the practice of public relations, has encouraged ethics codes and credentialing. Laws have been created to regulate public relations aimed at affecting public policy. These laws require lobbyists to register with the government.

■ Thinking Critically

1. What dynamics in modern society have driven the public relations industry's growth?

2. Why do public relations campaign planners need to be adroit in targeting media platforms for their messages?

3. How did theories about human nature and society help spawn public relations as a field in the late 1800s and early 1900s?

4. What impact does categorizing public relations as strategic communication have on the dialogic nature of traditional public relations?

5. Why might it be difficult to apply dialogic theory to advocacy?

6. What self-regulation practices would you propose to exorcise unethical practices from public relations?

■ Media Vocabulary

astroturfing (Page 280)

commonweal (Page 263)

crisis management (Page 274)

dialogic theory (Page 262)

government relations (Page 277)

greenwashing (Page 281)

image management (Page 273)

lobbying (Page 277)

media kit (Page 264)

media opportunities (Page 271)

media relations (Page 271)

news release (Page 264)

political communication (Page 279)

public relations (Page 262)

search advertising (Page 276)

social Darwinism (Page 265)

video news release (Page 264)

whitewashing (Page 281)

■ Media Sources

■ The industry's dominant trade journal is *PRWeek*.

■ Clarke L. Cayward, editor *Handbook of Strategic Public Relations and Integrated Marketing Communications*, 2nd edition. McGraw-Hill, 2012. Sixty-eight public relations practitioners and academics offer advice for business people to handle increasingly "ruthless" media.

■ Shannon A. Bowen, Brad Rawlins and Thomas Martin. *An Overview of the Public Relations Function*. Business Expert Press, 2010. The authors, representing a wide range of public relations experience, offer a primer for managers.

■ Kathleen Fearn-Banks. *Crisis Communications: A Casebook Approach, Fourth Edition*. Routledge, 2010. Fearn-Banks, a former journalist, and now an academic, offers case studies on crisis communication with news media, employees and consumers.

■ Naomi Oreskes and Erik M. Conway. *Merchants of Doubt: How a Handful of Scientists Obscured the Truth on Issues from Tobacco Smoke to Global Warming*. Bloomsbury, 2010. Oeskes, a historian, and Conway, a science writer, argue that science has been misused repeatedly for political and financial interests that have co-opted scientists and applied public relations techniques.

■ Kathryn Allamong Jacob. *King of the Lobby: The Life and Times of Sam Ward, Man-About-Washington in the Gilded Age*. Johns Hopkins, 2009. Jacob, a cultural historian on the post-Civil War era, profiles the public relations practitioner who perfected lobbying techniques to swoon Congress on behalf of banks, railroads and other clients.

■ Lawrence G. Foster. *Robert Wood Johnson and His Credo: A Living Legacy*. Lillian, 2008. Foster, a public relations executive at Johnson & Johnson, contributes to the reputation of the Johnson & Johnson co-founder for ethics in business practices.

■ Edward J. Lordan. "Defining Public Relations and Press Roles in the 21st Century," *Public Relations Quarterly* (Summer 2005), Pages 41–43. Lordan, a public relations scholar, examines the uneasy relationship between journalism and public relations.

■ Michael L. Kent and Maureen Taylor. "Toward a Dialogic Theory of Public Relations," *Public Relations Review* (February 2002), Pages 21–27. Kent and Taylor, both scholars, draw on a wide range of disciplines to argue for genuine dialogue as a basis for the moral practice of public relations.

■ Noel L. Griese. Arthur *W. Page: Publisher, Public Relations Pioneer, Patriot*. Anvil, 2001. Griese, a scholar and himself a public relations executive, draws on 80 boxes of Page's personal papers and also interviews with Page colleagues for a definitive biography.

■ John Stauber and Sheldon Rampton. *Toxic Sludge Is Good for You: Lies, Damn Lies and the Public Relations Industry*. Common Courage, 1995. Stauber and Rampton, media critics who focus on public relations, explore techniques for making counterintuitive cases on behalf of clients.

■ William Greider. *Who Will Tell the People: The Betrayal of American Democracy*. Touchstone, 1992. Grieder, of the *Nation* magazine, documents the rise of astroturfing with a focus on Bonner & Associates, a Washington lobby firm that specializes in operating front organizations for clients that seek to give a grassroots flavor to advocacy.

■ George S. McGovern and Leonard F. Guttridge. *The Great Coalfield War*. Houghton Mifflin, 1972. This account of the Ludlow Massacre includes the success of the Ivy Lee-inspired campaign to rescue the Rockefeller reputation but is less than enthusiastic about Lee's corporate-oriented perspective and sometimes shoddy fact gathering.

■ Ray Eldon Hiebert. *Courtier to the Crowd: The Story of Ivy Lee and the Development of Public Relations.* Iowa State University Press, 1966. Professor Hiebert's flattering biography focuses on the enduring public relations principles articulated, if not always practiced, by Ivy Lee.

■ Commission on the Freedom of the Press. *A Free and Responsible Press.* University of Chicago, 1946. Robert Hutchins led a group of intellectuals who laid out a landmark mandate for the press that included serving as a forum for the exchange of comment and criticism, as a means of projecting the opinions and attitudes of the groups in a society to one another, and as a way of reaching every member of the society by the currents of information, thought, and feeling that the press supplies. The commission also called for the press to provide a truthful, comprehensive account of the day's events in a context which gives them meaning.

■ Ivy Ledbetter Lee. *Human Nature and the Railroads.* E. S. Nash, 1915. Lee, the public relations pioneer, had railroads among early clients.

A Thematic Chapter Summary

Public Relations

To further deepen your media literacy here are ways to look at this chapter from the perspective of themes that recur throughout the book:

MEDIA ECONOMICS

Public pioneer Ivy Lee prescribed forthrightness and honesty.

The dark side of capitalism, un-mitigated greed, marked the rise of corporations into unprecedented wealth and power in the latter 1800s. Abusive practices, often from monopo-lies, included the pursuit of profit over and above any sense of social respon-sibility. The Populist movement, led by underclass farmers and laborers, caught the ear of government. Public policy reforms followed, forcing industry to find new ways to conduct itself. Public relations, using a model devised by Ivy Lee in 1906, guided corporations toward behavior that served their own good and also took note of the needs and interests of society's other constitu-ency groups.

MEDIA AND DEMOCRACY

Lobbyists defend their work as honest advocacy when done well.

Public relations ensures more diver-sity in public dialogue by giving an articulate voice to organizations. The best practice of public relations seeks win-win solutions on issues not only for the organization being represented but also for other constituencies with a stake in the issues. Public relations, practiced well, is honest advocacy in society's marketplace of ideas. One public relations activity, lobbying, goes to the heart of public policy by providing information and arguments to legislators in the creation of public policy. Lobbyists also work with govern-ment officials who put public policy into effect. Unethical and illegal lobby-ing activities, which sometimes make headlines, malign an otherwise honor-able public relations activity that helps democracy work.

ELITISM AND POPULISM

Charles Darwin may have shuttered at how his survival-of-the-fittest theory came to explain wealth and privilege.

The Industrial Revolution that trans-formed U.S. society in the decades following the Civil War created a drasti-cally two-tiered society—the haves and the have-nots. Many in the upper class, panged to varying degrees with guilt about their unprecedented wealth, drew on the survival-of-the-fittest theory of Charles Darwin, the new rage of the time, to justify their privileged position. They called it *social Darwinism*, which meant they had acquired their advantage of superior status by being the most fit. The theory was cast in terms of a religious theme that went something like this: It wasn't the fault of rich people that the Creator had imbued them with special gifts at amassing fortunes that enabled extravagant lifestyles. The notion was insulting to laborers, farmers and other ordinary people. A new political move-ment, populism, arose to give voice to the underprivileged "inferiors" who, according to social Darwinism, had been left behind. The populist movement inspired public policy changes that shook industry. Into this environment came public relations, as a way for industry to both listen to and communicate with the whole range of society's constituent groups.

MEDIA FUTURE

Next step in effective public relations: More listening, not just telling.

Public relations has a bum rap in many quarters. Take, for example, the derogatory phrase "It's only PR" to suggest something illusory and less than honest. The public relations profession has been working to repair its tarnished image, encouraging good practice through codes of ethics and accreditation. More needs to be done. Scholars are working on new theories to guide public relations practitioners. These include dialogics, which emphasizes genuine listening before developing positions on issues.

AUDIENCE FRAGMENTATION

Public relations practitioners, including those in political communication, know how to parse the mass audience for made-to-fit messages.

The concept of publics, groups within society that are identifiable and addressable, has grown more complex with the proliferation of special interest groups. People once identified themselves mostly as members of large groups, like political parties, religious denominations, ethnic communities and geographic areas. The old categories today have subcategories and subcategories within them, most with articulate leadership and their own channels of communication. This all adds layers of challenge for public relations practitioners in listening to the growing diversity of voices and designing campaigns to build support for mutually beneficial goals.

MEDIA TECHNOLOGY

Tylenol employed numerous techniques to assure people about its product safety after a terrorist lethally laced pills.

Not being a mass medium itself but relying on media to carry its messages, public relations has no technology unique to itself. But technology for other media, particularly the internet, has opened fascinating new wrinkles for the conduct of public relations. One is online news releases with links to blogs and a wide range of related sites. Called the social media news release, the innovation encourages interactive and ongoing communication. It makes public relations more than ever a two-way street for communication.

■ Advertising Outside the Box

If advertising had a guru, it would be Bob Greenberg. He was the first to talk about cell phones as a new advertising medium—the "third screen," he called it, coming after movies and television. In the fast-changing media environment, those insights were ages ago—at least a couple years.

Now Greenberg is into data visualization. He is encouraging advertising that invites consumers to track their own personal data and compare the numbers with others. Comparing your miles per gallon with other commuters can be a game—fun and engaging and made possible by, say, an auto manufacturer. Says Greenberg: "The profound effect of seeing

◄ **Bob Greenberg.** *His crystal ball sees advertising not in packaging ads inside entertainment and news but integrated into the digital age in which we now live.*

CHAPTER INSIGHTS

- Advertising is integral in consumer economies, democracies and mass media.

- Mass media makes advertising possible.

- Ad agencies and the media in which they advertise are closely linked.

- Advertisement placement in media outlets is determined by their media reach.

- Branding as an advertising strategy encompasses building large product lines around a particular product or service.

- Advertising tactics include lowest common denominators, positioning, redundancy and testimonials.

- New techniques include viral advertising, word-of-mouth testimonials or "buzz" advertising, and stealth.

your stats compared to someone else's is inspiring." Why should advertisers embrace data visualization? Because, says Greenberg, data visualization becomes part of the core customer experience of purchasing and using a product. He calls it "the ultimate motivation." The Greenberg lesson: Advertising is all about motivating consumers.

Greenberg shares his observations freely. But no mere armchair commentator, he practices post-mass media advertising at his R/GA agency in New York, part of the global Interpublic agency chain. R/GA designed the Nikeplus web site, which employs data visualization. Hardcore runners can track their distance, pace, time and calories burned as well as correspond with other runners. The customer's ability to compare themselves to others and to share this experience with others, he says, builds loyalty and sells products.

The era of entertainment that brought massive audiences to advertising messages is fast fading, Greenberg says. It's time to think outside the box.

Greenberg pities those ad agency execs who still pitch the 30-second television spot to clients because it's all they know. It's not that television, radio, magazines and newspapers are dead but that their heyday is past and their near-monopoly as carriers of advertising is fading fast. As Greenberg tells it, ad agencies that don't find new models to reach consumers are setting themselves up for extinction.

Greenberg's answer: Rather than ads being sandwiched into entertainment products, the ads themselves must be the entertainment. Greenberg has been called a media futurist, but there is evidence that the future is now. Samsung and Verizon have tripled their internet ad budgets. American Express has shifted away from network television. At R/GA, Greenberg has integrated information technologists, data analysts and what he calls "experience designers" into his staff. He must be doing something right. His staff has quintupled to 400. ■

Importance of Advertising

STUDY PREVIEW

Advertising is vital in a consumer economy. Without it people would have a hard time even knowing what products and services are available. Advertising, in fact, is essential to a prosperous society. Advertising also is the financial basis of important contemporary mass media.

Consumer Economies

Advertising is a major component of modern economies. In the United States, advertisers spend 2.4 to 2.9 percent of the gross domestic product to promote their wares. When the nation's production of goods and services is up, so is advertising spending. When production falters, as it did in the Great Recession of 2007 through 2009, many manufacturers, distributors and retailers pull back on advertising.

The essential role of advertising in a modern consumer economy is obvious if you think about how people decide what to buy. If a car manufacturer were unable to tout the virtues of its vehicles by advertising in mass media, people would have a hard time learning about the product, let alone knowing whether it is what they want.

Advertising and Prosperity

Advertising's phenomenal continuing growth has been a product of a plentiful society. In a poor society with a shortage of goods, people line up for necessities like food and clothing. Advertising has no role and serves no purpose when survival is the main concern. With prosperity, however, people have not only discretionary income but also a choice of ways to spend it. Advertising is the vehicle that provides information and rationales to help people decide how to enjoy their prosperity.

▲ **A Society of Choices.** *By presenting choices to consumers, advertising mirrors the democratic ideal of individuals choosing intelligently among alternatives. The emphasis is on individuals making up their own minds: Democrats or Republicans? Nike or Reebok? Subaru or Ford?*

Besides being a product of economic prosperity, advertising contributes to prosperity. By dangling desirable commodities and services before mass audiences, advertising can inspire people to greater individual productivity so that they can have more income to buy the things that are advertised.

Advertising also can introduce efficiency into the economy by allowing comparison shopping without in-person inspections of all the alternatives. Efficiencies also can result when advertising alerts consumers to superior and less costly products and services that have displaced outdated, outmoded and inefficient offerings.

Said Howard Morgens, when he was president of Procter & Gamble: "Advertising is the most effective and efficient way to sell to the consumer. If we should ever find better methods of selling our type of products to the consumer, we'll leave advertising and turn to these other methods." McGraw-Hill, which publishes trade magazines, has offered research showing that a salesperson's typical call costs $178, a letter $6.63 and a phone call $6.35. For 17 cents, says McGraw-Hill, an advertiser can reach a prospect through advertising. Although advertising does not close a sale for all products, it introduces products and makes the salesperson's job easier and quicker.

Here are estimates of how much the leading advertisers spend in U.S. mass media:

Procter & Gamble	$5.2 billion
AT&T	$3.2 billion
Verizon	$3.0 billion
General Motors	$3.0 billion
Time Warner	$3.0 billion
Ford	$2.5 billion
GlaxoSmithKline	$2.5 billion
Johnson & Johnson	$2.4 billion
Disney	$2.3 billion
Unilever	$2.2 billion

Advertising and Democracy

Advertising first took off as a modern phenomenon in the United States, which has given rise to the theory that advertising and democracy are connected. This theory notes that Americans, early in their history as a democracy, learned to hold individual opinions to participate in the political system. They looked for information so that they could evaluate their leaders and vote on public policy. This emphasis on individuality and reason paved the way for advertising: Just as Americans looked to mass media for information on political matters, they also came to look to media for information on buying decisions.

In authoritarian countries, by contrast, people tend to look to strong personal leaders, not reason, for ideas to embrace. This, according to the theory, diminishes the demand for information in these non-democracies, including the kind of information provided by advertising.

Advertising has another important role in most democratic societies in generating the majority of the operating revenue for newspapers, magazines, television and radio.

Without advertising, many of the media on which people in the United States rely for information, for entertainment and for the exchange of ideas on public issues would not exist as we know them.

- How is advertising an essential element in modern consumer economies?
- This is a chicken-or-egg question: Which predates the other—advertising or prosperity?
- How does advertising empower people living in a democratic society?

Origins of Advertising

STUDY PREVIEW

Advertising is the product of great forces that have shaped modern society, beginning with Gutenberg's movable type, which made mass-produced messages possible. Without mass media there would be no vehicle to carry advertisements to mass audiences. Advertising also is a product of the democratic experience; of the Industrial Revolution and its spin-offs, including vast transportation networks and mass markets, and of continuing economic growth.

Stepchild of Technology

Advertising is not a mass medium, but it relies on media to carry its messages. **Johannes Gutenberg**'s movable type, which permitted mass production of the printed word, made mass-produced advertising possible. First came flyers, then advertisements as newspapers and magazines were introduced. In the 1800s, when technology created high-speed presses that could produce enough copies for larger audiences, advertisers used these media to expand markets. With the introduction of radio, advertisers learned how to use electronic communication. Then came television.

Johannes Gutenberg
Progenitor of advertising media

Flyers were the first form of printed advertising. The British printer **William Caxton** issued the first printed advertisement in 1468 to promote one of his books. In America publisher **John Campbell** of the Boston *News-Letter* ran the first advertisement in 1704. The ad was a notice from somebody wanting to sell an estate on Long Island. Colonial newspapers listed cargo arriving from Europe and invited readers to come, look and buy.

William Caxton
Printed first advertisement

John Campbell
Published first ad in British colonies

Industrial Revolution

The genius of **Benjamin Day**'s New York *Sun*, in 1833 the first penny newspaper, was that it recognized and exploited so many changes spawned by the Industrial Revolution. Steam-powered presses made large press runs possible. Factories drew great numbers of people to jobs in cities that were geographically small areas to which newspapers could be distributed quickly. The jobs also drew immigrants who were eager to learn—from newspapers as well as other sources—about their adopted country. Industrialization, coupled with the labor union movement, created unprecedented wealth, with laborers gaining a share of the new prosperity. Although primitive by today's standards, a consumer economy was emerging.

Benjamin Day
His penny newspaper brought advertising to new level

A key to the success of Day's *Sun* was that, at a penny a copy, it was affordable for almost everyone. Of course, Day's production expenses exceeded a penny a copy. Just as commercial media do today, Day looked to advertisers to recoup the loss. As Day wrote in his first issue, "The object of this paper is to lay before the public, at a price within the means of everyone, all the news of the day, and at the same time afford an advantageous medium for advertising." Day and imitator penny press publishers sought larger and larger circulations, knowing that merchants would see the value in buying space to reach so much purchasing power.

National advertising took root in the 1840s as railroads, another creation of the Industrial Revolution, emerged. The railroads comprised new networks for mass distribution of manufactured goods. National brands developed, and their producers looked to magazines, also delivered by rail, to promote sales. By 1869 the rail network linked the Atlantic and Pacific coasts.

- How is advertising efficient for selling products and services?
- Compare the roles of Johannes Gutenberg, William Caxton and Benjamin Day in the emergence of advertising.
- How were railroads instrumental in the phenomenon of national advertising?

Advertising Agencies

STUDY PREVIEW | Central in modern advertising are the agencies that create and place ads on behalf of their clients. These agencies are generally funded by media in which they place ads. In effect, this makes agency services free to advertisers. Other compensation systems are also emerging.

MEDIAtimeline

ADVERTISING MILESTONES

FIRST AD
William Caxton promoted a book with first printed advertisement (1468)

PIVOTAL EVENTS

- Gutenberg invented movable metal type (1440s)
- First colonial newspaper (1690)
- Martin Luther (1483–1546)

NEW ERA OF COMMERCE
- Dutch East India Company founded (1602)
- King James Bible (1611)
- Pilgrims arrived at Plymouth Rock (1620)
- Coffeehouses popular among Boston mercantilists for exchanging commercial news (1640s)
- René Descartes wrote Meditations (1641)

The potential for advertising never dawned on Gutenberg

1400s–1600s

ADVERTISING MILESTONES

COLONIAL AD
Joseph Campbell included advertisements in his Boston *News-Letter* (1704)

WEDGWOOD
British china, first consumer brand name (1765)

Wedgwood china a branding pioneer

PIVOTAL EVENTS
- Benjamin Franklin (1706–1790)
- British Stamp Tax on colonies (1765)
- Revolutionary War (1775–1783)

1700s

ADVERTISING MILESTONES

PENNY PRESS
Benjamin Day created New York *Sun* as combination news, advertising vehicle (1833)

MAGAZINES
Godey's Lady's Book leading advertising vehicle (1840–1878)

AD AGENCY
Wayland Ayer opened first advertising agency, Philadelphia (1869)

WAR FOR READERS
Hearst and Pulitzer begin newspaper circulation war for advertisers (1896)

PIVOTAL EVENTS

- Penny press period (1833–)
- Henry Bessemer's mass production of superior steel (1858)
- Civil War (1861–1865)
- Transcontinental railroad (1869)

Ben Day's one-cent New York Sun was dependent on advertising

1800s

Pioneer Agencies

By 1869 most merchants recognized the value of advertising, but they grumbled about the time it took away from their other work. In that grumbling, a young Philadelphia man sensed opportunity. **Wayland Ayer,** age 20, speculated that merchants, and even national manufacturers, would welcome a service company to help them create advertisements and place them in publications. Ayer feared, however, that his idea might not be taken seriously by potential clients because of his youth and inexperience. So when Wayland Ayer opened a shop, he borrowed his father's name for the shingle. The father was never part of the business, but the agency's name, N. W. Ayer & Son, gave young Ayer access to potential clients, and the first advertising agency was born. The Ayer agency not only created ads but also offered the array of services that agencies still offer clients today:

- Counsel on selling products and services.
- Design services, that is, actually creating advertisements and campaigns.
- Expertise on placing advertisements in advantageous media.

Wayland Ayer
Founded first ad agency

ADVERTISING MILESTONES

ETHICS
Edward Bok of *Ladies' Home Journal* established advertising code (1919)

REGULATION
Congress created Federal Trade Commission to combat unfair advertising (1914)

BROADCAST CODE
NBC established code of acceptable advertising (1929)

AD COUNCIL
Media industries created predecessor to Ad Council (1942)

PIVOTAL EVENTS

- Women's rights movement succeeded in suffrage (1920)
- Great Depression (1930s)
- World War II (1941–1945)

Consumer economy in full swing by 20th century

1900–1949

ADVERTISING MILESTONES

BRANDS
David Ogilvy devised brand imaging (1950s)

TV ADS
Network television surpassed magazines as national advertising medium (1960s)

USP
Rosser Reeves devised unique selling proposition (1960s)

REGULATION
Federal crackdown on misleading claims (1980s)

PIVOTAL EVENTS

- Korean War (1950–1953)
- Vietnam War (1964–1973)
- Humans reached moon (1969)
- Carter presidency (1977–1981)

David Ogilvy: First-class image for branded products

1950–1999

ADVERTISING MILESTONES

STORE BRANDS
Store brands emerged as major challenge to brand names (2000s)

VIRAL
Ongoing story lines used to generate buzz (2000s)

WORD OF MOUTH
BzzAgency created as word-of-mouth agency (2001)

SUPER BOWL
NBC charged top advertiser $4 million for 30-second spot (2012)

Word-of-mouth advertising

PIVOTAL EVENTS

- George W. Bush presidency (2001–2009)
- 9/11 terrorist attacks (2001)
- Iraq War (2003–2011)
- Hurricane Katrina (2005)
- Great Recession (2007–2009)
- Obama presidency (2009–)

2000s

Full-service advertising agencies conduct market research for their clients, design.

The advertising industry is concentrated in a few global holding companies, ranked here by global revenue:

WWP (London)	$13.7 billion	141,000 employees
Omnicon (New York)	$13.4 billion	68,000 employees
Interpublic (New York)	$ 6.9 billion	40,000 employees
Publicis (Paris)	$ 4.5 billion	45,000 employees

Agency Compensation

Advertising agencies once earned their money in a standard way—15 percent of the client advertiser's total outlay for space or time. On huge accounts, like Procter & Gamble, agencies made killings.

Commissions. The 15 percent commission contract system broke down in the 1990s when U.S. businesses scrambled to cut costs to become more competitive globally. Today, according to a guesstimate by the trade journal *Advertising Age,* only 10 to 12 percent of agency contracts use a standard percentage. Agency compensation generally is negotiated. Big advertisers, like P&G, are thought to be paying 13 percent on average, but different agencies handle the company's brands, each with a separate contract. For competitive reasons all parties tend to be secretive about actual terms.

In one sense, advertising under the commission system is free for advertisers. Most media companies offer a 15 percent discount to ad agencies for ads placed by agencies. In effect, media companies induce agencies to place their clients' messages with them. Media companies and agencies prefer, however, to explain the discount as compensation for bulk purchases of time and space.

Performance. Commission contracts have been replaced largely by performance contracts. With these contracts, pioneered by Procter & Gamble, an advertiser pays an agency's costs plus a negotiated profit. In addition, if a campaign works spectacularly, agencies land bonuses.

A variation that Coca-Cola forced on agencies for 2010 contracts was to cover agency costs for a campaign with nothing additional if a campaign flopped but as much as 30 percent extra if a campaign met all targets. Agencies weren't pleased. One concern was that Coke was transferring all the risk for daring creativity to agencies. But Coke, with ad spending of $3 billion a year worldwide, held the upper hand in negotiating new contracts. Said Coca-Cola executive Sarah Armstrong: "We want our agencies to earn their profitability."

Bob Greenberg, chief executive at the advertising firm R/GA, predicted in a 2010 *AdWeek* article on the use of data visualization in advertising that "in the future, agencies will be paid based on their performance data and not on their hourly rates. That's a bar chart we can all look forward to seeing."

Equity. In the 1990s dot-com boom, a performance contract variation was to pay agencies with shares in the company. Equity contracts are chancy for agencies because an advertiser's success hinges on many variables, not just the advertising, but the return for an agency with a soaring client can be stratospheric.

APPLYING YOUR MEDIA LITERACY

- **What effects did moving the creation of advertising from the merchant to Wayland Ayer's advertising agency have on the merchant? The consumer?**
- **If you were an advertising agency's client, what compensation form would you prefer? Why?**

Placing Advertisements

STUDY PREVIEW The placement of advertisements is a sophisticated business. Different media have inherent advantages and disadvantages in reaching potential customers. So do individual publications, broadcast outlets, web sites and social media outlets.

Media Plans

Agencies create **media plans** to ensure that advertisements reach the right target audience. Developing a media plan is no small task. Consider the number of media outlets available: 1,400 daily newspapers in the United States alone, 8,000 weeklies, 1,200 general-interest magazines, 13,000 radio stations and 1,700 television stations. Other possibilities include direct mail, banners on web sites, billboards, blimps, skywriting and even printing the company's name on pencils.

Media buyers use formulas, some very complex, to decide which media are best for reaching potential customers. Most of these formulas begin with a factor called CPM, short for cost per thousand. If airtime for a radio advertisement costs 7.2 cents per thousand listeners, it's probably a better deal than a magazine with a 7.3-cent CPM, assuming that both reach the same audience. **CPM** by itself is just a starting point in choosing media. **Media reach** gauges the size of the audience exposed to the advertising for a particular medium. Other variables that media buyers consider include whether a message will work in a particular medium. For example, a Facebook profile works for clothing retailers looking to expand their online sales, but radio does not work for a product that lends itself to a visual pitch or sight gags.

Media buyers have numerous sources of data to help them decide where advertisements can be placed for the best results. The **Audit Bureau of Circulations,** created by the newspaper industry in 1914, provides reliable information based on independent audits of most dailies and major magazines. Nielsen, a survey organization originated to track television audiences, recently developed the Nielsen Online Campaign Ratings survey as a simpler way to measure the combined reach of television, web and mobile advertising. Arbitron conducts surveys of radio audiences. Standard Rate and Data Service publishes volumes of information on media audiences, circulations and advertising rates.

Conventional Placement Choices

Here are pluses and minuses of major advertising vehicles:

Newspapers. Advertisers recognize the hot relationship that media theorist Marshall McLuhan described between newspapers and their audiences. Readers are predisposed to consider information in advertisements seriously. The act of reading requires them to be focused. Also, studies show that many people look more to print media than to other media when they're ready to buy. Because newspapers are tangible, readers can refer back to advertisements just by picking up the paper a second time, which is not possible with ephemeral media like television and radio. Coupons are possible in print. Newspaper readers tend to be older, better educated and higher earning than television and radio audiences. Also, while advertisements need to be reserved weeks, even months ahead in some media, like network television, space for newspaper ads usually can be reserved as late as 48 hours ahead, and 11th-hour changes are possible.

However, newspapers are becoming less valuable for reaching the post-Baby Boomer generations. To the consternation of newspaper publishers, there has been an alarming drop in readership among young people. Unlike their parents, young adults are not picking up the newspaper habit as they mature.

media plans
Lay out where ads are placed

cost per thousand CPM
A tool to determine the cost-effectiveness of different media

media reach
Size of audience exposed to an advertisement through a particular medium

Audit Bureau of Circulations
Verifies circulation claims

▲ **Global Marketing.** *Knowing the following that Houston Rockets star Yao Ming has in his China homeland, the distributor for the Chinese beer Yanjing paid $6 million for Chinese-language billboards at the Rockets' arena. When Rockets games were broadcast in China, millions of viewers saw Yanjing signs. Also, the imported Yanjing beer picked up customers in Houston. With Yao Ming's retirement in 2011, what will Yanjing do now?*

MEDIAcounterpoints

■ Kids in Army Cross-Hairs?

Big Red One. *Has the Army gone too far in recruiting when kids are targeted for pitches?*

Alarms sounded at the Pentagon when the U.S. Army missed its recruiting goal of 80,000 new soldiers for the first time in years. Short 7,000, the Army launched multiple programs to restore its strength. New financial incentives were offered. The high school diploma requirement was dropped. Applicants with criminal records were accepted. Waivers were issued for bad physical and medical deficiencies. It all worked. Recruiters met goals the next few years.

But what of the long term?

The Army reshaped its marketing to create a stronger and positive impression with the next generation from which soldiers would be recruited. Among tactics:

- The online game America's Army, already with more than nine million registered users, was updated for a new release and a graphic novel added.

- Through an Army-approved licensing intermediary, the insignia of the historic First Infantry Division—Big Red One—was licensed to the retailer Sears for an apparel collection. Sizes even included those of boys. Prices began at $11.99 and topped at $120.

- Free graphic novels depicting military characters engaging in acts of bravery and demonstrating honor and integrity under stressful conditions are available on the America's Army web site.

The new marketing initiatives raised eyebrows. Was the Army softening a market of teen and even pre-pubescent kids? Was it right for the Army to glamorize itself to kids whose critical-assessment skills were still in formative stages? It was the same question that had been put to breakfast cereal makers for decades. Toy-makers had been similarly gigged for their ads. Were the promotions exploiting immature minds that could infer less than the whole truth of what products really delivered?

One critic of the new Army initiatives, Robert Weissman of Commercial Alert talked about "the infusion of militaristic trappings into children's culture."

The Army was ready for critics. The game America's Army was rated T, meaning teens can buy it but not pre-teens. Army marketing spokesperson Paul Boyce told the trade journal Advertising Age that the helicopter simulators at the Philadelphia mall exhibit were for kids 13 and older only. The target audience, Boyce said, was 18 to 25. Also, he said, the Big Red One apparel had no overt combat element—no fatigues, steel-toe boots or Kevlar helmets, just T-shirts, sweatshirts, jeans and jackets.

POINT

The reasoning power of children and even teenagers are in a developmental stage, Children must be protected from advertising and promotional campaigns that exploit their own vulnerabilities.

COUNTER POINT

Limits to protect children aren't practicable because limits work against access of adults and mature teen-agers to information and ideas. Anyway, who can oppose something as patriotic and noble as military service?

DEEPENING YOUR MEDIA LITERACY

EXPLORE THE ISSUE: Search for retailers selling the online game America's Army. Read the free graphic novels.

DIG DEEPER: Do you find any appeals to children, indirect or explicit, in these elements of the Army's marketing? If not, do you see how others might?

WHAT DO YOU THINK? Robert Weissman of Commercial Alert has argued against Army marketing that reaches kids: "You see the glamorization and romanticism of the military in a context that is targeted at kids who don't probably have broader vantage to understand that complexity of military operations." How do you respond?

Another drawback to newspapers is printing on newsprint, a relatively cheap paper that absorbs ink like a slow blotter. The result is that ads do not look as good as they do in slick magazines or on high-resolution computer, tablet and mobile screens. Slick, stand-alone inserts offset the newsprint drawback somewhat, but many readers pull the inserts out and discard them as soon as they open the paper. The use of paper itself, a finite natural resource, is also a factor.

Magazines.   As another print medium, magazines have many of the advantages of newspapers plus longer **shelf life,** an advertising term for the amount of time that an advertisement remains available to readers. Magazines remain in the home for weeks, sometimes months, which offers greater exposure to advertisements. People share magazines, which gives them high **pass-along circulation.** With slick paper and splashier graphics, magazines provide a more prestigious context for advertisements than newspapers. With precise color separations and enameled papers, magazine advertisements can be beautiful in ways that newspaper advertisements cannot. Magazines, specializing as they do, offer more narrowly defined audiences than do general-interest newspapers.

On the downside, magazines require reservations for advertising space up to three months in advance. Opportunities for last-minute changes are limited, often impossible.

Radio.   Radio stations with narrow formats offer easily identified target audiences. Time can be bought on short notice, with changes possible almost until airtime. Comparatively inexpensive, radio lends itself to repeated play of advertisements to drive home a message introduced in more expensive media like television. Radio also lends itself to jingles that can contribute to a lasting image.

However, radio offers no opportunity for a visual display, except when accessed online via a computer, tablet or mobile device. Radio is a mobile medium that people carry with them. The extensive availability of radio is offset, however, by the fact that people tune in and out. Another negative is that many listeners are inattentive. Also, there is no shelf life.

Television.   As a moving audio-visual medium, television offers special impact for advertising messages. Throughout its history, dating from the 1950s until recently, television has outpaced the growth of other media as an advertising vehicle. Today, the Internet is growing faster but remains a mere blip compared with network, cable and local television.

Drawbacks to placing ads on television include production costs. Because of cost, many advertisers have gone to shorter and shorter commercials. Historically, limited inventory was a problem for advertisers considering television. The networks, for example, had only so many ad slots available within and between programs and demand for slots outstripped availability. Slots for some hours were locked up months, even whole seasons, in advance. The networks historically used the short supply of slots to push rates to what every year seemed to be even more astronomical levels. The demand, however, is softening due to the continued fragmentation of television's audiences and the growth of new media outlets.

Because of the television audience's diversity, especially at local stations and major networks, targeting potential customers with any precision is difficult. Narrowly focused cable services like health, sport and fitness channels are an exception.

Online.   Literally thousands of internet sites serve niche audiences, enhancing the likelihood of reaching people with an inherent interest in specific products. For advertisers that choose the right sites, there is less waste than with traditional mass media, like the television networks that seek massive heterogeneous audiences. Some online sites have amassed gigantic databases on consumers that enable advertisers to custom-match their messages with likely consumers.

shelf life
How long a periodical remains in use

pass-along circulation
All the people who see a periodical

▲ **GEICO'S Rhetorical Question.** *Actor Mike McClone enters an empty room and asks: "Could Geico really save you 15 percent or more on car insurance?" McClone then asks a rhetorical question, like: "Does a 10-pound bag of flour make a really big biscuit?" It's an engagement ploy, followed by an amusingly absurd scene. The 15-second television commercials are part of multi-targeted campaigns for different consumer groups. The Geico ad has included its chatty gecko mascot, frustrated cavemen who can't get understanding, and Little Richard in campy self-mockery. Over five years Geico moved up to 7.6 percent of the competitive U.S. insurance market.*

Goods and services can be ordered directly from ads appearing on the internet, making the point of purchase only a few keystrokes away. For mail-order products, orders can be placed over the internet right from the ad. With other media, ads only whet the consumer's appetite. A phone call or a visit to a showroom is necessary—and lots of otherwise likely customers frequently don't take that next step.

Another advantage of internet advertising is cost. Except for high-demand sites, space is relatively inexpensive.

Some advertisers have experimented with consumer-created content on sponsored blog sites. An advantage of these post-your-own-clip blogs is the consumer interest created by the bizarre stuff that people post. The sites have a high level of credibility because of their free-for-all nature. But there is great risk. General Motors, for example, invited homemade clips about its Chevrolet Tahoe, a large sport-utility. The site ended up hosting TV spot-like messages from critics about the Tahoe as a gas-guzzler that was contributing to global warming. An advertiser that edits or shuts off negative input runs the risk of losing credibility.

Heavy consumer traffic on social networking sites like Facebook and YouTube attracts advertising. But these sites also carry risk because people can post pretty much whatever they want on their pages, including negative stuff on a product, which works against the effectiveness of the paid-for sponsored ads.

Among the five major media, here is how U.S. advertising dollars were spent, both nationally and locally, according to projections for 2010. It is important to note that online advertising is in second place with ad dollars more than doubled since 2005. Television is still number one, but ad dollars only increased one percent in the same timeframe.

Television	$63.9 billion
Online	$25.4 billion
Newspapers	$23.4 billion
Radio	$16.0 billion
Magazines	$ 9.2 billion

Search Engine Placement

The internet search engines Google, AOL, Yahoo and MSN for Microsoft, capitalizing on their super-fast hunt technology, have elbowed into the traditional placement service provided by advertising agencies. These search engines arrange for advertising space on thousands of web sites, many of them narrowly focused, like blogs, and place ads for their clients on the sites. Every blog visitor who clicks a **sponsored link** placed by the search engine provider will go to a fuller advertisement.

Google charges the advertiser a **click-through fee.** Google pays the site for every click-through. Google matches sites and advertisers—so a search for a new Porsche doesn't display ads for muffler shops.

Google also places what it calls "advertiser links" on search screens. The New York *Times,* for example, has a license to use Google technology when readers enter search terms on the *Times* site. The license allows Google to display ads of likely interest whenever a *Times* site reader conducts an internal site search. A search for *Times* coverage of Jamaican news, for example, will produce links to *Times* stories on Jamaica, as well as to advertisements for Caribbean travel elsewhere on the internet. If a *Times* reader clicks on an ad, Google pays the *Times* a click-through fee—from the revenue the advertiser paid to Google to place its ads.

Google is the major player in web advertising. Of the estimated advertisers' spending for online messages by 2009, Google had $23 billion. That was 99 percent of the company's revenue.

Gaming

To catch consumers who spend less time with television and more time with video games, advertisers have shifted chunks of their budgets to gaming. The potential is incredible. Half

sponsored link
On-screen hot spot to move to an online advertisement

click-through fee
A charge to advertisers when an online link to their ads is activated; also, a fee paid to web sites that host the links

◀ **Game Platform.** *Jeep has found video games a new advertising platform. Background billboards on Tony Hawk's Pro Skater 2 can be updated with new products either as new DVD editions are issued or with downloads for Internet-connected games.*

of Americans age 6 and older play games, and that elusive target for advertisers, men 18 and older, make up 26 percent of the gamers.

For an on-screen plug, advertisers pay typically $20,000 to $100,000 for a message integrated into the game. In gaming's early days, game makers and product markets worked directly with each other, but now many ad agencies have gaming divisions that act as brokers.

Game ads have advantages, particularly for online games. Messages can be changed instantly—a background billboard with a Pepsi ad can become a Chevy Volt ad or a movie trailer. One company, Massive, Incorporated, uses unseen interactive coding to identify gamers and adjust plugs that, for example, list stores near specific players and make geographic and other ad content adjustments. Nielsen, known mostly for television ratings, and game publisher Activision have an interactive system for tracking how many players see advertiser impressions—how many gamers see an ad and even how many recall an ad.

Although generally cost-effective for advertisers, online gaming has downsides. Online gaming ads can be problematic. Games can take months to develop, requiring far more lead time than advertisers usually have for rolling out a comprehensive multimedia campaign. For simple billboard messages, however, games have the advantage of being instantly changeable.

Established brands have created their own games, which appear on their web sites. In an early **advergame,** as these ads are called, the shoe manufacturer Nike created a soccer game at Nikefootball.com. Kraft Foods had an advergaming race at Candyland.com. A downside: Because advergames are accessible only through a brand's site, they don't make sense for emerging brands.

advergame
A sponsored online game, usually for an established brand at its own site

APPLYING YOUR MEDIA LITERACY

- What measures do advertisers look to in deciding where to place ads? Where does the information come from?
- If you choose only one media platform for advertising a new bubble gum, which would be your first choice? Which platform would be last? What knowledge drove your decisions?
- How quickly to you foresee online advertising platforms overtaking television platforms as the number one advertising media? What market conditions impacted your answer?
- What impact do you see digital status generators having on the nature of online advertising?

Brand Strategies

STUDY PREVIEW

Branding is a time-proven advertising strategy for establishing a distinctive name among consumers to set a product apart from competitors. The recent history of branding has moved beyond products into arrays of unrelated products. Special K is no longer just a break cereal. Now it's an extensive line of diet products. Branding also includes building lines of products around celebrity images.

Brand Names

Josiah Wedgwood, a well-to-do British potter, devised new heat controls for his kilns in 1765 and produced incredible new china. So impressed was the British Queen Charlotte that she consented to allow Wedgwood to call the product the Queen's China. Wedgwood became the first real consumer brand. Two and one-half centuries later the name lives on in bridal gift registries.

In the Wedgwood tradition, brand names still today designate a superior or unique product—sometimes. But branding also is sometimes just hokum. A modern reality is that most mass-produced products intended for large markets are essentially alike: Toothpaste is toothpaste is toothpaste. When a product is virtually identical to the competition, how can one toothpaste maker move more tubes?

By trial and error, tactics using the Wedgwood model were devised in the late 1800s to set similar products apart. One tactic, the **brand** name, aimed to make a product a household word. When it is successful, a brand name becomes almost the generic identifier, like Coke for cola and Kleenex for facial tissue.

Brand Images

David Ogilvy, who headed the Ogilvy & Mather agency, developed the **brand image** in the 1950s. Ogilvy's advice: "Give your product a first-class ticket through life."

Ogilvy created shirt advertisements with the distinguished Baron Wrangell, who really was a European nobleman, wearing a black eye patch—and a Hathaway shirt. The classy image was reinforced with the accoutrements around Wrangell: exquisite models

brand
A nongeneric product name designed to set the product apart from the competition

David Ogilvy
Championed brand imaging

brand image
Spin put on a brand name

▲ Josiah Wedgwood.

▲ **First Brand Name.** *When Queen Charlotte chose potter Josiah Wedgwood's new vitrified ceramic dinnerware in 1765, he extolled the royal endorsement on his stationery. Demand swelled. Soon Wedgwood was a brand name. And Wedgwood had a following for other china products, including an abolitionist medallion that became a rage in British fashion.*

of sailing ships, antique weapons, silver dinnerware. To some seeing Wrangell's setting, the patch suggested all kinds of exotica. Perhaps he had lost an eye in a romantic duel or a sporting accident.

Explaining the importance of image, Ogilvy once said: "Take whisky. Why do some people choose Jack Daniels, while others choose Grand Dad or Taylor? Have they tried all three and compared the taste? Don't make me laugh. The reality is that these three brands have different images which appeal to different kinds of people. It isn't the whisky they choose, it's the image. The brand image is 90 percent of what the distiller has to sell. Give people a taste of Old Crow, and tell them it's Old Crow. Then give them another taste of Old Crow, but tell them it's Jack Daniels. Ask them which they prefer. They'll think the two drinks are quite different. They are tasting images."

Whither Brand Names?

Perhaps prematurely, perhaps not, obituaries are being written for brand names—and brand-name advertising.

Store Brands.   Retailers are pushing **store brands,** on which they typically score 10 percent higher profits. Every time somebody buys Walmart's Ol' Roy dog chow, Purina and other brand-name manufacturers lose a sale. Walmart spends virtually nothing other than packaging costs for in-store displays to advertise Ol' Roy, which has knocked off Purina as top-seller. The store-brand assault has struck at a whole range of venerable brand names: Kellogg's, Kraft, Procter & Gamble and Unilever. Forrester Research, which tracks consumer trends, has predicted: "Walmart will become the new P&G."

Some brands remain strong, like automobile lines, but many manufacturers of consumer goods, whose advertising has been a financial mainstay of network television and magazines as well as newspapers and radio, have had to cut back on ad spending. P&G once spent $13.9 million advertising its Era, the first liquid laundry detergent but only $5.4 million a few years later. Some manufacturers have dropped out of the brand-name business. Unilever has only 200 brands left, compared to 1,600 in the mid-1990s.

store brands
Products sold with a store brand, often manufactured by the retailer. Also called *house brands* and *private labels*

◀ David Ogilvy.

◀ **First-Class Ticket.** *In one of his most noted campaigns, advertising genius David Ogilvy featured the distinguished chair of the company that bottled Schweppes in classy locations. Ogilvy realized how advertising creates impressions.*

Retail chains, led by Walmart, have the gigantic marketing channels to move great quantities of products without advertising expenses. Some retailers even own the factories. The Kroger chain owns 41 factories that produce 4,300 store-brand products for its grocery shelves.

Before the mega-retailers, brand names gave products an edge—with network television and national magazines carrying the messages. In those days the major networks—ABC, CBS and NBC—delivered messages to millions of consumers with greater effect than could small retailers. Not only are small retailers disappearing, but the networks also can't deliver what they used to. Television systems with 500 channels and the highly diverse web have divided and subdivided the audience into fragments. The ad agency Doremus has noted despairingly that "it's almost impossible to get your name in enough channels to build substantial awareness." Willard Bishop Consulting came to a similar conclusion from a study on network television, noting that three commercials could reach 80 percent of one target audience, 18-to 49-year-old women, in 1995. Only five years later that penetration level required 97 ads.

In an analysis of the phenomenon, *Fortune* magazine writer Michael Boyle said the big superstores are displacing brand-name advertising as the new direct connection to consumers. The new mass channel, he said, is the superstore.

branding
Enhancing a product image with a celebrity or already established brand name, regardless of any intrinsic connection between the product and the image

Branding. Brand names have taken on a new dimension. Today the concept of **branding** includes lending a recognized name to an array of unrelated products. Consider the Kardashian sisters who parlayed a tawdry, low-budget television reality series into modeling and endorsement franchises for products as wide-ranging as, can you believe, Quicktrim weight-loss solutions and Sugar Factory lollipops, not to mention numerous fashion lines, a burger chain, jewelry and sunless tanners. Originally, brand names were for products from a particular company, but the concept now includes unconnected products whose only

◀ **Sam Walton.**

◀ **Store Brands.** *Changes in retailing to one-stop super-stores have diluted the value of traditional brand names. Chains, meanwhile, have introduced their own brands. Walmart's Ol' Roy pet food and related pet products pick up on the name of company founder Sam Walton's favorite dog.*

connection is a name. Celebrities willing to objectify their image lend their names to arrays of products, giving the products a marketing cachet.

Advertising Tactics

STUDY PREVIEW

When the age of mass production and mass markets arrived, common wisdom in advertising favored aiming at the largest possible audience of potential customers. These are called lowest common denominator approaches, which tend to be heavy-handed so that no one can possibly miss the point. Narrower pitches, aimed at segments of the mass audience, permit more deftness, subtlety and imagination.

▲ **Cachet.** *Despite questionable talent, the Kardashian sisters Khloe, Kim and Kourtney found a following in a cable television reality series on their private lives. After garnering further attention with stunts and antics they found themselves celebutantes. Besides joint ventures with perfume lines and fashion lines, they each are celebrity endorsers on their own. Will salads from Carl's Jr. burger chain forever be associated with Kim in bed fondling dripping bites of salad as the camera closes in on her lips and cleavage. Still nibbling, she then sinks into a bubble bath.*

Lowest Common Denominator

Early brand-name campaigns were geared to the largest possible audience, sometimes called an LCD, or **lowest common denominator,** approach. The term *LCD* is adapted from mathematics. To reach an audience that includes members with IQs of 100, the pitch cannot exceed their level of understanding, even if some people in the audience have IQs of 150. The opportunity for deft touches and even cleverness is limited by the fact they might be lost on some potential customers.

Unique Selling Proposition.   LCD advertising is best epitomized in contemporary advertising by USP, short for **unique selling proposition,** a term coined by **Rosser Reeves** of the giant Ted Bates agency in the 1960s. Reeves' prescription was simple: Create a benefit of the product, even if from thin air, and then tout the benefit authoritatively and repeatedly as if the competition doesn't have it. A unique selling proposition need be neither hollow nor insulting, however. Leo Burnett, founder of the agency bearing his name, refined the USP concept by insisting that the unique point be real. For Maytag, Burnett took the company's slight advantage in reliability and dramatized it with the lonely Maytag repairman who turned into the longest running advertising character in the history of television.

Positioning.   Rather than pitching to the lowest common denominator, advertising executive **Jack Trout** developed the idea of **positioning.** Trout worked to establish product identities that appealed not to the whole audience but to a specific audience. The cowboy image for Marlboro cigarettes, for example, established a macho attraction beginning in 1958. Later, something similar was done with Virginia Slims, aimed at women.

lowest common denominator
Messages for broadest audience possible

unique selling proposition
Emphasizes a single feature

Rosser Reeves
Devised unique selling proposition (USP)

Jack Trout
Devised positioning

positioning
Targeting ads for specific consumer groups

Positioning helps to distinguish products from all the LCD clamor and noise. Advocates of positioning note that there are more and more advertisements and that they are becoming noisier and noisier. **Ad clutter,** as it is called, drowns out individual advertisements. With positioning, the appeal is focused and caters to audience segments, and it need not be done in such broad strokes.

ad clutter
So many competing ads that all lose impact

Campaigns based on positioning have included:

- Johnson & Johnson's baby oil and baby shampoo, which were positioned as adult products by advertisements featuring athletes.
- Alka-Seltzer, once a hangover and headache remedy, which was positioned as an upscale product for stress relief among health-conscious, success-driven people.

Redundancy Techniques

Advertising people learned the importance of redundancy early on. To be effective, an advertising message must be repeated, perhaps thousands of times. Redundancy is expensive, however. To increase effectiveness at less cost, advertisers use several techniques:

flight (or wave)
Intense repetition of ads

- **Barrages.** Scheduling advertisements in intensive bursts called **flights or waves.**
- **Bunching.** Promoting a product in a limited period, such as running advertisements for school supplies in late August and September.
- **Trailing.** Running condensed versions of advertisements after the original has been introduced, as automakers do when they introduce new models with multipage magazine spreads and follow with single-page placements.
- **Multimedia trailing.** Using less expensive media to reinforce expensive advertisements. Relatively cheap drive-time radio in major markets is a favorite follow-through to expensive television advertisements created for major events like the Super Bowl.

Repetition can be annoying, especially with heavy-handed, simplistic messages. Annoying or not, redundancy can work. The chairman of Warner-Lambert, whose personal products include Rolaids gastric-relief tablets, once joked that the company owed the American people an apology for insulting their intelligence with the redundant line that "R-O-L-A-I-D-S spells relief." Warner-Lambert, however, has never been apologetic to shareholders about Rolaids maintaining its market dominance.

Marshall McLuhan, the media theorist prominent in the 1960s, is still quoted as saying that advertising is important after the sale to confirm for purchasers that they made a wise choice. McLuhan's observation has not been lost on advertisers that seek repeat customers.

▲ **Over and Over and Over Again.** *Cheesy infomercials made Snuggies part of popular culture. Comedians tell jokes about them, YouTube videos parody the TV ads and internet sites like snuggiesightings.com are filled with fan postings about them. Redundancy establishes a product in the minds of consumers, and no matter how annoying, redundancy has proven to work to propel a product to success and maintain sales.*

Testimonials

Celebrity endorsements have long been a mainstay in advertising. Testimonials can be less than classy, though. Quarterback Joe Montana offered testimonials to a jock-itch potion, presidential candidate Bob Dole to an erectile-dysfunction prescription, former Surgeon General Everett Koop to an emergency-call device. Professional fund-raising, a growth industry, includes pleas from celebrity volunteers. For commercial products, however, testimonials are given only for compensation.

During Jimmy Carter's presidential administration in the 1970s, the Federal Trade Commission was among the federal agencies that cracked down on excessive business practices. The FTC saw testimonials getting out of hand and required that endorsers actually be users of the product. The commission also clamped down on implied expert endorsements, like actors wearing white coats that suggested they were physicians as they extolled the virtues of over-the-counter remedies. That led to one laughable FTC-ordered disclaimer that has endured as a comedy line: In the interest of full disclosure, one soap-opera star in a white frock opened an ad: "I'm not really a doctor but I play one on TV." Then he made the spiel.

Contemporary Techniques

STUDY PREVIEW

What goes around comes around. The original pre-media advertising, word-of-mouth, has new currency in techniques that go by the name *buzz communication*. The goal is to create buzz about a product. Many buzz campaigns originate on the internet with the hope of something virus-like. The term *viral advertising* has come into fashion.

▲ **Celebrity Ads.** *When pop performer Michael Jackson pitched Pepsi in a 1984 advertisement, celebrities began to abandon their historic disdain for celebrity endorsements. Pepsi followed its $5 million deal with Jackson with Madonna, Michael J. Fox, Ray Charles, Cindy Crawford and Britney Spears. Soon, everybody was doing it: Presidential candidate Bob Dole, the Kansas senator, extolled how Viagra worked for him.*

Advertising Clutter

Leo Bogart of the Newspaper Advertising Bureau noted that the number of advertising messages doubled through the 1960s and 1970s. Except during recessions, the trend continues. This proliferation of advertising creates a problem: too many ads. The problem has been exacerbated by the shortening of ads from 60 seconds in the early days of television to today's widely used 15-second format.

At one time the National Association of Broadcasters had a code limiting the quantity of commercials. The Federal Communications Commission let station owners know that it supported the NAB code, but in 1981, as part of the Reagan administration's deregulation, the FCC backed away from any limitation. In 1983 a federal court threw out the NAB limitation as a monopolistic practice.

Ad clutter is less of an issue in the print media. Many people buy magazines and newspapers to look at ads as part of the comparative shopping process. Even so, some advertisers, concerned that their ads are overlooked in massive editions like a 700-page bridal magazine are looking to alternative means to reach potential customers in a less cluttered environment.

The clutter that marks much of commercial television and radio today may be alleviated as media fragment further. Not only will demassification create more specialized outlets, such as narrowly focused cable television services, but there will be new media. The result will be advertising aimed at narrower audiences.

One measure of network television ad clutter is the average number of messages per commercial break, here including network program promotions:

ABC	7.1
CBS	6.3
NBC	6.2
Fox	6.0

MEDIAtomorrow

■ Automating Celebrity Endorsements

Celebrity for Sale. *Hakeem Nicks of the New York Giants is available as a television endorser for products with generic images like this. For a fee, advertisers can use his image and superimpose text and audio for their products. The result: A big name endorser for a local product. It's easy and quick through the ad agency Brand Affinity Technologies.*

What Do You Think?

Whose product endorsement would have greater influence on you: A top-tier recording artist, or a singer who makes the rounds of fairs and events in your region?

What do you see as Tiger Woods' future in product endorsements?

You may be seeing more advertising than ever with celebrity testimonials. Digital technology has enabled the ad agencies that create ads to find celebs for their clients' products by going online. Click, click, agencies can sign up celebs. The celebrity-on-tap service is from a Hollywood company, Brand Affinity Technologies, whose database lists 3,800 athletes and celebrities. Some are big-time, some of local renown, all ranked by many factors, including popularity, fan base and media exposure. An ad agency looking for a celebrity match for a client, say, the San Francisco car dealer Royal Motor, might choose San Francisco Giants pitcher Matt Cain from BAT's database.

A few more clicks and an email contract proposal goes to Cain. He has 96 hours to decide, thumbs up or thumbs down. If Cain agrees, the ad agency has access to all kinds of generic poses shot for BAT to use when building ads. Soon Cain's image can be mated electronically into product images. Indeed, Cain has been on billboards for Royal Motor throughout San Francisco.

The celebrity links can be for products as diverse as car dealers, burger joints and tax-prep services. For online ads, fees start at $15,000 for 30 days.

The BAT system has opened a new digital-driven avenue for celebrity endorsements. BAT's stock video and photo images can be packaged and repackaged. No talent agent necessary. Good-bye to time-devouring interviewing. Good-bye too to long-term commitments to stars, like golfer Tiger Woods, whose endorsements can backfire.

If a celebrity ends up in a scandal that could tarnish an advertiser's product, it's relatively quick and easy to replace the stock BAT image with another endorser. This is in contrast to the traditional practice of hugely expensively campaigns built entirely around a single star, like Nike's five-year $105 million deal with Woods before the golfer's sexual escapades ruined his attraction for testimonials.

Big name performers are in BAT's database of videos and photos, among them singer Alicia Keyes and Kings of Leon. But the BAT system has enabled lesser celebrities, some with only local followings, to translate their image into a second source of income, albeit for less than Tiger Woods. At his peak, Woods was rolling in $120 million a year.

In its commercial niche of the mass media, BAT's digital technology is contributing to the democratizing of mass communication. More people, in this case second-tier and even third-tier celebrities, have opportunities they didn't have before to become endorsement personalities.

Word-of-Mouth Advertising

Besides clutter, advertising as an industry still has to contend with its age-old credibility problem. Consumers are hardly blotters who absorb any line laid on them through mass media. Far more credible are stories from friends and acquaintances who have had a favorable experience with a product. Or an unfavorable experience.

Word-of-mouth testimonials, friends talking to friends, is strong advertising. But how does word-of-mouth **buzz advertising** get the buzz going? And how can the buzz be sustained? In the advertising industry's desperation in recent years to find new avenues for making pitches, buzzing has turned into an art. Several agencies specialize in identifying individuals with a large circle of contacts and introducing them to a product. These agents sample the product, generally being able to keep the samples for their help in talking them up with family, coworkers and anyone else in earshot. The agents file occasional reports, with the incentive of being eligible for prizes.

Advertisers also look more and more to social media sites, like Facebook and YouTube, to generate buzz. How does buzz stack up against traditional advertising media? Nobody knows, but it's cheap enough that advertisers have seen it as worth trying.

Viral Advertising

Related to buzzing is **viral advertising.** When successful, viral advertising spreads contagion-like through the population. Advertisers create clever clips that they hope will prompt visitors to pass them on to friends. People open messages from friends, which tangentially increases an ad's reach at low cost. Viral advertising works particularly well on the internet. Automakers were among the first to experiment with viral techniques. Ford promoted its SportKa in Europe with story lines designed to stir conversation and draw people in for other installments. BMW estimated that 55.1 million people saw its *For Hire* series. Honda could not have been happier with its *Cog* mini-story. Said a Honda executive: "I have never seen a commercial that bolted around the world like *Cog* in two weeks."

On the downside, however, advertisers can't cancel viral ads, which have a life of their own and can float around the interne for months, even years. An advertisement for beach

viral advertising
Media consumers pass on the message like a contagious disease, usually on the internet

◀ **Viral Advertising.** *Automakers have experimented with what's called "viral advertising," producing compelling action stories on the web that viewers will want to pass on, virus-like, to friends. Embedded in story lines like Ford's Evil Twin for its SportKa in Europe are product messages.*

MEDIApeople

■ Word of Mouth—or WOM, for Short

▲ Dave Balter.

They call Dave Balter the king of buzz. His BzzAgent company stirs up word-of-mouth promotion for products through networks of people he calls "influentials." These people are given a product to try and to talk up to friends and associates.

Out of Skidmore College with a psychology degree, Dave Balter set out to be a romance author. Sidetracked, he instead landed jobs on the periphery of advertising in direct marketing and promotion. In time, seeing the slipping effectiveness of traditional advertising, Balter toyed in his mind with promoting products by word-of-mouth. Today at his marketing company in Boston, he's known around the office as buzzagent Dave.

The company, BzzAgent, is at the vanguard of the explosive word-of-mouth segment of the advertising industry—WOM, for short. BzzAgent handles about 300 campaigns simultaneously. Clients include Dunkin' Donuts, Clinique, and Stonyfield Organic.

By age 40 Balter, an absolute believer in buzz, had founded the Word-of-Mouth Marketing Association and chaired the association's ethics committee. Balter was in the process of securing a patent on the buzz schemes he had devised at BzzAgent. In 2005 he cemented his place in the evolution of advertising with a book fittingly titled *Grapevine*. Later he introduced Blogger Network and Frogpond, a digital listing service, to further exploit the word-of-mouth applications of the internet.

The premise of Balter's system is the universally acknowledged fact that people are more influenced by people around them, no matter how much they're also immersed in traditional advertising messages. BzzAgent signs up volunteers who meet a profile of "influentials," as they're called, and matches them up with a client's products—latte, perfumes, cheese goodies, you name it—to sample and then chat up the products among family, friends, associates and anybody else. The buzzing is unscripted, mostly just everyday conversation, although many agents use the internet to spread the word. The buzz agents file reports on their buzzing and earn buzz points that can be redeemed for rewards. iPads go over well. So do cameras and books. Balter's agents constitute an army, as many as 117,000 at any one point.

Does buzz marketing work? Measures are elusive, but WOM is so cheap compared to buying space and time in traditional media that advertisers figure, what's to lose?

Anecdotal evidence of the effectiveness abounds. For example, the influential book-retailing trade journal *Publishers Weekly*, after receiving advance proofs of Balter's book *Grapevine*, issued a negative review that normally would be a death knell: "Balter's gee-whiz, narcissistic writing voice won't help win converts." But Balter also had put 2,000 copies into the hands of buzz agents. The book became a best-selling business title.

What do You Think?

Which products lend themselves to buzz promotion? Which do not?

If you were an executive at an automobile manufacturer, how much of your advertising budget would you risk on buzz tactics? Explain your reasoning.

What if the product were a new toothpaste? Or iPhone competitor? How would the product impact your marketing plan and budget?

vacations in Beirut would have been fine in 2005 but grotesquely inappropriate a year later with Israeli air attacks on Hezbollah targets in the city, mass evacuations and hundreds of casualties.

Under-the-Radar Advertising

Inundated with advertisements, over 6,000 a week on network television, many people tune out. Some do it literally with their remotes. Ad people are concerned that traditional modes, like television, are losing effectiveness. People are overwhelmed. Consider, for example, that a major grocery store carries 30,000 items, each with packaging that screams "Buy me." More commercial messages are there than a human being can handle. The problem is ad clutter. Advertisers are trying to address the clutter in numerous ways, including stealth ads, new-site ads and alternative media. Although not hidden or subliminal, stealth ads are subtle—even covert. You might not know you're being pitched unless you're attentive—really attentive.

So neatly can **stealth ads** fit into the landscape that people may not recognize they're being pitched. Consider the Bamboo lingerie company, which stenciled messages on a Manhattan sidewalk: "From here it looks like you could use some new underwear."

stealth ads
Advertisements, often subtle, in nontraditional, unexpected places

Sports stadiums like FedEx Field outside of Washington, D.C., work their way into everyday dialogue, subtly reinforcing product identity.

Not all stealth advertising is so harmless. In early 2007 some motorists in Boston began noticing suspicious-looking black boxes covered with lights and wires clamped to bridge supports near busy motorways. Roads were shut down and the bomb squad called in to remove what turned out to be battery-powered LED displays to advertise a show on the Cartoon Network. It was part of a campaign of "guerrilla marketing" carried out by Interference Inc., a marketing firm. Two artists, Peter Berdovsky and Sean Stevens, were arrested and charged with causing panic, a crime carrying a maximum penalty of five years. Although the charges were dropped, the public outrage over the hoax was so great that Cartoon Network's general manager was forced to resign. The network's parent company, Turner Broadcasting, paid more than $2 million restitution to the City of Boston.

Product Placement

In the 1980s advertisers began wiggling brand-name products into movie scripts, creating an additional although minor revenue stream for moviemakers. The practice, **product placement**, stirred criticism about artistic integrity, but it gained momentum. Fees zoomed upward. For the 2005 release of *The Green Hornet*, Miramax was seeking an automaker willing to pay at least $35 million for its products to be written into the script, topping the $15 million that Ford paid for its 2003 Thunderbird, Jaguar and Aston Martin lines to be in the James Bond movie *Die Another Day*.

product placement
Writing a brand-name product into a television or movie script

Later, placing products into television scenes gained importance with the advent of **TiVo** in 1999 and other devices that allow people to record shows and replay them commercial-free at their convenience. As of 2011, 1.7 million people used TiVo. In addition, cable and satellite companies offer similar devices to 24 million subscribes. This worries the television industry, whose business model was dependent on revenue from advertisers to which it guaranteed an audience for ads. With these replay devices, audiences no longer are trapped into watching commercials. Is the 30-second spot commercial doomed?

TiVo
A television recording and playback device that allows viewers to edit out commercials. A competing device is ReplayTV.

One response from the television and advertising industries has been more product placement deals that go beyond anything seen before. For a fee, products are being built into scripts not only as props but also for both implicit and explicit endorsement. For the 2010 season premiere of the Fox adventure-drama *24*, Apple paid $292,000 for 12 product placements and Pontiac $256,000 for eight. Advertisers spent an estimated $941 million for product placements on television in 2010.

How effective is product placement? The research company Arbitron surveyed moviegoers as they left theaters and found that 80 percent remembered ads shown at the beginning of the movie. Other media aren't close, recently spurring a 37 percent increase in

▲ **Scripted Plugs.** *Product placements have become a significant revenue stream in television, totaling $941 million a year. Programs with the most plugs: "The Biggest Loser," 6,248 in 2008; "American Idol," 4,636; and "Extreme Makeover: Home Edition," 3,371.*

movie ad revenue to $356 million in one year. Also, according to Arbitron, the notion that most people resent ads is mythical. Of viewers between ages 12 and 24, 70 percent weren't bothered by the ads.

Infomercials

infomercial
Program-length broadcast commercial

Less subtle is the **infomercial,** a program-length television commercial dolled up to look like a newscast, a live-audience participation show or a chatty talk show. With the proliferation of 24-hour television service and of cable channels, airtime is so cheap at certain hours that advertisers of even offbeat products can afford it. Hardly anybody is fooled into thinking that infomercials are anything but advertisements, but some full-length media advertisements are cleverly disguised.

'zine
Magazine whose entire content, articles and ads, pitches a single product or product line

A print media variation is the **'zine**—a magazine published by a manufacturer to plug a single line of products with varying degrees of subtlety. 'Zine publishers, including such stalwarts as IBM and Sony, have even been so brazen as to sell these wall-to-wall advertising vehicles at newsstands. One example was a splashy magazine called *Colors,* for which you originally paid $4.50. Once inside, you realized it was a thinly veiled ad for Benetton casual clothes. Benetton continues this concept online with its new collaborative website, *Colorslab: The Interactive Platform About the Rest of the World* and still masks the advertising nature of the publication.

Stealth advertisements try "to morph into the very entertainment it sponsors." wrote Mary Kuntz, Joseph Weber and Heidi Dawley in *Business Week.* The goal, they said, is "to create messages so entertaining, so compelling—and maybe so disguised—that rapt audiences will swallow them whole, oblivious to the sales component."

APPLYING YOUR MEDIA LITERACY

- **Why is clutter more of a problem in broadcast than in print media?**
- **Do you see media demassification easing the ad clutter problem?**
- **Who among your friends would make a good buzz agent? Why? How about you?**
- **From an advertiser's perspective, what are the pros and cons of going viral? Of going under the radar?**

■ Importance of Advertising   (Pages 289–291)

Modern consumer economies are driven by the demand stirred by advertising for products. The demand contributes to economic growth and prosperity. Also, because advertising brings attention to consumer choices, it fits well with the democratic notion of people making decisions individually on what serves their interests. The question can be asked whether advertising is a negative in consumer decision-making because it is aimed at selling products and not at promoting the common good. Conversely, it can be argued that prosperity is the common good. Despite the critics, the role of advertising is undeniable. Advertising comprises as much as 2.9 percent of the U.S. gross domestic product.

■ Origins of Advertising   (Pages 291–292)

The printing technology that developed from Johannes Gutenberg's movable metal type made possible the mass production of advertising messages. Actual advertising evolved slowly, but some 400 years later, when the Industrial Revolution was in full swing, advertising became integral in the nascent U.S. national consumer economy. Mass-produced products for far-flung markets were promoted through national advertising with ads in national magazines and in hundreds of local newspapers. Later, radio and television became part of the media mix through which manufacturers, distributors and retailers promoted their wares nationally and locally—and increasingly globally.

■ Advertising Agencies   (Pages 292–294)

Retailers and other advertisers tried managing their own promotions in the growing U.S. consumer economy in the 1870s. Gradually they farmed out the advertising to new agencies that specialized in creating advertising. These agencies also chose media outlets for reaching the most potential customers efficiently. Agencies charged for the services, generally as a percentage of the cost of the time or space purchased from media companies to carry the ads. More variations on this so-called commission system have been introduced in recent years.

■ Placing Advertisements   (Pages 295–299)

Advertisements don't appear magically in mass media. Media companies, dependent on advertising revenue, energetically court agencies and advertisers. Also, agencies and advertisers conduct extensive research before buying space and time to reach target consumers. Each type of media outlet has advantages.

■ Brand Strategies   (Pages 300–303)

Brand names became a vehicle for distinguishing a product from competitors in the late 1800s. Brand names have endured as an advertising strategy. For commodities, with products largely the same, advertisers linked brands with extraneous qualities—like racing excitement with

CHAPTER WRAP UP

Dodges, daring and adventure with Hathaway shirts, class with Grand Dad whisky. Today, it seems, everything is branded. Does a Paris Hilton watch keep better time than a Timex? In the media, CNN is promoted as a brand. So is Fox News. Each has its own cachet. Less glamorous than branding in promoting products are hard-sell pitches, especially those that refrain from going over anyone's head by using lowest common denominator messages that hammer away. Redundancy works in selling, which makes those hard-sell messages annoying but no less effective.

■ Advertising Tactics   (Pages 303–305)

Like all mass messages, advertising has the potential to reach the largest possible audience when it appeals to a lowest common denominator. Tactics include often grating, heavy-handed messages and repetition.

■ Contemporary Techniques   (Pages 305–310)

Modern life has become advertising saturated. On prime-time network television, dozens of 15-second spots drown each other out. Inundated, viewers zone out. The problem, called *ad clutter,* is a critical challenge for the advertisers that need somehow to get their messages across. The original pre-media advertising, word-of-mouth, is back. This time it's called *buzz communication.* The goal is to get people talking about a product. Many buzz campaigns originate on the internet with the hope of spreading virus-like. The term *viral advertising* has come into favor.

■ Thinking Critically

1. What is advertising's role in a capitalistic society? In a democracy? In mass media?

2. How has advertising evolved since the days of Johannes Gutenberg?

3. What is the role of advertising agencies in today's society?

4. Why do some ads appear in some media products and not in others?

5. Brand-name advertising is under siege somewhat. What affects whether a product loses its brand cachet?

6. What new advertising tactics are being devised? And how do they increase the visibility of the product they advertise?

7. What do you see as effective responses to the problem of ad clutter?

Media Vocabulary

ad clutter (Page 304)

advergame (Page 299)

Audit Bureau of Circulations (Page 295)

branding (Page 302)

click-through fee (Page 298)

flights (Page 304)

infomercial (Page 310)

lowest common denominator (Page 303)

media plans (Page 295)

media reach (Page 295)

pass-along circulation (Page 297)

positioning (Page 303)

product placement (Page 309)

shelf life (Page 297)

sponsored link (Page 298)

stealth ads (Page 309)

viral advertising (Page 307)

'zine (Page 310)

Media Sources

- James Othmer. *Adland: Searching for the Meaning of Life on a Brand Planet.* Doubleday, 2009. Othmer offers a memoir on a career as an advertising copywriter and advertising creative director and deals with the transition to digital marketing. A theme is the industry's influence on culture.

- Kit Yarrow and Jayne O'Donnell. *Gen Buy: How Tweens, Teens, and 20-Somethings Are Revolutionizing Retail.* Wiley, 2009. Yarrow, a consumer research scholar, and O'Donnell, a consumer-affairs journalist, examine marketing to people born between 1978 and 2000.

- Tom Reichert and Jacqueline Lamblase, editors. *Sex in Consumer Culture: The Erotic Content of Media and Advertising.* Erlbaum, 2006. Reichert and Lamblase, both professors, have collected quantitative and qualitative articles on gender differences and representation in mass media.

- Helen Katz. *Media Handbook: A Complete Guide to Advertising, Media Selection, Planning, Research and Buying,* third edition. Erlbaum, 2006. Katz, a media buying executive, assesses categories of media for advertising choices.

- Dave Balter and John Butman. *Grapevine: The New Art of Word-of-Mouth Marketing.* Portfolio, 2005. With chatty enthusiasm, Balter and Butman extol the cost-efficiency and also fun of buzz marketing as the next wave in advertising.

- Brian Dolan. *The First Tycoon.* Viking, 2004. This is a biography of Josiah Wedgwood, the mid-1700s English potter whose china became the first consumer brand name.

A Thematic Chapter Summary

ADVERTISING

To further deepen your media literacy here are ways to look at this chapter from the perspective of themes that recur throughout the book:

MEDIA TECHNOLOGY

For better or worse, mass media greases the consumer market for mass-produced products.

As a form of media message, advertising didn't take off quickly after Johannes Gutenberg's invention of movable metal type. But by the time the Industrial Revolution was transforming economies 400 years later, advertising became key to drawing customers to new mass-produced products. By then, in the latter 1800s, printing technology was advanced to the point that thousands of copies of a message could be distributed. Broadcasting, particularly the television networks, augmented the audience.

MEDIA ECONOMICS

While advertising spurs economic growth, it also encourages materialistic consumption.

Of all the messages that use mass media to reach huge audiences, advertising is the most obvious. It's in-your-face, sometimes shouting: "See me. Buy this." The core message of advertising smacks of a circus sideshow barker, but media magnification adds potency of which a circus barker could only dream. In the United States it's estimated that 2 percent of the gross domestic product goes to advertising. When advertising succeeds in exciting consumer demand and spending, it contributes to prosperity. Not unimportantly, advertising is the economic engine for the newspaper, magazine, radio and television industries and increasingly the internet. It is from these media outlets that advertisers buy time and space for their spiels.

MEDIA AND DEMOCRACY

In advertising, like democracy, the idea is that people make choices.

When democracy works well, people choose their common course through informed decision-making. This conceptually dovetails with the societal role of advertising, which provides people with information to make choices as consumers. The emphasis is on individuals reasoning their own way to conclusions about what's best. In some ways, however, advertising falls short. Ads seldom are aimed at even-handed and intelligent discourse but rather at a quick sell, often with emotional and one-sided appeals.

AUDIENCE FRAGMENTATION

Insurance company Geico has grown rapidly with multiple ad campaigns, geared to different audience segments.

Advertisers see no point in buying time and space in media outlets that don't deliver the likeliest customers. The American Association of Retired Persons, for example, doesn't recruit members through the magazine *Seventeen*. To deliver the audiences that advertisers want, media companies have narrowed the focus of their products to coincide with what advertisers are seeking. The mutual interests of media companies and advertisers have led to fragmentation of the mass audience into countless subsets. Even media products that continue in the tradition of seeking mega-audiences with something for everyone are dissected by advertisers and advertising agencies for modicums of difference. Demographically there are differences between CBS and Fox prime-time audiences. Likewise, advertisers know whether the Yahoo or the MSN.com homepage is better for delivering the customers they seek.

MEDIA FUTURE

Expect more innovative techniques to address the problem of ad clutter

Newspaper and magazine publishers delight when ads comprise 70 percent of the space in their publications. That's the max allowed by the U.S. Postal Service to qualify for discount mail rates. In television, networks can cram six to seven ads in sequence during single prime-time breaks. Consumers, overwhelmed by the quantity, tune out. This *ad clutter*, as it's called, is a major problem that the advertising industry needs to solve. A message lost in the clutter is wasted. One answer has been to find alternative media with better chances for ads to get attention. New tactics also include word-of-mouth campaigns. Another tactic, called *viral advertising*, offers compelling story lines continued through a series of ads. Stealth advertising is a tactic that puts messages where people least expect them, sometimes as time-proven as skywriting and chalked messages on sidewalks.

ELITISM AND POPULISM

Redundancy can create household words in the popular culture, like snuggie, and phrases, like, "Diamonds are forever."

Advertising messages generally are brief. A rule of thumb for billboards is no more than seven words. Any more than that, motorists going 60 mph will miss the message. The requirement for ads to be compact can make for cleverness, but it also can lead to simplistic "Buy me" exhortations that not only lack cleverness but are downright annoying. Worse is "buy me" in all caps, bold type and italics and followed by multiple exclamation marks. These are appeals to the lowest common denominator among consumers. On a populist-elitist scale, these LCD appeals, repeated to the point of being annoying, are at the populist extreme.

12 MASS AUDIENCES

■ Looking At Polls Through Different Glasses

Every election season was the same until 2008. No one, including the media, thought that predicting the results of an election could be done with much guaranteed accuracy. Nate Silver changed all that.

After graduating from the University of Chicago with a degree in economics, Silver got a job as an economic consultant. On the side, he began to work on something he called PECOTA, short for Player Empirical Comparison and Optimization Test Algorithm. It was a system for projecting the performance and careers of baseball players. The system turned the baseball world on its ear. Silver's methods were key in Michael Lewis's book *Moneyball*, which Hollywood made into a blockbuster film in 2011. By

▲ **Nate Silver.** *His data-based predictions on baseball and elections have made Silver the prognosticator to follow. The next step for Silver's techniques may be finding easy help in media decisions on which content will find large audiences. Which sitcom? Which pilot? Which manuscript? Which screenplay?*

CHAPTER INSIGHTS

- ● Sophisticated methods are used to measure and assess audiences.
- ● Statistics are a foundation for measuring mass audiences.
- ● Mass audience size is measured by pressruns, sales and surveys.
- ● Audience-measuring companies have gone digital to track media habits.
- ● Reactions of mass audiences are part of media content decision-making.
- ● Audience analysis includes demographics, geodemographics and psychographics.

then Silver was already managing partner of a Fantasy Baseball forecast company.

Just ahead of the 2008 elections Silver branched out from sports with a blog he called FiveThirtyEight.com, named after the number of votes in the Electoral College. Silver's blog received about 800 visits a day. Not especially notable. That changed when Silver began predicting primary election results around the country with stunning success.

Every other pundit was following the polls—the traditional way of tracking candidate electability. But taking a radically new approach, Silver used demographics that not only tracked but predicted. This was new stuff. Hitherto, pollsters had assiduously avoided predicting, knowing that their data were real-time and that lots can change between a poll and the election itself.

But Silver had created a model that took voting patterns from previous primaries and applied them to upcoming contests. He also found a way to predict a pollster's future performance based on how good it had been in the past. He analyzed all the presidential polling data back to 1952 and ran 10,000 computer simulations of the election every day based on historic data and current tracking polls.

His blog took off. Suddenly Silver was the pundit to follow. Silver correctly predicted the winners of every U.S. Senate contest and the winner of the presidential election in 49 states. *New York* magazine called him a "spreadsheet psychic" and a "number-crunching prodigy." *Time* magazine named him one of the World's 100 Most Influential People for 2009.

Silver says that it's the track record that counts. Whether he's looking at baseball stats or political polls, he focuses on their records. The numbers, he says, are unswayed by famous names or ideology. A numbers guy, he's uninterested in whether there's shock value in a prediction. He's definitely not interested in proving a point of view.

In 2010 Silver joined the New York *Times* as a columnist. His blog was incorporated into NYTimes.com where he shares his perspectives on a wide swath of issues relating to politics, culture and sports. In the buildup to the 2012 elections, Silver's site was attracting 600,000 visits a day. ■

Discovering Mass Audiences

STUDY PREVIEW

Mass media research has origins as folksy as eavesdropping on what people are talking about to decide what kind of stories to put in the newspaper. But today the research is sophisticated, with more at stake than ever—like which television programs survive and which get axed. Media research techniques overlap into many aspects of modern life, including marketing, politics and governance.

Audience Research Evolution

Stories abound about Joseph Pulitzer wandering the streets of New York and looking over shoulders to see what people were reading. Too, Pulitzer listened to what people were talking about. It was research, 1880s style. Indeed, his research was a building block of Pulitzer's success at building his New York *World* into a circulation leader. What about today? New local television anchors hired from out of town have their own variation on Pulitzer's audience research. They hang out at barbershops and eavesdrop at mall eateries. Woe be to a new anchor in Milwaukee who doesn't know what a bubbler is. Or in New Orleans who doesn't know a po'boy.

Today's media people have vast resources to learn about their audiences, albeit less colorful than hanging out at local eateries to hear what folks are discussing. There are data from research that can be sliced and diced into useful truths about audience. Lots of the research is census-like—income levels, educational attainment, religious and other affiliations. Other research focuses on attitudes and values or habits and motivations and reactions to new things.

The informal audience research of Joseph Pulitzer still has its place, but an entire industry today provides far more audience information than Pulitzer could gather in a lifetime of eavesdropping. Used well, the new data, gathered largely by surveys, can lead to successful decision-making in television programming and advertising campaigns and be a useful factor in choosing what makes news.

Survey Industry

George Gallup
Introduced probability sampling

Institute of American Public Opinion
Gallup polling organization

Public opinion surveying is a multi-billion a year business whose clients include major corporations, political candidates and the mass media. Today, just as in 1935 when **George Gallup** founded it, the **Institute of American Public Opinion** cranks out regular surveys for clients. Major news organizations hire survey companies to tap public sentiment regularly on specific issues.

About 1,000 companies and institutions are in the survey business in the United States, most performing advertising and product-related opinion research for private clients. During election campaigns, political candidates become major clients. There are dozens of other survey companies that do confidential research for and about the media. Their findings are important because they determine what kinds of advertising will run and where, what programs will be developed and broadcast, and which ones will be canceled. Some television stations even use such research to choose anchors for major newscasts.

These are major companies whose work is often cited as measures of public opinion and also media audiences:

Nielsen.   Nielsen Media Research is known mostly for its network television ratings although it does significant work tracking retail sales.

Arbitron.   Arbitron measures mostly radio audiences in local markets.

Gallup.   The Gallup Organization studies human nature and behavior and specializes in management, economics, psychology and sociology.

Pew.   The Pew Research Center is an independent opinion research group that studies attitudes toward the press, politics and public policy issues.

Harris.   Market research firm Harris Interactive Inc. is perhaps best known for the Harris Poll and for pioneering and engineering internet-based research methods.

Three of the largest polling companies–Nielsen, Harris and Arbitron–generate $7.3 billion a year in revenue. Industry totals are hard to come by because some companies are privately held and don't disclose their revenues. Organizations like Pew and Quinnipiac, as philanthropic and educational institutions, don't break out details of their finances.

APPLYING YOUR MEDIA LITERACY

- **How has audience research changed since the Pulitzer era?**
- **To whom do polling companies sell their information?**

Audience Measurement Principles

statistical extrapolation
Drawing conclusions from a segment of the whole

STUDY PREVIEW The effectiveness of mass media messages is measured through research techniques that are widely recognized in the social sciences and in business. These techniques include public opinion polling, which relies on statistical extrapolation that can be incredibly accurate. Sad to say, less reliable survey techniques also are used, sullying the reputation of serious sampling.

MEDIApeople

■ George Gallup

George Gallup was excited. His mother-in-law, Ola Babcock Miller, had decided to run for Secretary of State. If elected, she would become not only Iowa's first Democrat but also the first woman to hold the statewide office. Gallup's excitement, however, went beyond the novelty of his mother-in-law's candidacy. The campaign gave him an opportunity to pull together his three primary intellectual interests: survey research, public opinion and politics. In that 1932 campaign George Gallup conducted the first serious poll in history for a political candidate. Gallup's surveying provided important barometers of public sentiment that helped Miller to gear her campaign to the issues that were most on voters' minds. She won and was re-elected twice by large margins.

Four years after that first 1932 election campaign, Gallup tried his polling techniques in the presidential race and correctly predicted that Franklin Roosevelt would beat Alf Landon. Having called Roosevelt's victory accurately, Gallup had clients knocking at his door.

Gallup devoted himself to accuracy and in 1936 again predicted another Roosevelt victory. But he was bothered that his reliability had not been better. His method, quota sampling, could not call a two-way race within 4 percentage points. With quota sampling, a representative percentage of women and men was surveyed, as was a representative percentage of Democrats and Republicans, Westerners and Easterners, Christians and Jews, and other constituencies.

In 1948 Gallup correctly concluded that Thomas Dewey was not a shoo-in for president. Nonetheless, his pre-election poll was 5.3 percentage points off. So he decided to switch to a tighter method, probability sampling, which theoretically gives everyone in the population being sampled an equal chance to be surveyed.

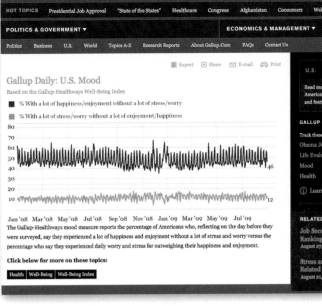

▲ Probability Sampling.

Data collection has become more sophisticated since George Gallup began polling in the 1930s. Polls today track changes in public attitudes over the several decades that data have been accumulated.

With probability sampling, there is no need for quotas because, as Gallup explained in his folksy Midwestern way, it was like a cook making soup: A cook knows if the soup is right by tasting just a teaspoonful, so long as it's been thoroughly stirred. One teaspoon is enough to test whether the ingredients are working. With the new method, Gallup's **statistical extrapolation** narrowed his error rate to less than 2 percentage points.

Even with improvements pioneered by Gallup, public opinion surveying has detractors. Some critics say that polls influence undecided voters toward the front-runner—a bandwagon effect. Other critics say that polls make elected officials too responsive to the momentary whims of the electorate, discouraging courageous leadership. George Gallup, who died in 1984, tirelessly defended polling, arguing that good surveys give voice to the "inarticulate minority" that legislators otherwise might not hear.

Gallup was convinced that public opinion surveys help to make democracy work.

▲ George Gallup.

What Do You Think?

How would you rank George Gallup's polling techniques as an agent of change in the quality of life? Think about the grass-roots ideals of American democracy. But go beyond politics to think about the marketing of consumer goods. What about cultural values such as art and literature?

Do you understand why Gallup emphasized he was taking snapshots of public opinion? Why was he cautious about claiming his survey results were predictive.

How would you respond to someone who says Nate Silver's methodology is eclipsing what Gallup pioneered? What do you think about the predictive aspect of Nate Silver's work?

Probability Sampling

Although polling has become a high-profile business, many people do not understand how questions to a few hundred individuals can indicate the mood of 300 million Americans. In the **probability sampling** method pioneered by George Gallup in the 1940s, four factors figure into accurate surveying, including sample size:

Sample Size. To learn how Layne College students feel about capital punishment, you start by asking one student. Because you can hardly generalize from one student to the whole student body of 2,000, you ask a second student. If both agree, you start developing a tentative sense of how Layne students feel, but because you cannot have much confidence in such a tiny sample, you ask a third student and a fourth and a fifth. At some point between interviewing just one and all 2,000 Layne students, you can draw a reasonable conclusion.

How do you choose a **sample size**? Statisticians have found that **384** is a magic number for many surveys. Put simply, no matter how large the **population** being sampled, if every member has an equal opportunity to be polled, you need ask only 384 people to be 95 percent confident that you are within 5 percentage points of a precise reading. For a lot of surveys, that is close enough. Here is breakdown that statisticians have used for decades for sample sizes that yield 95 percent confidence within 5 percentage points:

Population Size	Sample Size
500,000 or more	384
100,000	383
50,000	381
10,000	370
5,000	357
3,000	341
2,000	322
1,000	278

At Layne, with a total enrollment of 2,000, the sample size would need to be 322 students.

Sample Selection. Essential in probability sampling is **sample selection,** the process of choosing whom to interview. A good sample gives every member of the population being sampled an equal chance to be interviewed. For example, if you want to know how Kansans intend to vote, you cannot merely go to a Wichita street corner and survey the first 384 people who pass by. You would need to check a list of the state's 1,701,520 registered voters and then divide by the magic number, 384:

$$1,701,520/384 = 4,459$$

You would need to talk with every 4,459th person on the list. At Layne College, 2,000 divided by 322 would mean an interval of 6.2. Every sixth person in the student body would need to be polled.

Besides the right sample size and proper interval selection, two other significant variables affect survey accuracy: margin of error and confidence level.

Margin of Error. For absolute precision, every person in the population must be interviewed, but such precision is hardly ever needed, and the process would be prohibitively expensive and impracticable. Pollsters must therefore decide what is an acceptable **margin of error** for every survey they conduct. This is a complex matter, but in simple terms, you can have a fairly high level of confidence that a properly designed survey with 384 respondents can yield results within 5 percentage points, either way, of being correct. If the survey finds that two candidates for statewide office are running 51 to 49 percent, for example, the race is too close to call with a sample of 384. If the survey says that the candidates are running 56 to 44 percent, however, you can be reasonably confident who is ahead because, even if the survey is 5 points off on the high side for the leader, the candidate at the very least has 51 percent support (56 percent minus a maximum 5 percentage points for possible error).

---

probability sampling
Everyone in the population being surveyed has an equal chance to be sampled

sample size
Number of people surveyed

384
Number of people in a properly selected sample for results to provide 95 percent confidence that results have less than a 5 percent margin of error

population
Group of people being studied

sample selection
Process for choosing individuals to be interviewed

margin of error
Percentage that a survey may be off mark

At best, the trailing candidate has 49 percent (44 percent plus a maximum 5 percentage points for possible error).

Increasing the sample size will reduce the margin of error:

Population Size	Sample Size	Margin of Error
Infinity	384	5 percentage points
Infinity	600	4 percentage points
Infinity	1,067	3 percentage points
Infinity	2,401	2 percentage points
Infinity	9,605	1 percentage point

Professional polling organizations that sample U.S. voters typically use sample sizes between 1,500 and 3,000 to increase accuracy. Also, measuring subgroups within the population being sampled requires that each subgroup, such as men and women, Catholics and non-Catholics or Northerners and Southerners, be represented by 384 properly selected people.

Confidence Level.   With a sample of 384, pollsters can claim a relatively high 95 percent **confidence level,** that is, that they are within 5 percentage points of being on the mark. For many surveys, this is sufficient statistical validity. If the confidence level needs to be higher, or if the margin of error needs to be decreased, the number of people surveyed will need to be increased. In short, the level of confidence and margin of error are inversely related. A larger sample can improve confidence, just as it also can reduce the margin of error.

confidence level
Degree of certainty that a survey is accurate

Quota Sampling

Besides probability sampling, pollsters survey cross-sections of the whole population. This quota sampling technique gave Gallup his historic 1936 conclusions about the Roosevelt-Landon presidential race. With **quota sampling,** a pollster checking an election campaign interviews a sample that includes a quota of men and women that corresponds to the number of male and female registered voters. The sample might also include an appropriate quota of Democrats, Republicans and independents; of poor, middle-income and wealthy people; of Muslims, Jews and Protestants; of Southerners, Midwesterners and New Englanders; of the employed and unemployed; and other breakdowns significant to the pollster.

quota sampling
Demographics of the sample coincide with those of the whole population

Both quota sampling and probability sampling are valid if done correctly, but Gallup abandoned quota sampling because he could not pinpoint public opinion more closely than within 4 percentage points on average. With probability sampling, he regularly came within 2 percentage points.

Evaluating Surveys

Sidewalk interviews cannot be expected to reflect the views of the population. The people who respond to such polls are self-selected by virtue of being at a given place at a given time. Just as unreliable are call-in polls with 800 or 900 telephone numbers. These polls test the views only of people who are aware of the poll and who have sufficiently strong opinions to go to the trouble of calling in.

Journalists run the risk of being duped when special interest groups suggest that news stories be written based on their privately conducted surveys. Some organizations selectively release self-serving conclusions.

To guard against being duped, careful newsrooms insist on knowing methodology details before running poll stories. These are questions that reporters are instructed to ask:

- **How many people were interviewed and how were they selected?** Any survey of fewer than 384 people selected randomly from the population group has a greater margin for error than is usually tolerated.

- **When was the poll taken?** Opinions shift over time. During election campaigns, shifts can be quick, even overnight.

- **Who paid for the poll?** With privately commissioned polls, reporters should be skeptical, asking whether the results being released constitute everything learned in the survey. The timing of the release of political polls to be politically advantageous is not uncommon.

- **What was the sampling error?** Margins of error exist in all surveys unless everyone in the population is surveyed.

- **How was the poll conducted?** Whether a survey was conducted over the telephone, via the internet, or face-to-face in homes is important. Polls conducted on street corners or in shopping malls are not worth much statistically. Mail surveys are flawed unless surveyors follow up on people who do not answer the original questionnaires.

- **How were questions worded and in what order were they asked?** Drafting questions is an art. Sloppily worded questions yield sloppy conclusions. Leading questions and loaded questions can skew results. So can question sequencing.

Polling organizations get serious when someone misuses their findings. The Gallup organization once told the tobacco industry publicly to stop saying that a 1954 Gallup poll found that 90 percent of Americans were aware of a correlation between smoking and cancer. Not so, said Gallup. The question was "Have you heard or read anything recently that cigarette smoking may be a cause of cancer of the lung?" Ninety percent said that they were aware of a controversy, but, says Gallup, that doesn't necessarily mean those people believed there was a smoking-cancer correlation. Gallup threatened to go to court to refute the flawed conclusion if a tobacco company used it again in any wrongful-death lawsuit. Lydia Saad of Gallup told the *Wall Street Journal* that her organization gives people lots of latitude in interpreting its surveys. But this, Saad added, "really crosses the line."

MEDIAtimeline

MEDIA RESEARCH MILESTONES

INTUITION
Public opinion was largely measured intuitively and was generally irrelevant until advent of libertarianism and democracy

CATO'S PAPES
John Trenchard and Thomas Gordon fuel democratic thinking with widely read essays condemning tyranny (1720)

King James' treatise in defense of monarchy, on the wrong side of history

EXPERIMENT IN DEMOCRACY
United States founded as a democracy (1776)

THOMAS PAINE
Wrote *Common Sense* (1776) and *The Rights of Man* (1792)

PIVOTAL EVENTS

- American Revolution (1775–1783)
- French Revolution (1789–1799)

1700s

MEDIA RESEARCH MILESTONES

POLITICAL PRESS
Dominant publications were politically sponsored without strong advertising revenue (to 1833)

PENNY PRESS
Ben Day launched New York *Sun*, attracted a mass audience and advertisers (1833)

PIVOTAL EVENTS

- Jackson presidency (1833–1841)
- Morse's first telegraph message (1844)
- Mexican-American war (1846–1848)

1800–1849

MEDIA RESEARCH MILESTONES

NATIONAL MARKETS
Mass-produced consumer products enter national distribution (1880s)

AD AGENCIES
Advertising as industry takes form (1880s)

AUDIENCE CHECKS
Joseph Pulitzer based news judgments by eavesdropping on newspaper readers in the street (1880s)

BATTLING FOR ADVERTISERS
Great newspaper circulation war begins between Pulitzer and Hearst (1895)

PIVOTAL EVENTS

- Civil War (1861–1865)
- Transcontinental railroad completed (1869)

Intuitively gauging audience interests

1850–1899

It is with great risk that a polling company's client misrepresents survey results. Most polling companies, concerned about protecting their reputations, include a clause in their contracts with clients that gives the pollster the right to approve the release of findings. The clause usually reads: "When misinterpretation appears, we shall publicly disclose what is required to correct it, notwithstanding our obligation for client confidentiality in all other respects."

Latter-Day Straw Polls

The ABC and CNN television networks and other news organizations have dabbled, some say irresponsibly, with phone-in polling on public issues. These **straw polls** are conducted on the internet and via mobile devices too. While they can be fun, statistically they are meaningless.

straw polls
Respondents select themselves to be polled; unreliable indicator of public opinion

Just as dubious are the candid-camera features, popular in weekly newspapers, in which a question is put to people on the street. The photos of half a dozen individuals and their comments are then published, often on the editorial page. These features are circulation builders for small publications whose financial success depends on how many local names and mug shots can be crammed into an issue, but it is only coincidental when the views expressed are representative of the population as a whole.

These **roving photographer** features are at their worst when people are not given time to formulate an intelligent response. The result too often is contributions to the public babble, not public understanding. The result is irresponsible pseudo-journalism.

roving photographer
Statistically unsound way to tap public opinion

MEDIA RESEARCH MILESTONES

PRESS RUNS
Audit Bureau of Circulations created to verify circulation claims (1914)

RADIO
Archibald Crossley conducted first listenership survey (1929)

GALUP POLL
George Gallup used quota sampling in Iowa election (1932)

QUOTA SAMPLING
Gallup used quota sampling in presidential election (1936)

DEMOGRAPHICS
A. C. Nielsen conducted demographic listenership survey (1940s)

PROBABILITY SAMPLING
Gallup used probability sampling in presidential election (1948)

PIVOTAL EVENTS

- Radio emerged as commercial medium (late 1920s)
- Great Depression (1930s)
- World War II (1941–1945)
- Soviet–West Cold War (1945–1989)

1900–1949

MEDIA RESEARCH MILESTONES

VALS
Values and Life-Styles program introduced (1970s)

GEODEMOGRAPHICS
Jonathan Robbin introduced PRIZM geodemographics (1979)

PIVOTAL EVENTS

- Television emerged as commercial medium (early 1950s)
- Vietnam war (1964–1973)
- Humans reached moon (1969)
- Internet emerged as commercial medium (late 1990s)

1950–1999

New techniques for audience analysis

MEDIA RESEARCH MILESTONES

MORE MEDIA
Nielsen added measures of internet, iPod and cell phone devices (2006)

BILLBOARDS
Nielsen introduced cell phone-based Go Meters (2008)

TRACKING EYE MOVEMENTS
GazeHawk tracks eye movements on onscreen pages (2011)

TRACKING VOTER OPINION
New York *Times* hired Nate Silver for his new approach to tracking voter opinion (2010)

PIVOTAL EVENTS

- 9/11 terrorist attacks (2001)
- Iraq war (2003–2011)
- Hurricane Katrina (2005)
- Japan earthquake and tsunami (2011)

2000s

Visceral news judgment

- **What could make an election race too close to call?**
- **With what kind of audience research do you find quota sampling sufficient? For what would you prefer probability sampling?**
- **Why are straw polls statistically problematic?**

Measuring Audience Size

STUDY PREVIEW | To attract advertisers, the mass media need to know the number and kinds of people they reach. This is done for the print media by audits and for the broadcast media by surveys. For online media, heat mapping is a new tool. Although surveying is widely accepted for obtaining such data, some approaches are more reliable than others.

Newspaper and Magazine Audits

circulation
Number of readers of a publication

Audit Bureau of Circulations
Checks newspaper and magazine circulation claims

The number of copies a newspaper or magazine puts out, called **circulation,** is fairly easy to calculate. It is simple arithmetic involving data like pressruns, subscription sales and unsold copies returned from newsracks. Many publishers follow strict procedures that are checked by independent audit organizations, like the **Audit Bureau of Circulations,** to assure advertisers that the system is honest and circulation claims comparable.

The Audit Bureau of Circulations was formed in 1914 to remove the temptation for publishers to inflate their claims to attract advertisers and hike ad rates. Inflated claims, contagious in some cities, were working to the disadvantage of honest publishers. Today, most magazines and daily newspapers belong to ABC, which means that they follow the bureau's standards for reporting circulation and are subject to the bureau's audits.

Broadcast Ratings

ratings
Measurements of broadcast audience size

Nielsen Media Research
Surveys television viewership

Archibald Crossley
Conducted first polls on broadcast audience size

A. C. Nielsen
Founder of broadcast survey firm bearing his name

demographic
Characteristics of groups within a population being sampled, including age, gender and affiliations

Radio and television audiences are harder to measure, but advertisers have no less need for counts to help them decide where to place ads and to know what a fair price is. To keep track of broadcast audiences, a whole **ratings** industry, now with about 200 companies, has developed. **Nielsen Media Research** tracks media audiences like network television viewership, radio listenership and movie-goers.

Radio ratings began in 1929 when advertisers asked pollster **Archibald Crossley** to determine how many people were listening to network programs. Crossley checked a small sample of households and then extrapolated the data into national ratings, the same process that radio and television audience-tracking companies still use, though there have been refinements.

In the 1940s **A. C. Nielsen** showed up in the broadcasting ratings business. Nielsen began telling advertisers which radio programs were especially popular among men, women and children. Nielsen also divided listenership into age brackets: 18 to 34, 35 to 49, and 50-plus. These were called **demographic** breakdowns. When Nielsen moved into television monitoring in 1950, the company expanded audience data into more breakdowns. Today breakdowns include income, education, religion, occupation, neighborhood and even which products the viewers of certain programs use frequently.

While Archibald Crossley's early ratings were sponsored by advertisers, today networks and individual stations also commission ratings. The television networks pass ratings

Measuring Prime Time. *Every prime-time network show is ranked by audience in weekly Nielsens. In this week the leader, NCIS, earned a 14.1, which is called a rating. A rating is based on the number of television-equipped U.S. households tuned in nationwide, in this case 14.1 percent. Another television measure is called share. This week NCIS had a share of 22. In other words, of the television sets that were on, 22 percent had NCIS on.* ▶

	ABC	CBS	NBC	FOX	Univision	Telemundo	CW

MONDAY (10/31/2011–10/31/2011)

Time	ABC	CBS	NBC	FOX	Univision	Telemundo	CW
8:00	SCARED SHREKLESS(S)	HOW I MET YOUR MOTHER 7.4/13		TERRA NOVA 5.9/10	FAMILIA CON SUERTE MON 2.0/3	MI CORAZON INSISTE M 0.6/1	RINGER-10/31(SR) 0.5/1
8:30	DANCING WITH THE STARS 11.5/18	2 BROKE GIRLS 8.1/13					
9:00		TWO AND A HALF MEN 10.6/16	SING OFF 3.1/5	HOUSE 6.2/9	FUERZA DEL DESTINO MON 2.3/4	FLOR SALVAJE M 0.6/1	RINGER2-10/31(SR) 0.4/1
9:30		MIKE & MOLLY 8.3/13					
10:00	CASTLE 9.9/16	HAWAII FIVE-0 8.9/15	ROCK CENTER-B. WILLIAMS(P) 3.0/5		DON FRANCISCO PRESENTA MO 1.3/2	CASA DE AL LADO M 0.8/1	
10:30							

TUESDAY (11/01/2011–11/01/2011)

Time	ABC	CBS	NBC	FOX	Univision	Telemundo	CW
8:00	LAST MAN STANDING 6.8/11	NCIS 14.1/22		GLEE 6.5/10	FAMILIA CON SUERTE TUE 2.2/3	MI CORAZON INSISTE T 0.7/1	90210 1.3/2
8:30	MAN UP! 4.4/7		BIGGEST LOSER 12 4.5/7		FUERZA DEL DESTINO TUE 2.5/4		
9:00	DANCING W/STARS RESULTS 10.9/16	NCIS: LOS ANGELES		NEW GIRL 6.2/9		FLOR SALVAJE T 0.7/1	RINGER 1.6/2
9:30		11.5/17		RAISING HOPE 4.0/6	PROTAGONISTA TUES 1.3/2		
10:00	BODY OF PROOF 8.5/14	UNFORGETTABLE 9.1/15	PARENTHOOD 4.8/8			CASA DE AL LADO T 0.9/1	
10:30					AQUI Y AHORA TUE 1.3/2		

WEDNESDAY (11/02/2011–11/02/2011)

Time	ABC	CBS	NBC	FOX	Univision	Telemundo	CW
8:00	MIDDLE, THE 6.5/10	SURVIVOR: SOUTH PACIFIC	UP ALL NIGHT 4.1/7		FAMILIA CON SUERTE WED 2.1/3	MI CORAZON INSISTE W 0.7/1	RINGER-ENC(R) 0.8/1
8:30	SUBURGATORY 6.1/9	7.8/12	UP ALL NIGHT-8:30P(RP) 2.4/4	X-FACTOR-WED 7.7/12			
9:00	MODERN FAMILY 10.9/17	CRIMINAL MINDS 10.1/15	HARRY'S LAW 6.2/9		FUERZA DEL DESTINO WED 2.5/4	FLOR SALVAJE W 0.7/1	AMERICA'S TOP MODEL-11 1.8/3
9:30	HAPPY ENDINGS 5.3/8						
10:00	REVENGE 7.6/12	CSI 8.7/14	LAW AND ORDER:SVU 6.3/10		PROTAGONISTAS WED 1.0/2	CASA DE AL LADO W 0.9/2	
10:30							

THURSDAY (11/03/2011–11/03/2011)

Time	ABC	CBS	NBC	FOX	Univision	Telemundo	CW
8:00	CHARLIE'S ANGELS 3.9/6	BIG BANG THEORY, THE 11.2/18	COMMUNITY 3.0/5	X-FACTOR-THU 7.4/12	FAMILIA CON SUERTE THU 2.1/3	MI CORAZON INSISTE R 0.7/1	VAMPIRE DIARIES 2.7/4
8:30		RULES OF ENGAGEMENT 7.8/12	PARKS AND RECREATION 3.2/5				
9:00	GREY'S ANATOMY 8.8/13	PERSON OF INTEREST	OFFICE(PAE) 5.0/8	BONES(P) 7.8/12	FUERZA DEL DESTINO THU 2.5/4	FLOR SALVAJE R 0.7/1	SECRET CIRCLE 1.9/3
9:30		9.2/14	WHITNEY(PAE) 3.6/5				
10:00	PRIVATE PRACTICE 6.4/11	MENTALIST, THE 10.7/18	PRIME SUSPECT 4.2/7		PROTAGONISTAS THU 1.1/2	CASA DE AL LADO R 1.0/2	
10:30							

FRIDAY (11/04/2011–11/04/2011)

Time	ABC	CBS	NBC	FOX	Univision	Telemundo	CW
8:00	EXTREME MAKEOVER:HOME ED. 3.3/6	GIFTED MAN, A 6.1/11	CHUCK 2.5/4	KITCHEN NIGHTMARES 2.7/5	FAMILIA CON SUERTE FRI 2.0/3	MI CORAZON INSISTE F 0.7/1	NIKITA 1.5/3
8:30							
9:00	EXTREME MAKEOVER:HM ED-9P 3.8/6	CSI: NY 7.2/12	GRIMM 5.1/9	FRINGE 3.0/5	FUERZA DEL DESTINO FRI 2.4/4	FLOR SALVAJE F 0.6/1	SUPERNATURAL 1.5/3
9:30							
10:00	20/20-FRI 3.4/6	BLUE BLOODS 9.3/16	DATELINE FRI 3.1/5		PROTAGONISTAS FRI 1.2/2	CASA DE AL LADO F 0.9/2	
10:30							

SATURDAY (11/05/2011–11/05/2011)

Time	ABC	CBS	NBC	FOX	Univision	Telemundo	CW
8:00				COPS 2.2/4			
8:30			HARRY'S LAW-SAT(R) 2.4/7	COPS 2 2.4/4			
9:00	SAT NIGHT FOOTBALL© 1.9/3	HOME DEPOT PRIME CLG FTBL(S) 11.5/20	PRIME SUSPECT-SAT(R) 2.9/5	TERRA NOVA-ENCORE 1.3/2	SABADO GIGANTE SAT 1.4/2		
9:30						FUTBOL ESTELAR II 0.4/1	
10:00			LAW AND ORDER:SVU-SAT(R) 3.3/6				
10:30							

SUNDAY (11/06/2011–11/06/2011)

Time	ABC	CBS	NBC	FOX	Univision	Telemundo	CW
7:00	ONCE UPON A TIME SP-11/6(SR) 2.7/4	60 MINUTES 8.6/13	FOOTBALL NT AMERICA PT 2 3.4/5		ROSA DE GUADALUPE SUN 1.1/2		
7:30			FOOTBALL NT AMERICA PT 3 7.7/12	OT, THE 9.1/14		PA'LANTE CON CRISTINA 0.5/1	
8:00	ONCE UPON A TIME 8.2/12	AMAZING RACE 19 6.6/10		SIMPSONS 5.3/8			
8:30				ALLEN GREGORY 2.9/4	MIRA QUIEN BAILA 2 SUN 2.2/3		
9:00	DESPERATE HOUSEWIVES 7.1/10	GOOD WIFE, THE 7.2/11	NBC SUNDAY NIGHT FOOTBALL 13.3/21	FAMILY GUY 4.6/7			
9:30				AMERICAN DAD 3.5/5		MARAV MUNDO DE DISNEY(P) 0.4/1	
10:00	PAN AM 4.7/8	CSI: MIAMI 7.1/12			SAL Y PIMIENTA SUN 1.5/3		
10:30							

data on to advertisers immediately. Local stations usually recast the raw data for brochures that display the data in ways that put the stations in the most favorable light. These brochures are distributed by station sales representatives to advertisers. While advertisers receive ratings data from the stations and networks, major advertising agencies also have contracts with Nielsen, Arbitron and other market research companies to gather audience data to meet their specifications.

Criticism of Ratings

However sophisticated the ratings services have become, they have critics. Many fans question the accuracy of ratings when their favorite television program is canceled because the network finds the ratings inadequate. Something is wrong, say the fans, when the viewing preferences of a few thousand households determine network programming for the entire nation. Though it seems incredible to someone who is not knowledgeable about statistical probability, the sample base of major ratings services like Nielsen generally is considered sufficient to extrapolate reliably on viewership in the 116 million television-equipped U.S. households.

It was not always so. Doubts peaked in the 1940s and 1950s when it was learned that some ratings services lied about sample size and were less than scientific in choosing samples. A congressional investigation in 1963 prompted the networks to create the **Broadcast Ratings Council** to accredit ratings companies and audit their reports.

Ratings have problems, some inherent in different methodologies and some attributable to human error and fudging.

Discrepancies. When different ratings services come up with widely divergent findings in the same market, advertisers become suspicious. Minor discrepancies can be explained by different sampling methods, but significant discrepancies point to flawed methodology or execution. It was discrepancies of this sort that led to the creation of the Broadcast Ratings Council.

Slanted Results. Sales reps of some local stations, eager to demonstrate to advertisers that their stations have large audiences, extract only the favorable data from survey results. It takes a sophisticated local advertiser to reconcile slanted and fudged claims.

Sample Selection. Some ratings services select their samples meticulously, giving every household in a market a statistically equal opportunity to be sampled. Some sample selections are seriously flawed: How reliable, for example, are the listenership claims of a rock 'n' roll station that puts a disc jockey's face on billboards all over town and then sends the disc jockey to a teenage dance palace to ask about listening preferences?

Hyping. Ratings-hungry stations have learned how to build audiences during **sweeps** weeks in February, May, July and November when major local television ratings are compiled. Consider these examples of **hyping:**

- Integrating social media into programming—like CBS sports anchors and sitcom stars sending out Twitter feeds and maintaining Facebook presences during sweeps week.
- Radio giveaways often coincide with ratings periods
- Many news departments promote sensationalistic series for the sweeps and then retreat to routine coverage when the ratings period is over.
- Besides sweeps weeks, there are **black weeks** when no ratings are conducted. In these periods some stations run all kinds off-beat and dull programs that they would never consider running during a sweeps period.

Respondent Accuracy. With handwritten diaries, respondents don't always answer honestly. People have an opportunity to write that they watched *Masterpiece Theatre* on PBS instead of less classy fare. For the same reason, shock radio and trash television probably have more audience than the ratings show.

In a project to tighten measurement techniques, Nielsen gradually began eliminating diaries in local television markets in 2006. In the 10 largest markets, Nielsen redesigned its people meters, which measure both what network shows are being watched and who is in the room watching. Gradually Nielsen sought to eliminate diary-based

Broadcast Ratings Council
Accredits ratings companies

sweeps
When broadcast ratings are conducted

hyping
Intensive promotion to attract an audience during ratings periods

black weeks
Periods when ratings are not conducted

reporting in smaller markets too. In 2009 Nielsen further updated its people meter to track both internet and television viewing.

Zipping, Zapping and Flushing.   Ratings services measure audiences for programs and for different times of day, but they do not measure whether commercials are watched. Advertisers are interested, of course, in whether the programs between which their ads are sandwiched are popular, but more important to them is whether people are watching the ads.

This vacuum in audience measurements was documented in the 1960s when somebody with a sense of humor correlated a major drop in Chicago water pressure with the halftimes of televised football games. The drop became known as the **flush factor.** Football fans were getting off the couch by the thousands at halftime to go to the bathroom. Advertisers were missing many people because although viewers were tuned in, many were not watching the ads.

This problem has been exacerbated with the advent of handheld television remote controls and systems like TiVo. Viewers can zip from station to station to avoid commercials, and when they record programs for later viewing, they can zap out the commercials.

Engagement Ratings

In the quest to spend their advertising dollars to the greatest effect, some advertisers have taken a liking to **engagement ratings.** These are attempts to gauge how attentive people are to certain programs and ads. To be sure, engagement ratings are imprecise—a combination of data and intuitiveness.

Television Engagement.   Ford, for example, was won over to advertising its new F-series pickup trucks on Mike Rowes' *Dirty Jobs* on the Discovery Channel. It was not because *Dirty Jobs* was a ratings leader. In fact, the audience was not impressive in size. But the engagement metrics indicated that the viewers were deeply immersed in the show and were disproportionately 18- to 45-year-old men. That's an audience segment loaded with pickup buyers. By 2009 half of the 100 major advertisers on U.S. network television were pressing the networks for engagement ratings.

The research firm IAG pioneered engagement ratings in 2004 by asking viewers how well they recalled programs and ads. Within a year Toyota was using the data in negotiating rates with the networks. With the engagement ratings catching on, Nielsen put up $225 million in 2008 and bought IAG. The acquisition put Nielsen in a position to report not only how many households have their television sets tuned to certain programs but also how engaged they are—how much they're paying attention.

Engagement ratings can also be used to gauge the effectiveness of ads themselves. The ad agency Crispin Porter + Bogusky found that ads for the Volkswagen Jetta and Tiguan had 75 percent more viewers paying attention if an old VW Bug were a character in the ads.

Internet Engagement.   Nielsen actually had earlier experimented with engagement ratings on the internet. Until 2007 Nielsen had ranked web sites by page views. Because people race through views until they find what they want, the method missed engagement. To track what sites both attracted and kept web users, Nielsen switched in 2007 to checking how much time was spent at a site. Measuring web audiences, whatever the system, remains an inexact science, but advertisers now have a firmer feel for how many eyeballs their web advertising is reaching.

What difference did Nielsen's post-click counting method yield? Gaming company Electronic Arts suddenly was in the Top 10. Gamers stay at a game a while. Apple iTunes with its 90-second sampler of songs also moved up.

APPLYING YOUR MEDIA LITERACY

- **How do broadcasters and advertisers use ratings?**
- **What do engagement ratings measure? And how?**

Audience Measurement Techniques

STUDY PREVIEW

Traditional polling techniques included interviews and diaries, both of which were eclipsed by meters. Some devices tracked which billboards a person passes and how often. New devices track usage of new media forms, including the internet, the extension of television viewing beyond the living room, including smartphones, and also playback viewing with TiVo and similar devices.

Basic Tools

The primary techniques, sometimes used in combination, for measuring broadcast audiences are interviews, diaries and meters.

interviews
Face-to-face, mail, telephone survey technique

Interviews. In his pioneer 1929 listenership polling, Archibald Crossley placed telephone calls to randomly selected households. Although many polling companies use telephone **interviews** exclusively, they're not used much in broadcasting anymore. Also rare in broadcasting are face-to-face interviews. Although eyeball-to-eyeball interviewing can elicit fuller information, it is labor-intensive and relatively expensive.

diaries
Sampling technique in which respondents keep their own records

Diaries. Nielsen began using **diaries** in the 1950s. Instead of interviews, Nielsen mailed forms to selected families in major markets for them to list program titles, times and channels and who was watching. This was done in major sweep periods: February, May, July and November. Although diaries were cost-efficient, many viewers would forget their duty and then try to remember days later what they had watched. The resulting data were better than no data but rather muddy and gradually diaries are being phased out.

Meters. Meters were introduced in the 1970s as a supplement to diaries to improve accuracy. Some Nielsen families had their television sets wired to track what channel was on. Some were issued meters that household members could click so that Nielsen could determine for whom programs have their appeal—men, women, children, oldsters. Some set-top meters even traced who was watching by sensing body mass.

People Meters
Devices that track individual viewers

People Meters. In 1987 Nielsen introduced **People Meters.** These were two-function units, one on the television set to scan the channels being watched every 2.7 seconds and a handheld remote that monitored who was watching. With data flowing in nightly to Nielsen's central computers, the company generates next-day reports, called **overnights,** for the networks and advertisers.

overnights
Next-morning reports on network viewership

Portable Meters. In 2001 Nielsen and Arbitron jointly tested portable meters that people could carry around. The pager-size meters, were set to pick up inaudible signals transmitted with programs. The goal: to track away-from-home audiences at sports bars, offices and airports and, in the case of radio, cars. The "walking meters," as they are called, are now used primarily to track commuter radio habits.

Internet Audience Measures

Media Metrix
A service measuring internet audience size

A leading internet audience measuring company, **Media Metrix,** uses a two-track system to determine how many people view web sites. Media Metrix gathers data from 40,000 individual computers whose owners have agreed to be monitored. Some of these computers are programmed to track internet usage and report data back by e-mail. In addition, Media Metrix has lined up other computer users to mail in a tracking disc periodically. The Nielsen ratings company has set up a similar methodology. Other companies also are in the internet ratings business.

How accurate are internet ratings? Some major content providers, including CNN, ESPN and Time Warner, claim that the ratings undercount their users. Such claims go beyond self-serving comments because, in fact, different rating companies come

■ A Quest for Social Media Tools

Procter & Gamble spends $400 million a year on market research, more than any other company. Most goes into surveying markets and consumer preferences. But Joan Lewis, the market knowledge officer for the giant household-products manufacturer, sees new methods joining traditional number-crunching. By the year 2020 Lewis sees much more listening to social media.

Lewis says the quest for near-perfect statistical models has gone about as far as it can go. She likes the two-way communication that's possible between a consumer and a company through social media. It has an authenticity: "The more people see two-way engagement and being able to interact with people all over the world, I think the less they want to be involved in structured research."

Lewis's approach may be no surprise considering that she studied literature in college—not stats. And even though Lewis has spent her career in traditional market research and doesn't dismiss a continuing role for quantitative data-gathering, she see a dramatically larger role ahead for qualitative studies, especially relating to social media.

"If somebody has something to say to a company these days, there are lots of ways to do it—rather than wait to perhaps be included in a statistical probability sample," she says. "Besides, social media are quicker at tracking fast-changing consumer behavior and expectations."

The key, Lewis says, is finding tools sufficiently adroit to make sense of unstructured social media feedback and conversations. For marketing research, P&G is hiring people whom Lewis says don't fit the norm: "We need people who are agile and know how to learn." The future, as Lewis sees it, won't belong to people who merely know a bunch of traditional methods.

Looking forward, she says: "We need to be methodology agnostic." It's an error to believe in any single method, particularly survey research, as a solution with all the answers.

Researchers focus too much on process, details of validation and treating methods, she said. It's like the methodology has become an ideology requiring blind dogma-like allegiance. As an example, she cites extraordinary energy that goes into creating survey samples that are representative of an entire population. Lewis acknowledges that representative samples have a place, but, she says, there is also a lot to learn from social-media samples whether they're representative or not.

Joan Lewis. *Global consumer and market knowledge officer at Procter & Gamble.*

Lewis concedes too that social-media and engagement analytics need more sophistication, including standards for measurement and calibration. She cautions that qualitative research with social media, as opposed to statistical surveys, cannot be an excuse for shoddy or fuzzy research. "It's really been easy for people to take the idea that the world is changing as an excuse to do really poor work," she says.

Despite the calls of Lewis and others for new thinking about market research, traditional methods remain the workhorse of the industry.

Lewis notes that old methods just aren't up to the task with newer media. Most market studies today are built around well-known media like television, which, compared to social media, are static and in place: "There will never be another medium like TV again." Social media in particular presents challenges. With social media, the challenge is measuring something that's itself moving constantly and hard to measure with firm, clear metrics."

Accumulating massive mounds of data as a marketing and advertising tool doesn't work well with new social media.

POINT COUNTER POINT

Traditional quantitative research tools remain valuable in sorting and making sense of information however it is accumulated, whether by surveys or from social media.

DEEPENING YOUR MEDIA LITERACY

EXPLORE THE ISSUE: List prime-time network television shows this week or last. You can check zap2it.com or any of several online sources.

DIG DEEPER: List the advertisers on one of these leading shows.

WHAT DO YOU THINK? If you were one of these prime-time network advertisers, would you be shopping to buy time on another show? Or perhaps considering an alternate media platform?

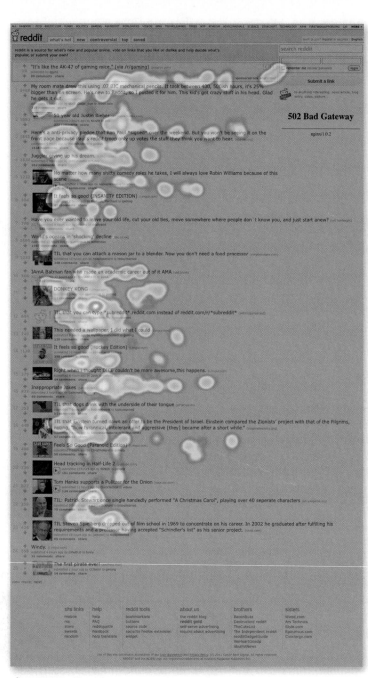

▲ **Eye-tracking.** *With new GazeHawk technology, a computer-mounted webcam tracks where eyes go on a web page. There is a common F pattern, as shown for a page for the social news website Reddit. The F pattern is different from the habits that readers have for newspapers and magazines. This GazeHawk-style research has a lot to tell us about crafting effective messages for online reading.*

Anytime Anywhere Media Measurement (A2/M2)
Nielsen plan to integrate audience measurements on a wide range of video platforms

heatmapping
Technology to track how people move through a web page

up with widely divergent ratings. The question is: Why can't the ratings companies get it right? The answer, in part, is that divergent data flow from divergent methodologies. Data need to be viewed in terms of the methodology that was used. Also, the internet ratings business undoubtedly is hobbled by methodology flaws that have yet to be identified and corrected.

Multimedia Measures

Recognizing that television viewers were increasingly mobile and less set-bound, Nielsen began remaking its ratings system in 2006 to measure the use of personal computers, video game players, iPods, cell phones and other mobile devices. Nielsen said the program, called **Anytime Anywhere Media Measurement,** or A2/M2 for short, represented a commitment to "follow the video" to whatever platform it goes for viewing. Nielsen's chief researcher, Paul Donato, put it this way: "The plan is to try to capture it all."

An initial step was creating a panel of 400 video iPod users to track the programs they download and watch. Nielsen also began fusing data from its television-tracking unit and its Nielsen/Net Ratings unit to measure the relation between conventional television viewing and web surfing with meters on both televisions and personal computers.

Mobile Audience Measures

Over-air networks tried addressing the audience leakage to DVD and TiVo-like devices when the Nielsen rating service introduced its Live Plus Seven measure in 2006. The new measure tracked live viewing plus any viewing within seven days. The networks built the extended period into their audience guarantees with advertisers. The network argument was that DVD and TiVo viewers are more affluent as a group and therefore worth more to advertisers. Advertisers balked. Advertisers argued that ads viewed after the fact have diminished value. Also, the new Nielsen gizmo for recording viewers didn't record ads that were skipped, which TiVo facilitates.

Advertisers were more comfortable with Nielsen's live-plus-same-day counts, which included DVD viewing before the next morning. Despite the issue over the counting period being spread out, Nielsen continued to install the new measuring devices. By 2007 about 18 percent of measured U.S. households were included.

APPLYING YOUR MEDIA LITERACY

- **What tools do ratings companies use to measure broadcast audiences?**
- **How much confidence do you have in internet site ratings?**
- **Do you see approaches like Nielsen's Live Plus Seven attractive to advertisers in this age of on-demand broadcasting?**

■ Heatmapping as an Audience Measure

Graphics people thought they had it all figured out. From a century of experience with magazines, they knew how to make an image pop off a page at a reader. They also knew that a billboard sponsor's name, perhaps logo too, should be subordinated to an eye-catching image. Research found newspapers readers' eyes were inexplicably attracted to the upper right of a front page, upper left inside.

▲ **GazeHawk Co-Founders.**
Joe Gershenson and Brian Krausz.

Then came internet-delivery of mass messages.

Old rules didn't seem right. Where does the eye go first in a word-centric onscreen page that's peppered with headlines, photos, moving graphics, links, ads? Are color blotches effective? Reverse type? Flashing messages? Do people's eyes move differently on word-centric pages? Do eyes behave differently on mobile devices than on traditional desktop computers? Without a body of principles to guide them, designers found themselves flying by the seat of their pants in crafting web pages.

Gradually new graphics principles are emerging, many of them from **heatmapping.** By tracking eye movements, a camera can tell where eyeballs land on a web page. And where they go next on the page and next. For analysis the tracks show like dyes superimposed over the web page on a separate screen.

Alas. The early specialized and unwieldy equipment for heatmapping was too expensive for most designers to measure the effectiveness of their designs. The equipment cost $40,000 per unit. In 2011 a Silicon Valley startup company, GazeHawk, exhibited a low-cost alternative—a webcam mounted atop a computer screen to track eye movements.

The co-founders of GazeHawk, Joe Gershenson and Brian Krausz, blog endlessly on their findings. They've confirmed a pattern identified by Jakob Nielsen, a scholar on human-computer interaction: On word-centric web pages, people look first at the top-left and read the first line. Then, they scan the second line. Then they glance down the left column, reading a little of each line. As they move further down the page, they read less text. As Gershenson and Krausz put it: "Retinal acuity drops off fast." On a heatmap the pattern, a blotchy F shape, is nearly universal. It's worth knowing, Gershenson and Krausz add, because most users will read only the first few sentences on a page: "Those sentences must have an impact." But competing visuals are a factor, which further complicates figuring out what works. Heatmapping tracks everything a pair of eyes does on a web page.

As magazine publishers move into tablet versions of their publications, heatmapping is helping create new models for subscriptions, design, content and advertising. Condé Nast, whose products include *Vanity Fair, Glamour, New Yorker* and *Wired,* has promised to give advertisers new metrics on iPad edition consumption—measures such as the number of times an ad in a digital edition was displayed and the average time that digital readers lingered on a page with a specific ad.

Traditional web audience measures like page views and click-throughs are done through tools like cookies, which has privacy issues. Privacy is not an issue with heatmapping, which can be done only with subjects who are aware that they're part of a test. Heatmapping cannot be nonconsensual. It would be difficult to calibrate a webcam to an eyeball without someone knowing it.

What Do You Think?

How might you use heatmapping if you were a student in media design?

Do you see heatmap technology ever becoming nonconsensual? Would that bother you?

Measuring Audience Reaction

STUDY PREVIEW

The television ratings business has moved beyond measuring audience size to measuring audience reaction. Researchers measure audience reaction with numerous methods, including focus groups, galvanic skin checks and prototypes.

Focus Groups

focus groups
Small groups interviewed in loosely structured ways for opinion, reactions

Television consulting companies measure audience reaction with **focus groups.** Typically, an interview crew goes to a shopping center, chooses a dozen individuals by gender and age, and offers them cookies, soft drinks and $50 each to sit down and watch a taped local newscast. A moderator then asks for reactions, sometimes with loaded and leading questions to open them up. It is a tricky research method that depends highly on the skill of the moderator. In one court case, an anchor who had lost her job as a result of responses to a focus group complained that the moderator had contaminated the process with prejudicial assertions and questions:

- "This is your chance to get rid of the things you don't like to see on the news."
- "Come on, unload on those sons of bitches who make $100,000 a year."
- "This is your chance to do more than just yell at the TV. You can speak up and say 'I really hate that guy' or 'I really like that broad.'"
- "Let's spend 30 seconds destroying this anchor. Is she a mutt? Be honest about this."

galvanic skin checks
Monitor pulse, skin responses to stimuli

Even when conducted skillfully, focus groups have the disadvantage of reflecting the opinion of the loudest respondent.

The Bedroom Project

Fascinating new research that lets you hear the thoughts and opinions of 18- to 28-year-olds.

The Bedroom Project
How Young Americans Use and Interact with Media

ARBITRON
jacobs media

▲ **Natural Habitat Interviews.** *To learn how young people used media and technology, Jacobs Media recognized shortcomings of traditional surveys. Focus groups also were ruled out. Instead, small teams of peer interviewers, all specially trained, went to visit young people where they do most of their media consultation, often in dorm rooms or bedrooms, and videotaped natural-habitat conversation that averaged two hours.*

Sit-Down Interviews

Surveying may need to shift to more personal methods. A growing number of people refuse to participate in telephone surveys. They covet their time. They resent the intrusion. There also is growing skepticism that surveys are not always seeking information or opinion but are sly marketing or opinion-manipulating tactics. This distrust extends beyond the telephone to internet and mail polls.

What eases the resistance to participate? One research company, Jacobs Media, recommends an introduction that promises the survey will be simple and fast, serve a worthy cause, and offer compensation for the participant's time.

Galvanic Skin Checks

Consulting companies hired by television stations run a great variety of studies to determine audience reaction. Local stations, which originate news programs and not much else, look to these consultants for advice on news sets, story selection and even which anchors and reporters are most popular—not who are the best journalists. Besides surveys, these consultants sometimes use **galvanic skin checks.** Wires are attached to individuals in a sample group of viewers to measure pulse and skin reactions, such as perspiration. Advocates of these tests claim that they reveal how much interest a newscast evokes and whether the interest is positive or negative.

These tests were first used to check audience reaction to advertisements, but today some stations look to them in deciding a range of questions, some relatively trivial, like whether to remodel a studio. A dubious use, from a

If It Bleeds, It Leads. *Audience researchers have found newscast ratings go up for stations that consistently deliver graphic video. This has prompted many stations to favor fire stories, for example, even if the fire wasn't consequential, if graphic video is available. The ratings quest also prompts these stations to favor crimes and accidents over more substantive stories, like government budgets, that don't lend themselves to gripping graphics.*

journalistic perspective, is using galvanic skin checks to determine what kinds of stories to cover and whether to find new anchors and reporters. The skin checks reward short, photogenic stories like fires and accidents rather than significant stories, which tend to be longer and don't lend themselves to flashy video. The checks also favor good-looking, smooth anchors and reporters, regardless of their journalistic competence. One wag was literally correct when he called this "a heartthrob approach to journalism."

Prototype Research

Before making major investments, media executives seek as much information as they can obtain in order to determine how to enhance a project's chances for success or whether it has a chance at all. This is known as **prototype research.**

prototype research
Checks audience response to a product still in development

Movie Screenings. Movie studios have previewed movies since the days of silent film. Today the leading screening contractors are units of Nielsen and OTX. Typically about 300 people, selected carefully to fit a demographic, watch the movie and fill out comment cards. Were they confused at any point? Did they like the ending? What were their favorite scenes? Would they recommend the movie to a friend? The audience usually is filmed watching the movie, and producers and studio executives later look for reactions on a split screen with the movie running. Usually 20 or so testers are kept after a screening as a sit-down focus group with the studio people listening in.

Screenings make a difference. How a movie is promoted can be shaped by the test audience's reactions. Paramount, for example. took the advice of a Nielsen screener and had Glenn Close's character in the thriller *Fatal Attraction* be murdered rather than commit suicide.

Many directors don't like their creative control contravened by test screenings. Some directors, indeed, have the clout to refuse screenings. Steven Spielberg famously forsakes them. The usual objection from directors is that they don't want to surrender creative control. Put another way, some directors see screenings as a way for studio executives to cover their backsides by claiming to their supervisors, if a movie flops, that they did all they could to ensure its success.

In recent years, screenings have been squeezed out because of tighter and tighter production schedules, especially when computer-generated imaging plays a big role in a movie. For *The Da Vinci Code* and *Pirates of the Caribbean: Dead Man's Chest*, both big summer releases, there were no screen tests. There was no time to line up preview audiences, let alone make any changes that might have bubbled up through the process.

Some studio execs also have cooled to screenings because of negative leaks that can derail promotion plans. In 2006 a blogger had posted a review of Oliver Stone's *World*

MEASURING AUDIENCE REACTION   333

Trade Center within hours of a screening in Minneapolis. One site, Ain't It Cool News, works at infiltrating screenings. The site editor at the time, Drew McSweeney, defends the crashing as a way to stunt executive interference in movies and return power to directors.

Publication Protoypes. When in 1982 Gannett decided to establish a new newspaper, *USA Today*, it created prototypes, each designed differently, to test readers' reactions. Many new magazines are preceded by at least one trial issue to sample marketplace reaction and to show to potential advertisers.

Advertising agencies, too, often screen campaigns before launch to fine-tune them.

Television Pilots. In network television a prototype can even make it on the air in the form of a **pilot.** One or a few episodes are tested, usually in prime time with a lot of promotion, to see whether the audience goes for the program concept. Some made-for-television movies actually are test runs to determine whether a series might be spun off from the movie.

pilot
A prototype television show that is given an on-air trial

APPLYING YOUR MEDIA LITERACY

- **Do you foresee a rise in sit-down interviewing for audience research?**
- **Why is analysis important in nonstatistical research with focus groups?**
- **If you were a television programming executive, would you make decisions based on galvanic skin checks?**
- **What role should an audience have in determining the mass media's literary content?**

Audience Analysis

STUDY PREVIEW

Traditional demographic polling methods divided people by gender, age and other easily identifiable population characteristics. Today, media people use sophisticated lifestyle breakdowns such as geodemographics and psychographics to match the content of their publications, broadcast programs and advertising to the audiences they seek.

Demographics

Early in the development of public opinion surveying, pollsters learned that broad breakdowns had limited usefulness. Archibald Crossley's pioneering radio surveys, for example, told the number of people who were listening, which was valuable to the networks and advertisers, but Crossley's figures did not tell how many listeners were men or women, urban or rural, old or young. Such breakdowns of overall survey data, called **demographics**, were developed in the 1930s as Crossley, Gallup and other early pollsters refined their work.

Today, if demographic data indicate that a presidential candidate is weak in the Midwest, campaign strategists can gear the candidate's message to Midwestern concerns. Through demographics, advertisers keen on reaching young women can identify magazines that will carry their ads to that audience. If advertisers seek an elderly audience, they can use demographic data to determine where to place their television ads.

While demographics remains valuable today, newer methods can break the population into categories that have even greater usefulness. These newer methods, which include cohort analysis, geodemography and psychographics, provide lifestyle breakdowns.

Cohort Analysis

cohort analysis
Demographic tool to identify marketing targets by common characteristics

Marketing people have developed **cohort analysis,** a specialized form of demographics, to identify generations and then design and produce products with generational appeal. Advertising people then gear media messages to the images, music, humor and other generational variables that appeal to the target cohort. The major cohorts are dubbed:

- **Generation Y** or the **Millennial Generation,** who came of age in the 1990s
- **Generation X,** who came of age in the 1980s.
- **Baby Boomers,** who came of age in the late 1960s and 1970s.

- **Postwar Generation,** who came of age in the 1950s.
- **World War II Veterans,** who came of age in the 1940s.

Cohort analysis has jarred the traditional thinking that as people get older, they simply adopt their parents' values. The new 50-plus generation, for example, grew up on Coke and Pepsi and, to the dismay of coffee growers, may prefer to start the day with cola—not the coffee their parents drank.

The Chrysler automobile company was early to recognize that baby boomers aren't interested in buying Cadillac-type luxury cars even when they have amassed the money to afford them. Chrysler determined that graying baby boomers preferred upscale Jeeps to the luxo-barge cars that appealed to the Postwar Generation.

Advertising people who use cohort analysis know that baby boomers, although now in their 60s, are still turned on by pizzas and the Rolling Stones. In short, many of the habits of their youth stick with a generation as it gets older. What appealed to the 30-something group a decade ago won't necessarily sail with today's 30-something set. David Bostwick, Chrysler's marketing research director, puts it this way: "Nobody wants to become their parents."

When the guerrilla war in Iraq began hurting U.S. military recruiting, the Pentagon desperately needed to fine-tune its message to reach the young men and women who were the most likely prospects to enlist. Applying analytical tools to its own existing data, the Pentagon identified ethnic, geographical and income cohorts that are more receptive to the military. The analysis also identified media for reaching these cohorts. Prospective Army recruits, for example, listen more to Spanish radio than the general population does. *Bassmaster* magazine is more the style of Air Force prospects. Marine prospects lean to *Car Craft, Guns & Ammo* and *Outdoor Life.*

Here are seven cohorts that the Pentagon identified to target their recruiting pitches:

Cohort	Urbanization	Ethnicity	Income
Beltway Boomers	Suburban	White/Asian	Upper-middle
Kids and Cul de Sacs	Suburban	White/Asian/Hispanic	Upper-middle
Big Sky Families	Town/rural	White	Midscale
Blue-Chip Blues	Suburban	White/black/Hispanic	Midscale
Shotguns and Pickups	Town/rural	White	Lower-middle
Suburban Pioneers	Suburban	White/black/Hispanic	Lower-middle
Bedrock America	Town/rural	White/black/Hispanic	Downscale

Geodemographics

While demographics, including cohort analysis, remain valuable today, new methods can break the population into categories that have even greater usefulness. These newer methods, which include geodemography, provide lifestyle breakdowns.

Computer whiz **Jonathan Robbin** provided the basis for more sophisticated breakdowns in 1974 when he began developing his **PRIZM** system for **geodemography**. From census data Robbin grouped every zip code by ethnicity, family life cycle, housing style, mobility and social rank. Then he identified 66 factors that statistically distinguished neighborhoods from each other. All this information was cranked through a computer programmed by Robbin to plug every zip code into one of 40 clusters. Here are the most frequent clusters created through PRIZM, which stands for Potential Rating Index for Zip Markets, with the labels Robbin put on them:

- **Blue-Chip Blues.** These are the wealthiest blue-collar suburbs. These make up about 6 percent of U.S. households. About 13 percent of these people are college graduates.

- **Young Suburbia.** Childrearing outlying suburbs, 5.3 percent of the U.S. population; college grads, 24 percent.

- **Golden Ponds.** Rustic mountain, seashore or lakeside cottage communities, 5.2 percen of the population; college grads, 13 percent.

- **Blue-Blood Estates.** Wealthiest neighborhoods; 51 percent college grads.

- **Money and Brains.** Posh big-city enclaves of townhouses, condos and apartments; college grads, 46 percent college grads.

Jonathan Robbin
Devised PRIZM geodemography system

PRIZM
Identifies population characteristics by zip code

geodemography
Demographic characteristics by geographic area

Psychographics

psychographics
Breaking down a population by lifestyle characteristics

VALS
Psychographic analysis by values, lifestyle and life stage

A refined lifestyle breakdown, **psychographics,** divides the population into lifestyle segments. One leading psychographics approach, the Values and Life-Styles program, known as **VALS** for short, uses an 85-page survey to identify broad categories of people:

- **Belongers.** Comprising about 38 percent of the U.S. population, these people are conformists who are satisfied with mainstream values and are reluctant to change brands once they're satisfied. Belongers are not very venturesome and fit the stereotype of Middle America. They tend to be churchgoers and television watchers.

- **Achievers.** Comprising about 20 percent of the population, these are prosperous people who fit into a broader category of inner-directed consumers. Achievers pride themselves on making their own decisions. They're an upscale audience to which a lot of advertising is directed. As a group, achievers aren't heavy television watchers.

- **Societally Conscious.** Comprising 11 percent of the population, these people are aware of social issues and tend to be politically active. The societally conscious also are upscale and inner-directed, and they tend to prefer reading to watching television.

- **Emulators.** Comprising 10 percent of the population, these people aspire to a better life but, not quite understanding how to do it, go for the trappings of prosperity. Emulators are status-seekers, prone to suggestions on what makes the good life.

- **Experientials.** Comprising 5 percent of the population, these people are venturesome, willing to try new things in an attempt to experience life fully. They are a promising upscale audience for many advertisers.

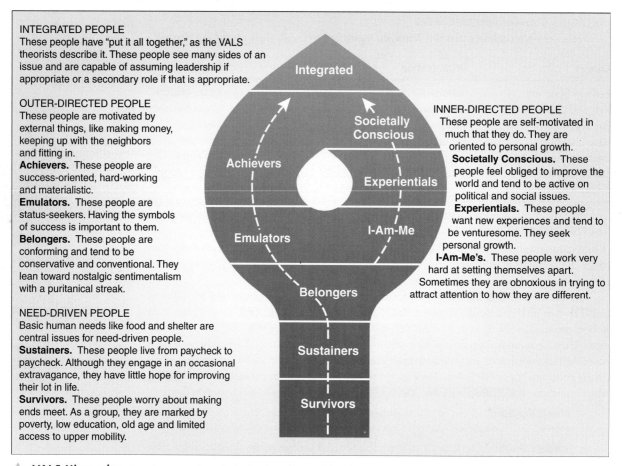

▲ **VALS Hierarchy.** *Developmental psychologists have long told us that people change their values as they mature. Today, many advertisers rely on the Values and Life-Style model, VALS for short, which was derived from developmental psychology, to identify potential consumers and to design effective messages. Relatively few advertising messages are aimed at survivors and sustainers, who have little discretionary income. However, belongers and people on the divergent outer-directed or inner-directed paths are lucrative advertising targets for many products and services.*

- **I-Am-Me's.** Comprising 3 percent of the population, these people work hard to set themselves apart and are susceptible to advertising pitches that offer ways to differentiate themselves, which gives them a kind of subculture conformity. SRI International, which developed the VALS technique, characterized a member of the I-Am-Me's as "a guitar-playing punk rocker who goes around in shades and sports an earring." Rebellious youth, angry and maladjusted, fit this category.

- **Survivors.** This is a small downscale category that includes pensioners who worry about making ends meet.

- **Sustainers.** These people live from paycheck to paycheck. Although they indulge in an occasional extravagance, they have slight hope for improving their lot in life. Sustainers are a downscale category and aren't frequent advertising targets.

- **Integrateds.** Comprising only 2 percent of the population, integrateds are both creative and prosperous—willing to try different products and ways of doing things, and they have the wherewithal to do it.

Applying psychographics is not without hazard. The categories are in flux as society and lifestyles change. SRI researchers who chart growth in the percentage of I-Am-Me's, experientials and the societally conscious project that they soon will total one-third of the population. Belongers are declining.

Another complication is that no person fits absolutely the mold of any one category. Even for individuals who fit one category better than another, there is no single mass medium to reach them. VALS research may show that achievers constitute the biggest market for antihistamines, but belongers also head to the medicine cabinet when they're congested.

APPLYING YOUR MEDIA LITERACY

- **What are common demographic breakdowns in survey research?**
- **Think about a person your grandparents' age and plug them into the VALS category that today fits them best. Discuss how you came to your conclusion.**

■ Discovering Mass Audiences (Pages 317–318)

Mass media research can be traced to newspaper entrepreneurs who eavesdropped on street corners to hear what was on people's minds-and then edited the next edition to pander to those interests. Today the research is sophisticated. For mass media companies, a lot is at stake in understanding the audience. Basic techniques include polling with many of the techniques used for surveying in marketing, politics and governance.

■ Audience Measurement Principles
(Pages 318–324)

Surveying for opinions plays a growing role in our society's public life, in public policy and in decisions about advertising and other media content. Survey techniques have become increasingly complex and statistically more reliable. Generally the best surveys use probability sampling, which statistically chooses respondents whose responses will coincide with the whole group. All surveys have caveats, however. Some surveys are hocus-pocus with no statistical reliability, including 800 number call-ins and people-on-the-street interviews.

■ Measuring Audience Size (Pages 324–327)

Advertisers long were victims of bogus circulation claims by newspapers and magazines, whose advertising rates were based on unverified audience rates. The Audit Bureau of Circulations largely cleaned up false claims beginning in 1914. ABC checked pressruns. Radio, then television audiences were not so easily measured. In 1929 Archibald Crossley used extrapolations from small samples to see how many people were tuned to network radio programs. The networks, of course, wanted the information to guide programming decisions. Today Nielsen is the largest player in television ratings.

■ Audience Measurement Techniques (Pages 328–331)

Traditional polling techniques include interviews and diaries. Meters have added new precision in recent years. Some new devices even track eye movement on the computer screen to gauge viewer interest.

■ Measuring Audience Reaction (Pages 332–334)

Special techniques have been devised to measure how audiences react to media messages. This includes focus groups to generate feedback on media content, like a television program, a publication redesign, and advertisements. Visceral effects can be tracked by charting heartbeat, brain activity and other physiological reactions as a message is being presented. The fate of a pilot for a television program can hang on these measures. So can an advertising campaign. Some movies are adjusted by analyzing audience reactions to pre-final cuts. Advisers to large-budget political candidates also use these techniques to hone messages to various blocs of voters.

■ Audience Analysis (Pages 334–337)

The imperative to match messages with audience has created a relatively new component of analysis. The historical breakdowns—demographics like age, gender and affiliations—have become much more sophisticated. Some analysis looks at media habits in highly defined neighborhoods in assessing how to craft media messages, particularly advertising and political spots. Called geodemographics, the method clusters people by income, education and geography. Psychographics looks at lifestyles and motivations. Some groupings include high achievers, followers, and convention-defiers.

■ Thinking Critically

1. Who has the greatest stakes in measuring mass media audiences?

2. What variables determine whether surveys based on probability sampling can be trusted?

3. How is the size of newspaper audiences measured? Radio? Television?

4. What lifestyle and media changes have prompted media survey companies to update their techniques? What are these new techniques?

5. How are audience reactions to mass media content measured? What results from these measurements?

6. What are techniques of audience analysis? How are data from these analyses used?

■ Media Vocabulary

384 (Page 320)

black weeks (Page 326)

cohort analysis (Page 334)

confidence level (Page 321)

demographic (Page 324)

diaries (Page 328)

engagement ratings (Page 327)

flush factor (Page 327)

focus groups (Page 332)

galvanic skin checks (Page 332)

geodemography (Page 332)

heatmapping (Page 331)

hyping (Page 326)

interviews (Page 328)

margin of error (Page 320)

overnights (Page 328)

pilot (Page 334)

probability sampling (Page 320)

prototype research (Page 333)

psychographics (Page 336)

quota sampling (Page 321)

ratings (Page 324)

sample selection (Page 320)

sample size (Page 320)

statistical extrapolation (Page 319)

straw polls (Page 323)

sweeps (Page 326)

VALS (Page 336)

■ Media Sources

■ Jakob Nielsen. *Eyetracking Web Usability.* New Riders Press, 2009. Nielsen, a human-computer interaction scholar, develops theories on the four components of web pages: text, graphics, motion, and sound.

■ Ken Auletta. *Googled: The End of the World as We Know It.* Penguin, 2009. Auletta, media critic, for the *New Yorker*, tracks Google from humble origins into an online powerhouse that displaced traditional media, then deals with its profit-driven quest to dominate media delivery and become a major advertising vehicle.

■ James Webster, Patricia Phalen and Lawrence W. Lichty. *Ratings Analysis: The Theory and Practice of Audience Research*, third edition. Erlbaum, 2006. The authors, all professors, discuss how to conduct audience research and how to make use of the findings.

■ Kenneth F. Warren. *In Defense of Public Opinion Polling.* Westview, 2001. Warren, a pollster, acknowledges that bad polling exists but explains and defends good practices and notes their growing role in democracy.

■ Dan Fleming, editor. *Formations: 21st Century Media Studies.* Manchester University Press, 2001. In this collection of essays, Fleming lays out the groundwork for students interested in advanced media studies.

A Thematic Chapter Summary

MASS AUDIENCES

To further deepen your media literacy here are ways to look at this chapter from the perspective of themes that recur throughout the book:

MEDIA TECHNOLOGY

Methods to measure media audiences have gone high-tech. Fewer telephone surveys. Fewer diaries.

Traditional techniques to measure media audiences focused on the advertising-supported mass media of newspapers, magazines, radio and television. For broadcast media these techniques have fallen short over time. The proliferation of television to follow people out of their homes—to dentists' waiting rooms and pizza joints, for example—left millions of viewing hours untracked. VCRs and DVDs complicated the tracking of audiences. And what of web browsing? Advertisers wanted wider and better measuring techniques to help them find the right media for their messages and to weigh competing advertising rates. Survey companies are introducing new gizmos to provide more detailed media usage data. These include A2/M2 devices, short for Anytime Anywhere Media Measurement, to track television viewing regardless of platform-over-air stations, cable, satellite, even the web.

MEDIA ECONOMICS

Advertisers would love to figure out how much of the media audience they buy is disinterested.

John Wanamaker, the department store magnate of 100 years ago, said he recognized that half of his advertising budget was wasted on reaching people who had no interest in shopping at his stores. Alas, he added, he didn't know which half. Today a major industry exists to help advertisers make informed decisions on where to place their advertising. For a fee, these survey companies provide data on audience size and breakdowns of demographics and lifestyle. Media companies use these data in choosing content that will attract the kinds of audiences that advertisers covet.

MEDIA AND DEMOCRACY

Nielsen's program-by-program television ratings help advertisers determine whether their dollars are being well spent.

Techniques for measuring media audiences were pioneered and honed by George Gallup's political polling in the 1930s. His core contribution, probability sampling, is the backbone of surveying today. The data are important for political candidates in shaping campaign strategies and tactics. Economic consultant Nate Silver found a way to predict a pollster's future performance based on how good the polls had been in the past using demographics that not only track but predict.

AUDIENCE FRAGMENTATION

Slicing and dicing the audience with demographics, psychographics, psychodemographics and who knows what's next.

Recent refinements in surveying have yielded data that provide advertisers with incredible tools for designing messages and then buying media time and space to reach their most likely customers. The Army, for example, has breakdowns to match its media buys with specific targets for recruiting ads on scales of an urban-rural lifestyle, ethnicity and socioeconomics. This goes beyond the broad categories of traditional demographics like age and gender. The use of these data, from techniques like geodemographics and psychographics, has prompted media companies to shape their products more precisely to match slivers of the mass audience with advertisers. This has furthered media demassification-the Cartoon Network for kids' breakfast cereals and HGTV for Home Depot, for example.

MEDIA EFFECTS

Why do media programmers favor so much violence and gore? Because advertisers know these things attract audiences — and potential customers.

Media companies that seek the biggest possible audiences, including over-air television stations, use research to identify what goes over with the most people. The result, say critics, has been a coarsening of what's on the air and a trend away from news and information that contributes to public understanding and participation in significant issues. Research has found, for example, that a roaring house fire with its visceral visuals attracts more viewers than a report on a municipal budget crisis. Wags have said of TV news: "If it bleeds, it leads." The obsession of many media products on celebrities is a reflection of offering what draws the largest viewership. Celeb news displaces what's more important. A proliferation of violence in movies and television also reflects what survey data say about audience preferences.

MEDIA TOMORROW

Political surveying has been turned on its head by Nate Silver's data-based predictions.

The rising star in applying statistical analysis as has never been before is Nate Silver. He taught baseball clubs how to hire players using statistics—and to win. Then to turned his methods to political campaigns and amassed an impressive record that does more than polling had ever done. He predicted results. The question is whether Silver's techniques can help media decision-makers make choices on programming and other content. Are the days waning for Russian roulette when advertisers choose where to spend their dollars.

13 MASS MEDIA EFFECTS

▪ Orson Welles

The boy genius Orson Welles was on a roll. By 1938, at age 23, Welles' dramatic flair had landed him a network radio show, *Mercury Theater on the Air*, at prime time on CBS on Sunday nights. The program featured adaptations of well-known literature. For their October 30th program, Welles and his colleagues decided on a scary 1898 British novel, H. G. Wells' *War of the Worlds*.

Orson Welles opened with the voice of a wizened chronicler from some future time, intoning an unsettling monologue. That was followed by an innocuous weather forecast, then hotel dance music. Then the music was interrupted by a news bulletin. An astronomer reported several explosions on Mars, propelling something at enormous velocity toward Earth. The bulletin over, listeners were transported back to the hotel orchestra. After

◀ **War of the Worlds.** *Young Orson Welles scared the living daylights out of thousands of radio listeners with the 1938 radio drama* War of the Worlds. *Most of the fright was short-lived, though. All but the most naïve listeners quickly realized that Martians really had not had the time within a one-hour real-time drama to devastate the New Jersey militia en route to wading the Hudson River to destroy Manhattan.*

CHAPTER INSIGHTS

- Scholars today believe that the effects of mass communication generally are cumulative over time.

- Mass messages are significant in helping children learn society's expectations.

- Most of the effects of mass communication are difficult to measure and predict.

- Mass communication binds large audiences culturally but also can reinforce cultural fragmentation.

- Some notions about the effects of mass messages, including subliminal messages, have been overstated.

- Scholars differ on whether media-depicted violence triggers aggressive behavior.

applause the orchestra started up again, only to be interrupted by a special announcement:

Seismologists had picked up an earthquake-like shock in New Jersey. Then it was one bulletin after another.

The story line accelerated. Giant Martians moved across the countryside spewing fatal gas. One at a time, reporters at remote sites vanished off the air. The Martians decimated the Army and were wading across the Hudson River. Amid sirens and other sounds of emergency, a reporter on a Manhattan rooftop described the monsters advancing through the streets. From his vantage point he described the Martians felling people by the thousands and moving in on him, the gas crossing Sixth Avenue, then Fifth Avenue, then 100 yards away, then 50 feet. Then silence.

To the surprise of Orson Welles and his crew, the drama triggered widespread mayhem. Neighbors gathered in streets all over the country, wet towels held to their faces to slow the gas. In Newark, New Jersey, people—many undressed—fled their apartments. Said a New York woman, "I never hugged my radio so closely.... I held a crucifix in my hand and prayed while looking out my open window to get a faint whiff of gas so that I would know when to close my window and hermetically seal my room with waterproof cement or anything else I could get a hold of. My plan was to stay in the room and hope that I would not suffocate before the gas blew away."

Researchers estimate that one out of six people who heard the program, more than 1 million in all, suspended disbelief and braced for the worst.

The effects were especially amazing considering that:

- An announcer identified the program as fiction at four points.
- Almost 10 times as many people were tuned to a popular comedy show on another network.
- The program ran only one hour, an impossibly short time for the sequence that began with the blastoffs on Mars, included a major military battle in New Jersey and ended with New York's destruction.

Unwittingly, Orson Welles and his *Mercury Theater* crew had created an evening of infamy and raised questions about media effects to new intensity. In this chapter you will learn what scholars believe to be true about the effects of the mass media on individuals and society. ∎

Effects Theories

STUDY PREVIEW

Early mass communication scholars assumed that the mass media were so powerful that ideas and even ballot-box instructions could be inserted as if by hypodermic needle into the body politic. It's called the bullet theory. Doubts arose in the 1940s about whether the media were really that powerful, and scholars began shaping their research questions on the assumption that media effects are more modest. Most scholars now look to long-term, cumulative media effects.

War of the Worlds
Novel that inspired a radio drama that became the test bed of the media's ability to instill panic

Orson Welles
His radio drama cast doubt on powerful effects theory

Bullet Theory

The first generation of mass communication scholars thought the mass media had a profound, direct effect on people. Their idea, called **powerful effects theory,** drew heavily on social commentator **Walter Lippmann**'s influential 1922 book *Public Opinion.* Lippmann argued that we see the world not as it really is but as "pictures in our heads." The "pictures" of things we have not experienced personally, he said, are shaped by the mass media. The powerful impact that Lippmann ascribed to the media was a precursor to the powerful effects theory that evolved among scholars over the next few years.

powerful effects theory
Theory that media have immediate, direct influence

Walter Lippmann
His *Public Opinion* assumed powerful media effects in 1920s

Harold Lasswell
His mass communication model
assumed powerful effects

Yale psychologist **Harold Lasswell,** who studied World War II propaganda, embodied the effects theory in his famous model of mass communication:

Who says what,
In which channel,
To whom,
With what effect.

At their extreme, powerful effects theory devotees assumed that the media could inject information, ideas and even propaganda into the public consciousness. The theory was explained in terms of a hypodermic needle model or **bullet model.** Early powerful effects scholars would agree that newspaper coverage and endorsements of political candidates decided elections.

bullet model
Another name for the overrated
powerful effects theory

The early scholars did not see that the hypodermic metaphor was hopelessly simplistic. They assumed, wrongly, that individuals are passive and absorb uncritically and unconditionally whatever the media spew forth. The fact is that individuals read, hear and see the same things differently. Even if they did not, people are exposed to many, many media—hardly a single, monolithic voice. Also, there is skepticism among media consumers that is manifested at its extreme in the saying "You can't believe a thing you read in the paper." People are not mindless, uncritical blotters.

third-person effect
One person overestimating the effect
of media messages on other people

W. P. Davison
Scholar who devised third-person
effect theory

A remnant of now-discredited perceptions that the media have powerful and immediate influence is called **third-person effect.** In short, the theory holds that people overestimate the impact of media messages on other people. Scholar **W. P. Davison** who came up with the concept, told a story about a community film board that censored some movies because they might harm people who watch them—even though the board members denied that they themselves were harmed by watching them. The theory can be reduced to this notion: "It's the other guy who can't handle it, not me."

Davison's pioneering scholarship spawned many studies. Most of the conclusions can be boiled down to these:

- Fears about negative impact are often unwarranted.
- Blocking negative messages is often unwarranted.

Minimalist Effects Theory

Paul Lazarsfeld
Found voters are more influenced by
other people than by mass media

Scholarly enthusiasm for the hypodermic needle model dwindled after two massive studies of voter behavior, one in Erie County, Ohio, in 1940, and the other in Elmira, New York, in 1948. The studies, led by sociologist **Paul Lazarsfeld** of Columbia University, were the first rigorous tests of media effects on elections. Lazarsfeld's researchers went back to 600 people several times to discover how they developed their candidate preferences. Rather than citing particular newspapers, magazines or radio stations, as had been expected, these people generally mentioned friends and acquaintances. The media had hardly any direct effect. Clearly, the hypodermic needle model was off-base, and the powerful effects theory needed rethinking. From that rethinking emerged the **minimalist effects theory,** which includes:

minimalist effects theory
Theory that media effects are mostly
indirect

two-step flow
Media affects individuals through
opinion leaders

opinion leaders
Influential friends, acquaintances

Two-Step Flow Model. Minimalist scholars devised the **two-step flow** model to show that voters are motivated less by the mass media than by people they know personally and respect. These people, called **opinion leaders,** include many clergy, teachers and neighborhood merchants, although it is impossible to list categorically all those who are opinion leaders. Not all clergy, for example, are influential, and opinion leaders are not necessarily in authority roles. The minimalist scholars' point is that personal contact is more important than media contact. The two-step flow model, which replaced the hypodermic needle model, shows that whatever effect the media have on the majority of the population is through opinion leaders. Later, as mass communication research became more sophisticated, the two-step model was expanded into a **multistep flow** model to capture the complex web of social relationships that affects individuals.

multistep flow
Media affects individuals through
complex interpersonal connections

Status Conferral. Minimalist scholars acknowledge that the media create prominence for issues and people by giving them coverage. Conversely, media neglect relegates issues and personalities to obscurity. Related to this **status conferral** phenomenon is **agenda-setting.** Professors **Maxwell McCombs** and **Don Shaw,** describing the agenda-setting phenomenon in 1972, said the media do not tell people *what to think* but tell them *what to think about.* This is a profound distinction. In covering a political campaign, explain McCombs and Shaw, the media choose which issues or topics to emphasize, thereby helping set the campaign's agenda. "This ability to affect cognitive change among individuals," say McCombs and Shaw, "is one of the most important aspects of the power of mass communication."

Narcoticizing Dysfunction. Some minimalists claim that the media rarely energize people into action, such as getting them to go out to vote for a candidate. Rather, they say, the media lull people into passivity. This effect, called **narcoticizing dysfunction,** is supported by studies that find that many people are so overwhelmed by the volume of news and information available to them that they tend to withdraw from involvement in public issues. Narcoticizing dysfunction occurs also when people pick up a great deal of information from the media on a particular subject—poverty, for example—and believe that they are doing something about a problem when they are really only smugly well-informed. Intellectual involvement becomes a substitute for active involvement.

Cumulative Effects Theory

In recent years some mass communication scholars have parted from the minimalists and resurrected the powerful effects theory, although with a twist that avoids the simplistic hypodermic needle model. German scholar **Elisabeth Noelle-Neumann,** a leader of this school, concedes that the media do not have powerful, immediate effects but argues that effects over time are profound. Her **cumulative effects theory** notes that nobody can escape either the media, which are ubiquitous, or the media's messages, which are driven home with redundancy. To support her point, Noelle-Neumann cites multimedia advertising campaigns that hammer away with the same message over and over. There's no missing the point. Even in news reports there is a redundancy, with the media all focusing on the same events.

Noelle-Neumann's cumulative effects theory has troubling implications. She says that the media, despite surface appearances, work against diverse, robust public consideration of issues. Noelle-Neumann bases her observation on human psychology, which she says encourages people who feel they hold majority viewpoints to speak out confidently. Those views grow in credibility when they are carried by the media, whether they really are dominant or not. Meanwhile, says Noelle-Neumann, people who perceive that they are in a minority are inclined to speak out less, perhaps not at all. The result is that dominant views can snowball through the media and become consensus views without being sufficiently challenged.

To demonstrate her intriguing theory, Noelle-Neumann has devised the ominously labeled **spiral of silence** model, in which minority views are intimidated into silence and obscurity. Noelle-Neumann's model raises doubts about the libertarian concept of the media providing a marketplace in which conflicting ideas fight it out fairly, all receiving a full hearing.

APPLYING YOUR MEDIA LITERACY

- In our cultural folklore, the magic bullet theory of mass communication effects remains alive and well. Identify an example in your recent experience and assess it.
- What layers of complexity did Paul Lazarsfeld add to our understanding of the effects of mass communication?
- Cull your own experience for an example of the spiral-of-silence model and explain how it worked.

status conferral
Media attention enhances attention given to people, subjects, issues

agenda-setting
Media tell people what to think about, not what to think

Maxwell McCombs and Don Shaw
Articulated agenda-setting theory

narcoticizing dysfunction
People deceive themselves into believing they're involved when actually they're only informed

Elisabeth Noelle-Neumann
Leading cumulative effects theorist

cumulative effects theory
Theory that media influence is gradual over time

spiral of silence
Vocal majority intimidates others into silence

▲ **Elisabeth Noelle-Neumann.** *Her spiral of silence theory sees people with minority viewpoints being discouraged into silence by louder majority views. These majority views sometimes come into dominance through media amplification. The more the dominance, the less these views are subject to continuing review and evaluation.*

Lifestyle Effects

STUDY PREVIEW

Mass media have a large role in initiating children into society. The socialization process is essential in perpetuating cultural values. For better or worse, mass media have accelerated socialization by giving youngsters access to information that adults kept to themselves in earlier generations. While the mass media affect lifestyles, they also reflect lifestyle changes that come about for reasons altogether unrelated to the mass media.

Socialization

Nobody is born knowing how to fit into society. This is learned through a process that begins at home. Children imitate their parents and brothers and sisters. From listening and observing, children learn values. Some behavior is applauded, some is scolded. Gradually this culturization and **socialization** process expands to include the influence of friends, neighbors, school and at some point the mass media.

In earlier times the role of the mass media came into effect in children's lives late because books, magazines and newspapers require reading skills that are learned in school. The media were only a modest part of early childhood socialization.

socialization
Learning to fit into society

MEDIAtimeline

MASS MEDIA EFFECTS MILESTONES

CATHARTIC THEORY
Aristotle dismissed notion that depictions of violence beget violence (350 B.C.)

POWERFUL EFFECTS THEORY
The media shape the pictures in our heads (1922)

MINIMALIST EFFECTS THEORY
Paul Lazarsfeld tested media effects on elections (1940s)

Aristotle saw depictions of violence positively

PIVOTAL EVENTS

- Greek Hellenistic period
- Right to vote for women (1920)
- Radio emerged as commercial medium (late 1920s)
- Great Depression (1930s)
- World War II (1941–1945)

MASS MEDIA EFFECTS MILESTONES

BOBO DOLL STUDIES
Albert Bandura concluded media cause violence (1960)

COGNITIVE DISSONANCE
Media depictions cause overt racism to fade (1960s)

Can mass media wipe out entire cultures?

CULTURAL IMPERIALISM
Herbert Schiller examined media's impact on indigenous cultures (1969)

PIVOTAL EVENTS

- Television emerged as commercial medium (early 1950s)
- Vietnam war (1964–1975)
- Humans reached moon (1969)

MASS MEDIA EFFECTS MILESTONES

AGENDA SETTING
Maxwell McCombs and Don Shaw showed that media set agendas, not opinions (1972)

CUMULATIVE EFFECTS THEORY
Elisabeth Noelle-Neumann theorized media effects (1973)

PIVOTAL EVENTS

- Unabomber Ted Kaczynski mailed first bomb in 17-year spree (1978)

Media campaigns affect behavior. Smoking becoming less acceptable

Pre-1950 · 1950–1969 · 1970–1979

Today, however, television and the internet are omnipresent from the cradle. A young person turning 18 will have spent more time watching television than in any other activity except sleep. Television and the internet have displaced much of the socializing influence that once came from parents. *Sesame Street* imparts more information on the value of nutrition than does Mom's admonition to eat spinach.

By definition, socialization is **prosocial.** American children learn that motherhood, baseball and apple pie are valued; that buddies frown on tattling; that honesty is virtuous; and that hard work is rewarded. The stability of a society is ensured through the transmission of such values to the next generation.

prosocial
Socialization perpetuates positive values

Living Patterns

The mass media both reflect lifestyles and shape them. The advent of television in the mid-1950s, for example, kept people at home in their living rooms in the evening. Lodge memberships tumbled. Wednesday-night vespers became an anachronism of earlier times. Television supplanted crossroads taverns in rural areas for socializing and keeping up-to-date.

Media and lifestyle are intertwined. To find and keep audiences, media companies adjust their products according to the changes caused by other changes. Department stores, a phenomenon in the 1880s, put shopping into the daily routine of housewives, giving rise to evening newspapers carrying store ads so that women could plan their

MASS MEDIA EFFECTS MILESTONES

INTERGENERATIONAL EAVESDROPPING
Joshua Meyrowitz observed that television was eroding childhood innocence (1985)

WHAT CAUSAL CONNECTION?
Scholar William McQuire: Studies flawed on violence causality (1986)

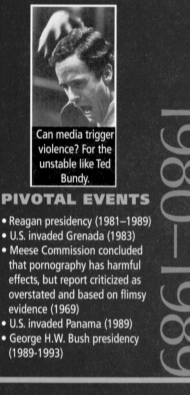

Can media trigger violence? For the unstable like Ted Bundy.

PIVOTAL EVENTS

• Reagan presidency (1981–1989)
• U.S. invaded Grenada (1983)
• Meese Commission concluded that pornography has harmful effects, but report criticized as overstated and based on flimsy evidence (1969)
• U.S. invaded Panama (1989)
• George H.W. Bush presidency (1989-1993)

1980–1989

PIVOTAL EVENTS

• Internet emerged as commercial medium (late 1990s)
• Federal agents held Ruby Ridge family in Idaho siege.
• Clinton presidency (1993–2001)
• FBI destroyed Waco religious compound in siege (1993)
• Oklahoma City federal building bombing (1995)
• Dolly the sheep born after cloning from adult cell (1997)
• The movie *Titanic* (1997)
• Columbine High School massacre (1997)

Need evidence that audiences like to see violence? Check out an evening of prime-time television.

1990–1999

MASS MEDIA EFFECTS MILESTONES

OFFENSIVE MASCOTS DEBATED
Nebraska *Journal Star* banned offensive sports mascots (2005)

PIVOTAL EVENTS

• George W. Bush presidency (2001–2009)
• 9/11 terrorist attacks (2001)
• Iraq war (2003–2011)
• Hurricane Katrina (2005)
• Great Recession (2007–2009)
• Obama presidency (2009–)
• BP Gulf oil disaster (2010)

Campaign against media stereotyping included ridding athletics of racial mascots

2000–

next day's shopping expeditions. Newspapers previously were almost all in morning publication.

A century later, with the growing influx of women into full-time, out-of-the-house jobs, newspapers dropped their evening editions. Today almost all U.S. newspapers have only morning publication. Other societal changes also contributed to the demise of evening newspapers. In the old industrial economy, most jobs were 7 a.m. to 3 p.m., which allowed discretionary evening time to spend with a newspaper. With the emergence of a service economy, with 9 a.m. to 5 p.m. jobs coming into dominance, the market for evening newspapers withered. Television, as an alternative evening activity, also squeezed into the available time for people to read an evening paper.

Intergenerational Eavesdropping

The mass media, especially television, have eroded the boundaries between the generations, genders and other social institutions that people once respected. Once, adults whispered when they wanted to discuss certain subjects, like sex, when children were around. Today, children "eavesdrop" on all kinds of adult topics by seeing them depicted on television, in movies, and on YouTube. Though meant as a joke, these lines ring true today to many squirming parents:

Father to a friend: My son and I had that father-and-son talk about the birds and the bees yesterday.
Friend: Did you learn anything?

Joshua Meyrowitz, a communication scholar at the University of New Hampshire, brought the new socialization effects of intergenerational eavesdropping to wide attention with his 1985 book, *No Sense of Place.* In effect, the old socially recognized institution of childhood, which had been protected from "grown-up issues" like money, divorce and sex, has disappeared. From television sitcoms, kids learn that adults fight and goof up and sometimes are just plain silly. Kids have front-row seats to the world of adults from tabloid television to trashy reality shows.

Television also cracked other protected societal institutions, such as the "man's world." Through television many women enter the man's world of the locker room, the fishing trip and the workplace beyond the home. Older mass media, including books, had dealt with a diversity of topics and allowed people in on the "secrets" of other groups, but the ubiquity of television and the internet and the ease of access to them accelerated the breakdown of traditional institutional barriers.

APPLYING YOUR MEDIA LITERACY

- **Why is mass communication a growing issue in child development?**
- **What examples can you offer of mass communication reflecting lifestyles? How about the opposite—lifestyles reflecting mass communication?**
- **How has modern media content eroded the innocence of childhood?**

▲ **Tobacco Warning.**
After 25 years of a government-required all-text health warning on cigarette packs, the U.S. Food and Drug Administration had planned to go graphic. The plan, to start in 2013, was for packs to carry gruesome depictions designed to steer young people away from tobacco. The labels in the proposed Smoking Can Kill You campaign were to be based on the premise that media campaigns can shape behavior. But the tobacco industry responded in 2011 by going to court against the labels. The industry claimed that the labels would coerce the companies to say things they don't want to say and thereby would infringe on their corporate rights of free speech.

Joshua Meyrowitz
Noted that media have reduced generational and gender barriers

Attitude Effects

STUDY PREVIEW When media messages rivet people's focus, public opinion can take new forms almost instantly. These quick cause-and-effect transformations are easily measured. More difficult to track are the effects of media messages on opinions and attitudes that shift over time—like customs and social conventions. Studies on role models and stereotype shifts seek to address these more elusive effects and how media messages can be manipulated to influence opinions and attitudes.

Influencing Opinion

How malleable are opinions? People, in fact, change their minds. In politics, the dominance of political parties shifts. Going into the 2008 election and again in 2012, polls found a growing disaffection with the Democratic and Republican parties. More people were calling themselves independents. Enthusiasm for products can spiral to success overnight and collapse just as fast. We know that people adjust their opinions, sometimes gradually, sometimes suddenly. Also, we know that media messages are important in these processes.

Some cause-and-effect is tracked easily. A horrendous event, like the unexpected Japanese attack on U.S. Navy facilities at Pearl Harbor in 1941, instantly transformed American public opinion. Before the attack, sentiment had been against armed resistance to Japanese and German expansionism. In an instant, a massive majority decided to go to war. In 2005 public confidence in the federal government bottomed with the failure to deal with the hurricane devastation in New Orleans and the Gulf coast. British Petroleum was gaining traction with its eco-friendly and green-theme "Beyond Petroleum" campaign until 2010 and its Gulf oil disaster. Such sudden shifts result from information carried by mass media, including statements from opinion leaders.

Causal explanations for gradual opinion shifts are elusive, although mass messages are a factor. What puts a company atop lists of most-admired brands? What makes the rest of the country view California as it does? Or New York? Or New Jersey? Many institutions, including state tourism agencies, budget millions of dollars to promote an image that they hope will be absorbed over time. One concentration of corporate image messages airs weekly on Sunday-morning television talk shows.

Scholars have puzzled for decades over how to measure the effects of media content on opinion. Except for major events that trigger sudden turnarounds, media effects on opinion are gradual.

Role Models

The extent of media influence on individuals may never be sorted out with any precision, in part because every individual is a distinct person and because media exposure varies from person to person. Even so, some media influence is undeniable. Consider the effect of entertainment idols as they come across through the media. Many individuals, especially young people casting about for an identity all their own, groom themselves in conformity with the latest heartthrob. This imitation, called **role modeling,** even includes speech mannerisms from whoever is hip at the moment. Let's not forget "yadda-yadda-yadda" from *Seinfeld*.

No matter how quirky, fashion fads are not terribly consequential, but serious questions can be raised about whether role modeling extends to behavior. Many people who produce media messages recognize their responsibility for role modeling. Whenever Batman and Robin leaped into their Batmobile in the campy 1960s television series, the camera always managed to show them fastening their seat belts. Many newspapers have a policy of mentioning in accident stories whether seat belts were in use. In the 1980s, as concern about AIDS mounted, moviemakers went out of their way to show condoms as a precaution in social situations. Now schoolyard bullying is portrayed less and less in a kids-will-be-kids spirit.

If role modeling can work for good purposes, such as promoting safety consciousness and disease prevention, it would seem that it could also have a negative effect. Some people linked the Columbine High School massacre in Littleton, Colorado, to a scene in the Leonardo DiCaprio movie *The Basketball Diaries*. In one scene, a student in a black trench coat executes fellow classmates. An outbreak of

role modeling
Basis for imitative behavior

▲ **Angry Birds Everywhere.** *Well into 2011, more than 12 million video game players had bought the addictive touchscreen game Angry Birds from Apple's App Store. And Finnish game-maker Roxio was expanding to Android devices. Outpacing game sales, however, were Angry Bird toys, T-shirts and themed what-have-you. Eleven million items had been sold, not counting Halloween costumes that were the season's top-seller. And the Christmas sales were only beginning, A television series next? Movies? Roxio is working on those too.*

MEDIAtomorrow

■ CIA's 'Ninja Librarians'

▲ **Hero of the Revolution.** *Social media were a key vehicle to amass people for the revolution that toppled the Egyptian regime in the Arab Spring of 2011. Here an art student at the University of Helwan paints the Facebook logo on a mural commemorating the revolution. Facebook postings, as well as Twitter chatter, have proven revealing to U.S. policy-makers in assessing and predicting unrest around the world.*

During the tumultuous Mideast unrest of 2011, the White House got a daily snapshot of the world built from tweets, Facebook updates, and traditional news media. The reports were prepared by the Open Source Center, a secretive agency of the CIA. Usually the reports ended up in President Barack Obama's daily intelligence briefings. The material answered questions from the president about threats and trouble spots.

The daily reports gave the president insight into world reaction to events like the Navy raid that killed Osama bin Laden and the end of the war in Iraq. Earlier the reports accurately predicted the regime-toppling uprising in Egypt. So too the reports predicted social media could be a Mideast game-changer.

Hardly anyone knew about the Open Source Center until the Associated Press was allowed inside late in 2011. That's when the world found out that the CIA analysts working at the OSC jokingly called themselves Ninja Librarians. The center's director, Doug Naquin, explained that a good open source officer was someone with a master's degree in library science and knowledge of multiple languages. The most successful analysts were likened to the heroine of *The Girl With the Dragon Tattoo:* "A quirky, irreverent computer hacker who knows how to find stuff other people don't know exists."

The Open Source Center started examining social media after the Twitter-sphere rocked the Iranian regime during Iran's Green Revolution of 2009. By 2011 there were days when the center checked as many as 5 million tweets—almost an unimaginable quantity of messages. The center also checked out Facebook updates, newspaper articles, television news channels, local radio stations, internet chat rooms—anything to which people overseas had access and could contribute openly. The ninjas cast their net widely, tracking things as disparate as Chinese internet access and the mood on the street in Pakistan. The traffic ranged from angry tweets to thoughtful blogs.

After a Navy team killed bin Laden, the center gathered information from Twitter for a snapshot of world public opinion. Because tweets can't be tracked geographically, the analysts broke the information down by language. The majority of tweets in Chinese were negative. So were most of the tweets in Urdu, the language of Pakistan. The Ninja Librarians had become a proven and useful tool in assessing grassroots world opinion—and certainly quicker than traditional assessments from U.S. embassies around world.

According to the AP, the CIA facility was set up in response to a recommendation by the 9/11 Commission. The identity of most employees is secret. So is the location.

The center's director, Doug Naquin, is the agency's public face. When AP reporter Kimberly Dozier asked him about his predictions for the next generation of social media. Naquin said it would probably be closed-loop, subscriber-only cell phone networks like those used by the Taliban terrorist organization to send messages among hundreds of followers. Those non-open source networks can be penetrated today only by technical eavesdropping by branches of U.S. intelligence, like the National Security Agency. But Naquin predicted his covert colleagues, the Ninja Librarians, will find ways to adapt. Just like the people they spy on do.

What Do You Think?

Is it proper for government agencies to eavesdrop on people using Twitter and Facebook?

What level of confidence would you place in the Open Source Center's daily snapshots of grassroots opinions in world trouble spots?

shootings followed other 1990s films that glorified thug life, including *New Jack City, Juice* and *Boyz N the Hood.*

Stereotypes

Close your eyes. Think "professor." What image forms in your mind? Before 1973 most people would have envisioned a harmless, absent-minded eccentric. Today, *The Nutty Professor* movie remake is a more likely image. Both the absent-minded and later nutty professor images are known as stereotypes. Both flow from the mass media. Although neither is an accurate generalization about professors, both have long-term impact.

Stereotyping is a kind of shorthand that can facilitate communication. Putting a cowboy in a black hat allows a movie director to sidestep complex character exploration and move quickly into a story line because moviegoers hold a generalization about cowboys in black hats: They are the bad guys—a stereotype.

stereotyping
Using broad strokes to facilitate storytelling

Newspaper editors pack lots of information into headlines by drawing on stereotypes held by readers. Consider the extra meanings implicit in headlines that refer to "Arab terrorists," a "Southern belle" or a "college jock." Stereotypes paint broad strokes that help create impact in media messages, but they are also a problem. A generalization, no matter how useful, is inaccurate. Not all Scots are tightfisted, nor are all Wall Street brokers crooked, nor are all college jocks dumb—not even a majority.

By using stereotypes, the mass media perpetuate them. With benign stereotypes there is no problem, but the media can perpetuate social injustice with stereotypes. In the late 1970s the U.S. Civil Rights Commission found that blacks on network television were portrayed disproportionately in immature, demeaning or comic roles. By using a stereotype, television was not only perpetuating false generalizations but also being racist. Worse, network thoughtlessness was robbing black people of strong role models.

Critics call for the media to become activists to revise demeaning stereotypes. Although often right-minded, such calls can interfere with accurate portrayals. Italian-Americans, for example, lobbied successfully against Mafia characters being identified as Italians. Exceptions like HBO's Soprano family remained irritants, however. In general, activists against stereotyping have succeeded. New sensitivities have set in.

Agenda-Setting and Status Conferral

Media attention lends a legitimacy to events, individuals and issues that does not extend to things that go uncovered. This conferring of status occurs through the media's role as agenda-setters. It puts everybody on the same wavelength, or at least a similar one, which contributes to social cohesion by focusing our collective attention on issues we can address together. Otherwise, each of us could be going in separate directions, which would make collective action difficult if not impossible.

Examples of how media attention spotlights certain issues abound. An especially poignant case occurred in 1998 when a gay University of Wyoming student, Matthew Shepard, was savagely beaten, tied to a fence outside of town and left to die. It was tragic, more than gay-bashing in that it was outright murder, and coverage of the event moved gay rights higher on the national agenda. Coverage of the gruesome death was an example of the media agenda-setting and of status conferral.

APPLYING YOUR MEDIA LITERACY

- **How frequently does mass communication trigger sudden and drastic changes in public opinion? Offer examples.**
- **From your experience, cite examples of role modeling on issues more consequential than fashion and fads.**
- **Although media-perpetuated stereotypes can be false, misleading and damaging, stereotypes are nonetheless essential in mass communication. Why?**
- **How does mass communication wield power through status conferral on some issues and neglect others?**

MEDIApeople

■ Stereotyping on Field and Court

At the Last Dance.
After the University of Illinois mascot Chief Illiniwek danced for the last time during a Fighting Illini halftime, students Kelby Lanning and Alison Perle couldn't conceal their lament at the passing of an era. The university retired Chief Illiiniwek after 71 years, deciding that the Indian-derived mascot was a demeaning stereotype.

▲ Kathleen Rutledge.

To people who criticize mass media for trafficking in misleading stereotypes, Kathleen Rutledge is a hero. When she was editor of the Lincoln, Nebraska *Journal Star*, Rutledge banned references to sports mascots and nicknames that many American Indians consider insulting. Readers of the *Journal Star*, circulation 76,300, no longer read about the Washington Redskins, just Washington. The Cleveland Indians' mascot, Chief Wahoo, whose weird grin irked many Indians, doesn't appear in the newspaper either.

Rutledge's policy change rankled some readers. In 500-some letters and e-mail messages, readers accused the newspaper of abandoning tradition and succumbing to the leftist politically correct agenda. Leftist? Hardly, responded Rutledge, noting that the *Journal Star* endorsed the self-proclaimed "compassionate conservative" George Bush for president in 2000. More than anything, the political tinge of some critics bespoke blind emotional attachments to tradition.

Can school nicknames and mascots have ill effects? Jesse Steinfeldt, an Indiana University psychology professor who has studied the issue, says that "a racially hostile education environment" can affect the self-esteem of Native American kids.

In 2005 the National Collegiate Athletic Association stepped up pressure on colleges to drop Indian nicknames. Eighteen schools were listed for using nicknames and imagery the NCAA considered "hostile or abusive." The University of North Dakota was blacklisted by the NCAA. The university resisted for years but eventually retired

its Fighting Sioux nickname and logo on order of the State Board of Higher Education.

In Kewaunee, Wisconsin, it was retired teacher Marsha Beggs Brown who pushed for change. A new state law went into effect in 2010 to eliminate race-based nicknames, logos and mascots. Seeing the law being ignored locally, Brown filed a complaint about the Kewaunee High School Indians. In the small town of 2,700, some people sent Brown anonymous letters and made unpleasant phone calls. She was snubbed. A popular t-shirt read: "Once an Indian, Always an Indian." Brown was motivated by a respect for all people: "There's just no refuting that these names harm children."

The Kewaunee school board asked the community for alternative names. Almost 200 ideas were submitted. In a community-wide vote, 1,400 ballots were cast to choose between the two finalists: River Bandits and Storm.

Not all Indian references are out, however. In Michigan the Mishicot Indians have granted permission to the Hannahville Potawatomi high school to use the name because the town is named for a chief from that tribe.

In Wisconsin in 2011, American Indian Cultural Support reported 45 schools still had mascots it considered offensive. Councilman Brandon Stevens of the Oneida Nation, the tribe closest to Kewaunee, sees an upside: "As long as there's debate, there's an avenue for education."

At Kewaunee High School it's now "Go Storm. Ride the Wind!"

What Do You Think?

Should sports teams be required to choose kinder, gentler mascots and nicknames so as not to offend?

Can a media ban on references to a controversial mascot be effective in reducing stereotyping?

Cultural Effects

STUDY PREVIEW

Mass media messages to large audiences can be culturally unifying, but media demassification, with messages aimed at narrower audiences, has had a role also in the fragmentation of society. On a global scale, media have imposed U.S. and Western values on the traditional values of other cultures. Even in countries with emerging media systems, the indigenous media continue to be influenced by media content from dominant cultures.

Values

Mass media are factors in shaping and reflecting contemporary values with the immense quantity of content that they carry. Often overlooked is that media also allow generations to share experiences, thoughts and values over the centuries.

Historical Transmission.   Human beings have a compulsion to pass on the wisdom they have accumulated to future generations. There is a compulsion, too, to learn from the past. In olden times, people gathered around fires and in temples to hear storytellers. It was a ritual through which people learned the values that governed their community. This is a form of **historical transmission.**

Five-thousand years ago the oral tradition was augmented when Middle Eastern traders devised an alphabet to keep track of inventories, transactions and rates of exchange. When paper was invented, clay tablets gave way to scrolls and eventually books, which became the primary vehicle for storytelling. Religious values were passed on in holy books. Military chronicles laid out the lessons of war. Literature provided lessons by exploring the nooks and crannies of the human condition.

Books remain a primary repository of our culture. For several centuries it has been between hard covers, in black ink on paper, that the experiences, lessons and wisdom of our forebears have been recorded for posterity. Other mass media today share in the preservation and transmission of our culture over time. Consider these archives:

historical transmission
Communication of cultural values to later generations

- **Paley Center for Media** in New York, with 120,000 television and radio performances, productions, debuts and series.
- **Library for Communication and Graphic Arts** at Ohio State University, whose collection includes editorial cartoons.
- **Vanderbilt Television News Archive** in Nashville, Tennessee, with 900,000 items from network nightly news programs and also special coverage such as political conventions and space shots.

Contemporary Transmission.   The mass media also transmit values among contemporary communities and societies, sometimes causing changes that otherwise would not occur. This is known as **contemporary transmission.** Anthropologists have documented that mass communication can change society. When Edmund Carpenter introduced movies to an isolated New Guinea village, the men adjusted their clothing toward the Western style and even remodeled their houses. This phenomenon, which scholars call **diffusion of innovations,** occurs when ideas move through the mass media. Consider the following:

contemporary transmission
Communication of cultural values to different cultures

diffusion of innovations
Process through which news, ideas, values and information spread

- **American Revolution.** Colonists up and down the Atlantic seaboard took cues on what to think and how to act from newspaper reports on radical activities, mostly in Boston, in the decade before the Declaration of Independence. These included inflammatory articles against the 1765 Stamp Act and accounts of the Boston Tea Party in 1773.
- **Music, fashion and pop culture.** In modern-day pop culture, the cues come through the media, mostly from New York, Hollywood and Nashville.
- **Third World innovation.** The United Nations creates instructional films and radio programs to promote agricultural reform in less developed parts of the world. Overpopulated areas have been targets of birth control campaigns.

Herbert Schiller. *Schiller sounded the alarm that Western culture, epitomized by Hollywood, was flooding the planet. The result, he said, was that traditions and values in other cultures were being drowned out. The phenomenon, called cultural imperialism, has been offset somewhat by the growth in media content originating in other countries and targeted at U.S. and other Western audiences.*

cultural imperialism
One culture's dominance over another

- **Demise of Main Street.** Small-town businesses are boarding up throughout the United States as rural people see advertisements from regional shopping malls, which are farther away but offer greater variety and lower prices than Main Street.

Scholars note that the mass media can be given too much credit for the diffusion of innovations. Diffusion almost always needs reinforcement through interpersonal communication. Also, the diffusion is hardly ever a one-shot hypodermic injection but a process that requires redundancy in messages over an extended period. The 1989 outburst for democracy in China did not happen because one Chinese person read Thomas Paine on a sunny afternoon, nor do rural people suddenly abandon their local Main Street for a Walmart 40 miles away. The diffusion of innovations typically involves three initial steps in which the mass media can be pivotal:

- **Awareness.** Individuals and groups learn about alternatives, new options and possibilities.
- **Interest.** Once aware, people need to have their interest further whetted.
- **Evaluation.** By considering the experience of other people, as relayed by the mass media, individuals evaluate whether they wish to adopt an innovation.

The adoption process has two additional steps in which the media play a small role: the trial stage, in which an innovation is given a try, and the final stage, in which the innovation is either adopted or rejected.

Cultural Imperialism

Nobody could provoke debate quite like Herbert Schiller, whether among his college students or in the whole society. He amassed evidence for a pivotal 1969 book, *Mass Communications and American Empire.* His argument: U.S. media companies were coming to dominate cultural life abroad. He called it **cultural imperialism.**

Schiller sensitized readers to the implications of exporting movies and other U.S. media products. He also put leading media companies on notice that Mickey Mouse in Borneo, no matter how endearing, had untoward implications for the indigenous culture. U.S. corporate greed, he said, was undermining native cultures in developing countries. He described the process as insidious. People in developing countries found U.S. media products so slickly produced and packaged that, candy-like, they were irresistible no matter the destruction they were causing to the local traditions and values that were fading fast into oblivion.

Plenty of evidence supported Schiller's theory. In South Africa, robbers have taken to shouting, "Freeze," a word that had no root in either Afrikaans or other indigenous languages. The robbers had been watching too much American television. A teen fashion statement in India became dressing like *Baywatch* characters, a fashion hardly in subcontinent tradition. In India, too, television talk shows began an American-like probing into private lives. Said media observer Shailja Bajpai: "American television has loosened tongues, to say nothing of our morals."

Schiller's observations were a global recasting of populist-elitist arguments. Populists, whose mantra is "Let the people choose," called Schiller hysterical. These populists noted that Hollywood and other Western media products weren't being forced on anyone. People wanted the products. Some elitists countered that traditional values, many going back centuries, were like endangered species and needed protection against Western capitalistic instincts that were smothering them pell-mell. Elitists noted too that the Western media content that was most attractive abroad was hardly the best stuff. *Rambo* was a case in point at the time that Schiller was becoming a best-selling author with his ideas.

Post-Schiller Revisionism.   Schiller's ideas took firmer hold in the 1990s as major U.S. and European media companies extended their reach. MTV and ESPN turned themselves into global brands. The Murdoch empire was flying high as his SkyTV satellite serviced virtually all of Asia plus similar ventures in Europe and Latin America. Hollywood was firmly in place as a reigning international icon. The largest U.S. newspaper, *USA Today,* launched editions in Europe and Asia.

At the same time, cracks were appearing in Schiller's model. Homegrown television production powerhouses in Latin America, like TV Globo in Brazil and Televisa in Mexico, were pumping programs into the United States. In Asia and the Middle East, Western programming ideas were being adapted to local cultures. Countless variations of *American Idol*, for example, from a growing number of independent companies in the Middle East, went on the air in Arabic countries. Pokémon wasn't invented in America, nor was Hello Kitty. Manga comics from Japan have mushroomed into $180 million in U.S. sales, roughly a third of comic sales.

Too, Western media products are adapted to local cultures. Profanities are edited from movies exported to Malaysia. For India, Spider-Man switched his crotch-hugging tights for the traditional billowing Hindu dhoti. He also wears pointy sandals.

By the first decade of the 21st century, the idea of a monolithic Western culture displacing everything else on the globe needed rethinking. Yes, Hollywood was still big globally, but other players were emerging.

Transcultural Enrichment. Turning the cultural imperialism model on its head has been the British-based Virgin Comics, a Johnny-come-lately to the comic book business. With London capital and Bangalore studios, comics with story lines from Indian religion and mythology have been launched in U.S. and other markets. Other themes were drawn from the epic Sanskrit poem *Ramayana*. Could this be called cultural counter-imperialism?

Adventurer-entrepreneur Richard Branson, who was one of the original masterminds behind Virgin Comics, now Liquid Comics, set his sights far beyond just another product on magazine racks. Aware that the sources for franchise movie series like *Superman*, *Batman*, *Spider-Man* and *X-Men* are nearing exhaustion, Branson looked to Indian mythology as a Next Big Thing. The comic *Sudhu*, about a Brit who discovers he was a Hindu holy man in a previous life, became a Virgin movie. John Woo, whose action films include *Reign of Assassin*, cocreated a China-themed story, *Seven Brothers*, for Virgin. Now a digital entertainment company, Liquid Comics uses numerous media platforms to offer films and graphic novels.

The Liquid Comics phenomenon is hardly isolated. Think Al-Jazeera, the Middle Eastern news channel that went global in 2006. Think the Chinese policy to become a global player in motion pictures. This can be seen as enriching. Scholar George Steiner has made the point that U.S. and European cultures are the richer for, not corrupted by, the continuing presence of Greek mythology from over 2,000 years ago. Sociologist Michael Tracey points to silent-movie comedian Charlie Chaplin, whose humor traveled well in other cultures: "Was it not Chaplin's real genius to strike some common chord, uniting the whole of humanity?"

▲ **Occupy Wall Street.** *When the loosely organized 99 Percenters began their demonstrations in 2011 against growing and concentrated wealth in the United States, they employed the media devices du jour to do their thing. One technique, in case of arrest, was a pre-programmed message to friends, family and perhaps an attorney that they had been arrested. The messages were sent from their GPS location before police could shut down their calls.*

APPLYING YOUR MEDIA LITERACY

- **How does mass communication connect us to the past, as well as help us resolve diverse contemporary values?**
- **Can transcultural communication be enriching even if also imperialist? Why or why not?**

Behavioral Effects

STUDY PREVIEW

The overstated magic bullet theory on how mass communication affects people has been perpetuated by advertising. The message is "buy me" or "test me" either immediately or soon. Manipulative advertising can have behavioral effects, although some techniques, like subliminal messages, are overrated and dubious.

MEDIAcounterpoints

■ Media in Immigration Debate

When Arizona Governor Jan Brewer met President Obama to discuss her state's controversial new immigration enforcement law in 2011, one of the protestors outside the White House snapped a photo and posted it on Twitter. Within minutes, the tweet was re-posted on the Illinois Coalition for Immigrant and Refugee Rights' own Twitter feed. Also effective in communicating the immigration cause, especially to people without internet access, has been a text messaging system run by the Reform Immigration for America campaign.

Social media also connect undocumented immigrant youth. They meet on Facebook and share their experiences, fears and hopes. At California State University, Fullerton, students started a Facebook group to protest the Arizona immigration enforcement bill. The group featured photos of members holding signs with the words, "Do I Look Like an Illegal?" The page started with five photos. Before the end of the year there were 1,600 members.

Activists claim that social media have allowed them to re-frame the immigration debate and put it into human terms—being able to see a face in a photo or a video has allowed people to identify with immigrants.

Media, however, have played a second and contradictory role in the U.S. immigration debate.

A report by the Brookings Institution, one of Washington's oldest think tanks, concluded that media make the search for compromise on immigration issues more difficult in Washington. The report examined how both traditional media and social media covered immigration going back to 1980 with a focus on the extended policy debates. Those debates collapsed. Why?

The Brookings report pointed to three tendencies in media coverage:

- Immigration is a story that has developed gradually over a long period of time. In contrast, media coverage has been episodic. The spikes of coverage have conditioned the public and policymakers to think of immigration as a sudden event, often tinged with crisis.
- Although illegal immigrants have never been more than a third of the foreign-born population in the United States, the government's efforts to control illegal immigration have dominated news

coverage. As a result, the public and policymakers associate the influx of foreign-born people with violations of the law, disruption of social norms, and government failures.

- Immigrants, policymakers and advocates have dominated the coverage, depriving the public of news about the labor market, employers and consumers, and the size and characteristics of immigrant flows—and overemphasized the role of government. Audiences with a negative attitude toward immigration who are deprived of this context can readily view immigrants as villains and themselves as victims. This leads to distrust of government.

▲ The Power of Tweeting.
Phone-snapped images of Lafayette Square protestors against immigration laws, near the White House, made the rounds quickly on Twitter. Similar protests with same message, "Do I Look Illegal," soon were mounted all around the country.

The Brookings report concluded that the media response to audience fragmentation and more competition for audience shares was to convey an air of crisis by pouncing on subjects, all with the goal of generating a surge in viewership. That, in turn, heightens public anxieties and impedes the development of consensus by focusing on political process and gamesmanship rather than the substance of the issues. The media narrative has left the issue open to exploitation by extremists on both sides.

Media give voice to strongly felt and well-defined views at either end of the immigration policy spectrum.

POINT

COUNTER POINT

Media tend to emphasize crime, crisis or controversy in covering immigration. This mischaracterizes a massive demographic event that has developed over decades and mostly through legal channels.

DEEPENING YOUR MEDIA LITERACY

EXPLORE THE ISSUE: Can you find an immigration story that explores issues instead of just reporting crime, crisis or controversy?

DIG DEEPER: What issues do you think are missing from the media's coverage of immigration?

WHAT DO YOU THINK? What kind of stories about immigration would you like to read? Do you think pundits add to the debate about immigration in the U.S.? Why hasn't new media done a better job than traditional media in coverage of the immigration debate in America?

Motivational Messages

The 1940s marked the beginning of a confusing period about the effects of mass communication that remains with us. Early magic bullet theories, challenged by Lazarsfeld and others, were falling apart. Even so, as World War II progressed, people had a growing uneasiness about how media might be affecting them. Sinister possibilities were evident in the work of Joseph Goebbels, the minister of propaganda and public enlightenment in Nazi Germany. His mantra for using the media: Tell lies often enough and loudly enough, and they'll be believed. In the Pacific the Japanese beamed the infamous Tokyo Rose radio broadcasts to GIs to lower morale. Then during the Korean war in the early 1950s, a macabre fascination developed with so-called brainwashing techniques used on U.S. prisoners of war. In this same period, the work of Austrian psychiatrist **Sigmund Freud,** which emphasized hidden motivations and repressed sexual impulses, was being popularized in countless books and articles.

No wonder, considering this intellectual context, that advertising people in the 1950s looked to the social sciences to find new ways to woo customers. Among the advertising pioneers of this period was **Ernest Dichter,** who accepted Freud's claim that people act on motivations that they are not aware of. Depth interviewing, Dichter felt, could reveal these motivations, which could then be exploited in advertising messages.

Dichter used his interviewing, called **motivational research,** for automotive clients. Rightly or wrongly, Dichter determined that the American male is loyal to his wife but fantasizes about having a mistress. Men, he noted, usually are the decision makers in purchasing a car. Then, in what seemed a quantum leap, Dichter equated sedans, which were what most people drove, with wives. Sedans were familiar, reliable. Convertibles, impractical for many people and also beyond their reach financially, were equated with mistresses—romantic, daring, glamorous. With these conclusions in hand, Dichter devised advertisements for a new kind of sedan without a center door pillar. The hardtop, as it was called, gave a convertible effect when the windows were down. The advertisements, dripping with sexual innuendo, clearly reflected Dichter's thinking: "You'll find something new to love every time you drive it." Although they were not as solid as sedans and tended to leak air and water, hardtops were popular among automobile buyers for the next 25 years.

Dichter's motivational research led to numerous campaigns that exploited sexual images. For Ronson lighters, the flame, in phallic form, was reproduced in extraordinary proportions. A campaign for Ajax cleanser, hardly a glamorous product, had a white knight charging through the street, ignoring law and regulation with a great phallic lance. Whether consumers were motivated by sexual imagery is hard to establish. Even so, many campaigns based on motivational research worked.

To some extent, mass communication can move people to action—at least, to sample a product. This, of course, is far short of brainwashing. Also, the effect is uneven—not everybody buys. And the effect can be short-lived if an advertised product fails to live up to expectations. Seen many pillarless sedans lately?

Subliminal Messages

Some concern about mass communication as a hidden persuader was whacky. In 1957, for example, market researcher **Jim Vicary** that he had inserted messages like "Drink Coca-Cola" and "Eat Popcorn" into movies. The messages were flashed too fast to be recognized by the human eye, but, Vicary claimed, were nonetheless recognized by the brain. Prompted by the **subliminal message,** he claimed that people flocked mid-movie to the snack bar. Vicary had impressive

Sigmund Freud
Austrian psyciatrist who theorized that the human mind is unconsciously susceptible to suggestion

Ernest Dichter
Pioneered motivational research

motivational research
Seeks subconscious appeals that can be used in advertising

Jim Vicary
Made dubious subliminal advertising claims

subliminal message
Cannot be consciously perceived

▲ **Flashed Message.** *Master political tactician Karl Rove knows how to get attention for his message. In a web ad opposing President Obama, 39 seconds into the ad, Rove flashed the word TAXES over the President's face for a split second. Rove knows there's no evidence that subliminal messages prompt people to action, but he knew too that reviving the discredited technique would prompt bloggers to pick up the ad and spread his anti-Obama message.*

numbers from his experiments, supposedly conducted at a New Jersey movie house. Coke sales increased 18 percent, popcorn almost 60 percent. Vicary's report stirred great interest, and also alarm, but researchers who tried to replicate his study found no evidence to support his claim.

Despite doubts about Vicary's claims, psychologists have identified a phenomenon they call **subception,** in which certain behavior sometimes seems to be triggered by messages perceived subliminally. Whether the effect works outside laboratory experiments and whether the effect is strong enough to prod a consumer to go out and buy are uncertain. Nevertheless, there remains a widespread belief among the general population that subliminal advertising works, and fortunes are being made by people who peddle various devices and systems with extravagant claims that they can control human behavior. Among these are the "hidden" messages in stores' sound systems that say shoplifting is not nice.

David Ogilvy, founder of the Ogilvy & Mather agency, once made fun of subliminal effects claims, pointing out the absurdity of "millions of suggestible consumers getting up from their armchairs and rushing like zombies through the traffic on their way to buy the product at the nearest store." The danger of "Go Taliban" being flashed during the *NBC Nightly News* is remote, and whether it would have any effect is dubious.

subception
Receiving subconscious messages that trigger behavior

APPLYING YOUR MEDIA LITERACY

- **What in the mid-20th century American experience contributed to the belief that mass communication can trigger radical changes in our behavior?**
- **Why does the fraudulent research of Jim Vicary persist as urban legend?**

Media-Depicted Violence

STUDY PREVIEW | Some individuals mimic the aggressive behavior they see in the media, but such incidents are exceptions. Some experts argue, in fact, that media-depicted violence actually reduces real-life aggressive behavior.

Learning About Violence

The mass media help to bring young people into society's mainstream by demonstrating dominant behaviors and norms. This prosocial process, called **observational learning,** turns dark, however, when children learn deviant behaviors from the media. In Manteca, California, two teenagers, one only 13, lay in wait for a friend's father in his own house and attacked him. They beat him with a fireplace poker, kicked him and stabbed him, and choked him to death with a dog chain. Then they poured salt in his wounds. Why the final act of violence—the salt in the wounds? The 13-year-old explained that he had seen it on television. While there is no question that people can learn about violent behavior from the media, a major issue of our time is whether the mass media are the cause of aberrant behavior.

observational learning
Theory that people learn behavior by seeing it in real life, in depictions

Individuals on trial for criminal acts occasionally plead that "the media made me do it." That was the defense in a 1974 California case in which two young girls playing on a beach were raped with a beer bottle by four teenagers. The rapists told police they had picked up the idea from a television movie they had seen four days earlier. In the movie a young woman was raped with a broom handle, and in court the youths' attorneys blamed the movie. The judge, as is typical in such cases, threw out media-projected violence as an unacceptable scapegoating defense and held the young perpetrators responsible.

Although the courts have never accepted transfer of responsibility as legal defense, it is clear that violent behavior in the media can be imitated. Some experts, however, say that the negative effect of media-depicted violence is too often overstated and that media violence actually has a positive side.

Media Violence as Positive

People who downplay the effect of media portrayals of blood, guts and violence often refer to a **cathartic effect.** This theory, which dates to ancient Greece and the philosopher **Aristotle,** suggests that watching violence allows individuals vicariously to release pent-up everyday frustration that might otherwise explode dangerously. By seeing violence, so goes the theory, people let off steam. Most advocates of the cathartic effect claim that individuals who see violent activity are stimulated to fantasy violence, which drains latent tendencies toward real-life violence.

In more recent times, scholar **Seymour Feshbach** has conducted studies that lend support to the cathartic effect theory. In one study, Feshbach lined up 625 junior-high school boys at seven California boarding schools and showed half of them a steady diet of violent television programs for six weeks. The other half were shown nonviolent fare. Every day during the study, teachers and supervisors reported on each boy's behavior in and out of class. Feshbach found no difference in aggressive behavior between the two groups. Further, there was a decline in aggression among boys who had been determined by personality tests to be more inclined toward aggressive behavior.

Opponents of the cathartic effect theory, who include both respected researchers and reflexive media bashers, were quick to point out flaws in Feshbach's research methods. Nonetheless, his conclusions carried a lot of influence because of the study's unprecedented massiveness—625 individuals. Also, the study was conducted in a real-life environment rather than in a laboratory, and there was a consistency in the findings.

Prodding Socially Positive Action

Besides the cathartic effect theory, an argument for showing violence is that it prompts people to engage in socially positive action. This happened after NBC aired *The Burning Bed*, a television movie about an abused woman who could not take any more and set fire to her sleeping husband. The night the movie was shown, battered-spouse centers nationwide were overwhelmed by calls from women who had been putting off doing something to extricate themselves from relationships with abusive mates.

On the negative side, one man set his estranged wife afire and explained that he was inspired by *The Burning Bed.* Another man who beat his wife senseless gave the same explanation.

Media Violence as Negative

The preponderance of evidence is that media-depicted violence has the potential to cue real-life violence. However, the **aggressive stimulation** theory is often overstated. The fact is that few people act out media violence in their lives. For example, do you know anybody who saw a murder in a movie and went out afterward and murdered somebody? Yet you know many people who see murders in movies and *don't* kill anyone.

We need to be careful when we talk about aggressive stimulation. Note, for example, the qualifiers used by scholar Wayne Danielson in summing up the conclusion of the 1995–1997 National Television Violence Study: Viewing violence on television tends to increase violent behavior in viewers, more in some situations and less in others. Increased violence can be found only when the circumstances are right and a tendency to imitate what weakens an inner resistance against engaging in violent behavior.

The study concluded that children may be more susceptible than adults to copying media violence, but that too was far, far short of a universal causal statement.

cathartic effect
People release violent inclinations by seeing them portrayed

Aristotle
Defended portrayals of violence

Seymour Feshbach
Found evidence for media violence as a release

aggressive stimulation
Theory that people are inspired to violence by media depictions

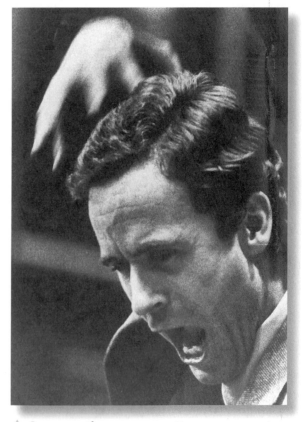

▲ **Scapegoating.** *On the eve of his execution, serial killer Ted Bundy claimed that his violence had been sparked by girlie magazines. Whatever the truth of Bundy's claim, scholars are divided about whether media depictions precipitate violent behavior. At one extreme is the view that media violence is a safety valve for people inclined to violence. At the other extreme is the aggressive stimulation theory that media violence causes real-life violence. The most prevalent thinking, to paraphrase a pioneer 1961 study on television and children, is that certain depictions under certain conditions may prompt violence in certain people.*

Why, then, do many people believe that media violence begets real-life violence? Some early studies pointed to a causal link. These included the 1960 **Bobo doll studies** of **Albert Bandura,** who showed children a violent movie and then encouraged them to play with oversize, inflated dolls. Bandura concluded that kids who saw the film were more inclined to beat up the dolls than were other kids. Critics have challenged Bandura's methodology and said that he mistook childish playfulness for aggression. In short, Bandura and other aggressive-stimulation scholars have failed to prove their theory to the full satisfaction of other scholars.

When pressed, people who hold the aggressive-stimulation theory point to particular incidents they know about. A favorite is the claim by serial killer Ted Bundy that *Playboy* magazine had led him to stalk and kill women. Was Bundy telling the truth? We will never know. He offered the scapegoat explanation on his way to the execution chamber, which suggests that there may have been other motives. The Bundy case is anecdotal, and anecdotes cannot be extrapolated into general validity.

An alternative to aggressive stimulation theory is a theory that people whose feelings and general view of the world tend toward aggressiveness and violence are attracted to violence in movies, television and other media depictions of violence. This alternative theory holds that people who are violent are predisposed to violence, which is far short of saying that the media made them do it. This leads us to the **catalytic theory,** which sees media-depicted violence as having a contributing role in violent behavior, not a triggering one.

Catalytic Theory

Simplistic readings of both cathartic and aggressive stimulation effects research can yield extreme conclusions. A careful reading, however, points more to the media having a role in real-life violence but not necessarily triggering it and doing so only infrequently—and only if several nonmedia factors are also present. For example, evidence suggests that television and movie violence, even in cartoons, is arousing and can excite some children to violence, especially hyperactive and easily excitable children. These children, like unstable adults, become wrapped up psychologically with the portrayals and are stirred to the point of acting out. However, this happens only when a combination of other influences is also present. Among these other influences are:

- **Whether violence portrayed in the media is rewarded.** In 1984 David Phillips of the University of California at San Diego found that the murder rate increases after publicized prizefights, in which the victor is rewarded, and decreases after publicized murder trials and executions, in which, of course, violence is punished.

- **Whether media exposure is heavy.** Researcher Monroe Lefkowitz studied upstate New York third-graders who watched a lot of media-depicted violence. Ten years later, Lefkowitz found that these individuals were rated by their peers as violent. This suggests cumulative, long-term media effects.

- **Whether a violent person fits other profiles.** Studies have found correlations between aggressive behavior and many variables besides viewing violence. These include income, education, intelligence and parental childrearing practices. This is not to say that any of these third variables cause violent behavior. The suggestion, rather, is that violence is far too complex to be explained by a single factor.

Most researchers note, too, that screen-triggered violence is increased if the aggression:

- **Is realistic and exciting,** like a chase or suspense sequence that sends adrenaline levels surging.

- **Succeeds in righting a wrong,** like helping an abused or ridiculed character get even.

- **Includes situations or characters** similar to those in the viewer's own experience.

All these things would prompt a scientist to call media violence a catalyst. Just as the presence of a certain element will allow other elements to react explosively but itself is not part of the explosion, the presence of media violence can be a factor in real-life violence but not be a cause by itself. This catalytic theory was articulated by scholars **Wilbur Schramm,** Jack Lyle and Edwin Parker, who investigated the effects of television on children and came up with this statement in their 1961 book *Television in the Lives of Our Children*, which has become a classic on the effects of media-depicted violence on individuals: "For *some* children under *some* conditions, *some* television is harmful. For *other* children under the same conditions, or for the same children under *other* conditions, it *may* be beneficial. For *most* children, under *most* conditions, *most* television is *probably* neither particularly harmful nor particularly beneficial."

Societally Debilitating Effects

Media-depicted violence scares far more people than it inspires people to commit violence, and this, according to **George Gerbner,** a leading researcher on screen violence, leads some people to believe the world is more dangerous than it really is. Gerbner calculated that 1 in 10 television characters is involved in violence in any given week. In real life the chances are only about 1 in 100 per *year.* People who watch a lot of television, Gerbner found, see their own chances of being involved in violence nearer the distorted television level than their local crime statistics or even their own experience would suggest. It seems that television violence leads people to think they are in far greater real-life jeopardy than they really are.

The implications of Gerbner's findings go to the heart of a free and democratic society. With exaggerated fears about their safety, Gerbner said, people will demand greater police protection. They are also likelier, he said, to submit to established authority and even to accept police violence as a trade-off for their own security.

Media Violence and Youth

Nobody would argue that Jerry Springer's television talk show is a model of good taste and restraint. In fact, the conventional wisdom is that such shows do harm. But do they? Two scholars at the University of Pennsylvania, Stacy Davis and Marie-Louise Mares, conducted a careful study of 292 high-school students in North Carolina, some from a city and some from a rural area, and concluded from their data that some talk shows may offend people but that evidence is lacking that teenagers are desensitized to aberrant or tawdry behavior.

One issue was whether talk-show viewing desensitizes teenagers to tawdry behavior. The conventional wisdom, articulated by many politicians calling for television reform, is that teenagers are numbed by all the antisocial, deviant and treacherous figures on talk shows. Not so, said Davis and Mares: "Heavy talk-show viewers were no less likely than light viewers to believe that the victims of antisocial behavior had been wronged, to perceive that the victim had suffered, or to rate the antisocial behavior as immoral."

Do talk shows undercut society's values? According to Davis and Mares, Davis and Mares concluded that talk shows actually are conservative. Studio audiences, they noted, boo guests who flout social norms and cheer those who espouse mainstream vales and behavior. These shows actually are "cautionary tales," Davis and Mares said. The result is that teenagers end up with heightened perceptions about how certain behaviors come about and the seriousness the social issues are.

Tolerance of Violence

An especially serious concern about media-depicted violence is that it has a numbing, callousing effect on people. This **desensitizing theory**, which is widely held, says not only that individuals are becoming hardened by media violence but also that society's tolerance for such antisocial behavior is increasing.

desensitizing theory
Tolerance of real-life violence grows because of media-depicted violence

Media critics say that the media are responsible for this desensitization, but many media people, particularly movie and television directors, respond that it is the desensitization that has forced them to make the violence in their shows even more graphic. They explain that they have run out of alternatives to get the point across when the story line requires that the audience be repulsed.

Some movie critics, of course, find this explanation a little too convenient for gore-inclined moviemakers and television directors, but even directors who are not inclined to gratuitous violence feel that their options for stirring the audience have become scarcer. The critics respond that this is a chicken-or-egg question and that the media are in no position to use the desensitization theory to excuse including more and more violence in their products if they themselves contributed to the desensitization. And so the argument goes on about who is to blame.

Desensitization is apparent in news also. In 2004 the New York *Times*, traditionally cautious about gore, showed a photo of victims' corpses hanging from a bridge in war-torn Iraq. Only a few years earlier there had been an almost universal ban on showing the bodies of crime, accident and war victims in newspapers and on television newscasts. Photos of U.S. troops torturing Iraqi prisoners, integral in telling a horrible but important story, pushed back the earlier limits. No mainstream media showed the videotaped beheading of U.S. businessman Nick Berg by terrorists in Iraq, but millions of people found the gruesome sequence online. This desensitizing did not come suddenly with the Iraq war and its aftermath, but the war has clearly established new ground rules.

It is undeniable that violence has had a growing presence in the mass media, which makes even more poignant the fact that we know far less about media violence than we need to. What do we know? Various theories explain some phenomena, but the theories themselves do not dovetail. The desensitizing theory, for example, explains audience acceptance of more violence, but it hardly explains research findings that people who watch a lot of television actually have heightened anxiety about their personal safety. People fretting about their own safety are hardly desensitized.

Violence Studies

The mass media, especially television and movies that deal in fiction, depict a lot of violence. Studies have found as many as six violent acts per hour on prime-time network television. In and of itself, that may seem a lot, but a study at the University of California, Los Angeles, operating on the premise that the issue should not be how much violence is depicted but the context in which it occurs, came to a less startling conclusion: Slapstick comedic violence shouldn't be lumped with graphic homicide in counting depictions of violence. Nor should a violent storm.

Violence Assessment Monitoring Project
Conducted contextual nonviolence studies and found less serious media depictions than earlier thought

The UCLA research, called the **Violence Assessment Monitoring Project,** concluded in its first year that distressing human violence was much less prevalent than earlier studies had counted. Of 121 prime-time episodes, only 10 had frequent violence and only eight had occasional violence. This was after comedic violence and nonhuman violence, such as hurricanes, were screened out. The next year, 1996, found violence in only five prime-time shows—half the number of the year before. Also, most of the shows didn't survive the season. In 1998, the number was down to two series.

William McQuire
Found most media violence research flawed

The UCLA study added sophistication to Gerbner's counting acts of media-depicted violence but still didn't assess whether the violence affected people. In 1986 scholar **William McQuire** reviewed the literature on mediated violence and found that hardly any of the studies' evidence was statistically reliable. The exception was controlled laboratory studies, for which the statistics were more meaningful but did not indicate much causality.

APPLYING YOUR MEDIA LITERACY

- **Why do the courts refuse to excuse violent criminals who blame their behavior on media-depicted violence?**
- **What variables contribute to a person's proneness for violence after an experience with media-depicted violence?**
- **Recall someone from your experience whose media experience has led to an elevated and unwarranted concern for their personal safety. What can be done about this?**
- **How can it be argued that media portrayals of deviant behavior discourage real-life deviance?**
- **What difficulty do researchers have in measuring violent media content?**

■ Effects Theories (Pages 343–345)

Early mass communication scholars assumed that media messages had powerful and direct impacts on people. At an extreme, the bullet theory said the media could immediately affect behavior. Further scholarship found that the bullet theory was simplistic and vastly overstated the effects of mass communication. This does not mean that the media are without effect but that the dynamics of the effects generally are gradual over time.

■ Lifestyle Effects (Pages 346–348)

In most of the world, mass media are integrated into people's lives from the cradle. In fact, media have a large role in initiating children into society by instilling cultural values. It is worth asking whether the media's role in childhood development is good, bad or neutral. The answer is not obvious. It can be said, however, that media reflect existing cultural values. This reflection, because values are in continuing flux, means that media content includes a rich mix of values. The mix includes traditional values as well as challenges to tradition.

■ Attitude Effects (Pages 348–352)

Mass messages bring information and opinions to large numbers of people, in effect setting an agenda and conferring status on issues. What is missed by the media generally doesn't get on the public radar. But what are the effects of media content on attitudes and opinions? Scholars know a lot about the effect of stereotypes, which, when repeated, can have a compounding effect. Also, there is a copycat factor, at least for superficial issues like fashion and style. Which celebrity haircut will be the rage tomorrow? On more significant issues, shifts in attitudes and opinions generally are gradual.

■ Cultural Effects (Pages 353–355)

Cultural values of dominant societies, as depicted in mass media content, have had unmistakable effects on developing societies. The extent of this so-called cultural imperialism can be debated, as can whether the effects are good, bad or nil. The export of dominant cultural values has been mitigated by the rise of indigenous media in developing countries, but there remains a lot of transcultural influence, some with content that imitates content from other countries and also the direct importation of content.

■ Behavioral Effects (Pages 355–358)

Advertising research has found ways to tap into consumer psyches, sometimes with tactics so subtle as to be unrecognized for what they are. Precise control on hidden persuasion, however, is impossible. The larger the audience, the more exponentially the degree of influence decreases. Even so, a mythology exists about the effect of hidden persuasion. The power of subliminal communication has never been demonstrated conclusively to be a trigger of behavior. This is not to say, however, that media content has no effect on behavior. Media depictions of unacceptable behavior, especially when widely publicized, can have a dampening effect on such behavior. Also, media campaigns that explicitly encourage certain behaviors, as in Ad Council public-service announcements, can have an impact, albeit one that is difficult to measure.

CHAPTER WRAP UP

Media-Depicted Violence (Pages 358–362)

Media-depicted violence has been around forever. Read any Shakespeare lately? Despite anecdotal stories and testimony that "the media made me do it," scholars have come up empty in confirming the claim that media-depicted violence causes mentally healthy people to commit real-life violence. In fact, there is a line of reasoning dating to Aristotle that says witnessing violence sways people away from committing violence. There are, however, people, including the mentally deranged, who are susceptible to what's called aggressive stimulation. Research goes both ways on whether children are moved to violence by seeing it. The classic study on the issue says some children may be affected some of the time in some circumstances. That hardly is a firm conclusion of a predictable causal effect.

▇ Thinking Critically

1. Why has the bullet theory of mass communication effects lost support? What has replaced the bullet theory?

2. How is the role of mass messages in childhood development changing?

3. What are examples of the influence of mass communication on attitudes and opinions?

4. How has advertising perpetuated myths about the effects of mass communication?

5. What continues to fuel magic bullet theory beliefs about immediate, powerful effects of mass messages, including subliminal messages?

6. Identify and discuss different ideas about the effects of media-depicted violence.

▇ Media Vocabulary

agenda-setting (Page 345)

aggressive stimulation (Page 359)

Bobo doll studies (Page 360)

bullet model (Page 344)

catalytic theory (Page 360)

cathartic effect (Page 359)

contemporary transmission (Page 353)

cultural imperialism (Page 354)

cumulative effects theory (Page 345)

desensitizing theory (Page 361)

diffusion of innovations (Page 353)

historical transmission (Page 353)

minimal effects theory (Page 344)

motivational research (Page 357)

multistep flow (Page 344)

narcoticizing dysfunction (Page 345)

observational learning (Page 358)

opinion leaders (Page 344)

powerful effects theory (Page 343)

prosocial (Page 347)

role modeling (Page 349)

socialization (Page 346)

spiral of silence (Page 345)

stereotyping (Page 351)

subception (Page 358)

subliminal messages (Page 358)

third person effect (Page 344)

two-step flow (Page 344)

■ Media Sources

■ Steven J. Kirsh. *Children, Adolescents, and Media Violence: A Critical Look at the Research,* 2nd edition. Sage, 2011. Kirsh, a child developmental psychologist, reviews research on the effects of media-related violence on children, including internet aggression, violent music, and teen suicide.

■ Catherine A. Luther, Carolyn Ringer Lepre and Naeemah Clark. *Diversity in U.S. Media.* Wiley-Blackwell, 2011. The authors, all scholars, examine the roots and evolution of how social groups are portrayed.

■ Dorothy G. Singer and Jerome L. Singer. *Handbook of Childen and the Media,* 2nd edition. Sage, 2011. The authors, both research psychologists, examine research on children's use of media, including smart phones, iPods, iPads, digital readers, social networks, and Skype, and the effects of cyber-bullying, sexting, and violent video games.

■ John Gosling. *Waging The War of the Worlds: A History of the 1938 Radio Broadcast and Resulting Panic.* McFarland, 2009. Includes original script. Gosling's almost life-long interest in the broadcast has led to a thorough review of the people behind the program and variations and translations in other countries

■ Cass R. Sunstein. *On Rumors. How Falsehoods Spread, Why We Believe Them, What Can Be Done.* Farrar, Straus & Giroux. 2009. Sunstein, a Harvard legal scholar, argues that internet communication has compounded the dangerous potency of rumors to undermine public confidence in political leadership and thus erode functioning democracy. Sunstein, an adviser to President Obama, offers examples, many political, in advancing his thesis.

■ Brenda R. Weber. *Makeover TV: Selfhood, Citizenship and Celebrity.* Duke University, 2009. Weber, a gender scholar, studied 2,000 television programs with self-reinvention themes for lessons on cultural desires and fears.

■ Lisa Blackman and Valerie Walkerdine. *Mass Hysteria: Critical Psychology and Media Studies.* Palgrave, 2001. Blackman and Walkerdine draw on numerous psychology theories to examine the relationship between psychology and the mass media.

A Thematic Chapter Summary

MASS MEDIA EFFECTS

To further deepen your media literacy here are ways to look at this chapter from the perspective of themes that recur throughout the book:

MEDIA EFFECTS

Elisabeth Noelle Neumann's Spiral of Silence theory offers sophisticated model for media effects.

Scholars know that mass messages don't have a sudden, bullet-like impact that affects behavior, but the idea of immediate, powerful media effects persists in our cultural mythology. A lot of the fears about the effects of media-depicted violence, for example, are drawn from the bullet theory. Scholars have come to the conclusion that the effects of mass messages are gradual, building up over time—a cumulative effect, not a bullet effect.

MEDIA AND DEMOCRACY

No matter how good the campaign speech, most voters look to respected acquaintances for guidance in voting.

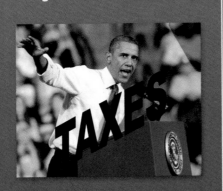

Pioneering studies by sociologist Paul Lazarsfeld in the 1940s discovered that most voters don't make their decisions based on campaign speeches, news accounts or advertisements. Lazarsfeld found that the greatest influence comes from opinion leaders with whom voters are in regular contact, like a respected neighbor, a teacher or a wizened uncle. He concluded that media messages are their most effective when they reach these opinion leaders, who then, often not recognizing their influence, shape how people around them vote.

MEDIA AND CULTURE

Mass communication can strengthen stereotypes, as with loose characterizations of immigrants—both legal and illegal—and also dismantle stereotypes

Media messages hardly are products of immaculate conception. They flow from their culture. Indeed, they are products of their culture. To find an audience, messages need to resonate fundamental values of the culture. Mass media products thus perpetuate existing values, although there can also be challenges to tradition in mass messages. But messages never can be so out of line that they won't find an audience. This process is called cultural transmission.

MEDIA GLOBALIZATION

Herbert Schiller cautioned that media-exported Western culture could wipe out indigenous values elsewhere

Media content can be pivotal when cultures collide. Scholar Herbert Schiller called it cultural imperialism when media content from economically, politically and militarily dominant parts of the world, such as the United States, finds audiences in less developed regions. Dominant values begin displacing native values, which can be lost forever. There is strong evidence of cultural imperialism at superficial levels—styles, fads, idioms. Contrarians note, however, that Schiller may have overstated his case. Not all displaced values are worth preserving, at least from a Western perspective. These include slavery, subjugation of women and suppression of free expression.

ELITISM AND POPULISM

What's the role of indigenous culture and values in a world that mass media have a role in homogenizing?

MAP OF FREEDOM 2006

The elitism-populism prism that explains some mass communication effects has global applications. Scholar Herbert Schiller has seen people in developing cultures as unschooled in media literacy. These people, Schiller said, are especially vulnerable to alien values that media from developed societies export. He called the phenomenon cultural imperialism. Although criticized in recent years, Schiller's idea explains a lot of the gradual global homogenization in values.

MEDIA ECONOMICS

Celebrities and other cultural icons motivate people toward buying their endorsed products.

Advertising has found success in associating products with celebrities and other people with bigger-than-life reputations and followings. Shortstop Derek Jeter is worth millions for helping sell Fords, geriatric actor William Shatner for the online travel service Priceline, Kim Kardashian for her product du jour. The role-model phenomenon, although hardly recent, especially worries traditionalists when cultural icons engage in errant behavior. Like it or not, rapper 50 Cent has a following that translates into retail sales of a clothing line.

CHAPTER 14
GOVERNANCE AND MASS MEDIA

■ Television Ads And Elections

To run for the U.S. Senate, the queen of World Wrestling's *Smackdown*, Linda McMahon, needed to reinvent herself. She put $50 million into her Senate campaign. All her own money. McMahon's company, the billion-dollar-a-year World Wrestling Entertainment Corporation created with her husband Vince McMahon, had made her rich. Although without gaining as much fame as WWE's Hulk Hogan and John Cena, Linda McMahon had put herself both in the ring and into a bitchy role in ringside antics beginning in 1999. She also acquired a reputation for business acumen as chief executive of WWE with moves like shifting wrestling from the facade of being a sport into a make-believe escapist fantasy with tawdry soap opera story lines. Then McMahon engineered an exorcism of the sleaze to expand WWE's audience to kids. The formerly TV-14 rating, which cautioned parents, became the less worrisome PG. Still, when McMahon decided to run for the U.S. Senate from Connecticut, many people couldn't rid the *Smackdown* images from their minds.

Could $50 million, mostly to buy advertising time on television, overcome McMahon's earlier low-brow television persona? Could she remake herself as worthy of high public office in a television-dominated political age? Apparently not. She lost. But she sure spent lots of money in trying. Only one-time Goldman Sachs investment executive Jon Corzine had spent more on a Senate campaign in all U.S. history, $60 million, almost all on television ads, in 2000. He won. For the 2012

◀ **Her Hat in the Ring.** *When wrestling exec Linda McMahon announced her candidacy for the U.S. Senate, she pledged $50 million of her own money to the campaign. Most was destined to buy television ad time. Can elections be bought? Not in this case. She lost. Is it better that candidates finance themselves rather than be beholden to deep-pocket contributors? What is the alternative in this age of expensive television campaigns that would otherwise preclude people of ordinary means from seeking high office?*

CHAPTER INSIGHTS

- A major role for media in a democracy was encapsulated in the term *Fourth Estate* introduced by British statesman Edmund Burke in 1787.

- Media influence governance by setting the agenda for political discussion.

- Strategies for U.S. government manipulation of mass media are as old as the Republic itself.

- Partisanship plays a role in mass media coverage of U.S. political campaigns.

- Corporate spending enables television to play a pivotal role in U.S. political campaigns.

presidential campaigns, the Democratic and Republican parties each were budgeting as much as $1 billion, a record.

The question: Can elections be bought with lots of expensive television ads? Blair Hull of Illinois spent $29 million in 2004, the third costliest Senate campaign in history, and lost. Michael Huffington of California spent $28 million in 1994 and lost. The lesson: Money alone cannot win an election. But neither can a successful campaign be waged without money to place television ads.

Historically the connection of politics and mass media was mostly limited to editorial endorsements. Every presidential candidate since Abraham Lincoln, for example, coveted an editorial endorsement from the influential New York *Times,* even while receiving neutral and dispassionate campaign coverage in the paper's news section. The only financial linkage between media and candidates was campaign checks written to newspaper and broadcast companies for ad space and time. Traditional journalism had insisted on a brick wall between newsrooms where coverage is decided and the editorial endorsement process as well as between the newsrooms and the company bookkeepers who collected advertising revenue. It was a business model that assured audiences that the news could be trusted as impartial and not bought.

Another dynamic for change, also troubling, may have been signaled when News Corporation, the media empire whose properties include Fox News, began channeling money into politics. In 2010 News Corporation donated $1.2 million to the Republican Governors Association. Pressed to explain the large donation, News Corporation chief executive Rupert Murdoch said that Republicans tended to support tax policies that were beneficial to his company. News Corporation donated an additional $1 million to the like-minded U.S. Chamber of Commerce, which funneled political donations almost wholly to Republican campaigns.

Such blatant cracks in the old brick wall built between newsrooms and politics and also between news corporations and politics were unprecedented. True, for years news corporations had made political donations but always for much smaller amounts that were almost always divided between the political parties—a kind of civic contribution to facilitate the working of the American political system.

It could be concluded that mass media corporations may be coming to see themselves as just another special interest, akin to the petroleum, banking and health industries that donate to buy the ears of candidates and keep them beholden once elected. Ever higher costs of mounting campaigns, including gargantuan purchases of television time, place candidates in positions to collect money from wherever and whomever they can.

In Connecticut, Linda McMahon was able to argue that she wasn't beholden to contributors. The $50 million she budgeted for her Senate campaign was entirely her own money. Touting herself as an incorruptible purist, McMahon made a case that she would be indebted only to the people of Connecticut—not well-heeled special interests. That raised another question: Should public office be limited only to those rich enough to buy enough television time to be elected?

The issues posed by the campaign of the wealthy *Smackdown* queen are among the subject of this chapter on media and governance and the interconnected U.S. election process. ■

Media Role in Governance

STUDY PREVIEW | The news media are sometimes called *the fourth estate* or *the fourth branch* of government. These terms identify the independent role of the media in reporting on the government. The media are a kind of watchdog on behalf of the citizens.

Fourth Estate

Medieval English and French societies were highly structured into classes of people called *estates.* The first estate was the clergy. The second was the nobility. The third was the common people. After Gutenberg, the mass-produced written word began emerging as a player in the power structure, but it couldn't be pigeonholed as part of one or another of the three estates. In time the press came to be called the **fourth estate.** Where the term

▲ **Edmund Burke.** *The British political philosopher Edmund Burke concocted the term fourth estate for the press. Pointing to reporters in the gallery, he told fellow members of Parliament: "There sits a* Fourth Estate *more important by far than them all." Burke was adding to the three recognized estates—the nobility, the clergy and the common people.*

fourth estate
The press as a player in medieval power structures, in addition to the clerical, noble and common estates

Edmund Burke
British member of Parliament who is sometimes credited with coining the term *fourth estate*

fourth branch
The press as an informally structured check on the legislative, executive and judicial branches of U.S. government

watchdog role
Concept of the press as a skeptical and critical monitor of government

equal time rule
Government requirement for stations to offer competing political candidates the same time period and the same rate for advertising

fairness doctrine
Former government requirement that stations air all sides of public issues

Don Burden
Radio station owner who lost licenses because he favored some political candidates over others

came from isn't clear, but **Edmund Burke,** a member of the British Parliament, used it in the mid-1700s. Pointing to the reporters' gallery, Burke said, "There sat a Fourth Estate more important by far than them all." The term is applied to all journalistic activity today. The news media report on the other estates, ideally with roots in none and a commitment only to truth.

The fourth-estate concept underwent an adaptation when the United States was created. The Constitution of the new republic, drafted in 1787, set up a balanced form of government with three branches: the legislative, the executive and the judicial. The republic's founders implied a role for the press in the new governance structure when they declared in the Constitution's First Amendment that the government should not interfere with the press. The press, however, was not part of the formal structure. This led to the press informally being called the **fourth branch** of government. Its job is to monitor the other branches as an external check on behalf of the people. This is the **watchdog role** of the press. As one wag put it, the founders saw the role of the press as keeping tabs on the rascals in power to keep them honest.

Government–Media Relations

Although the First Amendment says that the government shouldn't place restrictions on the press, the reality is that exceptions have evolved.

Broadcast Regulation. In the early days of commercial radio, stations drowned one another out. Unable to work out mutually agreeable transmission rules to help the new medium realize its potential, station owners went to the government for help. Congress obliged by creating the Federal Radio Commission in 1927. The commission's job was to limit the number of stations and their transmitting power to avoid signal overlaps. This the commission did by requiring stations to have a government-issued license that specified technical limitations. Because more stations were broadcasting than could be licensed, the commission issued and denied licenses on the basis of each applicant's potential to operate in the public interest. This criterion led to numerous requirements for broadcasters in radio and later television, to include public issues in their programming.

Congress tried to ensure even-handedness in political content through the **equal time rule.** If a station allows one candidate to advertise, it must allow competing candidates to advertise under the same conditions, including time of day and rates. The equal-time requirement is in the law that established the Federal Radio Commission and also the 1934 law that established its successor, the Federal Communications Commission. The rule has since been expanded to require stations to carry a response from the opposition party immediately after broadcasts that can be construed as political, like the president's State of the Union address.

From 1949 to 1987 the Federal Communications Commission also required stations to air all sides of public issues. The requirement, called the **fairness doctrine,** was abandoned in the belief that a growing number of stations, made possible by improved technology, meant the public could find plenty of diverse views. Also, the FCC figured the public's disdain for unfairness would undermine the ability of lopsided stations to keep an audience. The commission, in effect, acknowledged that the marketplace could be an effective force for fairness—without further need for a government requirement.

Abandonment of the fairness doctrine was part of the general movement to ease government regulation on business. This shift has eased the First Amendment difficulties inherent in the federal regulation of broadcasting. Even so, the FCC remains firmly against imbalanced political broadcasting. In 1975, for example, the commission refused to renew the licenses of stations owned by **Don Burden** after learning that he was using them on behalf of political friends. At KISN in Vancouver, Washington, Burden had instructed the news staff to run only favorable stories on one U.S. Senate candidate and only negative stories on the other. At WIFE in Indianapolis he ordered "frequent, favorable mention" of one U.S. senator. The FCC declared it would not put up with "attempts to use broadcast facilities to subvert the political process." Although the Burden case is almost a quarter-century old, the FCC has sent no signals that it has modified its position on blatant slanting.

Print Regulation.   The U.S. Supreme Court gave legitimacy to government regulation of broadcasting, despite the First Amendment issue, in its 1975 **Tornillo opinion.** Pat Tornillo, a candidate for the Florida legislature, sued the Miami *Herald* for refusing to print his response to an editorial urging voters to vote for his opponent. The issue was whether the FCC's fairness doctrine could apply to the print media—and the Supreme Court said no. As the Court sees it, the First Amendment applies more directly to print than to broadcast media.

This does not mean, however, that the First Amendment always protects print media from government interference. The Union Army shut down dissident newspapers in Chicago and Ohio during the Civil War. Those incidents were never challenged in the courts, but the U.S. Supreme Court has consistently said it could envision circumstances in which government censorship would be justified. Even so, the Court has laid so many prerequisites for government interference that censorship seems an extremely remote possibility.

Internet Regulation.   The internet and all its permutations, including chatrooms and web sites, are almost entirely unregulated in terms of political content. The massive quantities of material, its constant flux and the fact that the internet is an international network make government regulation virtually impossible. Even Congress' attempts to ban internet indecency in 1996 and again in 1999 fell apart under judicial review. The only inhibition on internet political content is through civil suits between individuals on issues like libel and invasion of privacy, not through government restriction—with the exception since 2005 on advertising purchases by candidates, political parties and related organizations.

Tornillo opinion
The U.S. Supreme Court upheld First Amendment protection for the print media even if they are imbalanced and unfair

APPLYING YOUR MEDIA LITERACY

- **What impact has the consolidation of ownership of the various media have on the assumption that the public can find a balance of diverse views on public issues?**
- **What do you see as today's U.S. equivalents of Edmund Burke's four estates?**
- **Is news coverage more catalytic or activist in public decision-making? How so?**

Media Effects on Governance

STUDY PREVIEW Media coverage shapes what we think about as well as how we think about it. This means the media are a powerful linkage between the government and how people view their government. A negative aspect is the trend of the media to pander to transitory public interest in less substantive subjects, like scandals, gaffes and negative events.

Agenda-Setting

A lot of people think the news media are powerful, affecting the course of events in god-like ways. It's true that the media are powerful, but scholars, going back to sociologist Paul Lazarsfeld in the 1940s and even Robert Park in the 1920s, have concluded that it's not in a direct tell-them-how-to-vote-and-they-will kind of way. Media scholars **Maxwell McCombs** and **Don Shaw** cast media effects succinctly when they said the media don't tell people *what to think* but rather *what to think about.* This has come to be called **agenda-setting.**

Civil Rights.   The civil rights of American blacks were horribly ignored for the century following the Civil War. Then came news coverage of a growing reform movement in the 1960s. That coverage, of marches and demonstrations by Martin Luther King Jr. and others, including film footage of the way police treated peaceful black demonstrators, got the larger public thinking about racial injustice. In 1964, Congress passed

Maxwell McCombs, Don Shaw
Scholars whose agenda-setting ideas further displaced powerful effect theory

agenda-setting
The process through which issues bubble up into public attention through mass media selection of what to cover

▲ **Agenda-Setting.** *At a time when the United States was denying military incursions into Pakistan, the mass media carried this photograph of a fragment of a U.S. drone shot down inside the nation's border. The media were setting an agenda that moved public dialogue from whether the Afghan war should be taken across the border to pursue al-Qaeda terrorists to whether the U.S defense and state departments should have lied about it. The root question: In a democracy, when if ever is government justified in lying to its citizens?*

CNN Effect
The ability of television, through emotion-raising video, to elevate distant issues on the domestic public agenda

framing
Selecting aspects of a perceived reality for emphasis in a mass media message, thereby shaping how the audience sees the reality

the Civil Rights Act, which explicitly forbade discrimination in hotels and eateries, government aid and employment practices. Without media coverage, the public agenda would not have included civil rights at a high enough level to have precipitated change as early as 1964.

Watergate. Had the Washington *Post* not doggedly followed up on a break-in at the Democratic Party's national headquarters in 1972, the public would never have learned that people around the Republican president, Richard Nixon, were behind it. The *Post* set the national agenda.

Sex Scandals. Nobody would have spent much time pondering whether President Bill Clinton engaged in sexual indiscretions if David Brock, writing in the *American Spectator* in 1993, had not reported allegations by Paula Jones. Nor would the issue have reached a feverish level of public attention without Matt Drudge's 1997 report about Monica Lewinsky in his online *Drudge Report.* More recently New York Governor Eliot Spitzer found no choice but to resign after the New York *Times* revealed he was a client of the Emperors Club VIP prostitution service.

By and large, news coverage does not call for people to take positions, but on the basis of what they learn from coverage, people do take positions. It's a catalytic effect. The coverage doesn't cause change directly but serves rather as a catalyst.

CNN Effect

Television is especially potent as an agenda-setter. For years, nobody outside Ethiopia cared much about the devastating famine there. Not even after four articles in the New York *Times* was there much response. The Washington *Post* ran three articles, and the Associated Press distributed 228 stories—still hardly any response. The next year, however, disturbing videos aired by BBC captured public attention and triggered a massive relief effort to ease starvation. Although a 2010 study found that much of the relief funds, perhaps 95 percent, ended up diverted to buy weapons for rebels, the fundraising itself was an example of the extraordinary effect of television, more than other media, to move people to action. Scholars looking at the agenda-setting effect of television vis-à-vis other media have focused on CNN, whose extensive coverage lends itself to study. As a result, the power of television to put faraway issues in the minds of domestic audiences has been labeled the **CNN Effect.**

Framing

Related to agenda-setting and the CNN Effect is a process called **framing,** in which media coverage shapes how people see issues. Because the Pentagon has allowed news reporters to accompany combat units in the Iraq and Afghan wars, there has been concern that the war coverage might be decontextualized. Critics foresaw coverage focusing on tactical encounters of the combat units, missing larger, strategic stories. In other words, highly dramatic and photogenic stories from combat units might frame the telling of the war story in terms of the minutiae of the conflict. Too, Pentagon war planners were aware that reporters living with combat units would, not unnaturally, see the story from the soldiers' perspective. The Pentagon, in fact, had carefully studied the 1982 war between Britain and Argentina, in which embedded British journalists were entirely reliant on the military not only for access to the battle zone but even for such basics as food. The resulting camaraderie gave a not unnatural favorable twist to coverage. As it turned out, scholars who analyzed Iraq war coverage concluded that the framing from

■ When Accuracy Isn't Truth

The Sherrod Injustice. *A video posted on a blog suggested that Shirley Sherrod was a racist in her federal leadership role in agriculture. The video excerpts, from a Sherrod speech, were accurate as far as they went but misrepresented her point 180 degrees.*

You might put Shirley Sherrod at a crossroads in 20th century U.S. racial history. In 1965, when Sherrod was 17, her father, a black farmer in Georgia, was shot dead in a dispute over a few cows. An all-white grand jury declined to indict the white farmer suspected in the case. Sherrod recognized it was impossible to seek justice for her father's death but pledged her life to seeking broad social reforms.

After college, Sherrod became an activist for black farmers wishing to reclaim their foreclosed farms. One day in 1986 a white farmer approached Sherrod's Federation of Southern Cooperatives for help, the first white farmer to do so. Sherrod was in a position to win revenge not against her father's killer but against someone else who was white—to get even, to be racist, to be less than fully helpful. Sherrod resisted the temptation and offered the white farmer the guidance he sought to keep his farm.

From time to time Sherrod told her story about overcoming racism, encouraging other black people also to do the right thing. The story was a classic morality tale and figured into Sherrod's rising prominence in agricultural circles. In 2009 she was appointed as a federal director of rural development.

Sherrod's dramatic story of discarding racism was largely unknown to mass audiences until a white blogger, Andrew Breitbart (pronounced BRATE-bart), posted parts of one of her speeches online. Breitbart, who specialized in provoking white fearfulness of black people, had chosen segments of the speech that told of Sherrod having the opportunity to be racist.

Things happened quickly. Breitbart had posted his out-of-context video excerpts about 9 a.m. The video went from his BigGovernment.com blog to YouTube. At 1:43 p.m. the Fox News site Fox Nation posted the misleading video with the headline "Obama Official Discriminates Against White Farmer." At 5:50 p.m., in taping his widely watched Fox talk show, host Bill O'Reilly presented Sherrod as a racist and demanded she resign immediately. All this occurred without anyone verifying the truthfulness of the Breitbrat report.

Meanwhile, top brass at the U.S. Agriculture Department forced Sherrod to resign. Sherrod was told she was being removed quickly to pre-empt Fox from smearing USDA as racist in the next news cycle.

The next day a tape of Sherrod's entire speech became available. Finally other news agencies put together the whole story and refuted the implication of racism. The Secretary of Agriculture rescinded Sherrod's dismissal. President Barrack Obama added his apologies and criticized his staff people for over-reacting to a blogger before establishing the facts. Fox first waffled that it had jumped the gun, shifting blame to the USDA for the injustice done to Sherrod. Eventually Fox apologized.

Breitbart, who strongly opposed the Obama presidency, said he posted the excerpts to counter claims from black groups that the nascent Tea Party, which he supported, was racist. In effect, Breitbart said he was bringing balance to the dialogue. Balance, Breitbart was saying, was more important than the accuracy of details.

POINT COUNTER POINT

Although literally accurate, Breitbart's excerpts were misleading and irresponsible. Sherrod's life was disrupted, her career jeopardized. The focus of Agriculture Secretary Tom Vilsack and President Barack Obama were distracted from other matters until the dust settled.

DEEPENING YOUR MEDIA LITERACY

EXPLORE THE ISSUE: What is Breitbrat's record as a political blogger? What qualifies BigGovernment.com or any blog to label itself a news and analysis source?

DIG DEEPER: Are Breitbrat's journalistic credentials strong enough for news organizations to pick up his material without verifying his truthfulness? Are any news reporter's?

WHAT DO YOU THINK? What restrictions would discourage irresponsible blogging and the explosive spreading of unfounded blog content through other media? What about licensing journalists, just as physicians, lawyers and accountants are licensed, to assure good practice?

MEDIAtomorrow

■ Hazards of Tracking Media Bias

An unresolved mass media issue is how to measure political bias in news reporting. After countless attempts to quantify bias, there is no firm consensus on how to do it. Might scholars just as well give up? No. They should keep trying. A continuing challenge for the years ahead, undoubtedly, will be the ongoing quest for gauges of media bias whose validity will be universally recognized.

At best, measuring bias clinically is perilous. Like ideas and values, bias doesn't lend itself to precise pigeon-holing.

A classic example of the perils was an ambitious project by political scientist Tim Groseclose and economist Jeff Milyo. They devised an elaborate study to rank news organizations on a liberal-to-conservative scale. Their methodology included these steps:

Groseclose and Milyo began by accepting the ideological ranking of members of Congress from a policy advocacy organization, Americans for Democratic Action, as reasonably accurate. For 2010 the ADA gave top liberal scores to 15 senators, all Democrats and one independent. Seventeen senators, all Republicans, received the highest conservative scores.

Political think tanks and advocacy groups then were ranked ideologically by how frequently they were cited in speeches by members of Congress. Cited most by liberals were the Brookings Institution, American Civil Liberties Union and National Association of Colored People. Cited most by conservatives were the Manhattan Institute, American Conservative Union and the Nixon Center.

Twenty-one research assistants then tracked 20 news organizations over 10 years to see the frequency that the think tanks and advocacy groups were cited in news stories. The more that liberal think tanks and advocacy groups appeared in news coverage, the more liberal a news organization was ranked.

Although carefully structured, the study's conclusions were far afield from conventional wisdom. Eighteen of the 20 media organizations scored left of center. The *Wall Street Journal,* scored extremely left, which seemed odd to most media observers because of the *Journal's* historically conservative editorials. Just as odd to conventional wisdom was that the primetime newscast on PBS, often lambasted by the right as leftist, came out politically centrist. Also centrist was the premier dinnertime newscast of Fox News, a network widely seen to have a right-wing perspective. The *Drudge Report,* a website known for a rightist tilt, also was ranked centrist.

How could the study have reached such conclusions? To justify the surprise ranking of the *Wall Street Journal* as liberal, Groseclose and Milyo explained that that they studied only news coverage, not opinion and editorial sections. About the *Drudge Report,* they said Matt Drudge's own lopsided right-wing reporting and commentary was offset by huge quantities of other content.

But the problems ran deeper. As other scholars and critics got into the nuts and bolts of the study, questions arose about assumptions in the methodology. For example, reporters in their quest for balanced reporting cite and quote all kinds of think tanks and advocacy groups. It's not an issue of agreeing or not, as Gloseclose and Milyo had assumed. In fact, the assumption of a reporter-source correlation runs counter to studies that reporters often over-reach for balance. On global warming, for example, many reporters have given scientists with outdated and sometimes even discredited views disproportional attention for arguments that warming isn't occurring or isn't human-driven—all in the name of including all sides.

Something was wrong too in assuming that a correlation exists between members of Congress and the think tanks and advocacy groups they mention in speeches. How can members of Congress debunk an ideologically rival organization without mentioning them?

No one challenges the sophistication of Groseclose and Milyo's work, but there are risks in quantifying anything as qualitative as bias. The variables involve countless judgments and assumptions that are subject to debate. Even so, scholars need to keep working on bias studies and improving them.

Left of Center	Right of Center
Wall Street Journal	ABC Good Morning America
New York *Times*	CNN NewsNight
CBS Evening News	PBS Newshour
Drudge Report	

▲ **Curious Findings.**
The Groseclose-Milyo study lumped media products into political categories that shook conventional wisdom.

What Do You Think?

Consider what criteria you would use to check ideological leanings of a news organization. Then look for whether there is a left or right slant in news coverage. If there is an opinion section, where biases are expected, do you see the bias extending into news coverage?

Is it reasonable for news audiences to expect centrist political coverage?

combat zones was largely, though not wholly, as the Pentagon had intended. The tone was favorable to the military and individual combat units. However, the reports from embedded reporters in the Iraq and Afghan wars were packaged in larger-perspective accounts that also include material from war protesters, mostly in Europe, and the fractured diplomatic front.

Partisan framing is the easiest to spot. Radio talkers like Rush Limbaugh and Glenn Beck are blatant at partisan framing. So are lots of bloggers. But news, though usually cast in a dispassionate tone, is also subject to framing. Framing cannot be avoided. Not everything about an event or issue can be compacted into a 30-second television story item, a 300-word blog or even a 3,000-word magazine article. Reporters must choose what to include and what not to. Whatever a reporter's choices, the result is a framing of how the audience will see the reality.

Media Obsessions

Although critics argue that the media are politically biased, studies don't support this. Reporters perceive themselves as middle-of-the-road politically, and by and large they work to suppress personal biases. Even so, reporters gravitate toward certain kinds of stories to the neglect of others, and this flavors coverage.

Presidential Coverage. News reporters and editors have long recognized that people like stories about people, so any time an issue can be personified, so much the better. In Washington coverage, this has meant focusing on the president as a vehicle for treating issues. A study of the *CBS Evening News* found that 60 percent of the opening stories featured the president. Even in non-election years, the media have a near-myopic fix on the White House. This displaces coverage of other important government institutions, like Congress, the courts, and state and local government.

Conflict. Journalists learn two things about conflict early in their careers. First, their audiences like conflict. Second, conflict often illustrates the great issues by which society is defining and redefining its values. Take, for example, capital punishment, abortion or gay marriage. People get excited about these issues because of the fundamental values involved.

Part of journalists' predilection for conflict is that conflict involves change—whether to do something differently. All news involves change, and conflict almost always is a signal to the kind of change that's most worth reporting. Conflict is generally a useful indicator of newsworthiness.

Scandals. Journalists know too that their audiences like scandal stories—a fact that trivializes political coverage. Talking about the coverage of Bill Clinton early in his presidency, political scientists Morris Fiorina and Paul Peterson said: "The public was bombarded with stories about Whitewater, Vince Foster's suicide, $200 haircuts, parties with Sharon Stone, the White House travel office, Hillary Clinton's investments, and numerous other matters that readers will not remember. The reason you do not remember is that, however important these matters were to the individuals involved, they were not important for the overall operation of government. Hence, they have been forgotten."

No matter how transitory their news value, scandal and gaffe stories build an audience, which explains their increased coverage. Robert Lichter and Daniel Amundson, analysts who monitor Washington news coverage, found policy stories outnumbered scandal stories 13 to 1 in 1972 but only 3 to 1 in 1992. During that same period, news media became more savvy at catering to audience interests and less interested in covering issues of significance. This also led to more negative news being covered. Lichter and Amundson found that negative stories from Congress outnumbered positive stories 3 to 1 in 1972 but 9 to 1 in 1992.

Horse Races. In reporting political campaigns, the news media obsess over reporting the polls. Critics say this treating of campaigns as **horse races** results in substantive

horse race
An election campaign treated by reporters like a game—who's ahead, who's falling back, who's coming up the rail

▲ **Presidents and Reporters.** *In populous political entities, the best shot for the people to be heard by political leadership is through mass media. News reporters are surrogates for the public. Reporters seek information that citizens need to know and want to know.*

issues being underplayed. Even when issues are the focus, as when a candidate announces a major policy position, reporters connect the issue to its potential impact in the polls.

Brevity. People who design media packages, such as a newspaper or newscast, have devised presentation formats that favor shorter stories. This trend has been driven in part by broadcasting's severe time constraints. Network anchors have complained for years that they have to condense the world's news into 23 minutes on their evening newscasts. The result: short, often superficial treatments. The short-story format shifted to many newspapers and magazines, beginning with the launch of *USA Today* in 1982. *USA Today* obtained extremely high story counts, covering a great many events by running short stories—many only a half-dozen sentences. The effect on political coverage has been profound.

sound bites
The actual voice of someone in the news, sandwiched into a correspondent's report

The **sound bites** in campaign stories, the actual voice of a candidate in a broadcast news story, dropped from 47 seconds in 1968 to 10 seconds in 1988 and have remained short. Issues that require lengthy explorations, say critics, get passed up. Candidates, eager for airtime, have learned to offer catchy, clever capsules that are likely to be picked up rather than articulate, thoughtful, persuasive statements. The same dynamic is apparent in *USA Today*-style brevity.

Some people defend brevity, saying it's the only way to reach people whose increasingly busy lives don't leave them much time to track politics and government. In one generalization, brevity's defenders note that the short attention span of the MTV generation can't handle much more than 10-second sound bites. Sanford Ungar, the communication dean at American University, applauds the news media for devising writing and reporting styles that boil down complex issues so that they can be readily understood by great masses of people. Ungar makes a distinction between being superficial, which he says would be a disservice, and being concise. Nothing wrong with making a point concisely, he says.

While many news organizations have moved to briefer and trendier government and political coverage, it's unfair to paint too broad a stroke. The New York *Times*, the

Washington *Post* and the Los Angeles *Times* have resisted the trend to scrimp on coverage even while budget pressures have forced staff cuts. Even *USA Today* has begun to carry more lengthy articles on government and politics. The television networks, which have been rapped the most for sound-bite coverage, also offer in-depth treatments outside of newscasts—such as the Sunday-morning programs.

Candidates have also discovered alternatives to their words and views being condensed and packaged. Not uncommon are candidate appearances on the Oprah Winfrey, Jay Leno and David Letterman shows, and even the Daily Show with Jon Stewart.

APPLYING YOUR MEDIA LITERACY

- **What examples of the CNN Effect do you see in your campus news media?**
- **What factors make it unreasonable to expect the media to be comprehensive in reporting news?**
- **How are audiences short-changed by sound bites and other media tools that are used for brevity?**

Government Manipulation

STUDY PREVIEW | Many political leaders are preoccupied with media coverage because they know the power it can have. Over the years they have developed mechanisms to influence coverage to their advantage.

Influencing Coverage

Many political leaders stay up nights figuring out ways to influence media coverage. James Fallows, in his book *Breaking the News,* quoted a Clinton White House official: "When I was there, absolutely nothing was more important than figuring out what the news was going to be.... There is no such thing as a substantive discussion that is not shaped or dominated by how it is going to play in the press."

The game of trying to outsmart the news media is nothing new. Theodore Roosevelt, at the turn of the 20th century, chose Sundays to issue many announcements. Roosevelt recognized that editors producing Monday newspapers usually had a dearth of news because weekends, with government and business shut down, didn't generate much worth telling. Roosevelt's Sunday announcements, therefore, received more prominent play in Monday editions. With typical bullishness, Roosevelt claimed that he had "discovered Mondays." Compared to how sophisticated government leaders have become at manipulating press coverage today, Roosevelt was minor league.

Trial Balloons and Leaks

To check weather conditions, meteorologists send up balloons. To get an advance peek at public reaction, political leaders float **trial balloons.** When Richard Nixon was considering shutting down radio and television stations at night to conserve electricity during the 1973 energy crisis, the idea was floated to the press by a subordinate. The reaction was so swift and so negative that the idea was shelved. Had there not been a negative reaction or if reaction had been positive, the president himself would have unveiled the plan as his own.

Trial balloons are not the only way in which the media can be used. Partisans and dissidents use **leaks** to bring attention to their opponents and people they don't much like. In leaking, someone passes information to reporters on condition that he or she not be identified as the source. While reporters are leery of many leakers, some information is so significant and from such reliable sources that it's hard to pass up.

It's essential that reporters understand how their sources intend information to be used. It is also important for sources to have some control over what they tell

trial balloon
A deliberate leak of a potential policy, usually from a diversionary source, to test public response

leak
A deliberate disclosure of confidential or classified information by someone who wants to advance the public interest, embarrass a bureaucratic rival or supervisor, or disclose incompetence or skullduggery

▲ **Palin Control Tactic.** *Alaska Governor Sarah Palin suffered interview disasters as a 2008 candidate for vice president, frequently displaying shallow acumen on issues, processes and even facts. But her populist message found followers. They booked her for big-buck speeches after the election. Gun-shy of the press from her campaign experience, Palin insisted that event organizers buffer her from reporters. Largely she succeeded in controlling media coverage by limiting it to videotaping her speeches to enthusiastic crowds and stonewalling the journalists.*

reporters. Even so, reporter-source relationships lend themselves to abuse by manipulative government officials. Worse, the structures of these relationships allow officials to throttle what's told to the people. As political scientists Karen O'Connor and Larry Sabato have said: "Public officials know that journalists are pledged to protect the confidentiality of their sources, and therefore the rules can sometimes be used to an official's own benefit." Such manipulation is a regrettable, though unavoidable, part of the news-gathering process.

Stonewalling

When Richard Nixon was under fire for ordering a cover-up of the Watergate break-in, he went months without a news conference. His aides plotted his movements to avoid even informal, shouted questions from reporters. He hunkered down in the White House in a classic example of **stonewalling.** Experts in the branch of public relations called political communications generally advise against stonewalling because people infer guilt or something to hide. Nonetheless, it is one way to deal with difficult media questions.

A variation on stonewalling is the **news blackout.** When U.S. troops invaded Grenada, the Pentagon barred the press. Reporters who hired runabout boats to get to the island were intercepted by a U.S. naval blockade. While heavy-handed, such limitations on media coverage do, for a limited time, give the government the opportunity to report what's happening from its self-serving perspective.

Another variation on stonewalling is to encourage media attention while avoiding accountablity. This became high art with Sarah Palin, who was John McCain's 2008 presidential running mate. After the election, Palin resigned as Alaska's governor "in the best interest of the state" and to allow her "to more effectively advocate for issues of importance" to her... Palin found herself a favorite of the fledgling Tea Party movement and popular as a speaker at right-wing events. She was a crowd-pleaser but often demonstrated quantum gaps in logic and not infrequent historical and civics inaccuracies. At some events, Palin insisted there be no reporters. At others, she insisted that she be shielded from any reporter questions and even audience questions. The no-interview policy reduced the vulnerability that Palin had experienced in sit-down interviews during the 2008 campaign.

APPLYING YOUR MEDIA LITERACY

- How do political leaders use news flow to their advantage? How can this approach backfire?
- What role do reporters play in the dissemination of negative information about their sources' political opponents?
- How have internet-based media affected the government's ability to leak information?
- Look for recent news examples in which reporters have been spurned in requests for interviews or told "no comment." Do your examples qualify as stone-walling?

■ Being of One Mind

Barack Obama has no discomfort invoking Christian scripture in his oratory. But the line in his inaugural address, about it being time to end partisanship and "put away childish things," from the Gospel of Paul, was crafted into the speech by Jon Favreau. Jon who? At age 27, after service as news aide to Massachusetts Senator John Kerry, Favreau had joined the Obama White House staff as chief speech-writer.

Favreau, "Favs" to his friends, got his start writing speeches at age 23. Just after college, he had volunteered for the 2004 John Kerry presidential campaign. For the Democratic National Convention, Favreau was assigned to check the keynote speech written by the little-known Illinois Senator Barack Obama to avoid redundancies with Kerry's acceptance. Favreau helped Obama rewrite an overlapping line.

When Obama began putting together his own presidential bid in 2007, he sat down with Favreau in the Senate cafeteria. Obama had no questions about Fav's resume, impressive though it was—college valedictorian, lots of civic and political activism, the Kerry campaign. Obama wanted to know Favreau's theory of speech-writing. As Favreau recalls his response: "A speech can broaden the circle of people who care about this stuff. How do you say to the average person that's been hurting, 'I hear you, I'm there'?"

As Favreau sees it, the key to good speeches that resonate powerfully through the mass media is not trickery with words but a quality message. Favreau applauded Obama as in tune with mass audiences in his 2004 Democratic keynote speech. "When I saw you at the convention, you basically told a story about your life from beginning to end, and it was a story that is the larger American narrative. People applauded you not because you had an applause line but because you touched something in the party and the country that people had not touched before."

No one challenges that Obama's strengths include his oratory, but even a consummate speech-giver needs help for dozens upon dozens of public statements a week. Not every script is spectacular oratory. But for the president of the United States, every utterance is crucial—even five-minute ceremonial appearances, condolences at a death, opening lines for news conferences, reactions to breaking news.

As Obama's speech-writer, Favreau isn't alone. He has two assistants. Their job, like that of any speechwriter, is not to put words into their boss's mouth but to know the boss so well they can help craft messages with which the president is comfortable and that will settle well with multiple audiences. When Favreau joined the Obama campaign, he wrote down everything the senator said and worked to absorb it—the words, the ideas, the rhythm. Favreau said he has found inspiration in works of Franklin Roosevelt, John and Bobby Kennedy, and Martin Luther King Jr. He consulted with legendary Ronald Reagan speechwriter Peggy Noonan.

Day-to-day Favreau and Obama have a close collaboration, which Favreau has explained this way: "What I do is sit down with him for half an hour. He talks, and I type everything he says. I re-shape it. I write. He writes. I reshape it. That's how we get a finished product."

Pressures can be heavy. Ahead of a major event, Favreau not uncommonly spends 16-hour days poring over Obama policy statements, speeches, news coverage, commentary, and history. It was that kind of backgrounding that inspired Favreau to take an old Obama campaign line, "Yes We Can," and turn it into a catchphrase for the 2008 bid for the presidency. It was how he crafted the Gospel of Paul and "putting away childish things" into the Obama inaugural.

To concentrate, Favreau sometimes bolts the intensity of the White House for the anonymity of a quiet corner in a nearby coffee house with his laptop. Caffeine is a core in his regimen: Red Bulls, double espressos, diet colas. He can't remember ever sleeping more than six hours at night. For crunch projects Favreau is up until 3, then again at 5.

▲ **Jon Favreau.**
At 27, as Barack Obama's speech-writer, Favreau became second only to James Fallows as the youngest presidential speech-writer in U.S. history. Fallows served two years for Jimmy Carter in the 1970s.

What Do You Think?

What characteristics make a successful speechwriter?

Is it disingenuous for a public figure to have a ghost writer?

What career path opportunities can you learn from Jon Favreau?

Political Campaigns

STUDY PREVIEW

Elections are a key point in democratic governance, which explains the scrutiny that news media coverage receives. Also, the partisanship inherent in a campaign helps ensure that media missteps are identified quickly. Some criticism of media is of news, other of advertisements that media are paid to carry.

Campaign Coverage

Critics fault the news media for falling short in covering political campaigns. These are frequent criticisms:

Issues. Reporters don't push hard enough for details on positions or ask tough questions on major issues, and instead accept generalities. They need to bounce one candidate's position off other candidates, creating a forum of intelligent discussion from which voters can make informed choices.

Agenda. Reporters need to assume some role in setting a campaign agenda. When reporters allow candidates to control the agenda of coverage, reporters become mere conduits for self-serving news releases and images from candidates. **Pseudo-events**

pseudo-event
A staged event to attract media attention, usually lacking substance

MEDIAtimeline

GOVERNANCE AND MASS MEDIA MILESTONES

FOURTH ESTATE
Edmund Burke coined term *Fourth Estate* for press (1787)

AGENDA-SETTING
Scholars identified agenda-setting as media role (1920s)

Edmund Burke sees press as watchdog

FEDERAL COMMUNICATIONS COMMISSION
Regulatory agency FCC created to regulate broadcast industry (1935).

PIVOTAL EVENTS

- John Milton argued that government should not hinder free expression (1644)
- United States government began functioning under a constitution with elected representation (1789)
- Civil War (1861–1865)

Pre-1950

GOVERNANCE AND MASS MEDIA MILESTONES

CAMPAIGN COMMERCIALS
First political television ad, for Dwight Eisenhower (1952)

TELEVISION GOVERNANCE
President Kennedy started televised news conferences (1961)

PIVOTAL EVENTS

- Television industry moves into media dominance (1960s)
- Kennedy presidency (1961–1963)
- Vietnam war with on-scene reporting on television (1964–1973)
- Nixon presidency (1969–1974)

Television makes a premium on photogenic public figures like JFK

1950–1969

GOVERNANCE AND MASS MEDIA MILESTONES

WATERGATE
Watergate scandal unseated President Nixon, demonstrating watchdog media function (1974)

SUPREME COURT DECISION
Boston bank won court approval to finance ads against a ballot initiative (1977)

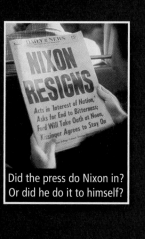
Did the press do Nixon in? Or did he do it to himself?

1970–1979

with candidates, like visits to photogenic flag factories, lack substance. So do staged **photo ops.** Reporters need to guard against letting such easy-to-cover events squeeze out substantive coverage.

Interpretation. Campaigns are drawn out and complicated, and reporters need to keep trying to pull together what's happened for the audience. Day-to-day spot news isn't enough. There also needs to be explanation, interpretation and analysis to help voters see the big picture.

Inside coverage. Reporters need to cover the machinery of the campaigns—who's running things and how. This is especially important with the growing role of campaign consultants. Who are these people? What history do they bring to a campaign? What agenda?

Polling. Poll results are easy to report but tricky and inconsistent because of variations in methodology and even questions. News operations should report on competing polls, not just their own. In tracking polls, asking the same questions over time for consistency is essential.

Depth. With candidates going directly to voters in debates and talk show appearances and on blogs, reporters need to offer something more than what voters can see and hear for themselves. Analysis and depth add a fresh dimension that is not redundant to what the audience already knows.

Instant feedback. Television newsrooms have supplemented their coverage and commentary with instant mobile texting and e-mail feedback from viewers. Select messages are flashed on-screen within minutes. In some programs a reporter is assigned to analyze

photo op
Short for "photo opportunity." A staged event, usually photogenic, used to attract media attention.

GOVERNANCE AND MASS MEDIA MILESTONES

WATCHDOG
Presidential aspirant Gary Hart withdraws after news reporters catch him in dalliance (1988)

NBC's Richard Engel today continues tradition of live reporting on Middle East turmoil

PIVOTAL EVENTS

- CNN founded as 24/7 news channel (1980)
- Reagan presidency (1981–1989)
- First test-tube baby born (1981)
- Mysterious disease AIDS reported (1982)
- George H.W. Bush presidency (1989–1993)

1980–1989

GOVERNANCE AND MASS MEDIA MILESTONES

WAR LIVE
CNN's Peter Arnett, John Holliman and Bernard Shaw report live as Baghdad under aerial attack (1991)

BLOGOSPHERE
Matt Drudge launched *Drudge Report* website (1994)

MORE CABLE NEWS
Rupert Murdoch launched Fox News with conservative political slant; MSNBC launched (1996)

PIVOTAL EVENTS

- Web emerged as a powerful internet tool (1990s)
- Bruce Ableson's Open Diary a model for modern blogging (1998)
- First Iraq war (1991)
- Tiananmen Square massacre (1991)
- News broke of sexual relations between White House intern Monica Lewinsky and President Clinton (1998)

1990–1999

GOVERNANCE AND MASS MEDIA MILESTONES

ATTACK ADS
Political attack ads of new intensity called *swiftboating.* (2004)

ADVERTISING CAMPAIGN SPENDING
Presidential campaigns of Barack Obama and John McCain spend $1 billion-plus (2008)

Victim of free-for-all blogging

TELEVISION CAMPAIGN SPENDING
Total political campaign spending for television tops $3 billion (2008)

MEDIA BLOGS
Potential of blogs as media agenda-setters demonstrated in Shirley Sherrod firing (2010)

PIVOTAL EVENTS

- World Trade Center and other terrorist attacks in United States (2001)
- Afghan war (2001–)
- Iraq war (2003–2011)
- Corporations win court approval for unrestricted political campaign donations (2010)

2000–

incoming messages and identify trends. Informal polling is done using mobile text messaging. While all this makes for "good television," the comments are statistically dubious as indicators of overall public opinion. Too much can be read into them.

Attack Ads

negative ads
Political campaign advertising, usually on television, in which candidates criticize the opponents rather than emphasizing their own platforms

The 2004 presidential campaign spawned **negative ads** in unprecedented quantity. With little regard for facts or truth, Republicans loosely connected to the Bush campaign, under the banner of Swift Boat Veterans for Truth, ripped at the war-hero record of Democratic candidate John Kerry. Then there was the entry in a campaign advertising contest that likened George W. Bush to Hitler, which an anti-Bush group, moveon.org, let sit on its web site for days.

Negativism is not new in politics. An 1884 ditty that makes reference to Grover Cleveland's illegitimate child is still a favorite among folk singers. Negativism took center stage in 1952 when the Republican slogan "Communism, Corruption, Korea" slammed outgoing President Truman's Korea policy. Two hunkered-down soldiers, portrayed by actors, were lamenting a shortage of weapons. Then one soldier was killed, and the other charged courageously into enemy fire. The **attack ad** demonstrated the potency of political advertising in the new medium of television.

attack ads
A subspecies of negative ads, especially savage in criticizing an opponent, many playing loosely with context and facts

527 status
For political support groups that independently create and finance campaign advertising

527 Financing. The 2004 wave of attack ads was mostly from shadowy groups not directly affiliated with candidates or parties. These groups operated under what was called **527 status** in the federal campaign law, status as an American tax-exempt organization. Unlike the parties and candidates, the 527s were allowed to collect unlimited money independently. The 527s had raised an incredible $240 million within a month of Election Day. Although there was widespread disgust at the nastiest 527 ads, experts who tracked polls concluded they had significant influence. When Congress reconvened in 2005, there were cries for reforms to curb the influence of the 527 organizations. Nothing happened. As recently as July 2010 Congress voted on the Disclose Act as an attempt to force transparency on political advertising by outside groups and corporations. It did not pass.

Making Light. Amid the 2004 campaign negativity, Senator Russ Feingold of Wisconsin took a different tack—humor. Just as commercial advertising relies largely on evoking chuckles, Feingold did the same and won re-election. Whether easygoing self-deprecation and deft fun-poking are antidotes that will displace attack ads, or at least reduce their role, may be determined by whether future candidates and their advisers have a good sense of humor and also decency and good taste.

APPLYING YOUR MEDIA LITERACY

- **List common criticisms of political campaign news coverage from most to least offensive as you see it. How do you justify your rankings?**
- **What recent actions have been taken by government to address negative political advertising? How effective have these attempts been?**

Media and Campaign Finance

STUDY PREVIEW | Mass media, especially television and the internet, have become central in U.S. elections that choose the leaders for governance. Laws for broadcasting have attempted to create a level playing field for candidates, but the pressure on candidates to raise money for expensive television ads have created numerous avenues to tilt the field. Special interests, including corporations, labor unions and ideologues, have been willing partners.

Television Buys

Except for candidates for dogcatcher, office-seeking takes big bucks. Barrack Obama and John McCain together spent more than $1 billion, a record, for the presidency in 2008. Most of candidate budgets go to buying television time. For 2012 the totals for presidential campaigns were expected to approach $2 billion if not more.

The momentum that television advertising can give a campaign is undeniable although not without risk. Some advertising backfires. An ill-advised ad tactic, especially in the panicky last days of a campaign, can undermine a candidacy. Even so, the question remains whether an equal playing field can be maintained when some candidates are in a position to vastly outspend their rivals. One solution is Norway's. Political advertising is banned. France has strict limitations.

Broadcast Legal Requirements

Even before television, Congress recognized the potential of broadcasting to affect elections. Two sections of federal law addressed the issue early, creating a framework for the later essentiality of television in political campaigns.

Section 312. Commercial radio and television stations must allow candidates for the presidency and the U.S. Senate and House to buy time to sell themselves to voters. The law, in **Section 312** of Title 47 of U.S. Code, itself is vague, requiring "reasonable access" to "reasonable amounts of time." Because stations' licenses to broadcast would be in jeopardy for non-compliance, stations don't push for firm definitions of "reasonable."

Section 312
Requires broadcasters to carry ads for federal candidates

Section 315. Stations are forbidden from favoring any candidate over another by denying advertising time. **Section 315** specifies that a station that gives access to the airwaves to one candidate must give equal opportunities to competing candidates. The sections 312 and 315 requirements generally mean equal time at equal rates at equivalent times of day. Further,

Section 315
Requires stations to sell equal time to competing candidates

▲ **Meg Whitman.** *After leaving eBay wealthy as the chief executive, she waged the costliest campaign for a governorship in U.S. history. Whitman pledged $100 million of her own money and picked up roughly another $100 million from other sources. Does the cost of campaigning, mostly for television advertising, exclude less well-heeled people from seeking leadership roles in the U.S. democracy?*

stations cannot edit or censor candidate ads. To be clear, stations are not required to give free time to candidates just because a competing candidate has bought time.

Notable is that the law explicitly excludes news. Congress did not want the Federal Communications Commission, the government regulatory agency for broadcasting, to get messed up in First Amendment issues by imposing government rules on news judgment. There is no access or equal opportunity requirement for newscasts, on-the-spot news coverage or news interviews. News documentaries also are excluded so long as the candidate's role is incidental. The law makes a point, however, that stations are expected to operate in the public interest and "to afford reasonable opportunity for the discussion of conflicting views of issues of public importance."

Although political advertising dominates the airwaves during campaign months, it isn't all profitable bliss for stations. Because stations are required to carry ads for federal candidates, the available spots in programming for commercials can fill up, squeezing out regular local advertisers. Station managers know that some local advertisers shift to other media when stations turn them away. Some of these advertisers find unexpected success elsewhere and don't come back to the station after election day or begin dividing their ad budgets among competing media.

Internet Legal Requirements

The Federal Elections Commission floundered at first on regulating political campaigning on the internet but, for most intents and purposes, ended up applying the same rules as for other media. Restrictions on advertising apply to candidates and political parties and to groups that advertise in coordination with candidates or parties. There are, however, no restrictions on online campaign news and comments by internet news services, bloggers or citizens acting on their own.

Campaign Finance

Another factor in the media-political mix are federal and state laws that cap campaign donations. Laws also require that candidates publicly report all but the smallest donors and how much they donate. The disclosures, reported quarterly, give voters valuable information about special interests to which candidates may be indebted.

The pressure on candidates to raise money to buy television time has spawned a wink-wink-nudge-nudge environment with gaping loopholes. Caps are a joke. Corporations with special interests in shaping pubic policy in their interests informally encourage their executives to donate individually, even with spouses, children and others making donations in their own names. A $2,400 cap, in effect, can be doubled, tripled and, who knows, multiplied manifold through something akin to illegal **straw donor** schemes.

The mosaic of methods that have been devised to funnel donations into campaigns include **political action committees.** These committees, PACs for short, number more than 4,000. These came into being when federal law forbade corporations and unions from donating to campaigns directly. PACs can collect from affinity groups, like corporate executives, managers and shareholders, and pass the funds onto to candidates. Unions also create PACs. The largest PAC is the American Federation of State, County and Municipal Employees, a labor union, which has given as much as $9 million in an election year, almost all to Democrats. The telecommunications company AT&T typically gives $3 million, divided between Democrats and Republicans. PACs account for about 30 percent of all Congressional campaign spending.

A less regulated form of PACs are groups with 527 status, which escape Federal Election Commission regulation because they don't donate to candidates. Instead, 527s spend their funds to influence elections. This is legal so long as they don't coordinate their activities with a candidate or a party. These tax-exempt groups, whose name comes from Title 527 in federal tax law, have become vehicles for attack ads. Candidates can distance themselves from sometimes outlandish 527 ads and do so with plausible deniability. These 527s attained unprecedented visibility with the group Swift Boat Veterans for Truth, created in 2004, to question the credibility and patriotism of Democratic presidential candidate John Kerry. The term **swiftboating** came into the vocabulary for

straw donor
A person who uses someone else's money to make a political contribution

political action committee (PAC)
Creations of corporations, labor unions and ideological organizations to collect money to support candidates

swiftboating
Smear campaigns, generally by 527s

smear campaigns. Kerry was slow to respond to the attacks, which analysts feel factored into his loss. A lesson was that attack ads need to be countered quickly and even louder, which means the purchase of more costly television time.

The 527s also exist on the political left. The 527 organization MoveOn became a major player in 2004, spending more than $10 million on television advertising. Later, MoveOn shifted back to PAC status and accepted FEC regulation. This came after Democratic presidential candidate Barrack Obama discouraged free-wheeling 527s in order to coordinate his 2008 campaign.

Corporate Spending

Restrictions on corporate political spending have exceptions. For example, some political organizations have no restrictions. Such it was that Rupert Murdoch's News Corporation gave $1 million in 2010 to the Republican Governors Association. The donation was no-strings-attached, with the governors' association, not News Corporation doling out the money to candidates needing funds. It's a laundering in some respects but unregulated by the Federal Election Commission.

The role of corporate funding in campaigns has widened through court decisions. It was a landmark in 1977 when **First National Bank of Boston** won a battle to support a referendum on the Massachusetts ballot by buying ads. The U.S. Supreme Court affirmed earlier rulings that free speech belongs to corporations, like individuals, and that this includes the right to spend money on ballot initiatives that are in their corporate interests. The opinion raised concern that wealthy corporations could tilt the playing field and overwhelm less well-financed interests on the other side of a ballot issue.

The Supreme Court went a step further in 2010. In deciding the **Citizens United** case, the Court held that corporations can directly buy television time to support and oppose candidates. After the Court decision there were indications that corporations were stepping up their political campaign budgets, some going with direct donations.

Other corporations were sticking with covert political involvement, channeling funds to organizations like the U.S. Chamber of Commerce, which doesn't disclose its donors. The Chamber pledged $75 million for 2010 elections, mostly to pro-business Republican candidates. American Crossroads, created by Republican strategists Karl Rove and Ed Gillespie, pledged $450 million to ads for GOP candidates and against Democrats. Americans for Prosperity, founded by petroleum heir David Koch, a libertarian purist, budgeted $26 million for opponents of federal economic stimulus legislation and against stimulus supporters.

First National Bank of Boston
Litigant in U.S. Supreme Court decision allowing corporations to advertise for and against ballot initiatives *(FNB v. Bellotti,* 1977)

Citizens United
U.S. Supreme Court decision allowing corporations to buy advertising directly for and against political candidates (*Citizens United v. Federal Election Commission*, 2010)

APPLYING YOUR MEDIA LITERACY

- **How would U.S. elections change if the Norwegian model of no political advertising was instituted? Would the nation have better governance?**
- **What would subjecting all mass media to campaign advertising requirements like those for broadcasting do to the U.S. political campaign process?**
- **Explain whether attack ads help voters make better decisions.**

■ Media Role in Governance   (Pages 369–371)

The U.S. democratic system relies on the mass media as an outside check to keep government accountable to the people. The concept has many labels, including the press as a fourth branch of government. The similar label *fourth estate* comes from feudal European times. A more modern variation characterizes the press as a watchdog on government. The concept has given rise to the informally put goal of "keeping them honest." The First Amendment gives an autonomous role to the press, although government regulation exists, particularly of broadcasting, as an anomaly.

■ Media Effects on Governance   (Pages 371–377)

For lack of time and space to report all that might be reported, the media are selective in their coverage. What makes the news ends up on the public's agenda. The rest misses radar screens. This reality has been described in numerous variations, including agenda-setting, the CNN Effect and framing. What it all means is that we are dependent on the intelligence and goodwill of news people to use good judgment in their news choices. News people can be faulted for their focus on easily told aspects of stories, for superficiality, and for missing stories worth telling. Competition among news sources helps correct the worst shortcomings.

■ Government Manipulation   (Pages 377–379)

Political leaders quickly learn techniques to influence if not manipulate news coverage in their favor. Floating ideas, sometimes with plausible deniability as to their source, is one method for peeking at how the media and the public might respond on an issue. It's called the *trial balloon*. Leaks of explosive information to the press, sometimes intended to damage reputations, are another method of bending the news media for ulterior motives.

■ Political Campaigns   (Pages 380–382)

The same factors that lead to formulaic and superficial government news coverage extend also to political campaigns. Issues take a backseat to the latest poll numbers, reducing campaigns to a kind of horse-race caricature. Polls are important, but no less is citizens' thorough attention to candidates' character and positions. Besides news coverage, the mass media carry advertisements paid for by candidates and their supporters and, also, sometimes attack ads from opponents who can get really nasty and are not always accurate or honest. Dealing with the worst negative advertising is an unresolved issue. Everybody talks about it, but not much is being done.

■ Media and Campaign Finance   (Pages 382–385)

Television advertising has proven a potent megaphone for political candidates. It's also costly. The reality is that candidates need larger and larger budgets to buy television time, which has given special interests an opening to donate funds and win the ear of candidates. These donors include corporations, even entire industries, and mega-labor unions and ideologically obsessed organizations. Attempts to regulate campaign financing so there is an even playing field among all candidates, rich and poor, have been wrought with loopholes.

Thinking Critically

1. How might the role of media in governance change if the charging of fees for political advertising were eliminated?

2. What impact has media agenda-setting of public policy had on how news is covered in the United States?

3. How can mass media address governmental attempts to manipulate media content?

4. How can deficiencies in media coverage of political campaigns be corrected?

5. Would restrictions on political campaign advertising on television, even a total ban, enhance the U.S. governance system?

Media Vocabulary

527 status (Page 382)

agenda-setting (Page 371)

attack ads (Page 382)

CNN Effect (Page 372)

equal time rule (Page 370)

fairness doctrine (Page 370)

fourth branch (Page 370)

fourth estate (Page 369)

framing (Page 372)

political action committees (Page 384)

Section 312 (Page 383)

Section 315 (Page 383)

swiftboating (Page 384)

Tornillo opinion (Page 371)

watchdog role (Page 370)

Media Sources

- Kate Kenski, Bruce W. Hardy and Kathleen Hall Jamieson. *The Obama Victory: How Media, Money and Messages Shaped the 2008 Election.* Oxford, 2010. The authors, all scholars, offer a comprehensive empirically-based analysis that is informed also by interviews with Obama and McCain campaign insiders.

- Kate Kaye. *Campaign '08: A Turning Point for Digital Media.* Kate Kaye, 2009. Kaye, a journalist on marketing news, offers a breezy account of the McCain and Obama media strategies.

- Paul S. Ryan. "527s in 2008: The Past, Present and Future of 527 Organizational Political Activity Regulation," *Harvard Journal on Legislation* (Summer 2008), Pages 461–506.

- Costas Panagopoulos, editor. *Politicking Online: The Transformation of Election Campaign Communications.* Rutgers University Press, 2009. Panagopoulos has collected observations from fellow political scientists on new media applications in election campaigns and their effect on democracy.

- Alex S. Jones. *Losing the News: The Future of the News that Feeds Democracy.* Oxford, 2009. Jones, a Pulitzer Prize winning author, argues that entertainment has squeezed the amount of news in the media and is corroding the media's role in democracy.

- Craig Crawford. *Attack the Messenger: How Politicians Turn You Against the Messenger.* Littlefield, 2005. Crawford, a *Congressional Quarterly* columnist, examines White House policies in the Bush administrations to undermine the mainstream news media.

A Thematic Chapter Summary

GOVERNANCE AND MASS MEDIA

To further deepen your media literacy here are ways to look at this chapter from the perspective of themes that recur throughout the book:

MEDIA TECHNOLOGY

Television creates a premium on photogenic public figures like JFK. How would William Howard Taft, elected long before television in 1912, and weighing 312 pounds, fare today?

The role of television and other visual media in politics is undeniable. Could the portly William Howard Taft, who won the presidency in pre-television 1912, be elected president today? Taft carried 321 pounds. In 1960, John Kennedy's calm command of issues won over voters in a televised debate as his opponent, Richard Nixon, sweated in obvious discomfort in the studio lights. Kennedy won. Since the earliest days of the republic, political candidates and leaders have used leading media technology to seek public support. Newspapers were the medium of choice back then. Newspapers were joined by radio in the 1930s, when President Franklin Roosevelt combined the novelty of the emerging medium and a public yearning for leadership to solve the Great Depression. As a political tool, radio came of age during Roosevelt's four terms. In 1960, Senator John Kennedy exuded confidence, some said charisma, on television. He won the presidency.

MEDIA AND ECONOMICS

Candidates for national office and governorships need to spend heavily for television time and market themselves on television on par with toothpaste and cellphone companies. Where's the money come from? More and more, the internet.

A former Vermont governor, Howard Dean, relied on the Internet to raise funds for his 2004 presidential bid and to spread his message. Dean washed out in later primaries. Nonetheless, he wrote the how-to book for other candidates on the potential of the latest mass medium and of blogging. In a 2010 bid to be governor of California, former eBay executive Meg Whitman spent close to $200 million. Estimates pegged the 2012 presidential election at close to $2 billon.

ELITISM AND POPULISM

In pre-libertarian England, Edmund Burke saw the press as powerful as the nobility, clergy and commoners—a fourth estate.

British political philosopher Edmund Burke put a name to the role of the news media in the political life of a democratic society. Burke called the press a *fourth estate*, every much as powerful as the nobility, the clergy and the common people as institutions that influence the course of events. The founders of the United States saw the press as a conduit for information and ideas, back and forth between the people and the elected leadership. In the United States the press came to be called a *fourth branch* of government, in addition to the executive, legislative and judicial branches, but functioning outside the structure of the constituted branches.

MEDIA AND DEMOCRACY

Did the mass media falter in its watchdog function when swiftboating became a political campaign tool? Presidential candidate John Kerry lost after opponents manufactured lies about his Navy record in a swiftboat firefight.

Mass media have essential roles in democracy, including that of watchdog. Theoretically immune to government control under the U.S. Constitution, the media are like an outside auditor to assure that the government is accountable to the people. The media accountability system, however, lacks the precision of audits in the sense of bookkeeping and works unevenly. Working against the accountability system is that political leaders have mastered tools for influencing news coverage to their advantage. Also, the media sometimes falter in their watchdog function.

MEDIA FUTURE

When a U.S. Senate campaign costs $50 million or more, as did Linda McMahon's, are spending caps in order? Presidential candidate John Kerry lost after opponents manufactured lies about his Navy record in a swiftboat firefight. With the Obama presidential campaign budgeted to spend $1 billion in 2012 and Republicans in the same ballpark, most of it for television advertising, campaign spending reform is a bigger issue than ever. The costs have forced candidates into a financial dependency on big donors, many with self-serving public policy agendas. Existing limits on campaign spending donations are so big that deep-pocket donors could drive truckloads of cash through. Major advertising, for example, is funded by shadowy partisan organizations that support some candidates but have no direct ties to the candidates. Solutions? One proposal is to give candidates free time for advertising on television, the most-used medium.

MEDIA AND CULTURE

Do the tricks and techniques that make for celebrity always translate into political leadership?

Lifestyle changes wrought by mass media technology don't settle easily with everyone. In political life, candidates and leaders with squeaky voices and shrill pitches don't come across effectively. Some candidates are simply wary of new media technology. When CNN first attempted to employ live YouTube questions in a presidential debate, one candidate. Mitt Romney, declined to participate. He said he preferred questions from professional journalists and characterized YouTube questions as "disrespectful." Romney bowed to the new technology a few days later and accepted the then-new format of taking voter questions live from YouTube.

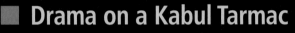

15 MASS MEDIA GLOBALIZATION

■ Drama on a Kabul Tarmac

The leading Afghan media executive Saad Mohseni was flying home from an international business trip when he got word that police had raided his Tolo TV network headquarters. Three Tolo TV staff members had been dragged off, others had been beaten. Mohseni had escaped arrest, but when the police learned that his plane was due to land shortly they went to the Kabul airport. Positioned on the tarmac, the police were armed, ready and poised to make the arrest.

Why the fuss? The Afghanistan attorney general, Abdul Jabar Sabet, a religious traditionalist, had been riled by the Tolo TV network. In short, Sabet didn't like the news. Even more troubling to Sabet were imported soap operas with female actors, some without scarves. What directly precipitated the raid on Tolo's headquarters was the attorney general's rage at the limited television coverage given to a four-hour speech he had delivered to Parliament. Some recall that Sabet was berserk with anger. He summoned the Tolo TV reporter who covered the speech and demanded an apology. The reporter ignored the command. His anger rising, Sabet sent 50 police to the Tolo TV headquarters to arrest Mohseni as the network's

◀ **Kabul Politics.** *Afghan police, here holding a journalist at the site of a suicide attack, are powerful armed tools in political power struggle. An example: The nation's attorney general, a religious traditionalist, was irked at something he saw on Tolo television and sent 50 police to arrest the network's owner, who was flying home from abroad. The nation's vice president, a friend of the media executive, then sent 20 of his bodyguards to the airport. The media executive ended up a tertiary player in the tense drama. In the end, the vice president's contingent of bodyguards prevailed. Everybody went home.*

CHAPTER INSIGHTS

- Philosophical premises explain differences between countries with free and controlled mass media.

- The principle of a free mass media is hard to keep in the crisis of war.

- Online media have created tools for fundamental changes in human governance and commerce.

- Governments can use mass media to reach people in other countries.

- Generalizations about Arab mass media are hazardous.

- Dynamics are in place to move China out of heavy-handed media censorship.

chief executive. The raid, however, did not catch Mohseni who was airborne somewhere between Dubai and Kabul.

From his airplane, Mohseni alerted his friend the Afghan vice president to his plight. The vice president dispatched 20 bodyguards to the airport to protect Mohseni. It was a standoff—the vice president's bodyguards versus the attorney general's police force. Finally the police backed off. The attorney general did too, apparently realizing that his instinctive bullying could backfire. For one thing, the Tolo television network, although an infant enterprise, clearly had a popular following. Also, as attorney general, Sabet was the nation's chief law enforcement officer. It must have dawned on him at some point that raiding the offices of Tolo TV was a violation of Afghanistan's constitutional guarantee against government interference with mass media.

To many high level Afghan leaders, including Sabet, the transition from a feudal warlord tradition to democracy was hard. Even President Hamid Karzai was uneasy about Tolo TV. Mohseni's concept of news was unabashed truth-seeking and truth-telling that included occasional interviews with out-of-favor Taliban leaders. Karzai once lectured Mohseni: "You better fix up your TV station." Mohseni shot back: "When you fix your Cabinet, I will fix my TV station." Mohseni was being pointed about the pressure that Karzai was receiving from Afghan mullahs and religious traditionalists among his advisers. The conversation became horribly awkward. Karzai softened, aware both that Tolo TV was growing in popularity and also, as Mohseni reminded him, that despite Afghan tradition and

indeed recent practice, the current national constitution, dating to 2003, protected media freedom.

Mohseni's Tolo television venture has been waged against incredible odds. Feudal warlords had run the region for centuries. The people, impoverished, never developed much beyond tribal-cohesion-type structures, and the economy fell far short of a modern national economy that could attract advertisers as a financial base for mass media. The only thing that has ever come close to giving Afghanistan an identity was the Islamic faith. Even so, Afghan Islamism was a mish-mash of secular customs layered confusingly with religious doctrine. When single-minded Taliban religious purists took over the country in 1996, the already-scant radio programming was decreed to be only unending calls to prayer amid religious chants.

The United States invaded Afghanistan in 2001 and ousted the Taliban, which fueled a painful modernization. In the mayhem, Saad Mohseni, an expatriate living in Australia, saw an opportunity to return to his native country and make a mark. His vision, formed while living in Australia and Europe, was for a robust and free media that Afghanistan had never had. Mohseni wanted to help draw his feudal homeland into the 21st century. His vision was also to make money.

A decade later Mohseni is on his way, except for the money part, which continues to be a struggle. The harder hurdles, the ones taking courage, have been avoiding prison and worse. Powerful mullahs who had dictated taste, decorum and morality for centuries had a stake in preserving old ways. ■

Mass Media and Nation-States

STUDY PREVIEW

The world's nations and media systems fall into competing, philosophically irreconcilable systems. Authoritarianism places confidence in political and sometimes theocratic leadership for governance. In contrast, libertarianism emphasizes the ability of human beings to reason their own way to right conclusions and therefore believes humans are capable of their own governance. Democracy and a free mass media are in the libertarian tradition.

Authoritarianism

Throughout mass media history, **authoritarian** political systems have been the most common. The powerful monarchies were authoritarian. In 1529, **King Henry VIII** of England outlawed imported publications because many presses were producing materials that bordered on sedition and treason. Also authoritarian were Nazi Germany and Franco's Spain in the 1900s. The Soviet Union had its own twist on authoritarianism. Today, dictatorships

authoritarianism
Top-down governance such as a monarchy or dictatorship

Henry VIII
English king whose censorship epitomized early authoritarianism

and theocracies continue the tradition. A premise of authoritarian systems is that the government is infallible, which places its policies beyond questioning. The media's role in an authoritarian society is subservience to government.

Censorship.   Authoritarian regimes have found numerous ways, both blatant and subtle, to control mass media. Censorship is one. The most thorough censorship requires that manuscripts be read by government agents before being printed or aired. To work, **pre-publication censorship** requires a government agent in every newsroom and everywhere else that mass media messages are produced. Such thorough censorship is hardly practicable, although governments sometimes establish censorship bureaucracies during wartime to protect sensitive military information and to ban information that runs counter to their propaganda. Most authoritarian regimes have opted instead for post-publication action against dissidents. The effect of the execution of a media person who strayed beyond what's acceptable can be chilling to like-minded people.

Authoritarian Effectiveness.   Authoritarian controls can have short-term effectiveness, but truth is hard to suppress for very long. In Franco's Spain, which was allied with Germany in World War II, the news media were mum for years about Nazi atrocities against Jews. Despite the media blackout, the Spanish people were aware of the Holocaust. People do not receive all their information through the mass media. Especially if people have come to distrust the accuracy or thoroughness of an authoritarian medium, they pay special attention to alternative sources. They talk to travelers. They read contraband publications. They listen secretly to trans-border newscasts. They tap into the internet. In recent years, China has created the largest censorship apparatus in history to maintain ideological control, complete with electronic and internet monitoring and intercepts, but the system leaks. It's an open question whether the Chinese will come to recognize the futility of pre-publication censorship, as have earlier authoritarian-minded regimes.

pre-publication censorship
Authorities preview material before dissemination

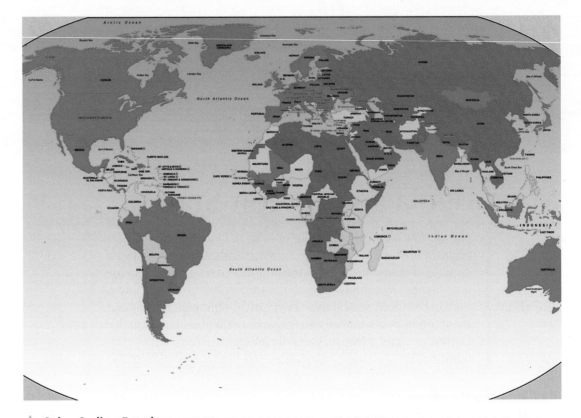

▲ **Color-Coding Freedom.** *Freedom House, which tracks the freedom of the news media worldwide, reports relatively few countries where news and information flow freely within and across their borders. Green shows countries that Freedom House regards as free, yellow as partly free, and purple as not free. The number of free countries has grown over 20 years from 31 percent to 40 percent.*

Global Authoritarianism. Authoritarianism dies hard. The organization Freedom House, which monitors press freedom worldwide, lists 45 nations that deny a broad range of freedoms. The eight worst-rated countries include Cuba and North Korea, both Marxist-Leninist regimes. Turkmenistan and Uzbekistan in central Asia are ruled by dictators with roots in the Soviet period. Until 2011 and the Arab Spring revolutions, Libya was on the list. So was Syria, where, despite the Arab Spring, the dictatorial president was mercilessly resisting a freedom movement. Sudan is under leadership that has elements of both radical Islamism and military juntas. Burma has a tightly controlled military dictatorship. Tibet, although not a country but a region under Chinese jurisdiction, rates among the bottom-most territories.

Authoritarian Premises. Authoritarian media systems make sense to anyone who accepts the premise that the government, whether embodied by a monarch or a dictator, is right in all that it says and does. Such a premise is anathema to most people in democracies today, but merely 400 years ago it was mainstream Western thought. **King James VI** of Scotland, who later became James I of England, made an eloquent argument for the **divine right of kings** in 1598. He claimed that legitimate monarchs were anointed by an the Almighty and thereby were better able to express righteousness and truth than anyone else. By definition, therefore, anybody who differed with the monarch was embracing falsity and probably heresy.

The authoritarian line of reasoning justifies suppression of ideas and information on numerous grounds:

- Truth is a monopoly of the regime. Commoners can come to know truth only through the ruler, who in King James' thinking had an exclusive pipeline to the Almighty. Advocates of authoritarianism hold little confidence in individuals.

- Challenges to government are based on falsity. It could not be otherwise, considering the premise that rulers are infallible.

- Without strong government, the stability necessary for society to function may be disrupted. Because challenges to government tend to undermine stability and because challenges are presumed to be false to begin with, they must be suppressed.

To the authoritarian mind, media people who support the government are purveying truth and should be rewarded. The unfaithful, those who criticize, are spreading falsity and should be banished. It all makes sense if King James I was right about his divine right theory.

▲ **Divine Right.**
King James I, who fancied himself a scholar, wrote a treatise in 1598 that claimed monarchies were legitimate because of a pipeline to God. His theory, called the divine right of kings, is a classic defense for authoritarian political and media systems.

King James I
Articulated the divine-right-of-kings theory

divine right of kings
Proper decisions follow the monarch's will, which is linked to the Almighty

▲ **Authoritarian Execution.** *Authoritarian governments prevent mass media criticism of their policies with numerous methods, including execution. In authoritarian England, the Crown made spectacles of executions. Here, a crowd gathered in 1619 to witness the execution of John de Barneveld, which had a chilling effect on other people who might have challenged the Crown.*

▲ Marketplace of Ideas.

A marital spat and a confrontation with the king led John Milton to write Areopagitica *in 1644. The tract challenged royal authority on intellectual and moral grounds and paved the way for libertarianism. Milton made a case that everyone should be free to express ideas for the consideration of other people, no matter how traitorous, blasphemous, deleterious or just plain silly. It was a strong argument against restrictions on free speech.*

John Milton
Early libertarian thinker

marketplace of ideas
An unbridled forum for free inquiry
and free expression

Enlightenment
A movement emphasizing reason and
individualism

self-righting process
Although people make occasional
errors in truth-seeking, they eventually
discover and correct them

Thomas Paine
Revolutionary War pamphleteer
who defined libertarianism for
common readers

Thomas Jefferson
Among libertarian drafters of
Declaration of Independence

natural rights
Inherent human rights, including
self-determination

First Amendment
The free-expression section of
the U.S. Constitution

Libertarianism

Libertarian thinkers, in contrast to authoritarians, have faith in the ability of individual human beings to come to know great truths by applying reason. This distinction is the fundamental difference between libertarian and authoritarian perspectives.

Marketplace of Ideas. An English writer, **John Milton**, was the pioneer libertarian. In his 1644 pamphlet *Areopagitica*, Milton made a case for free expression based on the idea that individual human beings are capable of discovering truth if given the opportunity. Milton argued for a free and open exchange of information and ideas—a **marketplace of ideas**. Just as people at a farmers' market can pinch and inspect a lot of vegetables until they find the best, so can people find the best ideas if they have a vast array from which to choose. Milton's marketplace is not a place but a concept. It exists whenever people exchange ideas, whether in conversation, letters or the printed word.

Milton was eloquent in his call for free expression. He saw no reason to fear any idea, no matter how subversive, because human beings inevitably will choose the best ideas and values. He put it this way: "Let Truth and Falsehood grapple: whoever knew Truth put to the worse in a free and open encounter." Milton's line is perhaps the greatest insight in the period in intellectual history called the **Enlightenment**. Milton reasoned that people would gain confidence in their ideas and values if they tested them continually against alternative views. It was an argument against censorship. People need to have the fullest possible choices in the marketplace if they are going to go home with the best product, whether vegetables or ideas. Also, bad ideas should be present in the marketplace because, no matter how objectionable, they might contain a grain of truth.

Milton and his libertarian successors acknowledged that people sometimes err in sorting out alternatives, but these mistakes are corrected as people continually reassess their values against competing values in the marketplace. Libertarians see this truth-seeking as a never-ending, life-long human pursuit. Over time, people will shed flawed ideas for better ones. This is called the **self-righting process**.

First Amendment. Libertarianism took strong root in Britain's North American colonies in the 1700s. Pamphleteer **Thomas Paine** stirred people against British authoritarianism and incited them to revolution. The rhetoric of the Enlightenment was clear in the Declaration of Independence, which was drafted by libertarian philosopher **Thomas Jefferson**. His document declares that people have **natural rights** and are capable of deciding their own destiny. No king is needed. There is an emphasis on liberty and individual rights. Libertarianism spread rapidly as colonists rallied against Britain in the Revolutionary War.

Not everyone who favored independence was a firm libertarian. When it came time to write a constitution for the new republic, there was a struggle between libertarian and authoritarian principles. The libertarians had the greater influence, but sitting there prominently were Alexander Hamilton and a coterie of individuals who would have severely restricted the liberties of the common people. The constitution that resulted was a compromise. Throughout the Constitution, an implicit trust of the people vies with an implicit distrust. Even so, the government that emerged was the first to be influenced by libertarian principles, and so began "the great experiment in democracy," as it's been called.

By the time the Constitution was ratified, it had been expanded to include the **First Amendment**, which bars government from interfering in the exchange of ideas. The First Amendment declares that "Congress shall make no law... abridging the freedom of speech, or of the press."

In practice there have been limits on both free speech and free expression since the beginning of the republic. Legal scholars debate where to draw the line when the First Amendment comes into conflict with other civil rights, such as the right to a fair trial. Even so, for 200 years the First Amendment has embodied the ideals of the Enlightenment. The United States clearly is in the libertarian tradition, as are the other Western-style democracies that followed.

Global Libertarianism. On its scale of *Free* and *Not Free*, the Freedom House organization, which tracks freedom globally, says that democracy and freedom are the dominant trends in Western and East-central Europe, in the Americas, and increasingly in the Asia-Pacific region. In the former Soviet Union, Freedom House says the picture remains mixed.

MEDIAtomorrow

■ The Inexorability of Innovation

The low cost of digitized media has accelerated economic development in parts of the world where governments have made forward-thinking policy commitments.

Proactive Public Policy. India is a model. The government has taken a lead in linking remote villages with the rest of the world through wireless technology. Villagers and farmers who once had to walk several miles to pay their power bills now go to a "knowledge center," where desktop computers connect to the internet. Villagers now pay their bills online. "Knowledge centers" are being installed in all 237,000 villages in India large enough to have a governing unit.

The India experience is a model for extending mass media links into isolated poverty-ridden areas in Africa and elsewhere. Farmers can learn market prices for corn to decide when it's best to sell. Faraway doctors can diagnose illnesses through telemedicine and other systems. The Indian government also wants personal laptop computers within everyone's means. The national minister for human resource development, Kapil Sibal, set a target of $35 for a new laptop design. The Linux-based devices include an internet browser, a multimedia player, a PDF reader, and video-conferencing ability. University students were in line to receive the first units in 2011.

▲ **Computers for Everyone.** *India has set a target of $35 for a computer that is within almost everyone's means. The minister for human resource development, Kapil Sibal, says the Linux-based device includes an internet browser, a multimedia player, a PDF reader, and video conferencing ability. University students were in line to receive the first units in 2011.*

Leadership Blogging. Media-savvy government leaders have taken to blogging in efforts at two-way communication with their constituents. Russian President Dmitry Medvedev, for example, started a blog that he proclaimed was a platform for public debate. He maintains the blog himself. Medvedev later opened a Twitter account both in English and Russian for **microblogging.** Not all political leaders, however, assign a priority to the time that blogging and tweeting takes.

Candidates for public office have found blogging and tweeting essential for campaigning. This has been especially true in the United States, where bloggers frequently find mainstream media picking up their online comments and amplifying them to a larger audience. A downside risk, of course, is when off-the-top-of-the-head blog lines and tweets miss the mark and become embarrassing. Few have inspired more guffaws than Alaska political figure Sarah Palin's malapropisms, portmanteaus and naïveté, perhaps most famously her 2010 call for her followers to *refudiate* plans for a mosque a few blocks from the World Trade Center site in New York.

Media Inexorablity. Not all governments are forward-thinking or media-conscious. A persistent lesson from history is that the spread of media innovations can be slowed but not stopped. Authoritarian rulers as disparate as Henry VIII in 16th-century England and Francisco Franco in 20th-century Spain tried censorship and control. In the end they failed. Even so, there remain regimes that miss the potential of media innovations and instead attempt to suppress them.

In China, entrepreneurs were faster than the government in sensing the potential of digitized media in the hands of the people. Entrepreneurs opened internet cafes, where people could rent time on computers and browse the internet. The internet-cafe business peaked in 2009 with 140,000 internet cafes. The Chinese government, censorious by instinct, has since been playing catch-up to gain control. Filtering software helps block out sites the government doesn't trust. Police look over shoulders to check what people are browsing. Censors monitor messages.

What happened next further demonstrates that media innovation is difficult to suppress. Chinese entrepreneurs went underground. People began patronizing so-called black cafes that suddenly were flourishing. How many? Who knows?

What Do You Think?

What history lessons would you impress on leaders in China about online access policies?

If you were a candidate for public office, what campaign role would you choose for an online presence?

What do you think about the China model for protecting minors by barring them from internet cafes?

microblogging
online exchange forum, typically
of sentence fragments

In Africa, free societies and electoral democracies are a minority despite recent progress. The Middle East has experienced gains for freedom, although the region as a whole overwhelmingly consists of countries that Freedom House rates as *Partly Free* or *Not Free*.

APPLYING YOUR MEDIA LITERACY

- **What obstacles do libertarian media systems face?**
- **How does an authoritarian media system support authoritarian political systems?**
- **Are libertarian media and political systems inexorably linked? Are there any exceptions?**

War as a Libertarian Test

STUDY PREVIEW

From the fog of war can come defining clarity on the irreconcilable clash between authoritarianism and libertarianism. The trials of combat, with national survival at issue, can put even the greatest democracies to a test of their libertarian ideals. Expedience can lead to contradictory policies—such as censorship and suppression of dissent.

Combat Reporting

The ordeal of combat is perhaps the greatest test not only of personal courage but also of democratic nations' commitment to their ideals. In crisis situations, with national survival at issue, can a government allow unfettered news coverage? The struggle for an answer is rooted deeply in the American experience.

Civil War. The war between the states was the first war to have a large contingent of reporters accompanying the armies, about 500. After some fumbling with how to deal with the reporters, the secretary of war, **Edwin Stanton**, ordered that stories go to censors to delete sensitive military matters. In general, the system worked from Stanton's perspective. Toward the end of the war General William Sherman marched all the way from Chattanooga, Tennessee, through hostile Georgia to the sea at Savannah, a nine-month campaign, without a hint in the press to tip off the Confederacy.

Edwin Stanton
U.S. secretary of state who organized Civil War censorship of sensitive military news

World War II. In World War II, correspondents wore uniforms with the rank of captain and usually had a driver and a Jeep. The reporters generated lots of field coverage, but the reporting, reflecting the highly patriotic spirit of the times, as evident in the reporters wearing military uniforms, was hardly dispassionate and sometimes propagandist.

Vietnam. Reporters had great freedom in reporting the Vietnam war in the 1960s and 1970s. Almost at will, reporters could link up with South Vietnamese or U.S. units and go on patrols. The result, dubbed **rice-roots reporting**, included lots of negative stories on what was, in fact, an unsuccessful military campaign unpopular among many soldiers and a growing majority at home. For the first time the reporting was filmed for television, with networks pumping gruesome footage into living rooms across the nation on the evening news, deepening opposition to the war.

rice-roots reporting
Uncensored field reporting from the Vietnam war

Commanders didn't like negative reports, which some blamed for losing the public's support for the war. In the end, demoralized, the United States withdrew in defeat—the first war in its history the nation had lost.

Grenada. For the next wars, relatively quick incursions, the Pentagon had new rules. In 1983, when the United States took over the Caribbean nation of Grenada, a naval blockade kept reporters out. Secretly planned, the war surprised the news media. Scrambling to get on top of the story but barred from the action, enterprising reporters hired small boats to run the blockade but were intercepted.

Major newspapers, the networks and news agencies protested loudly at being excluded from covering the Grenada invasion. Acknowledging that the policy had ridden roughshod over the democratic principles on which the United States was founded, with an informed electorate essential for the system to work, the Pentagon agreed to sit down with news media leaders to

▲ **Last U.S. Combat Soldiers.** *When the U.S. Army Stryker vehicles carried the last combat brigade out of Iraq, NBC foreign correspondent Richard Engel was embedded aboard. Combat-embedded journalists face risks to provide coverage, although the overnight Stryker convoy took no fire nor encountered any improvised mines that marked the Iraq war.*

▲ Richard Engel.

devise new ground rules. The result was a **pool system**, in which a corps of reporters would be on call on a rotating basis to be shuttled to combat areas on short notice for the next quick war.

pool system
Reporters chosen on a rotating basis to cover an event to which access is limited

Embedded Reporters

The Iraq war, beginning in 2003, was covered by journalists like no other. The U.S. government, after flip-flopping on rules for war correspondents for 50 years, seemed to recognize the futility of trying to manipulate information in the digital age. Months before the invasion, the Pentagon chief for media relations, **Victoria Clarke**, invited news organizations to send reporters to special combat mini-courses to get up to speed—and also into physical shape—to go to war with combat units. Commanders were told to let the cameras roll whenever the journalists wanted.

Victoria Clarke
Designed policy to embed war reporters in combat units

The embed system was fine-tuned as the war ground on. Even so, the system had problems. A military unit with an embedded reporter needed to assign additional soldiers to address security. If a reporter was wounded, resources had to be diverted from the mission to evacuate the reporter. This became a growing issue in the Iraq war. More than 100 reporters were mortally wounded. Bureau chiefs for U.S. news organizations in Baghdad left it to individual reporters to decide whether to embed with a combat unit.

APPLYING YOUR MEDIA LITERACY

- **How does war-time news reporting challenge the notion that the mass media should be free of government restrictions?**
- **What impact does the embedding of news reporters have on the combat units to which they are assigned?**

Online Global Reform

STUDY PREVIEW | Online global communication has evolved quickly to challenge the most powerful structures that the human species has created. These structures include nation-states and mega-corporations and their traditional mode of operations, including secrecy. With online tools, independent organizations like WikiLeaks are torpedoing government and corporate secrecy as contrary to the public good.

Whither Nation-States

The impact of digital global communication raises questions about whether media-driven obsolescence is settling in on the **nation-state** model around which human existence has been organized for centuries. The internet is not licensed by any government. Putting the internet further beyond government regulation is the reality that almost anyone on the planet is equipped to post their opinions uncensored. The overwhelming flood of information from innumerable sources is baffling the leadership of many traditional nation-states. To be sure, some governments, notably China but also Iraq and Myanmar, have attempted internet censorship through blockages but with limited success.

Nothing better illustrates the potential of the internet to force humans into new governance structures than **WikiLeaks.org**, which, with no single home base, calls itself "multi-jurisdictional." In other words, WikiLeaks is beyond any single government's regulation. The site, created by social activist **Julian Assange**, encourages anyone aware of wrong-headedness, or, worse, wrong-doing, in government to submit internal documents that indict things that are contrary to the public good or that need at least to be part of the public dialogue on major issues. Revealing government secrets is called **principled leaking** by Assange. Among WikiLeaks revelations:

- Before the 2007 national elections in Kenya, WikiLeaks documented $3 billion in government corruption. Assange claims the revelations swung the vote by a significant 10 percent: "This led to enormous changes in the constitution and the establishment of a more open government."

MEDIAtimeline

GLOBAL MASS MEDIA MILESTONES

CENSORSHIP
Henry VIII placed limits on imported publications; licensing followed (1529)

AUTHORITARIANISM JUSTIFIED
James I claimed kings held a divine right to rule (1598)

PIVOTAL EVENTS

- Printing presses throughout Europe (1500–)
- Martin Luther initiates Protestant Reformation (1517)

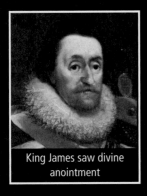

King James saw divine anointment

1500s

GLOBAL MASS MEDIA MILESTONES

AREOPAGITICA
John Milton argued for robust discourse in seeking truth (1644)

PIVOTAL EVENTS

- Age of Science, Age of Reason, Enlightenment

Milton would let Truth and Falsehood grapple

1600s

GLOBAL MASS MEDIA MILESTONES

JOHN PETER ZENGER
A jury of his New York peers found Zenger innocent of seditious libel (1735)

FIRST AMENDMENT
U.S. Constitution barred government control of press (1791)

PIVOTAL EVENTS

- Benjamin Franklin (1705–1790)
- Stamp Tax imposed on colonies (1765)
- Washington presidency (1787–1797)
- Revolutionary War (1776–1781)
- French Revolution (1789–1799)
- Alien and Sedition Acts (1798)

1700s

- WikiLeaks released a graphic video of a U.S. helicopter crew shooting and killing 13 people, including a Reuters news photographer and driver, in a 2007 attack on Baghdad. For three years the U.S. military refused to release the horrific video, which documented mistaken targeting of civilians. But someone with access to the video gave it to WikiLeaks.

- About 109,000 classified documents on the Afghanistan war, all field reports from military units and intelligence sources, fell into WikiLeaks' hands and were released en masse on the internet, followed by 392,000 more documents on the Iraq war few weeks later. The documents confirmed that the Talibani fighting U.S. troops were receiving support from inside supposedly American-friendly Pakistan and that war-profiteering was rampant. There also were other messy war details that the U.S. government had been suppressing or downplaying.

Historically, secrecy has been essential in statecraft among nation-states. Over the centuries, leaked documents have been occasional and serious problems in international relations. These problems, however, were merely nettlesome compared with the new age that WikiLeaks epitomizes. With advanced cryptology and procedures to protect the identity of whistle-blowers, WikiLeaks proved to be an unrelenting thorn in the side of governments. Since its founding in 2006, WikiLeaks has released thousands of secret government documents a year. WikiLeaks has expert analysts who sort through submissions to test their validity. In some cases the experts black out information to protect individuals, like soldiers in the battlefield and the families of spy-agent informants.

The question: Can nation-states as we know them survive the accelerating flow of government secrets online?

GLOBAL MASS MEDIA MILESTONES

CIVIL WAR
U.S. government limited war reporting (1862)

PIVOTAL EVENTS

- Morse invented telegraph (1844)
- U.S. Civil War (1861–1865)
- Lincoln presidency (1861–1965)
- Mathew Brady photographers recorded Civil War (1861–1865)
- Spanish-American War (1898)
- Lincoln presidency (1861–1965)

Pro-war journalistic muscle flexed against Spain

GLOBAL MASS MEDIA MILESTONES

GLOBAL SHORTWAVE
British Broadcasting Corporation created (1927)

Voice of America as a Cold War tool

UNIFORMED JOURNALISTS
U.S. government credentialed reporters (1942)

AIRWAVE PROPAGANDA
U.S. created Voice of America (1942)

SATELLITE BROADCASTING
CNN launched a 24/7 news channel, later went global (1976)

REPORTER POOLS
Government allowed coverage of Panama invasion through reporter pools (1989)

EMBEDS
Reporters embedded with combat units (1993)

AL-JAZEERA
Qatar sheik created Al-Jazeera news channel (1996)

PIVOTAL EVENTS

- World War II (1941–1945)
- Soviet–Western rivalry triggered Cold War (1945)
- Vietnam war (1964–1973)
- Soviet empire imploded (1989)
- Persian Gulf war (1991)

GLOBAL MASS MEDIA MILESTONES

CHINESE CENSORSHIP
China installed filters on incoming internet communication (2001)

PAN-ARAB MEDIA
Dubai launched media enterprise for multinational audiences (2003)

WIKILEAKS
Online site launched to reveal government, corporate secrets (2005)

Julian Assange: Openness gone too far?

PIVOTAL EVENTS

- 9/11 terrorist attacks (2001)
- Afghan war (2001–)
- Iraq war (2003–2011)
- Thousands of classified Afghan war documents leaked online (2010)
- BP oil spill in Gulf of Mexico (2010)

1800s

1900s

2000s

Saaed w/camera
There's one, yeah.
Oh yeah.
Hotel Two-Six; Crazyhorse One-Eight.
Oh, yeah, look at those dead bastards.
Saaed
Yeah, we won't shoot anymore.
Oh yeah, look at that. Right through the windshield!
Ha ha!
Running with child #2

Horrors of War. *When a botched helicopter attack killed innocents in a Baghdad public square, including two news reporters, the U.S. Army refused to release its video. Somebody with access gave the video to WikiLeaks, which posted it online. Once online, materials cannot be censored or recalled, making it extremely difficult for governments to control their messaging to rally support.*

■ WikiLeaks: New Age of Openness?

Worldwide, Julian Assange is driving governments and corporations crazy. Assange, an Australian, has designed unprecedented encryption coding to protect internet messages from being decoded—much like the coding banks and retailers use to prevent criminals from eavesdropping on transactions. Except Assange's coding is better. The coding, coupled with procedures and protocols for gathering and evaluating leaked documents, has enabled Assange's brainchild, the WikiLeaks. org site, to post thousands of secret government and corporate materials online and protect the whistleblowers who leaked the documents.

The most massive WikiLeaks post, in 2010, was 501,000 military field reports and other classified documents on the Afghan and Iraq wars. The White House denounced the disclosure. Spokesperson Robert Gibbs accused WikiLeaks of endangering the lives of U.S. and allied soldiers as well as intelligence sources. Gibbs said that the enemy Taliban would comb through the documents to identify people who are cooperating with American and international forces and go after them. Tellingly, Gibbs acknowledged that the U.S. government was helpless: "We can do nothing but implore the person that has those classified, top secret documents not to post anymore." In London, Assange said that WikiLeaks had an additional 15,000 documents to post but was redacting names and information that could lead to assassinations. WikiLeaks also was following its usual practice of checking document postings, many of them provided anonymously, for authenticity. Assange takes pride that bogus documents have never made it through WikiLeaks screening.

What drives Assange? He believes that powerful institutions, particularly governments and corporations, should operate openly and transparently. Secrecy, he says, provides a cover for fraud and abuse. He sees WikiLeaks as a means for accountability: "The public scrutiny of otherwise unaccountable and secretive institutions forces them to consider the ethical implications of their actions."

As a teenager in Australia, Assange mastered hacking into computers of the giant Canadian telecom company Nortel to test for security flaws, which he found. He was arrested and pleaded guilty to 24 counts of hacking.

His college record is checkered but suggests strong interests in physics, philosophy, neuroscience and human rights. Mostly, though, he is self-taught.

At age 26 Assange helped invent Rubberhose, an online cryptograph program, for human rights activists to protect their data in the field from un-friendly agencies. He built the Rubberhose concept into WikiLeaks.

From Amnesty International, Assange has won a media award for exposing extra-judicial killings in Kenya. He has been honored with an Economist Index on Censorship award. The Sam Adams Award, from a group of retired U.S. Central Intelligence Agency officials, has gone to Assange for integrity and ethics in whistle-blowing.

To be sure, Assange is a crusader. Also, he acknowledges himself a cynic on the behavior of major institutions. He makes his case that large corporations are akin to the worst authoritarian governments with few reins on their power. In corporations, he says:

- The right to vote does not exist for employees, customers and others—except for shareholders who, like landowners of yore, have voting power in proportion to ownership.
- All power issues from a central committee.
- There is no balancing division of power. No Fourth Estate. No juries. Innocence is not presumed.
- Failure to submit to any order may result in instant firing, akin to exile in nation-states.
- Corporate freedom of speech? What freedom of speech?
- Freedom of association? Even romances usually are forbidden without higher approval.
- The economy of corporations is centrally planned. It's top-down, nothing grassroots about it.
- Pervasive surveillance of movement and electronic communication is the corporate norm.
- Corporate society is heavily regulated. Employees, Assange notes, are told when, where and how many times a day they can go to the toilet.
- Internal opposition groups, such as unions, are banned, kept under surveillance or marginalized as much as possible.

Clearly Assange has deep disdain for corporate as well as government secrecy. It's no surprise that he characterizes WikiLeaks as a vehicle for "principled leaking."

WikiLeaks is essential, Assange says. He talks about the world having not only many authoritarian governments in power but also a growing authoritarian tendencies in democracies, not to mention the greater and greater role in global affairs played by corporations that have nil accountability to the people: "The need for openness and transparency is greater than ever." Noting that WikiLeaks has no commercial or national interests, Assange calls his organization "the first intelligence agency of the people."

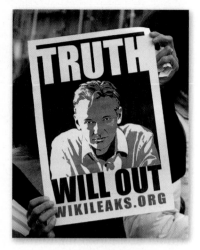

▲ Julian Assange.

In Spain and elsewhere, demonstrators have rallied in support of freedom of speech and against prosecution of WikiLeaks founder Julian Assange. Governments have been so upset that they mounted a financial stranglehold by pressuring banks to refuse to forward donations from WikiLeaks supporters to help fund the operation. Governments have also targeted Assange himself through a variety of legal actions, some as irrelevant to leaks as allegations of sexual misconduct.

What Do You Think?

Why do you think that U. S. federal agents attend when Julian Assange speaks at high-tech and human rights conferences?

What impact, if any, has WikiLeaks' policy of disclosure had on U. S. national security? Has it made governance more difficult?

What alternatives to secrecy do governments of nation-states and corporations have?

Whither Mega-Corporations

The immensity of global corporations has given them an economic might that puts them largely beyond accountability except to their profit-driven ownerships. Corporate recklessness in pursuit of profits, including inattentiveness to human well-being and survival of the planet, surfaces with increasing regularity. As an example, the 2010 Gulf of Mexico oil disaster found British Petroleum was not only ignoring safety standards but government regulators were signing off on the BP compliance reports without checking veracity of the company's claims. The result: A major assault on the environment and a resulting devastation to human livelihoods, including the Gulf fishing and hospitality industries. This is not to mention the BP employees who died on the drill rig that exploded, triggering the massive oil discharge that lasted 100 days. Ironically, the BP disaster was within the regulatory jurisdiction of the United States, the most powerful nation-state. This raises the question of whether mega-corporations are accountable to anyone except themselves.

The power of multinational mega-corporations is worrisome. With revenue of over $200 billion a year, British Petroleum generates more money than the economy of many nations. Without naming BP, Julian Assange of WikiLeaks puts the situation succinctly and bleakly: "Through governmental corruption, political corporation or manipulation of the judicial system, abusive corporations are able to gain control over the defining government—the sole right to deploy coercive force." Weak governments are especially susceptible, he says. But the problem is not limited to small countries with feeble governments. In the aftermath of the BP Gulf of Mexico disaster, it was learned that the U.S. government agency responsible for oil industry regulation was riddled with cronyism and corruption. Major corporations make huge lobbying investments to influence U.S. laws and regulations. BP alone spends $3.6 million a year on Washington lobbying.

Traditional mass media organizations have not done well in exposing corporate excesses. The media lack the resources, including enough reporters to get inside major corporations and track what goes on. The task is even more difficult because of corporate secrecy and coercive demands that knowledgeable employees hold their silence: Talk or be fired—or worse if you buy into corporate plotting and Hollywood-style intrigue.

The internet, however, has opened avenues for well-motivated corporate insiders to blow the whistle. Online sites like WikiLeaks, for example, accept internal corporate documents and have created mechanisms to protect leakers from retribution by cloaking their identity. Assange at WikiLeaks sees a cleansing result: "Public disclosure can lead to reforms."

▲ **Corporate Recklessness.** *The immensity of the clean-up project after the Gulf of Mexico drilling explosion demonstrated the resources of mega-corporations like British Petroleum. These companies operate with a culture of secrecy except when their recklessness is exposed. Online sites like WikiLeaks operate on a premise that disclosing inside documents on corporate policies and practices can force reforms.*

APPLYING YOUR MEDIA LITERACY

- Besides reforming their practices, do governments and corporations have any recourse to deal with online disclosures of their secret documents?
- How can the nation-state model for governance and international relations survive with organizations like WikiLeaks intent on full disclosure?

Trans-Border Soft Diplomacy

STUDY PREVIEW

Mass media are important in statecraft. Governments have beamed radio broadcasts across borders to bypass hostile governments and reach foreign audiences directly. The Radio Free Europe and Radio Liberty projects of the U.S. government date to the Cold War. More recent projects are Radio and Televisión Martí for Cuban audiences and Radio Farda for Arab audiences. The United States also subsidizes in-country media as part of its soft diplomacy in nation-building.

Afghanistan Media-Building

After Afghanistan was invaded and the government overthrown in 2001, billions of U.S. dollars were invested to create a favorable climate for a new governance infrastructure. Millions of these dollars have gone to nurture a fledgling Afghan mass media. The **U.S. Agency for International Development** gave $228,000 to the Mohseni family, which had returned to Afghanistan, to start the country's first privately owned radio station. The Mohseni family put up the additional $300,000 that was necessary. Since then, USAID has further subsidized the Mohseni enterprise, known as the Moby Group. The group has grown to include the Arman radio and Tolo television national networks, media production companies, an ad agency, a magazine and internet cafes. Competing media companies also have come into existence in post-invasion Afghanistan, but Moby dominates.

The U.S. initiatives in Afghanistan became part of a broad foreign policy initiative called **nation building**, which includes foreign aid to nurture essential services for a modern society like police protection, postal delivery, electricity grids and, of course, a mass media. The media aid, called **soft diplomacy**, furthers U.S. foreign policy goals of leaving behind a sustainable society. The aid mostly is quietly administered, which minimizes accusations that the United States is propagandizing. There is no overt U.S. control on content. With Moby, USAID's only on-air visibility for years was sponsorship of one Saturday night program, *On the Road*. A friendly, young reporter traveled the country by Jeep to interview Afghans about their lives and customs, which, in USAID's eyes, contributed to a desperately needed sense of nationhood. At half an hour, USAID's *On the Road* comprised less than one-half of one percent of the 112 hours a week of Moby's Tolo TV network programming.

Under the earlier Taliban government, television had been banned in Afghanistan. Radio was confined to prayer calls and religious music. By 2011 the country had 17 television stations that didn't exist before. One radio network, Salam Watandar, funded party by USAID, was feeding diverse programming to 42 stations. The network manager, Masgood Farivar, told reporter Ken Auletta of the *New Yorker* magazine this about USAID's soft diplomacy: "The media is a huge success story. It has contributed to nation-building and democracy by educating the public. If the Taliban came back to power, they could not ban television."

Trans-Border Propaganda

In contrast to U.S. soft-diplomacy media initiatives in Afghanistan are trans-border direct-to-the-people broadcasts. **Radio Farda**, for example, aims 24-hour broadcasts in the Persian language Farsi at Iran and regions that are hostile to the United States. Farda transmits from facilities in the Czech Republic with full U.S. control over content but with the on-air presence leaving the impression of being independent. Ostensibly the goal is to present information on U.S. positions on issues that are distorted by government-controlled local media in Farsi-speaking regions. Programming also projects American culture sympathetically. Critics call Farda soft-sell propaganda. The U.S. State Department counters that Farda is a balance to what repressed people hear from their own governments.

Radio Farda is patterned on earlier U.S. government-sponsored trans-border media like **Radio Martí**, which has targeted Cuba since 1975. Neither Farda nor Martí are new as weapons in the U.S. propaganda arsenal. During most of the Cold War, the U.S.

U.S. Agency for International Development (USAID)
Government agency that administers non-military foreign aid

nation building
Encouraging governance and infrastructure systems in developing countries

soft diplomacy
Government's low-key initiatives to create a favorable context for foreign relations. Includes direct-to-the-people media messages.

Radio Farda
U.S. government Farsi language service aimed at Iran and Iraq

Radio and Televisión Martí
U.S. propaganda station aimed at Cuba

Central Intelligence Agency secretly funded **Radio Free Europe** and **Radio Liberty**, which beamed signals into Central Europe and Russia under the guise of citizen and expatriate sponsorship. Funding became transparent in 1972 when the U.S. Congress began open appropriations. In spy-speak, Radio Free Europe and Radio Liberty eventually came out of the cold. Radio Farda is part of the RFE/RL operation.

Voice of America

Many countries, the United States included, have global media voices that, unlike Farda, Martí and RFE/RL, produce station programming for distribution in other countries. The **Voice of America**, launched in 1942 as a shortwave service, has evolved into a broad-based source of programming for radio and television stations and cable networks worldwide. The global popularity of American jazz has been attributed to Voice of America. Today VOA broadcasts by satellite and on FM, AM, and shortwave radio frequencies and posts on the internet in both streaming media and downloadable formats.

The VOA mission: To promote a positive image of the United States. News is largely in the fact-oriented and balanced U.S. tradition. This has created occasional problems, as happened when VOA aired parts of an interview with a Taliban leader, terrorist Mullah Omar Mohammad, along with clips from U.S. President George W. Bush. Critics saw the reporting as giving terrorists a platform. VOA defended itself and won praise among journalists for presenting both sides.

Other countries have similar national voices, including BBC World Service, China Radio International, Deutsche Welle, Radio Australia, Radio Canada International, Radio France Internationale, Voice of Indonesia, and Voice of Russia. U.S. stations pick up programming from these nationally sponsored foreign services, all of which also have internet presences and some with television too.

Trans-Border Blockages

With varying intensity, authoritarian regimes try to block information from sources they see as unfavorable. In Iran the militia-like Revolutionary Guard jams radio signals. The British Broadcasting Corporation's Farsi service is a frequent target. The Iranian Administration for Culture and Islamic Guidance controls blogs with robots and human censors and blocking. In addition, the agency hires hundreds of agents to saturate blogs with the government's own message.

The Castro regime in Cuba has jammed Radio Martí, apparently with some effectiveness. Twenty years after Radio and Televisión Martí were founded under President Reagan, a federal study found that that less than 1 percent of Cubans watched or listened. Despite slick production and $500 million in U.S. government support over its first 20 years, Televisión Martí has been dubbed "the world's least watched news station."

During the Cold War, the Soviet Union and its bloc jammed incoming radio and television signals. Even so, Radio Free Europe and Radio Liberty claimed significant audiences. Today many repressed countries have developed their own media systems that vie for ears and eyes with trans-border propaganda. Some countries, most notably China with its so-called **Golden Shield firewall**, have tackled incoming internet communications with sophisticated interception technology. The Chinese, in fact, have attempted pre-publication censorship on an unprecedented scale.

Chinese censorship is partly automated. Internet postings are machine-scanned for words and terms like *human rights*, *Taiwan independence* and *Falun Gong* (a forbidden religious movement) and, postings including such phrases are dropped from further routing. The system also catches other terms that signal forbidden subjects, like *oral sex* and *pornography.*

No one outside the government has numbers on the extent of human involvement in censorship, but there appears to be significant human monitoring at work. Western organizations, including Reporters Without Borders, occasionally test the Chinese system by posting controversial messages, some with terms that machines can easily spot, some with trickier language. Postings with easy-to-catch terms like *Falun Gong* never make it. Postings with harder-to-spot language but nonetheless objectionable content last a bit longer, although seldom more than an hour, which suggests a review by human eyes.

■ Legitimacy of Trans-Border Media Output

▲ **Aerial Messaging.** *Tethered two miles above the Florida Keys, helium-filled blimps have been transmission platforms for Televisión Martí to send messages to Cuba. The messages, say critics, are intent on fomenting an overthrow of the Castro government. Martí also transmits television signals at Cuba from C120 cargo planes over international waters and from orbiting satellites.*

By treaty most nations, including the United States, have agreed to honor each other's sovereignty over broadcasting within their borders. The treaties exclude shortwave broadcasts. Traditional shortwave global operations like BBC World Service and the Voice of America operate within treaty terms.

Then there is Radio and Televisión Martí, established in 1983, which the U.S. government beams at Cuba. Since 1985 Radio Martí has used powerful transmitters on the U.S. mainland to force programming into Cuba, much of it themed in opposition to the island strongman dictator Fidel Castro. The Castro government has protested to the International Telecommunications Union, a unit of the United Nations, which supervises broadcast treaties. Cuba claims that Martí signals interfere with its island stations, not to mention its national sovereignty. In response the United States ignored the complaints and kept on broadcasting.

The intrusion issue became sharper in 1990, when Televisión Martí was launched. Because television signals have relatively short range, Martí floated a transmitter in a blimp 10,000 feet over the Florida Keys and within 100 miles of the Cuba capital of Havana. In addition, U. S. Air Force cargo planes flew low-speed circles with a second transmitter on board. Orbiting satellites also carried a Martí transmitter. It was a patchwork arrangement—blimps were pulled down for maintenance, and during storms the C130 planes flew only a few hours at a time. Also, satellite positions did not make 24/7 broadcasting possible. With its complex efforts for getting Martí television signals to Cuba, it was undeniable that the United States was intentionally intruding on Cuban airwaves, unlike the Radio Martí transmissions which reached countries all around the Caribbean and, it could be argued, although disingenuously, were only incidentally reaching Cuba.

In 2007 the ITU declared the Martí transmissions from aircraft a clear and illegal treaty violation.

POINT **COUNTER POINT**

Delegates to the 2007 World Radio Communication Conference, under the auspices of the ITU, were plain in their resolution: A broadcast station "that functions on board an aircraft and transmits only to the territory of another administration without its agreement cannot be considered in conformity with the radio communications requirements."

Defenders of Martí have their own arguments. These include the policy commitment of the United States, as well as the United Nations, to protecting human rights. A Cuban-born member of the U.S. Congress, Ileana Ros-Lehtinen, is adamant that Martí expand "the flow of uncensored information about the dictatorship's brutality and human rights abuses."

DEEPENING YOUR MEDIA LITERACY

EXPLORE THE ISSUE: How does Radio Martí fit into the history of U.S.-Cuba relations since the 1959 Cuban Revolution led by Fidel Castro?

DIG DEEPER: How does the station determine what issues should interest Cubans? What can you determine about the tenor of the content of Radio Martí's news and commentaries?

WHAT DO YOU THINK? How binding should a nation's treaty obligations be? Consider the argument that Castro's Cuba is a threat to U.S. national security. If Cuba is a threat, does that override treaty obligations, including those governing international broadcasting? What about a role for international broadcasting in the moral imperative to encourage and protect human rights?

Who are these censors? How many are there? The consensus among experts outside the country is that China, whose internet users number 100 million-plus, must be a massive censorship bureaucracy. A rare peek into the system appeared in a 2005 interview in *Nanfang Weekend* with a censor in Siquan, Ma Zhichun, whose background is in journalism. Ma discusses his job as an *internet coordinator* in the municipal External Propaganda Office, where, without identifying himself online as a government agent, he guides discussions in the government's favor. Ma is part of elaborate mechanisms to keep online dialogue on the right track, particularly in chatrooms, but like thousands of other propaganda officers throughout the country, Ma is in a position to spot banned postings and report them.

APPLYING YOUR MEDIA LITERACY

- What characterizes the different broadcast and internet services funded by the U.S. government for audiences in other countries?
- Which types of services are most effective in the short term? In the long term? Least effective?
- Which types of services are most worthy of government funding?

Arab Media Systems

STUDY PREVIEW | Media in Islamic regions do not fit a single mold. These media operate in diverse political systems, some driven by theologies that themselves are inconsistent. Others are pragmatically oriented to create pan-Arabic mass audiences. Among the most successful is Al-Jazeera.

▲ **Control Room.** *The Al-Jazeera control room in Qatar is staffed by a mix of former British Broadcasting Corporation employees and Arabian journalists. Al-Jazeera's reporting during the U.S.-led war on Iraq displeased President Bush, who, according to British press reports, suggested to British Prime Minister Tony Blair in 2004 that the network's headquarters be bombed.*

Diverse Media Structures

Media systems of the nations comprising Islam-dominated regions are as diverse as the nations themselves. These nations span from northern Africa to southeast Asia. Many resemble classic authoritarian systems, some being among the planet's last theocracies with clerics dominating public policy. Variations, however, are significant. Islamic dogma ranges widely among sects vying for dominance. The civil war into which Iraq fell during the U.S. occupation, for example, was a clash of different traditions and strains of Islam going back centuries. In contrast, in the sheikdom of Dubai, whose governance resembles a monarchy, economic growth has trumped divisive issues with overt pan-Arabic attempts to accommodate diverse traditions.

Media systems in some Arabic areas reflect values from periods of overbearing European dominance, mixed with resurgent indigenous traditions and values. Some of this Western influence continued long after this dominance had ended. In the 1990s, for example, the British Broadcasting Corporation, with a history of international broadcasting in the region, spent two years setting up an Arab-language service. Obstacles led BBC to abandon the project in 1996. But, seeing a vacuum, the government of the tiny Gulf state of Qatar, already committed to creating itself as a regional media center, created a 24/7 television news service, modeled on U.S.-based CNN. Sheikh **Hammad bin Khalifa** put up the money. Thus, **Al-Jazeera** was born, which today has been ranked the world's 19th best-known brand.

Al-Jazeera

Al-Jazeera picked up its journalistic tradition largely by hiring Brits who had been with the abandoned BBC project. For the Middle East, the approach was fresh—home-grown live coverage of breaking news told dispassionately and as thoroughly as possible, no holds barred. Viewers glommed to the channel. Call-in shows were uncensored. Arabs suddenly had an avenue to unload on their governments, many of them despotic and unevenly responsive to public needs.

Al-Jazeera was applauded in the West as a voice for democracy and reform. But things changed after Arab terrorists killed thousands of people in New York City and Washington in 2001. As the United States responded by moving toward war in Iraq, the Arab perspective inherent in Al-Jazeera included independent reporting that sometimes was at odds with U.S. portrayals. Commentary was from all sides, including insurgents to whom the U.S. government wanted to deny a voice. According to news reports, in a 2004 meeting with the British prime minister, U.S. President George W. Bush stepped out of the U.S. libertarian tradition in an unguarded moment and suggested bombing Al-Jazeera's headquarters in Qatar. For whatever reason, it never happened.

Meanwhile, Al-Jazeera's reporting continued in the BBC tradition, seeking multiple perspectives to get at the facts and truth. The reporting carried a high price to intolerant factions that claimed their own monopolies on truth. Twice Al-Jazeera bureaus were bombed, including a 2001 U.S. aerial attack on the Al-Jazeera bureau in Baghdad. Several Arab governments banned Al-Jazeera, although with little effect. The audience, already 50 million in 2000, has continued to grow.

So has Al-Jazeera's influence. In 2003 the network entered a news-sharing agreement with BBC. CNN began carrying Al-Jazeera video feeds. Also, Al-Jazeera launched an English-language network in 2006 to extend its global reach. In 2010 mobile web services and Al-Jazeera English on Facebook were launched. The English language anchors have familiar faces, some formerly with CNN, Sky News and BBC.

Media as Terrorism Tool

Islamic radicals including the terrorist group Al-Qaeda have adapted low-cost digital media to their needs. During the U.S. presence in Iraq, insurgents learned to plan multicamera, high-resolution video shots of large-scale attacks on U.S. forces. The videos were quickly edited into hyped narratives and spliced with stock clips of snipers felling U.S. soldiers, all with backgrounds of religious music or martial chants. The videos were meant to inspire triumphal passions. The videos, sold in Baghdad markets, were fundraisers for the cause. More potently, they made the rounds on video cell phone incredibly quickly. Within minutes after an attack, video was in virtually unlimited circulation on handheld devices.

The adroit use of technology—all it takes is a laptop—figures into internecine tensions. A ghoulish sectarian video of a Sunni militiaman sawing off the head of a Shiite prisoner with a five-inch knife stirred Sunni emotion. The Shiites, of course, have no monopoly on the new tools of the information and propaganda war. When secretly shot video of the hanging of Iraqi leader Saddam Hussein, close up, his neck cracked in the noose, leaked onto the internet, incensed Shiites rioted in Anbar province.

New media can give underdogs an identity against forces that are superior by traditional measures. In Fallujah, an insurgent stronghold northwest of Baghdad, the United States created a multimillion-dollar campaign with traditional public relations and **propaganda** tools to win over the people. The other side, however, carried the day. To honor the U.S.-deposed dictator Saddam Hussein, the people renamed a major thoroughfare the Street of the Martyr Saddam Hussein.

Dubai Media Incorporated

As a nation, Dubai might seem a mere speck of sand on the Persian Gulf—674,000 people, only 265,700 in its main city. From under the sand, though, has come oil that has brought spectacular wealth to the tiny emirate. But what will happen when the wells run dry? Resources extractable from the earth inevitably run out.

The government has set a deliberate course to create a post-oil financial infrastructure. The plan includes lavish hotels to transform Dubai into a tourism magnet. Beaches line the Gulf for miles, easily only a day's flight from major population centers in Europe, south Asia and, of course, the rest of the Arab world.

And so much sunshine. Could Dubai also become the Arabian Hollywood? It was California sunshine, after all, that drew the infant U.S. filmmaking industry from the East Coast to Hollywood early in the 1900s. The more sunshine, the more days for outdoor shooting. With moviemaking could come a host of related media industries—particularly television.

Hammad bin Khalifa
Founder of Al-Jazeera television news network

Al-Jazeera
Qatar-based satellite news channel for Arab audiences; now global

propaganda
Widespread promotion of particular ideas, doctrines usually loose with truth or designed to promote a distinctly partisan or sectarian view

The brainstorming that began with a tourist-oriented Dubailand complex mushroomed. In 2003 the government converted its Ministry of Information into **Dubai Media Incorporated** to run the nation's television system. DMI is a quasi-government agency but is set up to operate like a private company. Ninety-seven billion dollars, much of it borrowed, which created a fiscal crisis in 2009, has gone into construction. More than 1,000 television and film companies have taken up residence, availing themselves of the sunshine and also the government's tax-free incentives.

Dubai Media Incorporated, with audience goals far beyond the emirate's borders, operates four television channels. These include an Arab-language general entertainment channel. The channel became the most-watched pan-Arabian satellite station, second only to the older Saudi-owned, London-based MBC. The Dubai Sports Channel, the only 24-hour Arab sports channel, has exclusive rights to the World Cup of horse racing. Arab soccer also is exclusive. An English-language service carries mostly movies and imported programs. In addition, a local channel aims at audiences within the United Arab Emirates, of which Dubai is part.

In the culturally and religiously fractured Arab region, Dubai TV and its competitors are on a tightrope in choosing content. Hussein Ali Lootah, chief executive, sees Dubai TV's greatest achievement in introducing Gulf-oriented programming that has not alienated Arabs on the Mediterranean. Creativity is within the bounds of local sensitivities, he says. For news, Dubai TV avoids hard-hitting journalism like Al-Jazeera's by having a deliberately friendly, informal approach. On magazine and talk shows there is more analysis, less polemics.

On the English-language One TV, programs and movies are chosen because they are "relevant and sensitive to our culture," says manager Naila Al-awadhi. Shows are subtitled and promoted in Arabic.

Dubai TV claims 50 percent market penetration, which means a reach of 100 million Arabs across the region. Dubai TV's pre-2004 predecessor earned less than $4 million. Two years later the gross reached $40 million. DMI claims English-language One TV can reach 70 million Arab households.

APPLYING YOUR MEDIA LITERACY

- **How warranted is criticism of Al-Jazeera for picking up propagandist tapes from master terrorists like Osama bin Laden?**
- **What obstacles do pan-Arab media companies have in maximizing their audiences to build advertising revenue streams and stay in business? Do these companies have a future?**

China Media

STUDY PREVIEW | The struggle between freedom and tyranny plays and replays itself out with the mass media offering case studies on broader issues. Among major nations, China has suppressed challenges to government authority with the most labor-intensive censorship initiative in history.

Chinese Policy

Chinese authorities were less than amused at the free-wheeling satire of someone on the internet going by the name Stainless Steel Mouse. The Mouse was tapping out stinging quips about ideological hypocrisy among the country's communist leaders. When government agents tracked the commentaries to **Liu Di**, a psychology major at a Beijing university, they jailed her for a year without charges. Finally, figuring the publicity about the arrest would be enough to chill other freethinkers into silence, the authorities let Liu Di go—on the condition that she not return to her old ways.

The government's rationale has been articulated at the highest levels. In a speech, translated to English by the official Chinese government news agency Xinhua, former President Jiang Zemin put the necessity of absolute government control this way: "We must be vigilant against infiltration, subversive activities, and separatist activities of international and domestic hostile forces. Only by sticking to and perfecting China's socialist political system can we achieve the country's unification, national unity, social stability, and economic development. The Western mode of political systems must never be copied."

Chinese Censorship

The rise of a market economy in China has loosened the financial dependence of newspapers on the ruling Communist Party. Competing for readers in this emerging marketplace, the predictable and dull propagandist thrust of many newspapers has begun to dim. More reporting is appearing, for example, on disasters and other previously off-limits spot news. Suppression is no longer so easily done, now that a journalistic dragon is stirring.

In entertainment, the government discourages what it sees as a creeping intrusion of Western values. In a clampdown on racy radio gab and, lo and behold, orange-tinted hair on television, the State Administration for Radio, Film and Television issued an edict: Enough. To television hosts, the order was no vulgarity. That includes "overall appearance." Specifically forbidden: "multicolor dyed hair" and "overly revealing clothing." There also are new bans on things sexual. Violence, murder and horrors are out until 11 p.m. So too are "fights, spitting, littering and base language."

The restrictions, which are periodically issued as media stray, are consistent with the communist notion that government and media are inseparably linked in moving the society and culture to a better future. As the Chinese put it, the media are the *houshe*, the throat and tongue, of the ruling Communist Party.

Chinese nationalism takes unexpected turns. Broadcasters, for example, periodically are instructed to use only Mandarin. Foreign words, including Westernisms like *OK* and *yadda-yadda*, are not allowed. Not allowed either are dialects from separatist Taiwan. Also, a strict cap was put on imported soap operas and martial arts programs for television. Imports can't constitute more than 25 percent of the total of such programs.

The internet has become the largest focus of Chinese censorship. Never before in human history has a government employed censorship on so large a scale. Past authoritarian regimes have relied almost wholly on post-publication sanctions with severe penalties against wayward printers and broadcasters to keep others in line. The Chinese, however, are engaging in pre-publication censorship on an unprecedented scale.

Some government control is subtle. Throughout the country the government has thousands of agents, called internet coordinators. These coordinators guide chatroom discussions in the government's favor but never identify themselves as government propagandists. These agents, of course, are in a position to report people whose postings are not on the right track. Although a lot of Chinese government control of internet postings is invisible, some is overt. Because internet users are required to use a government-issued personal identification number to log on, citizens know they're subject to being monitored. Operators of blog sites, which number 4 million, need to register with the government. Cybercafes, which have been woven into the lifestyles of many Chinese, must be licensed. At cybercafes, cameras look over users' shoulders for what's on-screen. Police spend a lot of time in cafes looking over shoulders too.

APPLYING YOUR MEDIA LITERACY

- **What is a counterargument to the Chinese government's position that unbridled journalism can disrupt social and political stability?**
- **As a traveler in China, how would China's policies impact the way you would engage in internet communication?**

▲ **"You Write, We Jail."**
Government agents arrested college student Liu Di for her internet essays, some of which mocked the government. Agents jailed her in a cell with a convicted murderer. After a year she was released subject to "permanent surveillance." She was told never to speak to foreign journalists.

Emergency Response Law
Chinese limits on news reporting of disasters, ostensibly to ensure social stability

embeds
News reporters who are with military units on missions

prior censorship
Government review of content before dissemination

firewall
A block on unauthorized access to a computer system while permitting outward communication

Next Carrying Network (CN2)
Fast Chinese internet protocols built on new technical standards; incompatible with other protocols

■ Mass Media and Nation-States   (Pages 391–396)

The world's nations and media systems can be measured on a scale of media freedom. At one extreme are nations in a libertarian tradition, which accords high levels of autonomy and independence to the mass media. Libertarianism emphasizes the ability of human beings to reason their own way to right conclusions and therefore believes humans are capable of their own governance. Democracy and a free mass media are in the libertarian tradition. At the other extreme are authoritarian nations with top-down leadership in control, sometimes overtly and onerously, sometimes less so. Libertarianism and authoritarianism are philosophically irreconcilable systems, a fact that explains many divisions in the world.

■ War as a Libertarian Test   (Pages 396–397)

For all of its attractions for Americans, whose traditions are libertarian, the concept has had a rough history. U.S. leadership hasn't always been responsive to the idea of grassroots governance nor to the ideal of a free press as embodied in the nation's Constitution. In times of war, even little wars like Grenada, leadership consistently has declared that national survival trumps free expression and a free press. The trials of combat put even the greatest democracies to the test of libertarian ideals. Contradictory policies result, including censorship and suppression of dissent.

■ Online Global Reform   (Pages 397–402)

The secrecy that has been a core tool in statecraft and corporate policy is under new assault by online activists. Mechanisms have been devised by WikiLeaks.org, among other sites, to acquire classified and secret documents and post them. The goal of the activists is to force openness, transparency and accountability. Neither governments nor corporations have found ways to counter the leaks, in part because the internet is global and also because the sites have mechanisms to assure the anonymity of whistleblowers. The question is whether nation-states or mega-corporations can keep doing business as usual.

■ Trans-Border Soft Diplomacy   (Pages 403–406)

As part of its nation-building programs in developing countries, the United States finances start-up mass media. The greatest spending is in countries deemed critical to U.S. interests, like Afghanistan. The goal of nation-building is a self-sustaining national infrastructure, which, of course, includes functional broadcasting and web systems. Historically the United States and other nations too have been heavy-handed in international broadcasting. Trans-border programming beamed into hostile countries was designed to turn people against their governments. This was a Cold War tactic from the 1940s through the implosion of the Soviet Union in the 1990s.

◼ Arab Media Systems (Pages 406–408)

Although most nations in Islam-dominated regions are authoritarian, they also are diverse. Some are theocracies for all practical purposes, even when internal Islamic sects are hardly of one mind. Some of these countries, however, have moved beyond religion and pragmatically sought to be part of the modern world. Examples include the Qatar-based Al-Jazeera news network that seeks pan-Arabic, even global mass audiences. Media production centers, notably in Lebanon and Dubai but also elsewhere, are cultivating trans-border and trans-cultural Arab and Islamic audiences.

◼ China Media (Pages 408–409)

China's emergence as a global economic power hinges in part on its ability to tightly control mass media. Government policy is to let nothing interfere with the stability necessary for the nation's economic engine to remain in high gear. The government has created the largest pre-publication censorship apparatus in human history, called the Chinese Firewall, to monitor and censor incoming communication. Within the country, both entertainment and news media are kept in check—although signs of loosening appear from time to time.

◼ Thinking Critically

1. How can the necessities of national survival during wartime be meshed with the democratic commitment to free expression and an unbridled mass media?

2. What are the risks and benefits of whistleblowers having anonymous access to online media, and how might the disclosure of internal information from major governmental and commercial structures impact their ability to function?

3. Explain the potential benefits soft diplomacy with subsidized media in unfriendly regions has over trans-border propaganda like Radio Liberty and Martí?

4. What media models would you propose for future use in Arab regions and why?

5. Examining the heavy-handed censorship continuing in China, what impact do you see it having on the country's ability to establish itself as a major world power?

CHAPTER WRAP UP

Media Vocabulary

authoritarianism (Page 391)

divine right of kings (Page 393)

embeds (Page 409)

Emergency Response Law (Page 409)

Enlightenment (Page 394)

firewall (Page 409)

First Amendment (Page 394)

Golden Shield Firewall (Page 404)

marketplace of ideas (Page 394)

nation-building (Page 403)

nation-state (Page 398)

natural rights (Page 394)

Next Carrying Network (CN2) (Page 409)

pool system (Page 397)

pre-publication censorship (Page 392)

principled leaking (Page 398)

prior censorship (Page 409)

rice-roots reporting (Page 396)

self-righting process (Page 394)

soft diplomacy (Page 403)

Media Sources

- Scholarly journals that carry articles on foreign media systems and issues include the *International Communication Bulletin.*

- Tal Samuel-Azran. *Al-Jazeera and U.S. War Coverage.* Peter Lang, 2010. Samuel-Azran, an Israeli journalist and scholar, argues that U.S. government efforts to discredit and marginalize Al-Jazeera have undercut cross-cultural debate and understanding.

- Stephen Cushion and Justin Lewis, editors. *The Rise of 24-Hour News Television: Global Perspectives.* Peter Lang, 2010. Cushion and Lewis, both British scholars, have collected articles and essays on the effect of 24-hour news channels on journalism and democracy.

- Glenn Greenwald. "How Propaganda is Disseminated: WikiLeaks Edition," Salon.com (October 17, 2010). Greenwald, a political columnist, offers a case study on U.S. government officials discrediting contrarian views with anonymous and false but not-immediately verifiable leaks to the news media, knowing the leaks will gain traction and escape being exposed as false until government objectives are achieved.

- Charles Hirschkind. *The Ethical Soundscape: Cassette Sermons and Islamic Counterpublics.* Columbia University Press, 2006. Hirschkind, an anthropologist whose interests bridge media and religion, examines the role of cassette sermons in the daily lives of Muslims in the Middle East.

- William A. Hachten and James F. Scotton. *World News Prism: Challenges of Digital Communication,* 8th edition. Wiley-Blackwell, 2011. The authors, both widely published on global media issues, include updates on traditional and evolving social media in the Middle East.

- Michael S. Sweeney. *Secrets of Victory: The Office of Censorship and the American Press and Radio in World War II.* University of North Carolina Press, 2001. Sweeney, a scholar, examines the U.S. government's World War II censorship program and attempts to explain its success. Sweeney, once a reporter himself, draws on archival sources.

A Thematic Chapter Summary

MASS MEDIA GLOBALIZATION

To further deepen your media literacy here are ways to look at this chapter from the perspective of themes that recur throughout the book:

MEDIA TOMORROW

Julian Asssange saw government and corporate secrecy as Establishment tools that work against the commonweal.

Global online communication makes it harder to keep secrets than ever before. Nation-states are losing a tool of statecraft. Organizations like WikiLeaks use anonymous drop boxes and encryption to encourage whistleblowers to post classified documents online. Internal documents of mega-corporations are vulnerable too. Sites that post documents make a case that they are encouraging openness, transparency and accountability to the public. These leaks, once out, are impossible to censor or call back. As a result, governments and corporations may need to find new ways of doing their work. An alternative is for people to find new ways to organize governance and commerce. What the future needs may be outside-the-box thinking.

MEDIA ECONOMICS

Al-Jazeera. The pan-Arab news channel has become the world's fifth most-recognized brand.

Advertising revenue goes to the media that amass audiences that advertisers covet. This financial incentive has become a factor in burgeoning broadcast services in Islamic-dominated regions. The 24-hour Arab television news service Al-Jazeera, for example, was designed to attract a pan-Arab audience that never existed before. Other Middle East enterprises have the same goal, some aiming for global audiences.

MEDIA AND DEMOCRACY

Under authoritarian Chinese regime, Liu Di paid a price for speaking out: Jail.

The democratic ideal of government enacting the will of the people requires an informed populace. The ideal is from the philosophical school of libertarianism, which holds that people can reach good conclusions through the open exchange of ideas. This principle was articulated by the English poet and novelist John Milton in 1644. Libertarianism became the philosophical basis for the form of democracy pioneered by the United States when it was a new country in the late 1700s.

MEDIA EFFECTS

The greening of the planet by Freedom House, which tracks global press freedom, has been gradual but steady for 20 years. Russia wobbles. Most of Asia and Africa have consistently been in the authoritarian tradition.

Although media effects are difficult to measure, governments, including that of the United States, have invested heavily in directly reaching people in other countries to encourage political reforms if not outright revolt. The United States became heavily involved in trans-border broadcasting during World War II with Voice of America. VOA and similar services continued into the Cold War with programming aimed at the Soviet Union and Eastern Europe. Today variants are targeting people in Cuba, Arab nations and wherever it suits U.S. national policy. Governments of target nations hardly see these projects as benign. Attempts are made to block incoming programs.

ELITISM AND POPULISM

Authoritarian James I and libertarian John Milton.

What a conversation King James and John Milton would have had. The scholarly British king defended monarchical systems as divine and thus beyond criticism. Two generations later, Milton made the case for libertarianism in *Areopagitica*. Authoritarian government systems are elitist. A monarch or a coterie of governing elite are presumed to hold answers that common folks can't recognize without guidance. This monopoly on knowing what's best includes social policies, cultural affairs and other matters, including media content. In contrast, libertarianism has confidence in individual human beings. Given enough time to sort through even the most complex issues, according to libertarians, people individually and collectively will reach correct conclusions. To work well, libertarianism requires that mass media be an uncensored forum for people to gather information and exchange ideas.

CHAPTER 16 MEDIA LAW

■ Shaking Up Hollywood

By age 12, Jon Lech Johansen had written his first computer program. That made him a wunderkind of sorts. But nobody foresaw that he would, while still a teenager, devise programs that would shake the billion-dollar Hollywood movie industry to its core. His genius also would make him a folk hero to millions of movie-lovers worldwide.

Jon-Lech, as he came to be lionized in his native Norway, began his trek to notoriety unwittingly. He loved movies. By 15 he owned 360 DVDs. Some he bought at jacked-up Norwegian prices because Hollywood's geographical coding prevented European computers from playing U.S.-issued versions. Other DVDs he bought from U.S. sources, and with coding he invented, he played them on his computer. It all was perfectly legal in Norway. He recalls reveling at

◄ **Waiting for the Judge.** *Jon Lech Johansen waits for his case to begin in a Norway court. The U.S. movie industry had gone after DVD-Jon, as he came to be called, for publishing code that enabled others to copy disks. He was acquitted.*

CHAPTER INSIGHTS

- Copyright law protects intellectual property, with a lot of twists wrought by emerging technology.

- The heart of U.S. mass media law is the First Amendment's guarantee of free expression.

- The First Amendment has come to be applied more broadly over the years.

- Anyone falsely slandered by the mass media may sue for libel.

- The courts have addressed indecency as an issue by defining *obscenity* and *pornography* differently.

his accomplishment when he first ripped copies of *The Matrix* and *The Fifth Element*.

"Why shouldn't others share my enjoyment?" he asked himself. A week later, he posted his coding on the internet.

Hollywood went ballistic, recognizing that Jon-Lech's coding could be used to bypass the encrypting that prevented their DVD movies from being easily swapped through file-sharing. The revenue loss could be devastating. The Motion Picture Association of America pushed Norwegian authorities to act. Police raided the Johansen home, confiscated Jon-Lech's computer, and put him through seven hours of interrogation. Confident he had done nothing wrong, Jon-Lech even gave police the password to his computer.

Johansen thus found himself at the vortex of a continuing struggle between the rights of megamedia conglomerates that own creative material and the rights of individuals to do what they want with products they buy—in this case copying DVDs, and also music, to play on any number of their own devices.

For the trial, Hollywood executives flew to Oslo to argue that Johansen had unleashed software that facilitated movie piracy and could leave the movie industry in ruins. Johansen responded that he had committed no wrongdoing, let alone piracy, and that he had a fundamental human right of free expression to share his coding however he wanted. In effect, he said: "Go after the pirates, not me." Jon-Lech fancied himself a consumer advocate, allowing people to use their DVD purchases as they wanted—on computers at home, on laptops on the road, on handheld devices anywhere else. The court agreed. In fact, when the prosecution appealed, the court agreed again.

In the run-up to the trial, Jon-Lech supporters worldwide distributed T-shirts and neckties printed with his software. In the May Day parade in Oslo, backers carried a banner "Free DVD-Jon." Meanwhile, more than 1 million copies of his anti-DVD encryption software had been downloaded from Johansen's site.

For better or worse, depending on your perspective, Norway later revised its laws to forbid software that could be used to undermine copyright protections. The United States had done this earlier at the behest of giant media companies. But the issue lives on, as you will discover in this chapter on mass media law. This includes the most pressing media law dilemma in the early 21st century—the protection of intellectual property. ∎

Intellectual Property

STUDY PREVIEW | Products produced by mass media companies go by the legal name of *intellectual property*. Copyright law protects ownership rights to intellectual property. Other rights, including consumer rights and free expression rights, have arisen to challenge the long-held supremacy of copyright. Mass media companies are worried.

Copyright

Copyright has been around since the beginning of the Republic. The founders wrote copyright law into the Constitution. When Congress first convened in 1790, the second law to be passed was for copyright. The whole idea was to encourage creativity. With creative work classified as property, creative people have a legal right to derive income from their works by charging for their use. An author, for example, can charge a book publisher a fee for publishing the book. Actually, it's a little more complicated, but that's the idea. The goal was to guarantee a financial incentive for creative people to keep creating. Why? The rationale was that a society is richer for literature and music and other creative works. Inventions, which are covered by patents, are a separate area of **intellectual property** law. But the idea is the same.

copyright
Protects the ownership rights of creative works, including books, articles and lyrics

intellectual property
Creative works

Permissions. Copyright law allows creators to control their creation. They can sell it, lease it, give it away or just sit on it. Copyright law is the vehicle through which creative people earn a livelihood, just as someone in the trades, like a carpenter earning money from carpentry or a landlord earning money by renting out real estate. Creators of intellectual property grant **permissions** for the use of their work, usually for a fee. Freelance photographers, as an example, charge magazines that want to use their photographs. Composers charge music publishers that want to issue their music.

permissions
Grant of rights for a second party
to use copyright-protected work

Assignments. As a practical matter, most photographers, composers, authors and other creators of intellectual property don't have the expertise or means to exploit the commercial potential of their work. Simon & Schuster, for example, can better market a hot murder mystery than can its best whodunit author. Imagine Jay-Z without Def Jam. Or a Mark Burnett eco-adventure show without CBS. Although there are notable Lone Rangers, the resources of major media companies make it attractive for the creators of intellectual property to sell or assign their rights to a media company. In exchange for the **assignment** of their rights, the originating creator usually receives a flat fee or a percentage of the eventual revenue.

assignment
Transfer of ownership interest in a
piece of intellectual property

Also, media companies hire creative people whose work, as part of their employment, belongs automatically to the company.

For media companies, these rights are a treasure trove. It's their product. It's what they have to sell. No surprise, media companies vigilantly guard the studio's intellectual property against theft, or **piracy**, as they call it. Hollywood studios each have dozens of attorneys who monitor for **infringements** of their copyrights. So do music companies. Magazines and newspapers are increasingly active in identifying infringements. Not uncommonly, media companies go to court against anyone who expropriates their property without permission and without paying a fee.

piracy
Theft of copyright-protected material

infringement
A violation of copyright

Consumer Rights

Predictably, mass media companies overreact when a threat to their tried-and-true business models presents itself. This has been no more true than in frenzied, almost Luddite attempts by media companies to apply copyright law to shield their old and comfortable ways of doing business. Time and again, media companies, wedded to the past, have failed to think outside the box and exploit new technologies. In fact, not since the glory days of RCA, which prided itself on research and development under David Sarnoff, have the established media companies been on the technological cutting edge.

Recent history has shown media companies merely making tepid applications of technology for modest advantages in efficiency. Then, wham, they find their existence on the verge of being upended by innovators who are seeing new basic infrastructures and saying to hell with old business models. Consider the recorded music industry in the Napster and Grokster cases, and the book industry in the Google case.

Grokster. In the 1990s, the music recording industry, entrenched in its traditional ways of doing business, was in a frenzy with music-swapping software sales eroding profits dramatically. First with Napster, then other peer-to-peer music-sharing services, people were bypassing the retail CD bins. Napster was the first to hit the dust, in a 2001 federal court case. Then came the case against **Grokster**, another peer-to-peer service. Grokster argued that its software was neutral as to the rights and wrongs of copyright law. Yes, said Grokster, there could be misuses but the recording industry's legal target should be the misusers—not Grokster.

Grokster
Involved in U.S. Supreme Court case
that said promoting the illegal copying
of intellectual property is an infringement on copyright

In deciding the case in 2005, the Supreme Court noted that Grokster had explicitly promoted the copyright-infringement potential of its software. It was right there in the company's own advertising. The ads were self-incriminating, the Court said. Grokster was out of business. The lesson is that infringement-enabling devices are all right as long as infringement isn't encouraged.

◀ **Download Confrontation.**
Among young people, emotions run high about music. A widely held view is that access to music should be free. When the U.S. Supreme Court was hearing the Grokster case over software intended to facilitate music downloads without the permission of copyright holders, protesters displayed their disdain for the record industry's initiative to shut down file-sharing.

In any event, the music recording industry was shaken by Napster and look-alike systems like Grokster. The end result, after the legal battles, was that the industry came out of its decades-old buffered ways, which had been shielded by copyright law, and embraced the new technology. Even by the time of the Grokster decision, the German-owned global media giant Bertelsmann had bought the remnants of Napster to find ways to market its music online. Also, Apple's online music store, iTunes, introduced in 2002, was an instant success. Other online music sales outlets cropped up, sponsored by record makers, to capitalize on new technology—not to fight it or continue into denial about the technology-wrought new digital downloading reality.

Google. The book industry, also entrenched in old ways, missed the potential of digital technology. Except for back-shop production efficiencies and minor forays with e-books, publishers had to be dragged kicking and screaming into the 21st century, like the movie and recording industries before them. Google was the reason.

Fueled with untold revenues from its massively successful search engine in the early 2000s, Google expanded rapidly into new ventures. In 2005, Google executives talked five major libraries into allowing it to digitize their entire collections, 15 million books in the English language. The goal, then, was to create a single online index system, the **Google Books Library Project**, with worldwide free access.

Google Books Library Project
Digitizes 15 million English-language books for online index access by Google

Publishers first bristled, then sued. The publishers' claim was that their intellectual property interests would be jeopardized through free online access to copyright-protected works not yet in the public domain.

Google and the Association of American Publishers reached a settlement in 2009. Almost immediately other groups including the Authors Guild as well as industry groups in other countries questioned the settlement and raised objections of their own. These issues may create new parameters on the protections afforded by copyright law. Whatever the outcome, the case further illustrates that mass media companies are less in control of the technology that is reshaping the world than are companies and individuals who specialize in the research and creative thinking that brings about technical revolution.

CHECKING YOUR MEDIA LITERACY

- **How have the consumer rights movement and the copyright community collided?**
- **What lessons about copyright can be derived from the Grokster decision?**
- **What are the copyright issues in the Google library project?**

MEDIAcounterpoints

■ The Price of Free Music

Imagine opening an urgent e-mail from the Recording Industry Association of America accusing you of illegally downloading hundreds of songs onto your computer. Indeed, you have used a file-sharing program you found on the internet to build your music collection. By doing this, the e-mail charges, you have violated federal copyright law. The law, you're reminded, grants rights to an artist, publisher or distributor for exclusive publication, production, sale or distribution of artistic work. The message from the RIAA is threatening: Settle now for several thousand dollars or we'll see you in federal court.

A hoax? Not for several hundred college students who have received these "prelitigation" e-mails. Most students settle, despite feeling that they were unfairly singled out. After all, it's estimated that more than half of all college students illegally download copyrighted music and movies. As one 20-year-old student who recently received the RIAA e-mail explained: "I knew it was illegal, but no one got in trouble for it."

Copyright infringements continue to cost the artistic community billions of dollars. And with less money to reward creativity, artists may be less able to support themselves financially, and the companies that distribute their art will be less willing to invest in the endeavors as a matter of diminishing return. This is a line of reasoning embedded in Article 1, Section 8, of the U.S. Constitution: "The Congress shall have power.... to promote the progress of science and useful arts, by securing for limited times to authors and inventors the exclusive right to their respective writings and discoveries."

A second argument against copyright infringement is that piracy hurts honest people. The piracy forces higher prices for artistic goods, like music, so that creators and rights holders can offset their losses to piracy.

IF YOU CAN'T SEE THAT ILLEGAL DOWNLOADING IS STEALING

THEN KEEP READING

1 2 3 4 5 6 7

If you download music illegally, you are stealing music.

Every month, thousands of students face university disciplinary action or lawsuits and fines that cost thousands of dollars.

Legal downloading doesn't cost much. The choice is yours. Pay a little now or a lot more later.

RIAA

Developed by university students for the RIAA.

▲ **Piracy Not Nice.** *The recording industry, crippled by revenue losses from music file-swapping, has gone after downloaders, mostly college students, for copyright infringement. Legal settlements can run into thousands of dollars.*

Only a chump would pay for something that is available free. If a law is widely ignored it is archaic. It is time for copyright laws to go. Everybody's doing it. Or just about everybody.

POINT

COUNTER POINT

Stealing someone else's work is hard to justify. It's all the worse with the intellectual property because the theft discourages creativity that enriches the culture and the lives of everyone.

DEEPENING YOUR MEDIA LITERACY

EXPLORE THE ISSUE: Think of web sites that allow people to download music or movies legally.

DIG DEEPER: Do you think the lawsuits brought by the recording industry will solve the problem of illegal downloading? Are there alternatives? Would legislation help? How about education programs starting in grade school?

WHAT DO YOU THINK? Individuals who download music may not be the only ones being sued. Media giant Viacom has sued YouTube because its users can illegally upload Viacom movies. Is it just a matter of time before individual YouTube users are also sued for sharing copyrighted media without permission?

Free Expression

STUDY PREVIEW

A core American value is that the government cannot impede free expression, which, of course, extends to mass communication. Although the U.S. Constitution bars government censorship, the courts have allowed exceptions. These exceptions include utterances that could undermine national security in wartime. In general the Supreme Court has expanded the prohibition on censorship over the years.

Distrust of Government

In colonial times as ill feeling grew against British authority, before the formation of the United States, a critical mass of libertarians ascended into leadership roles. These people were still in critical leadership roles when the Revolutionary War ended. These included many luminaries of the time—Thomas Jefferson, Benjamin Franklin, James Madison and John Adams. Their rhetoric excoriated the top-down authoritarian British governance system.

In drafting the Constitution for the new republic, the founders, mindful of their experience as part of the British empire, were firm in their distrust of governmental authority. Also, they exalted the ability of people individually and collectively to figure out their way to the best courses of action through free inquiry and free expression in an unregulated marketplace of ideas. No surprise, the Constitution they put together prohibited government from interfering in free expression. The prohibition is in the Constitution's **First Amendment:** "Congress shall make no law-abridging the freedom of speech or of the press." The amendment, a mere 45 words, also prohibits government from interfering in religion. Also, it guarantees people the right to complain about the government and demand that wrongs be righted. Most relevant for media people are the free speech and free press clauses, which can be summed up as the **free expression provision**.

Implicit in the First Amendment is a role for mass media as a watchdog guarding against government misdeeds and policies. In this respect, in news as well as in other content areas, media are an informal **fourth branch of government**—in addition to the executive, judicial and legislative branches. Media have a role in governance to, in effect, ensure that the government is accountable to the people.

First Amendment
Prohibits government interference in free expression, religion and individual and public protests against government policies

free expression provision
First Amendment ban against government abridgment of freedom of speech and freedom of the press

fourth branch of government
The mass media

First Amendment Rediscovered

As ironic as it seems, merely seven years after the Constitution and the First Amendment were ratified, Congress passed laws to limit free expression. People were jailed and fined for criticizing government leaders and policies. These laws, the **Alien and Sedition Acts** of 1798, ostensibly were for national security at a time of paranoia about a French invasion. One of the great mysteries in U.S. history is how Congress, which included many of the same people who had created the Constitution, could pass the Alien and Sedition acts that so contradicted the anti-censorship provision of the First Amendment.

The fact, however, is that nobody paid much attention to the First Amendment for more than 100 years of the nation's history. The First Amendment was a nice idea but complicated. Nobody wanted to tackle tough questions, such as in the case of the 1798 laws, or whether exceptions to free expression were needed in times of war or a perceived threat of war.

Many states, meanwhile, had laws that explicitly limited freedom of expression. The constitutionality of these laws too went unchallenged.

Not until 1919 did the U.S. Supreme Court decide a case on First Amendment grounds. Two Socialists, husband and wife **Charles Schenck and Elizabeth Baer**, had been arrested by federal agents for distributing an antiwar pamphlet. They sued, contending that the government had violated their free-expression rights as guaranteed by the First Amendment. The Supreme Court turned down their appeal, saying that censorship is reasonable during a war,. But for the first time the justices acknowledged in the case, usually called *Schenck* v. *U.S.*, that Freedom from government restraint is a civil right of every citizen.

Alien and Sedition Acts
1798 laws with penalties for free expression

Charles Schenck, Elizabeth Baer
Principal plaintiffs in 1919 U.S. Supreme Court opinion decided on First Amendment grounds

Numerous other censorship cases also flowed from World War I. In 1925 the Court overruled a New York state law under which antiwar agitator **Benjamin Gitlow** had been arrested. Gitlow lost his case, but importantly, the Court said that state censorship laws in general were unconstitutional.

Prior Restraint

Near v. Minnesota
U.S. Supreme Court case that barred
government interference with free expression in advance

prior restraint
Prohibiting expression in advance

On a roll with the First Amendment, the Supreme Court in 1931 barred the government in most situations from silencing someone before an utterance. In **Near v. Minnesota**, the Court banned **prior restraint.** The case began after a sheriff padlocked the Minneapolis scandal sheet under a state law that forbade "malicious, scandalous and defamatory" publications. The great libertarian John Milton, who had articulated the marketplace of ideas concept in 1644, would have shuddered at the law. So did the U.S. Supreme Court. In a landmark decision against government acts to pre-empt free expression before it occurs, the Court ruled that any government unit at any level is in violation of the First Amendment if it suppresses a publication because of what might be said in the next issue.

Nobody would much defend Near's paper, the *Saturday Press,* just Near's right to write whatever he wanted. Stories were peppered with bigoted references to "niggers," "yids," "bohunks" and "spades." The court did say, however, that prior restraint might be justified in extreme situations. But exceptions must be extraordinary, such as life-and-death situations in wartime.

Clarence Brandenburg
Ku Klux Klan leader whose conviction
was overturned because his speech
was farfetched

Since the *Near* case, the Supreme Court has moved to make it even more difficult for the government to interfere with freedom of expression. In an important case, from the perspective of free-expression advocates, the Court overturned the conviction of a white racist, **Clarence Brandenburg**, who had been jailed after a Ku Klux Klan rally in the woods outside Cincinnati. Brandenburg had said hateful and threatening things, but the Court, in a landmark decision in 1969, significantly expanded First Amendment protection for free expression. Even the advocacy of lawless actions is protected, according to the Brandenburg decision, as long as it's unlikely that lawlessness is imminent and probable. This is called the **Incitement Standard**. The distinction is that advocacy is protected up to the moment that lawlessness is incited. According to the Incitement Standard, authorities can justify silencing someone only if:

Incitement Standard
A four-part test to determine whether
an advocacy speech is constitutionally
protected

- The statement advocates a lawless action.
- The statement aims at producing lawless action.
- Such lawless action is imminent.
- Such lawless action is likely to occur.

Unless an utterance meets all four tests, it cannot be suppressed by the government.

Allowable Abridgments

In its wisdom the U.S. Supreme Court has avoided creating a rigid list of permissible abridgments to freedom of expression. No matter how thoughtfully drafted, a rigid list could never anticipate every situation. Nonetheless, the Supreme Court has discussed circumstances in which censorship is sometimes warranted.

National Security. The federal government jailed dozens of antiwar activists during World War I. Many appealed, prompting the U.S. Supreme Court to consider whether the First Amendment's prohibition against government limitations should be waived in wartime. At issue in the *Schenck* case were anti-war pamphlets aimed at recently drafted men. The pamphlets made several points:

- The draft violated the 13th Amendment, which prohibits slavery, and being drafted is like enslavement.
- The draft was unfair because clergy and conscientious objectors, like Quakers, were exempted.
- The war was being fought for the profit of cold-blooded capitalists, who, the leaflets claimed, controlled the country.
- Draftees should join the socialists and work to repeal the draft law.

As the government prosecutor saw it, the leaflets encouraged insubordination and disloyalty in the military, even mutiny. The Supreme Court agreed that the government can take exceptional prerogatives when the nation is at war. Schenck and Baer lost.

Since *Schenck* in 1919 the Court has repeated its point that national security is a special circumstance in which government restrictions can be justified. Even so, the Court's thinking has evolved in specifics, and many scholars believe that Schenck and Baer today would have prevailed. Support for this assessment of the Court's revised thinking came in an important 1972 case, during the Vietnam war, when the Court overruled the government for threatening the New York *Times* for a series of articles drawn from classified defense documents. In the so-called **Pentagon Papers** case, the Court said that the people's right to know about government defense policy was more important than the government's claim that the *Times* was jeopardizing national security.

Besides actions by the executive branch of government to infringe on free expression before the courts can respond, as in the Pentagon Papers case, the legislative branch sometimes creates laws that remain in force until the courts can act. Immediately after the 9/11 terrorist attacks on New York and Washington in 2001, for example, the Bush administration quickly drafted multipronged legislation to give authorities more power to track terrorists. Congress concurred and passed the **Patriot Act** by an overwhelming majority. Civil libertarians objected to provisions that allowed federal agents to ignore constitutionally guaranteed citizen rights, but Congress reasoned simply: Better to be safe than sorry.

The book industry mobilized against a provision that allowed federal agents to go into bookstores, unannounced and without close judicial oversight, and confiscate customer records to see who had bought books that might be used to aid or promote terrorism. The

Pentagon Papers
Case in which the government attempted prior restraint against the New York *Times*

Patriot Act
2001 law that gave federal agents new authority to pre-empt terrorism

▲ **Martyred Political Prisoner.** *Eugene Debs, a Socialist Party leader, had run four times for the presidency, in 1900, 1904, 1908 and 1912. He ran a fifth time, in 1920—this time from prison. Here, party officials pose with Debs at the prison after notifying him that he had been nominated. He had been sent to jail for making an antiwar speech, a conviction that was upheld by the U.S. Supreme Court because of special national security considerations in time of war. Debs' 1920 campaign photograph showed him in prison garb with bars in the background—the martyred political prisoner. He won almost 1 million votes. A year later, President Warren Harding pardoned Debs, who by then was aged and ailing.*

provision also allowed agents to go into libraries to see who had been reading what. To book publishers, authors, librarians and indeed all civil liberty advocates, the implications were alarming. They launched a massive lobbying effort to rescind parts of the Patriot Act that could chill citizen inquiry and expression. Their point was that the law's effect would be to discourage people from reading works on a secret list of seditious literature. In time, as post-9/11 hysteria eased, the provision was rescinded.

Public Endangerment. In the Schenck case, the eloquent Justice **Oliver Wendell Holmes** wrote these words: "The most stringent protection of free speech would not protect a man in falsely shouting 'Fire' in a crowded theater and causing panic." His point was that the First Amendment's ban on government abridgment of freedom of expression cannot be applied literally. Holmes was saying that reasonable people agree that there must be exceptions. Since then, lesser courts have carved out allowable abridgments. Some have been endorsed by the Supreme Court. On other cases the Court has been silent, letting lower-level court decisions stand.

In a 1942 New Hampshire case, the police were upheld in jailing **Walter Chaplinsky**, who had taken to the streets to deride religions other than his own as "rackets." Somebody called the police. Chaplinsky then turned his venom on the marshal who showed up, calling him, in a lapse of piety, "a God-damned racketeer" and "a damned fascist." From these circumstances emerged the **Fighting Words Doctrine**. The Court said someone might be justified taking a poke at you for using "fighting words," with perhaps a riot resulting. Preventing a riot was a justification for halting someone's freedom of expression. Again, whether courts today would uphold Chaplinsky being silenced is debated among legal scholars. Nonetheless, the Fighting Words Doctrine from *Chaplinsky* remains as testimony to the Court's willingness to consider public safety as a value that sometimes should outweigh freedom of expression as a value.

The courts also accept time, place and manner limits by the government on expression, using the **TPM Standard**. Cities can, for example, ban newsracks from busy sidewalks where they impede pedestrian traffic and impair safety, as long as the restriction is content-neutral—an important caveat. A newspaper that editorializes against the mayor cannot be restricted while one that supports the mayor is not.

Oliver Wendell Holmes
Justice who wrote that shouting "Fire!" in a crowded theater would be justification for abridgment of freedom of speech rights

Walter Chaplinsky
Namesake for the case in which the Fighting Words Doctrine was defined

Fighting Words Doctrine
The idea that censorship can be justified against inciting provocation to violence

TPM Standard
Government may control the time, place and manner of expression as long as limits are content-neutral

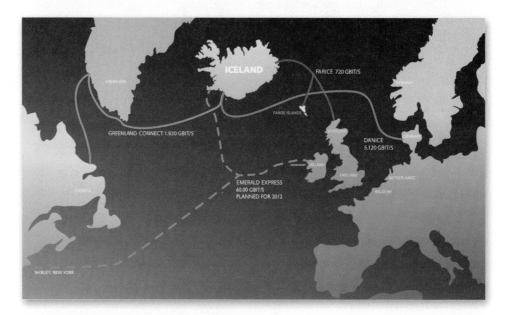

▲ **Wired to Iceland.** *Undersea fiber optic cables place Iceland geographically at a hub of internet connections from Europe and North America. With the country's emerging legal climate to bar government shutdowns of computers servers, might Iceland become a global center for mass communication?*

■ Iceland: New Transparency Model?

▲ **Birgitta Jónsdóttir.** *After a banking collapse in Iceland, poet Birgitta Jónsdóttir crusaded for new transparency in banking and government and other institutions and won election to Parliament. Her election gave her a forum to make tiny Iceland, population 300,000 in the North Atlantic, a centerpiece in a transparency-based New Information Order.*

Icelanders were angry. They had taken national pride in the growing international presence of their home-grown Kaupthing Bank. Then without warning, Kaupthing collapsed. The impact was horrendous on the Icelandic economy, not to mention the shattered national pride. The collapse saddled the island-nation with $128 billion in debts, an incredible $400,000 per citizen. The crisis rippled through the economy. Unemployment tripled. Angry Icelanders wanted to know: "How did this happen?"

Big-time banking is a mystery to ordinary folks, which fueled suspicion when things went so wrong. Suspicions worsened when, 10 months later, the avuncular television news anchor Bogi Ágústsson went on the air to report that an exposé on the Kaupthing meltdown could not be aired. The Kaupthing bank, as well as the London bank Barclay and Lucerne trader Trafigura had won a court injunction to suspend media reports drawn from the bank's own books. Ágústsson told viewers, however, that they could visit the web site WikiLeaks.org to read the documents.

WikiLeaks had posted shocking stuff. The documents detailed that Kaupthing had funneled more than $6 billion into sweetheart loans to some of the bank's owners individually and to companies that they owned.

WikiLeaks instantly attained a Robin Hood aura for putting the people's information needs ahead of the Establishment. WikiLeaks founder Julian Assange was asked to keynote a Reykjavik conference on free expression. Poet Birgitta Jónsdóttir, an outspoken Assange supporter, was elected to Parliament. Jónsdóttir pushed through a document favoring legal protection for WikiLeaks' revelation of corporate and government secrets and to shield leakers from prosecution. An international award, modeled on the Nobel Prize, was set up for work for freedom of expression.

Jóndóttir sees Iceland becoming a magnet for media companies, including whistler-blowers like WikiLeaks, that are looking for a place to locate their computer servers without laws elsewhere that interfere with the free flow of information. Media companies might even relocate their headquarters and editing staffs to Iceland to avoid laws in other countries against transparency. Jóndóttir's vision is to prove anti-transparency laws elsewhere futile. She believe that Iceland can force a global shift to transparency—no more secrecy that can shield wrongdoers from public scrutiny. Eventually Jóndóttir sees full openness on institutional transactions that traditionally have been cloistered from public scrutiny and accountability—a New Information Order.

Could Iceland indeed become a safe haven for WikiLeaks and similar organizations, like OpenLeaks.org, SaharaReporters.com, Transparency.org and Thailinks.info, which now play a cat-and-mouse game with authorities in many countries?

A piece of the Jóndóttir vision is the Thor Data Center. In 2011 an abandoned aluminum factory 10 miles outside Reykjavik was reopened as a global host site for computer servers. The server farm, with 1,000 servers at its launch, draws cheap energy from Iceland's natural thermal basins and dammed rivers. Arctic currents, which keep the annual median 50 degrees, provide low-cost cooling that is essential for high-volume computer servers that generate tremendous heat. Besides drawing clients from all over the world, the Thor server farm is key to reviving Iceland's economy after the Kaupthing bank meltdown.

- How would you establish the argument that free expression was too complex an issues for the Supreme Court to tackle in the first 130 years of the existence of the United States? Or was it just that free expression was too much a hot potato?
- What are the allowable exceptions to the First Amendment prohibition on government interference with free expression? What is the basis for these exceptions?
- In the wake of 9/11, would you have shared the objections of the book industry, librarians and civil libertarians to the Patriot Act's Section 215?
- Can you give an example of the TPM standard allowing government to ban a publication's distribution?

Broadening Protection

STUDY PREVIEW

The U.S. Supreme Court's initial First Amendment decisions involved political speech. The justices had no problem applying protections against government interference to political discourse, which is essential in democracy. It became apparent, however, that a fence cannot easily be erected between political and nonpolitical discourse. Gradually, First Amendment protections have been broadened.

Political Expression

The strides of the U.S. Supreme Court in the 20th century for free expression were limited to political expression at first. The justices saw free exchanges of political ideas as necessary for a functioning democracy. Entertainment and advertising initially were afforded no First Amendment protection. They were considered less important to democracy than political expression. New cases, however, made it difficult to draw the line between political and nonpolitical expression.

Random House
Fought against censorship of James Joyce's *Ulysses*

John Woolsey
Judge who barred import law censorship of *Ulysses*

Literature.   A 1930 tariff law was used as an import restriction to intercept James Joyce's *Ulysses* at the docks because of four-letter words and explicit sexual references. The importer, **Random House**, went to court, and the judge ruled that the government was out of line. The judge, **John Woolsey**, acknowledged "unusual frankness" in *Ulysses* but said he could not "detect anywhere the leer of the sensualist." The judge, who was not without humor, made a strong case for freedom in literary expression: "The words which are criticized as dirty are old Saxon words known to almost all men, and, I venture, to many women, and are such words as would be naturally and habitually used, I believe, by the types of folks whose life, physical and mental, Joyce is seeking to describe. In respect to the recurrent emergence of the theme of sex in the minds of the characters, it must always be remembered that his locale was Celtic and his season Spring."

Woolsey was upheld on appeal, and *Ulysses*, still critically acclaimed as a pioneer in stream-of-consciousness writing, remains in print today.

Grove Press
Fought against censorship of D. H. Lawrence's *Lady Chatterley's Lover*

Postal restrictions were used against a 1928 English novel, *Lady Chatterley's Lover*, by D. H. Lawrence. The book had been sold in the United States in expurgated editions for years, but in 1959 **Grove Press** issued the complete version. Postal officials denied mailing privileges. Grove sued and won.

In some respects the Grove case was *Ulysses* all over again. Grove argued that Lawrence, a major author, had produced a work of literary merit. Grove said the explicit, rugged love scenes between Lady Chatterley and Mellors the gamekeeper were essential in establishing their violent yet loving relationship, which was the heart of the story. The distinction between the *Ulysses* and *Lady Chatterley* cases was that one ruling was against the customs service and the other against the postmaster general.

Entertainment.　　Courts had once claimed movie censorship as involving something unworthy of constitutional protection. But movies can be political. Witness the series of documentaries by Michael Moore in recent years. Or poignant political and social commentaries like Clint Eastwood *J. Edgar,* Andrew Niccol's *In Time* and Tate Taylor's *The Help* in 2011.

It had been in 1952 that the Supreme Court widened First Amendment protection to movies in striking down a local ban on a controversial movie, *The Miracle,* in which a simple woman explained that her pregnancy was by St. Joseph. Some Christians saw the movie as blasphemy. The Court found, however, that government could not impede the exploration of ideas under the Constitution's guarantee that expression should be free of government control.

Advertising.　　Advertising, called **commercial speech** in legal circles, also was not easily separated from political speech, as the Supreme Court discovered in a libel case out of Alabama. The case originated in an advertisement carried by the New York *Times* to raise money for the civil rights cause. The ad's sponsors included negative statements about Montgomery, Alabama, police. Being an ad, was this commercial speech? Or, being in a public policy issue, was it political speech? In the 1964 landmark case *New York Times* v. *Sullivan,* the Court found the ad to be political speech and began opening the door for First Amendment protection of advertising—although the process of full protection for advertising remains a work in progress.

Emotive Speech.　　Polite society has never been particularly tolerant of vulgarities, but what if the vulgarity is clearly political? The issue was framed in the Vietnam war-protest era when a young man showed up at the Los Angeles courthouse wearing a jacket whose back carried a message: "Fuck the Draft." Paul Robert Cohen was sent to jail for 30 days. The Supreme Court overturned the conviction. Justice John Harlan wrote that linguistic expression needs to allow for "inexpressible emotions," sometimes called **emotive speech.** As one wag put it: Cohen wouldn't have been arrested if his jacket had said, "The Heck with Conscription" or "I Really Don't Like the Draft Very Much." Instead Cohen chose to use more charged language—the F-word. His jacket conveyed the depths of his feelings about the draft. Justice Harlan said: "One man's vulgarity is another's lyric. Words are often chosen as much for their emotive as their cognitive force."

Hate Speech.　　Emotions run high on First Amendment issues when expression is obnoxious or even vile. The Supreme Court, however, takes the position that a society that is free and democratic cannot have a government that silences somebody just because that person's views don't comport with mainstream values. In effect, the Court says that people need to tolerate a level of discomfort in a society whose core principles value freedom of expression.

This point, made in the *Brandenburg* case, has come up in Court decisions against **hate speech** laws that grew out of the political correctness movement of the 1990s. Especially notable was *R.A.V.* v. *St. Paul.* Several punks had burned a cross, KKK style, on the lawn of a black family in St. Paul, Minnesota. The punks, all of them white, were caught and convicted under a municipal ordinance against so-called "hate speech." One of them, identified only as R.A.V. in court documents, appealed to the U.S. Supreme Court on First Amendment grounds. The Court found that the ordinance was aimed at the content of the expression, going far beyond allowable time, place or manner restrictions. The decision was a slap at the political correctness movement's attempts to discourage language that can be taken offensively.

Broadcast Regulation

Early commercial radio was a horrendous free-for-all. Government licensing was a joke. Stations went on the air at any frequency with as much wattage as they wanted. As the number of stations grew, they drowned each other out. To end the cacophony

▲ **Joey Johnson.** *Flag-burning protester whose conviction was overturned on First Amendment grounds.*

and create a workable national radio system, Congress established the Federal Radio Commission in 1927 to facilitate the orderly development of the new radio industry. A no-nonsense licensing system was put in place with licenses going to stations that could best demonstrate they would operate in "the public interest, convenience and necessity."

Wait a minute? Government licensing based on performance sure smacks of government regulation. What about the First Amendment?

public airwaves
Concept that broadcast should be subject to government regulation because the electromagnetic spectrum is a public asset

To sidestep the First Amendment issue, Congress embraced the concept that the airwaves, which carried radio signals, were a public asset and therefore, somewhat like a public park, were subject to government regulation for the public good. The **public airwaves** concept was useful for justifying regulation of the 1927 chaos on the airwaves, but it also was problematic. Some stations that lost licenses made First Amendment objections, but the courts declined to address the inherent constitutional contradictions. The radio industry overall was pleased with the new federal regulatory structure. The system, today under the Federal Communications Commission, later was expanded to television.

Over time many early restrictions have been relaxed. No longer, for example, are stations expected to air public affairs programs as a condition for license renewal. Although the FCC talks tough about on-air indecency, old bans have become loosened with the times.

APPLYING YOUR MEDIA LITERACY

- **What are arguments for and against First Amendment protection for four-letter and related vulgarities, flag-burning and hate speech?**
- **How has government regulation of broadcasting been justified when regulation of print media is clearly unconstitutional?**

■ Challenging Broadcast Regulation

John Brinkley and his bride arrived in Milford, Kansas, population 200, in 1917 and rented the old drug store for $8 a month. Mrs. Brinkley sold patent medicines out front, while Brinkley consulted with patients in a back room. One day an elderly gentleman called on "Dr. Brinkley" to do something about his failing manhood. As the story goes, the conversation turned to Brinkley's experience with goats in the medical office of the Swift meat-packing company in Omaha a job he had held for barely three weeks. Said Brinkley, "You wouldn't have any trouble if you had a pair of those buck glands in you." The operation was performed in the back room, and word spread. Soon the goat gland surgeon was charging $750 for the service, then $1,000, then $1,500. In 1918 Brinkley, whose only credentials were two mail-order medical degrees, opened the Brinkley Hospital. Five years later he set up a radio station, KFKB, to spread the word about his cures.

Six nights a week, Brinkley extolled the virtues of his hospital over the air. "Don't let your doctor two-dollar you to death," he said. "Come to Dr. Brinkley." If a trip to Milford was not possible, listeners were encouraged to send for Brinkley compounds. Soon the mail-order demand was so great that Brinkley reported he was buying goats from Arkansas by the boxcar. "Dr. Brinkley" became a household word. *Radio Digest* awarded Brinkley's KFKB its Golden Microphone Award as the most popular radio station in the country. The station had received 356,827 votes in the magazine's write-in poll. Brinkley was a 1930 write-in candidate for governor. Harry Woodring won with 217,171 votes to Brinkley's 183,278, but Brinkley would have won had it not been for misspellings that disqualified thousands of write-in ballots.

Also in 1930 the KFKB broadcast license came up for renewal by the Federal Radio Commission, which had been set up to regulate broadcasting. The American Medical Association wanted the license revoked. The medical profession had been outraged by Brinkley but had not found a way to derail his thriving quackery. In fact, Brinkley played to the hearts of thousands of Middle America listeners when he attacked the AMA as "the meat-cutter's union." At the license hearing, Brinkley argued that the First Amendment guaranteed him freedom to speak his views on medicine, goat glands and anything else he wanted. He noted that Congress had specifically forbidden the FRC to censor. It would be a censorious affront to the First Amendment, he said, to take away KFKB's license for what the station put on the air. Despite Brinkley's arguments, the FRC denied renewal.

▲ **John Brinkley.** *Eager for publicity, John Brinkley obliges a photographer by placing a healing hand on a supposedly insane patient he is about to cure. Broadcasting such claims from his Kansas radio station, Brinkley developed a wide market for his potions. Because of his quackery, he lost the station in a significant First Amendment case.*

Brinkley challenged the denial in federal court, and the case became a landmark on the relationship between the First Amendment and U.S. broadcasting. The appeals court sided with the FRC, declaring that broadcast licenses should be awarded for serving "public interest, convenience and necessity." It was appropriate, said the court, for the commission to review a station's programming to decide on renewal. Brinkley appealed to the U.S. Supreme Court, which declined to hear the case. The goat gland surgeon was off the air, but not for long. In 1932 Dr. Brinkley, proving himself unsinkable, bought a powerful station in Villa Acuna, Mexico, just across the Rio Grande from Del Rio, Texas, to continue peddling his potions. By telephone linkup from his home in Milford, Brinkley continued to reach much of the United States until 1942, when the Mexican government nationalized foreign-owned property.

What Do You Think?

How do you explain the skirting of First Amendment issues in early court decisions about federal regulation of broadcasting?

Do you see a problem in a government agency establishing the requirements for a license to broadcast?

Can you defend the broadcast licensing standard of "public interest, convenience and necessity"?

Defamation

STUDY PREVIEW

When the mass media carry disparaging descriptions and comments, they risk being sued for libel. The media have a strong defense if the disparagement was accurate. If not, there can be big trouble. Libel is a serious matter. Not only are reputations at stake when defamation occurs but losing a suit can be so costly that it can put a publication, broadcast or internet organization out of business.

Libel as a Concept

If someone punched you in the face for no good reason, knocking out several teeth, breaking your nose and causing permanent disfigurement, most courts would rule that your attacker should pay your medical bills. If your disfigurement or psychological upset causes you to lose your job, to be ridiculed or shunned by friends and family or perhaps to retreat from social interaction, the court would probably order your attacker to pay additional amounts. Like fists, words can cause damage. If someone writes false, damaging things about you, you can sue for **libel**. Freedom of speech and the press is not a license to say absolutely anything about anybody.

If a libeling statement is false, the utterer may be liable for millions of dollars in damages. The largest jury award to date, in 1997 against the *Wall Street Journal*, was almost twice the earnings that year of the *Journal*'s parent company. The award was reduced substantially on appeal, but the fact remains that awards have grown dramatically in recent years and can hurt a media company seriously.

Reckless Disregard

Elected officials have a hard time winning libel suits today. Noting that democracy is best served by robust, unbridled discussion of public issues and that public officials are inseparable from public policy, the U.S. Supreme Court has ruled that public figures can win libel suits only in extreme circumstances. The Court has also said that people who thrust themselves into the limelight forfeit some of the protection available to other citizens.

The key Court decision in developing current U.S. libel standards originated in an advertisement carried by the New York *Times* in 1960. A civil rights group escalated its antisegregationist cause by placing a full-page advertisement in the *Times*. The advertisement accused public officials in the South of violence and illegal tactics against the civil rights struggle. Although the advertisement was by and large truthful, it was marred by minor factual errors. Police Commissioner L. B. Sullivan of Montgomery, Alabama, filed a libel action saying that the errors damaged him, and he won $500,000 in an Alabama trial. On appeal to the U.S. Supreme Court, the case, **New York Times v. Sullivan**, became a landmark in libel law. The Supreme Court said that the importance of "free debate" in a democratic society generally was more important than factual errors that might upset and damage public officials. To win a libel suit, the Court said, public officials needed to prove that damaging statements were uttered or printed with the knowledge that they were false. The question in the *Sullivan* case became whether the *Times* was guilty of "**reckless disregard** of the truth." The Supreme Court said it was not, and the newspaper won.

Questions lingered after the *Sullivan* decision about exactly who was and who was not a public official. Lower courts struggled for a definition, and the Supreme Court eventually changed the term from *public official* to *public figure*. In later years, as the Court refined its view on issues raised in the *Sullivan* case through several decisions, it remained consistent in giving mass communicators a lot of room for error, even damaging error, in discussing government officials, political candidates and publicity hounds.

- **Government officials.** All elected government officials and appointed officials with high-level policy responsibilities are public figures as far as their performance in office is

Margin glossary

John Brinkley
Radio quack who challenged government regulation of radio

libel
A written defamation

New York Times v. *Sullivan*
Libel case that largely barred public figures from the right to sue for libel

reckless disregard
Supreme Court language for a situation in which public figures may sue for libel

concerned. A member of a state governor's cabinet fits this category. A cafeteria worker in the state capitol does not.

- **Political candidates.** Anyone seeking public office is subject to intense public scrutiny, during which the courts are willing to excuse false statements as part of robust, wide-open discussion.

- **Publicity hounds.** Court decisions have gone both ways, but generally people who seek publicity or intentionally draw attention to themselves must prove not only inaccuracy but also "reckless disregard of the truth" if they sue for libel.

How far can mass communicators go in making disparaging comments? It was all right, said a Vermont court, when the Barre *Times Argus* ran an editorial that said a political candidate was "a horse's ass, a jerk, an idiot and a paranoid." The court said open discussion on public issues excused even such insulting, abusive and unpleasant verbiage. Courts have generally been more tolerant of excessive language in opinion pieces, such as the Barre editorial, than in fact-based articles

Comment and Criticism

People flocked to see the **Cherry Sisters**' act. Effie, Addie, Jessie, Lizzie and Ella toured the country with a song-and-dance act that drew big crowds. They were just awful. They could neither sing nor dance, but people turned out because the sisters were so funny. Sad to say, the Cherry Sisters took themselves seriously. In 1901, desperate for respect, the sisters vowed to sue the next newspaper reviewer who gave them a bad notice. That reviewer, it turned out, was Billy Hamilton, who included a lot of equine metaphors in his piece for the Des Moines *Leader*: "Effie is an old jade of 50 summers, Jessie a frisky filly of 40, and Addie, the flower of the family, a capering monstrosity of 35. Their long skinny arms, equipped with talons at the extremities, swung mechanically, and anon waved frantically at the suffering audience. The mouths of their rancid features opened like caverns, and sounds like the wailings of damned souls issued therefrom. They pranced around the stage with a motion

Cherry Sisters
Complainants in a case that barred performers from suing critics

◀ **Fair Comment and Criticism.** *Upset with what an Iowa reviewer had written about their show, the Cherry Sisters sued. The important 1901 court decision that resulted said that journalists, critics and anybody else can say whatever they want about a public performance. The rationale was that someone who puts on a performance for public acceptance has to take a risk also of public rejection.*

that suggested a cross between the *danse du ventre* and the fox trot—strange creatures with painted faces and hideous mien. Effie is spavined, Addie is stringhalt, and Jessie, the only one who showed her stockings, has legs with calves as classic in their outlines as the curves of a broom handle."

The outcome of the suit was another setback for the Cherrys. They lost in a case that established that actors or others who perform for the public must be willing to accept both positive and negative comments about their performance. This right of **fair comment and criticism**, however, does not make it open season on performers in aspects of their lives that do not relate to public performance. The *National Enquirer,* for example, could not defend itself when entertainer Carol Burnett sued for a story that described her as obnoxiously drunk at a restaurant. The story was false. Carol Burnett abstains from alcohol. The pivotal issue, however, was that Burnett, although a performer, was in no public or performing role at the restaurant. This distinction between an individual's public and private lives also has been recognized in cases involving public officials and candidates.

fair comment and criticism
Doctrine that permits criticism of performers, performances

APPLYING YOUR MEDIA LITERACY

- **How many people can you name who fall into a gray area that was created by *New York Times v. Sulllivan* between pubic figure and private figure? Discuss their ambiguous status.**
- **Disparaging comments about an individual are legally protected in mass communication in some situations but not others. Consider a celebrity. What's off-limits? What's not?**

MEDIAtimeline

Celebrated and ridiculed vaudeville troupe

MASS MEDIA LAW MILESTONES

INTELLECTUAL PROPERTY
Congress passed first copyright law (1790)

FREE EXPRESSION
Revolutionary War (1776–1781)

FIRST AMENDMENT
States ratified First Amendment to U.S. Constitution (1791)

PIVOTAL EVENTS

- Alien and Sedition Acts (1798)

MASS MEDIA LAW MILESTONES

CENSORSHIP
Wartime newspapers closed (1864–1865)

PIVOTAL EVENTS

- Civil War (1861–1865)

Opposition newspapers padlocked on Lincoln's watch

MASS MEDIA LAW MILESTONES

CHERRY SISTERS
Iowa Supreme Court ruled that performers must accept criticism of performances (1901)

PRIOR RESTRAINT
Justice Oliver Wendell Holmes coined "Fire!" in a crowded theater example for prior restraint (1919)

BOOK BAN
Court overruled import restriction against *Ulysses* (1930)

LANDMARK CASE
U.S. Supreme Court banned prior restraint in *Near* v. *Minnesota* (1931)

1700S

1800S

1900–1949

Indecency

STUDY PREVIEW | Despite the First Amendment's guarantee of freedom of expression, the U.S. government has tried numerous ways during the past 100 years to regulate obscenity and pornography.

Pornography Versus Obscenity

Through U.S. history, governments have attempted censorship of various sorts at various levels of jurisdiction. But since the courts overruled a government effort to ban James Joyce's classic novel *Ulysses* in the 1930s, much has occurred to discourage censorship.

The U.S. Supreme Court has ruled that **pornography**, material aimed at sexual arousal, cannot be stopped. Import and postal restrictions, however, still can be employed against obscene materials. So how is obscenity different from pornography? The court said that government can restrict sexually explicit mass media content if the answer is yes to *all* of the following questions:

- Would a typical person applying local standards see the material as appealing mainly for its sexually arousing effect?

- Is the material devoid of serious literary, artistic, political or scientific value?

- Is sexual activity depicted offensively, in a way that violates state law that explicitly defines offensiveness?

pornography
Sexually explicit depictions that are protected from government bans

PIVOTAL EVENTS

- World War I (1914–1918)
- Right to vote extended to women (1920)
- Great Depression (1930s)
- World War II (1941–1945)

First Amendment guarantees sometimes fudged in wartime

MASS MEDIA LAW MILESTONES

SULLIVAN CASE
U.S. Supreme Court ruled that public figures can sue for libel only if media were reckless (1964)

Nixon legacy includes failed First Amendment showdown

OBSCENITY
U.S. Supreme Court ruled that local community standards determine obscenity (1968)

NATIONAL SECURITY
U.S. Supreme Court banned prior restraint in Pentagon Papers case (1971)

PIVOTAL EVENTS

- Civil rights movement (1960s)
- Humans reached moon (1969)
- Vietnam war (1964–1973)
- Nixon resigns presidency (1974)

MASS MEDIA LAW MILESTONES

DOWNLOAD PIRACY
Recording industry won case against Grokster and other Internet file-swap enablers (2005)

PIVOTAL EVENTS

- 9/11 terrorist attacks (2001)
- Iraq war (2003–2011)
- Hurricane Katrina (2005)
- Obama presidency (2009–)
- Supreme Court removes limits on corporate political donations (2010)

Napster-like file-swaps outlawed

1950–1999

2000s

Protecting Children

Although the Supreme Court has found that the First Amendment protects access to pornography, the Court has stated on numerous occasions that children must be protected from sexually explicit material. It's a difficult double standard, as demonstrated by 1996 and 1999 federal forays into systematically regulating media content with communications decency laws. Without hearings or formal debate, Congress created the laws to keep smut away from children who use the internet. Although hardly anyone defends giving kids access to indecent material, the laws had two flaws: the difficulty of defining **indecency** and the impossibility of denying questionable material to children without restricting freedom of access for adults.

Before a Philadelphia federal appeals court that reviewed the 1996 Communications Decency Act, witnesses from the Justice Department testified that the law went ridiculously far. The law, they said, required them to prosecute for certain AIDS information, museum exhibits, prize-winning plays and even the *Vanity Fair* magazine cover of actress Demi Moore nude and pregnant.

Access. When it reviewed the 1996 Communications Decency Act, the U.S. Supreme Court noted that the internet is the most democratic of the media, enabling almost anyone to become a town crier or pamphleteer. The court said that enforcing the law would necessarily inhibit freedom of expression of the sort that has roots in the revolution that resulted in the creation of the Republic and the First Amendment. The 7-2 decision purged the law from the books.

How, then, are government bans of indecency on radio and television justified but not on the internet? Justice John Stevens, who wrote the majority Supreme Court opinion, said the internet is hardly "invasive broadcasting." The odds of people encountering pornography on the internet are slim unless they're seeking it, he said. Underpinning the Court's rejection of the **Communications Decency Act** was the fact that the internet lends itself to free-for-all discussions and exchanges with everybody participating who wants to. Other media, however, are dominated by carefully crafted messages aimed at people whose opportunity to participate in dialogue with the message producers is so indirect as to be virtually nil.

Even while politicians and moralists rant at indecency, people seem largely unperturbed by the issue. The V-chip, required by a 1996 law to be built into every television set, allows parents to block violence, sexual explicitness and vulgarity automatically. Although the V-chip was widely praised when it became a requirement, hardly anybody uses it.

In 2006, when Congress was in a new dither over objectionable content, movie industry lobbyist Jack Valenti came out of retirement to lead a $300 million campaign to promote the V-chip. Valenti made the point that stiff fines being levied against broadcasters for indecency are unnecessary because people already have the tool they need to block it, if they want: Turn it off.

indecency
Term used by the Federal Communications Commission to encompass a range of words and depictions improper on public airwaves

Communications Decency Act
Failed 1996 and 1999 laws to keep indecent content off the Internet

APPLYING YOUR MEDIA LITERACY

- **How are obscenity and pornography different?**
- **What is the difficulty of enforcing indecency restrictions for children but not adults?**

■ Intellectual Property   (Pages 417–420)

Copyright law protects mass communicators and other creative people from having their creative work used without their permission. It's an issue of property rights. Also, copyright law encourages creativity in society with a profit incentive for creative people. They can charge for the use of their work. The financial structure of mass media industries has been built around the copyright concept. Time and again technology has challenged media control over copyrighted content, most recently with downloaded music and video.

■ Free Expression   (Pages 421–426)

The First Amendment to the U.S. Constitution guarantees freedom to citizens and mass media from government limitations on what they say. The guarantee has solid roots in democratic theory. Even so, the U.S. Supreme Court has allowed exceptions. These are mostly commonsense exceptions. They include utterances that could undermine national security in wartime. In general, however, the Supreme Court has expanded the prohibition on censorship over the years, all in the libertarian spirit articulated by John Milton in the 1600s.

■ Broadening Protection   (Pages 426–429)

The U.S. Supreme Court addressed First Amendment issues for the first time after World War I and had little problem in declaring that government limitations were unacceptable for political discourse, albeit with specific exceptions. It turned out, however, that political speech has lots of crossover with literature, entertainment and advertising. Over time, the Supreme Court has broadened First Amendment protection into these additional areas of expression—although less exuberantly than for political issues. An odd exception has been broadcasting, for which the Court has never squarely addressed the contradictions between federal regulation and the First Amendment.

■ Defamation   (Pages 430–432)

Someone who is defamed can sue for libel. This generally is not a constitutional free expression issue but a civil issue. If the defamation was false and caused someone to suffer public hatred, contempt or ridicule, civil damages can be awarded by the courts. Judgments can be severe, sometimes approaching $100 million. The courts have found some defamations excusable. The landmark *New York Times* v. *Sullivan* decision of 1964 makes it difficult for public figures to recover damages unless there has been reckless disregard for truth. Also, performers cannot sue for criticism of their performances, no matter how harsh.

CHAPTER WRAP UP

■ Indecency   (Pages 433–434)

Indecency revolts many people, but the U.S. Supreme Court in struggling with the issue has said, in effect, that indecency like beauty is in the eye of the beholder. The Court says the media are guaranteed freedom to create pornography and citizens are guaranteed freedom of access. However, sexually explicit material that goes too far—obscenity, the Court has called it—cannot be tolerated. But the Court has never devised a clear distinction between pornography, which is protected, and obscenity, which it says is not. In both categories, however, the Court has endorsed laws to punish purveyors of sexually explicit material to children.

■ Thinking Critically

1. What is the rationale underlying copyright law?

2. Why is the First Amendment important to mass media in the United States?

3. What was the direction of court interpretation of the First Amendment in the 1900s?

4. Who can sue for libel? And who can be sued successfully and under what situations?

5. How are obscenity and pornography different?

■ Media Vocabulary

assignment (Page 418)

commercial speech (Page 427)

copyright (Page 417)

emotive speech (Page 427)

fair comment and criticism (Page 432)

Fighting Words Doctrine (Page 424)

First Amendment (Page 421)

free expression provision (Page 421)

hate speech (Page 427)

Incitement Standard (Page 422)

indecency (Page 434)

infringement (Page 418)

intellectual property (Page 417)

libel (Page 430)

permissions (Page 418)

piracy (Page 418)

pornography (Page 433)

prior restraint (Page 422)

public airwaves (Page 428)

reckless disregard (Page 430)

TPM standard (Page 424)

Media Sources

- Richard J. Peltz. *The Law of Access to Government.* Carolina Academic Press, 2011. This casebook deals with federal and state freedom of information law and executive policy.

- John Denvir. *Freeing Speech: The Constitutional War over National Security.* New York University, 2010. Denvir, a constitutional lawyer, argues a redefining of the presidency has enabled presidents to initiate offensive military action without an active or informed role for Congress or the public. He favors felony prosecution and impeachment of presidents and their surrogates who intentionally or recklessly make false statements on national security issues.

- Roy L. Moore, Carmen Maye and Erik L. Collins, *Advertising and Public Relations Law,* second edition. Routledge, 2010. The authors cover a wide of range of issues, including the varying degrees of First Amendment protection for commercial speech.

- Lawrence Lessig. *Remix: Making Art and Commerce Thrive in a Hybrid Economy.* Penguin, 2008. Lessig, a leading theorist on intellectual property, calls for loosening copyright restrictions that he sees as inhibiting creativity.

- Uta Kohl. *Jurisdiction and the Internet: Regulatory Competence over Online Activity.* Cambridge, 2007. Kohl, a British scholar, examines issues of transnational regulation through defamation or contract law, obscenity standards, gambling or banking regulation, pharmaceutical licensing requirements or hate speech.

- Robert J. Wagman. *The First Amendment Book.* Paros, 1991. This lively history of the First Amendment is a solid primer on the subject.

- Clark R. Mollenhoff. "25 Years of *Times* v. *Sullivan,*" *Quill* (March 1989), pages 27–31. A veteran investigative reporter argues that journalists have abused the landmark *Sullivan* decision and have been irresponsibly hard on public figures.

- Fred W. Friendly. *Minnesota Rag: The Dramatic Story of the Landmark Supreme Court Case That Gave New Meaning to the First Amendment.* Random House, 1981. A colorful account of the *Near* v. *Minnesota* prior restraint case.

A Thematic Chapter Summary

MEDIA LAW

To further deepen your media literacy here are ways to look at this chapter from the perspective of themes that recur throughout the book:

MEDIA TECHNOLOGY

Feelings run strong on the recording and movie industries' call for court protection against downloading and file-swapping that threatens their franchises.

New technologies keep creating new mass media legal issues. The first home video recording equipment in the 1970s, Betamax, raised questions of whether people have a legal right to duplicate copyright-protected movies. Despite Hollywood's objections, the answer of the U.S. Supreme Court was yes. For more than a century, photography has created poignant privacy questions that nobody ever thought about before. The problem with copyright law is that lawmakers are no better than the rest of us at seeing what future technology will bring. Copyright law has been revisited over and over in the history of the Republic, most recently because of internet-related issues like unauthorized downloading that have shaken media industries.

MEDIA ECONOMICS

Jon Lech Johansen became Hollywood's Norwegian nightmare with software that cracked regional coding for movies.

At the core of mass media infrastructure is copyright law, which gives exclusive rights to creative people to profit from their creations. The internet has broken the control of media companies on distribution of their creations. Anybody with a few pieces of low-cost, easy-to-use computer equipment can distribute media content for free downloading by anyone on the planet. Most threatened have been the recording and movie industries, which have scrambled in the courts for protection of assets under copyright law. Both industries have cast the issue as economic survival.

MEDIA AND DEMOCRACY

Edmund Burke had the idea right: The press as a Fourth Estate.

The democratic ideal of self-governance through grassroots political participation requires that people have full access to information. The ideal also requires that people have the freedom to sort through and hash out the facts to arrive at the best possible public policy. The First Amendment to the U.S. Constitution guarantees these freedoms of inquiry and expression to all citizens and to the mass media. The guarantee, however, is limited only to a ban on government interference in inquiry and expression. Citizens who feel wronged can seek compensation from other citizens and corporate entities, including media companies. Also, the courts have carved out some areas, including national security, in which the government can restrict access to and sharing of information.

MEDIA AND CULTURE

George Carlin's dirty words OK on air? Depends on the time of day.

The polarizing Culture Wars that have divided American society in recent years are not new except in their shrill intensity. Sexual explicitness is a hot-button cultural issue that goes way back. The U.S. Supreme Court has barred government interference with adult access to sexually explicit material. The Court has said that the access is a right under the free expression guarantee of the First Amendment, but the Court also has created limits. Some of these limits are clear, like protecting children. Some are vague, like the distinction between pornography, which is acceptable, and obscenity, which is not. In short, though, the mass media have had growing latitude in dealing with sexuality through the First Amendment.

ELITISM AND POPULISM

Public figures must take criticism as well as praise.

Elected and appointed governing elites have been largely stripped of the ability to sue their critics. In a landmark 1964 decision, *New York Times* v. *Sullivan,* the U.S. Supreme Court ruled that a democracy requires full and robust citizen discourse on public policy issues. The Court said that defamations that occur in this discourse are excusable, except for egregious and intentional untruths. The *Sullivan* decision gave new leeway for criticism of political leadership to the people and also to the media. The decision also opened up the range of negative comments on a broad range of other public figures.

MEDIA FUTURE

John Brinkley's First Amendment argument dead-ended.

Our understanding of the First Amendment is evolving. It's been clear since the U.S. Supreme Court began examining the First Amendment after World War I that discussion of political issues must be protected for democracy to function. But numerous practices, also endorsed by the courts, leave many contradictions unresolved. For example, the government in 1927 gave itself the authority to decide who could broadcast and who couldn't. Criteria for a broadcast license still include on-air performance expectations, a kind of government content control that the Court would never countenance for print media. Also not addressed squarely by the courts so far are a wide range of government restrictions on advertising.

CHAPTER 17 ETHICS

■ Does Illegal Equal Immoral?

Jim DeFede, a hard-hitting Miami *Herald* investigative reporter, was home late in the afternoon when his phone rang. It was an old friend, Arthur Teele Jr., former city and county commissioner. Teele was distraught that another newspaper had outed him for trysts with a transvestite prostitute. "What did I do to piss off this town?" Teele asked. The transvestite allegation had followed 26 charges of fraud and money laundering. Teele said he was being smeared by prosecutors. He was afraid the transvestite story would hurt him with "the ministers and the church."

◀ **Jim DeFede.** *Reflexively, Miami* Herald *columnist Jim DeFede did what seemed right when a suicidal friend called: He taped the call. But in Florida taping a call without permission is against the law. But does being illegal make an act necessarily wrong? Such are the issues that make ethics essential to understand.*

CHAPTER INSIGHTS

- Mass media ethics codes cannot anticipate all moral questions.

- Audiences help shape media ethics.

- Media people draw on numerous, sometimes inconsistent moral principles.

- Some media people see ethics as process-based, others as outcome-based.

- Potter's Box is a useful tool to sort through ethics issues.

- Some media people confuse ethics, law, prudence and accepted practices.

- Dubious media practices confound efforts to establish universal standards.

Worried about his friend's anguish, DeFede turned on his telephone recorder to record Teele's pain. He also asked if Teele wanted to go public about the prosecutors using the media to smear him. Teele said no, but the discussion meandered back and forth to a potentially explosive story for which Teele said he had documents. A couple hours later, Teele called and said he was leaving the documents for DeFede. Then he hung up, put a pistol to his head, and shot himself dead.

DeFede briefed his editor, Judy Miller, who told him to write a front-page story. In the meantime, higher executives at the *Herald* realized that DeFede had violated a state law that forbade taping a telephone conversation without permission. Over Miller's objections, publisher Jesus Diaz Jr. and corporate attorney Robert Beatty and two other corporate executives decided to fire DeFede—even though the *Herald* had once fought the Florida law, even though anyone who calls a reporter implicitly

is consenting to being quoted, even though tape recording is just a more detailed form of note-taking—and even though, in this case, *Herald* executives decided to draw on DeFede's notes from the taped conversation to be used in a story on the suicide.

If indeed DeFede had acted unethically, then how about the fact that the *Herald* drew on his information from the phone call? And how's this for a twist to make the issue murkier? The state's attorney cleared DeFede of violating the anti-recording statute. Also, only 12 states, including Florida, have such a law. If what DeFede did was unethical in Florida, is it less so in the 38 states that don't have such restrictions?

Clearly, the law and ethics don't coincide lockstep, which is a major issue in media ethics. In this chapter you will learn tools that have been developed through the centuries to sort through complexities posed by dilemmas of right and wrong. ■

The Difficulty of Ethics

STUDY PREVIEW

Mass media organizations have put together codes of ethics that prescribe how practitioners should go about their work. Although useful in many ways, these codes neither sort through bedeviling problems that result from conflicting prescription. Nor do codes help much when the only open options are negative.

Prescriptive Ethics

The mass media abound with **codes of ethics.** The earliest was adopted in 1923, the **Canons of Journalism** of the American Society of Newspaper Editors. Advertising, broadcast and public relations practitioners also have codes. Many newcomers to the mass media make an erroneous assumption that the answers to all the moral choices in their work exist in the prescriptions of these codes, a stance known as **prescriptive ethics.** While the codes can be helpful, ethics is not so easy.

The difficulty of ethics becomes clear when a mass communicator is confronted with a conflict between moral responsibilities to different concepts. Consider:

Privacy. The code of the Society of Professional Journalists prescribes that reporters will show respect for the dignity, privacy, rights and well-being of people "at all times." The SPJ prescription sounds excellent, but moral priorities such as dignity and privacy sometimes seem less important than other priorities. The public interest, for example, overrode privacy in 1988 when the Miami *Herald* staked out presidential candidate Gary Hart overnight when he had a woman friend in his Washington townhouse. Or in 2011 when the media reported allegations that a leading presidential hopeful, Herman Cain, was a serial cheater on his wife.

Timeliness. The code of the Radio-Television News Directors Association prescribes that reporters be "timely and accurate." In practice, however, the virtue of accuracy is

code of ethics
Statement that defines acceptable, unacceptable behavior

Canons of Journalism
First media code, 1923

prescriptive ethics
Follow the rules and your decision will be the correct one

jeopardized when reporters rush to the air with stories. It takes time to confirm details and be accurate—and that delays stories and works against timeliness.

Fairness.   The code of the Public Relations Society of America prescribes dealing fairly with both clients and the general public. However, a persuasive message prepared on behalf of a client is not always the same message that would be prepared on behalf of the general public. Persuasive communication is not necessarily dishonest, but how information is marshaled to create the message depends on whom the public relations person is serving.

Conflict of Duties

Media ethics codes are well-intended, often helpful guides, but they are simplistic when it comes to knotty moral questions. These inherent problems become obvious if you consider how the various duties of mass communicators can conflict. Media ethicist Clifford Christians and others have examined, for example, conflicts in duties to audience, to employer, to society, to the profession and to self.

Duty to Self.   Self-preservation is a basic human instinct, but is a photojournalist shirking a duty to subscribers by avoiding a dangerous combat zone?

Self-aggrandizement can be an issue too. Many college newspaper editors are invited, all expenses paid, to Hollywood movie premieres. The duty-to-self principle favors going: The trip would be fun. In addition, it is a good story opportunity, and being a free favor, it would not cost the newspaper anything. However, what of an editor's responsibility to readers? Readers have a right to expect writers to provide honest accounts that are not colored by favoritism. Can a reporter write fairly after being wined and dined and flown across the continent by movie producers who want a gung-ho story about a weak flick?

Even if reporters rise above being affected and are true to conscience, there are the duty-to-employer and the duty-to-profession principles to consider. The newspaper and the profession itself can be tarnished by audience suspicions that a reporter has been bought off, whether or not the suspicions are unfounded.

Duty to Audience.   Television programs that re-enact violence are popular with audiences, but do they do a disservice because they frighten many viewers into inferring that the streets are more dangerous than they really are?

Tom Wicker of the New York *Times* tells a story about his early days as a reporter in North Carolina. He was covering a divorce case involving one spouse chasing the other with an ax. Nobody was hurt physically, and everyone who heard the story in the courtroom had a good laugh, except the divorcing couple. It was ribald human comedy. Everyone in the courtroom laughed at the account. In writing his story, Wicker captured the darkly comedic details so skillfully that his editor put the story on the front page. Wicker was proud of the piece until the next day when the woman in the case visited him. Worn-out, haggard, hurt and angry, she asked, "Mr. Wicker, why did you think you had a right to make fun of me in your paper?"

The lesson stayed with Wicker for the rest of his career. He had unthinkingly hurt a fellow human being for no better reason than to evoke a chuckle, or perhaps a belly laugh, from his readers. For Wicker, the duty-to-audience principle would never again transcend his moral duty to the dignity of the subjects of his stories. Similar ethics questions involve whether to cite AIDS as a contributor to death in an obituary, to identify victims in rape stories, or to name juveniles charged with crimes.

Duty to Employer.   Does loyalty to an employer transcend the ideal of pursuing and telling the truth when a news reporter discovers dubious business deals involving the parent corporation? This is a growing issue as the mass media become consolidated into fewer gigantic companies owned by conglomerates.

In a classic case, the executive producer of the NBC *Today* show, Marty Ryan, ordered a reference to General Electric deleted from an affiliate-provided news story on untested and sometimes defective bolts in jet engines manufactured by GE. The owner of NBC at the time was GE. At ABC television, which is part of the Disney empire, newscasts tread lightly on negative events at Disney theme parks.

■ Fighting the Wrong-Headed Rape Stigma

▲ Charlie Gay.
Editor Charlie Gay sees no choice in the practice of good journalism but to include the names of victims in rape stories.

Unusual among U.S. newspapers, the Shelton, Washington, *Journal* printed the names of rape victims and even got into X-rated details in covering trials. The former publisher, Charlie Gay, knew the policy ran against the grain of contemporary news practices. It's also, he said, "good basic journalism."

Most newsrooms shield the names of rape victims, recognizing a notion, flawed though it is, that victims invite the crime. This stigma sets rape apart from other crimes, or at least so goes one line of thinking. Thus, naming should be at the victim's discretion, not a journalist's. To that, Charlie Gay said balderdash. Silence and secrecy only perpetuate stigmas, he said. As he sees it, only with the bright light of exposure can wrong-headed stigmas be cleansed away.

Gay said the journalist's duty is to tell news fully and fairly. Not to name the accuser while naming the accused would be unfair. Gay's point is that not naming both is "stacking everything against the accused."

In a speech to the Shelton Rotary Club, Gay defended the Journal's reporting of crimes and trials: "We're not trying to protect one party or make judgments about one party." The ideal to Gay is full, fair, detailed stories that inform without prejudicing.

The *Journal's* victim-naming policy rankled many readers. Letters flooded the opinion page with every rape case. The newspaper was picketed. Critics tried organizing an advertiser boycott and called on readers to cancel subscriptions.

At one point the state legislature responded. After lengthy debate about whether naming names should be outlawed, the legislature decided to bar reporters from naming child victims. The law was later ruled unconstitutional. It violated the First Amendment because government was abridging freedom of the press. The flap, however, demonstrated the intensity of feelings on the subject.

Police, prosecutors and social workers generally want names withheld, saying that some victims won't come forward for fear of publicity. Gay was blunt about that argument: The job of the press is to report the news, not to make the job of government easier. He said it is the job of government agents, including police and social workers, to persuade victims to press charges.

Although decidedly with a minority view, Gay had some support for including names and gripping detail in reporting sex crimes. Psychologist Robert Seidenberg, for example, believes that rape victims may be encouraged to report the crime by reading the accounts of victims with whom they can relate because details make compelling reading that helps them sort through their own situation more clearly.

Duty to the Profession.   At what point does an ethically motivated advertising agency person blow the whistle on misleading claims by other advertising people?

Duty to Society.   Does duty to society ever transcend duty to self? To the audience? To the employer? To colleagues? Does ideology affect a media worker's sense of duty to society? Consider how Joseph Stalin, Adolf Hitler and Franklin Roosevelt would be covered by a highly motivated communist. Or by a fascist journalist? Or by a libertarian journalist?.

Are there occasions when the duty-to-society and duty-to-audience principles are incompatible? Nobody enjoys seeing the horrors of war, for example, but journalists may feel that their duty to society demands that they go after the most grisly photographs of combat to show how horrible war is and, thereby, in a small way, contribute to public pressure toward a cessation of hostilities and eventual peace.

APPLYING YOUR MEDIA LITERACY

- How do ethics codes sometimes fail in helping media people make right decisions?
- If you were a college newspaper editor, would you accept an all-expenses-paid trip to a Hollywood movie premiere? Explain the pros and cons of your decision.

Media Ethics

STUDY PREVIEW | Media ethics is complicated by the different performance standards that mass media operations establish for themselves. This is further complicated by the range of expectations in the mass audience. One size does not fit all.

Media Commitment

A single ethics standard is impossible to apply to the mass media. Nobody holds Steven Colbert and the Comedy Channel to the same standard as the New York *Times.* Why the difference? Media ethics, in part, is a function of what a media operation promises to deliver to its audience. Some media have a commitment to tongue-in-cheek news context. Some are patently fun-and-games. The New York *Times,* on the other hand, considers itself a "newspaper of record." There is a big difference.

For years CNN touted accuracy in its promotional tagline: "News You Can Trust." Explicitly, the network promised to deliver truthful accounts of the day's events. CNN was establishing a standard for audience expectations. A lapse, like a misleading story—especially if intentional or the result of sloppiness—would represent a broken promise and an ethics problem.

A media organization's commitments may be implicit. Disney, for example, has cultivated an image of wholesome products with which the whole family can be comfortable. It's a commitment: No smut here.

Audience Expectations

The audience brings a range of ethics expectations to different media sources, which further thwarts any attempt at one-size-fits-all media ethics. From a book publisher's fantasy science-fiction imprint, readers have far different expectations than they do from politico. com, which, except for plainly labeled opinion, is expected to deliver unmitigated nonfiction.

A range in the type of messages purveyed by the mass media also bespeaks a variety of ethics expectations. Rarely is falsity excusable, but even the courts allow puffery in advertising. The news releases that public relations people produce are expected, by their nature, to be from a client's perspective, which doesn't always coincide with the perspective that people expect of a news reporter.

Media messages in the fiction story tradition don't unsettle anyone if they sensationalize to emphasize a point. Sensationalistic exaggeration in a serious biography, however, is unforgivable.

- **How does a media organization's self-concept guide decision-making in ethics?**
- **What is the role of audience expectations in media ethics?**
- **Why do ethics expectations differ among media organizations?**

Moral Principles

STUDY PREVIEW

Concern about doing the right thing is part of human nature. And over the centuries, leading thinkers have developed a great number of enduring moral principles. The mass media, like other institutions and also like individuals, draw on these principles, but this does not always make moral decisions easy. The principles are not entirely consistent, especially in sorting through dilemmas.

Golden Mean

Writing almost 2,400 years ago, the Greek philosopher **Aristotle** devised the **Golden Mean** as a basis for moral decision making. The Golden Mean sounds simple and straightforward: Avoid extremes and seek moderation. Modern journalistic balance and fairness are founded on this principle.

The Golden Mean's dictate, however, is not as simple as it sounds. As with all moral principles, application of the Golden Mean can present difficulties. Consider the federal law that requires over-the-air broadcasters to give equal opportunity to candidates for public office. If one candidate buys 30 seconds at 7 p.m. for $500 the station is obligated to allow other candidates for the same office to buy 30 seconds at the same time for the same rate. On the surface this application of the Golden Mean, embodied in federal law, might seem to be reasonable, fair and morally right, but the issue is far more complex. The equality requirement, for example, gives an advantage to candidates who hold simplistic positions that can be expressed compactly. Good and able candidates whose positions require more than a sound bite to explain are disadvantaged, and society is damaged when inferior candidates win public office.

"Do Unto Others"

The Judeo-Christian principle of "**Do unto others** as you would have them do unto you" appeals to most people. Not even the do-unto-others prescription is without problems, however. Consider the photojournalist who sees virtue in serving a mass audience with a truthful account of the human condition. This might manifest itself in portrayals of great emotions, like grief. But would the photojournalist appreciate being photographed herself in a grieving moment after learning that her own infant son had died in an accident? If not, her pursuit of truth through photography for a mass audience would be contrary to the "do-unto-others" dictum.

Categorical Imperatives

About 200 years ago, German philosopher **Immanuel Kant** wrote that moral decisions should flow from thoroughly considered principles. As he put it, "Act on the maxim that you would want to become universal law." He called his maxim the **categorical imperative**. A categorical imperative, well thought out, is a principle that the individual who devised it would be willing to apply in all moral questions of a similar sort. In a way, Kant recast the Judeo-Christian "do unto others" admonition but more intellectually and less intuitively.

Kant's categorical imperative does not dictate specifically what actions are morally right or wrong. Moral choices, says Kant, go deeper than the context of the immediate issue. He encourages a philosophical approach to moral questions, with people using their intellect to identify principles that they, as individuals, would find acceptable if applied universally.

Kant does not encourage the kind of standardized approach to ethics represented by professional codes. His emphasis, rather, is on hard thinking. The point has been put

Aristotle
Advocate of the Golden Mean

Golden Mean
Moderation is the best course

▲ **Aristotle.** *The Greek thinker Aristotle told his students 2,400 years ago that right courses of action avoid extremes. His recommendation: moderation.*

"Do unto others"
Judeo-Christian principle for ethical behavior

Immanuel Kant
Advocated the categorical imperative

categorical imperative
A principle that can be applied in any and all circumstances with moral certitude

▲ **John Stuart Mill.** *He saw decisions as ethical if the ascertainable outcomes were good.*

▲ **John Rawls.** *He favored putting a blind eye to all issues except rightness and wrongness. The veil of ignorance, he called it.*

John Stuart Mill
Advocated utilitarianism

principle of utility
Best course bestows the most good for the most people

John Dewey
Advocate of pragmatism

pragmatic ethics
Judge acts by their results

John Rawls
Advocated egalitarianism

veil of ignorance
Making decisions with a blind eye to extraneous factors that could affect the decision

this way by scholar Patricia Smith, writing in the *Journal of Mass Media Ethics*: "A philosophical approach to ethics embodies a commitment to consistency, clarity, the principled evaluation of arguments and unrelenting persistence to get to the bottom of things."

Utilitarian Ethics

In the mid-1800s British thinker **John Stuart Mill** declared that morally right decisions are those that result in "happiness for the greatest number." Mill called his idea the **principle of utility**. It sounds good to many of us because it parallels the democratic principle of majority rule, with its emphasis on the greatest good for the greatest number of people.

By and large, journalists embrace Mill's utilitarianism today, as evinced in notions like the *people's right to know*, a concept originally meant to support journalistic pursuit of information about government, putting the public's interests ahead of government's interests. The right-to-know mantra, however, has come to be almost reflexively invoked to defend pursuing very personal information about individuals, no matter what the human toll. Utilitarianism has its difficulties.

Pragmatic Ethics

John Dewey, an American thinker who wrote in the late 1800s and early 1900s, argued that the virtue of moral decisions had to be judged by their results. Like other ethics systems, Dewey's **pragmatic ethics** has problems. One is that people do not have crystal balls to see for sure whether their actions will have good consequences—no matter how well thought out. Almost always there are unanticipated consequences.

Egalitarian Ethics

In the 20th century, philosopher **John Rawls** introduced the **veil of ignorance** as an element in ethics decisions. Choosing a right course of action, said Rawls, requires blindness to social position or other discriminating factors. This is known as **egalitarianism**. An ethical decision requires that all people be given an equal hearing and the same fair consideration.

To Rawls, a brutal slaying in a poor urban neighborhood deserves the same attention as a similarly brutal slaying in an upscale suburb. Moral decisions must be blind to race, ethnicity, sexuality and other differentiating factors among people, unless, of course, other factors are relevant. In the same sense, all other things being equal, a crime against property, like a $20,000 bank burglary, is no more newsworthy than a $20,000 bank embezzlement. Bank robbery, however, with human beings in immediate jeopardy, is another and hardly parallel issue.

Social Responsibility

The **Hutchins Commission**, a learned group led by intellectual **Robert Hutchins** that studied the U.S. mass media in the 1940s, recommended that journalists and other media people make decisions that serve society responsibly. For all its virtues the **social responsibility** system, like all ethics systems, has difficulties. For one thing, decision-makers can only imperfectly foresee the effects of their decisions. It is not possible to predict with 100 percent confidence whether every decision will turn out to be socially responsible. Also, well-meaning people may differ honestly about how society is most responsibly served.

APPLYING YOUR MEDIA LITERACY

- **What are strengths and weaknesses of Aristotle's Golden Mean?**
- **Was Immanuel Kant merely restating the much older "Do unto others" maxim? Explain your thinking.**
- **How is John Stuart Mill's utilitarianism attractive to people in modern democracies?**
- **What is the problem of using outcomes to determine media ethical behavior?**
- **How realistic is the egalitarianism of John Rawls in guiding media behavior?**
- **Who decides what's socially responsible media behavior as set out by Robert Hutchins?**

Process versus Outcome

STUDY PREVIEW | The various approaches to ethics fall into two broad categories: deontological ethics and teleological ethics. Deontologists say people need to follow good rules. Teleologists judge morality not by the rules but by the consequences of decisions.

Deontological Ethics

The Greek word *deon*, which means "duty," is at the heart of **deontological ethics,** which holds that people act morally when they follow good rules. Deontologists feel that people are duty-bound to identify these rules.

Deontologists include people who believe that biblical scripture holds all the answers for right living. Their equivalent among media practitioners are those who rely entirely on codes of ethics drafted by organizations they trust. Following rules is a prescriptive form of ethics. At first consideration, ethics might seem as easy as following the rules, but not all questions are clear-cut. In complicated situations, the rules sometimes contradict each other. Some cases are dilemmas with no one right option—only a choice among less-than-desirable options.

Deontological ethics becomes complicated, and also more intellectually interesting, when individuals, unsatisfied with other people's rules, try to work out their own universally applicable moral principles.

Here are some major deontological approaches:

- **Divine command theory.** This theory holds that proper moral decisions come from obeying the commands of God, with blind trust that the consequences will be good. A variation, the divine right of kings theory, is that monarchs are divinely appointed and thus deserve allegiance.

- **Secular command theory.** This theory is a nonreligious variation that stresses allegiance to a dictator or other political leader from whom the people take cues when making moral decisions. There has been no more prominent example than Kim Jong-Il, who was designated North Korea's *Supreme Leader* in a 2009 revision of the nation's constitution.

- **Libertarian theory.** This theory stresses a laissez-faire approach to ethics: Give free rein to the human ability to think through problems, and people almost always will make morally right decisions.

- **Categorical imperative theory.** This theory holds that virtue results when people identify and apply universal principles.

Robert Hutchins
Called for the new media to emphasize its social responsibility, not only its freedom

egalitarianism
Treat everyone the same

Hutchins Commission
Advocated social responsibility as goal and result of media activities

social responsibility
Making decisions that serve society responsibly

deontological ethics
Good actions flow from good processes

divine command theory
Proper decisions follow God's will

secular command theory
Holds that authorities legitimately hold supreme authority although not necessarily with a divine authority

libertarian theory
Given good information and time, people ultimately make right decisions

▲ **Immanuel Kant.**
Kant emphasized using good processes as the route to good choices.

▲ **John Dewey.**
Dewey's pragmatism measures wise decisions by their outcome.

MEDIAtomorrow

■ Truth in the News Blogosphere

In India's news media, no story was too trivial about the pending visit of Barrack Obama. One story told of animal-catchers being hired to shield Obama from mischievous monkeys in a park across from his hotel. There was a story too on crews scaling palm trees to knock down coconuts, lest one conk the American president on the head.

Among the stories was one that all the arrangements would cost the United States government $200 million a day—a whopping figure. The war in Afghanistan was running only $190 million. The staggering figure was from an Indian provincial source, who was not named in the story, but described as "privy to arrangements." Knowing that Indians were hungry for anything about the Obama visit, the news agency Press Trust of India distributed the story to 450 newspapers in India. There the story might have stayed. But in the United States the *Drudge Report* web site, without any fact-checking, posted a link to an Indian television schannel carrying the Press Trust story.

Michele Bachmann. *In her 2012 presidential bid, Minnesota member of Congress Michele Bachmann acquired a reputation for looseness with facts. From podium to podium she passed on things she picked up from blogs and chitchat as truth. One was a claim that childhood vaccinations against certain cancers caused mental retardation. In millions of inoculations there was no medical evidence to support the claim. But Bachmann, after hearing a mother's moving anecdotal claim, made it a point in her bid for higher office—until news reporters pressed her and she had no choice but to back down.*

Any reporter covering Washington would have recognized the absurdity of the $200 million figure. But in the untamed blogosphere, it is ideology—not facts—that often drives stories. And the numbers on the cost of the presidential visit to India fit into a right-wing blogosphere scenario of government-spending-gone-mad. The story, as they say, then went viral. The facts assumed further partisan fluidity in the retellings in the blogosphere.

When anti-Obama radio talk-show rambler Rush Limbaugh picked up the story, he had it that 40 airplanes were assigned to the trip. Limbaugh doesn't do any journalistic legwork of his own but reads lots of blogs. Meanwhile, the numbers grew Pinocchio-like. Limbaugh had said that 507 hotel rooms had been booked. Back in the blogosphere the number was suddenly 570. The Obama entourage swelled to 3,000.

Absurdities piled unchecked on absurdities. Limbaugh, for example, said the Navy was assigning 34 ships including an aircraft carrier to support the trip. Quite a feat for a Navy with a total of 288 ships spread all over the globe. It doesn't take a genius to do the math. Thirty-four ships would be 12 percent of the Navy, many of whose vessels are in port at any given time, some even dry-docked.

One frequent critic of Obama in Congress, Michele Bachmann of Minnesota, used the $200 million figure as an example of government lavishness. By this point, as Bachmann had it, the number of rooms booked at the Taj Mahal Palace hotel had swelled to "over 870." Fact: The Taj has only 565 rooms. In interviewing Bachmann, CNN's Anderson Cooper pressed her on her sources: "Well these are the numbers that have been coming out in the press." Well, kinda, depending in how loosely the word *press* is defined.

What should be done? There seems to be no mechanisms in place to encourage accuracy among reckless bloggers and quasi-mainstream radio-talkers, even public officials. The ready access to information doesn't seem to be encouraging fact-checking prior to citation. These people feed on unconfirmed information so long as it fits a partisan narrative, then pass the bad stuff on. Repeated and repeated, these inaccuracies compound exponentially. They assume a life of their own as if fact, the accuracies wandering, sometimes deliberately, further and further from reality.

What Do You Think?

Should responsible bloggers organize and create an ethics code, much as did the American Society of Newspaper Editors in 1923? Would it need to be a global initiative? How might it be enforced?

Rush Limbaugh. *Not only do some candidates for elected office recklessly pick up blog-embroidered information, so do some media people. In the 2012 elections, the issue became more intense. Do facts matter? Do media people, including bloggers and radio talk-show hosts like Rush Limbaugh, have a responsibility for accuracy? Do public officials?*

Teleological Ethics

Unlike deontological ethics, which is concerned with the right actions, teleological ethics is concerned with the consequences of actions. The word **teleology** comes from the Greek word *teleos*, which means "result" or "consequence."

Teleologists see flaws in the formal, legalistic duty to rules of deontologists, noting that great harm sometimes flows from blind allegiance to rules.

Here are some major teleological approaches:

- **Pragmatic theory.** This theory encourages people to look at human experience to determine the probable consequences of an action and then decide its desirability.

- **Utilitarian theory.** This theory favors decisions that benefit more people than they damage—the greatest good for the greatest number.

- **Social responsibility theory.** This theory judges actions by the good effect they have on society.

teleology
Good decisions are those with good consequences

Situational Ethics

Firm deontologists see two primary flaws in teleological ethics:

- Imperfect foresight.

- Lack of guiding principles.

Despite these flaws, many media practitioners apply teleological approaches, sometimes labeled **situational ethics**, to work through moral issues. They gather as much information as they can about a situation and then decide, not on the basis of principle but on the facts of the situation. Critics of situational ethics worry about decisions governed by situations. Much better, they argue, would be decisions flowing from principles of enduring value. With situational ethics the same person might do one thing one day and on another day go another direction in a similar situation.

Consider a case at the *Rocky Mountain News* in Denver. Editors learned that the president of a major suburban newspaper chain had killed his parents and sister in another state when he was 18. After seven years in a mental hospital the man completed college, moved to Colorado, lived a model life and became a successful executive at the suburban chain. The *Rocky Mountain News* decided not to make a story of it. Dredging up the man's past, said a News official, would serve no purpose except to "titillate morbid curiosity" or maliciously damage an otherwise solid citizen.

However, when the *Rocky Mountain News'* chief competitor, the Denver *Post*, revealed the man's past, the *News* reversed itself and published a lengthy piece of its own. Why, *The*

situational ethics
Make ethics decisions on the basis of situation at hand

Post, in breaking the story, had suggested that *News* editors knew about the man's past and had decided to protect him as a fellow member of the journalistic fraternity. *News* editors denied that their motivation was to protect the man. To prove it, they reconsidered their decision and published a story on him. The *News* explained its change of mind by saying that the situation had changed. *News* editors, concerned that their newspaper's credibility had been challenged, thought that printing a story would set that straight. Of less concern, suddenly, was that the story would titillate morbid curiosity or contribute to the destruction of a successful citizen. It was a classic case of situational ethics.

Flip-flops on moral issues, such as what happened at the *Rocky Mountain News*, bother critics of situational ethics. The critics say that decisions should be based on deeply rooted moral principles—not immediate, transient facts or changing peripheral contexts.

APPLYING YOUR MEDIA LITERACY

- As a media consumer, would you rather that media people followed deontological or teleological ethics? Why?
- What are plusses and minuses of situational ethics to sort through dilemmas?

Potter's Box

STUDY PREVIEW | Moral problems in the mass media can be so complex that it may seem there is no solution. Although ideal answers without any negative results may be impossible, a process exists for identifying a course of action that integrates an individual's personal values with moral principles and then tests conclusions against loyalties.

Four Quadrants

Ralph Potter
Ethicist who devised Potter's Box

Potter's Box
Tool for sorting through the pros and cons of ethics questions

A Harvard Divinity School professor, **Ralph Potter**, devised a four-quadrant model for sorting through ethics problems. Each quadrant of the square-like model, called **Potter's Box**, poses a category of questions. Working through these categories helps to clarify issues and leads to a morally justifiable position. These are the quadrants of Potter's Box:

Situation. In Quadrant 1 the facts of the issue are decided. Consider a newsroom in which a series of articles on rape is being developed and the question arises of whether to identify rape victims by name. Here is how the situation could be defined: The newspaper has access to a young mother who has been abducted and raped and who is willing to describe the assault in graphic detail and to discuss her experience as a witness at the assailant's trial. Also, the woman is willing to be identified in the story.

Values. Moving to Quadrant 2 of Potter's Box, editors and reporters identify the values that underlie all the available choices. This process involves listing the positive and negative values that flow from conscience. One editor might argue that full, frank discussion on social issues is necessary to deal with them. Another might say that identifying the rape victim by name might discourage others from even reporting such a crime. Other positions:

- Publishing the name is in poor taste.
- The newspaper has an obligation to protect the victim from her own possibly bad judgment in allowing her name to be used.
- The purpose of the rape series can be accomplished without using the name.
- Readers have a right to all the relevant information that the newspaper can gather.

An editor who is torn between such contrary thoughts is making progress toward a decision by at least identifying all the values that can be posited.

Principles. In Potter's Quadrant 3, decision-makers search for moral principles that uphold the values they identified in Quadrant 2. John Stuart Mill's principle of utility, which favors the majority over individuals, would support using the victim's name because it could add

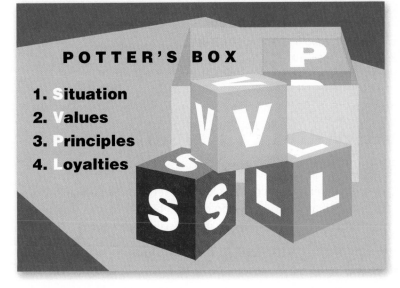

POTTER'S BOX

1. **S**ituation
2. **V**alues
3. **P**rinciples
4. **L**oyalties

◀ **Potter's Box.** *Potter's Box offers four categories of questions to help develop morally justifiable positions. Ralph Potter, the divinity professor who devised the categories, said to start by establishing the facts of the situation. Next, identify the values that underpin the options, recognizing that some values may be incompatible with others. Then, consider the moral principles that support each of the values. Finally, sort through loyalties to all the affected interests. Potter's Box is not a panacea, but it provides a framework for working through ethics issues in a thorough way.*

poignancy to the story, enhancing the chances of improved public sensitivity, and perhaps even lead to improved public policy, all of which, Mill would say, outweigh the harm that might come to an individual. On the other hand, people who have used Immanuel Kant's ideas to develop inviolable operating principles—categorical imperatives—look to their rule book: We never publish information that might offend readers. One value of Potter's Quadrant 3 is that it gives people confidence in the values that emerged in their debates over Quadrant 2.

Loyalties. In Quadrant 4 the decision-maker folds in an additional layer of complexity that must be sorted through: loyalties. The challenge is to establish a hierarchy of loyalties. Is the first loyalty to a code of ethics, and if so, which code? Or is the first loyalty to readers, and if so, which ones? To society? To the employer? To self? Out of duty to self, some reporters and editors might want to make the rape series as potent as possible, with as much detail as possible, to win awards and bring honor to themselves and perhaps a raise or promotion or bigger job in another newsroom. Others might be motivated by their duty to their employer: The more detail in the story, the more newspapers it will sell. For others their duty to society may be paramount: The newspaper has a social obligation to present issues in as powerful a way as possible to spur reforms in general attitudes and perhaps public policy.

▲ **Ralph Potter.**

Intellectual Satisfaction

Potter's Box does not provide answers. Rather, it offers a process through which the key elements in ethics questions can be sorted out.

Also, Potter's Box focuses on moral aspects of a problem, leaving it to the decision-maker to examine practical considerations separately, such as whether prudence supports making the morally best decision. Moral decisions should not be made in a vacuum. For example, would it be wise to go ahead with the rape victim's name if 90 percent of the news audience would become so offended that they would launch a boycott of everything coming out of your newsroom?

Other practical questions can involve the law. If the morally best decision is to publish the name but the law forbids it, should media go with the name anyway? Can journalistic virtue ever transcend the law? Is it worth it to publish the name to create a First Amendment issue? Are there legal implications, like going to jail or piling up astronomical legal defense costs?

Is it worth it to go against generally accepted practices and publish the victim's name? Deciding on a course of action that runs contrary to tradition, perhaps even contrary to some ethics codes, could mean being ostracized by other media people who might have gone another way in dealing with the same dilemma. Being right can be lonely. But there is consolation with Potter's Box as a vehicle to know you thoroughly considered the facts and all the competing values, principles and loyalties. This is an intellectual satisfaction.

- You are a news reporter. A candidate for mayor tells you that the incumbent mayor is in cahoots with organized crime. What a bombshell story! Use Potter's Box to decide whether to rush to tell the story.

Ethics, Law and Practicality

STUDY PREVIEW | Right and wrong are issues in both ethics and law, but ethics and law are different. Obedience to law, or even to professional codes of ethics, will not always lead to moral action. There are also times when practical issues can factor into decisions on ethics.

Ethics and Law

Ethics is an individual matter that relates closely to conscience. Because conscience is unique to each individual, no two people have exactly the same moral framework. There are, however, issues about which there is consensus. No right-minded person condones murder, for example. When there is a universal feeling, ethics becomes codified in law, but laws do not address all moral questions. It is the issues of right and wrong that do not have a consensus that make ethics difficult: Was it morally right for *USA Today* to initiate coverage of tennis superstar Arthur Ashe's AIDS? Ashe regarded his disease as a private matter, but, expecting that *USA Today* would be making a story of it, he called a news conference and made a painful and tearful announcement that he had contracted the disease from a blood transfusion.

Ethics and law are related but separate. The law will allow a mass media practitioner to do many things that the practitioner would refuse to do ethically. Since the 1964 *New York Times* v. *Sullivan* case, for example, the U.S. Supreme Court has allowed mass media to cause tremendous damage to public officials, even with false information. However, rare is the journalist who would intentionally push the *Sullivan* latitudes to their limits to pillory a public official.

The ethics decisions of an individual mass media practitioner usually are more limiting than the law. There are times, though, when a journalist may choose to break the law on the grounds of ethics. Applying John Stuart Mill's principle of "the greatest good," a radio reporter might choose to break the speed limit to reach a chemical plant where an accident is threatening to send a deadly cloud toward where her listeners live. Breaking a speed limit might seem petty as an example, but it demonstrates that obeying the law and obeying one's conscience do not always coincide.

Accepted Practices

Just as there is no reliable correlation between law and ethics, neither is there one between accepted media practices and ethics. What is acceptable at one advertising agency to make a product look good in photographs might be unacceptable at another. Even universally **accepted practices** should not go unexamined, for unless accepted practices are examined and reconsidered on a continuing basis, media practitioners can come to rely more on habit than on principles in their work.

Prudence and Ethics

Prudence is the application of wisdom in a practical situation. It can be a leveling factor in moral questions. Consider the case of Irvin Lieberman, who had built his *Main Line Chronicle* and several other weeklies in the Philadelphia suburbs into aggressive, journalistically excellent newspapers. After being hit with nine libel suits, all costly to defend,

accepted practices
What media do as a matter of routine, sometimes without considering ethics implications

prudence
Applying wisdom, not principles, to an ethics situation

Lieberman softened the thrust of his newspapers. He decided to abandon hard-hitting investigative journalism. It was more important, he said, to stay in business so he could feed his family than to rack up huge legal bills.

Courageous pursuit of morally lofty ends can, as a practical matter, be foolish. Was Irvin Lieberman exhibiting moral weakness by bending to the chilling prospect of more libel suits? Or was he being prudent? Those questions can be debated forever. The point, however, is that prudence cannot be ignored as a factor in moral decisions.

APPLYING YOUR MEDIA LITERACY

- How do law and ethics guide media behavior differently?
- What is the problem of "We always did it that way" as a guide for ethical media behavior?
- Should prudence ever trump ethics?

Unsettling Media Issues

STUDY PREVIEW | Many standard media practices press the line between right and wrong, which muddies clear-cut standards that are universally applicable and recognized. There is further muddiness because many ethics codes confuse unethical behavior with behavior that may appear unethical but is not necessarily so.

Plagiarism

Perhaps the most fiercely loyal media fans are those who read romance novels and swear by a favorite author. In an internet chatroom romance writer Janet Dailey found herself boxed into an admission that she had plagiarized from rival writer Nora Roberts. There is no scorn like that of creative people for those who steal their work. Roberts was "very, very upset." HarperCollins recalled Dailey's book that contained the plagiarism, and Roberts' fans, many of them long-time Dailey detractors, began a hunt for other purloined passages. They found them.

What is **plagiarism**? Generally, it's considered passing off someone else's creative work as your own, without permission. It's still plagiarism even if the original is changed a tad, as was Dailey's loose paraphrasing.

The fact that Dailey's 93 books over 20 years had sold an average of more than 2 million each made the scandal all the juicier. In the end Roberts proposed a financial settlement, and the proceeds went to promote literacy.

Everyone agrees that plagiarism, a form of thievery, is unethical, but the issue is not simple. The fact is that many media people draw heavily on other people's ideas and work. Think about sitcom story lines that mimic each other or the bandwagons of movies that follow an unexpected hit with an oddball theme that suddenly becomes mainstream. Journalists, most of whom consider themselves especially pristine compared to their media brethren, have standard practices that encourage a lot of "borrowing."

Among factors that make journalists uncomfortable when pressed hard on plagiary questions are:

- Institutionalized exchanging of stories
- The role of public relations in generating news stories
- Monitoring the competition
- Subliminal memory and innocent recall

This all is further complicated by a cut-and-paste mentality that has been facilitated by digitized messages on the internet. A whole new generation is missing a level of

plagiarism
Using someone else's work without permission or credit

MEDIAcounterpoints

■ Plagiarism: Should We Care?

As Chris Anderson explains it, his plagiarism was a confluence of events that nobody intended, himself included. For his book *Free*, Anderson had picked up passages from entries in the online reference work Wikipedia. A book reviewer for the literary journal *Virginia Quarterly Review* spotted similarities in wording and cross-checked the manuscript against Wiki entries.

How could this happen? Anderson, chief editor of *Wired* magazine, is no intellectual slouch inclined to stealing other people's work. For years he had been a respected thinker on information issues. His book *The Long Tail* had charted new territory in contemporary thinking about economics in the digital age.

About the plagiarism charge, Anderson said: "My screwups." He explained that he used footnotes, a standard practice, in his manuscript. The book's editors, however, wanted each footnote to include the date and hour that Anderson consulted the source material. Anderson thought all that would be "clumsy and archaic" and pointless. To sidestep his editors' insistence on timestamps, Anderson wove attributives into the manuscript. His goal: A seamless read. But under the deadline pressure, Anderson said, he missed inserting some of the in-text credits he had intended.

After the uncredited passages were revealed, Anderson's publisher, Hyperion, accepted quickly inserted footnotes into the online edition. Hyperion also promised to include the notes in print edition reprints.

But the damage was done. Purists on footnoting had a new field day with Anderson's lapse.

▲ **Chris Anderson.** *Ironically, Anderson practices traditional footnoting, even though in his book* Free *he argued that information cannot be sealed up forever. In effect, he was saying that the conventions of identifying sources are impossible to maintain in the digital age, whatever their virtue may be. The irony is all the more so because of lapses that deleted some footnotes in the book and brought down the traditionalist establishment on Anderson.*

Traditionalists make the case that it's only right that scholars and other people who create new intellectual property acknowledge those on whose work they draw. To traditionalists it's a moral issue—the right thing to do. Traditionalists call it theft to expropriate someone else's work without permission or even a credit.

POINT COUNTERPOINT

To attempt to restrain the free flow of information is to place artificial human limitations that ultimately will fail. So why fight the inevitable? Old-style conventions like footnoting should be seen as dams that deny the free exchange of information and ideas by artificially slowing the process.

DEEPENING YOUR MEDIA LITERACY

EXPLORE THE ISSUE: Restraints on using other people's intellectual property in your own work have a moral foundation. Simply put, it's not nice to claim someone else's work as your own—not even to let it be inferred.

DIG DEEPER: The U.S. Constitution indirectly speaks to plagiarism. The Constitution protects creators on intellectual property, including authors, poets, composers and lyricists, from losing their work to copiers. Consult Article I, Section 8, Clause 8 of the Constitution and then put the rationale of the nation's founders into contemporary language. Also, explain what the constitutional language means.

WHAT DO YOU THINK? Has digital technology rendered the traditional moral imperative against plagiarism obsolete?

sensitivity to traditionally recognized rights of people who create or own intellectual property to control its reuse.

Some creative work, like scholarship, requires that information and ideas be attributed to their sources. Scholars have made footnoting a high art. Journalists are not so strict, as shown by story-swapping through the Associated Press. The AP picks up stories from its members and distributes them to other members, generally without any reference to the source. Some publications and broadcasters do not even acknowledge AP as the intermediary.

Conditioned by more than 150 years of the AP's being a journalistic model and under pressure to gather information quickly, many journalists have a high tolerance for "borrowing." When the Chicago *Tribune* was apologizing for a story cribbed from the Jerusalem *Post*, for example, one of the writer's colleagues defended the story: "Everybody rewrites the Jerusalem *Post*. That's how foreign correspondents work."

Incredible as it seems, journalistic tolerance for plagiarism once even allowed radio stations to pilfer the local newspaper for newscasts. Sometimes you could hear the announcer turning the pages. A sad joke that acknowledged this practice was that some stations bought their news at 50 cents a copy, which was cheaper than hiring reporters to cover the community. So pervasive was the journalistic tolerance for "borrowing" that few newspapers protested even mildly when their stories were pirated.

Misrepresentation

Janet Cooke's meteoric rise at the Washington *Post* unraveled quickly the day after she received a Pulitzer Prize. Her editors had been so impressed with her story "Jimmy's World," about a child who was addicted to heroin, that they had nominated it for a Pulitzer Prize. The gripping tale began: "Jimmy is 8 years old and a third-generation heroin addict, a precocious little boy with sandy hair, velvety brown eyes and needle marks freckling the baby-smooth skin of his thin brown arms." Janet Cooke claimed that she had won the confidence of Jimmy's mother and her live-in male friend, a drug dealer, to do the story. Cooke said she had promised not to reveal their identities as a condition for her access to Jimmy.

The story, which played on the front page, so shocked Washington that people demanded that Jimmy be taken away from his mother and placed in a foster home. The *Post* declined to help authorities, citing Cooke's promise of confidentiality to her sources. The mayor ordered the police to find Jimmy with or without the newspaper's help. Millions of dollars in police resources went into a door-to-door search. After 17 days the police gave up knocking on doors for tips on Jimmy. Some doubts emerged at the *Post* about the story, but the newspaper stood behind its reporter.

Janet Cooke, 25 when she was hired by the *Post*, had extraordinary credentials. Her résumé showed a baccalaureate degree, *magna cum laude*, from Vassar; study at the Sorbonne in Paris; a master's degree from the University of Toledo; abilities in several languages; and two years of journalistic experience with the Toledo *Blade*. Said Ben Bradlee, editor of the *Post*: "She had it all. She was bright. She was well-spoken. She was pretty. She wrote well." She was also black, which made her especially attractive to the *Post*, which was working to bring the percentage of black staff reporters nearer to the percentage of blacks in the newspaper's circulation area.

Six months after "Jimmy's World" was published, the Pulitzer committee announced its decision and issued a biographical sheet on Janet Cooke. The Associated Press, trying to flesh out the biographical information, spotted discrepancies right away. Janet Cooke, it turned out, had attended Vassar for one year but had not graduated with the honors she claimed. The University of Toledo had no record of awarding her a master's. Suddenly, doubts that had surfaced in the days immediately after "Jimmy's World" was published took on a new intensity. The editors sat Cooke down and grilled her on the claims on which she was hired. No, she admitted, she was not multilingual. The Sorbonne claim was fuzzy. More important, they pressed her on whether there was really a Jimmy. The interrogation continued into the night, and finally Janet Cooke confessed all: There were no confidential sources. There was no Jimmy. She had fabricated the story. She resigned. The *Post*, terribly embarrassed, returned the Pulitzer.

Janet Cooke
Classic case of representing fiction as truth

In cases of outright fabrication, as in "Jimmy's World," it is easy to identify the lapses in ethics. When Janet Cooke emerged briefly from seclusion to explain herself, she said that she had been responding to pressures in the *Post* newsroom to produce flashy, sensational copy. Most people found the explanation unsatisfying, considering the pattern of deception that went back to her falsified résumé.

There are **misrepresentations**, however, that are not as clearly unacceptable. Much debated are the following:

Staging News. To attract favorable attention to their clients, public relations people organize media events, a practice known as **staging news**. The events are designed to be irresistible to journalists. Rallies and demonstrations on topical issues, for example, find their way onto front pages, magazine covers and evening newscasts because their photogenic qualities give them an edge over less visual although sometimes more significant events. The ethics question is less important for publicists, who generally are up front about what they are doing. The ethics question is more serious for journalists, who claim that their job is to present an accurate, balanced account of a day's events but who regularly overplay staged events that are designed by publicists to be photogenic and easy to cover.

Re-Creations. Some television **reality programs** feature **re-enactments** that are not always labeled as such. Philip Weiss, writing in *Columbia Journalism Review*, offered this litany: shadows on the wall of a woman taking a hammer to her husband, a faceless actor grabbing a tin of kerosene to blow up his son, a corpse in a wheelbarrow with a hand dangling, a detective opening the trunk of a car and reeling from the stench of a decomposing

misrepresentations
Deception in gathering or telling information

staging news
Creating an event to attract news media attention and coverage

reality programs
Broadcast shows with a nonfiction basis

Re-enactments
Re-creating real events

MEDIAtimeline

ETHICS MILESTONES

ARISTOTLE
The Golden Mean (400 B.C.)

JESUS CHRIST
"Do unto others as you would have them do unto you" (20)

PIVOTAL EVENTS

• Greek defeat of Persians at
  Marathon (490 B.C.)
• Athenian democracy (430 B.C.–)
• Roman domination of
  Mediterranean (250–300 B.C.)

Aristotle's Golden Mean

EARLY ERAS

ETHICS MILESTONES

IMMANUEL KANT
Categorical imperatives (1785)

PIVOTAL EVENTS

• Johannes Gutenberg's movable metal type (1440s)
• Martin Luther launched Reformation (1517)
• Age of Science, Age of Reason began (1600s–)
• Isaac Newton's natural laws (1687)
• Industrial Revolution (1760s–)
• Revolutionary War (1776–1781)

Kant, less intuitive on ethics, more intellectual

1700S

body. Although mixing re-creations with strictly news footage rankles many critics, others argue that it helps people understand the situation. The same question arises with docudramas, which mix actual events and dramatic re-creations.

Selective Editing.   The editing process, by its nature, requires journalists to make decisions on what is most worth emphasizing and what is least worth even including. In this sense, all editing is selective, but the term **selective editing** refers to making decisions with the goal of distorting. Selective editing can occur in drama too, when writers, editors and other media people take literary license too far and intentionally misrepresent.

selective editing
Misrepresentation through omission and juxtaposition

Fictional Methods.   In the late 1960s many experiments in media portrayals of people and issues came to be called the **new journalism.** The term was hard to define because it included so many approaches. Among the most controversial were applications of fiction-writing methods to topical issues, an approach widely accepted in book publishing but suddenly controversial when it appeared in the news media. Character development became more important than before, including presumed insights into the thinking of people being covered. The view of the writer became an essential element in much of this reporting. The defense for these approaches was that traditional, facts-only reporting could not approach complex truths that merited journalistic explorations. The profound ethics questions that these approaches posed were usually mitigated by clear statements to the audience about what the writer was attempting. Nonetheless, it was a controversial approach to the issues of the day and remains controversial. There remains no defense, however, when the fictional approach was complete fabrication passing itself off as reality, as in "Jimmy's World."

new journalism
Mixing fiction techniques with nonfiction

ETHICS MILESTONES

JOHN STUART MILL
Utilitarianism (1865)

YELLOW PRESS
Sensationalism grew as factor in news (1890s)

PIVOTAL EVENTS

• Morse invented telegraph (1844)
• Darwin's seminal work on human evolution (1859)
• U.S. Civil War (1861–1865)
• Railroad link of Atlantic and Pacific coasts (1869)
• Wayland Ayer founded first advertising agency (1869)

Maine explosion fit jingoism of Hearst and Pulitzer

1800s

ETHICS MILESTONES

JOHN DEWEY
Pragmatism (1903)

NEWS ETHICS
Upton Sinclair exposed newsroom abuses in *The Brass Check* (1919)

ETHICS CODE
American Society of Newspaper Editors adopted first media ethics code (1923)

SOCIAL RESPONSIBILITY
Hutchins Commission urged media to be socially responsible (1947)

ETHICS AS PROCESS
Ralph Potter devised quadrants as a model to deal with dilemmas (1965)

JOHN RAWLS
The veil of ignorance (1971)

PIVOTAL EVENTS

• Right to vote extended to women (1920)
• Great Depression (1930s)
• Netscape browser ignited the Internet as a mass medium (1997)

1900s

ETHICS MILESTONES

POLITICAL ADVERTISING
False, misleading negative ads include the Swiftboat attacks on presidential candidate John Kerry by supporters of George W. Bush (2004)

Ideology, sloppiness undermine the internet's potential

MEDIA SCAPEGOATING
Faltering presidential candidates Rick Perry, Herman Cain, Newt Gingrich, Ron Paul claim media skewed coverage (2011)

INTERNET
Plagiarism swelled with growing access to digitized media (2000s)

PIVOTAL EVENTS

• 9/11 terrorist attacks (2001)
• Iraq war (2003–2011)
• Hurricane Katrina (2005)
• George W. Bush presidency (2001–2009)
• Great Recession (2007–2009)
• Barack Obama presidency (2009–)

2000s

Gifts, Junkets and Meals

Upton Sinclair
Author of *The Brass Check*

In his 1919 book *The Brass Check,* a pioneer examination of newsroom ethics, **Upton Sinclair** told how newspeople took bribes to put stories in the paper. Today all media ethics codes condemn gifts and certainly bribes. Even so, there are still people who curry favor with the mass media through gifts, such as a college sports publicist who gives a fifth of whisky at Christmas to a sportswriter as a gesture of goodwill. Favors can take many forms: media-appreciation lunches; free trips abroad, known as **junkets**, especially for travel writers; season passes to cover the opera; discounts at certain stores.

junket
Trip with expenses paid by someone who may expect favors in return

Despite the consistent exhortation of the ethics codes against gifts, favors, free travel and special treatment and privileges, there is nothing inherently wrong in taking them if they do not influence coverage and if the journalist's benefactor understands that. The problem with favors is more a practical one than one of ethics. Taking a favor may or may not be bad, but it *looks* bad. Many ethics codes do not make this important distinction. One that does is the code of the Associated Press Managing Editors, which states: "Journalists must avoid impropriety and *the appearance of impropriety* as well as any conflict of interest or *the appearance of conflict.* They should neither accept anything nor pursue any activity that might compromise or *seem to compromise* their integrity." The APME admonitions at least recognize the distinction between the inherent wrongness of impropriety, which is an ethics question, and the perception that something may be wrong, which is a perception that is unwise to encourage but is not necessarily unethical.

freebies
Gifts for which the giver may expect favors in return

While ethics codes are uniform in prohibiting **freebies**, as gifts and favors are called, many news organizations accept free movie, drama, concert and other tickets, as well as recordings, books and other materials for review. The justifications are usually that their budgets allow them to review only materials that arrive free and that their audiences would be denied reviews if the materials had to be purchased: "Newsroom budgets are tight, you know." A counterargument is that a news organization that cannot afford to do business right should not be in business. Many news organizations insist on buying tickets for their reporters to beauty pageants, sports events and other things to which there is an admission fee. A frequent exception occurs when a press box or special media facility is available. With recordings, books and free samples, some media organizations return them or pass them on to charity to avoid any appearance that they have been bought off.

When junkets are proposed, some organizations send reporters only if they can pay the fare and other expenses. The Louisville *Courier-Journal* is firm. If a reporter accompanies a sports team on a bus or plane to a far-away game, the paper pays a pro-rata share of the cost. At some news organizations, an exception is made by some news organizations for trips that they could not possibly arrange on their own, such as covering a two-week exercise at sea aboard a Navy ship.

Some media organizations address the issue of impropriety by acknowledging favors. Many quiz shows say that "promotional consideration" has been provided to companies that give them travel, lodging and prizes. Just as forthright are publications that state that reviews are made possible through season passes or free samples. Acknowledging favors does not remove the questions, but at least it is up front.

APPLYING YOUR MEDIA LITERACY

- **How have traditional media practices muddied a strict view of plagiarism?**
- **Can staging and even fictionalizing have a legitimate role in news? How about in long-form journalism like biographies?**
- **As a news editor, how would you handle a proposal from the National Guard to ferry a reporter in a Guard aircraft to hometown unit training exercises? "Just have the reporter bring a pad, pencil and camera," says the Guard public relations officer. "We'll provide lodging, field meals, flak jackets and everything else—even a souvenir T-shirt and Guard baseball cap."**

◼ The Difficulty of Ethics (Pages 441–444)

Media people have no shortage of ethics codes. Every professional organization has one. This multitude of ethics codes makes it easy for people to infer that ethical behavior is a simple matter of learning and obeying the rules. But they are missing the complexity of moral issues. No prescriptive code, cast in broad terms as they must be, can replace a good mind and the application of broad, universal principles.

◼ Media Ethics (Pages 444–445)

Mass communicators try to do good in an often-confusing combination of obligations. One fundamental obligation, for example, is to serve the audience. But who decides what serves the audience best? The editors of the New York *Times* and the *National Enquirer* could debate endlessly on that. Imagine the conflict of advertising-supported media when the interests of advertisers and listeners don't coincide. That's been the crux of ethics debates on sugary, fat-laden snacks marketed to kids.

◼ Moral Principles (Pages 445–446)

Philosophers have struggled over the centuries to devise overarching principles to sort through moral dilemmas. In the 1700s Immanuel Kant proposed *categorical imperatives*—broad principles that everyone would see as acceptable for dealing with any and all situations. The Kant idea is not prescriptive as much as it is a call for thorough consideration, clarity of thinking, and consistency.

◼ Process versus Outcome (Pages 447–450)

Nothing better demonstrates the complexity of ethics than the conflict between deontologists and teleologists. Deontologists emphasize creating good rules. As deontologists see it, following good rules results in good behavior. Whoa, say the teleologists. They can cite all kinds of well-intentioned rules that backfired in particular situations. Teleologists argue that behavior can be judged better by the results. A third school of ethicists approach each moral dilemma from scratch. The idea is to consider the facts of a situation without any larger or philosophical framework. Critics of situational ethics note, however, that no two human minds work alike. Without agreed-upon principles, people end up with very different ideas of how to handle a dilemma. Not everyone can be right.

◼ Potter's Box (Pages 450–452)

By definition, a moral dilemma has no perfect solution. That's what makes a dilemma a dilemma. A useful process for working through problems, called Potter's Box, is to start with the facts and apply values and principles—and then to sort through loyalties that affect everyone involved. Potter's Box emphasizes not rules but an intellectual process in finding answers.

■ Ethics, Law and Practicality (Pages 452–453)

Ethics and law often are confused. The confusion is no better illustrated than by someone claiming to have been ethical for following a law. Ethics is not so simple. Think about the long history of whistleblowers who have violated national security laws and been lauded as heroes for exposing wrongheaded government practices. Sometimes ethics is confused with standard and accepted practices in a profession. The fact, however, is that accepted practices need continuing reconsideration as to their efficacy. Mimicking old ways of doing things may or may not be practicing good behavior.

■ Unsettling Media Issues (Pages 453–458)

Many standard media practices border on the shady. None is more problematic than plagiarism. Everybody condemns plagiarism as thievery and dishonesty, but a tremendous amount of "borrowing" occurs in creating media content. The rash of movies picking up on a blockbuster theme is one example. It's similar with misrepresentation, which is easy to condemn. But what about John Howard Griffin, a white man who dyed his skin black and traversed the South in the 1950s to see racial injustices, which helped trigger the civil rights movement? Griffin misrepresented himself. Was it the right thing to do? Or was it wrong?

■ Thinking Critically

1. Why can't ethics codes anticipate all moral questions? Does this limit the value of media ethics codes?

2. How do media audiences influence media ethics?

3. What are legacy principles to help media people sort through dilemmas.

4. How can process-based or outcome-based ethics systems yield different guidance on media behavior?

5. Why is Potter's Box more satisfying than a code of ethics?

6. How is law different from ethics? From accepted practice? From prudence?

7. Discuss dubious mass media practices that run counter to many moral principles.

Media Vocabulary

accepted practices (Page 452)

canons of journalism (Page 441)

categorical imperative (Page 445)

code of ethics (Page 441)

deontological ethics (Page 447)

divine command theory (Page 447)

Do Unto Others (Page 445)

egalitarianism (Page 446)

freebies (Page 458)

Golden Mean (Page 445)

junket (Page 458)

libertarian theory (Page 447)

misrepresentations (Page 456)

new journalism (Page 457)

plagiarism (Page 453)

Potter's Box (Page 450)

pragmatic ethics (Page 446)

prescriptive ethics (Page 441)

principle of utility (Page 446)

prudence (Page 452)

reality programs (Page 456)

re-enactments (Page 456)

secular command theory (Page 447)

selective editing (Page 457)

situational ethics (Page 449)

social responsibility (Page 446)

staging news (Page 456)

teleology (Page 449)

veil of ignorance (Page 446)

Media Sources

■ Dan Gillmor. *Mediactive*. Lulu.com, 2010. Gillmor, a technology journalist and scholar, says good media habits can help consumers avoid the traps of passive media consumption.

■ Howard Good and Sandra L. Borden, editors. *Ethics and Entertainment: Essays on Media Culture and Media Morality.* McFarland, 2010. A wide-ranging collection of scholarship and thinking on ethics in media entertainment.

■ Thomas Bivins. *Mixed Media: Moral Distinctions in Advertising, Public Relations and Journalism.* Erlbaum, 2004. Professor Bivins stresses identifying the impact of ethics decisions in choosing courses of action.

■ Clifford G. Christians, Kim B. Rotzoll and Mark Fackler. *Media Ethics,* sixth edition. Longman, 2002. These scholars are especially good at describing Kant's categorical imperative and other philosophical systems on which media ethics can be based.

■ Ralph B. Potter. "The Structure of American Christian Responses to the Nuclear Dilemma, 1958–1963." Potter describes what came to be known as Potter's Box, in his Harvard University doctoral dissertation in 1965.

A Thematic Chapter Summary

MASS MEDIA ETHICS

To further deepen your media literacy, here are ways to look at this chapter from the perspective of themes that recur throughout the book:

MEDIA **TECHNOLOGY**

Relying on internet information as accurate has posed problems for Congresswoman Michele Bachmann.

Changing technology through the history of the mass media has posed ethics challenges that never could have been anticipated earlier. A growing contemporary issue is a lack of sensitivity among a new generation whose practices include wholesale cutting of internet material and pasting it into their own work without credit. Plagiarism has always been a difficult issue for the mass media, especially with the vagaries imposed by deadlines and the continuing repackaging of material. For better or worse, media people have agreed upon all kinds of conditions and rules for swapping information. Even these accepted practices cause purists in some academic fields to shudder—"Egads! No footnotes?" The issue is becoming more critical with broadening acceptance of the rampant copying that's facilitated by digitization. Old ways of doing things need to be reconsidered.

MEDIA **ECONOMICS**

Finding alternatives to advertising as a revenue stream could avoid some ethics issues of obligations. But how would advertising-dependent media stay in business?

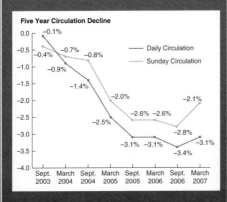

Five Year Circulation Decline

Legend: — Daily Circulation — Sunday Circulation

Advertising-dependent media have an obligation to advertisers as their financial supporters. But media also have obligations to other interests and values, including to their readers, to their owners and, let's not forget, to the truth. Weighing these obligations can expose all kinds of moral dilemmas. Consider a magazine that is financially dependent on ads for dubious Viagra substitutes. To turn away the ads could mean the magazine goes belly-up. What kind of service is that to readers who would benefit from the magazine's articles?

MEDIA **ETHICS**

New technology enables just about anybody to contribute to the media marketplace, which means many new mass communicators are unschooled about the Hutchins Commission call for social responsibility.

In 1947 a blue-ribbon task force of intellectuals headed by Robert Hutchins placed a premium on the media acting in socially responsible ways. The Hutchins ideas came to be embraced by the media, albeit with notable exceptions. But the media are no longer the easily identified companies that had the equipment and means to reach huge audiences. New technology has enabled just about anyone to enter the media marketplace, many who never heard of the Hutchins Commission and are completely oblivious to the Hutchins legacy.

MEDIA AND DEMOCRACY

How much biographical background do voters need to know about candidates?

For democracy to work as it should, people need accurate, timely and useful information. Ethical media conduct includes providing full reports, but are there no limits? During the 2000 presidential campaign, when an intrepid reporter in Maine unearthed a nearly 30-year-old drunken driving conviction against George H. W. Bush, the Bush campaign people were irate and used words like *irrelevant, unfair* and *smear.* Others saw evidence of Bush not owning up to his past. They argued that he had wanted to conceal his record, which they saw as a character flaw that voters should know about.

ELITISM AND POPULISM

The usual route to a media career once included schooling with attention to the ethicists. Now anyone with a computer and a modem is job-ready. Or maybe not?

Digitization has given almost everyone a mass media megaphone. Look around you. Who doesn't have the capability to set up a Facebook page or become a blogger? This democratization of the mass media has triggered a need to reassess the rules by which traditional media have operated. Ethical conduct, for example, had been conditioned over the centuries and decades by conventions of copyright and widely accepted bounds on defamation, privacy and decency adopted by media organizations and the trained professionals who crafted media messages. These conventions were fortified by a broad range of institutions, including journalism schools and other career-oriented educational programs. Today, nobody needs a degree to blog or go on Facebook.

MEDIA TOMORROW

Hard thinking has no substitute in addressing dilemmas.

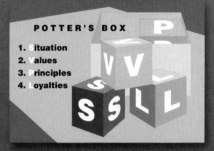

Professional media associations will continue to tweak their ethics codes, especially to address issues that could never have been anticipated because of changes wrought by technology and evolving values in society. These codes will place pressure on media people who operate at the fringes of appropriate behavior, but, lacking the force of law, will wield influence mostly through moral persuasion. On complex issues with conflicting duties, the codes will continue to have limited roles in finding answers. Only through hard thinking can moral dilemmas be addressed and even then not to universal satisfaction.

index

A

A2/M2 (*See* Anytime Anywhere Media Measurement)
AAP (*See* Association of American Publishers)
ABC, 60–61, 75, 132, 146, 150, 323
abolition, 300
abortion, 18
Abramoff, Jack, 277, 279
Academy Awards, 156
accepted practices, 452
The Accordion, 247
accredited in public relations (APR), 281
Adams, John, 421
ad clutter, 304–305
adult entertainment, 243–244
Advanced Research Projects Agency Networks (ARPAnet), 43, 179
advergame, 299
advertiser-to-consumer business model, 100
advertising (*See also* public relations, and advertising)
   attack, 382
   barrages, 304
   brand strategies for, 300–303
   bunching, 304
   celebrity, 304–306
   clutter, 304–305
   consumer economies and, 289
   democracy and, 290–291
   elections and, 368–369
   ethics, 462
   free expression, 427
   games, 190
   gaming, 298–299
   importance of, 289–291, 311
   Industrial Revolution and, 291
   innovative, 315
   Internet, 184, 188–189, 297–298
   magazine, 99, 297
   mass media entertainment, 242, 314
   mass media violence effects, 341
   media economics, 314
   in media finances, 58, 72
   media plans, 295
   milestones, 292–293
   multimedia trailing, 304
   negative, 382
   newspaper, 88, 90, 295, 297
   newspaper industry financial framework with, 86–87
   online game, 189–190, 299
   origins/history, 291, 311
   outside the box, 288–289
   placement, 295–299, 311
   political campaign, 383–384
   prosperity and, 289–290
   public relations, 263–264
   radio, 127–128, 136, 297
   search engines and, 177, 276, 298
   small-screens quality of, 162
   targeted marketing, 188
   as technology stepchild, 291
   television, 150–151, 165, 170, 297, 383–384
   TiVo and television, 165, 309
   trailing, 304

advertising agencies, 292, 311
   compensation, 294
   largest, 294
   pioneer, 293–294
advertising tactics
   LCD, 303–304
   redundancy techniques, 304, 315
   testimonials, 304–305
advertising techniques
   buzz, 307–308
   clutter, 304–305
   infomercial, 310
   new, 305–310
   product placement, 309–310
   stealth, 309
   under-the-radar, 309
   viral, 307, 309
   word-of-mouth, 307
A&E network, 2–3
aerial messaging, 405
affiliates, 133
Afghanistan
   censorship, 390
   media-building, 403
Afghan Star, 391
agenda-setting
   civil rights, 371–372
   mass media attitude effects, 351
   media governance effects, 371–372
   political campaign, 372
   television, 372
   Watergate, 222, 224, 372
   White House sex scandals, 372
Age of Mass Communication, 10, 29–30, 32
aggregation news, 217, 219
aggregation sites, 217, 219
aggregator, 217, 219
aggressive stimulation theory, 359
Agnew, Spiro, 213
Ahmadinejad, Mahmoud, 9
airplay, 121–122
Alien and Sedition Acts, 421
alliterate, 110
all-news radio, 133–134
All Things Considered (ATC), 134–135, 143
AM (*See* amplitude modulation)
Amazon.com, 166, 187, 190
American Idol, 180, 310, 355
American Public Media (APM), 136
American Revolution, 353
America Online (AOL), 62, 176
AMM (*See* Association of Magazine Media)
amplification, 48
amplitude modulation (AM), 129
ancient communication, 5–6
Anderson, Chris, 454
Andreessen, Marc, 45, 176, 196
Android, 177
animated films, 153–154, 158
Anytime Anywhere Media Measurement (A2/M2), 330
AOL (*See* America Online)
AP (*See* Associated Press)
APM (*See* American Public Media)
Apple Computer, 109, 172–173
Apps, 46
APR (accredited in public relations), 281

Arab media systems, 411
   diverse media structures, 406
   Dubai Media Incorporated, 407–408
   Al-Jazeera, 220, 355, 406–407, 414
   Tolo TV, 390–391, 403
   war coverage, 407
Arab Spring, 15, 350
Arbitron, 131, 309, 318
Areopagitica (Milton), 394
Aristotle, 190, 359, 445
Arledge, Roone, 242
Army marketing, 296
ARPAnet (*See* Advanced Research Projects Agency Networks)
artistic values, mass media entertainment, 245, 248–254
Assange, Julian, 398, 401–402, 414
assignment, 418
Associated Press (AP), 65, 211, 321–322
Association of American Publishers (AAP), 77
Association of Magazine Media (AMM), 77
astroturfing, 77–78, 280
ATC (*See* All Things Considered)
AT&T, 61, 152
   Bell Labs, 42
attack ads, 382
auction sites, 186–187
audience (*See also* mass audiences)
   authentic performance and, 236
   ethics duty to, 442
   high/middle/low-culture, 251
   news and fragmentation of, 209–210
   news perceptions about, 215
   niche, 20, 98
   sub-mass, 19
   television fragmentation of, 171, 209–210
audience analysis, 338
   cohort analysis, 334–335
   demographics, 324, 334–335
   geodemographics, 335
   psychographics, 336–337
audience measurement
   audits of magazines, 324
   audits of newspapers, 324
   broadcast ratings, 324–325
   engagement ratings, 327
   radio, 324
   ratings criticism, 326–327
   size, 324–327, 338
   television, 324–327
audience measurement principles, 337
   latter-day straw polls, 323
   probability sampling, 319–321
   quota sampling, 321
   survey evaluation, 321–323
audience measurement techniques, 338
   basic tools, 328
   heatmapping, 330–331
   Internet audience measures, 328, 330
   mobile audience measures, 330
   multimedia measures, 330
   social media tools, 329
   tracking technology, 329–331
audience reaction measurement, 338

   focus groups, 332
   galvanic skin checks, 332–333
   prototype research, 333–334
   sit-down interviews, 332
   television, 332
audience research
   evolution, 317–318
   survey industry, 318
Audit Bureau of Circulations, 295, 324
audits, 324
auteur, 248
authentic performance
   audience and, 236
   feedback and, 236
   media technology *vs.*, 236
authoritarianism, England, 391, 415
authoritarian mass media
   censorship, 392
   control effectiveness, 392
   corporations and, 401
   global, 393
   premises, 393
auxiliary enterprise, 74
Ayer, Wayland, 293

B

Baby Boomers, 334
Bachmann, Michele, 448
Baer, Elizabeth, 421, 423
Baer, George, 265
Balboni, Philip, 65
Balter, Dave, 308
Bandura, Albert, 360
Bardeen, Jack, 43
Barnum, P. T., 268, 271
barrages, advertising, 304
Barstow, David, 224
BAT (*See* Brand Affinity Technologies)
Bazin, Andre, 248
BBC (*See* British Broadcasting Company)
Beck, Glenn, 375
Beckman, Richard, 100
behavioral targeting, 188–189
Bennett, James Gordon, 200–201, 203, 241
Bennett Model
   compelling events, 201–202
   components, 201–202
   deadline-driven, 202
   deadline haste, 203
   dullness, 203
   manipulation in, 204
   McCarthy case study, 204–205
   missed trends, 203
   objectivity, 202, 211–212
   problems in, 203–204
   questions unasked, 204
   sourcing, 202
   superficiality of, 203
   veiling reporter, 202
Bergman, Ingmar, 248
Berliner, Emile, 36
Bernays, Edward, 273–274
Berners-Lee, Tim, 44, 196, 219
Bernstein, Carl, 222, 224

equal time rule, 370
equity contract, 294
e-reader, 109
essays, 96–97
ethics (*See also* media ethics; moral principles)
  advertising, 462
  audience duty, 442
  codes of, 441
  deontological, 447
  difficulty of, 441–444, 459
  egalitarian, 446
  employer duty, 442, 444
  law and, 452–453, 460
  milestones, 456–457
  newspaper, 216
  news release and, 264
  Potter's Box, 450–451, 459
  pragmatic, 446, 449
  prescriptive, 441–442
  profession duty, 444
  prudence and, 452–453
  public relations, 278
  radio, 441–442
  self duty, 442
  situational, 449–450
  social media, 462
  social responsibility, 446, 449
  teleological, 449
  television, 441–442
  utilitarian, 446, 449
ethnocentrism, 212
exhibition business
  box office and, 163
  d-cinema, 166
  movie-house chains, 163, 165
  overexpansion/constriction, 165
  release windows and, 166
  streaming, 166
  theater rise/decline, 153
extremism, mass media entertainment *vs.*, 250–251
ExxonMobil, 199, 280

F

Facebook, 7, 17, 307
  Arab Spring and, 15, 350
  behavioral targeting of, 188–189
  Like button, 188
  origins of, 56–57, 183
  privacy issues with, 189
  success and impact of, 184
fair comment and criticism, 431–432
Fairness Doctrine, 162, 370
Fallows, James, 378
Falun Gong (forbidden religious movement), 404
Falwell, Jerry, 113
family media ownership, 66–67
Fanning, Shawn, 124, 142
Farnsworth, Philo, 37, 39–40, 42
fashion, 260–261
Favreau, Jon, 379
FCC (*See* Federal Communications Commission)
feature films
  CGI, 158
  color, 158
  talkies, 157–158

Federal Communications Act (1934), 150
Federal Communications Commission (FCC), 61, 125, 150, 162, 370–371, 428
Federal Elections Commission, 384–385
Federalist Papers, 67
Federal Radio Act (1927), 70, 125, 150
Federal Radio Commission, 70, 77, 428
Federal Trade Commission (FTC), 304–305
feedback, 6
  authentic performance and, 236
  mass audiences and, 6–7
Feingold, Russ, 382
Feshbach, Seymour, 359
fiber-optic cables, 42
Fighting Words Doctrine, 424
file-swapping
  copyright and, 420
  recording industry and, 124
film (*See also* movie(s))
  festivals, 158, 160
  literacy, 10
  narrative, 157
Filo, David, 179
filter, 49
finances (*See* media finances)
Fink, Sheri, 224
firewall, 404, 409
First Amendment, 113, 127, 211, 370–371, 394, 429, 438
  evolution of, 439
  free expression provision, 421–422
First National Bank of Boston, 385
527 financing, 382, 385
527 status, 382, 385
Flaherty, Robert, 158
flash mobs, 237
Flickr, 184
flight (wave), 304
flush factor, 327
FM (*See* frequency modulation)
focus groups, 332
forbidden religious movement (*See* Falun Gong)
foreign movies, 247
fourth branch of government, 370, 388, 421
fourth estate, 369–370
Fox, Michael J., 49
Fox News, 63, 161
Fox television, 2, 63, 243
framing, 372, 376
Franken, Al, 60–61
Franklin, Benjamin, 88
freebies, 458
Freedom House, 392–393, 415
Freedom of Information Act, 183
free expression, 435
  advertising and, 427
  allowable abridgments, 422–424
  broadcast regulation, 427–429, 435
  broadening protection, 424–429
  distrust of government and, 421
  in entertainment, 427
  First Amendment rediscovered and, 421–422

Iceland transparency and, 425–426
  landmarks, 422
  literature and, 426
  national security and, 422–424
  newspapers and, 113
  Patriot Act and, 423–424
  political expression, 426–427
  political prisoner, 423
  prior restraint and, 422
  provision, 421–422
  public endangerment and, 424
French New Wave, 248
frequency modulation (FM), 129
Freud, Sigmund, 357
FTC (*See* Federal Trade Commission)
fund drives, 73–74
fund-raising, 280

G

Gallup, George, 318–319, 340
Gallup Organization, 318, 322
galvanic skin checks, 332–333
games
  advertising, 190
  new media landscape with, 189–190
  role-playing, 189
gaming
  advertising, 298–299
  future of, 246
  video, 245–246
gaming media content, 254
  censorship and, 245
  as growing entertainment form, 245
  impact of, 246
Gannett, 60, 94
Gannett, Frank, 60
Gans, Herbert, 212, 251
Garrett, Paul, 272
gatekeepers, 48, 217
gatekeeping, 217, 222
Gay, Charlie, 443
GazeHawk, 330–331
Geffen, David, 156
Geico, 297
General Electric, 60–61
General Motors, 272, 298
Generation X, 334
Generation Y, 334
genres, 106–108, 115, 157–162, 234, 237–238, 259
geodemography, 335
geosynchronous orbit, 40
Gerbner, George, 361
Gershenson, Joe, 331
Ghonim, Wael, 15
Gibbs, Robert, 401
Giffords, Gabby, 18
gifts, and media ethics, 458
Gingrich, Newt, 63
Ginsberg, Sam, 244
Gitlow, Benjamin, 422
global mass media (*See also* Arab media systems; China media)
  censorship, 405
  media and terrorism, 407

mega-corporations and, 402
  milestones, 398–399
  nation-state mass media, 391–394, 396, 398–399, 410
  war as libertarian test and, 396–397, 410
  war coverage, 396–397
  WikiLeaks, 398–399, 401–402, 414, 425
Global News Enterprises, 65
global warming, 198–199
Godard, Jean Luc, 248
Golden Mean, 445
Golden Shield, 404
Gone with the Wind, 108
Google, 74, 196
  book industry and, 109
  Books Library Project, 190–191, 419
  Chinese tensions with, 26–27, 181, 197
  click-through fee, 298
  history, 178
  news alerts, 219
  search engine, 177–178, 298
  sponsored link, 298
  targeted marketing of, 188
Gordy, Berry, 123
Gore, Al, 47, 147
Gould, Chester, 54
governance and mass media milestones, 380–381
government
  distrust of, 421
  fourth branch of, 370, 388, 421
government-media links (*See also* media governance effects; media governance role)
  broadcast economics, 69–70
  favored tax treatment, 70, 72
  funding, 72–73
  government communication policy, 68–69
  government operated media, 70
  government role debate, 67–72, 79
  historic, 67–69
  postal subsidies, 67–69
government media manipulation, 377, 386
  influencing coverage, 378
  stonewalling, 378, 380
  trial balloons/leaks, 378
  war coverage, 378
government relations, 277
Grant, Hugh, 71
Grapevine (Balter), 308
graphic novels, 9
Great Depression, 272
Great Moon Hoax, 216–217
Greenberg, Bob, 288–289
greenwashing, 281
Grenada, 396–397
Griffith, D. W., 164, 240–241, 245, 248
Grokster, 418–419
Groseclose, Tim, 374–375
group communication, 5–6
Grove, Andy, 76, 78
Grove Press, 426
Gutenberg, Johannes, 24, 28–29, 74, 291, 314
  printing technology legacy, 29–30
Gutenberg Bible, 29

nonstop coverage, 221–222
Nook, 109
No Sense of Place (Meyrowitz), 348
novels
    cell phone, 182
    technology eclipsing, 11
NPR (*See* National Public Radio)
Nupedia, 84

O

Obama, Barack, 18, 63, 350, 356–357, 373, 379, 385, 448
objectivity, 202, 211–212
obscenity, 244, 433
observational learning, 358
Occupy Wall Street, 355
Office of War Information, 269
Ogilvy, David, 290, 300–301, 358
Old Crow, 301
oligopoly, 75
Omidyar, Pierre, 186–187
on-demand radio, 138
one paper towns, 209
Ong, Walter, 45
online archives, 193
    digital storage, 190
    Google Books Library Project, 190–191, 419
    news record, 191
    Wikipedia, 84–85, 106, 191
online books, 190–191
online commerce, 192–193
    auction sites, 186–187
    mail order, 187
    product downloads, 187
    sales sites, 186
online domination, 193
    amassing target audiences, 188
    behavioral targeting, 188–189
online games, 193
    advertising, 190, 299
    audience, 189–190
    role-playing, 189
    video, 189–190
online global reform, 397–402, 410
online portals, 192
    browser, 176–177
    walled garden, 176
open editing, 84–85
Open Source Center, 350
opinion leaders, 344
over-air television
    cable networks and, 151–152
    networks and cable networks, 151
    stations and cable companies, 151–152
    stations and satellite television, 152
overnights, 328
ownership structures (*See* media ownership structures)

P

Pacifica case, 244
PACs (*See* political action committees)
Page, Arthur, 270
Page, Larry, 177–178
Paine, Thomas, 394

Paley Center for Media, 353
Palin, Sarah, 378, 380
Panahi, Jafar, 247
Pandora, 72, 120–121, 137
paper reels, 31
Paramount, 147–148, 155
Paramount decision (1948), 149, 153
Park, Robert, 371
Parker, Edwin, 361
Parker, Sean, 59
Parsons, Ed, 41
partisan press, 211
Pashto movie industry, 250–251
pass-along circulation, 297
passed links, 185
Patriot Act, 423–424
payola, 122
paywall, 90–91
PBS (*See* Public Broadcasting Service)
Pearl Jam, 240
PECOTA (*See* Player Empirical Comparison and Optimization Test Algorithm)
Penguin, 104
Pennsylvania Railroad, 267
penny papers, 86–87
penny press, 86, 206, 211
Pentagon Papers, 93, 423
People, 225
people meters, 328
performance
    authentic, 236
    live, 236
    as mass media entertainment, 236–237, 253
    mediated, 236–237
performance contract, 294
permissions, 418
Perry, Tyler, 144–145
persistence of vision, 35
personality profiles, 97
persuasion, 16–17
Pew Research Center, 318
P&G (*See* Procter & Gamble)
philanthropy, media, 73
Phillips, Sam, 239
phonograph, 36, 121
photography, 33, 35
photojournalism, 97
photo-op, 382
physical filter, 49
Picard, Robert, 65, 67
Pickford, Mary, 148
pilots, television, 334
piracy
    movie, 416–418
    music, 418–420
plagiarism
    book, 453
    complications with, 453
    Internet, 454
    swapping stories, 455
Playboy, 97
Player Empirical Comparison and Optimization Test Algorithm (PECOTA), 316–317
playlist, 122
Podcast Alley, 137
podcasting, 138
    evolution, 137

political action committees (PACs), 384–385
political bias, media, 374–375
political campaign, 386
    advertising, 383–384
    agenda setting, 372
    attack ads, 382
    coverage, 318, 381–382
    framing, 372, 376
    Internet fundraising, 388
    mass media shaping, 366
    media obsessions, 376
    sound bites, 377
    television's impact on, 388
political communication, 279–280, 287
political expression, 426–427
political lobbying (*See* lobbying)
political music, 239–240
political speech writing, 379
poll, straw, 323
polling (*See also* audience measurement)
    companies, 318
    journalism standards for, 321–322
    misrepresentation in, 323
    misuse of, 322–323
    political campaign coverage, 318, 382
    Silver's innovative techniques for, 316–317
pool system, 397
pop art
    case against, 252
    as evocative, 252
    revisionism, 252–253
    as societal unifier, 252
popular art, high art as, 253
population, 320
populist, elitist values v., 251, 258
pornography, 244, 433
portable devices (*See* small-screens)
portable meters, 328
positioning, 303
Postal Act (1789), 67
Postal Act (1845), 68
Postal Act (1879), 68
postal subsidies
    government communication policy, 67
    postal favoritism, 67–69
    second-class rates, 68
post-print culture, 111, 113, 115
Postwar Generation, 335
Potter, Ralph, 450–451
Potter's Box, 450–451, 459
powerful effects theory, 343
pragmatic ethics, 446, 449
A Prairie Home Companion, 136
pre-publication censorship, 392
prescriptive ethics, 441–442
presidential coverage, 376
Presley, Elvis, 239
press
    colonial, 206
    partisan, 211
    penny, 86, 206, 211
    watchdog role, 213
    yellow, 206
presses
    high-speed, 31
    rotary, 31

principled leaking, 398
principle of utility, 446
printing technology, 28, 51
    Chinese, 30
    Gutenberg's legacy with, 29–30
    Industrial Revolution effects, 30–32
    movable metal type, 28–29, 54
    print-visual integration, 32
print-less democracy, 111, 113
print media, 114(*See also* book; magazine; newspaper(s))
    decline and Internet, 90–91
    differentiating, 87
    milestones, 102–103
    regulation, 371
    'zine, 310
print-on-demand, 109
prior censorship, 409
prior restraint, 422
privacy, Facebook and, 189
PRIZM, 335
proactive media relations, in India, 395
probability sampling, 319
    confidence level, 321
    margin of error, 320
    sample selection, 320
    sample size, 320
Procter & Gamble (P&G), 294, 301, 329
product placement, 309–310
Progressive, 113
promotion, 271, 273
propaganda
    trans-border, 403–404
    war, 407
ProPublica, 74, 111
prosocial, 347
protest music, 239–240, 259
prototype research, 333–334
PRSA (*See* Public Relations Society of America)
prudence, and ethics, 452–453
pseudo-event, 381
psychographics, 336–337
psychological filter, 49
public
    airwaves, 428
    endangerment and free expression, 424
    figure, 430
public broadcasting, 129
Public Broadcasting Act (1967), 135
Public Broadcasting Service (PBS), 74, 150
    public television and, 150
public domain, 104, 190
"public interest, convenience and necessity," 125
Publick Occurrences, 206, 230
Public Opinion (Lippmann), 343
public opinion surveying, 318
public radio, 135–136
public relations
    advocacy, 277–280, 286
    agencies, 262
    commonweal and, 263
    defining, 262
    ethics, 278
    external, 270

Photo Credits

2: Mandi Wright/MCT/Newscom; 6(l): Hemis/Alamy; 6(r): Library of Congress; 7(r): Courtesy Scott McCloud; 7(l): JEWEL SAMAD/AFP/Getty Images/Newscom; 9: Courtesy Scott McCloud; 9: Courtesy Scott McCloud; 11: Bob Peterson/Time Life Pictures/Getty Images; 13: Courtesy The Atlantic; 15: Matthias Toedt/dpa/picture-alliance/Newscom; 16(t): STR/AFP/Getty Images/Newscom; 16(b): REUTERS/Suhaib Salem /Landov; 17: Library of Congress; 18(r): JEWEL SAMAD/AFP/Getty Images/Newscom; 18: NY Daily News/Getty Images; 19: Gregory Urquiaga KRT/Newscom; 20: Shalom TV. As seen on Shalom TV, America's National Jewish Cable Television Network.; 24: Courtesy Scott McCloud; 24(m): © Bettmann/CORBIS; 24(r): Library of Congress; 25(m): Shalom TV. As seem on Shalom TV, America's National Jewish Cable Television Network.; 25(l): Mandi Wright/MCT/Newscom; 25(tr): Juan Ocampo/UPI/Newscom; 26: */Kyodo/Newscom; 29: North Wind Picture Archives; 31: Public Domain; 32(m): SIPA USA-KT/SIPA/Newscom; 32(r): SIPA USA-KT/SIPA/Newscom; 32(l): © SSPL/The Image Works; 33(l): AP Photo/Mathew B. Brady; 33(r): The Granger Collection, New York; 34: REUTERS/Rick Wilking; 36: Library of Congress; 37: © Bettmann/CORBIS; 38: Francisco Cruz/SuperStock; 38(l): North Wind Picture Archives; 38(m): Public Domain; 39(m) Victor Habbick Visions/Photo Researcher, Inc. 39(m): Victor Habbick Visions/Photo Researcher, Inc.; 39(r): © Corbis RF; 41(l): Victor Habbick Visions/Photo Researcher, Inc.; 41(r): © Shahidul Alam/Drik/Majority World/The Image Works; 43(r): Files/Lucent Technologies Agence France Presse/Newscom; 43(l): © Corbis RF; 44: AP Photo/Lefebvre Communications, HO; 45: Courtesy Saint Louis University; 54(r): REUTERS/Rick Wilking; 54(m): Victor Habbick Visions/Photo Researcher, Inc.; 54(tl): North Wind Picture Archives; 54(bl): Hilde Vanstraelen/iStockphoto; 55(l): © Corbis RF; 55(r): AP Photo/Mathew B. Brady; 56: Ian Dagnall/Alamy; 61: Jonathan Ernst/Reuters; 63: WILLIAM WEST/AFP/GETTY IMAGES/Newscom; 64(r): Melanie Stetson Freeman/Christian Science Monitor/Getty Images; 64(l): World History Archive/Alamy; 68(l): Lebrecht Music and Arts Photo Library/Alamy; 68(r) Public Domain; 69(r): Jonathan Ernst/Reuters; 69(l): Douglas Graham/Roll Call Photos/Newscom; 70: © Bettmann/CORBIS; 71: Russell Boyce/Reuters; 77(b): Douglas Graham/Roll Call Photos/Newscom; 77(t): Scott J. Ferrell/Congressional Quarterly/Newscom; 82(m): WILLIAM WEST/AFP/GETTY IMAGES/Newscom; 82(l): Melanie Stetson Freeman/Christian Science Monitor/Getty Images; 82(r): Lebrecht Music and Arts Photo Library/Alamy; 83(r): Jonathan Ernst/Reuters; 83(m): Douglas Graham/Roll Call Photos/Newscom; 83(l): Dean Musgrove/ZUMA Press/Newscom; 84: © Rick Friedman/Corbis; 86(l): © Bettmann/CORBIS; 86(r): North Wind Picture Archives;

89(l): Public Domain; 89(r): © akg-images/The Image Works; 92: The New York Times; 95: STAN HONDA/AFP/Getty Images/Newscom; 96: Popperfoto/Getty Images; 98(r): Bob Landry/Time & Life Pictures/Getty Images; 98(l): Alfred Eisenstadt/Getty Images/Time Life Pictures; 100: Phil McCarten/Reuters; 101(r): Studio 101/Alamy; 101(l): Keith Bedford/Reuters; 102(l): North Wind Picture Archives; 102(m): Library of Congress; 102(r): Popperfoto/Getty Images; 103(t): -/AFP/Getty Images/Newscom; 103(bl): North Wind Picture Archives; 103(bm): Alfred Eisenstadt/Getty Images/Time Life Pictures; 103(br): © Rick Friedman/Corbis; 105: Paul Souders/Getty Images; 107: National Association of College Stores; 110: Art Directors & TRIP/Alamy; 112: Carolyn Cole/Los Angeles Times/ContourPhotos.com; 118(m): Studio 101/Alamy; 118(l): Public Domain; 118(r): SuperStock, Inc.; 119(m): Art Directors & TRIP/Alamy; 119(l): Library of Congress; 119(r): North Wind Picture Archives; 120: Brendan McDermid/Reuters; 124(t): George DeSota/Getty Images Inc.; 124(b): AP Wide World Photos; 126: ZUMA Press/Newscom; 128: The Print Collector/Heritage/AGE fotostock; 130(l): The Print Collector/Heritage/AGE fotostock; 131: Courtesy Everett Collection; 132: AP Wide World Photos; 133: AP Wide World Photos; 135: Yana Paskova/The New York Times/Redux Pictures; 137: Courtesy Everett Collection; 142(l): George DeSota/Getty Images Inc.; 142(r): ZUMA Press/Newscom; 142(m) Victor Habbick Visions/Photo Researcher, Inc.; 143(l): AP Wide World Photos; 143(r): Yana Paskova/The New York Times/Redux Pictures; 144: Soul Brother/FilmMagic/Getty Images; 146(l): Richard Foreman/ABC via Getty Images; 146(r): Ron Wolfson/WireImage for 20th Century Fox Studios/Getty Images; 148(l): Everett Collection; 148(r): Photofest; 154(l): Getty Images Inc. -Hulton Archive Photos; 154(m): AP Wide World Photos; 155(l): © Bettman/Corbis; 155(r): Dean Musgrove/ZUMA Press/Newscom; 156: Walt Disney Studios Motion Pictures/Courtesy Everett Collection; 159: Paramount Pictures/LucasFilm/Amblin Entertainment/Santo Domi/Album/Newscom; 160: NBC/Meet the Press via Getty Images; 161: Photos 12/Alamy; 162: Jonathan Ernst/Reuters; 164: Photos 12/Alamy; 166: Enrique Marcarian/Reuters; 170(l): Victor Habbick Visions/Photo Researcher, Inc.; 170(r): Walt Disney Studios Motion Pictures/Courtesy Everett Collection; 170(m): NBC/Meet the Press via Getty Images; 171(r): David Pearson/Alamy; 171(l): Jonathan Ernst/Reuters; 172: David Pearson/Alamy; 174(r): Greg Tarczynski/Polaris/Newscom; 174(l): © Shahidul Alam/Drik/Majority World/The Image Works; 175: David Pearson/Alamy; 176: Robert Burroughs/Getty Images; 178: AP Photo/Randi Lynn Beach; 181: Guo Yifu/Xinhua/Photoshot/Newscom; 182: Jeremy Sutton-Hibbert/Alamy; 184(t): Kimihiro Hoshino/AFP/Getty Images/Newscom; 184(bl): David Brabyn/